THEORY OF PRODUCTION

This book contains a systematic and comprehensive analytical treatment of the theory of production in a long-period framework. Given the scope of investigation, the methods employed, and the results derived, this study is of interest to all economic theorists. Professors Kurz and Salvadori explore economic systems in which commodities are produced by means of labor, natural resources, and produced means of production. They investigate the relationship between production, income distribution, and relative prices for stationary or growing economies characterized by free competition. Specific chapters deal with joint production, fixed capital (including the joint utilization of machines), scarce natural resources (both renewable and exhaustible), heterogeneous labor, the problem of capital, and alternative theories of distribution. The historical origins of the concepts used from the time of the classical economists onward are also discussed in considerable detail.

Theory of production

A long-period analysis

HEINZ D. KURZ
University of Graz

AND

NERI SALVADORI
University of Pisa

CAMBRIDGE
UNIVERSITY PRESS

338
K96t

Published by the Press Syndicate of the University of Cambridge
The Pitt Building, Trumpington Street, Cambridge CB2 1RP
40 West 20th Street, New York, NY 10011–4211, USA
10 Stamford Road, Oakleigh, Melbourne 3166, Australia

First published 1995

Printed in the United States of America

Library of Congress Cataloging-in-Publication Data
Kurz, Heinz Dieter
Theory of production : a long-period analysis / Heinz D. Kurz, Neri
Salvadori.
p.   cm.
Includes bibliographical references and index.
ISBN 0-521-44325-3
1. Production (Economic theory). I. Salvadori, Neri. II. Title.
HB241.K868   1994
338 – dc20   94-1879
                                                          CIP

A catalog record for this book is available from the British Library.

ISBN 0-521-44325-3 hardback

To Gabriele and Rosa Lucia

Contents

Contents

Preface

This book deals with the theory of production from a long-period perspective. It is concerned with the inseparable problems of production and distribution, and, since the two are connected via the theory of value (or price), also with the latter. The method of analysis adopted in the book is that of "long-period positions" of the economic system, characterized by a uniform rate of profit on the supply prices of capital goods and uniform rates of remuneration of all factor services which are of homogeneous quality, such as certain kinds of labor or land services. In accordance with a long-standing tradition in economics, the tendency toward a uniformity of these rates is taken to result in conditions of "free competition," that is, the absence of significant barriers to entry or exit. Until recently, this method of analysis was generally adopted: developed by the classical economists from Adam Smith to David Ricardo, it was applied by such diverse authors as Karl Marx and all major marginalist economists including Léon Walras, Alfred Marshall, John Bates Clark, Eugen von Böhm-Bawerk, and Knut Wicksell (see Chapters 1 and 14). It is only since the late 1920s that this method has been challenged by the then emerging methods of "intertemporal" and "temporary equilibrium," which their advocates consider more general and powerful tools of analysis than the traditional "long-period" method. For the reasons given in Chapter 14 we do not share this conviction.

With this orientation the book and standard microeconomic theory have some ground in common. The reader familiar with microeconomics knows that in conditions of perfectly competitive markets the role of firms in the long run is just that of minimizing average unit costs, given the total amount of output of the industry as a whole. Hence, in a long-period setting an analysis of the behavior of the single firm is superfluous. Because of its concern with the long period, firms will play no role in the present book. On the contrary, a large part of it will be devoted to a discussion of the problem of the choice of technique of cost-minimizing producers. As will be argued in Chapter 1, this does not imply that returns to scale have to be assumed to be constant. (Notwithstanding this, constant returns will for simplicity be assumed whenever we shall deal with systems that grow.)

In dealing with certain issues, such as single production, joint production, fixed capital, and land, the book attempts to be as complete as it was possible to us. In other fields (for example, the treatment of exhaustible resources in Chapter 12) we restrict ourselves to indicating ways of dealing with certain problems that might prove fruitful. The book attempts to lead the reader to the frontiers of research in long-period analysis and provides him or her both with the analytical concepts and the technical tools to do original research. This does not imply, however, that the book is inaccessible to beginners because of insurmountable conceptual and technical barriers to entry. Chapters 2 and 3 introduce into the analysis in terms of simple one- and two-commodity models which even the novice should be able to master without difficulties. These chapters prepare the student for the more demanding parts of the book. (It goes without saying that the advanced student may skip these chapters.) The mathematical requirements (from Chapter 4 onward) have been kept within the widely known elements of linear algebra. For the convenience of the reader a mathematical appendix has been added which contains all the tools and theorems used in the main text.

In addition to its concern with analytical economics the book reflects our interest in the history of the economic ideas and concepts referred to. This interest materializes both in chapters that are mainly historical, such as Chapters 1 and 13–15, and in the historical notes appended to the predominantly analytical Chapters 2–12. It hardly needs to be emphasized that we do not claim that these notes exhaust the historical material that is pertinent to the different issues under consideration. However, the notes contain some hints as to the origins and developments of the concepts used which allow the reader to locate the place of the analysis developed in the history of our subject and to see whether and where this history is characterized by continuity, or otherwise. Hence, the book should also be of interest to historians of economic thought. Further, in the historical notes we inform the reader about our more immediate intellectual debts by referring him or her to the contemporary sources we used in elaborating the argument in the main text.

From this follows that there is a wide range of possible uses of the book. It is suitable as a textbook in graduate and post-graduate courses on the theory of production, prices, distribution, capital, growth, and general equilibrium. Some parts of it can be used in courses on intermediate microeconomics to supplement the main text(s). The book, or parts of it, can be used in courses on mathematical economics and on the history of economic thought. Finally, the book can serve as a reference work in the fields covered.

A few words should be said on the gestation of the book. Its first lines were written in 1985 when one of the authors, Neri Salvadori, started to work on a book on joint production meant to serve as a complement to Luigi Pasinetti's *Lectures on the Theory of Production*, which is exclusively devoted to single production (cf. Pasinetti, 1977). It turned out that Christian Bidard, Université de Paris X, Nanterre, was engaged in a similar project and proposed to merge efforts. However, due to differences in opinion the two authors eventually decided to give up the idea of writing the book together. In the meantime Christian Bidard has published his book (Bidard, 1991; the readers will easily recognize that Bidard's Chapters 1 and 2 and our Chapters 2 and 3 have common progenitors). Heinz Kurz working on related issues joined the project in 1989. While the two authors have written all the chapters together and share full responsibility for each single word, there was a division of labor among the authors in preparing first drafts of the chapters. Heinz Kurz drafted Chapters 1 (excluding Sections 2 and Subsection 3.4), 11, 13 (excluding Section 8), 14, 15 (excluding Section 2 and some of the historical notes), all the historical notes of the remaining chapters, Sections 5 and 7 of Chapter 2, Section 4 of Chapter 3, Subsection 4.2 of Chapter 4, and Section 7 of Chapter 7. Neri Salvadori drafted all the other sections.

The material contained in this book was used in classes given at the Universities of Bremen, Catania, Denver, Graz, Paris X at Nanterre, Pisa, Santiago de Compostela, and the New School for Social Research, New York. We owe our students several observations leading to improvements in the argument and its presentation. We take this opportunity to thank them for their attentiveness.

Over the long gestation period of this book we accumulated many debts of gratitude to friends and colleagues who gave us valuable comments and suggestions. Since our records are in all probability incomplete, the following attempt to inform the reader about our debts will be incomplete too. We apologize to those who are not mentioned but ought to be in what follows. Christian Bidard, Luciano Boggio, Jean Cartelier, Antonio D'Agata, Guido Erreygers, Duncan Foley, Rainer Franke, Giuseppe Freni, Pierangelo Garegnani, Christian Gehrke, Harvey Gram, Geoff Harcourt, Mark Knell, Ulrich Krause, Christian Lager, Lynn Mainwaring, Michio Morishima, Edward Nell, Alessandro Roncaglia, Paul Samuelson, Bertram Schefold, Ian Steedman, Stefano Zamagni, and two anonymous referees of Cambridge University Press, who kindly read earlier versions of some of the chapters and gave us valuable and in some cases very detailed comments. We thank them all. In six seminars held at the Istituto di ricerca sulla Dinamica dei Sistemi Economici (IDSE), Milan, in February and March 1992, we had the opportunity to present Chapters 1–10 and 13. We are grateful to IDSE and to the scholars who attended the meetings for their helpful observations and criticisms. We would like to mention in particular Gilberto Antonelli, Luciano Boggio, Luigi Filippini, Giorgio Gilibert, Peter Kalmbach, Ferdinando Meacci, Pier Carlo Nicola, Luigi Pasinetti, Giovanni Pegoretti, Pier Luigi Porta, Lionello Punzo, Alberto Quadrio Curzio, Andrea Salanti, Ian Steedman, Giovanni Vaggi, and Paolo Varri. We were also able to present some of the material contained in this book in seminars in various universities and at conferences held in many different places. We thank those who kindly invited us and thus were responsible for involving us in stimulating discussions which were of great help in sharpening our argument. Special thanks go to Giuseppe Freni who illuminated several aspects of Chapter 12 and provided a number of exercises for this chapter; to Pierangelo Garegnani for valuable discussions especially of some of the problems raised in Chapter 14; to Harvey Gram who, for Cambridge University Press, read the final typescript and made detailed suggestions to improve the text; to Lynn Mainwaring for scrutinizing Chapters 2–6; to Carlo Panico who put at our disposal his expert knowledge while writing Section 3 of Chapter 15 and the corresponding historical notes; to Salvatore Rao for his help with the mathematical appendix; and to Ian Steedman for his encouragement and advice during all the years the book was in preparation. It goes without saying that all remaining errors and omissions are entirely our responsibility. Finally, we should like to express our sincere thanks to Scott Parris, the economics editor of the American branch of Cambridge University Press, for his continuous support and assistance. It is hard for us to imagine a collaborator more congenial than he was.[1]

Economics is known as the "dismal science." We cannot confirm this judgment. Despite the hardship we encountered in finishing the manuscript, our collaboration was a continuous source of pleasure and excitement. Indeed, given all the fun we had while writing the following lines we were at times inclined to think that economics is a laughing matter. Our wives, Gabriele and Rosa Lucia, for perfectly good reasons may not quite share this view. Yet without their understanding it is doubtful that this book would ever have been completed. This is another reason to dedicate the result of our joint effort to them.

H.D.K. and N.S.

[1] Neri Salvadori also thanks the MURST (the Italian Ministry of University and Technological and Scientific Research) for financial support.

A reader's guide

As has been pointed out in the Preface, there is a range of possible uses of the book. The following diagram is perhaps of some help to guide the reader through the book. Numbers indicate chapters; A1 refers to Sections 1–3 of the mathematical appendix, A2 to Section 4 of the same appendix. Solid decreasing (horizontal) arrows connect chapters whose consecutive

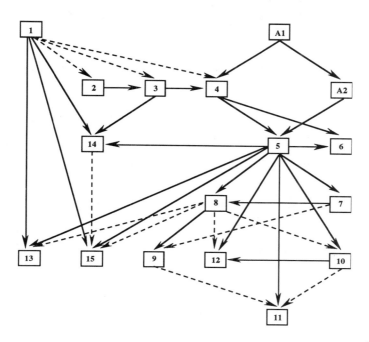

reading is necessary (useful) in order to understand other chapters that come later. Dashed decreasing arrows go from chapters, which have to be read first in order to understand *all* aspects of other chapters, to the latter, while many aspects of these can be understood without a prior knowledge of the former.

1

Free competition and long-period positions

This book is concerned primarily with the investigation of economic systems that are characterized by a uniform rate of profit and uniform rates of remuneration for each particular kind of "primary" input in the production process, such as different kinds of labor and natural resources. These economic systems and the corresponding prices are to be understood as reflecting characteristic features of a capitalist market economy in an ideal way: they express the pure logic of the relationship between value and distribution in such an economic system. The prices are taken to fulfil the condition of *reproduction*: they allow producers to cover just costs of production (including, as things may be, the provisions of the producers and profits at the "ordinary" rate of return on the value of capital advanced at the beginning of the uniform period of production). These prices have aptly been called "prices of production"; we might also talk of "prices of *re*production."

The classical as well as the early neoclassical economists did not consider these prices as purely ideal or theoretical; they saw them rather as "centers of gravitation," or "attractors," of actual or market prices. In their view a tendency toward a uniform rate of profit (and uniform rates of remuneration paid to the proprietors of the different primary factors of production) would prevail in the presence of free competition, that is, in the absence of significant and lasting barriers to entry or exit. This tendency was envisaged to be the result of the actions of profit-seeking producers concerned with minimizing costs of production. Hence the tendency toward a uniform rate of profit and that toward a *cost-minimizing system of production* were seen to be two sides of the same coin. The prices under consideration were therefore also called "natural," "normal" or "ordinary prices." They were conceived of as expressing the persistent, non-accidental and non-temporary forces governing the economic system, and were thus

1

distinguished from "actual" or "market" prices, which reflected all kinds
of influences, many of an accidental and temporary nature. In the literature,
the economic systems under consideration are also known as "normal"
or "long-period positions" of the economy.

This chapter is devoted to a discussion of the historical roots of the
analytical method adopted and the concepts used in this book. Section 1
argues that it was particularly Adam Smith who deserves the credit for
having provided a clear formulation of the method of normal or long-
period positions, which revolves around the concept of a *uniform* rate of
profit. In addition, Smith made important contributions to the development
of the classical analysis of the production and distribution of social wealth.
David Ricardo and Karl Marx built on the foundations laid by Smith
and, like him, sought to explain all shares of income other than wages in
terms of the residual or "surplus" left after the wage goods in the support
of laborers and what is necessary for the replacement of the used up means
of production have been deducted from the annual output. Hence, it is a
characteristic feature of the classical theory of value and distribution that
wages are taken to be given, that is, exogenous to the present analysis.
In this view relative prices are envisaged as a mere reflection of the rule
according to which the surplus is distributed in the form of profits (and
rents) among different sectors (and different proprietors of natural resources,
such as land). Section 2 investigates whether and under what circumstances
the assumption of a uniform rate of profit is admissible. Section 3 points
out that fundamentally the same long-period method of analysis was
adopted by the leading exponents of the so-called marginalist revolution
in the last third of the nineteenth century. In terms of content, it is shown
that a characteristic feature of the marginalist or "neoclassical" approach
consists in the fact that all kinds of incomes are explained *symmetrically*:
wages, profits, and rents are taken to be determined by the forces of supply
and demand in regard to the services of the respective "factors of
production," labor, "capital," and land. Léon Walras's general equilibrium
analysis and Alfred Marshall's partial equilibrium analysis exemplify this
argument. The role of demand (functions) in the neoclassical theory of
price and distribution is put into sharp relief in a brief discussion of the
"non-substitution theorem," which states that under certain conditions
relative prices are independent of the pattern of demand. As regards
Marshall's partial analysis it is argued that while there is no way of evading
Sraffa's criticism of it (cf. Sraffa, 1925, 1926), other features of Marshallian
analysis are perhaps worth retaining. In particular, it is shown that the
long-period method can deal with economies of scale, provided these are
external to firms. Section 4 gives an account of the sets of assumptions
that underlie the investigation of the various problems in the following

chapters. Section 5 provides some further historical material, in particular it is shown that the classical economists Adam Smith and David Ricardo were not the first to make some kind of distinction between natural and market prices.

1. **The English classical economists and Marx**

Adam Smith in *The Wealth of Nations*, published in 1776, put forward the view that surplus originated from production in general and not from agricultural production alone, as earlier authors had maintained. He conceived of profits as a second component of the surplus together with the rent of land. In conditions of free competition a rate of profit tending to equality across all sectors was assumed to obtain. This perspective defined the frame within which the classical theory of value and distribution was elaborated.

1.1. *Adam Smith (1723–1790)*

The attempt to come to grips with what are considered the fundamental forces governing "commercial society" is well expressed in Smith's distinction between "market price" and "natural price." The former is defined as follows: "The actual price at which any commodity is commonly sold is called its market price. It may either be above, or below, or exactly the same with its natural price" (*WN*, I.vii.7). Smith adds:

> The market price of every particular commodity is regulated by the proportion between the quantity which is actually brought to market, and the demand of those who are willing to pay the natural price of the commodity, or the whole value of the rent, labour, and profit, which must be paid in order to bring it thither. Such people may be called the effectual demanders, and their demand the effectual demand (*WN*, I.vii.8).

How does Smith define natural price?

> When the price of any commodity is neither more nor less than what is sufficient to pay the rent of land, the wages of labour, and the profits of the stock employed in raising, preparing, and bringing it to market, according to their natural rates, the commodity is then sold for what may be called its natural price (*WN*, I.vii.4).

The natural price must of course also repay the raw materials consumed and the wear and tear of fixed capital. Yet on the grounds that the prices of the means of production are likewise made up of wages, profits and rent plus the capital used up, Smith concluded that "the price of every commodity finally resolves itself into some or other, or all of those three parts" (*WN*, I.vi.10; see also Vaggi, 1987b).

Before continuing the discussion, the following observations should be made. First, while the notion of the market price is most certainly not a theoretical variable, it is neither a purely empirical one, but involves some degree of abstraction (cf. Roncaglia, 1990). Second, and in line with what has just been said, Smith was not of the opinion that market prices should or could be the object of systematic economic analysis. Being subject to the impact of a multiplicity of "accidental" factors interfering with the fundamental forces at work, market prices, by their very nature, defy an explanation that is sufficiently general. Third, Smith's concept of "effectual demand" refers to a single definite point in the price-quantity space, and not to a demand schedule as in later theory (cf. Garegnani, 1983b).

One of the novelties of *The Wealth of Nations* is the clarity with which the concept of "profits" is defined and their role in an explanation of relative prices is seen. While in earlier authors the term "profits" was generally a catch-all for various types of entrepreneurial incomes, in particular the wages of management, Smith maintained:

> The profits of stock, it may perhaps be thought, are only a different name for the wages of a particular sort of labour, the labour of inspection and direction. They are, however, altogether different, are regulated by quite different principles, and bear no proportion to the quantity, the hardship, or the ingenuity of this supposed labour of inspection and direction. They are regulated altogether by the value of the stock employed, and are greater or smaller in proportion to the extent of this stock (*WN*, I.vi.6).

Here Smith gives a clear statement of the notion of the *general* rate of profit, which was to become the pivotal concept around which classical economic analysis revolved. The natural price is defined in terms of it, since that price is taken to yield the capital owner "the ordinary rate of profit in his neighbourhood" (*WN*, I.vii.5) and is thus "the lowest at which he is likely to sell them [his goods] for any considerable time; at least where there is perfect liberty, or where he may change his trade as often as he pleases" (*WN*, I.vii.6).

When the quantity of any commodity supplied falls short of effectual demand, the market price will rise above the natural price, and *vice versa* when the quantity exceeds effectual demand. Smith points out that any deviation of the market price from the natural price is of necessity associated with the deviation of at least one of the component parts of the price from its natural level, defined at the normal levels of the rent per acre, the rate of profit and the wage rate, respectively. Smith, however, is of the opinion that fluctuations in market prices "fall chiefly upon those parts ... which resolve themselves into wages and profit. That part which resolves itself into rent is less affected by them" (*WN*, I.vii.18). The deviations will prompt landowners, capitalists and workers to reallocate their land, capital, and labor with the consequence that the quantity brought to the market tends to suit itself to the effectual demand. This is but another way of saying that the market price tends to adapt to the natural price. Smith concludes:

> The natural price, therefore, is, as it were, the central price, to which the prices of all commodities are continually gravitating. Different accidents may sometimes keep them suspended a good deal above it, and sometimes force them down even somewhat below it. But whatever may be the obstacles which hinder them from settling in this center of repose and continuance, they are constantly tending towards it (*WN*, I.vii.15).

Thus, in Smith the natural or normal levels of relative prices and outputs are taken to be known independently of the interplay of "demand and supply." The latter only explains the fluctuations of actual prices (and quantities) around their normal levels.[1] The gravitation of market levels of prices to their normal levels in conditions of free competition is one and the same thing as the gravitation of the distributive variables:

> The whole of the advantages and disadvantages of the different employments of labour and stock must, in the same neighbourhood, be either perfectly equal or continually tending to equality. If in the same neighbourhood, there was any employment evidently either more or less advantageous than the rest, so many people would crowd into it in the one case, and so many would desert it in the other, that its advantages would soon return to the level of other employments. This at least would be the case in a society where things were left to follow their natural course, where there was perfect liberty, and where every man was perfectly free both to chuse what occupation he thought proper, and to change it as often as he thought proper. Every man's interest would prompt

---

[1] In the report of 1762–3 of Smith's *Lectures on Jurisprudence* we read: "The market price ... sinks or rises in the same manner as the naturall one, being intimately connected with it, altho the circumstances which regulate the naturall price seem to be noways connected with those which regulate the market price" (*LJ* (A), vi.81).

him to seek the advantageous, and to shun the disadvantageous employment (*WN*, I.x.1).

The tendency for the rate of profit to become uniform does not presuppose an invariant set of technical alternatives from which producers can choose, but makes itself felt also in circumstances in which there is technological change, that is, in which new products or new methods of production become available:

> The establishment of any new manufacture, of any new branch of commerce, or of any new practice in agriculture, is always a speculation, from which the projector promises himself extraordinary profits. These profits sometimes are very great, and sometimes, more frequently, perhaps, they are quite otherwise; but in general they bear no regular proportion to those of the other old trades in the neighbourhood. If the project succeeds, they are commonly at first very high. When the trade or practice becomes thoroughly established and well known, the competition reduces them to the level of other trades (*WN*, I.x.b.43).

Not least because of product and process innovations relative natural prices are bound to change in the course of time. They vary with the natural rates of wages, profit, and rent, which in turn vary according to whether the society is in an "advancing, stationary, or declining condition" (*WN*, I.vii.33).

Finally, in chapter X of book I of *The Wealth of Nations*, Smith discusses five principal circumstances arising from the nature of the employments of labor and capital that can account for permanent inequalities of wage rates and rates of profit. He however sees evidence that, at least with regard to profitability the relevant circumstances, that is, "the agreeableness or disagreeableness of the business and the risk or security with which it is attended" (*WN*, I.x.b.34) are not that important.[2]

As regards the explanation of exchange values, Smith appears to have held a pure labor theory of value in only one page in chapter VI of book I of *The Wealth of Nations*:

> In that early and rude state of society which precedes both the accumulation of stock and the appropriation of land, the proportion between the quantities of labor necessary for acquiring

---

[2] This view is shared by Ricardo and Marx, whose main concern, therefore, is also with the *general* rate of profit; see Ricardo (*Works* I, chs. IV and VI) and Marx ([1894] 1959, chs. IX and X). We shall deal with this problem in Chapter 11.

different objects seems to be the only circumstance which can afford any rule for exchanging them for one another (*WN*, I.vi.1).

This passage is immediately followed by the famous deer and beaver example, which describes the specific rule of barter for this hypothetical economy.[3] However, as soon as the "early and rude state of society" is left behind, Smith contends that the value of a commodity is no longer regulated by the quantity of labor required for its production. "As soon as stock has accumulated in the hands of particular persons" and "as soon as the land of any country has all become private property," the price of commodities is arrived at by summing up the wages, profit and rent paid in its production: "Wages, profit, and rent, are the three original sources ... of all exchangeable value" (*WN*, I.vi.5, 8, and 17). Sraffa (1951, p. xxxv) characterized Smith's approach as an "adding-up theory of prices."

1.2. David Ricardo (1772–1823)

While Smith had a clear understanding of the tendency for the rate of profit to uniformity in competitive conditions, he had failed to provide a consistent and logically sound solution to the problem of how the level of the rate of profit was determined. It is this problem which was a main focus of Ricardo.

In terms of economic method Ricardo expresses full agreement with Adam Smith. In chapter IV of *On the Principles of Political Economy, and Taxation*, the first edition of which was published in 1817, he praises Smith for having "most ably treated" all that concerns the question of natural versus market prices. Ricardo's discussion of the issue is essentially a lucid summary of Smith's argument with perhaps a single, but important difference. This concerns the greater emphasis given to the decisions of profit-seeking capital owners in general and of the members of the "monied class," that is, financial capitalists, in particular. Ricardo starts out quite conventionally:

> Whilst every man is free to employ his capital where he pleases, he will naturally seek for it that employment which is most advantageous; he will naturally be dissatisfied with a profit of 10 per cent., if by removing his capital he can obtain a profit of 15 per cent. This restless desire on the part of all the employers

---

[3] Smith's argument has generally been interpreted as being concerned with the exchange relationships in a system with single-product processes of production. It can be shown, however, that with regard to the case under consideration he was concerned with *joint* production; see the historical notes in Chapter 8.

of stock, to quit a less profitable for a more advantageous business, has a strong tendency to equalize the rate of profits of all, or to fix them in such proportions, as may in the estimation of the parties, compensate for any advantage which one may have, or may appear to have over the other (*Works* I, pp. 88–9).

Ricardo adds that it is "perhaps very difficult to trace the steps by which this change is effected" (ibid., p. 89). What can be said, though, is that the adjustment process does not require capitalists to absolutely change their business. Relative changes in the employment of capital will do. It is in this context that Ricardo draws attention to the role of monied men and bankers. These are possessed of "a circulating capital [i.e. liquid funds] of a large amount," and since "there is perhaps no manufacturer, however rich, who limits his business to the extent that his own funds alone will allow: he has always some portion of this floating capital, increasing or diminishing according to the activity of the demand for his commodities" (ibid., p. 89). Because of this "floating capital," Ricardo surmises, profit rate deviations are reduced more rapidly: "we must confess that the principle which apportions capital to each trade in the precise amount that is required, is more active than is generally supposed" (ibid., p. 90). Ricardo summarizes the argument:

It is then the desire, which every capitalist has, of diverting his funds from a less to a more profitable employment, that prevents the market price of commodities from continuing for any length of time either much above, or much below their natural price. It is this competition which so adjusts the exchangeable value of commodities, that after paying the wages for the labour necessary to their production, and all other expenses required to put the capital employed in its original state of efficiency, the remaining value or overplus will in each trade be in proportion to the value of the capital employed (ibid., p. 91).

On the premise that the argument holds good, and on the further premise that a general analysis of market prices would be impossible anyway, it appears to be perfectly sensible to set aside altogether the "temporary effects" produced by "accidental causes," and to focus on "the laws which regulate natural prices, natural wages and natural profits, effects totally independent of these accidental causes" (ibid., p. 92).

Ricardo criticized Smith's explanation of these normal levels of prices and the distributive variables as erroneous. Since in Ricardo's view the problem of income distribution "is the principal problem in Political Economy" (*Works* I, p. 6), his main concern was with elaborating a coherent theory of the rate of profit, based on the concept of surplus: "Profits come out of the surplus produce" (*Works* II, pp. 130–1; similarly I, p. 95). The development of Ricardo's thoughts on the matter can be divided into four steps (cf. Sraffa, 1951, pp. xxxi–xxxiii; see also Garegnani, 1984, and De Vivo, 1987). These steps reflect Ricardo's consecutive attempts to simplify the problem of distribution.

The first step consisted of eliminating the problem of the rent of land in terms of the theory of extensive rent developed in Ricardo's *Essay on the Influence of a Low Price of Corn on the Profits of Stock*, published in 1815 (see *Works* IV). This allowed him to focus attention on marginal, that is, no-rent, land: "By getting rid of rent, which we may do on the corn produced with the capital last employed, and on all commodities produced by labour in manufactures, the distribution between capitalist and labourer becomes a much more simple consideration" (*Works* VIII, p. 194). The theory of extensive rent also provided the basis for a first criticism of what Ricardo called Smith's "original error respecting value" (*Works* VII, p. 100), that is, the latter's doctrine that "the natural price itself varies with the natural rate of each of its component parts, of wages, profit, and rent" (*WN*, I.vii.33). As Ricardo stressed in the *Principles*, the price of "corn is not high because a rent is paid, but a rent is paid because corn is high" (*Works* I, p. 74).

In Sraffa's interpretation the second step consisted of trying to get rid of the problem of value by assuming the "corn model": with seed corn as the only capital good and wages paid in terms of corn, the rate of profit obtained in corn production can be ascertained directly as a ratio of quantities of corn – that of the surplus product to the corn capital advanced – without any need of having recourse to prices. With corn entering the production of all other commodities (as the only wage good and possibly also as an input) the prices of these commodities would have to adjust such that the same competitive rate of return could be earned in their production. Sraffa stresses: "Although this argument is never stated by Ricardo in any of his extant letters and papers, he must have formulated it either in his lost 'papers on the profits of Capital' of March 1814 or in conversation [with Malthus]" (1951, p. xxxi; on the controversy about Sraffa's "corn model" interpretation, see the historical notes in Chapter 3).

Yet Ricardo had to accept Malthus's objection that there is no industry in which the composition of the product is exactly the same as that of the capital advanced. It is here that the theories of distribution based on the concept of social surplus are confronted with the problem of value. For, in physical terms the general rate of profit is the ratio between the social surplus and the social capital. Since the two aggregates of heterogeneous commodities generally differ in composition, they cannot be compared unless they are expressed as *value* magnitudes. Therefore, in a third step, in the *Principles* Ricardo presented a theory of value according to which the exchange values of commodities are regulated by the quantities of labor needed directly and indirectly in their production. The surplus product and the social capital, that is, the two magnitudes whose ratio gives the general rate of profit, could thus be "measured" in terms of embodied labor. Hence, what was to become known as the "labor theory of value" was introduced by Ricardo precisely in order to overcome the analytic difficulty encountered in his attempt to explain profits in terms of the surplus product left after making allowance for the cost of production, including the wages of productive workers.

The assumption that commodities are exchanged according to the quantities of labor "embodied" allowed Ricardo to dispel the idea, suggested by Adam Smith's notion of price as a sum of wages and profit (and rent), that the wage rate and the rate of profit can be determined *independently* of each other.[4] The constraint binding changes in the two distributive variables, or rather the quantity of labor embodied in the aggregate of wage goods, or "necessary consumption," and the rate of profit, is clearly stated in the following passages: "Profits, it cannot be too often repeated, depend on wages; not on nominal, but real wages" (*Works* I, p. 143); and "the greater the portion of the result of labour that is given to the labourer, the smaller must be the rate of profits, and vice versa" (*Works* VIII, p. 194). Therefore, in Ricardo's view Smith had abandoned the labor quantity rule of value prematurely; "as if, when profits and rent were to be paid, they would have some influence on the relative value of commodities, independent of the mere quantity of labour that was necessary to their production" (*Works* I, p. 23, n.)

However, Ricardo soon realized that the principle that the quantity of labor bestowed on the production of commodities regulates their exchangeable value cannot be sustained as a "general rule" of value: it is "considerably modified by the employment of machinery and other fixed and durable capital" (*Works* I, p. 30). For, with different proportions of (direct) labor to means of production in different industries, and with different durabilities of these means of production, relative prices would not only depend on the quantities of total labor "embodied" in the various commodities, but also on the level of the rate of profit, and would change with that level. This is so because with compound interest the weight of

---

[4] It should be noted however that in several places Smith showed his clear awareness of the inverse wage-profit relation; see the evidence provided in Subsection 1.1 of Chapter 15.

the profit component in prices depends on the rate of profit.[5] Ricardo's search for a measure of value that is "invariable" with respect to changes in distribution, that is, variations in the real wage rate and the associated contrary variations in the rate of profit, may be considered as the final step in Ricardo's efforts to simplify the theory of distribution. The measure of value that he was in search of was meant to corroborate his conviction that the laws of distribution "are not essentially connected with the doctrine of value" (*Works* VIII, p. 194).[6]

Ricardo's finding that relative prices depend on the distribution of the product between wages and profits might be regarded as finally confirming Smith's doctrine of value. However, this would be a misunderstanding. As Ricardo recalls in section VI of chapter I of the *Principles*, "On an invariable measure of value," Adam Smith "maintained that a rise in the price of labour would be uniformly followed by a rise in the price of all commodities." Yet this cannot be sustained, as Ricardo's third main criticism of Smith's doctrine of value makes clear:

> I hope I have succeeded in showing, that there are no grounds for such an opinion, and that only those commodities would rise which had less fixed capital employed upon them than the medium in which price was estimated, and that all those which had more, would positively fall in price when wages rose (*Works* I, p. 46).

While Ricardo was well aware that the principle of the quantity of labor embodied cannot serve as a "general rule" of value, in one place he called it "the nearest approximation to truth" (*Works* VIII, p. 279). He therefore felt justified in developing his analysis in terms of that hypothesis.

1.3. Karl Marx (1818–1883)

Karl Marx praised Ricardo for having elaborated the labor theory of value, which in his view was the most powerful instrument in Political Economy, but accused him of not having seen that the deviations of prices from labor values did not require "modifications" of the "law of value" but could be explained on the very basis of that law.

The account of the competitive process given by Marx appears to be largely consistent with that of Smith and Ricardo. Chapter X of Volume III of *Capital*, published posthumously by Friedrich Engels in 1894, is devoted

---

[5] This problem will be dealt with in Section 3 of Chapter 4. Additional elements will be provided in Section 1 of Chapter 6.

[6] For a detailed discussion of Ricardo's search for an "invariable" measure of value, see Kurz and Salvadori (1993a).

to the "Equalisation of the General Rate of Profit through Competition."
There we read that

> capital withdraws from a sphere with a low rate of profit and
> invades others, which yield a higher profit. Through this incessant
> outflow and influx, or, briefly, through its distribution among the
> various spheres, which depends on how the rate of profit falls
> here and rises there, it creates such a ratio of supply to demand
> that the average profit in the various spheres of production
> becomes the same (Marx, [1894] 1959, p. 195).

In a later chapter Marx stresses that "this movement of capitals is
primarily caused by the level of market-prices, which lift profits above the
general average in one place and depress them below it in another" (ibid.,
p. 208). He points out that various circumstances may impede the mobility
of capital and labor and thus slow down the speed of the equalization of
the rates of profit, or, in extreme cases, even prevent it from happening
altogether. He adds, however:

> As soon as capitalist production reaches a certain level of deve-
> lopment, the equalisation of the different rates of profit in individual
> spheres to general rate of profit no longer proceeds solely through
> the play of attraction and repulsion, by which market-prices
> attract or repel capital. After average prices, and their correspond-
> ing market-prices, become stable for a time it reaches the *con-
> sciousness* of the individual capitalists that this equalisation
> balances *definite differences*, so that they include these in their
> mutual calculations (ibid., p. 209).[7]

Marx concludes: "Average profit is the basic conception, the conception
that capitals of equal magnitude must yield equal profits in equal time
spans. This, again, is based on the conception... that every individual
capital should be regarded merely as a part of the total social capital"
(ibid., p. 209). Marx calls the price including the general rate of profit the
"price of production" and remarks that "it is really what Adam Smith
calls *natural price*, Ricardo calls *price of production*, or *cost of production*,
and the physiocrats call *prix nécessaire*, because in the long run it is a
prerequisite of supply, of the reproduction of commodities in every
individual sphere" (ibid., p. 198).

Marx proceeds in two steps to determine the general rate of profit and
relative prices; Ladislaus von Bortkiewicz (1906–7, II, p. 38) aptly dubbed
Marx's approach "successivist" (as opposed to "simultaneous"). In a first

---

[7] Unless otherwise stated, all emphases in references are the authors'.

step he specifies the rate of profit as the ratio between the (labor) value of the economy's surplus product, or "surplus value," *s*, and the (labor) value of social capital, *C*, consisting of a "constant capital" (means of production), *c*, and a "variable capital" (wages), *v*, that is,

$$\text{(value) rate of profit} = \rho = \frac{s}{C} = \frac{s}{c+v}. \tag{1.1}$$

In Marx's view it is here that the labor theory of value is indispensable, because it allegedly allows the determination of the rate of profit independently of, and prior to, the determination of relative prices.

In a second step this (value) rate of profit, ρ, is then used to calculate prices, starting from sectoral costs of production, or "cost prices," measured in terms of labor values. This is the famous problem of the "Transformation of Values of Commodities into Prices of Production" in chapter IX of part II of volume III of *Capital* (Marx, [1894] 1959). With p_i as the price of one unit of the *i*th commodity, and c_i and v_i as the corresponding constant and variable capitals, and setting aside the problem of fixed capital, we have, following Marx's procedure,

$$p_i = (1 + \rho)(c_i + v_i), \tag{1.2}$$

$i = 1, 2, \ldots, n$, where *n* is the number of commodities. With the c_i's, v_i's, and ρ given, the "prices of production" seem to be fully determined.

Marx's "successivist" procedure to determine the general rate of profit and relative prices cannot be sustained. A first and obvious error concerns the fact that in the above price equations (1.2) the constant and variable capitals ought to be expressed in price terms rather than in value terms. Marx was aware of this slip in his argument (cf. Marx, [1894] 1959, pp. 164–5; see also pp. 206–7), but apparently thought that it could easily be remedied. Yet once the necessary corrections are carried out it becomes clear that it cannot be presumed that the "transformation" of values into prices of production is relevant with regard to single commodities only, while it is irrelevant with regard to commodity aggregates, such as the surplus product or the social capital, the ratio of which gives the rate of profit. In other words, it cannot generally be excluded that the assumed "*redistribution*" of the surplus value involves a deviation of the price expressions of the surplus product and the social capital from their value expressions in the same way as it involves a deviation of the prices of single commodities from their values. Hence, there is no presumption that the "price" rate of profit, *r*, equals the "value" rate, ρ. Marx's equation (1.1) cannot, therefore, be correct in general. Since the rate of profit cannot be determined before knowing the prices of commodities, and since the prices cannot be determined before knowing the rate of profit, prices and the rate of profit have to be determined *simultaneously* rather than successively. This finding is implicitly confirmed by the analysis presented in Chapter 4 below, which deals with economic systems with any number of commodities. It is demonstrated that relative prices and the rate of profit, given the real wage rate, can be determined only simultaneously. In Section 3 of that chapter the special case will be dealt with in which the labor theory of value holds, that is, is able to explain relative prices. For a detailed criticizm of Marx's value-based analysis, see Steedman (1977a).

1.4. Characteristic features of the classical approach to the theory of value and distribution

Scrutiny shows that the contributions to the theory of value and distribution of "classical" derivation share a common feature, the many differences between different authors notwithstanding: in investigating the relationship between the system of relative prices and income distribution they start from the same set of *data*. These data concern the "system of production" in use, characterized, as it is, by

(i) the technical conditions of production of the various commodities,
(ii) the size and composition of the social product, and
(iii) the ruling wage rate(s).

The treatment of wages as an independent variable and of other distributive variables, profits in particular, as dependent residuals exhibits a fundamental *asymmetry* in the classical approach to the theory of value and distribution.[8]

In correspondence with the underlying long-period competitive position of the economy the capital stock is assumed to be fully adjusted to these data, in particular to the given levels of output. Hence the "normal" desired pattern of utilization of plant and equipment would be realized and a uniform rate of return on its supply price obtained. Setting aside the problem of rent, "natural" prices are considered the medium of distributing the social surplus in the form of profits between different sectors of the economy and thus different employments of capital. It turns out that these data, or independent variables, are sufficient to determine the unknowns, or dependent variables, that is, the rate of profit and relative prices. No additional data are needed to determine these unknowns. Thus the classical authors separated the determination of profits and prices from that of

---

[8] As will be seen in Section 3, this asymmetry involves a major difference between classical analysis and neoclassical, or marginalist, analysis which attempts to determine all distributive variables *symmetrically*. See also Chapters 14 and 15.

quantities, taken as *given* in (i) and (ii) above. The latter were considered as determined in another part of the theory, that is, the analysis of accumulation and economic and social development.

The classical authors were not only concerned with studying the properties of a *given* system of production. They were also investigating which methods of production will be chosen by profit-seeking entrepreneurs from a set of technical alternatives at their disposal. When the *problem of the choice on technique* is considered, the above set of data has to be extended to include

(iv) the quantities of different qualities of land available.[9]

2. Some formal analysis

The arguments of Smith, Ricardo, and Marx concerning the assumed tendency toward a uniform rate of profit can be summarized as follows:

Statement 1.1. A capitalist withdraws (parts of) his capital from one sector and employs it in another if and only if a higher rate of profit is expected to be earned by doing so.

Statement 1.2. There is no movement of capital from one sector to another if and only if the rate of profit is uniform.

The reader might be inclined to think that Statement 1.2 is a consequence of Statement 1.1. In order to investigate the relation between the two statements, let M be the set of sectors of the economy, let r_{ih} be the rate of profit actually obtained by capitalists who are incumbents in sector h, and let r_{eh} be the rate of profit that a new entrant expects to obtain in sector h. Statement 1.1 is equivalent to

Statement 1.3. If and only if $r_{ih} < r_{ek}$, capital moves from sector h to sector k.

A consequence of Statement 1.3 is:

Statement 1.4. There is no movement of capital from one sector to another if and only if $r_{ih} \geq r_{ek}$ (each h, k in M, $h \neq k$).

Statement 1.4 is not equivalent to Statement 1.2. However, one can easily prove the following

---

[9] The classical economists also took as given the (known) stocks of depletable resources, such as mineral deposits; see, for example, the chapter, "On the Rent of Mines" in Ricardo's *Principles* (*Works* I, ch. III). In what follows we shall set aside this problem; see, however, the historical notes in Chapter 12.

Proposition 1.1. If the following Statement 1.5 holds, then Statement 1.4 implies Statement 1.2.

Statement 1.5. For each h in M, $r_{ih} = r_{eh}$.

Proof of Proposition 1.1. Obviously, $r_{ih} \geq r_{ek} = r_{ik} \geq r_{eh} = r_{ih}$.   Q.E.D.

Therefore, if Statement 1.5 holds, then the uniformity of the rate of profit would be a consequence of Statement 1.1, and the classical and Marxian argument in support of such a uniformity would be well founded. Hence we need to determine the conditions which ensure that Statement 1.5 holds. If all firms have access to all known methods of production and if the set of these methods of production available to each single firm is independent of the size of the firm itself, then there is no problem in assuming that Statement 1.5 holds. In fact, the new entrant will utilize exactly the same method of production utilized by the firms in that sector *prior to the entry of the newcomer*.

Yet if some firms are characterized either (i) by internal division of labor, depending on the size of each individual firm, or (ii) by overhead charges to be paid by each individual firm, or (iii) by any other economy internal to each individual firm, then the presence of a new firm in one of the sectors whose firms are characterized by one of these features implies that the whole output of the sector is to be shared among a greater number of producers. As a consequence, if prices and total quantities produced are unchanged, the unit costs cannot be expected to be constant after a new entry. Thus, if sector h is one of these sectors, then $r_{ih} > r_{eh}$ and the rate of profit need not be uniform. Similarly, if one or more firms have access to some methods of production which are inaccessible to other firms, and if these former firms are incumbents in one of the sectors where they have that special access, they may obtain a larger rate of profit than the other firms.

However, the cases just mentioned do not belong to the domain of *free competition*. Indeed, if a firm has access to a method of production that is not available to other firms, it has a monopolistic power in the respective market. And if a few firms have such special access, they have an oligopolistic power in the market. Similarly, if the set of methods of production available to each single firm expands with the size of the firm itself, then there is a tendency of firms to merge and to form a monopoly.[10]

---

[10] If the set of available processes is restricted when the firm is larger, then the firm will prefer to be a multi-plant firm, each plant being utilized at the optimum size; except for some discontinuity, constant returns to scale within the firm would hold. This procedure cannot, however, be followed when the set of available processes expands indefinitely with the size of the firm.

Although the classical economists were well aware of forms of market different from free competition, they dealt with them in a rather cavalier way under the heading of "monopoly." There is no doubt that their major concern was with universal free competition. If we wish to follow them in this respect, then we have to admit that the following assumptions hold.

Assumption 1.1. All firms have access to all known methods of production.

Assumption 1.2. The set of these methods of production available to each single firm is independent of the size of the firm itself.

The reader might be of the opinion that the rate of profit is uniform only if returns to scale are constant. But this would be a misconception. What is required by assuming a uniform rate of profit is that returns are constant *within the single firm*. No problem arises if the set of methods of production available to all firms changes with the quantities of commodities produced in the economy.

This fact can be clarified with reference to the Ricardian theory of rent (cf. Subsection 1.2), which presupposes that some sector, that is, agriculture, uses a natural resource which is in short supply. Each single firm has access to all known processes and no single firm is constrained in the utilization of resources. The problem is that the size of the economy as a whole (or, if resources are specific to industries, the size of the industry utilizing one such resource) determines whether a resource is fully utilized or not. Total production of some commodities could be increased only

   (i) by utilizing some other resource which is not in short supply; or
  (ii) by substituting a method of production with another which produces the same commodity but utilizes a smaller amount per unit of output of the resource in short supply; or
 (iii) by substituting a method of production with another which produces the same commodity but utilizes a smaller amount of a commodity directly or indirectly produced with the resource in short supply.

In these cases a rent on the resource in short supply obtains, and the level of this rent is such that firms are indifferent with respect to the resource (cf. case (i)) or to the method of production utilized (cf. cases (ii) and (iii)). An analysis of these cases is provided in Section 1 of Chapter 10.

The fact that *returns external to firms* (that is, the case in which the size of one or more industries matters in determining the methods of production available to single firms) do not spell trouble for the hypothesis of a uniform rate of profit can also be clarified in terms of the following interpretation of Adam Smith's famous analysis of the division of labor in the first three chapters of book I of *The Wealth of Nations*. In chapter I Smith puts into sharp relief how powerful a device the division of labor is to increase labor productivity, and analyzes in some detail its different features: (i) the improvement of the dexterity of workers; (ii) the saving of time which is otherwise lost in passing from one sort of work to another; and (iii) the invention of specific machines (cf. *WN*, I.i.6–8). In chapter II he argues that there is a certain propensity in human nature "to truck, barter and exchange one thing for another," which itself seems to be rooted in "the faculties of reason and speech," that gives occasion to the division of labor (*WN*, I.ii.1–2). In chapter III Smith completes the argument by stressing that the division of labor is limited by the extent of the market: a larger market generates a larger division of labor among people and, therefore, among firms, and a larger division of labor generates a larger productivity of labor for all firms.

Despite the presence of increasing returns, Smith interestingly retains the concept of a uniform rate of profit. Applying the above considerations to Smith's argument, the latter can be said to be implicitly based on the hypothesis that each single firm operates at constant returns, while total production is subject to increasing returns. Even though some examples provided by Smith appear to relate more to the division of labor *within* firms than to the division of labor *among* firms, Smith seems to be correct in sustaining that some of the activities which were originally a part of the division of labor within the firm may eventually become a different "trade" or "business," so that the division of labor *within* the firm is but a step toward the division of labor *among* firms. In the example of pin-making at the beginning of chapter I, Smith points out that "in the way in which this business is now carried on, not only the whole work is a peculiar trade, but it is divided into a number of branches, of which the greater part are likewise peculiar trades" (*WN*, I.i.3).

As regards the question of returns, the structure of the book is as follows. In Chapters 2–9, if the rate of growth is assumed to be zero, then the set of available processes may be taken to depend on the vector of quantities of gross outputs produced. In this case prices and the wage rate are determined as functions of the rate of profit *and* the vector of gross outputs. In all these cases the relationship between changes in produced quantities on the one hand and prices and the wage rate on the other is not actually studied. In Chapter 10, however, in which it is assumed that there are no causes for variable returns other than land being in short supply, this relationship can actually be determined. If a positive rate of growth is assumed and if returns are not constant, then prices are changing over time, and a different framework has to be adopted. Elements of this different kind of framework are provided in Chapter 12.[11]

Finally, a few further observations on the problem of "gravitation" of market prices to "natural" prices appear to be appropriate. The discussion of this problem in Smith and the authors following him is based on two main propositions (cf. Boggio, 1987). First, the market price depends on the difference between current supply and "effectual demand," where the latter is defined as "the demand of those who are willing to pay the natural price of the commodity" (Smith, *WN*, I.vii.8). If the difference is positive, negative, or zero, then the market price is taken to be lower, higher, or equal to the natural price. Second, the difference between market and natural price triggers movements of capital (and labor) and, as a consequence, adjustments in the composition of production: the output of a commodity increases (decreases) if the market price is above (below) the natural price. In this view the constellation in which actual outputs equal "effectual demands" and actual prices are at their "natural" levels is a center of gravitation. The notion of gravitation and the related concept of a uniform rate of profit were basically adopted by all economists up to the 1920s and were abandoned only later (see Section 5 of Chapter 14).

In recent years the problem of gravitation has become an important topic of research which has led to new insights into the dynamic behavior of the economic system; see, in particular, Caminati and Petri (1990) and the summary statement of results and open questions in this area of research by Boggio (1992). The majority of the models and analyses in this area are devoted to the question whether a given system of production exhibits local asymptotic stability. While few people will deny that it is interesting to know whether or not small deviations of market prices from "natural" prices tend to zero as time moves on indefinitely, the economist would of course like to know more. His ultimate concern in regard to the problem under consideration is whether, in an ever-changing world characterised by ongoing technical progress, the depletion of natural resources etc., natural prices act as centers of gravitation which make themselves felt *quickly*. On the other hand, asking for *convergence* of market prices to natural prices, as is done in many studies on the subject, is, in all probability, asking for too much. As we have seen in Section 1, the classical economists were less demanding: in their view gravitation involves market prices "oscillating" around their natural levels, which may

[11] It deserves to be stressed that the analysis developed in Chapter 12 is far from being complete; in fact it provides but first steps in an area which until now has not been explored systematically.

perhaps be translated as meaning that market prices never move "too far away" from natural prices. These remarks suffice to indicate how intrinsically complex the issue of gravitation is. A proper answer to it would seem to contain, of necessity, an answer to many economic questions which are as yet unsolved. Hence, while in some analyses the problem of gravitation is seen in a way that is overly simplistic, there is the opposite danger of overburdening it with demands that are hard to meet. It should then be clear that there is no fear that the issue of gravitation will be settled in the foreseeable future. In this state of affairs the observation that rates of profit never seem to deviate "too much" from one another may prompt one to start from the "stylized fact" of a uniform rate of profit, that is, adopt the long-period method. This is what has been done in this book.

3. **The traditional neoclassical approach**

Major neoclassical authors considered the gist of the new theory to consist of a generalization of the classical theory of intensive rent. For example, in lesson 39 of his *Eléments d'économie politique pure*, Walras accuses Ricardo and his followers of having failed to develop "a unified general theory to determine the prices of all productive services in the same way" ([1874] 1954, p. 416). Walras contends that such a theory can be elaborated by generalizing the principle of *scarcity*, which the classical economists had limited to natural resources only, to all factors of production including "capital."

3.1. Characteristic features of neoclassical long-period analysis

It is important to note that the early neoclassical economists, including Jevons (1871), Léon Walras (1874), Eugen von Böhm-Bawerk (1889), Alfred Marshall (1890), Knut Wicksell (1893, 1901), and John Bates Clark (1899), fundamentally adopted the same *method* of analysis as the classical economists. That is, they were concerned with explaining the normal rate of profit and normal prices: the concept of long-period "equilibrium" is the neoclassical adaptation of the classical concept of normal positions. For example, in Marshall's *Principles of Economics* it is stated:

> The actual value at any time, the market value as it is often called, is often more influenced by passing events, and by causes whose action is fitful and short lived, than by those which work persistently. But in long periods these fitful and irregular causes in large measure efface one another's influence so that in the long run persistent causes dominate value completely ([1890] 1977, p. 291).

The long-period method, or, as he preferred to call it, the "static method," was also very clearly advocated by Ludwig von Mises:

> One must not commit the error of believing that the static method can only be used to explain the stationary state of an economy, which, by the way, does not and never can exist in real life; and that the moving and changing economy can only be dealt with in terms of a dynamic theory. The static method is a method which is aimed at studying changes; it is designed to investigate the consequences of a change in *one* datum in an otherwise unchanged system. This is a procedure which we cannot dispense with (Mises, 1933, p. 117).

And Böhm-Bawerk, in agreement with the classical authors, suggested that the investigation of the permanent effects of changes in what are considered the dominant forces shaping the economy should be carried out by means of comparisons among long-period equilibria. These comparisons are taken to express the "principal movement" entailed by a variation in the basic data of the economic system (cf. Böhm-Bawerk, [1889] 1959, vol. 2, p. 380).

The adoption of the long-period method was not, by itself, prejudicial as to the content of the theory. This can be seen when we turn to the forces which the traditional neoclassical approach conceptualized in order to determine normal income distribution and the associated system of relative prices. The basic novelty of the new theory consisted of the following: While the classical approach conceived the real wage as determined prior to profits and rent, in the neoclassical approach all kinds of incomes were explained simultaneously and *symmetrically* in terms of the "opposing forces" of supply and demand with regard to the services of the respective "factors of production," labor, "capital," and land. It was the seemingly coherent foundation of these notions in terms of *functional* relationships between the price of a service (or good) and the quantity supplied or demanded elaborated by the neoclassical theory that greatly contributed to the latter's success.

The data or independent variables from which neoclassical theory typically begins its reasoning are the following. It takes as given

(i) the initial endowments of the economy and the distribution of property rights among individual agents;
(ii) the preferences of consumers; and
(iii) the set of technical alternatives from which cost-minimizing producers can choose.

As regards the specification of "initial endowments," we have to distinguish between the "original" factors of production, such as different kinds of labor and different kinds of land, and a factor called "capital." While there appears to be agreement among the advocates of the new theory that the "original" factors of production have to be given in kind, that is, given quantities measured in terms of the respective factors' own natural units, there are two different treatments of the economy's "endowment" with a factor called "capital." First, there is the treatment of "capital" as a single magnitude; second, there is the treatment of "capital" as a given set of physical stocks of capital goods. Major representatives of the first alternative include Jevons, Böhm-Bawerk, Marshall, and Wicksell, whereas Walras adopted the second alternative.

In this section we shall briefly discuss the contributions of Walras and Marshall; in addition, we shall touch upon the neoclassical "non-substitution theorem." The two authors have been chosen because their analyses represent the two extreme versions in which neoclassical long-period theory is available: the *general* equilibrium version, or Walrasian theory, and the *partial* equilibrium version, or Marshallian theory. The interest in Walras's contribution also lies in the fact that he was initially of the opinion that starting from an arbitrary set of given amounts of heterogeneous capital goods would not contradict the notion of a long-run equilibrium characterized by a uniform rate of profit. A deeper assessment of neoclassical theory is provided in Chapter 14; see especially Section 1 of that chapter.

3.2. *Léon Walras (1834–1910)*

In parts II and III of his *Eléments d'économie politique pure*, first published in 1874, Walras is concerned with the model of a pure exchange economy. In his view the problem of exchange constitutes the first major problem of the "mathematical theory of social wealth" that he sought to elaborate. It is only in part IV that the production of consumption (or "income") goods is introduced, which is taken to constitute the second major problem. In that part Walras brings together his solution of the problem of exchange, that is, the *"law of offer and demand,"* and his solution of the problem of production, that is, the *"law of the cost of production or of cost price."* His concern is with showing "how the determination of the price of products is founded on the first of these laws, while the determination of the price of productive services is founded on the second" (Walras, [1874] 1954, p. 211).

In lesson 20 (ibid., pp. 239–40) Walras describes the system of general equilibrium in terms of four sets of equations: (i) equations giving the offers of productive services of different kinds of land, of different kinds of persons, and of different kinds of durable capital goods as functions of relative prices; (ii) equations giving the demands for consumption goods as functions of relative prices; (iii) equations expressing equilibria between the quantities of the different services offered and the quantities demanded; and (iv) equations expressing equality between the prices of the various consumption goods and their respective costs of production. It is assumed that all goods are produced by means of single product processes of production exhibiting fixed coefficients; that is, the amounts of productive services required per unit of output are taken as given and constant. Counting unknowns and equations, Walras arrives at the conclusion that "a theoretical solution" to "the same problem which is solved in practice in the market by the mechanism of free competition" has been found (ibid., pp. 241–2).

Walras notes that in this conceptualization the problem of the choice of technique is set aside for simplicity.[12] It is admitted that this is a rather strong assumption, since what is actually observed is that "in the making of a product, it is possible to employ more or less of some productive services, say land-services, provided that correspondingly less or more of other productive services, say labour or capital services, are employed." It is contended, however, that the existence of alternative methods of production poses no serious analytic difficulties: "The respective quantities of each of the productive services which...enter into the making of a single unit of each of the products are determined, along with the prices of the productive services, by the condition that the cost of production of the products be a minimum" (ibid., p. 240). A discussion of cost *minimization* is, however, postponed to a later part of the book. Hence, there is a striking parallel to the approach of the classical economists who also start with analyzing an economic system using a given set of methods of production, or technique, and address the problem of the choice of technique only subsequently.

The problem of the production and reproduction of capital goods utilized in the production process is not dealt with until part V of the *Eléments*, "Theory of Capital Formation ['Capitalisation'] and Credit." In the introduction to part V Walras makes it clear that "the determination of the prices of capital goods is the third major problem of the mathematical theory of social wealth" (ibid., p. 267). The emphasis is on "capital goods proper," that is, fixed capital as opposed to "personal capital" and "landed capital."

---

[12] It is also assumed that there are no circulating capital goods, for example, raw materials. Circulating capital goods are taken into account in the fourth edition of the *Eléments* in a way which is analogous to the one in which fixed capital is treated (cf. Walras, [1879] 1954, §205).

The price of a durable capital good is seen to depend on the price of its services, which covers (i) the wear and tear of the capital good, that is, its depreciation; (ii) the insurance of the capital good; and (iii) the net income the capital good yields to its proprietor. To show this relationship, suppose (ii) is insignificant, and let P_i be the price of one unit of capital good i ($i = 1, 2, \ldots, l$), π_i the corresponding price of its service, or "gross income," and d_i the depreciation charge which is taken to be proportional to the price of the capital good, that is, $d_i = h_i P_i$, with h_i as a given proportionality factor, $0 < h_i < 1$.[13] The *net* income is then given by $\pi_i - d_i = \pi_i - h_i P_i$. Walras stresses:

> It is ... readily seen that the values of capital goods are rigorously proportional to their net incomes. At least this would have to be so under certain normal and ideal conditions when the market for capital goods is in equilibrium. Under equilibrium conditions the ratio $[(\pi_i - h_i P_i)/P_i]$, or the rate of net income, is the same for all "capital goods" (ibid., pp. 268–9).

As with the classical economists, "normal" or "ideal" conditions of the economic system, characterized by a uniform rate of return on the supply price of capital goods, were important to Walras. The "rate of net income" was equivalent to the classical term "rate of profit" r and can be written as

$$r = \frac{\pi_i - h_i P_i}{P_i}, \tag{1.3}$$

or, solved for P_i,

$$P_i = \frac{\pi_i}{r + h_i} \tag{1.4}$$

($i = 1, 2, \ldots, l$). As Walras emphasizes, the prices of capital goods proper are not only subject to a uniform rate of (net) return, they are also subject to the "law of cost of production," which involves that "in equilibrium their selling price and their cost of production are equal" (ibid., p. 271). Taking the prices of the l different kinds of capital services, π_i ($i = 1, 2, \ldots, l$), the prices of the m different kinds of labor services, ω_j ($j = 1, 2, \ldots, m$), and the prices of the n different kinds of land services, θ_k ($k = 1, 2, \ldots, n$), as given, and starting from given coefficients of production per unit of output of the different capital goods, a_{si}, b_{sj}, and c_{sk} ($s = 1, 2, \ldots, l$), the price of

---

[13] Walras's treatment of the depreciation of durable instruments of production cannot be sustained; see the historical notes in Chapter 7.

one unit of capital good s has to satisfy the following equation

$$P_s = \frac{\pi_s}{r + h_s} = \Sigma_i a_{si}\pi_i + \Sigma_j b_{sj}\omega_j + \Sigma_k c_{sk}\theta_k. \tag{1.5}$$

Equation (1.5) may also be written as

$$P_s = \Sigma_i (r + h_i) a_{si} P_i + \Sigma_j b_{sj}\omega_j + \Sigma_k c_{sk}\theta_k. \tag{1.6}$$

Taking into account the production of capital goods proper necessitates the adaptation of the other sets of equations mentioned above. In particular, the rate of net income, r, has now to be included among the set of relative prices determining the offer of productive services and the demand for consumption goods.

The problem of *capitalization*, as Walras calls it, involves $l + 1$ additional unknowns: $P_1, P_2, \ldots, P_l$, and r. With (1.5) we have l additional equations. Hence there is one equation too few. Walras attempts to close the system in terms of an equation giving the equilibrium between gross savings and gross investment. He assumes that a quantity K_i of capital good i is produced $(i = 1, 2, \ldots, l)$, and that the total value of all newly produced capital goods, expressed in terms of the numeraire, equals the amount of gross savings, S. The latter is equal to the excess of the value of the services offered over the value of the consumption goods demanded, or, in other words, the excess of income over consumption (cf. ibid., p. 273). It is simultaneously determined with the demand for the u different consumption goods and thus depends on the prices of these goods, $\mathbf{p} = (p_1, p_2, \ldots, p_u)$, the prices of the different types of productive services, $\pi = (\pi_1, \pi_2, \ldots, \pi_l)$, $\omega = (\omega_1, \omega_2, \ldots, \omega_m)$ and $\theta = (\theta_1, \theta_2, \ldots, \theta_n)$, and the rate of net income, r. In equilibrium we have

$$S(\mathbf{p}, \pi, \omega, \theta, r) = \Sigma_i K_i P_i. \tag{1.7}$$

With (1.7) Walras thinks that he has found the additional equation that renders his system of general equilibrium (including the formation of capital) determinate.

It is beyond the scope of this book to discuss in detail the merits and demerits of Walras's general equilibrium analysis (see, however, the further observations on Walras's approach in Subsection 2.4 of Chapter 14). Here a few additional remarks must suffice. If there is only one labor service, that is, $m = 1$, if land services are not in short supply, that is, $\theta_k = 0$ $(k = 1, 2, \ldots, n)$, and if "fixed" capital is actually circulating capital, that is, $h_i = 1$ $(i = 1, 2, \ldots, l)$, then the set of equations (1.6) for $s = 1, 2, \ldots, l$ is nothing else than the set of equations investigated in Chapter 4 of the present book. Moreover, in Chapters 7 and 9 fixed capital will be introduced in a set of equations which are analogous to equations (1.6). The land services in short supply will then be introduced in Chapter 10. Plurality of labor services is finally considered in Chapter 11.

The pivotal role of the explanation of income distribution for neoclassical analysis as a whole can be exemplified in terms of the way in which the prices of goods are determined. It is frequently maintained that the main novelty of the marginalist doctrine consists in the introduction of consumer preferences centered around the notion of marginal utility, and thus demand conditions, into economic analysis. However, as the brief overview of Walras's model with a single fixed coefficients technique of production should have made clear, in it the demand for goods can affect prices only to the extent to which it affects income distribution. For, in equilibrium the price of a good equals its cost of production, that is, the sum total of the prices paid for all the productive services expended in its production. Hence, the demand for goods can exert its influence on the prices of goods only via its impact on the demand for productive services relative to their supply, and thus via its impact on the prices of these services, that is, income distribution. If this influence of demand on distribution is ruled out *ex hypothesi* as is the case in the neoclassical "non-substitution theorem," in which the rate of profit is taken to be given and constant, then it should come as no surprise, given the other assumptions underlying this theorem, that relative prices are independent of demand.

3.3. The "non-substitution theorem": a special case of neoclassical analysis

The "non-substitution theorem" states that under certain specified conditions, and taking the rate of profit (rate of interest) as given from outside the system, relative prices are independent of the pattern of final demand. The "non-substitution theorem" is of particular interest in the present context since, as was already mentioned, it puts into sharp relief the role of demand in neoclassical analysis.

The original formulation of the theorem assumes (i) constant returns to scale, (ii) a single primary factor of production only (homogeneous labor) and (iii) no joint production, that is, circulating capital only (see Arrow, 1951, Georgescu-Roegen, 1951, Koopmans, 1951a, and Samuelson, 1951). The theorem was received with some astonishment by authors working in the neoclassical tradition since it seemed to flatly contradict the importance attached to consumer preferences for the determination of relative prices. As Samuelson wrote: "From technology and the interest rate alone, *and completely without regard to the demand considerations* ... [,] price relations can be accurately predicted as constants" (1966b, p. 530). This astonishment is all the more understandable, since several "classroom" neoclassical models, for didactical reasons, are based precisely on the set of simplifying assumptions (i)–(iii) underlying the theorem, *without* however arriving at the conclusion that demand does not matter.

This latter observation should have raised doubts as to the validity of the widely held opinion that it is first and foremost the *special modeling of production* on which the theorem hinges. In order for demand to exert an influence on the price of a good the supply function must not be horizontal. Then how do neoclassical models that are subject to constant returns to scale, no joint production, and homogeneous labor arrive at an upward sloping supply curve? The upward slope of the supply curve reflects the increase in the relative price of the productive service which is required in a relatively high proportion in the production of the good. For example, if the good under consideration happens to be produced with a relatively high proportion of labor to "capital," that is, a high "labor intensity," then an increase in the demand for the good, that is, a rightward shift of the demand schedule, would lead to a rise in the relative price of the good due to an increase in the wage rate relative to the rate of profit. This change in relative prices of productive services is ultimately traced back to changes in the relative scarcity of the factors, labor and "capital," the endowment of which is assumed to be given.

It is therefore not so much assumptions (i)–(iii) which account for the theorem: it is rather the hypothesis that the rate of profit (or, alternatively, the wage rate) is given and independent of the level and composition of output. This hypothesis is completely extraneous to the neoclassical approach and in fact assumes away the role played by one set of data from which that analysis commonly begins: given initial endowments (see Subsection 3.1). While assumptions (i)–(iii) affect only the degree of generality of the neoclassical theory, the assumption of a given rate of profit radically transforms the substance of that theory. With the endowment side chopped off, the concept of "scarcity" of factors of production loses the significance usually attributed to it in neoclassical explanations of relative prices. Hence, the demand for goods, and thus preferences, can no longer exert an influence on prices via the derived demand for factor services which are available in given supply: prices of goods are independent of demand because income distribution is assumed to be independent of demand. The importance of the "non-substitution theorem" should thus be seen in the fact that it contributes to a clarification of the role of consumer preferences and thus demand for the neoclassical theory of distribution and relative prices.

It goes without saying that in the framework of classical analysis with its different approach to the theory of value and distribution, a characteristic feature of which is the non-symmetric treatment of the distributive variables (see Subsection 1.4), there is nothing unusual or exceptional about the "non-substitution theorem".

3.4. Alfred Marshall (1842–1924)

It was Marshall's contention that because of the impossibility of controlled experiment in economics and of the complexity of its material, "the function of analysis and deduction ... is not to forge a few long chains of reasoning, but to forge rightly many short chains" ([1890] 1977, p. 638). This methodological position led Marshall, at least in a first step of the analysis, to focus attention exclusively on the interaction of demand and supply in a single market, taking the prices of all other goods as given and constant. It is to be understood, however, that partial equilibrium analysis is legitimized only in proportion to the extent to which it is able to approximate the results which could be obtained in a general framework that takes full account of all the interdependencies that partial analysis sets aside.

The usual (short-period) partial equilibrium argument can be summarized as follows. A change in one market (for example, a shift in the demand curve for bread) has an effect first on the equilibrium of that market (for example, a change in the price and in the quantity of bread produced) and second on other markets as a consequence of the change in the price and the quantity determined in the market where the original change took place (for example, a shift in the demand for flour used to produce bread, and in the demand for biscuits, a bread substitute). If it can be assumed that the effects on other markets are of a second order of magnitude with respect to the effect obtained on the equilibrium of the market where the original change took place, and if these effects of the second order of magnitude are assumed to be so small that they can be neglected, at least at a first stage, then the demand and supply curves of a given market can be considered, with respect to small variations, as being independent both of each other and of the demand and supply curves of all other commodities. The partial equilibrium analysis can be considered but a transitional step to an understanding of all the interdependencies as they are portrayed by a fully general equilibrium analysis.

Marshall's partial equilibrium approach to price determination was designed in large part as a tool that is practicably applicable to concrete issues. It was combined with *period analysis* which distinguished between different lengths of "the particular time we have in view" ([1890] 1977, p. 369). The distinction between different lengths of time that are allowed for the supply side to adjust to the demand side is intended to clarify the respective roles of (marginal) utility and thus "demand" on the one hand, and cost of production and thus "supply" on the other, in determining prices. Marshall in fact distinguishes between four kinds of equilibria:

> In each, price is governed by the relations between demand and supply. As regards *market* prices, Supply is taken to mean the stock of the commodity in question which is on hand, or at all events 'in sight'. As regards *normal* prices, when the term Normal is taken to relate to *short* periods..., Supply means broadly what can be produced for the price in question with the existing stock of plant, personal and impersonal, in the given time. As regards *normal* prices, when the term Normal is to refer to *long* periods..., Supply means what can be produced by plant, which itself can be remuneratively produced and applied within the given time; while lastly, there are very gradual or *Secular* movements of normal price, caused by the gradual growth of knowledge, of population and of capital, and the changing conditions of demand and supply from one generation to another (ibid., pp. 314–15).

In the discussion that follows only a brief exposition of partial equilibrium analysis will be provided. Moreover, we shall be concerned more with the standard microeconomic textbook version of partial analysis rather than Marshall's own approach. This procedure appears to be justified in terms of the importance of the former in contemporary economics; it is not implied that the textbook version is a completely faithful representation of Marshall's analysis.

Marshall's concept of "long-period normal price" apparently bears a close resemblance to what Adam Smith and Ricardo called "natural price" and Torrens and Marx called "price of production." As in the earlier authors, the realization of the "normal" price in Marshall is a prerequisite to the long-run reproduction of commodities in each individual sector. This interpretation seems to be at odds with Marshall's view that in a situation of perfect competition *profits* vanish in the long period. However, it has to be kept in mind that in Marshallian language *profit* is what is called *extra profit* in the language of the classical economists, whereas what they called *profit* is called *interest* by Marshall. And since the rate of interest is assumed to be uniform throughout the economy, no profit (in the Marshallian sense) means, in the language of the classicals (which it is the language adopted in the remainder of this book), that the rate of profit is uniform.

Let us now have a closer look at the Marshallian treatment of the problem of production and prices. Take the short-period analysis of the *firm* first. Since the firm is assumed to be a price taker and profit maximizer, and assuming single production, the firm chooses to produce that quantity of a particular commodity at which the short-period marginal cost equals the price, provided the average variable cost is not higher than the price. As a consequence, the short-period supply curve of the firm coincides with that part of the short period marginal cost curve which is not below the average variable cost curve. The short-period supply curve of the industry is the sum of all the firms' supply curves, since in the short period the firms in existence are taken as given. The price is determined at the point in which the industry supply curve cuts the demand curve facing that industry.

The long-period analysis is a little more complicated. Take the long-period equilibrium of the *firm* first. Once again, since the firm is a price taker and profit maximizer, it chooses to produce that quantity at which the long-period marginal cost equals the price, provided that the average cost is not higher than the price. But in the long period firms can enter into or exit from the market: if the price were higher than the long-period minimum average cost, then the incumbent firms would obtain a profit (that is, extra profit) and new firms would enter into that industry. Conversely, if the price were lower than the long-period minimum average cost, then the incumbent firms would obtain a loss and therefore would leave that industry. Hence, the only price which can be an equilibrium price for the firm is that which equals the long-period minimum average cost.

Turning to the long-period equilibrium of the *industry*, the picture is complicated by the fact that the industry in question may be a *variable cost industry*. That is, the long-period average cost of each firm may depend on the size of the industry itself. In fact, if the industry is a constant cost industry, then the long-period average cost curve of each firm is independent of the size of the industry and, as a consequence, the long-period equilibrium price cannot diverge from *the* minimum of the long-period average cost curve of each firm in the industry:[14] the long-period supply curve of the industry is a horizontal line and demand can only determine the quantity produced by the industry in a long-period equilibrium.

Conversely, if the industry is a variable cost industry, then the long-period average cost curve of each firm depends on the size of the industry and, as a consequence, for each quantity of product supplied by the industry there is a long-period average cost curve for each firm. All the average cost curves relative to the firms in an industry share the same

---

[14] All average cost curves relative to the firms in an industry have the same minimum since all the firms have access to the same processes. If a firm utilizes a resource not utilized by another firm, the rent paid for that resource must be such that the average cost curves relative to the two firms have the same minimum, otherwise all firms want either to utilize or to not utilize that resource.

minimum value, and such a minimum is the long-period equilibrium price for the firms within that industry supplying that quantity. At a higher quantity supplied by the industry, the long-period average cost curve of the firms in the industry will be higher or lower depending on whether the industry is an increasing or a decreasing cost industry. As a consequence, the long-period supply curve of the industry is an increasing or a decreasing schedule depending on whether the industry is an increasing or a decreasing cost industry. Both price and quantity produced by the industry in a long-period equilibrium are determined at the point in which the industry supply curve cuts the demand curve facing that industry.

In the mid 1920s Piero Sraffa (1925, 1926) criticized the analysis of variable cost industries within the framework of partial equilibrium. The main issue consists in the following: it cannot be excluded that a change in the quantity produced by a variable cost industry *at the same time* entails a change in the costs of firms in *other* industries as it entails a change in the costs of firms in the industry in which the change in the quantity produced took place. A typical example is that in which the same quality of land is used to produce two different commodities, say apples and pears. An increase in the production of apples, for example, may lead to a rise in the cost function of the producers of apples because of an increase in the rent paid for the use of land. But this rise in rent would likewise affect the cost function of the producers of pears. The changes in costs would be of the same order of magnitude in both industries, so that it would seem to be illegitimate to disregard the changes in the cost functions of firms outside the industry in which the quantity produced has changed (that is, pears), while taking into account the changes obtained in the cost functions of firms inside the industry only in which the variation in quantity took place (that is, apples).

When a change in the quantity produced by a variable cost industry does not entail a change in the costs of firms in other industries, the variable costs are *internal to the industry*. A typical example is that in which returns are decreasing because land is in short supply and each quality of land is specific to the production of one commodity only. If the (dis)economies responsible for variable costs are external to the firm and internal to the industry, variations in the quantity produced by one industry may affect the cost functions of the firms outside that industry only as a consequence of the change in the equilibrium price and quantity of the commodity produced by the industry in which the variation took place. As was mentioned above, this would be an effect of the second order of magnitude only, the presence of which, it could be contended, is compatible with using the *ceteris paribus* clause. (See also the recent exchange between Panico, 1991, and Samuelson, 1991.)

As is well known, in 1926 Sraffa suggested retaining partial equilibrium analysis. This was possible, however, at the cost of abandoning the concern with the free competition form of markets only: in order to be able to preserve the partial framework the analysis had to be limited to the study of economies internal to the firm. Sraffa's proposal was taken up by several authors and triggered a rich literature on market forms which bloomed during the 1930s. Yet this is not the only possible way of coping with Sraffa's critique of the Marshallian analysis. There is an alternative route that could be followed, which consists in retaining the concern with the free competition form of markets but abandoning partial analysis. This is the route followed by Sraffa (1960; see also Section 8 of Chapter 13).

The route taken by Sraffa does not preclude the preservation of several elements of the Marshallian analysis, provided these are modified appropriately, that is, adapted to the general framework of the analysis. This can be illustrated as follows. For example, assume single production and let $\mathbf{q}$ be the vector of quantities of commodities produced in the different industries. (If n is the number of commodities, then $\mathbf{q} \in \mathbb{R}^n$.) For a given $\mathbf{q}$ the processes available to firms are given irrespective of the question of returns with respect to industries, returns within firms being constant because of the assumption of free competition. The choice of technique analyzed in Chapter 5 of this book can be carried out so that a unique price vector $\mathbf{p}$ ($\mathbf{p} \in \mathbb{R}^n$) and a unique wage rate w can be determined for each given level of the rate of profit r once a numeraire has been specified (that is, the price vector and the wage rate associated with the cost-minimizing technique at the rate of profit r). Since this operation can be performed for any (feasible) vector $\mathbf{q}$, the analysis of Chapters 4 and 5 of this book will determine a function[15]

$$(\mathbf{p}, w) = G(\mathbf{q}, r), \tag{1.8}$$

where a vector of gross outputs $\mathbf{q}$ is feasible if there are techniques available that allow its production. If, following Marshall, we were prepared to introduce demand functions for all the n commodities, and if some regularity properties hold,[16] we could determine $\mathbf{p}, \mathbf{q}$, and w as functions of r. However, we most certainly cannot follow Marshall in determining the rate of profit in terms of the supply of and the demand for a factor

---

[15] This is so only if all commodities are produced. If only some commodities are produced the relationship between $(\mathbf{p}, w)$ and $(\mathbf{q}, r)$ is a correspondence (cf. Section 3 of Chapter 5).

[16] Let $\mathbf{q} = F(\mathbf{p}, w, r)$ designate the demand function, then we need that for each r the function $G(F(\mathbf{p}, w, r), r)$ has a unique fixed point in the $(\mathbf{p}, w)$ space.

called "capital" because of the results of the debate in the theory of capital dealt with in Chapter 14.

The procedure just sketched is of course little more than a hint that waits to be explored. Indeed, little is known about the form of function (1.8). What is clear, however, is that it depends on the kind of returns prevailing in the economy. Thus, with constant returns to scale throughout, function (1.8) is a constant function with respect to $\mathbf{q}$. In Chapter 10 the problem of the scarcity of natural resources, such as land, will be studied; hence in this case function (1.8) will reflect returns only insofar as they are connected with the presence of one or several natural resources in short supply. Further remarks on this problem will be provided in Section 5 of Chapter 10; a general analysis of function (1.8) is, however, beyond the scope of this book.

4. Preview of the argument and its premises

The argument in this book is developed for a closed economy (but see Section 6 of Chapter 5) characterized by conditions of production that are compatible with *free competition*, that is, economies of scale other than those that are external to the firm are precluded. It will be assumed throughout that commodities are produced by means of commodities and that there is a *production period* of uniform length; the production period is the time that elapses between the application of inputs and the availability of output(s), that is, time is considered a discrete variable.

The different steps of the following analysis are subject to different sets of assumptions. Whenever the economic system under consideration is assumed to be growing, it will be taken to grow along a *steady-state* growth path with all endogenous variables expanding according to a given and constant growth rate; this state of affairs is also known as a "quasi-stationary economic system." As was mentioned in Section 2 steady-state growth requires *constant returns to scale* throughout the economy. Otherwise the analysis of Chapters 2–9 is compatible with nonconstant returns to scale to the extent mentioned above.

With the exception of Chapter 11 it will be assumed that there is only *homogeneous labor*. Labor will be assumed to be the only visible primary input in production throughout Chapters 2–9. This does not mean, of course, that natural resources are taken to be entirely absent: it means only that they are assumed to be *nonscarce*. This assumption is removed in Chapter 10 with regard to *land*, and in Chapter 12 with regard to *exhaustible* and *renewable resources*. The introduction of exhaustible and renewable resources (plus some additional issues) poses problems which cannot adequately be tackled in terms of the long-period method that proves to be so powerful in dealing with the other problems studied in this book. This is so because in the presence of these types of resources it can no longer be presumed that the price of a commodity obtained as an output at the end of the production period is the same as the price of that commodity serving as an input at the beginning of the production period. Hence, the concept of *static* price systems has to be dispensed with in these cases.

Single production will be postulated in Chapters 2–6. Chapter 2 will be devoted to a *one*-commodity world, the discussion of which is motivated by the fact that several of the concepts developed in this framework, *but not all* the results derived, also apply, *cum grano salis*, to the more general models dealt with in the subsequent chapters. Chapter 3 discusses two-commodity models, whereas Chapter 4 is concerned with models with any number of commodities. In the latter case, other than in the one- and two-commodity cases, the problem of the choice of technique is dealt with in a separate chapter, Chapter 5. Chapter 6 provides alternative descriptions of a *technique*. Chapters 7–9 are dedicated to an investigation of systems with cases of *joint production*. The case of pure joint production is analyzed in Chapter 8, while Chapters 7 and 9 deal with *fixed capital* and *jointly utilized items of fixed capital*, respectively. Chapter 10 introduces the problem of scarcity in terms of a treatment of the classical case of *land*, that is, the case in which the services of indestructible means of production which are available in short supply are required in the production of some commodities. Chapter 11 addresses the problem of heterogeneous labor and Chapter 12 deals with some other cases which involve the scarcity of certain means of production.

So much for the assumptions regarding the conceptualization of production. As regards "demand" the following will be assumed. When each industry is a single-product industry, that is, in Chapters 2–6, the commodities required for consumption are taken to be known. In the simple fixed capital model of Chapter 7 we need to know which of the finished goods are consumed, while used machines are assumed not to be consumed. In the more general fixed capital model of Chapter 9 the assumption added is that investment is such that a uniform (and nonnegative) rate of growth obtains. The assumptions concerning "demand" are more difficult in the case of joint production and land, that is, in Chapters 8 and 10. It will be assumed that either the vector of net outputs, or the vector of consumption, or the consumption patterns of workers and capital owners are given. The growth rate will be assumed to be uniform and nonnegative in Chapter 8, whereas in Chapter 10 the economy will be taken to be stationary.

The most important proximate sources of inspiration for the present inquiry are the contributions to economic analysis by Piero Sraffa (1898–1983) and John von Neumann (1903–1957). While the former was explicitly concerned with reviving the "standpoint... of the classical economists from Adam Smith to Ricardo" (Sraffa, 1960, p. v), the latter can be said to have indirectly contributed to this task. This is the reason why an entire chapter, Chapter 13, is devoted to these authors and other major scholars contributing to the classical tradition.

Chapter 14 investigates the traditional, that is, long-run equilibrium, neoclassical analysis and shows, with reference to the controversy in the theory of capital, that the attempt to determine the distribution of income in a symmetrical way in terms of the supply and demand for factors or rather factor services is ill-conceived. The assumption of a given value or physical endowment of the economy with "capital," by means of which neoclassical authors try to close the system, turns out to be the "Achilles heel," so to speak, of the entire approach. Since the neoclassical procedure leads into a blind alley, in Chapter 15 alternative approaches to the determination of income distribution will be explored.

5. Historical notes

5.1. The importance of contributions to the development of classical Political Economy before Adam Smith lies more in the concepts and method put forward than in specific analytic propositions. The idea that it is possible and useful to distinguish the actual or market price that can be observed at a certain place and a certain time from some kind of ideal value or price can be traced back far into history. It played an important role in scholastic economic thought, which flourished during the Middle Ages. The "just price," the *justum pretium*, was that price which fulfilled some criteria of fairness in exchange. It was postulated more as a range of prices rather than as a fixed level. To some scholastic authors the just price had to cover necessary costs of production incurred by the producer plus his means of subsistence at a level considered adequate, given the producer's place in society.

The just price doctrine was anchored in the requirement of justice in exchange as set forth by Aristotle and in the principle of reciprocity: "do to others as you want them to do to you" (see, for example, de Roover, 1958, and, in particular, Langholm, 1992). It may even be conjectured that the definition of reciprocity in Aristotle foreshadows the idea of a competitive, that is, uniform, rate of return. In a famous passage from which the following sentence is taken, the ratio of the flow of output to the asset which generates that flow is equalized across sectors: "There will, then, be reciprocity when the terms have been equated so that as [the assets of the] farmer [are]...to [the assets of the] shoemaker, the amount [flow] of the shoemaker's work is to that [flow] of the farmer's work for which it exchanges" (Aristotle, Works, 1133, 5–30).

The idea of some kind of ideal prices, that is, prices fulfilling certain requirements or norms, kept fascinating intellectuals throughout the centuries. As we shall see in Chapter 13, it surfaced again, for example, in Robert Remak's concept of "superposed prices" (Remak, 1929). With his concept Remak intended to contribute to the debate about the feasibility of a socialist society, with a planned economy as its basis. The possibility of calculating a system of ideal prices which could serve as the basis for a rational allocation of resources was frequently seen to be a necessary prerequisite of the socialist alternative to capitalism. This explains the substantial effort made by some economists in the twenties and thirties to demonstrate that a rational calculation of costs and prices under socialism was possible. More recently, concepts of ideal prices are encountered in Luigi Pasinetti's "natural prices" (Pasinetti, 1981b) and in Francis Seton's "eigenprices" (Seton, 1992).

5.2. William Petty is the author of the famous dictum "that Labour is the Father and active principle of Wealth, as Lands are the Mother" (Petty, [1662] 1986, p. 68). Marx considered him the founder of classical Political Economy (cf. Marx, [1867] 1954, p. 85, fn. 2). As early as the *Treatise of Taxes and Contributions*, his first economic work, published in 1662, Petty put forward a clear notion of the social surplus. He expressed the agricultural surplus as corn output minus necessary corn input, including the necessary subsistence of laborers, and identified it with the rent of land. He wrote with regard to a single producer:

> Suppose a man could with his own hands plant a certain scope of Land with Corn, that is could Digg, or Plough, Harrow, Weed, Reap, Carry home, Thresh and Winnow so much as the Husbandry of this Land requires and had withal Seed wherewith to sowe the same. I say, that when this man hath subducted his seed out of the proceed of his Harvest, and also, what himself hath both eaten and given to others in exchange for Clothes, and other Natural necessaries: that the remainder of Corn is the natural and true Rent of the Land for that year: and the *medium* of seven years, or rather of so many years as make up the Cycle, within which Dearths and Plenties make their revolution doth give the ordinary Rent of the Land in Corn (Petty, [1662] 1986, p. 43).

Petty pointed out that given the means of subsistence per person, the surplus can also be expressed in terms of the extra number of people that could be maintained by a given number of laborers engaged in the production of necessaries given the socio-technical conditions of production, including the length of the working day. The difference between the total (adult) population of a country and that number of laborers is closely related to what Petty called the "Natural & Intrinsic strength of any Country" and of the "King's power," since it gives the number of those that "may be employed to luxury Ornament War Sciences, Superstitions & c" (cf. Matsukawa, 1977, pp. 45–7).

Petty regarded the cost of production of commodities as the main cause for determining their true or "natural value," which was seen to measure the difficulty of acquiring them. While the "natural value" expresses the "permanent Causes" governing the price of things, the "accidental value" also reflects the "contingent Causes" ruling in a particular situation (Petty, [1662] 1986, pp. 51 and 90). His main concern was, of course, with the "natural" magnitudes.

5.3. Richard Cantillon, who was greatly influenced by Petty's work, distinguished between market price and "intrinsic value" of a commodity. Of the latter he writes in his *Essai sur la nature du commerce en général*, published posthumously in 1755, that it "is the measure of the quantity of Land and of Labour entering into its production, having regard to the fertility or produce of the Land and to the quality of Labour" (Cantillon, 1755, p. 29; similarly p. 107). Market prices may deviate from natural prices or "intrinsic values" due to a mismatch of demand and actual production. This deviation is reflected in differences in entrepreneurial rates of return which will prompt producers to reallocate their capital. In this way market prices will tend to equality with "intrinsic values" which themselves are taken to be invariant (an idea which anticipates Adam Smith's idea of market prices oscillating around and gravitating toward natural prices):

> There is never a variation in intrinsic values, but the impossibility of proportioning the production of merchandise and produce in a State to their consumption causes a daily variation, and a perpetual ebb and flow in Market Prices. However, in well organised Societies the Market Prices of articles whose consumption is tolerably constant and uniform do not vary much from the intrinsic value (ibid., p. 31).

In Cantillon profits are clearly distinguished from wages; even the notion of a uniform rate of profit can be said to surface, albeit in embryonic form. According to Antoin Murphy (1986, pp. 252–3)

> it is quite clear in the *Essai* that he [Cantillon] considered intrinsic value to comprise the costs of the factors of production plus normal profit. As such it equates with the long-term equilibrium price determined in a competitive market. Cantillon recognized that if the market price was above or below intrinsic value, then

factor resources were directed into or out of the production of the commodity until the increased or reduced supply brought the market price into line with its intrinsic value.

5.4. The view that only agriculture can generate a surplus, a *produit net*, was most clearly expressed by Quesnay and his followers. It was around the concept of net product that Quesnay's entire economic analysis and not the *Tableau économique* alone was built: in particular, it was taken to hold the key to an explanation of the distribution of income in contemporary France. In the *Tableau* the first systematic expression of the concept of production as a circular flow is introduced: the production of commodities by means of commodities. While in the different versions of the *Tableau* Quesnay identified agricultural surplus with rent, in some of his other writings, most notably in his entries *Grains* and *Hommes* to the *Encyclopédie* (cf. INED, 1958, vol. 2, p. 475), he took into account that a part of the surplus goes to the farmers. The presence of profits, or rather gains, leads to the physiocratic notion of *bon prix*.

The physiocrats distinguished between fundamental price, *prix fondamental*, and market price. The former covers, first, total technical costs, at some normal level, incurred by the farmer in the production of one unit of corn, that is, wages, raw materials and the wear and tear of fixed capital; and, second, the rent the tenant has to pay to the landlord. Therefore, the fundamental price is seen to depend both on the technical conditions of production in farming and the rule which fixes that part of income, which is distributed in the form of rent. It may thus be considered a kind of "natural" price, referring to agricultural products and corresponding to zero profits. As Quesnay stressed in his contribution *Hommes* to the *Encyclopédie*, the fundamental price is the lowest price at which the producer can sell the commodity: it gives the minimum level of the market price (cf. ibid., p. 555). While the fundamental price is taken to change only slowly in correspondence to changes in normal cost of production or permanent changes in the terms at which land is leased, the market price may vary rapidly, expressing *inter alia* the influence of a variety of factors of a more or less short-lived nature.

The fundamental price does not include a pure profit of the farmer. In contradistinction to it the "good price," *bon prix* or *valeur vénale*, is that price which would obtain in conditions of free competition; it is assumed to exceed the fundamental price and thus yield to the farmer a profit (cf. ibid., p. 529). However, Quesnay did not provide an argument establishing a tendency of the actual price towards the good price. Hence in his doctrine, as in the doctrines of his close followers, profits do not constitute another necessary component of the price of commodities alongside the rent of land. On Quesnay's analysis see also Meek (1962), Cartelier (1976), and Vaggi (1987a, 1988); on the relationship between Quesnay's theory of price and the medieval doctrine of "just price," see Beer (1939).

5.5. Anne Robert Jacques Turgot assumed that the entire economic system is essentially organized in a capitalist way in his *Réflexions sur la formation et la distribution des richesses*, written in 1766 but not published till 1769–70 in serial form in the *Ephémérides*. This becomes clear in his description of the system's social stratification. He points out that "the Class of Cultivators, like that of Manufacturers, is divided into two orders of men, that of the Entrepreneurs or Capitalists who make all the advances, and that of the ordinary Workmen on wages" (Turgot, 1766a, p. 155). Turgot retained Quesnay's distinction between fundamental and market price, but redefined the former as cost of production including profits on the capital advanced. Hence prices of manufactures are *normally* taken to comprise a pure return on the entrepreneur's capital on the grounds that capital would otherwise be withdrawn from industry and employed in agriculture (cf. ibid., p. 154). From the latter observation it is of course only one step to the supposition that in competitive conditions there will be a tendency toward the equalization of the *rate* of profit across sectors (see also Meek, 1973, and Groenewegen, 1971, 1977). This step is indeed indicated by Turgot, who conceives of the emergence of a uniform rate of return as the outcome of the competitive process, with profit seeking entrepreneurs as the main actors:

> As soon as the profits resulting from an employment of money, whatever it may be, increase or diminish, capitals turn in that direction or withdraw from other employments, or withdraw and turn towards other employments, and this necessarily alters in each of these employments, the relation between the capital and the annual product (Turgot, 1766b, p. 87).

Closely connected with this is the tendency of market prices toward fundamental values. In his *Observations sur le mémoire de Saint Péravy*, published in 1767, Turgot stresses that while the fundamental value is fairly stable, the market price of a commodity is governed by "supply and demand" and liable to "very sudden fluctuations" though "not in any essential proportion to the fundamental value": the market price "has a tendency to approach it [the fundamental value] continually, and can never move far away from it permanently" (Turgot, 1767, p. 120, n. 16).

5.6. There has been some controversy whether Adam Smith or Turgot should be credited with the elaboration of an analysis of the emerging industrial capitalism (cf. Groenewegen, 1969). What is important is that there is evidence that Smith's theory of profit and normal values was already well on its way by the time of his Glasgow lectures in the academic year 1762–63 (see Smith, *LJ* (A), especially pp. 353–63). Therefore, it is doubtful that Turgot, as is customarily held, could have exerted a great influence on Smith concerning these matters during Smith's stay in Paris between the end of 1765 and October 1766. As Walsh and Gram note, "the major influence may have been the other way" (1980, p. 41).

5.7. The description of gravitation of market prices to natural prices given by Smith and those following him looks both simple and plausible. However, it cannot be considered a fully satisfactory treatment of the subject. There are particular difficulties the earlier authors were not aware of. For example, it cannot be presumed that a positive (negative) difference between market and natural price is equivalent to an above (below) normal rate of profit, since the positive (negative) difference between the respective prices of the inputs entering into the production of the commodity under consideration may be even larger (cf. Steedman, 1984b). The question close at hand is whether such a possibility does not prevent the ultimate tendency of the market price to gravitate toward the natural level, by causing the output of the commodity to decrease, thereby raising the market price even more. Garegnani (1990b) has put forward the following argument in support of "gravitation." Taking a system in which each commodity enters (directly or indirectly) into the production of all commodities, when a negative deviation of the market price of a particular commodity is accompanied by a positive deviation of the rate of profit, then the same opposition of signs cannot be true for at least one of the means of production that enter directly or indirectly into that commodity. For that means of production both the rate of profit and the market price deviation will have to be negative. Hence, the fall in its output will tend to raise its market price, leading directly or indirectly to a fall in the rate of profit of the commodity. This fall in the rate of profit will then reverse "the initial 'perverse' rise in output" (ibid, p. 331).

5.8. The abandonment of the classical approach and the development of a radically different theory was motivated by the deficiencies of the received cost or labor-based theories of value. The kind of arguments put forward against the classical approach can be exemplified in terms of some of William Stanley Jevons's criticisms leveled at the classical authors in his *Theory of Political Economy*, first published in 1871.

According to Jevons the basic framework of the classical approach to the theory of value and distribution was unsatisfactory because it started from the premise of given output levels. This is considered an inadmissible procedure. Hence, even taking the natural wage as given, which itself is regarded as being a problematic assumption, "the doctrine is radically fallacious; it involves the attempt to determine two unknown quantities from one equation" (Jevons, [1871] 1965, p. 258): profits *and* the level of output. In order to ascertain the output levels a theory of "demand" based on the concept of the "degree of utility," Jevons's terms for marginal utility, is required. The necessity of a theory of demand is best illustrated with regard to cases of joint production, which, in Jevons's opinion, "form the general rule, to which it is difficult to point out any clear or important exceptions" (ibid., p. 198). The classical economists are said to have turned a blind eye to joint production and therefore have failed to distinguish between commodities and "discommodities," that is, "substances or things which possess the quality of causing inconvenience or harm" (ibid., p. 58). This distinction presupposes the introduction of *utility–disutility* considerations into the analysis, which in the upshot will lead to a theory of "demand." (This judgement does not do justice to authors such as Smith or Marx, who were well aware of the empirical importance of joint production and who tried to deal with it analytically: see the historical notes in Chapter 8.)

5.9. For assessments of Walras's theory, see, in particular, Garegnani (1960, part II, chs. II and III, 1990a), Jaffé (1971), Morishima (1977), Walker (1983, 1987), Van Daal et al. (1985), Weintraub (1985) and Eatwell (1987). See also Chapter 14 below.

5.10. For a summary discussion of the non-substitution theorem, see Salvadori (1987d). For an assessment of the importance of the theorem within neoclassical analysis, see Garegnani (1987, pp. 563–4) and Kalmbach and Kurz (1986a, pp. 245–9). See also the historical notes in Chapters 5 and 7.

2

A one-commodity model

In this chapter the mathematical properties of a model in which only one commodity is produced by means of itself and homogeneous labor will be studied.[1] While this model is exceedingly simple from the mathematical point of view, it is difficult from the conceptual one. The economic system contemplated is a highly abstract one in which it is assumed that only one commodity is produced; it is assumed that this commodity is produced by means of itself and homogeneous labor. The only relative price dealt with is the real wage rate. This model is introduced for illustrative purposes only. However, several of the concepts developed in this chapter and some of the results derived carry over, with some modifications, to the more general models dealt with in the subsequent chapters.

The structure of the present chapter is as follows. In Section 1 the technical conditions of production are described and discussed. Section 2 introduces the concept of viability. Section 3 deals with growth and consumption opportunities, Section 4 with the distribution of the product between workers and capital owners. Two alternative views concerning the connection between the growth–consumption and the wages–profits aspects of the system under consideration are discussed in Section 5, in which saving and investment behavior is introduced. Section 6 is devoted to the problem of the choice of technique. Section 7 deals with alternative conceptualizations of the relationship between distribution and growth. Section 8 provides some historical notes, Section 9 contains some exercises.

---

[1] In this chapter as well as in Chapters 3 to 9 it will be assumed throughout that natural resources are non scarce. Therefore the problem of rent paid to the proprietors of these resources does not arise.

42

1. **Technology**

Consider an economy which produces only "corn." At the beginning of the production period, which is taken to be equal to a year, corn is sowed by laborers and at the end of the period the crop is harvested. Hence corn is the only produced means of production (seed-corn) and the only means of subsistence (food) to support the population. The production technique can be represented, in abstract terms, as follows:

$$a^* \text{ bushels of corn} \oplus l^* \text{ hours of labor} \to b^* \text{ bushels of corn.}$$

The symbol "$\to$" stands for the "black box" in which laborers working for l^* hours at a given intensity of work are transforming a^* bushels of corn into b^* bushels of corn during the yearly production cycle. The symbol "$\oplus$" in the present context indicates that both inputs, that is, corn and labor, are required to produce the given output of corn. The period of production separates the moment when the sowing starts from the moment when the harvesting is accomplished.

It is convenient to set b^* equal to unity. This can be done in two ways. The first consists in changing the physical unit in terms of which corn is measured from bushels to what may be called "b^*-units." We then have:

$$\frac{a^*}{b^*} b^*\text{-units of corn} \oplus l^* \text{ hours of labor} \to 1\ b^*\text{-unit of corn}$$

Obviously, the old and the new relationship describe exactly the same economy, even though they use different units of account. Moreover, no assumption about returns to scale is required in the switch from bushels to b^*-units.

The second possibility assumes constant returns to scale in the economy under consideration. With this assumption the production technique can be represented as:

$$\frac{a^*}{b^*} \text{ bu. of corn} \oplus \frac{l^*}{b^*} \text{ hours of labor} \to 1 \text{ bu. of corn}$$

While the first alternative has the advantage of not requiring any assumption about returns, it cannot be used if the quantities produced change. The second alternative, however, requires such an assumption, but allows variations in the quantity produced. In this book, constant returns to scale will be assumed whenever it is necessary for analytical convenience.

To simplify the notation, the two previous representations of the technology are rewritten in Table 2.1. In the following discussion the reader will adopt whichever interpretation is applicable to the particular

Table 2.1

inputs			outputs
corn	labor		corn
a	l	$\rightarrow$	1

case dealt with ($a = a^*/b^*$ in both cases; and $l = l^*$ in the first case or $l = l^*/b^*$ in the second).

In the present context, in which there is only one kind of capital good, corn, and only one kind of primary input in the production technique, homogeneous labor, the *capital intensity* or *capital-labor ratio* of the technology used can easily be ascertained: it is given by a/l. Similarly, the (net) *output-labor ratio*, or *labor productivity*, and the net *output-capital ratio* are given by $(1 - a)/l$ and $(1 - a)/a$, respectively.

2. Viability

An economy is said to be *viable* if the technology at its disposal allows it to reproduce itself (assuming labor to be available at no cost). Hence, the notion of viability used in the present book refers to the technical conditions of production only, whereas the provision of the means of subsistence needed in support of the population is not a part of it. Therefore, the viability of the system as it is defined here is a necessary but not sufficient condition of the survival of the economy. Keeping this in mind, an economy whose technology is described in Table 2.1 is viable if and only if

$$a \leqslant 1.$$

If $a = 1$, the economy is *just viable* since it can reproduce itself, but in order to do so the entire harvest has to be sowed. If $a < 1$, the economy produces a *surplus* over what is needed as seed-corn and the harvest can be divided in two parts: a and $(1 - a)$. The first part can be used for reproduction purposes, while the second may be devoted to other purposes.

3. Growth and consumption

The surplus can be used either for consumption or for accumulation. If the surplus or parts of it are saved and invested the economy will grow. Let g denote the growth rate and c the consumption per unit of labor employed, or, for short, *consumption per head* or *per capita*, then g and c must satisfy the following equation (assuming constant returns to scale):

$$(1 + g)a + cl = 1, \tag{2.1}$$

that is, one unit of output is used in part for consumption (*cl*), in part for reproduction (*a*), and in part for growth (*ga*). Equation (2.1) implies that

$$c = \frac{1 - (1 + g)a}{l}.$$

The *maximum growth rate*, G, is the growth rate corresponding to $c = 0$, that is, when the whole surplus is saved and invested:

$$G = \frac{1 - a}{a}.$$

Obviously, G equals the net output per unit of capital. The *maximum consumption per head* compatible with the given technological conditions, C, is the level of c corresponding to $g = 0$, that is, when the whole surplus is consumed:

$$C = \frac{1 - a}{l}.$$

Obviously, C equals the net output per unit of labor.

4. Wages and profits

The surplus is distributed to people as income. Assume that only two classes exist: workers and farmer-capitalists, receiving wages and profits, respectively. Let *w* denote the wage per hour in terms of corn, or, for short, the wage rate, and assume that wages are paid *post factum*, that is, at the end of the production period. Let *r* denote the rate of profit, or the proportion of profits to the capital advanced at the beginning of the production period, which in the present case consists of seed-corn only. With free competition among laborers there will be a tendency for wage rates to equalize throughout the economy. Moreover, since all farmer-capitalists are assumed to have access to the same technology, this implies that there will also be a tendency for the rates of profit to become uniform throughout the economy, that is, the establishment of a *general rate of profit*. On these premises w and r must satisfy the following equation (constant returns to scale need not be assumed):

$$(1 + r)a + wl = 1, \tag{2.2}$$

that is, one unit of gross output minus the capital used up (*a*) constitutes the net output $(1 - a)$, which is distributed as wages (*wl*), in proportion to labor, and as profits (*ra*), in proportion to the value of capital. Equation

(2.2) implies that

$$w = \frac{1 - (1 + r)a}{l}.$$

The wage rate (the rate of profit) depends both on the technical conditions of corn production, that is, a and l, and on the rate of profit (the wage rate).

The general concept underlying the present approach to the theory of income distribution is that of *normal* or *long-period positions* of the economy. These are conceived as centers around which the economy is assumed to gravitate, given the competitive tendency toward a uniform rate of profit and a uniform rate of remuneration for each particular kind of "primary" input in the production technique, such as homogeneous labor in the present case.

A comparison of equations (2.1) and (2.2) reveals immediately that the relationship between c and g on the one hand and the relationship between w and r on the other have exactly the same form. This fact is referred to in the literature as the *duality* of the two relationships. In particular, the *maximum rate of profit*, R, corresponding to $w = 0$, is equal to the maximum growth rate,

$$R = \frac{1 - a}{a},$$

and the *maximum wage rate*, W, corresponding to $r = 0$, is equal to the maximum level of consumption per head,

$$W = \frac{1 - a}{l}.$$

5. Saving and investment

In Section 3 the problem of consumption and growth was dealt with by treating consumption per head c or the growth rate g as given. Similarly, in Section 4 the problem of distributing the net product between wages and profits was dealt with by considering the wage rate w or, alternatively, the rate of profit r as exogenously determined. These two spheres, that is, what is known as the quantity system and the price and distribution system, respectively, are connected via the explicit introduction of some hypothesis concerning saving and investment behavior. This problem will be dealt with in some detail in Chapter 15. Here it suffices to illustrate the connection under discussion in terms of a simple example. The example chosen is rather prominent in the literature on growth and distribution, since according to the way in which it is interpreted, it is generally considered as conveying the essence of either the classical or the post-Keynesian economists' view on the matter. Assume for simplicity that workers do not save, whereas capitalists save a proportion s of profits, where $0 < s \leqslant 1$. The saving function can therefore be written

$$S = sP,$$

where S is total savings and P total profits. On the further assumption that total savings and total net investment are equal, we have

$$I = sP,$$

where I denotes investment, that is, in the present case, the amount of corn which will be added to the seed-corn advances at the beginning of the next production cycle to increase the overall level of production.

Dividing both sides of this equation by the capital (seed-corn) (K) advanced at the beginning of the current period gives

$$g = sr \tag{2.3}$$

or

$$r = \frac{g}{s}, \tag{2.3'}$$

where g is the rate of accumulation (I/K), which is equal to the rate of growth of output, under constant returns to scale, and r is the rate of profit (P/K). Accordingly, the rate of growth is proportional to the rate of profit, with s as the proportionality factor.

The condition that saving equals investment can have two interpretations. According to the *classical* approach to the theory of accumulation from Adam Smith to David Ricardo this condition is equivalent to what became known as "Say's Law", that is, the proposition that there cannot be a "general glut" of commodities. Since all savings are assumed to become investment, the negative impact of saving on aggregate demand is instantaneously and exactly offset by the positive impact of additional investment. The classical view can therefore be characterized as follows: given the rate of profit, which in turn is seen to depend on the historically and socially given wage rate, and the capitalists' propensity to save (and invest), the rate of accumulation is determined. A completely different point of view is taken by the *post-Keynesian* approach to the theory of growth and distribution advocated, among others, by Nicholas Kaldor and Joan Robinson. According to this approach it is investment which generates an equivalent amount of savings via changes in the distribution of income between wages and profits. The post-Keynesian view thus considers the

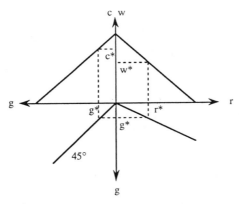

Figure 2.1

rate of profit as being determined by a given rate of growth of investment demand and given saving behavior.

Figure 2.1 illustrates the two views. According to the first interpretation it is the wage rate which is given at a level $w = w^*$, whereas according to the second interpretation it is the rate of accumulation which is given at the level $g = g^*$. From the w–r relationship (c–g relationship) depicted in quadrant I (II) we get the associated level of the rate of profit $r = r^*$ (consumption per head $c = c^*$), which, via the accumulation function (saving function) (2.3) depicted in quadrant IV, translates into a rate of growth $g = g^*$ (rate of profit $r = r^*$). In quadrant II (I) the c–g relationship (w–r relationship) is plotted, which gives the level of $c = c^*$ ($w = w^*$) relative to the growth rate (rate of profit). Other things being equal, a higher (lower) wage rate is associated with a lower (higher) rate of profit, a lower (higher) rate of accumulation and thus rate of growth, and a higher (lower) level of consumption per head. Similarly, a higher (lower) rate of accumulation is associated with a lower (higher) level of consumption per head, a higher (lower) rate of profit, and a lower (higher) wage rate.

6. Choice of technique

Up til now it has been assumed that only one technique to produce corn, denoted as (a, l), is known. We shall now relax this premise and assume that z different techniques, denoted as $(a_1, l_1), (a_2, l_2), \ldots, (a_z, l_z)$, are available from which the farmer-capitalists can choose. This is the problem of the choice of technique.

Let w^* and r^* be the ruling wage rate and rate of profit, respectively. If

$$(1 + r^*)a_j + w^*l_j < 1 \quad (\geqslant 1)$$

then technique (a_j, l_j) is (is not) able to pay extra profits at $w = w^*$ and $r = r^*$. On the contrary, if

$$(1 + r^*)a_j + w^* l_j > 1 \quad (\leqslant 1)$$

then technique (a_j, l_j) does (does not) incur extra costs at $w = w^*$ and $r = r^*$. If a technique is able to pay extra profits, then profit maximizing capitalists would operate it to obtain the extra income.

A *long-period position* is defined as a position such that nobody can get extra profits and the productive process can be performed; that is,

$$(1 + r^*)a_i + w^* l_i = 1 \quad \text{some } i \tag{2.4a}$$

$$(1 + r^*)a_j + w^* l_j \geqslant 1 \quad \text{each } j. \tag{2.4b}$$

Any technique which does not incur extra costs can be operated and at least one of them is; all the others cannot.

Obviously, the long period wage rate and rate of profit cannot both be given from outside. Let us assume therefore that the long period rate of profit r^* is given and let us determine the long period wage rate w^*. In order to do so let us define w_j as the wage rate which can be paid with technique (a_j, l_j) at the rate of profit r^*. Hence

$$(1 + r^*)a_j + w_j l_j = 1 \quad \text{each } j. \tag{2.5}$$

Then, we obtain from (2.4) and (2.5)

$$(1 + r^*)a_i + w^* l_i = (1 + r^*)a_i + w_i l_i \quad \text{some } i$$

$$(1 + r^*)a_j + w^* l_j \geqslant (1 + r^*)a_j + w_j l_j; \quad \text{each } j$$

that is,

$$w^* = w_i \quad \text{some } i$$

$$w^* \geqslant w_j \quad \text{each } j.$$

Therefore

$$w^* = \max\{w_j | j \in J\},$$

where J is the set of all existing techniques. Another way to look at the same problem is that

$$w^* = \min\{w \in \mathbb{R} | w \geqslant w_j, j \in J\}.$$

If, on the contrary, the long period wage rate w^* is given, the long period rate of profit r^* is determined in a similar way. In fact we define r_j as the rate of profit which can be paid with technique (a_j, l_j) at the wage rate w^* and we follow the same procedure as above in order to obtain

$$r^* = r_i \quad \text{some } i$$

$$r^* \geqslant r_j \quad \text{each } j.$$

Therefore

$$r^* = \max\{r_j | j \in J\},$$

or

$$r^* = \min\{r \in \mathbb{R} | r \geqslant r_j, \quad j \in J\}.$$

Thus, for a given wage rate (or, alternatively, a given rate of profit) the technique chosen in the long period coincides with the technique which yields the highest rate of profit (wage rate). Hence, if the (linear) $w-r$ relationships relative to all techniques available are drawn in the same diagram, the $w-r$ relationship relative to the whole economy is given by the outer envelope of all of them. The latter is known as the *wage–profit frontier*, or, for short, the *wage frontier*.

The wage–profit frontier $w = F(r)$ can be obtained either as a solution of a minimum problem,

$$F(r) = \min w$$

$$\text{s. to } w \geqslant \frac{1 - (1 + r)a_j}{l_j} \quad \text{all } j,$$

or as a maximum problem,

$$F(r) = \max w$$

$$\text{s. to } w \in W,$$

where

$$W = \left\{ w_j \in \mathbb{R} \,\middle|\, w_j = \frac{1 - (1 + r)a_j}{l_j}, \quad j \in J \right\}.$$

In the following chapters the first way to obtain the wage frontier will be called the *direct approach* and the second will be called the *indirect approach*. In Figure 2.2 it is assumed that there are four techniques: $z = 4$. Technique 3 is clearly inferior and will not be adopted irrespective of the level of the wage rate (rate of profit). The heavy line gives the relationship between the long-period levels of the wage rate in terms of corn and the rate of profit for the entire economy; it is constituted by the relevant segments of the $w-r$ relationships associated with techniques 1, 2, and 4, respectively. For example, with the rate of profit given at a level $r = r'$,

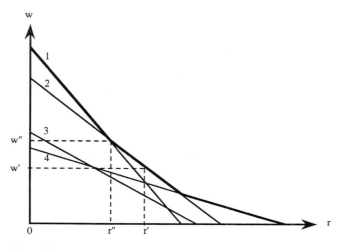

Figure 2.2

technique 2 will be chosen and the wage rate corresponding to this level of the rate of profit is $w = w'$. It is also possible that at a given wage rate (rate of profit) more than one technique is cost minimizing. This is, for example, the case at a level of the wage rate $w = w''$: at this level both techniques 1 and 2 are equiprofitable. The intersection of the w–r relationships associated with two techniques on the wage frontier is called a *switchpoint*.

7. Distribution and growth

In Section 5 it was argued that in steady-state analysis with planned investment equal to planned saving, the price and the quantity system are connected by the saving function. In this section we shall illustrate the involved relationship between income distribution and growth in the case in which there is a choice of technique in terms of a diagram which has the corn capital input per unit of labor employed, or capital intensity, k, on the abscissa and the net output per unit of labor employed, or (net) labor productivity, y, on the ordinate.

For technique i the two magnitudes are given by $y_i = (1 - a_i)/l_i$ and $k_i = a_i/l_i$, respectively, $i = 1, 2, \ldots, z$. In Figure 2.3, in correspondence with Figure 2.2, four techniques are depicted, that is, $z = 4$. In this type of diagram the pair (k_i, y_i) denotes technique i. The problem of the choice of technique can now be illustrated as follows. Given the real wage rate, w, from outside the system means fixing a value for w on the ordinate. Assume $w = w'$. Then we have, from the equation giving the rate of profit

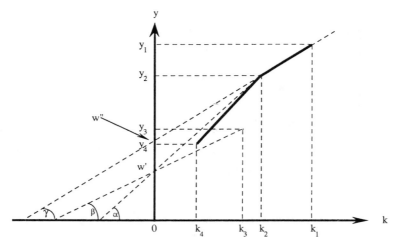

Figure 2.3

compatible with a given technique i at wage rate w',

$$r_i = \frac{y_i - w'}{k_i} \quad \text{all } i.$$

Thus, in Figure 2.3 the rate of profit associated with technique 2 is given by $\tan \alpha$, whereas the rate of profit associated with technique 3 is given by $\tan \beta$; the rates of profit associated with techniques 1 and 4 can easily be ascertained by the reader. Obviously, at the given wage rate $w = w'$, technique 2 yields the highest rate of profit, $r = r'$, and is thus the technique that minimizes costs: it defines the long-period position at the going wage rate w'. It cannot of course be ruled out that at a given level of the corn wage more than one technique satisfies the criterion of cost minimization. For example, in Figure 2.3 this is the case with a wage rate $w = w''$: both techniques 1 and 2 yield the same rate of profit, $r = r'' = \tan \gamma$, which is higher than the rates of profit attainable with any single other technique. Using the terminology introduced in Section 6, $w = w''$ represents a switchpoint wage rate at which the two techniques 1 and 2 are equiprofitable.[2]

With corn as the only capital good and the corn wage rate changing

---

[2] As the analysis in the preceding sections has made clear, the argument could also be carried out on the assumption that the rate of profit rather than the real wage rate is given from outside the system. Fixing the rate of profit means fixing the slope of the line intersecting the y-axis. Cost minimization then involves maximizing the real wage rate compatible with the technical alternatives, given r.

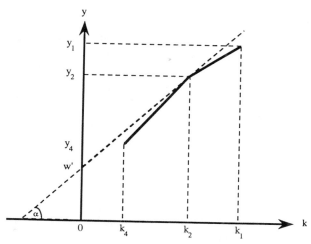

Figure 2.4

hypothetically from zero to its maximum value compatible with the given technical alternatives, the set of cost-minimizing techniques can be expressed in terms of a *per capita* corn "production function." It is given by the bold lines, made up of techniques 1, 2, and 4. (Technique 3 is inferior irrespective of the level of the real wage rate or, alternatively, of the level of the rate of profit.)

The graph of Figure 2.3 can now be used to illustrate anew the difference between the "classical" and the "post-Keynesian" approach to the theory of distribution and growth; this is done in Figure 2.4. To simplify matters, assume that all wages are consumed and capitalists save a portion s of their profits as in Section 5. In classical analysis the real wage rate is given from outside the system of production, say at $w = w'$. Cost minimization involves maximizing the rate of profit, that is, the slope of the straight line intersecting the y-axis at $y = w'$ and passing through a point defining a technique. In this way also the growth rate is maximized, since it is determined by equation (2.3); in Figure 2.4 $r = r' = \tan \alpha$. In contradistinction, in post-Keynesian analysis the rate of accumulation and growth is given exogenously, say at $g = g'$, whereas the rate of profit and the wage rate are determined endogenously: $r = r' \equiv g'/s$ (cf. equation (2.3')), and $w = w'$ is determined as in Figure 2.4 by the intersection with the y-axis of the highest straight line with slope $r' = \tan \alpha$ passing through a point defining a technique.[3]

---

[3] For a more general and detailed treatment of the difference between the two theories see Chapter 15.

8. Historical notes

8.1. One-commodity models of the kind presented in this chapter, or of a similar kind, abound in the economics literature. They are a familiar work horse in the macroeconomic theory of growth and distribution. However, in much of the literature it is assumed that the capital used in production is not circulating but fixed capital of an everlasting, that is, perennial, nature. (See Chapter 7 and especially Chapter 9.)

8.2. Newman (1962), in a review article on the first part of the book by Sraffa (1960), has utilized the idea of changing the physical unit in terms of which a commodity is measured such that the gross output of the commodity equals unity, while the scale of its production remains unaltered. This device was designed to shed light on Sraffa's claim that his argument does not rest "on a tacit assumption of constant returns in all industries" (Sraffa, 1960, p. v). (See also Subsection 8.3 of Chapter 13.)

8.3. In the above it has been assumed that wages are paid at the end of the production period, that is, *post factum* or *post numerandum*. The classical economists and Marx, however, reckoned wages as a part of total capital to be advanced at the beginning of the revolving (yearly) cycle of production. Accordingly, wages were taken to be paid *ante factum* or *ante numerandum*. For a justification of considering wages to be paid at the end of the period, see Sraffa (1960, pp. 9–10). (A further elaboration of Sraffa's treatment of wages will be provided in the historical notes to Chapter 3.)

Clearly, if wages were to be paid *ante factum*, equation (2.2) in Section 4 would have to be replaced by

$$(1 + r)(a + wl) = 1, \tag{2.2'}$$

and the equation giving the $w–r$ relationship would read:

$$w = \frac{1 - (1 + r)a}{(1 + r)l}.$$

Therefore, while with *post factum* payment of wages the $w–r$ relationship relative to a given technique is a straight line (see Figure 2.1), with *ante factum* payment it is an hyperbola which is convex to the origin with asymptotes at $r = -1$ and $w = -a/l$. A similar argument could be developed with regard to the $c–g$ relationship dealt with in Section 3.

8.4. The constraint binding changes in the distributive variables, in particular the real wage rate and the rate of profit, was discovered (though not consistently demonstrated) by Ricardo: "The greater the portion of the result of labour that is given to the labourer, the smaller must be the rate of profits, and vice versa" (Ricardo, *Works*, vol. VIII, p. 194). Similarly, Ricardo in his *Notes on Malthus* emphasized: "Mr. Malthus I believe would find it difficult to show that there can be any fall in the rate of profits unless there be a real rise in the value of labour when a larger proportion of the whole produce ... is devoted to the payment of wages" (*Works*, vol. II, pp. 61–2). Ricardo was thus able to dispel the idea, generated by Adam Smith's notion of price as a sum of wages and profits (and rents) (cf. *WN*, I.vi), that the wage rate and the rate of profit are determined independently of each other.

Since then the inverse relationship between the two distributive variables played an important role in long-period analysis of both classical and neoclassical descent. In more recent times it was referred to by Samuelson (1957), who later dubbed it "factor price frontier" (cf. Samuelson, 1962). Hicks (1965, p. 140, n. 1) objected that this term is unfortunate, since it is the earnings (quasi-rents) of the proprietors of capital goods rather than the rate of profit which are to be considered the "factor price" of capital (services). A comprehensive treatment of the problem under consideration within a classical framework of analysis was provided by Sraffa (1960); see also Pasinetti (1977), Lippi (1979), Mainwaring (1984), Goodwin and Punzo (1987), Woods (1990), Bidard (1991), and particularly Chapters 3 and 4 in this book. The relationship is also known as the "optimal transformation frontier" (Bruno, 1969) and the "efficiency frontier" (Hicks, 1973).

8.5. The duality of the w–r relationship and the c–g relationship in steady-state capital and growth theory has been demonstrated, among others, by Bruno (1969), Spaventa (1970), von Weizsäcker (1971), Hicks (1973), and in more general terms by Burmeister and Kuga (1970), Morishima (1971), Fujimoto (1975), and Craven (1979).

8.6. Historical notes on the post-Keynesian approach to the theory of distribution and growth will be provided in Chapter 15.

8.7. With a continuum of techniques available to produce corn, the production function need not, as in Figures 2.3 and 2.4, consist of a series of straight lines, but may be continuously differentiable (see exercises 9.4 and 9.5). The assumption that there is a continuously differentiable production function is prominent in the neoclassical literature on growth and distribution. See, for example, Solow's growth model (Solow, 1956), which centers around a function that is linear homogenous and can be written in terms of per capita output as a function of per capita capital.

Table 2.2

inputs			outputs
corn	labor		corn
$\frac{1}{2}$	1	$\rightarrow$	1
$\frac{1}{4}$	2	$\rightarrow$	1
$\frac{3}{8}$	$\frac{1}{9}$	$\rightarrow$	1
$\frac{1}{4}$	$\frac{1}{4}$	$\rightarrow$	1

9. Exercises

9.1. Determine the w–r relationships of the Table 2.2 techniques.

9.2. Determine the wage frontier relative to the set of techniques described in exercise 9.1.

9.3. Show that the choice of technique as analyzed in Section 6 does not depend on the assumption of a finite number of techniques. [*Hint*: Introduce a set of indices J; J may be countable or uncountable; then techniques can be denoted as (a_j, l_j) for $j \in J$. Then....]

9.4. (Calculus) Let $J = \{j \in \mathbb{R} \mid 4 \leqslant j \leqslant 5\}$ and let (a_j, l_j), $j \in J$, be techniques such that $a_j = j/10$ and $l_j = 1/10j$. Determine the wage frontier. [*Hint*: Use calculus and show first that if $0 \leqslant r \leqslant 0.25$, then $j = 10/(2(1+r))$, whereas if $0.25 \leqslant r \leqslant 1.50$, then $j = 4$. Then...]

9.5. (Calculus) Let $J = \{j \in \mathbb{R} \mid j > 0\}$ and let (a_j, l_j), $j \in J$, be techniques such that $a_j = j/10$ and $l_j = 1/10j$. Determine the wage frontier. [*Hint*: See the hint for the previous exercise.]

9.6. (Calculus) Calculate the y–k relationship analogous to that of Figure 2.3, that is, the per capita production function, relative to the previous two exercises.

9.7 (Calculus) Calculate the r–k relationship relative to exercises 9.4 and 9.5.

9.8. Show that if (a, l) is a technique producing a surplus ($a < 1$), then the amount of corn which needs to be sowed in order to obtain a surplus of exactly one unit of corn is $a/(1 - a)$. How much labor is employed?

9.9. As is well known, Adam Smith in the *The Wealth of Nations* distinguished between "productive" and "unproductive" labor. According to him, "some both of the gravest and most important, and some of the most frivolous professions" must be ranked among the latter: "churchmen, lawyers, physicians, men of letters of all kinds [including the authors of books on economics]; players, buffoons, musicians, opera-singers, opera-dancers, &c." (*WN*, II.iii.2). In the present exercise call the labor provided by workers directly engaged in the production of corn "productive" and the labor provided by all other workers "unproductive". Assume that each worker (productive or unproductive) consumes an amount b of corn and that $(a + bl) < 1$. Determine the maximum number of unproductive workers for each productive worker employed.

3

Two-commodity models

In this chapter, we will discuss models of economies in which it is assumed that two commodities are produced. The present chapter can thus be seen as an introduction to Chapters 4, 5, and 6 which deal with the general case of an economy producing n commodities.

A complete discussion of all possibilities of the two-sectoral case will be provided, subject to the following two assumptions: (i) the production of any commodity requires some material input(s); (ii) the two-commodity economy cannot be represented as if it consisted of two separate economies, each producing and using just one of the two commodities. The purely theoretical cases in which any of the two assumptions is violated are without any interest. A violation of assumption (i) would imply that some commodity is produced by labor only. If assumption (ii) were to be violated, this case could be interpreted as two economies which are technically completely disconnected. Most of the analysis in this book is carried out in terms of these two fundamental premises.[1]

In Section 1 a first simple case will be discussed, in which both corn and silk are produced by means of corn, while silk is not used as a means of production, hereafter called the corn–silk model. Section 2 will analyze a case in which both corn and iron are produced either directly or indirectly by means of corn and iron, that is, the roles of the two commodities in production are symmetrical (corn–iron model). Section 3 deals with the case, in which corn is used both in its own production and in the production of beans, whereas beans enter only into their own production (corn–beans model). Similar to the corn–silk model, the roles of the two commodities

---

[1] It should be noted that we have not yet introduced natural resources. When natural resources will be taken into account we will consider cases, in exercises 7.5 and 7.9 of Chapter 10, in which no commodity is required as an input.

Table 3.1

	inputs		outputs	
	corn	labor	corn	silk
corn process	a_c^* bu.	l_c^* hours →	b_c^* bu.	-
silk process	a_s^* bu.	l_s^* hours →	-	b_s^* sq. feet

in the corn–beans model are non symmetrical. This model raises some difficult problems which are further discussed in Section 6. In Section 4 it will be shown that the three cases under consideration cover all possible cases compatible with assumptions (i) and (ii). The discussion stresses the importance of the distinction between *basic* and *non-basic* commodities introduced in Section 2 of this chapter.

While in the initial sections it will be assumed that there is only one way to produce each of the two commodities, in Section 5 this assumption will be removed. The ensuing problem of the choice of technique will be discussed both for the case in which the two commodities are basic and the case in which one of them is non-basic. In this context the concept of a *cost-minimizing* technique will be introduced. Section 6 reconsiders the case in which the non-basic commodity enters into its own production. Section 7 traces the historical origins of the more important ideas and concepts dealt with in the chapter and relates the present discussion to recent contributions to the problems under consideration.

1. A first simple case

Consider a simple economy with only two commodities, corn and silk, both of which are produced by means of corn, whereas silk is not used as a means of production. Table 3.1 summarizes the technical features of the two production processes. Accordingly, b_c^* bushels of corn are produced by workers working for l_c^* hours and using up a_c^* bushels of corn; similarly, b_s^* square feet of silk are produced by workers working for l_s^* hours and using up a_s^* bushels of corn.

The gross quantities of the two products can again be set equal to unity. Thus in Table 3.2 a_s denotes either "b_c^*-units" of corn (and is equal to (a_s^*/b_c^*)), if we define b_c^* bushels as the new physical unit of corn, or the amount of corn in terms of bushels of corn needed to produce one square foot of silk (and is thus equal to (a_s^*/b_s^*), if returns to scale are constant. Similarly for a_c (which in both cases is equal to (a_c^*/b_c^*)), l_c and l_s ($l_j = l_j^*$ in the former case, and $l_j = (l_j^*/b_j^*)$ in the latter; $j = c, s$). In the following it will be assumed that $a_c a_s > 0$.

Table 3.2

	inputs			outputs	
	corn	labor		corn	silk
corn process	a_c bu.	l_c hours	→	1	-
silk process	a_s bu.	l_s hours	→	-	1

1.1. Viability

The economy is able to reproduce itself (assuming labor to be available at no cost), that is, it is *viable*, if and only if there are two real numbers Y_c and Y_s such that

$$Y_c \geqslant Y_c a_c + Y_s a_s, \qquad (3.1a)$$

$$Y_c \geqslant 0, \quad Y_s \geqslant 0, \quad Y_c + Y_s > 0. \qquad (3.1b)$$

Y_c and Y_s may be interpreted as (virtual) intensities of operation of the corn process and of the silk process, respectively. Since inequality (3.1a) implies that Y_c is positive if inequalities (3.1b) are satisfied, the inequalities (3.1) are equivalent to

$$Y_c \geqslant Y_c a_c + Y_s a_s,$$

$$Y_c > 0, \quad Y_s \geqslant 0.$$

That is, the economy is viable if and only if there is a real number Y_s/Y_c such that

$$1 \geqslant a_c + \frac{Y_s}{Y_c} a_s, \quad \frac{Y_s}{Y_c} \geqslant 0,$$

that is,

$$\frac{1 - a_c}{a_s} \geqslant \frac{Y_s}{Y_c} \geqslant 0.$$

Hence, the economy is viable if and only if

$$a_c \leqslant 1. \qquad (3.2)$$

Thus, the silk-process plays no role in assessing whether the economy is viable (if $a_c = 1$, then the economy is *just viable* and silk cannot be produced, that is, $Y_s = 0$).

1.2. Growth and the concept of sub-system

If the economy is able to produce a surplus and the whole surplus is invested, then silk is not produced and the maximum growth rate, G, is determined by the equation

$$a_c(1 + G) = 1.$$

If only a part of the surplus is invested, there is room for consumption. Let q_c and q_s be the amounts of corn and silk, respectively, which are consumed. Moreover, let Y_c and Y_s be the intensity of operation of the corn process and the silk process, respectively. Then the following equations need to be satisfied:

$$Y_c = (1 + g)(Y_c a_c + Y_s a_s) + q_c$$

$$Y_s = q_s.$$

We may distinguish between three cases according to whether only corn, only silk, or both commodities are consumed. In the following discussion we shall determine the quantities of the two commodities forming the gross product, that is, those quantities which go to replace the means of production and those which together form the surplus or net product of the system, given the rate of growth g. It should be noted that the respective quantity systems fulfilling these requirements are defined with respect to a given growth rate g, that is, the net product generally consists both of consumption and investment goods; these systems will be referred to as *sub-systems*.

The fictitious economy in which consumption consists of one unit of a commodity is the *sub-system* of that commodity. In the following discussion Y_c^c and Y_s^c (Y_c^s and Y_s^s) will denote the *gross products of corn and silk of the corn sub-system (silk sub-system)* at the given rate of growth g (subscripts refer to sectors, superscripts to sub-systems).

(i) If $g < G$ and consumption consists of one unit of corn, then the gross products of corn and silk, Y_c^c and Y_s^c, are determined by

$$Y_c^c a_c(1 + g) + 1 = Y_c^c$$

$$Y_s^c = 0,$$

that is,

$$Y_c^c = \frac{1}{1 - (1 + g)a_c}$$

$$Y_s^c = 0.$$

(ii) If $g < G$ and consumption consists of one unit of silk, then the gross products of corn and silk, Y_c^s and Y_s^s, are determined by

$$Y_c^s a_c (1 + g) + Y_s^s a_s (1 + g) = Y_c^s$$

$$Y_s^s = 1,$$

which implies

$$Y_c^s = \frac{(1 + g)a_s}{1 - (1 + g)a_c}$$

$$Y_s^s = 1.$$

(iii) If $g < G$ and consumption consists of q_c units of corn and q_s units of silk, then the gross product of corn is equal to $q_c Y_c^c + q_s Y_c^s$ and the gross product of silk is equal to $q_c Y_s^c + q_s Y_s^s = q_s$. Of course, Y_c^c and Y_c^s depend on g (which must be less than G).

Notice that whenever $g < G$, $q_c \geqslant 0$, $q_s \geqslant 0$, and $q_c + q_s > 0$ it is possible to calculate the gross quantities of corn and silk such that net consumption consists exactly of q_c units of corn and q_s units of silk.

1.3. Prices

Let p_s be the amount of corn which is exchanged for one unit of silk, that is, the price of silk in terms of corn. If the rate of profit, r, is assumed to be uniform, then the following equations must be satisfied (it is still assumed that wages are paid *post-factum* and that w is the wage in terms of corn):

$$1 = (1 + r)a_c + wl_c$$

$$p_s = (1 + r)a_s + wl_s,$$

or, rearranging,

$$w = \frac{1 - (1 + r)a_c}{l_c}$$

$$p_s = \frac{l_s + (1 + r)(a_s l_c - a_c l_s)}{l_c}.$$

The maximum rate of profit, R, which corresponds to $w = 0$, is determined by the corn process only, and is equal to the maximum growth rate:

$$R = \frac{1 - a_c}{a_c} = G.$$

The wage rate as a function of the rate of profit is also determined by the corn process only; but this is no longer true if the wage rate and prices are measured in terms of some combination of both goods.

Table 3.3

	material inputs			outputs	
	corn	iron	labor	corn	iron
corn process	a_{cc}^* bu.	a_{ci}^* lbs.	l_c^* hours $\rightarrow$	b_c^* bu.	-
iron process	a_{ic}^* bu.	a_{ii}^* lbs.	l_i^* hours $\rightarrow$	-	b_i^* lbs.

Table 3.4

	material inputs			outputs	
	corn	iron	labor	corn	iron
corn process	a_{cc}	a_{ci}	l_c $\rightarrow$	1	-
iron process	a_{ic}	a_{ii}	l_i $\rightarrow$	-	1

2. A model with two basic commodities

In the previous section, the roles of corn and of silk were not symmetrical: corn entered into the production of silk, but silk did not enter into the production of corn. In this section we will discuss a model in which the roles of the two commodities are symmetrical.

Suppose that corn and iron are produced as in Table 3.3. The quantities b_c^* and b_i^* will again be set equal to unity in Table 3.4, implying either a mere change in the physical units in which corn and iron are measured or constant returns to scale. Accordingly, a_{hk} ($h, k = c, i$) denotes either the b_k^*-units of commodity k necessary to produce one b_h^*-unit of commodity h (therefore $a_{hk} = (a_{hk}^*/b_k^*)$), or the quantity of commodity k necessary to produce one unit of commodity h, both measured in their original units, bushels and pounds, respectively (therefore $a_{hk} = (a_{hk}^*/b_h^*)$). Correspondingly, $l_k = l_k^*$ in the former case and $l_k = (l_k^*/b_k^*)$ in the latter.

2.1. Basic and non-basic commodities

A commodity h will be said to enter directly (indirectly) into the production of commodity k, if

$$a_{kh} > 0 \ (a_{kh} = 0 \text{ and } a_{kj}a_{jh} > 0),$$

where $h, k, j =$ corn, iron. A commodity h will be said to enter directly or indirectly into the production of commodity k, if

$$a_{kh} + a_{kc}a_{ch} + a_{ki}a_{ih} > 0.$$

A commodity which enters directly or indirectly into the production of all commodities is a *basic* commodity; otherwise it is a *non-basic* commodity.

In Section 1, silk was non-basic, whereas corn was basic. In this section it will be assumed that both corn and iron enter directly or indirectly into the production of both commodities, that is,

$$a_{cc} + a_{cc}^2 + a_{ci}a_{ic} > 0$$

$$a_{ic} + a_{ic}a_{cc} + a_{ii}a_{ic} > 0$$

$$a_{ci} + a_{cc}a_{ci} + a_{ci}a_{ii} > 0$$

$$a_{ii} + a_{ic}a_{ci} + a_{ii}^2 > 0.$$

Obviously, all the previous inequalities are satisfied if and only if

$$a_{ci}a_{ic} > 0. \tag{3.3}$$

2.2. Viability

An economy has been said to be viable if it is able to reproduce itself. In the present context this means that there are two real numbers Y_c and Y_i, such that

$$Y_c \geqslant Y_c a_{cc} + Y_i a_{ic}, \tag{3.4a}$$

$$Y_i \geqslant Y_c a_{ci} + Y_i a_{ii}, \tag{3.4b}$$

$$Y_c \geqslant 0, \quad Y_i \geqslant 0, \quad Y_c + Y_i > 0. \tag{3.4c}$$

Since inequality (3.3) holds, (3.4a) implies that if Y_i is positive then Y_c is positive, and (3.4b) implies that if Y_c is positive then Y_i is positive. Therefore if at least one of the Y's is positive, then both are. Hence, inequalities (3.4) are equivalent to

$$Y_c(1 - a_{cc}) \geqslant Y_i a_{ic}, \tag{3.5a}$$

$$Y_i(1 - a_{ii}) \geqslant Y_c a_{ci}, \tag{3.5b}$$

$$Y_c > 0, \quad Y_i > 0. \tag{3.5c}$$

From inequality (3.5a), taking account of inequalities (3.5c) and (3.3), one obtains that

$$1 - a_{cc} > 0 \tag{3.6a}$$

$$\frac{Y_c}{Y_i} \geqslant \frac{a_{ic}}{1 - a_{cc}}. \tag{3.6b}$$

Similarly, from (3.5b),

$$1 - a_{ii} > 0 \tag{3.6c}$$

$$\frac{1 - a_{ii}}{a_{ci}} \geqslant \frac{Y_c}{Y_i}. \tag{3.6d}$$

Therefore inequalities (3.4) are consistent if and only if (3.6a) and (3.6c) hold and there is a real number Y_c/Y_i such that

$$\frac{1 - a_{ii}}{a_{ci}} \geqslant \frac{Y_c}{Y_i} \geqslant \frac{a_{ic}}{1 - a_{cc}}.$$

Hence the economy is viable if and only if

$$1 - a_{cc} > 0$$

$$\frac{1 - a_{ii}}{a_{ci}} \geqslant \frac{a_{ic}}{1 - a_{cc}},$$

that is,

$$1 - a_{cc} > 0 \tag{3.7a}$$

$$(1 - a_{cc})(1 - a_{ii}) - a_{ci}a_{ic} \geqslant 0. \tag{3.7b}$$

Inequality (3.6c) is not mentioned since it is a consequence of inequalities (3.7). Inequalities (3.7) are the analog of inequality (3.2) of the corn–silk model analyzed in the previous section.

2.3. The maximum rate of profit

Let p_i be the price of one unit of iron in terms of corn. Then, if a uniform rate of profit is assumed, and if the wage rate is set equal to zero, the following equations hold:

$$(1 + R)a_{cc} + (1 + R)a_{ci}p_i = 1 \tag{3.8a}$$

$$(1 + R)a_{ic} + (1 + R)a_{ii}p_i = p_i, \tag{3.8b}$$

where R is the *maximum rate of profit*. Further on, in order to be sensible from an economic point of view, it is required that

$$p_i > 0, \quad R \geqslant 0. \tag{3.8c}$$

In this subsection it will be proved that system (3.8) has one and only one solution. To simplify the exposition, let us set

$$\lambda = \frac{1}{1 + R}. \tag{3.9}$$

Because of (3.9) system (3.8) can be rewritten as

$$a_{cc} + a_{ci}p_i = \lambda, \tag{3.10a}$$

$$a_{ic} + a_{ii}p_i = \lambda p_i, \tag{3.10b}$$

$$p_i > 0, \quad 0 < \lambda \leqslant 1. \tag{3.11}$$

System (3.10) is equivalent to the following system:

$$a_{ci}p_i^2 + (a_{cc} - a_{ii})p_i - a_{ic} = 0 \tag{3.12a}$$

$$\lambda = a_{cc} + a_{ci}p_i. \tag{3.12b}$$

The equation of the second order (3.12a) certainly has two distinct real solutions in that its discriminant is

$$(a_{cc} - a_{ii})^2 + 4a_{ci}a_{ic} > 0.$$

Moreover, since $a_{ci} > 0$ and $-a_{ic} < 0$, we obtain from Descartes's rule that equation (3.12a) has one positive and one negative solution.[2] Also, equation (3.12b) implies that the solution for λ associated with the positive p_i is positive and is larger than the other one. Hence system (3.10) has a single solution which satisfies the first two inequalities of (3.11).

---

[2] Descartes's rule connects the variations or permanences of the signs of the coefficients of algebraic equations to the signs of the solutions of the same equations. In the present context we are only interested in Descartes' rule concerning equations of the second degree. Let a second degree equation be expressed in its canonical form:

$$ax^2 + bx + c = 0.$$

With regard to coefficients a and b (b and c) call it a "variation" if $ab < 0$ ($bc < 0$) and a "permanence" if $ab > 0$ ($bc > 0$). Descartes's rule maintains that to each variation corresponds a positive solution and to each permanence a negative solution. Moreover, if a variation precedes a permanence (a permanence precedes a variation), then the solution with the largest absolute value is positive (negative). As is well known, the solutions to an equation of second degree expressed in its canonical form are given by

$$x_1 = \frac{-b - \sqrt{b^2 - 4ac}}{2a}, \quad x_2 = \frac{-b + \sqrt{b^2 - 4ac}}{2a}$$

and thus

$$x_1 + x_2 = -\frac{b}{a}, \quad x_1 x_2 = \frac{c}{a}.$$

If $ab < 0$ (a variation), then the sum of the solutions is positive, that is, the solution with the largest absolute value is positive. The reverse is true if $ab > 0$ (a permanence). In the case of two variations or two permanences $ac > 0$, which implies that $x_1 x_2 > 0$. Therefore, the solutions of the equation have the same sign. In the case of a variation and a permanence (independently of the order) $ac < 0$, $x_1 x_2 < 0$, and the solutions of the equation have opposite signs.

System (3.10) is also equivalent to the following system:

$$\lambda^2 - (a_{cc} + a_{ii})\lambda + (a_{cc}a_{ii} - a_{ci}a_{ic}) = 0 \qquad (3.13a)$$

$$p_i = \frac{\lambda - a_{cc}}{a_{ci}}. \qquad (3.13b)$$

The above argument proves that the solution to equation (3.13a) with the higher absolute value satisfies the first two inequalities of (3.11), whereas the other does not. In order to complete the proof of the existence of a unique solution to system (3.8) it has to be shown that the third inequality in (3.11), $\lambda \leqslant 1$, is also satisfied. In the following discussion we shall show that the economy is viable if and only if the solutions to equation (3.13a) are smaller than or equal to one: the economy is able to produce a surplus if these solutions are smaller than one, and it is just viable if of the two solutions the one with the higher absolute value is equal to one. To do this, let us put

$$\theta = 1 - \lambda \qquad (3.14)$$

and prove that $\theta \geqslant 0$. We obtain from equations (3.13a) and (3.14):

$$(1 - \theta)^2 - (a_{cc} + a_{ii})(1 - \theta) + (a_{cc}a_{ii} - a_{ci}a_{ic}) = 0,$$

that is,

$$\theta^2 - [2 - (a_{cc} + a_{ii})]\theta + [(1 - a_{cc})(1 - a_{ii}) - a_{ci}a_{ic}] = 0. \qquad (3.15)$$

Hence, if and only if the economy is able to produce a surplus, that is, if and only if both inequalities (3.7) are satisfied as strict inequalities, we obtain from Descartes's rule that both solutions to equations (3.15) are positive. As a consequence $\lambda < 1$ and $R > 0$ if and only if the economy is able to produce a surplus. If the economy is just viable, that is, if the weak inequality (3.7b) is satisfied as an equation, then either

$$\theta = 0, \quad \lambda = 1, \quad R = 0 \quad \text{and} \quad p_i = \frac{1 - a_{cc}}{a_{ci}};$$

or

$$\theta = 2 - (a_{cc} + a_{ii}), \quad \lambda = a_{cc} + a_{ii} - 1, \quad R = \frac{2 - (a_{cc} + a_{ii})}{(a_{cc} + a_{ii}) - 1},$$

and

$$p_i = \frac{a_{ii} - 1}{a_{ci}},$$

where $-1 \leqslant a_{cc} + a_{ii} - 1 < 1$. Only the first alternative has an economic rationale, since in the second p_i is negative. Thus, the maximum rate of profit is nonnegative, if and only if the economy is viable: $R > 0$ if and only if the economy is able to produce a surplus; $R = 0$ if and only if the economy is just viable.

2.4. Prices

Equations (3.8) determine the price of iron when $r = R$. With $r < R$, the following equations hold:

$$(1 + r)a_{cc} + (1 + r)a_{ci}p_i + wl_c = 1 \qquad (3.16a)$$

$$(1 + r)a_{ic} + (1 + r)a_{ii}p_i + wl_i = p_i, \qquad (3.16b)$$

where the wage rate, w, and the price of iron, p_i, are measured in terms of corn. For each given r such that $0 \leqslant r \leqslant R$, equations (3.16) constitute a linear system in p_i and w whose solution is

$$w = \frac{1 - (a_{cc} + a_{ii})(1 + r) + (a_{cc}a_{ii} - a_{ci}a_{ic})(1 + r)^2}{(1 + r)a_{ci}l_i + [1 - (1 + r)a_{ii}]l_c} \qquad (3.17a)$$

$$p_i = \frac{[1 - (1 + r)a_{cc}]l_i + (1 + r)a_{ic}l_c}{(1 + r)a_{ci}l_i + [1 - (1 + r)a_{ii}]l_c}. \qquad (3.17b)$$

Equation (3.17a) is known as the *w–r relationship*. From equations (3.8a) and (3.8b), and taking into account inequalities (3.3) and (3.8c), we obtain

$$1 - (1 + R)a_{cc} > 0$$

$$1 - (1 + R)a_{ii} > 0.$$

This is enough to prove that if $-1 \leqslant r \leqslant R, p_i$, as defined by equation (3.17b), and the denominator of the fraction in equation (3.17a) are positive. Moreover, since the equation (3.13a) has no solution greater than $1/(1 + R)$, then

$$\left(\frac{1}{1 + r}\right)^2 - (a_{cc} + a_{ii})\left(\frac{1}{1 + r}\right) + (a_{cc}a_{ii} - a_{ci}a_{ic}) > 0,$$

for $-1 < r < R$. Thus, $w > 0$ if $0 \leqslant r < R$ and $w = 0$ if $r = R$.

When there is a variation in the rate of profit r, the wage rate w also varies. Let us assume that r and w move in the same direction, for example, they increase simultaneously. Then equation (3.16a) requires that p_i falls, but equation (3.16b) rewritten as

$$\frac{1}{p_i}[(1 + r)a_{ic} + wl_i] = 1 - (1 + r)a_{ii}$$

requires that p_i rises. Hence we have a contradiction. Thus r and w cannot move in the same direction, that is, w is a decreasing function of the rate of profit.

2.5. Growth

When the economy produces a surplus, then the gross product exceeds what is necessary for simple reproduction, and there is room both for consumption and accumulation. Since constant returns are assumed when growth is considered, we have

$$(Y_c a_{cc} + Y_i a_{ic})(1 + g) + q_c = Y_c \tag{3.18a}$$

$$(Y_c a_{ci} + Y_i a_{ii})(1 + g) + q_i = Y_i, \tag{3.18b}$$

where g, q_c, and q_i are the rate of growth, the consumption of corn, and the consumption of iron, respectively. The maximum growth rate, G, is determined by the system

$$(Y_c a_{cc} + Y_i a_{ic})(1 + G) = Y_c, \tag{3.19a}$$

$$(Y_c a_{ci} + Y_i a_{ii})(1 + G) = Y_i, \tag{3.19b}$$

$$G \geqslant 0, \quad Y_c > 0, \quad Y_i > 0. \tag{3.19c}$$

Because of the second inequality in (3.19c), equations (3.19a) and (3.19b) can be rewritten as

$$(1 + G)a_{cc} + (1 + G)a_{ic} \frac{Y_i}{Y_c} = 1$$

$$(1 + G)a_{ci} + (1 + G)a_{ii} \frac{Y_i}{Y_c} = \frac{Y_i}{Y_c}.$$

This system looks similar to system (3.8) and is in fact identical to it up to a permutation of a_{ci} and a_{ic} and different symbols are used to identify the unknowns. We use this remarkable fact to avoid repeating the demonstration that there exists a unique nonnegative solution to system (3.19) and that $G = R$ (see exercise 8.5).

Let $0 < g < G$, and consider the two extreme cases concerning equations (3.18). In the first case $q_c = 1$ and $q_i = 0$, that is, only (one unit of) corn is consumed, while in the second case $q_c = 0$ and $q_i = 1$, that is, only (one unit of) iron is consumed. Let us call Y_c^c and Y_i^c (Y_c^i and Y_i^i) the solutions to equations (3.18) in the former (latter) case. We obtain that

$$Y_c^c = \frac{1 - (1 + g)a_{ii}}{\Delta(g)}$$

$$Y_i^c = \frac{(1 + g)a_{ci}}{\Delta(g)}$$

Table 3.5

	material inputs			outputs	
	corn	beans	labor	corn	beans
corn process	a_{cc}	0	l_c →	1	–
beans process	a_{bc}	a_{bb}	l_b →	–	1

$$Y^i_i = \frac{1 - (1 + g)a_{cc}}{\Delta(g)}$$

$$Y^i_c = \frac{(1 + g)a_{ic}}{\Delta(g)},$$

where

$$\Delta(g) = (a_{cc}a_{ii} - a_{ci}a_{ic})(1 + g)^2 - (a_{cc} + a_{ii})(1 + g) + 1.$$

Note that $\Delta(g) > 0$ if $0 \leqslant g < G$, and $\Delta(g) = 0$ if $g = G$. In the general case we obtain that the solutions to system (3.18) are

$$Y_c = q_c Y^c_c + q_i Y^i_c$$

$$Y_i = q_c Y^c_i + q_i Y^i_i.$$

It is remarkable that if $0 \leqslant g < G$, then whichever nonnegative values q_c and q_i assume, there always exists a nonnegative solution to system (3.18). Y^c_c and Y^c_i (Y^i_c and Y^i_i) are the gross products of the corn (iron) *sub-system*.

3. Non-basic commodities reconsidered

The previous section has dealt with a two-commodity model where both commodities were basic. Section 1 has dealt with a two-commodity model where corn was basic and silk was non-basic. A non-basic enters neither directly nor indirectly into the production of a basic commodity, otherwise it would be a basic. But a non-basic could enter either directly or indirectly into the production of a non-basic commodity. Silk, in the model in Section 1, did not enter into the production of any commodity. This section will introduce a two-commodity model where one commodity is basic and the other is non-basic but enters into the production of itself.

Let us suppose that corn and beans are produced as in Table 3.5, where units can be measured in their original units (bushels and pounds) or in b^*_j-units ($j = c, b$).

It is assumed that

$$a_{bb}a_{bc}a_{cc} > 0,$$

so that corn enters into the production of both corn and beans, but beans enter only into the production of themselves.

Following the procedure adopted in Subsection 1.1 of the present chapter, the reader can easily check that the economy is viable if and only if three exists a real number Y_b/Y_c such that

$$\frac{1 - a_{cc}}{a_{bc}} \geqslant \frac{Y_b}{Y_c} \geqslant 0,$$

$$\frac{Y_b}{Y_c}(1 - a_{bb}) \geqslant 0,$$

that is, if and only if

$$a_{cc} \leqslant 1.$$

We already encountered this condition in the corn–silk model. In order to determine the maximum growth rate G, consider the following system:

$$(Y_c a_{cc} + Y_b a_{bc})(1 + G) = Y_c, \tag{3.20a}$$

$$Y_b a_{bb}(1 + G) = Y_b, \tag{3.20b}$$

$$G \geqslant 0, \quad Y_c \geqslant 0, \quad Y_b \geqslant 0, \quad Y_c + Y_b > 0. \tag{3.20c}$$

If in equation (3.20a) Y_b is positive, then Y_c is positive. Hence, system (3.20) can be written as follows:

$$(1 + G)a_{cc} + (1 + G)a_{bc}\frac{Y_b}{Y_c} = 1, \tag{3.21a}$$

$$(1 + G)a_{bb}\frac{Y_b}{Y_c} = \frac{Y_b}{Y_c}, \tag{3.21b}$$

$$\frac{Y_b}{Y_c} \geqslant 0, \quad G \geqslant 0. \tag{3.21c}$$

If $Y_b/Y_c = 0$, then inequalities (3.21a) and (3.21b) are satisfied if and only if

$$G = \frac{1 - a_{cc}}{a_{cc}}.$$

If $Y_b/Y_c > 0$, then system (3.21) is satisfied if and only if

$$a_{bb} > a_{cc}$$

$$G = \frac{1 - a_{bb}}{a_{bb}}$$

$$\frac{Y_b}{Y_c} = \frac{a_{bb} - a_{cc}}{a_{bc}}.$$

Therefore, if $a_{bb} \leqslant a_{cc}$,

$$G = \frac{1 - a_{cc}}{a_{cc}},$$

and if $a_{bb} > a_{cc}$,

$$G = \max\left\{\frac{1 - a_{cc}}{a_{cc}}, \frac{1 - a_{bb}}{a_{bb}}\right\} = \frac{1 - a_{cc}}{a_{cc}}.$$

Thus, the maximum rate of growth G is still determined by the technical conditions to produce corn only.

The sectoral intensity levels of the corn and beans sub-systems are

$$Y_c^c = \frac{1}{1 - (1 + g)a_{cc}}$$

$$Y_b^c = 0$$

$$Y_c^b = \frac{(1 + g)a_{bc}}{[1 - (1 + g)a_{bb}][1 - (1 + g)a_{cc}]}$$

$$Y_b^b = \frac{1}{1 - (1 + g)a_{bb}}.$$

Thus, beans can be produced only if $g < G^*$, where

$$G^* = \min\left\{\frac{1 - a_{cc}}{a_{cc}}, \frac{1 - a_{bb}}{a_{bb}}\right\}.$$

Obviously $G^* \leqslant G$. If $G^* = G$, that is, $a_{bb} \leqslant a_{cc}$, no difficulty arises; but if $G^* < G$ and beans are requested for consumption, then the growth rate cannot be greater than or equal to $G^* < G$. A similar difficulty arises with respect to the price system. The reader can easily calculate that

$$w = \frac{1 - (1 + g)a_{cc}}{l_c}$$

$$p_b = \frac{[1 - (1 + r)a_{cc}]l_b + (1 + r)a_{bc}l_c}{[1 - (1 + r)a_{bb}]l_c}.$$

Hence, the maximum rate of profit, R, is still determined by the corn technology alone,

$$R = \frac{1 - a_{cc}}{a_{cc}} = G.$$

But if $a_{bb} > a_{cc}$, then the price of beans is not determined for $r = R^* \equiv G^*$ and is negative for $R^* < r \leqslant R$. Thus, if a non-basic enters into the production of itself, the nice results of Sections 1 and 2 do not need to hold unless one assumes that

$$a_{bb} < a_{cc}.$$

A possible solution to this problem will be presented in Section 6.

4. A complete taxonomy

To conclude the discussion so far we can now provide a complete taxonomy of possible cases in the two-sectoral framework. In the preceding sections, which dealt with the corn–silk, the corn–iron, and the corn–beans model, respectively, what was at issue was the question whether the respective coefficients were positive or nil. For the sake of simplifying the comparison of the different cases, we shall refer to commodities 1 and 2, respectively.

The technology of an economy can be fully described in terms of six coefficients: two coefficients refer to the direct labor input in the two sectors of the economy, four coefficients refer to the means of production used in each of the sectors. In the present context we are only interested in the technical coefficients relating to the means of production and whether they are positive or nil. Representing each technique in terms of a matrix the rows of which relate to the technical conditions of production in sector 1 and sector 2, respectively, we have

$$\begin{bmatrix} a_{11} & a_{12} \\ a_{21} & a_{22} \end{bmatrix}.$$

Since we are not interested in the magnitudes of the coefficients which are positive, we have only two kinds of entries: those relating to positive coefficients which are indicated by the sign "+", and those relating to coefficients which are nil indicated by the sign "0". The complete set of cases can be grouped as follows:

$$\begin{bmatrix} 0 & 0 \\ 0 & 0 \end{bmatrix} \tag{3.22a}$$

$$\begin{bmatrix} + & 0 \\ 0 & 0 \end{bmatrix}, \begin{bmatrix} 0 & + \\ 0 & 0 \end{bmatrix}, \begin{bmatrix} 0 & 0 \\ 0 & + \end{bmatrix}, \begin{bmatrix} 0 & 0 \\ + & 0 \end{bmatrix} \tag{3.22b}$$

$$\begin{bmatrix} + & + \\ 0 & 0 \end{bmatrix}, \begin{bmatrix} 0 & 0 \\ + & + \end{bmatrix}, \begin{bmatrix} + & 0 \\ 0 & + \end{bmatrix} \tag{3.22c}$$

$$\begin{bmatrix} + & 0 \\ + & 0 \end{bmatrix}, \begin{bmatrix} 0 & + \\ 0 & + \end{bmatrix} \tag{3.22d}$$

$$\begin{bmatrix} 0 & + \\ + & 0 \end{bmatrix} \tag{3.22e}$$

$$\begin{bmatrix} 0 & + \\ + & + \end{bmatrix}, \begin{bmatrix} + & + \\ + & 0 \end{bmatrix} \tag{3.22f}$$

$$\begin{bmatrix} + & 0 \\ + & + \end{bmatrix}, \begin{bmatrix} + & + \\ 0 & + \end{bmatrix} \tag{3.22g}$$

$$\begin{bmatrix} + & + \\ + & + \end{bmatrix}. \tag{3.22h}$$

Indeed, (3.22a) gives the case with no positive elements; (3.22b) all cases with a single positive element; (3.22c)–(3.22e) all cases with two positive elements; (3.22f)–(3.22g) all cases with three positive elements; and (3.22h) the case with only positive elements.

As was mentioned in the introductory passage to this chapter, our analysis is subject to two fundamental assumptions. These two assumptions imply that there is at least one basic commodity. Hence, cases (3.22a)–(3.22c) need not be considered. All the remaining cases have been investigated in terms of the models dealt with in Sections 1–3: (3.22d) is covered by the corn–silk model; (3.22g) is covered by the corn–beans model; all other cases fall under the corn–iron model.

5. Choice of technique

Up til now it has been assumed that there is only one way to produce each of the two commodities. In this section this assumption will be removed. In order to do so the following concepts are defined. A *method* or *process of production*, or, for short, a *process*, to produce commodity j ($j = 1, 2$) is defined as the triplet (a_{j1}, a_{j2}, l_j), where a_{ji} ($i = 1, 2$) gives the quantity of commodity i needed per unit of output of commodity j, and l_j gives the corresponding direct labor input.[3] The set of all available processes is sometimes called a *technology*.

In general not all available processes will actually be operated. If the processes actually operated match social requirements for consumption and investment, and if the prices and wage rate determined by these processes at a given, uniform rate of profit r are such that no producer can obtain a higher rate of profit by operating another process, then the economy will be said to be a *long-period position at rate of profit r*.

---

[3] In the previous sections of this chapter we could do without the definition of a process, since in each sector or industry there was only one process and reference to sectors was enough.

Obviously, a long-period position is a position of rest, given the data of the problem, including the level of the rate of profit. (It should be noted that instead of the rate of profit, the wage rate could be taken as given from outside the system. This would modify the above definition of a long-period position in an obvious way.)

5.1. The model with two basic commodities

Assume that there are u processes to produce corn and v processes to produce iron, where both u and v are finite numbers. These processes are referred to as

$$(a_{cc}^{(h)}, a_{ci}^{(h)}, l_c^{(h)}) \quad h = 1, 2, \ldots, u$$

$$(a_{ic}^{(k)}, a_{ii}^{(k)}, l_i^{(k)}) \quad k = 1, 2, \ldots, v.$$

In addition, assume that

$$a_{ci}^{(h)} > 0, \quad a_{ic}^{(k)} > 0 \quad \text{each } h, \text{ each } k. \tag{3.23}$$

Let w, r, and p_i denote the ruling wage rate, rate of profit, and iron price, respectively. Then, processes $(a_{cc}^{(h)}, a_{ci}^{(h)}, l_c^{(h)})$ and $(a_{ic}^{(k)}, a_{ii}^{(k)}, l_i^{(k)})$ are *(are not) able to pay extra profits* if

$$(1 + r)a_{cc}^{(h)} + (1 + r)a_{ci}^{(h)}p_i + wl_c^{(h)} < 1 \quad (\geq 1)$$

$$(1 + r)a_{ic}^{(k)} + (1 + r)a_{ii}^{(k)}p_i + wl_i^{(k)} < p_i \quad (\geq p_i),$$

and they *do (do not) incur extra costs* if

$$(1 + r)a_{cc}^{(h)} + (1 + r)a_{ci}^{(h)}p_i + wl_c^{(h)} > 1 \quad (\leq 1)$$

$$(1 + r)a_{ic}^{(k)} + (1 + r)a_{ii}^{(k)}p_i + wl_i^{(k)} > p_i \quad (\leq p_i),$$

respectively. If a process is able to pay extra profits, producers would seek to adopt the new process in order to obtain the extra profits, and if they succeeded in doing so, the resulting rate of profit in the particular industry would be higher than r. It should also be noticed that because of assumption (3.23) none of the two commodities can be produced without the other also being produced. Therefore, in a long-period position at least one process to produce each of the two commodities has to be operated. Hence, the pair (w, p_i) is a *long-period position at rate of profit r*, if the rate of profit r, the wage rate w, and the price of iron p_i are such that no process is able to pay extra profits and that there is at least one process producing corn and at least one process producing iron that do not require extra costs. Accordingly, (w, p_i) represents a long-period position at the rate of profit r if

$$(1 + r)a_{cc}^{(s)} + (1 + r)a_{ci}^{(s)}p_i + wl_c^{(s)} = 1 \quad \text{some } s \tag{3.24a}$$

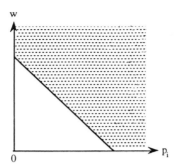

Figure 3.1

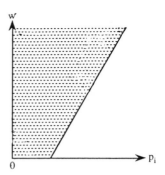

Figure 3.2

$$(1 + r)a_{ic}^{(t)} + (1 + r)a_{ii}^{(t)}p_i + wl_i^{(t)} = p_i \quad \text{some } t \qquad (3.24b)$$

$$(1 + r)a_{cc}^{(h)} + (1 + r)a_{ci}^{(h)}p_i + wl_c^{(h)} \geqslant 1 \quad \text{each } h \qquad (3.24c)$$

$$(1 + r)a_{ic}^{(k)} + (1 + r)a_{ii}^{(k)}p_i + wl_i^{(k)} \geqslant p_i \quad \text{each } k. \qquad (3.24d)$$

Processes $(a_{cc}^{(s)}, a_{ci}^{(s)}, l_c^{(s)})$ and $(a_{ic}^{(t)}, a_{ii}^{(t)}, l_i^{(t)})$ are operated, while processes which incur extra costs are not.

Let us now check whether system (3.24) allows for solutions. In order to do this, let us fix the rate of profit at $r = r^*$. Then each of the inequalities (3.24c) can be plotted in a (p_i, w) plane as in Figure 3.1. Processes for which $1 < (1 + r^*)a_{cc}$ can be left out of consideration. Similarly, each of the inequalities (3.24d) can be plotted as in Figure 3.2. Note that the decreasing straight line in Figure 3.1 cuts the vertical axis at a positive value, whereas the increasing straight line in Figure 3.2 cuts the vertical axis at a negative value. Figure 3.3 contains all inequalities (3.24c) and (3.24d) with $u = v = 3$. Obviously, a point in the diagram must be determined such that:

(a) it is an intersection between a decreasing and an increasing line (equations (3.24a) and (3.24b)), and
(b) it is not below any of the lines in the diagram.

Because of equation(s) (3.24a) and inequalities (3.24c), the long-period wage rate has to be located on the upper envelope of all the decreasing lines. Because of equation(s) (3.24b) and inequalities (3.24d), the long-period wage rate has to be located on the upper envelope of all the increasing lines. Therefore, on the assumption that at least one increasing line cuts a decreasing one in the positive quadrant, there is one and only one point satisfying (3.24). It coincides with the point with the highest w among those satisfying condition (a), and with the point with the lowest

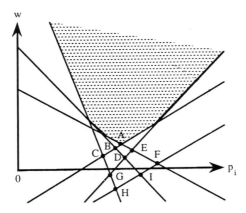

Figure 3.3

w among those satisfying condition (b). In Figure 3.3 the point under consideration is point A.

Obviously, a similar argument could be developed in the case in which the wage rate rather than the rate of profit is given from outside the system. It should be noted that in this case the no extra profits condition gives rise to lines which are not straight.

5.2. Another way to look at the same problem

Define a *technique* as a set of two processes consisting of one process producing corn and the other iron. In Figure 3.3 each point where a decreasing line intersects an increasing one represents the wage rate and the iron price of a technique when the rate of profit is r^*. Points A, B, C, D, E, F, refer to techniques which can sustain the rate of profit r^*, points G, H, I refer to techniques whose maximum rate of profit is lower than r^*. A technique is said to be *cost minimizing* at a rate of profit r^* if at the corresponding wage rate and iron price no known process is able to pay extra profits.

Figure 3.4 is useful to prove that for a given rate of profit the following propositions hold.

Proposition 3.1. If a process α is able to pay extra profits at the prices of technique β, then there is a technique γ which can pay a wage rate larger than that paid by technique β.

Proof. The wage rate and the price of iron associated with technique β are represented in Figure 3.4 by point A. Hence the relation between w and p_i relative to process α at $r = r^*$ intersects the line AD by hypothesis.

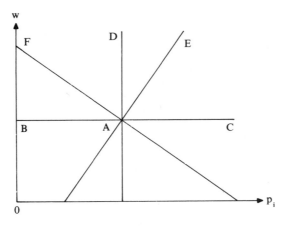

Figure 3.4

If this relation is a decreasing line (that is, process α produces corn), it will intersect line AE at a point above and to the right of A. If, on the contrary, this relation is an increasing line (i.e., process α produces iron), it will intersect line AF at a point above and to the left of A.   Q.E.D.

Proposition 3.1 is sufficient to sustain that each technique which at the given rate of profit r^* is able to pay the highest possible wage rate is cost-minimizing at that rate of profit. The following Proposition 3.2 precludes the case in which a technique which is not able to pay the highest possible wage rate can be a technique which minimizes costs.

Proposition 3.2. If technique α is able to pay a larger wage rate than technique β, then there is a process in technique α which is able to pay extra profits at the wage rate and iron price of technique β.

Proof. The wage rate and the iron price of technique β are represented in Figure 3.4 by point A. Hence, the wage rate and the iron price of technique α are represented by points which are either located in quadrant CAD or in quadrant BAD. In the first case, the process which produces corn if technique α is used will pay extra profits at prices relative to technique β. In the second case, the process which produces iron if technique α is used will pay extra profits at prices relative to technique β.
                                                                    Q.E.D.

Proposition 3.3. If both techniques α and β are cost-minimizing at the rate of profit r^*, then the iron price corresponding to $r = r^*$ is the same for both techniques.

Proof. The wage rate and the iron price of technique β are represented in Figure 3.4 by point A. Since both techniques α and β pay the same wage rate, the wage rate and the iron price of technique α are given either by point A, or by a point located on AC (excluding point A), or by a point located on AB (excluding point A). In the second case, the process which produces corn if technique α is used will pay extra profits at prices of technique β. In the third case, the process which produces iron if technique α is used will pay extra profits at prices of technique β. It follows that the wage rate and the iron price of technique α are of necessity given by point A. Q.E.D.

While Propositions 3.1–3.3 are important in themselves, they can also be utilized to prove the following theorem.

Theorem 3.1:

    (a) If there is a technique which has a positive p_i and a positive wage rate w for $r = r^*$, then there is a cost-minimizing technique at the rate of profit r^*.

    (b) A technique which yields a positive price p_i^* and a nonnegative wage rate w^* for $r = r^*$ minimizes costs at the rate of profit r^* if and only if no other technique allows a wage rate higher than w^* for $r = r^*$.

    (c) If there is more than one technique which minimizes costs at a rate of profit r^*, then these techniques yield the same wage rate and the same p_i^* at $r = r^*$.

Proof. The "only if" part of statement (b) is a direct consequence of Proposition 3.2. The "if" part is a consequence of Proposition 3.1. Statement (c) is equivalent to Proposition 3.3. Statement (a) is a direct consequence of statement (b) since the number of processes is finite.

Q.E.D.

Thus, if the w–r relationships relative to all techniques available are drawn in the same diagram (see Figure 3.5), the outer envelope represents the *wage–profit frontier* for the whole technology. The points on the wage–profit frontier at which two techniques are cost-minimizing are called *switch points*. If a technique is cost-minimizing at two disconnected ranges of the rate of profit and not so in between these ranges, we say that there is a *reswitching* of technique. Exercise 8.15 provides an example of reswitching, while exercises 8.16 and 8.17 contain some additional statements on the matter.

5.3. A model with a basic and a non-basic commodity

Consider the simple corn–silk model as it was analyzed in Section 1 of this chapter, with several processes to produce corn and several

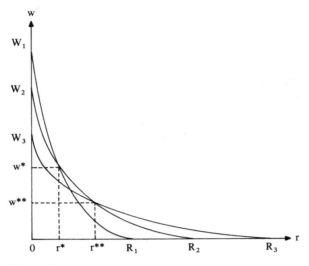

Figure 3.5

processes to produce silk. Moreover, assume

$$a_{cc}^{(h)} > 0, \quad a_{cs}^{(h)} = 0 \quad \text{each } h$$

$$a_{sc}^{(k)} > 0, \quad a_{ss}^{(k)} \geqslant 0 \quad \text{each } k.$$

Figure 3.6 is the analog of Figure 3.3 in this case: the horizontal lines refer to corn processes, the increasing lines refer to silk processes. The reader can easily check that in a long-period position

$$w = w^*.$$

If silk is produced in a long-period position, then

$$p_s = p_s^*.$$

The cost-minimizing technique can be determined in a two stages procedure. First, find the corn-process which is able to pay the largest wage rate, given the rate of profit. Second, find the silk process which, at the given rate of profit and wage rate, minimizes the price of silk.

Silk, by assumption, is a non-basic in each technique and therefore does not need to be produced if nobody wants it for consumption. Assume that silk is not consumed if its price is larger than or equal to $p_s^{**} < p_s^*$. Hence, any p_s, such that $p_s^{**} \leqslant p_s \leqslant p_s^*$, is a feasible silk price in a long-period position, since there is no need to produce silk and the operation of no silk process would yield extra profits.

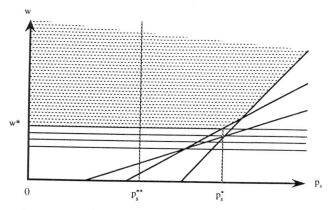

Figure 3.6

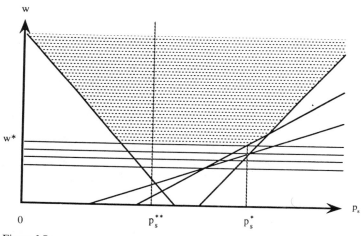

Figure 3.7a

Assume now that silk is basic in some technique, that is, there is a process producing corn by means of silk. Figures 3.7 reproduce Figure 3.6 when such a process is introduced. Figure 3.7a illustrates the case in which there is no change in the final result since the price of silk is too high to allow the new corn process to cover costs and yield a profit at the given rate. In the case illustrated in Figure 3.7b the range of feasible long-period levels of p_s is reduced since now $p_s^{***} \leqslant p_s \leqslant p_s^*$ must hold, because if $p_s^{**} < p_s < p_s^{***}$ the corn producing process utilizing silk is paying extra profits. Figure 3.7c illustrates the case in which silk must be

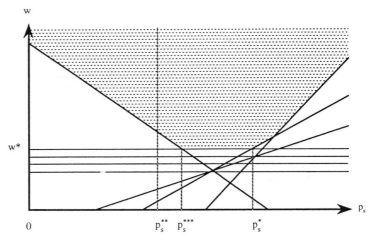

Figure 3.7b

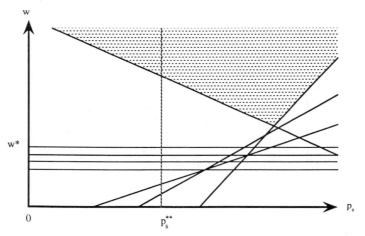

Figure 3.7c

produced because it is basic in the cost-minimizing technique, even though it is not consumed. Note that in the last case there is also an increase in the wage rate.

6. Self-reproducing non-basics reconsidered

In Section 3 some problems concerning self-reproducing non-basics were introduced. A problem which arises is the following: can a cost-minimizing technique exhibit the problems envisaged in that section? Consider first the case in which the non-basic is not required for consumption. A solution can possibly be obtained by changing the definition of a *technique* in order to allow for techniques made up of one process (producing the consumed commodity and *not utilizing* the non-consumed one as an input) and techniques made up of two processes (one producing the consumed commodity and *utilizing* the non-consumed one as an input, and one producing the non-consumed commodity). According to this definition of a technique a non-consumed commodity is contained in the description of a technique only if it is basic in that technique (in a two commodity world). In the more general case analyzed in Chapter 5, this is the solution explored in Subsection 3.3 of that chapter. This solution has many advantages, but it has the disadvantage that the price of the non-basic which is not consumed cannot be determined.

If one wishes to determine both prices one might take recourse to the following reasoning. In the case in which beans are not consumed, they do not need to be produced. This fact can be formalized in terms of an assumption concerning the free disposal of beans. Assume that for each process producing corn which does not utilize beans there is another process with the same output and the same inputs plus some beans included among its inputs. This second process would involve extra costs (extra profits) if the first process were utilized and the price of beans were positive (negative); furthermore, it will determine a zero price for beans when the two processes are in the same technique. Hence by taking all these processes into consideration the price of beans cannot be negative in a cost-minimizing technique. Figure 3.8a illustrates this point: the cost-minimizing technique is made up of two processes producing corn, one is the real process, which does not utilize beans, the other is a fictitious process utilizing some beans; only the first process is operated, whereas the second process contributes to determine a zero price for beans. Note that the technique made up of real processes would only determine a negative price for beans, p_b^*. In the more general case analyzed in Chapter 5, this solution is mentioned in Subsection 3.4 of that chapter.

If, on the contrary, beans are requested for consumption, they must be produced, but they cannot. The problem consists of the fact that if beans are produced their price, p_b, would have to be equal to p_b^*, which is negative. But then in a long-period position beans cannot be required for consumption. A simple solution is obtained if there is a p_b^{**} such that beans are not consumed if their price is larger than or equal to p_b^{**}. In fact, in this case any $p_b \geq p_b^{**}$ would be a feasible price in a long-period position. This solution is illustrated in Figure 3.8b.

Thus the problem envisaged in Section 3 is solved in the following cases.

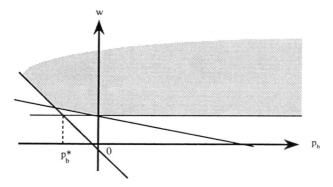

Figure 3.8a

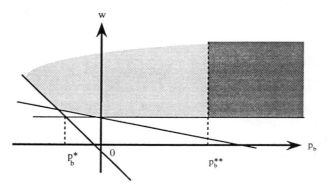

Figure 3.8b

If beans are not consumed, then either their price is ignored or the free disposal assumption implies a zero price anyway. If beans are consumed, then an assumption on consumption which asserts that at high prices beans are not consumed is enough to obtain a long-period solution. Further remarks on this problem will be made in Section 1 of Chapter 12 (see also the historical notes to this chapter and Section 4 of Chapter 5).

7. Historical notes

7.1. The assumption that the production of any commodity requires some material input is a common hypothesis in general equilibrium theory; in input–output analysis it assumes the character of an empirical fact. For a discussion of this assumption, which is also known as the "impossibility of the land of cockaigne," see, for example, Koopmans (1957, Subsection 3.5).

7.2. The concept of the *sub-system* has been introduced by Sraffa (1960, Appendix A); the concept of the vertically integrated industry developed by Pasinetti (1965, 1973) is closely related to it. The underlying idea is that the actual economic system can be envisaged as composed of a set of smaller self-reproducing systems, the net product of each of which consists of only a part of the net product of the system as a whole. According to Sraffa's definition, the net product of a sub-system consists of only one kind of commodity, whereas in the preceding discussion in Subsections 1.2 and 2.5 it was assumed that the net product consists both of the consumption good(s) and those quantities of the means of production needed directly and indirectly as (net) investment goods to allow the respective sub-system to grow at the given rate of growth.

Early forms of the concept of the sub-system or that of vertical integration can be found in the writings of the classical authors. For example, Ricardo in Chapter 31, "On Machinery", of his *Principles* refers to "a capitalist... [who] carries on the joint business of a farmer, and a manufacturer of necessaries" (*Works*, vol. I, p. 388). Each year the capitalist advances his capital consisting of fixed capital and "circulating capital in the support of labour", that is, food and necessaries. It is assumed "that the capitalist's capital is every year put into its original state of efficiency, and yields a profit" (op. cit. p. 388). In physical terms, the profit consists of the surplus product of food and necessaries. See also the historical notes of Chapter 6.

7.3. The distinction between basics and non-basics has been introduced by Sraffa (1960, § 6). According to him, in systems without a surplus "all commodities ranked equally, each of them being found both among the products and among the means of production; as a result each, directly or indirectly, entered the production of all the others.... But now there is room for a new class of 'luxury' products which are not used, whether as instruments of production or as articles of subsistence, in the production of others." Shortly after, Sraffa adds that the new class of luxury products extends "to such 'luxuries' as are merely used in their own reproduction" (ibid., pp. 7–8). The reference is to a system in which wages are regarded "as consisting of the necessary subsistence of the workers and thus entering the system on the same footing as the fuel of the engines or the feed for the cattle" (ibid., p. 9). In accordance with this assumption wages are taken to be paid *ante factum*, that is, at the beginning of the production period. Hence, as in the approach adopted by the classical economists the wages of labor are reckoned among the capital advanced at the beginning of the production period.

As is alluded to by Sraffa, in such a framework the distinction between basics and non-basics is closely related to the classical authors' distinction between "necessaries" and "luxuries." In Adam Smith's *The Wealth of Nations*, for example, we read: "Consumable commodities are either necessaries or luxuries. By necessaries I understand, not only the commodities which are indispensably necessary for the support of life, but whatever the custom of the country renders it indecent for creditable people, even of the lowest order, to be without.... Under necessaries therefore, I comprehend, not only those things which nature, but those things which the established rules of decency have rendered necessary to the lowest rank of people. All other things I call luxuries." Smith continues that, given real wages, "the [money] wages of labour are every where regulated ... by the average price of the necessary articles of subsistence; ... so that the labourer may still be able to purchase that quantity of those necessary articles" (Smith, *WN*, V.ii.k.3–4), which constitute his real wage bundle. Hence, while the classical concept of "necessaries" refers to necessary consumption goods only, which are almost identified with wage goods, Sraffa's concept of "basics," as it is used in §6 of his book, includes both the necessary subsistence goods of workers and all the different kinds of means of production needed directly and indirectly in the production of these goods. Basically the same distinction is to be found, for example, in the analyses of Dmitriev ([1898] 1974), von Bortkiewicz (1906–7, 1907), and von Charasoff (1910): von Charasoff actually uses the term "Grundprodukte" (basic products) for those products "which are indispensable in the production of all products" (see also Subsection 2.2 in Chapter 13).

In §§8–9 of his book Sraffa explains why he deems it convenient to abandon the classical economists' view of wages as a part of the yearly advances of capital, and assumes instead that wages are paid *post factum*. He points out that "the drawback of this course is that it involves relegating the necessaries of consumption to the limbo of non-basic products" (1960, p. 10). Accordingly, the distinction between basics and non-basics is now exclusively decided in terms of the technological features of the system of production under consideration, while the "established rules of decency" (Adam Smith) with respect to necessary consumption no longer play a role. See Roncaglia (1978, ch. 3) on this too.

7.4. The distinction between wage goods and luxury goods in classical economics is important in the context of ascertaining the determinants of the general rate of profit. The independence of the rate of profit from the conditions of production of luxury goods was emphasized by Ricardo. For example, in the chapter "On Foreign Trade" of the *Principles* he pointed out: "but if the commodities obtained at a cheaper rate, by the extension of foreign commerce, or by the improvement of machinery, be exclusively the commodities consumed by the rich, no alteration will take place in the rate of profits" (*Works* I, p. 132). This idea has been given a clear two-sectoral expression by Pasinetti (1960). As Pasinetti recalls in his paper, Sraffa had pointed out to him that the property of the independence of the rate of profit from the conditions of production of luxury goods "was first discovered by Ladislaus von Bortkiewicz" (ibid., p. 85, fn.); reference is to von Bortkiewicz (1907). Hence there is evidence that Sraffa was familiar with some of the writings of von Bortkiewicz. It should be added, though, that von Bortkiewicz elaborated on the formalization of the classical theory of value and distribution provided by Dmitriev ([1898] 1974) and openly recognized the latter's achievements, which include the statement of the property just referred to. See also Section 2 of Chapter 13.

7.5. In his Introduction to the first volume of Ricardo's *Collected Works* (cf. *Works* I, pp. xxxi-xxxii) Sraffa put forward an interpretation of Ricardo's early approach to the theory of the rate of profit which became known as the "corn-ratio" theory of profits or the "corn model." This interpretation was reiterated in Appendix D of his book, "References to the Literature" (Sraffa, 1960, p. 93). The starting point of this interpretation is the conclusion arrived at by Ricardo in his *Essay on the Influence of a low Price of Corn on the Profits of Stock*, published in 1815, that "it is the profits of the farmer that regulate the profits of all other trades" (*Works* IV, p. 23). According to Sraffa, the "rational foundation" of the "basic principle" of the determining role of the profits of agriculture was that "in agriculture the same commodity, namely corn, forms both the capital (conceived as composed of the subsistence necessary for workers) and the product; so that the determination of profit by the difference between total product and capital advanced, and also the determination of the ratio of this profit to the capital, is done directly between quantities of corn without any question of valuation." Sraffa added: "It follows that if there is to be a uniform rate of profit in all trades it is the exchangeable values of the products of *other* trades ... relatively to corn ... that must be adjusted so as to yield the same rate of profit as has been established in the growing of corn; since in the latter no value changes can alter the ratio of product to capital, both consisting of the same commodity" (Sraffa, 1951, p. xxxi; Sraffa's emphasis). In terms of the notions developed in his 1960 book, in the corn model "corn is the sole 'basic product' in the economy under consideration" (Sraffa, 1960, p. 93). In parentheses Sraffa added: "It should perhaps be stated that it was only when the Standard system and the distinction between basics and non-basics had emerged in the course of the present investigation that the above interpretation of Ricardo's theory suggested itself as a natural consequence" (ibid.).

Sraffa was careful to stress that this model was "never stated by Ricardo in any of his extant letters and papers." Yet although direct evidence is missing, Sraffa saw enough indirect evidence in support of the claim that Ricardo "must have formulated it either in his lost 'papers on the profits of Capital' of March 1814 or in conversation" (1951, p. xxxi). There are particularly two pieces of evidence referred to by Sraffa. The first is Malthus's objection to Ricardo that "we can never properly refer to a material rate of produce" in his letter of 5 August 1814 (cf. *Works* IV, p. 117), interpreted by Sraffa as "no doubt an echo of Ricardo's own [corn ratio] formulation". The second is the *Essay on Profits* in which Ricardo conducted his analysis on the assumption of given *corn* value inputs to agriculture even though conditions of production deteriorate as corn production is increased and less fertile plots of land are cultivated. Sraffa takes the analysis in the *Essay* to "reflect" the "corn ratio" argument, since "both capital and the 'neat produce' are expressed in corn, and thus the profit per cent is calculated without need to mention price" (Sraffa, 1951, p. xxxii), that is, he sees the numerical example in the *Essay* to refer to corn quantities. It is interesting to note that the "basic principle" which Sraffa ascribes to Ricardo was clearly spelled out by Robert Torrens (1820, p. 361) who called it a "general principle" and acknowledged his indebtedness to Ricardo's inquiry into the laws by which the rate of profit is determined; see also Section 1 of Chapter 13.

The "corn-ratio" interpretation has given rise to a debate that is still going on, in which Sraffa's qualifications added to his interpretation have not always been carefully taken into account. Contributions to the debate came from Hollander (1973a, 1975, 1979, 1982, 1983, 1986, 1993), Eatwell (1975), Roncaglia (1978, 1982), Faccarello (1982, 1983), Garegnani (1982, 1983a, 1984), Langer (1982), Bharadwaj (1983), Peach (1984, 1986, 1993), De Vivo (1985, 1986), Prendergast (1986a, 1986b), and Skourtos (1991). Peach (1993, ch. 2) has challenged Sraffa's interpretation of Ricardo's *Essay*. In his view the analysis in it "was in fact based on the corn valuation of *heterogeneous* inputs on the assumption that all prices remain constant: any 'reflection' of a 'corn model' analysis is wholly superficial" (ibid., p. 85). The "tacit assumption of *constant* prices" (ibid., p. 75) attributed to Ricardo by Peach would indeed seem to provide an alternative explanation to Sraffa's. However, by the time of the *Essay* Ricardo clearly saw that due to diminishing returns in agriculture the price of manufactures will fall relatively to corn, which squarely contradicts the assumption of constant prices. Hence, unless one is prepared to accuse Ricardo of having overlooked this when composing the *Essay*, which Peach is (ibid., p. 74), Sraffa's interpretation appears to hold the ground as the best available.

7.6. The problems arising due to the existence of self-reproducing non-basics ("beans" in Section 3) have been first discussed by Sraffa (1960, Appendix B). They have been the central issue of an exchange of letters between Sraffa and Peter Newman, published as an appendix to an article by Bharadwaj (1970); see also Newman (1962) and Zaghini (1967).

The solution suggested by Sraffa in Appendix B of his book reads as follows: "It is perhaps as well to be reminded here that we are all the time concerned merely with the implications of the assumption of a uniform price for all units of a commodity and a uniform rate of profits on all the means of production. In the case under consideration, if the rate of profits were at or above 10% [$= R^*$] it would be impossible for these conditions to be fulfilled. The 'beans' could however still be produced and marketed so as to show a normal profit if the producer sold them at a higher price than the one which, *in his book-keeping*, he attributes to them as means of production" (Sraffa, 1960, p. 91; emphasis added).

If it is assumed that *in his book-keeping* the beans producer refers to prices which are different from the prices in the market, then this argument seems unacceptable to us. In fact, beans producers would prefer to sell the whole harvest at the market to enter into another business, whereas nobody can enter into the beans industry because if somebody did, he would have to buy beans at the market price, that is, at a higher price than the one he could attribute to them as means of production.

Parrinello (1983) has interpreted the previous quotation by Sraffa in the sense that the price of beans at the time of the harvest is higher than the price of beans at the time of sowing. The short-period problem referred to in this interpretation is investigated in Section 1 of Chapter 12. The long-period consequence of this analysis is the solution suggested in Section 6.

7.7. The solution to the problem of the choice of technique developed in Subsection 5.1 can be connected with the von Neumann tradition; the solution developed in Subsection 5.2 is more closely related to the Sraffian tradition. Important contributions to the latter are collected in Steedman (1988a). Contributions to the former are reviewed by Morgenstern and Thompson (1976). (See also the historical notes of Chapters 5 and 8.) The possibility of reswitching of techniques played an important role in the capital controversies in the sixties and seventies; we shall come back to it in

Chapter 14. Here it suffices to draw attention to the fact that in the corn–silk model this possibility does not exist (see Morishima, 1966, 1969).

7.8. Conditions (3.7) as well as conditions (4.4) in Chapter 4 are also known as the Hawkins–Simon conditions; see Hawkins (1948) and Hawkins and Simon (1949).

8. Exercises

8.1. Show that in the two-commodity case commodity j is non-basic if and only if $a_{ij} = 0$ $(i \neq j)$.

8.2. Show that inequalities (3.7) imply inequality (3.6c).

8.3. An economy is said to be profitable if there are nonnegative prices (not both zero) that give rise to nonnegative profits on the assumption that labor is free. In the model of Section 2 the economy is profitable if and only if there exist prices p_c and p_i such that

$$p_c \geqslant a_{cc}p_c + a_{ci}p_i,$$
$$p_i \geqslant a_{ic}p_c + a_{ii}p_i,$$
$$p_c \geqslant 0, \quad p_i \geqslant 0, \quad p_c + p_i > 0.$$

Prove that the economy of Section 2 is profitable if and only if it is viable.

8.4. Prove that if the economy viable there is a solution to system (3.19). [*Hint*: Follow a procedure similar to that used in the text to show that there is a solution to system (3.8); set $\mu = (1/(1 + G))$.]

8.5. Prove that $G = R$, as asserted in Subsection 2.5. [*Hint*: Show that the second degree equation in μ obtained by exercise 8.4 is equivalent to equation (3.13a) in λ.]

8.6. Choose a process to produce corn and a process to produce iron from those given in Table 3.6. Determine the w–r relationship and the p_i–r relationship. Repeat the same exercise for each possible choice of processes.

8.7. Derive the w–r relationship if wages are paid *ante factum*. Is the p_i–r relationship changed because of this change in the assumptions?

8.8. Prove that the p_i–r relationship (3.17b) is increasing (decreasing) if and only if

$$\frac{a_{ic}l_c + a_{ii}l_i}{a_{cc}l_c + a_{ci}l_i} > \frac{l_i}{l_c}, \quad \left(\frac{a_{ic}l_c + a_{ii}l_i}{a_{cc}l_c + a_{ci}l_i} < \frac{l_i}{l_c}\right).$$

8.9. Prove that the w–r relationship (3.17a) is strictly concave (convex) to

Table 3.6

	material inputs		labor		outputs	
	corn	iron			corn	iron
(1)	0	$\frac{1}{2}$	1	$\rightarrow$	1	0
(2)	$\frac{1}{4}$	0	2	$\rightarrow$	0	1
(3)	$\frac{3}{8}$	$\frac{1}{9}$	1	$\rightarrow$	1	0
(4)	$\frac{1}{4}$	$\frac{1}{4}$	2	$\rightarrow$	0	1
(5)	0	$\frac{1}{4}$	$\frac{1}{4}$	$\rightarrow$	1	0
(6)	$\frac{1}{4}$	$\frac{3}{8}$	1	$\rightarrow$	1	0

the origin if and only if

$$\frac{a_{ic}l_c + a_{ii}l_i}{a_{cc}l_c + a_{ci}l_i} > \frac{l_i}{l_c}, \quad \left(\frac{a_{ic}l_c + a_{ii}l_i}{a_{cc}l_c + a_{ci}l_i} < \frac{l_i}{l_c}\right).$$

8.10. Give an economic interpretation of the case in which

$$\frac{a_{ic}l_c + a_{ii}l_i}{a_{cc}l_c + a_{ci}l_i} = \frac{l_i}{l_c}.$$

8.11. Throughout this chapter corn has always been the standard of value, that is, the numeraire. Show the effects of a different numeraire on the results of the previous two exercises. [*Hint:* Let p_c be the price of corn and add the equation

$$d_c p_c + d_i p_i = 1,$$

where d_c and d_i are arbitrary positive numbers; clearly, in this case the numeraire is assumed to consist of d_c units of corn and d_i units of iron.]

8.12. Take processes (1) and (2) from Table 3.6 and determine a special numeraire such that the w–r relationship is a straight line. [*Hint:* Solve first exercise 8.11.]

8.13. Is it in general possible to determine a special numeraire such that the w–r relationship is a straight line? [*Hint:* Solve first exercise 8.11.]

8.14. Determine the wage frontier for the technology given in Table 3.6.

8.15. (Garegnani, 1966) Let the technology be defined by the Table 3.7 processes. Show that processes (1) and (2) are operated if $0 \leqslant r \leqslant 0.1$ and $0.2 \leqslant r \leqslant R$, whereas processes (2) and (3) are operated if $0.1 \leqslant r \leqslant 0.2$, where $R \cong 0.378$.

Table 3.7

	material inputs			outputs	
	iron	corn	labor	iron	corn
(1)	-	$\frac{379}{423}$	$\frac{89}{10}$ →	1	—
(2)	$\frac{1}{2}$	$\frac{1}{10}$	$\frac{9}{50}$ →	—	1
(3)	$\frac{1}{4}$	$\frac{5}{12}$	$\frac{3}{2}$ →	—	1

Table 3.8

	material inputs			outputs	
	corn	iron	labor	corn	iron
(1)	—	$\frac{2}{5}$	$\frac{1}{2}$ →	1	—
(2)	—	$\frac{1}{5}$	$\frac{3}{5}$ →	1	—
(3)	$\frac{2}{5}$	—	$\frac{1}{2}$ →	—	1
(4)	$\frac{1}{10}$	—	$\frac{1}{10}$ →	—	1

8.16. (Woods, 1988) Let corn be the numeraire and assume that technique α has a convex $w–r$ relationship and that technique β has a concave $w–r$ relationship. Show that if they have a process in common, then they cannot have two switch points. [*Hint*: At switch points prices are equal; then utilize the results of exercises 8.8 and 8.9.]

8.17. (Bruno, Burmeister, and Sheshinksi, 1966) Let α and β be two techniques with one process in common. Show that the two techniques have not more than two switch points. [*Hint*: Let (3.17a) and (3.17b) be related to technique α; then at a switch point these functions have to satisfy also the process of technique β which is not in α: a second degree equation arises.]

8.18. (Fujimoto, 1983) Consider the Table 3.8 technology and assume that $r = 1$. Show that if only the first three processes are known, then the cost-minimizing technique consists of processes (2) and (3), whereas if all four processes are known, then the cost-minimizing technique consists of processes (1) and (4). Comment on these results.

8.19. Draw the analog of Figure 3.3 when the wage rate instead of the rate of profit is given. [*Hint*: Lines are not straight.]

8.20. As in exercise 9.9 of Chapter 2, call *productive* the labor provided by workers directly involved in the production of corn and *unproductive* the labor provided by all other workers. Assume that each worker (productive or unproductive) consumes an amount b_c of corn and an amount b_i of iron. Let $h_{st} = a_{st} + l_s b_t$ $(s, t = c, i)$ and assume that

$$1 - h_{cc} > 0$$
$$(1 - h_{cc})(1 - h_{ii}) - h_{ci} h_{ic} \geq 0.$$

Determine the maximum number of unproductive workers for each productive worker employed. [*Hint:* $Y_c, Y_i, g, q_c,$ and q_i of equations (3.18) must be such that

$$Y_c l_c + Y_i l_i = L$$
$$q_c = b_c (L + N)$$
$$q_i = b_i (L + N),$$

where L is the number of productive workers and N is the maximum number of unproductive workers.]

8.21. Discuss the inequality conditions mentioned in exercise 8.20.

4

Models with any number of commodities

In this chapter models with any number of commodities will be analyzed. Moreover, it will be assumed that there is the same number of processes as there are commodities and that each process produces only one of these commodities. This implies that both joint production and the problem of the choice of technique are set aside. Chapter 3 has shown the importance of the distinction between basic and non-basic commodities. These concepts have to be defined in the present context (see Subsection 1.1). The following discussion is subject to two premises:

(i) there is at least one basic commodity, and
(ii) labor is required directly or indirectly in the production of all commodities, that is, at least one basic commodity is produced by employing a positive amount of labor.[1]

The structure of the chapter is as follows. In Section 1 a model with only basic commodities will be investigated, while Section 2 will deal with models with both basic and non-basic commodities. Section 3 is dedicated to an analysis of the labor theory of value which figured prominently in early contributions to the theory of value and distribution. Section 4 will turn to a discussion of alternative standards of value or *numeraires*. Section 5 draws attention to earlier contributions to the theory of single production and Section 6 contains some exercises.

It should be mentioned that Chapter 6, which is concerned with providing alternative descriptions of a "technique," can be considered a

---

[1] This assumption is less restrictive than the assumption that labor enters directly into the production of each commodity. It allows for example the case of wine maturing in a cellar.

supplement to the present chapter. The discussion of the concept of the sub-system will be postponed until Chapter 6 in which a generalization will be provided.

1. A model with only basic commodities

Let the different commodities be $1, 2, \ldots, n$. Let $a_{ij}^*(i, j = 1, 2, \ldots, n)$ be the quantity of commodity j needed to produce the quantity b_{ii}^* of commodity i, $b_{ii}^* > 0$, and let l_i^* be the corresponding input of labor. If the a_{ij}^*'s and the l_i^*'s are assembled to constitute the square matrix $\mathbf{A}^*$ and the vector $\mathbf{l}^*$, respectively, and the b_{ii}^*'s are the diagonal elements of the diagonal matrix $\mathbf{B}^*$, then production can be represented as

$$\mathbf{A}^* \oplus \mathbf{l}^* \to \mathbf{B}^*.$$

As usual, it is convenient to set $b_{ii}^* = 1$, i.e. $\mathbf{B}^* = \mathbf{I}$:

$$\mathbf{A} \oplus \mathbf{l} \to \mathbf{I}.$$

As in the previous two chapters, this can be obtained either by assuming constant returns to scale:[2]

$$\mathbf{A} = \mathbf{B}^{*-1}\mathbf{A}^*, \quad \mathbf{l} = \mathbf{B}^{*-1}\mathbf{l}^*,$$

or by measuring commodities in b_{ii}^*-units:

$$\mathbf{A} = \mathbf{A}^*\mathbf{B}^{*-1}, \quad \mathbf{l}^* = \mathbf{l}.$$

1.1. Basic and non-basic commodities

We start from the following definitions. Commodity j enters *directly* into the production of commodity i if and only if

$$a_{ij} > 0.$$

Commodity j enters *indirectly* into the production of commodity i if and only if there is a sequence of z indices $i_1, i_2, \ldots, i_z$ $(z \geqslant 1)$ such that

$$a_{ii_1} a_{i_1 i_2} \cdots a_{i_z j} > 0,$$

that is, if and only if there is a natural number z such that

$$\mathbf{e}_i^T \mathbf{A}^{z+1} \mathbf{e}_j = \sum_{i_1 = 1}^{n} \sum_{i_2 = 1}^{n} \cdots \sum_{i_z = 1}^{n} a_{ii_1} a_{i_1 i_2} \cdots a_{i_z j} > 0,$$

---

[2] Note that matrices $\mathbf{B}^{*-1}\mathbf{A}^*$ and $\mathbf{A}^*\mathbf{B}^{*-1}$ are similar (see Subsection A.1.9 of the Mathematical Appendix).

where e_i and e_j are the ith and the jth unit vectors, respectively (see exercise 6.1). Since z can be reduced to $n-1$ at most (see exercise 6.1), we can assert that commodity j enters indirectly into the production of commodity i if and only if

$$e_i^T(A^2 + \cdots + A^n)e_j > 0,$$

(see exercise 6.1). Thus, commodity j enters *directly or indirectly* into the production of commodity i if and only if

$$e_i^T(A + A^2 + \cdots + A^n)e_j > 0.$$

A *basic commodity* (or, for short, a *basic*) is a commodity which enters directly or indirectly into the production of all commodities, that is, commodity j is basic if and only if

$$(A + A^2 + \cdots + A^n)e_j > 0.$$

A *non-basic commodity* (or, for short, a *non-basic*) is a commodity which is not basic.

Throughout Section 1 it will be assumed that all commodities are basic, that is,

$$A + A^2 + \cdots + A^n > 0. \tag{4.1}$$

Non-basic commodities will be considered in Section 2.

It is easily shown (exercise 6.2) that with more than one commodity inequality (4.1) holds if and only if matrix A is *indecomposable*, that is, if and only if it is not possible to interchange the rows and the corresponding columns of matrix A to reduce it to the form

$$A = \begin{bmatrix} A_{11} & 0 \\ A_{21} & A_{22} \end{bmatrix},$$

where A_{11} and A_{22} are square sub-matrices and 0 is a zero sub-matrix.

1.2. Viability

An economy has been said to be *viable* if it is able to reproduce itself (assuming labor to be available at no cost), that is, in the present context, if there is a vector x such that

$$x^T \geqq x^TA \tag{4.2a}$$

$$x \geqslant 0. \tag{4.2b}$$

In this subsection we want to determine some properties connected with viability. Since matrix A is indecomposable we can utilize the Perron–Frobenius Theorems for indecomposable nonnegative matrices (cf. Section

A.3.2 of the Mathematical Appendix). Let the economy be viable, then there are vectors **x** and **b** such that

$$\mathbf{x} \geqslant \mathbf{0}, \quad \mathbf{b} \geqslant \mathbf{0}, \quad \mathbf{x}^T(\mathbf{I} - \mathbf{A}) = \mathbf{b}^T. \tag{4.3}$$

If $\mathbf{b} = \mathbf{0}$ (that is, the economy is just viable) then Theorem A.3.6 ensures that the largest real eigenvalue of matrix **A** is equal to 1. If $\mathbf{b} \geqslant \mathbf{0}$ (that is, the economy is able to produce a surplus), let **a** be a nonnegative vector such that $\mathbf{x}^T\mathbf{a} = 1$. Thus, the equation in (4.3) is equivalent to

$$\mathbf{x}^T[\mathbf{I} - (\mathbf{A} + \mathbf{ab}^T)] = \mathbf{0}^T,$$

that is, the largest real eigenvalue of matrix $(\mathbf{A} + \mathbf{ab}^T) \geqslant \mathbf{A}$ is equal to 1 as a consequence of Theorem A.3.6. Thus, the largest real eigenvalue of matrix A is less than 1 because of statement (f) of Theorem A.3.5.

On the other hand, if the largest real eigenvalue of matrix **A** is not larger than 1 (equal to 1, less than 1), then the economy is viable (just viable, able to produce a surplus). In fact, let λ and **x** be the largest real eigenvalue and the associated left eigenvector respectively. Then

$$\lambda \mathbf{x}^T = \mathbf{x}^T \mathbf{A},$$

that is,

$$\mathbf{x}^T(\mathbf{I} - \mathbf{A}) = (1 - \lambda)\mathbf{x}^T,$$

which implies inequalities (4.2), since $\mathbf{x} > \mathbf{0}$.

Finally, Theorems A.3.4 and A.3.7 allow us to assert that an economy is viable (just viable, able to produce a surplus) if and only if

$$1 - a_{11} > 0 \tag{4.4.1}$$

$$\det\left(\begin{bmatrix} 1 - a_{11} & -a_{12} \\ -a_{21} & 1 - a_{22} \end{bmatrix}\right) > 0 \tag{4.4.2}$$

....

$$\det(\mathbf{I} - \mathbf{A}) \geqslant 0 \quad (\det(\mathbf{I} - \mathbf{A}) = 0, \quad \det(\mathbf{I} - \mathbf{A}) > 0). \tag{4.4.n}$$

Inequalities (4.4) constitute the generalization of inequalities (3.7).

1.3. The maximum rate of profit

Let **p** be the price vector of the economy when the standard of value is taken to be equal to a bundle of commodities constituted by d_1 units of commodity $1, d_2$ units of commodity $2,\ldots$, and d_n units of commodity n. If a uniform rate of profit is assumed, and if the wage rate is set equal to zero, then the following equations must be satisfied

$$(1 + R)\mathbf{Ap} = \mathbf{p} \tag{4.5a}$$

$$\mathbf{d}^T\mathbf{p} = 1, \tag{4.5b}$$

where $\mathbf{d}^T = (d_1, d_2, \ldots, d_n)$ and R is the maximum rate of profit. In order to be sensible from an economic point of view, it is also required that

$$\mathbf{p} \geqslant \mathbf{0} \tag{4.5c}$$

$$R \geqslant 0. \tag{4.5d}$$

Statements (a)–(c) of Theorems A.3.5 demonstrate that a solution to system (4.5a)–(4.5c) exists and is given by

$$\mathbf{p} = \bar{\mathbf{p}}$$

$$R = \frac{1-\lambda}{\lambda},$$

where λ is the largest real eigenvalue of matrix $\mathbf{A}$ and $\bar{\mathbf{p}}$ is the associated right eigenvector normalized in such a way that equation (4.5b) is satisfied. Moreover, Theorem A.3.6 guarantees that such a solution is unique. Finally, inequality (4.5d) holds if $\lambda \leqslant 1$, that is, if the economy is viable.

1.4. The price system

Equations (4.5) determine the price vector when $r = R$ and $w = 0$. When $-1 \leqslant r < R$, then

$$\mathbf{p} = (1 + r)\mathbf{Ap} + w\mathbf{l} \tag{4.6a}$$

$$\mathbf{d}^T\mathbf{p} = 1. \tag{4.6b}$$

Since $[\mathbf{I} - (1 + r)\mathbf{A}]^{-1} > \mathbf{0}$ because of statement (d) of Theorem A.3.2 and statement (e) of Theorem A.3.5, equation (4.6a) can be written

$$\mathbf{p} = w[\mathbf{I} - (1 + r)\mathbf{A}]^{-1}\mathbf{l}, \tag{4.7}$$

and, taking into account equation (4.6b), we get

$$w\mathbf{d}^T[\mathbf{I} - (1 + r)\mathbf{A}]^{-1}\mathbf{l} = 1,$$

that is,

$$w = \frac{1}{\mathbf{d}^T[\mathbf{I} - (1 + r)\mathbf{A}]^{-1}\mathbf{l}}. \tag{4.8a}$$

Equation (4.8a) gives the trade-off between the wage rate measured in terms of the commodity defining the standard of value and the rate of profit, known as the w–r relationship. Substituting (4.8a) in (4.7) gives

$$\mathbf{p} = \frac{1}{\mathbf{d}^T[\mathbf{I} - (1 + r)\mathbf{A}]^{-1}\mathbf{l}}[\mathbf{I} - (1 + r)\mathbf{A}]^{-1}\mathbf{l}. \tag{4.8b}$$

*1.5. Prices and the wage rate as differentiable functions
of the rate of profit*

Let $\dot{\mathbf{p}}$ and $\dot{w}$ denote the vector of derivatives of prices and the derivative of the wage rate with respect to r, respectively. Thus, equations (4.6) imply that

$$\dot{\mathbf{p}} = \mathbf{Ap} + (1 + r)\mathbf{A}\dot{\mathbf{p}} + \dot{w}\mathbf{l} \tag{4.9a}$$

$$\mathbf{d}^T\dot{\mathbf{p}} = 0. \tag{4.9b}$$

This subsection is devoted to the determination of $\dot{\mathbf{p}}$ and $\dot{w}$. We need to distinguish between two cases: (i) $-1 \leqslant r < R$ and (ii) $r = R$.

Case (i): In this case equation (4.9a) implies

$$\dot{\mathbf{p}} = [\mathbf{I} - (1 + r)\mathbf{A}]^{-1}[\dot{w}\mathbf{l} + \mathbf{Ap}], \tag{4.10}$$

and as a consequence of equations (4.9b)

$$\mathbf{d}^T[\mathbf{I} - (1 + r)\mathbf{A}]^{-1}[\dot{w}\mathbf{l} + \mathbf{Ap}] = 0,$$

that is,

$$\dot{w} = -\frac{\mathbf{d}^T[\mathbf{I} - (1 + r)\mathbf{A}]^{-1}\mathbf{Ap}}{\mathbf{d}^T[\mathbf{I} - (1 + r)\mathbf{A}]^{-1}\mathbf{l}} \, (<0). \tag{4.11a}$$

From equations (4.10) and (4.11a) it follows that

$$\dot{\mathbf{p}} = [\mathbf{I} - (1 + r)\mathbf{A}]^{-1}$$
$$\times \left\{ \mathbf{Ap} - \frac{1}{\mathbf{d}^T[\mathbf{I} - (1 + r)\mathbf{A}]^{-1}\mathbf{l}} \mathbf{l}\mathbf{d}^T[\mathbf{I} - (1 + r)\mathbf{A}]^{-1}\mathbf{Ap} \right\},$$

that is, because equation (4.8b) holds,

$$\dot{\mathbf{p}} = (\mathbf{I} - \mathbf{pd}^T)[\mathbf{I} - (1 + r)\mathbf{A}]^{-1}\mathbf{Ap}. \tag{4.11b}$$

Case (ii): In this case equation (4.9a) can be rewritten as:

$$[\mathbf{I} - (1 + R)\mathbf{A}]\dot{\mathbf{p}} = \mathbf{Ap} + \dot{w}\mathbf{l}. \tag{4.12}$$

Let $\mathbf{x}$ be the left eigenvector of matrix $\mathbf{A}$ associated to the eigenvalue $1/(1 + R)$ normalized in such a way that $\mathbf{x}^T\mathbf{l} = 1$. Equation (4.12) has solutions if and only if

$$\dot{w} = -\mathbf{x}^T\mathbf{Ap} \, (<0) \tag{4.13a}$$

because of the Fredholm Alternative (Theorem A.2.1). Let $\mathbf{p}^*$ be one of those solutions, then all solutions are given by

$$\mathbf{p}^* + \theta\mathbf{p},$$

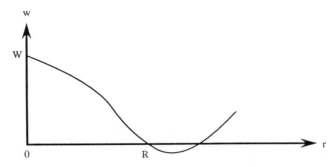

Figure 4.1

where θ is any real number, since $\mathbf{p}$ is such that

$$[\mathbf{I} - (1 + R)\mathbf{A}]\mathbf{p} = \mathbf{0}.$$

Since equation (4.9b) holds, θ must satisfy the equation

$$\mathbf{d}^T[\mathbf{p}^* + \theta\mathbf{p}] = \mathbf{0},$$

that is,

$$\theta = -\mathbf{d}^T\mathbf{p}^*.$$

Hence,

$$\dot{\mathbf{p}} = \mathbf{p}^* - \mathbf{p}\mathbf{d}^T\mathbf{p}^* = (\mathbf{I} - \mathbf{p}\mathbf{d}^T)\mathbf{p}^*. \qquad (4.13b)$$

It is worth pointing out that $\dot{w} < 0$ irrespective of the numeraire chosen.

1.6. The wage rate as the independent variable

In Subsections 1.3–1.5 the price system was analyzed on the assumption that $0 \leqslant r \leqslant R$. In this subsection we shall consider the wage rate as the independent variable. This completes the analysis of the dependency of prices on distribution also in another respect. This is best illustrated in terms of Figure 4.1. From the previous analysis we know that the w–r relationship is decreasing in the range $0 \leqslant r \leqslant R$. Yet it may be increasing for some $r > R$. As a consequence for some scalar $w \geqslant 0$ there may exist a scalar $r > R$ such that equations (4.6) have a solution (see exercise 6.6). However, it will be shown that in the latter case at least one price has to be negative if $0 \leqslant w \leqslant W \equiv 1/(\mathbf{d}^T(\mathbf{I} - \mathbf{A})^{-1}\mathbf{l})$ (see also exercise 6.10).

Because of equation (4.6b), equation (4.6a) can be written as

$$\mathbf{p} = (1 + r)\mathbf{A}\mathbf{p} + w\mathbf{l}\mathbf{d}^T\mathbf{p},$$

that is,

$$(\mathbf{I} - w\mathbf{l}\mathbf{d}^T)\mathbf{p} = (1 + r)\mathbf{A}\mathbf{p}.$$

Since (cf. exercise 6.7)

$$(\mathbf{I} - w\mathbf{l}\mathbf{d}^T)^{-1} = \mathbf{I} + \frac{w}{1 - w\mathbf{d}^T\mathbf{l}}\mathbf{l}\mathbf{d}^T, \tag{4.14}$$

if $w \leqslant W(< 1/\mathbf{d}^T\mathbf{l})$, then $(\mathbf{I} - w\mathbf{l}\mathbf{d}^T)^{-1} \geqslant 0$. Moreover, matrix $(\mathbf{I} - w\mathbf{l}\mathbf{d}^T)^{-1}\mathbf{A}$ is indecomposable (cf. exercise 6.9), and

$$\mathbf{p} = (1 + r)(\mathbf{I} - w\mathbf{l}\mathbf{d}^T)^{-1}\mathbf{A}\mathbf{p}. \tag{4.15}$$

Let $\lambda^{PF}(\mathbf{B})$ be the largest real eigenvalue of matrix $\mathbf{B}$, then equation (4.15) implies that

$$r = \frac{1 - \lambda^{PF}((\mathbf{I} - w\mathbf{l}\mathbf{d}^T)^{-1}\mathbf{A})}{\lambda^{PF}((\mathbf{I} - w\mathbf{l}\mathbf{d}^T)^{-1}\mathbf{A})}.$$

Finally, Theorem A.3.6 of the Mathematical Appendix ensures that for $0 \leqslant w \leqslant W$ there is one and only one eigenvalue of matrix $(\mathbf{I} - w\mathbf{l}\mathbf{d}^T)^{-1}\mathbf{A}$ associated with a semipositive eigenvector. Hence, there is one and only one rate of profit r for which equations (4.6) have a nonnegative solution, which is in fact positive. Consequently, one also has $0 \leqslant r \leqslant R$. Notice that since $\lambda^{PF}((\mathbf{I} - w\mathbf{l}\mathbf{d}^T)^{-1}\mathbf{A})$ is an increasing function of w (because of statement (f) of Theorem A.3.5; see also equation (4.14)), r is a decreasing function of w.

1.7. Growth
Assume that the economy is growing at a uniform growth rate g. Let f_i $(i = 1, 2, \ldots, n)$ be the amount consumed of commodity i and let $\mathbf{f}^T = (f_1, f_2, \ldots, f_n)$. Then, denoting the vector of the quantities produced of the different commodities by $\mathbf{q}^T = (q_1, q_2, \ldots, q_n)$, we have

$$\mathbf{q}^T = (1 + g)\mathbf{q}^T\mathbf{A} + \mathbf{f}^T. \tag{4.16}$$

The maximum growth rate, G, is determined by the system

$$(1 + G)\mathbf{q}^T\mathbf{A} = \mathbf{q}^T \tag{4.17a}$$

$$\mathbf{q} \geqslant 0. \tag{4.17b}$$

System (4.17) has a unique solution (up to a scalar transformation) (cf. statements (a)–(c) of Theorem A.3.5 and Theorem A.3.6):

$$\mathbf{q} = \mathbf{q}^*$$

$$G = \frac{1 - \lambda}{\lambda},$$

where $\mathbf{q}^*$ is a left eigenvector associated with the largest real eigenvalue of matrix $\mathbf{A}$, λ. Obviously, $G = R$.

Furthermore, if $g < G$, then the matrix $[\mathbf{I} - (1 + g)\mathbf{A}]$ is invertible and

$$[\mathbf{I} - (1 + g)\mathbf{A}]^{-1} > 0$$

(cf. statement (d) of Theorem A.3.2 and statement (e) of Theorem A.3.5). Hence,

$$\mathbf{q}^T = \mathbf{f}^T[\mathbf{I} - (1 + g)\mathbf{A}]^{-1}$$

and $\mathbf{q} > 0$ if $\mathbf{f} \geqslant 0$.

Let us now assume that $\mathbf{f} = c\mathbf{b}$, where c is a scalar to be determined and $\mathbf{b}$ is a given semipositive vector. Moreover, let us determine c on the premise that exactly one unit of labor is used, that is,

$$\mathbf{q}^T \mathbf{l} = 1.$$

Accordingly, we obtain from equation (4.16)

$$1 = \mathbf{q}^T \mathbf{l} = c\mathbf{b}^T[\mathbf{I} - (1 + g)\mathbf{A}]^{-1}\mathbf{l},$$

that is,

$$c = \frac{1}{\mathbf{b}^T[\mathbf{I} - (1 + g)\mathbf{A}]^{-1}\mathbf{l}}. \qquad (4.18)$$

The significance of equation (4.18) is the following. If commodities are consumed in proportion to the entries of vector $\mathbf{b}$, and the bundle of commodities $\mathbf{b}$ is the unit of consumption, then c represents *consumption per head* as a function of the growth rate g. That is, it gives the number of units of consumption per unit of labor employed as a function of the growth rate.

If vector $\mathbf{b}$ is a function of prices, then it is not always possible to separate the quantity system from the price system. It is perhaps of some interest to illustrate this proposition in terms of a special case, that is, in which commodities are still consumed in given proportions, but these proportions are different for workers and for capitalists. No attempt will be made to define consumption per head which would necessarily be in value terms. (See, however, exercises 6.20 and 6.21.)

Assume that workers consume commodities in proportion to vector $\mathbf{b}_w$ and capitalists consume in proportion to vector $\mathbf{b}_c$. Then,

$$\mathbf{q}^T = (1 + g)\mathbf{q}^T\mathbf{A} + \frac{[W + (r - g)K_w]}{\mathbf{b}_w^T\mathbf{p}}\mathbf{b}_w^T + \frac{(r - g)K_c}{\mathbf{b}_c^T\mathbf{p}}\mathbf{b}_c^T,$$

where $W = w\mathbf{q}^T\mathbf{l}$, K_w is the capital owned by workers (since they save) which is assumed to equal $\theta w \mathbf{q}^T \mathbf{l}$ (where θ depends on r, g, and workers' consumption habits: a formal expression for θ will be provided in Chapter 15), and $K_c = \mathbf{q}^T \mathbf{A} \mathbf{p} - \theta w \mathbf{q}^T \mathbf{l}$ is the capitalists' own capital. In fact $[W + (r - g)K_w]/\mathbf{b}_w^T \mathbf{p}$ is the number of workers' consumption units which workers can afford, whereas $(r - g)K_c/\mathbf{b}_c^T \mathbf{p}$ is the number of capitalists' consumption units which capitalists can afford. Of course, we are interested only in the cases in which $K_c = \mathbf{q}^T \mathbf{A} \mathbf{p} - \theta w \mathbf{q}^T \mathbf{l} > 0$ and $r > g$.[3]

In order to show that with the present assumptions on consumption the price and quantity system cannot be separated, let us divide the economy in two subsystems, one producing the workers' consumption basket $\mathbf{b}_w$ and the other producing the capitalists' consumption basket $\mathbf{b}_c$:

$$\mathbf{z}^T = (1 + g)\mathbf{z}^T \mathbf{A} + \frac{[1 + \theta(r - g)]w(\mathbf{z}^T \mathbf{l} + \mathbf{x}^T \mathbf{l})}{\mathbf{b}_w^T \mathbf{p}} \mathbf{b}_w^T \tag{4.19a}$$

$$\mathbf{x}^T = (1 + g)\mathbf{x}^T \mathbf{A} + \frac{(r - g)[\mathbf{z}^T \mathbf{A} \mathbf{p} + \mathbf{x}^T \mathbf{A} \mathbf{p} - \theta w(\mathbf{z}^T \mathbf{l} + \mathbf{x}^T \mathbf{l})]}{\mathbf{b}_c^T \mathbf{p}} \mathbf{b}_c^T. \tag{4.19b}$$

Obviously, $\mathbf{z} + \mathbf{x} = \mathbf{q}$ and capitalists' capital is positive if and only if $\mathbf{x} \geqslant 0$. We obtain from equations (4.19) that

$$\mathbf{z}^T = \alpha \mathbf{b}_w^T [\mathbf{I} - (1 + g)\mathbf{A}]^{-1} \tag{4.20a}$$

$$\mathbf{x}^T = \beta \mathbf{b}_c^T [\mathbf{I} - (1 + g)\mathbf{A}]^{-1}, \tag{4.20b}$$

where α and β are scalars to be determined. Capitalists' capital is positive if and only if $\beta/\alpha > 0$. Since equations (4.19) are homogeneous and linear in $(\mathbf{z}, \mathbf{x})$, only the ratio β/α can be determined. In order to do so, multiply both sides of equation (4.19b) by $\mathbf{p}$:

$$\mathbf{x}^T \mathbf{p} = (1 + g)\mathbf{x}^T \mathbf{A} \mathbf{p} + (r - g)[\mathbf{z}^T \mathbf{A} \mathbf{p} + \mathbf{x}^T \mathbf{A} \mathbf{p} - \theta w(\mathbf{z}^T \mathbf{l} + \mathbf{x}^T \mathbf{l})].$$

Since $\mathbf{p}$ satisfies equation (4.6a), the last equation can be rearranged as

$$(1 + r)\mathbf{x}^T \mathbf{A} \mathbf{p} + w\mathbf{x}^T \mathbf{l} = (1 + g)\mathbf{x}^T \mathbf{A} \mathbf{p}$$
$$+ (r - g)[\mathbf{z}^T \mathbf{A} \mathbf{p} + \mathbf{x}^T \mathbf{A} \mathbf{p} - \theta w(\mathbf{z}^T \mathbf{l} + \mathbf{x}^T \mathbf{l})],$$

that is,

$$[1 + \theta(r - g)]w\mathbf{x}^T \mathbf{l} = (r - g)(\mathbf{z}^T \mathbf{A} \mathbf{p} - \theta w \mathbf{z}^T \mathbf{l}).$$

---

[3] If $r = g$ capitalists' consumption is zero and therefore the model reduces to the one given in equations (4.16)–(4.18). With $r < g$ investors would get from production less than what they put into it.

Since x and z satisfy equations (4.20), the last equation implies

$$\frac{\beta}{\alpha} = \frac{(r-g)\mathbf{b}_w^T[\mathbf{I}-(1+g)\mathbf{A}]^{-1}(\mathbf{Ap}-\theta w\mathbf{l})}{[1+\theta(r-g)]w\mathbf{b}_c^T[\mathbf{I}-(1+g)\mathbf{A}]^{-1}\mathbf{l}},$$

which depends on prices, but is independent of the chosen numeraire. Note that $\beta/\alpha \geq 0$ if and only if

$$\mathbf{b}_w^T[\mathbf{I}-(1+g)\mathbf{A}]^{-1}(\mathbf{Ap}-\theta w\mathbf{l}) \geq 0. \tag{4.21}$$

2. Models with basic and non-basic commodities

We now turn to a system which exhibits both basics and some non-basics. In this case matrix A is reducible and can be transformed by the same permutation of rows and of columns in the following "canonical" form (see Subsection A.3.2 in the Mathematical Appendix):

$$\mathbf{A} = \begin{bmatrix} \mathbf{A}_{11} & \mathbf{0} & \cdots & \mathbf{0} \\ \mathbf{A}_{21} & \mathbf{A}_{22} & \cdots & \mathbf{0} \\ \cdot & \cdot & \cdots & \cdot \\ \cdot & \cdot & \cdots & \cdot \\ \cdot & \cdot & \cdots & \cdot \\ \mathbf{A}_{s1} & \mathbf{A}_{s2} & \cdots & \mathbf{A}_{ss} \end{bmatrix},$$

where $\mathbf{A}_{11}$ is a semipositive square indecomposable matrix and $\mathbf{A}_{hh}$ $(h = 2, 3, \ldots, s)$ is a square indecomposable matrix (a zero matrix consisting of one element only is indecomposable). Obviously more than one canonical form of a given matrix may exist. For instance, the following two matrices can be considered two canonical forms of the same matrix:

$$\begin{bmatrix} \mathbf{A}_{11} & \mathbf{0} & \mathbf{0} \\ \mathbf{A}_{21} & \mathbf{A}_{22} & \mathbf{0} \\ \mathbf{A}_{31} & \mathbf{0} & \mathbf{A}_{33} \end{bmatrix}, \begin{bmatrix} \mathbf{A}_{11} & \mathbf{0} & \mathbf{0} \\ \mathbf{A}_{31} & \mathbf{A}_{33} & \mathbf{0} \\ \mathbf{A}_{21} & \mathbf{0} & \mathbf{A}_{22} \end{bmatrix}.$$

Let us define groups of commodities:

$$I_h = \left\{ i \in \mathbb{N} \,\middle|\, \sum_{k=0}^{h-1} \text{ord}(\mathbf{A}_{kk}) < i \leq \sum_{k=0}^{h} \text{ord}(\mathbf{A}_{kk}) \right\}, \quad h = 1, 2, \ldots, s$$

where $\text{ord}(\mathbf{A}_{ii})$ is the order of the square matrix $\mathbf{A}_{ii}$ $(i = 1, 2, \ldots, s)$ and $\text{ord}(\mathbf{A}_{00}) = 0$. The commodities of group I_h $(h = 2, 3, \ldots, s)$ enter neither directly nor indirectly into the production of the commodities of groups $I_1, I_2, \ldots, I_{h-1}$. Therefore the commodities of groups $I_2, I_3, \ldots, I_s$ are non-basic, whereas the commodities of group I_1 are the only commodities that can be basic. To assume that there exists at least one basic commodity is equivalent to assuming that

$$\mathbf{A}_{21} \geq \mathbf{0} \tag{4.22.1}$$

$$(A_{31}, A_{32}) \geqslant 0 \tag{4.22.2}$$

. . . .

$$(A_{s1}, A_{s2}, \ldots, A_{s,s-1}) \geqslant 0. \tag{4.22.s-1}$$

If $\mathrm{ord}(A_{11}) = 1$ then $A_{11} > 0$. $\tag{4.23}$

If inequality (4.22.h–1) does not hold, then none of the commodities in $I_1 \cup I_2 \cup \cdots \cup I_{h-1}$ enters directly or indirectly into the production of the commodities in I_h. Hence no commodity can be basic. Conversely, if inequality (4.22.h–1) holds, then at least one commodity in $I_1 \cup I_2 \cup \cdots \cup I_{h-1}$ enters directly into the production of at least one commodity in I_h and, since A_{hh} is indecomposable, directly or indirectly into the production of all commodities in I_h. Therefore, if the commodities in I_1 enter directly or indirectly into the production of the commodities in $I_1 \cup I_2 \cup \cdots \cup I_{h-1}$, then they also enter directly or indirectly into the production of the commodities in I_h. Thus, if and only if inequalities (4.22) hold we have that if commodities in group I_1 enter directly or indirectly into their own production they are basic commodities. Finally, (4.23) guarantees that if the order of matrix A_{11} is equal to 1, then the only commodity in group I_1 enters directly into its own production. If $\mathrm{ord}(A_{11}) > 1$, the indecomposability guarantees that the commodities in group I_1 enter directly or indirectly into their own production. Matrix A_{11} represents the basic part of the economy.

The distinction between basic and non-basic commodities is important because the former exhibit various properties which do not carry over to the latter. In the remainder of this section the following six properties will be analyzed in some detail:

    (i) basic commodities are indispensable; they have to be (re)produced irrespective of the composition of the net product (non-basics are not indispensable: in the special case in which the net output vector consists of basics only, no non-basic will be produced);

   (ii) the viability of the economy depends exclusively on the conditions of production of the basic commodities and is independent of the conditions of production of the non-basics;

 (iii) the maximum rate of growth of the economy is determined by the conditions of production of the basic commodities and is independent of the conditions of production of the non-basics;

 (iv) if the numeraire consists of basic commodities only, the prices of basics are determined independently of the prices of non-basics and thus do not depend on the conditions of production of the latter (the prices of non-basics, on the contrary, always depend on the conditions of production of the basics);

(v) if the numeraire consists of basic commodities only, the relationship between the wage rate and the rate of profit is determined by the conditions of production of basics only and does not depend on the conditions of production of non-basics;

(vi) the relative prices of basics are definite and positive for all values of the rate of profit between zero and the maximum rate of growth (some non-basics may not have this property).

2.1. Indispensability

Let vector $\mathbf{x} \geqslant \mathbf{0}$ be such that

$$\mathbf{x}^T \geqslant \mathbf{x}^T \mathbf{A}. \tag{4.24}$$

Partition vector $\mathbf{x}$ in such a way that $\mathbf{x}^T = (\mathbf{x}_1^T, \mathbf{x}_2^T, \ldots, \mathbf{x}_s^T)$, where $\mathbf{x}_j$ is a subvector with the same number of rows as matrix $\mathbf{A}_{jj}$. Now inequality (4.24) can be written as

$$\mathbf{x}_1^T[\mathbf{I} - \mathbf{A}_{11}] \geqslant \mathbf{x}_2^T \mathbf{A}_{21} + \mathbf{x}_3^T \mathbf{A}_{31} + \cdots + \mathbf{x}_s^T \mathbf{A}_{s1} \tag{4.25.1}$$

$$\mathbf{x}_2^T[\mathbf{I} - \mathbf{A}_{22}] \geqslant \mathbf{x}_3^T \mathbf{A}_{32} + \cdots + \mathbf{x}_s^T \mathbf{A}_{s2} \tag{4.25.2}$$

. . . .

$$\mathbf{x}_s^T[\mathbf{I} - \mathbf{A}_{ss}] \geqslant \mathbf{0}^T, \tag{4.25.s}$$

from which $\mathbf{x}_1 > \mathbf{0}$ follows because of inequalities (4.22). This proves proposition (i). In order to clarify this point, let us begin by observing that if $\mathbf{x}_h \geqslant \mathbf{0}$ it follows that $\mathbf{x}_h > \mathbf{0}$ because of the irreducibility of matrix $\mathbf{A}_{hh}$ (see Lemma A.3.7). If $h > 1$, then because of inequality (4.22.h–1) there is a natural number $k < h$ such that $\mathbf{x}_h^T \mathbf{A}_{hk} \geqslant \mathbf{0}$; hence $\mathbf{x}_k > \mathbf{0}$ because of the irreducibility of matrix $\mathbf{A}_{kk}$. Reiterating the same kind of argument one arrives at the conclusion that $\mathbf{x}_1 > \mathbf{0}$.

2.2. Viability

An economy is viable if it is able to reproduce itself, that is if there is a vector $\mathbf{x}$ such that

$$\mathbf{x}^T \geqslant \mathbf{x}^T \mathbf{A} \tag{4.26a}$$

$$\mathbf{x} \geqslant \mathbf{0}. \tag{4.26b}$$

Partitioning the vector $\mathbf{x}$ as in the previous subsection, inequality (4.26a) can be written as inequalities (4.25). From this it immediately follows that the economy is viable if and only if

$$\mathbf{x}_1^T[\mathbf{I} - \mathbf{A}_{11}] \geqslant \mathbf{0}^T \tag{4.27a}$$

$$\mathbf{x}_1 \geqslant \mathbf{0}. \tag{4.27b}$$

This proves proposition (ii). In order to clarify this point, it has to be shown that inequalities (4.26) admit solutions if and only if inequalities (4.27) admit solutions. Note first that inequality (4.27a) follows immediately from inequality (4.25.1), while inequality (4.27b) is a direct consequence of inequalities (4.26) and the indispensability of basic commodities. Now, if inequalities (4.27) admit a solution, inequalities (4.25) will certainly admit one too: it suffices to set $x_j = 0$ ($j = 2, 3, \ldots, s$).

If an economy is just viable, then no non-basic can be produced. Because of this we assume throughout Section 2 that the economy is able to produce a surplus.

2.3. The maximum rate of growth

In Section 3 of Chapter 3 we have seen that with self-reproducing non-basics the following problem may arise: there is more than one G such that there is a semipositive vector x such that $x^T[I - (1 + \rho)A] = 0^T$. Hence the following definition of the maximum rate of growth seems more suitable:

$$G = \max\{\rho | \rho \in \mathbb{R}, \exists x \geqslant 0 : x^T[I - (1 + \rho)A] \geqslant 0^T\}. \tag{4.28}$$

G is the maximum rate of growth. Let us set $x^T = (x_1^T, x_2^T, \ldots, x_s^T)$, where x_j is a subvector with the same number of rows as matrix A_{jj}, then the last inequality in formula (4.28) can be written as

$$x_1^T[I - (1 + \rho)A_{11}] \geqslant (1 + \rho)[x_2^T A_{21} + x_3^T A_{31} + \cdots + x_s^T A_{s1}] \tag{4.29.1}$$

$$x_2^T[I - (1 + \rho)A_{22}] \geqslant (1 + \rho)[x_3^T A_{32} + \cdots + x_s^T A_{s2}] \tag{4.29.2}$$

$$\ldots\ldots\ldots\ldots\ldots\ldots\ldots\ldots\ldots\ldots\ldots\ldots\ldots \qquad \ldots\ldots\ldots$$

$$x_s^T[I - (1 + \rho)A_{ss}] \geqslant 0^T. \tag{4.29.s}$$

Let λ_1 be the largest real eigenvalue of submatrix A_{11}. If we set $\rho = (1 - \lambda_1)/\lambda_1$ in (4.28), and let x_1 be the eigenvector of A_{11} associated with λ_1, and $x_j = 0$ for all $j = 2, 3, \ldots, s$, then a solution to inequalities (4.29) is obtained. Hence $G \geqslant (1 - \lambda_1)/\lambda_1$. Moreover, any other solution to inequalities (4.29) with $x \geqslant 0$ implies $x_1 > 0$ (because of the indispensability of basic commodities) and that the vector $x_1^T[I - (1 + \rho)A_{11}]$ is semipositive. Due to proposition (d) of Theorem A.3.5 of the Mathematical Appendix this implies a value of ρ smaller than $(1 - \lambda_1)/\lambda_1$. Hence

$$G = \frac{1 - \lambda_1}{\lambda_1},$$

which proves proposition (iii).

2.4. The price system

Prices are determined by equations (4.6). Partition vectors $\mathbf{p}, \mathbf{l}$, and $\mathbf{d}$ in such a way that

$$
\mathbf{p} = \begin{bmatrix} \mathbf{p}_1 \\ \mathbf{p}_2 \\ \vdots \\ \mathbf{p}_s \end{bmatrix}, \quad
\mathbf{l} = \begin{bmatrix} \mathbf{l}_1 \\ \mathbf{l}_2 \\ \vdots \\ \mathbf{l}_s \end{bmatrix}, \quad
\mathbf{d} = \begin{bmatrix} \mathbf{d}_1 \\ \mathbf{d}_2 \\ \vdots \\ \mathbf{d}_s \end{bmatrix},
$$

where $\mathbf{p}_j, \mathbf{l}_j$, and $\mathbf{d}_j$ are subvectors with the same number of columns as $\mathbf{A}_{jj}$. Then equations (4.6) can be expanded as

$$\mathbf{p}_1 = (1+r)\mathbf{A}_{11}\mathbf{p}_1 \qquad\qquad\qquad\qquad + w\mathbf{l}_1 \qquad (4.30.1)$$

$$\mathbf{p}_2 = (1+r)(\mathbf{A}_{21}\mathbf{p}_1 + \mathbf{A}_{22}\mathbf{p}_2) \qquad\qquad + w\mathbf{l}_2 \qquad (4.30.2)$$

$$\cdots\cdots\cdots\cdots\cdots\cdots\cdots\cdots\cdots\cdots\cdots\cdots\cdots\cdots\cdots\cdots\cdots\qquad \cdots\cdots$$

$$\mathbf{p}_s = (1+r)(\mathbf{A}_{s1}\mathbf{p}_1 + \mathbf{A}_{s2}\mathbf{p}_2 + \cdots + \mathbf{A}_{ss}\mathbf{p}_s) + w\mathbf{l}_s \qquad (4.30.s)$$

$$\mathbf{d}_1^T\mathbf{p}_1 + \mathbf{d}_2^T\mathbf{p}_2 + \cdots + \mathbf{d}_s^T\mathbf{p}_s = 1. \qquad (4.31)$$

If it is assumed that the numeraire consists of basic commodities only, that is, $\mathbf{d}_j = 0$ for all $j > 1$, the prices of basics and the wage rate are determined by equations (4.30.1) and (4.31) in a way which is entirely analogous to the one analyzed in Subsections 1.3 and 1.4. Prices of basics and the wage rate are defined and positive for $0 \leqslant r < G$, since from statement (d) of Theorem A.3.2 and statement (e) of Theorem A.3.5 it follows that matrix $[\mathbf{I} - (1+r)\mathbf{A}_{11}]^{-1}$ is invertible for $0 \leqslant r < G$ and

$$[\mathbf{I} - (1+r)\mathbf{A}_{11}]^{-1} > \mathbf{0}.$$

Conversely, Theorem A.3.1 ensures that matrix $[\mathbf{I} - (1+r)\mathbf{A}]$ is invertible with a semipositive inverse for $0 \leqslant r < G^*$, where

$$G^* = \sup\{\rho \in \mathbb{R} \mid \exists \mathbf{x} \geqslant \mathbf{0} : \mathbf{x}^T[\mathbf{I} - (1+\rho)\mathbf{A}] > \mathbf{0}^T\}.$$

Obviously, $G^* \leqslant G$.

In the above, propositions (iv)–(vi) have been proved. The analysis of the system of prices when $G^* < G$ and $G^* \leqslant r < G$ will be carried out in the following subsection.

2.5. $G^* \leqslant r < G$

At the very beginning of this section we have seen that commodities can be divided in groups on the basis of a canonical form of matrix $\mathbf{A}$. Since more than one canonical form is possible, in the following we will assume that if group I_h and group I_k can be interchanged, then we order the groups in such a way that $h < k$ if the largest real eigenvalue of sub-matrix $\mathbf{A}_{hh}$ is not larger than the largest real eigenvalue of submatrix $\mathbf{A}_{kk}$. Let

$$G_j^* = \sup\{\rho \in \mathbb{R} | \exists \mathbf{x} \geqslant \mathbf{0} : \mathbf{x}^T[\mathbf{I} - (1 + \rho)\mathbf{A}] \geqslant \mathbf{0}^T, x_j > 0\}$$
$$j = 1, 2, \ldots, s.$$

Obviously, $G^* \leqslant G_j^* \leqslant G$ and $G_1^* = G$. Call the commodities in the subsets $I_j (j \geqslant 2)$ such that $G_j^* = G^{(1)} \equiv G$ *non-basics of the first degree*. Then, from an investigation of inequalities (4.29) it is obtained that if the commodities in I_j are non-basics of the first degree, then the largest real eigenvalue of matrix $\mathbf{A}_{jj}$ is not larger than $1/(1 + G)$.

Moreover, non-basics which are not of the first degree cannot enter directly or indirectly into the production of non-basics of the first degree, that is, $\mathbf{A}_{ji} = \mathbf{0}$ for each i such that I_i is a group of non-basics which are not of the first degree. Hence if there are non-basics of the first degree, there is a natural number $u_1, 2 \leqslant u_1 \leqslant s$, such that the set of non-basics of the first degree is $I_2 \cup I_3 \cup \cdots \cup I_{u_1}$. Moreover, if $u_1 < s$, then the largest real eigenvalue of matrix $\mathbf{A}_{u_1 + 1, u_1 + 1}$ is larger than $1/(1 + G)$.

If $u_1 < s$ (that is, $G^* < G$), call the commodities in the subsets $I_j (j > u_1)$ such that $G_j^* = G^{(2)} \equiv G_{u_1 + 1}^*$ *non-basics of the second degree*. Once again one can easily obtain from inequalities (4.29) that if the commodities in I_j are non-basics of the second degree, then the largest real eigenvalue of matrix $\mathbf{A}_{jj}$ is not larger than $1/(1 + G^{(2)})$. Moreover, non-basics which are not of the first or second degree cannot enter directly or indirectly into the production of non-basics of the first degree, i.e., $\mathbf{A}_{ji} = \mathbf{0}$ for each i such that I_i is a group of non-basics which are not of the first or of the second degree. Hence there exists a natural number $u_2, u_1 < u_2 \leqslant s$, such that the set of non-basics of the second degree is $I_{u_1 + 1} \cup I_{u_1 + 2} \cup \cdots \cup I_{u_2}$.[4] Moreover, if $u_2 < s$, then the largest real eigenvalue of matrix $\mathbf{A}_{u_2 + 1, u_2 + 1}$ is larger than $1/(1 + G^{(2)})$.

If $u_2 < s$ (that is, $G^{(2)} < G^*$), non-basics of the third degree can be defined in a similar way, and so on until the non-basics of the zth degree; $G^{(z)} = G^*$, $u_z = s$.

The concepts introduced in this subsection allow us to assert that if $0 \leqslant \rho < G^{(j)}$, then the matrix $[\mathbf{I} - (1 + \rho)\mathbf{B}_j]$ is invertible and

$$[\mathbf{I} - (1 + \rho)\mathbf{B}_j]^{-1} \geqslant \mathbf{0},$$

---

[4] If u_1 does not exist, then $1 < u_2 \leqslant s$ and the set of non-basics of the second degree is $I_2 \cup I_3 \cup \cdots \cup I_{u_2}$.

where

$$
\mathbf{B}_j =
\begin{bmatrix}
\mathbf{A}_{11} & \mathbf{0} & \cdots & \mathbf{0} \\
\mathbf{A}_{21} & \mathbf{A}_{22} & \cdots & \mathbf{0} \\
\cdot & \cdot & \cdots & \cdot \\
\cdot & \cdot & \cdots & \cdot \\
\mathbf{A}_{u_j 1} & \mathbf{A}_{u_j 2} & \cdots & \mathbf{A}_{u_j u_j}
\end{bmatrix}.
$$

Because of this result the following can be said. If the numeraire consists only of basics or non-basics of the first degree, that is, $\mathbf{d}_j = \mathbf{0}$ for each $j > u_1$, then the prices of basics and of non-basics of a degree not larger than j ($j = 1, 2, \ldots, z$) are defined and positive for $0 \leqslant r < G^{(j)}$. Note that if the numeraire also consists of non-basics of the jth degree, it may not be possible to ascertain prices at rates of profit larger than or equal to $G^{(j)}$. Therefore, it is convenient to adopt a numeraire consisting of basic commodities only.

2.6. Growth

The results presented in Subsection 1.7 can easily be generalized to the model with basic and non-basic commodities. One has just to pay attention to the fact that if non-basics of degree j are consumed, then the growth rate g must be lower than $G^{(j)}$.

2.7. A final remark

All the nice properties of basic systems (all prices are positive; the composition of consumption does not cause difficulties in answering the question whether an economy can grow at rate g) hold if and only if all non-basics are of the first degree only, that is, if $G^* = G$ (see also exercise 6.14). As has already been hinted at in Section 6 of Chapter 3, a possible solution to the difficulties mentioned can be indicated with respect to cost-minimizing techniques. This solution will be discussed in Section 4 of Chapter 5, after the possibility of a choice of technique has been introduced.

3. The labor theory of value

The theory of prices presented in the previous sections is frequently characterized as "classical," although the classical economists never stated it in this way, partly because the necessary mathematics were developed much later. Some important steps in the early development of the classical approach to the theory of value have been summarized in Sections 1 and 2 of Chapter 1. Here we shall focus attention on the concept of "quantity of labor embodied," or "labor value," and related concepts, and the question when the "labor theory of value" is able to explain relative normal prices. We are not concerned with the (in)famous problem of the "transformation" of labor values in prices of production.

Let $\mathbf{v}$ be the vector of the quantities of labor "embodied" in the different commodities, or (*labor*) *values* (following Marx's terminology). Then $\mathbf{Av}$ is the vector of the values of the means of production. Accordingly,

$$\mathbf{v} = \mathbf{Av} + \mathbf{l}, \tag{4.32}$$

and thus

$$\mathbf{v} = (\mathbf{I} - \mathbf{A})^{-1}\mathbf{l}. \tag{4.33}$$

Comparing equations (4.7) and (4.33) shows that prices are proportional to values if the rate of profit is zero.

If prices are proportional to values also at a positive level of the rate of profit, then the same price vector recurs at two different rates of profit. It can be demonstrated that if this is so, prices are proportional to values irrespective of the level of the rate of profit. In order to prove this, consider the following two equations:

$$\mathbf{p} = (1 + r')\mathbf{Ap} + w'\mathbf{l} \tag{4.34a}$$

$$\mathbf{p} = (1 + r'')\mathbf{Ap} + w''\mathbf{l}, \tag{4.34b}$$

where $r' \neq r''$ and $w' \neq w''$. Subtracting (4.34b) from (4.34a) gives

$$0 = \Delta r\mathbf{Ap} + \Delta w\mathbf{l},$$

where $\Delta r = r' - r''$ and $\Delta w = w' - w''$. As a consequence

$$\mathbf{Ap} = \alpha\mathbf{l}, \tag{4.35}$$

where $\alpha = -\Delta w/\Delta r$, and

$$\mathbf{p} = (1 + r')\alpha\mathbf{l} + w'\mathbf{l} \equiv \beta\mathbf{l}. \tag{4.36}$$

Hence,

$$\beta\mathbf{Al} = \alpha\mathbf{l},$$

that is,

$$\mathbf{Al} = \lambda\mathbf{l},$$

where $\lambda = \alpha/\beta$. Thus, the (direct) labor input vector $\mathbf{l}$ is an eigenvector of matrix $\mathbf{A}$. Since vector $\mathbf{l}$ is positive, λ is the highest real eigenvalue of matrix $\mathbf{A}$ and therefore $\mathbf{l}$ is proportional to the price vector corresponding to the maximum rate of profit. If a surplus can be produced, then $\lambda < 1$;

as a consequence,

$$(\mathbf{I} - \mathbf{A})\mathbf{l} = (1 - \lambda)\mathbf{l}.$$

It follows

$$\mathbf{l} = (1 - \lambda)(\mathbf{I} - \mathbf{A})^{-1}\mathbf{l} = (1 - \lambda)\mathbf{v},$$

that is, the labor input vector is proportional to the value vector. Substituting (4.35) and (4.36) in (4.6a) yields

$$\beta\mathbf{l} = (1 + r)\alpha\mathbf{l} + w\mathbf{l}.$$

Hence

$$w = \beta - (1 + r)\alpha,$$

that is,

$$w = \beta[1 - (1 + r)\lambda].$$

This proves that the price vector is invariant with respect to changes in the rate of profit, that the relationship between the wage rate and the rate of profit is linear, and that the price vector is proportional to the labor input vector and to the value vector. The argument proves also that α and β may depend on the choice of the numeraire, but are independent of r; obviously λ depends only on the elements of matrix $\mathbf{A}$.

We conclude this section by showing that the following statements are equivalent:

(i) the labor theory of value holds;
(ii) $\exists \gamma \colon \mathbf{p} = \gamma\mathbf{v}$;
(iii) the price vectors relative to two different levels of the rate of profit are equal;
(iv) the price vector is independent of the rate of profit;
(v) $\exists \beta \colon \mathbf{p} = \beta\mathbf{l}$;
(vi) $\exists \lambda \colon \mathbf{l} = (1 - \lambda)\mathbf{v}$;
(vii) $\exists \lambda \colon \mathbf{A}\mathbf{l} = \lambda\mathbf{l}$;
(viii) $\exists \alpha \colon \mathbf{A}\mathbf{p} = \alpha\mathbf{l}$;
(ix) whatever the numeraire is, the relation between the wage rate and the rate of profit is a straight line; that is, if commodity i is the numeraire, then there is β_i such that

$$w = \beta_i[1 - (1 + r)\lambda]$$

whatever is i.

Those among the following implications which are not obvious have already been established.

$$(ix)$$
$$\Uparrow$$
$$(iii) \Rightarrow (viii) \Rightarrow (v) \Rightarrow (iv) \Rightarrow (iii)$$
$$(vii) \Rightarrow (vi) \Rightarrow (ii)$$

Therefore, in order to prove that statements (ii)–(ix) are all equivalent we just need to show that statement (ix) implies any of the others. Since the maximum rate of profit $R = (1 - \lambda)/\lambda$, if statement (ix) holds, then there is a positive number β_i such that

$$[1 - (1 + r)\lambda]\beta_i \mathbf{e}_i^T [\mathbf{I} - (1 + r)\mathbf{A}]^{-1}\mathbf{l} = 1, \quad (i = 1, 2, \ldots, n)$$

each r. That is, there is a diagonal matrix $\mathbf{D}$ with elements on the main diagonal all positive such that, for all r,

$$[1 - (1 + r)\lambda]\mathbf{D}[\mathbf{I} - (1 + r)\mathbf{A}]^{-1}\mathbf{l} = \mathbf{e}. \tag{4.37}$$

Since identity (4.37) holds for $r = -1$,

$$\mathbf{D}^{-1}\mathbf{e} = \mathbf{l}.$$

Hence equation (4.37) implies

$$[1 - (1 + r)\lambda][\mathbf{I} - (1 + r)\mathbf{A}]^{-1}\mathbf{l} = \mathbf{D}^{-1}\mathbf{e} = \mathbf{l}.$$

Thus

$$[1 - (1 + r)\lambda]\mathbf{l} = [\mathbf{I} - (1 + r)\mathbf{A}]\mathbf{l},$$

that is,

$$\lambda\mathbf{l} = \mathbf{A}\mathbf{l},$$

which is statement (vii). Finally, statements (i)–(ix) are all equivalent since statement (ii) is nothing else than a different way to state statement (i).

4. The choice of a numeraire

The concept of the *numeraire* introduced in Section 1 is well known in economic theory. The numeraire is chosen by the theorist and does not depend on "observed facts." However, some numeraires have useful properties which can be utilized by the theorist. This section is devoted to an analysis of three special numeraires because of the useful properties they have. We shall first deal with the unit of consumption as numeraire, then Adam Smith's "labour commanded" measure of value, and finally Sraffa's "Standard commodity."

4.1. The unit of consumption

In Subsection 1.7 the unit of consumption has been introduced. If it is assumed that commodities are consumed in proportion to vector

b, we may define the *consumption per unit of labor employed* (or, for short, *consumption per head*) as the number of units of consumption produced (directly or indirectly) by one unit of labor. With **b** as the commodity bundle that serves as the *unit of consumption*, consumption per head is the scalar c for which there is a vector **q** such that

$$\mathbf{q}^T = (1 + g)\mathbf{q}^T\mathbf{A} + c\mathbf{b}^T \tag{4.38a}$$

$$\mathbf{q}^T\mathbf{1} = 1. \tag{4.38b}$$

If we adopt the unit of consumption also as the standard of value or numeraire, we have

$$\mathbf{p} = (1 + r)\mathbf{A}\mathbf{p} + w\mathbf{l} \tag{4.39a}$$

$$\mathbf{b}^T\mathbf{p} = 1. \tag{4.39b}$$

By solving these two sets of equations we obtain

$$w = \frac{1}{\mathbf{b}^T[\mathbf{I} - (1 + r)\mathbf{A}]^{-1}\mathbf{l}}$$

$$c = \frac{1}{\mathbf{b}^T[\mathbf{I} - (1 + g)\mathbf{A}]^{-1}\mathbf{l}}.$$

Thus, in the case where both consumption per head and wages are measured in terms of the unit of consumption, the relationship between the wage rate and the rate of profit turns out to be identical to the relationship between consumption per head and the growth rate.

The adoption of the unit of consumption as numeraire allows us to illustrate, in a simple diagram (see Figure 4.2), some basic aspects of the system of national accounting of the economy under consideration. Let us define

$$y = \mathbf{q}^T(\mathbf{I} - \mathbf{A})\mathbf{p}$$

and

$$k = \mathbf{q}^T\mathbf{A}\mathbf{p}.$$

Obviously, y gives the value of net income per head and k the value of capital per head (where *per head* actually means *per unit of labor employed*). Multiplying equation (4.38a) by **p** and rearranging terms we get

$$y = gk + c. \tag{4.40}$$

Multiplying equation (4.39a) by $\mathbf{q}^T$ and rearranging terms we get

$$y = rk + w. \tag{4.41}$$

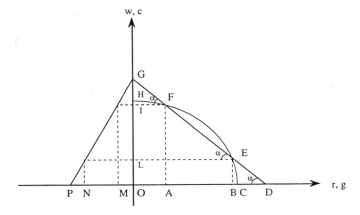

Figure 4.2

According to equation (4.40) income per head equals investment per head (gk) plus consumption per head. Analogously, equation (4.41) means that income per head equals profits per head (rk) plus wages per head. From (4.40) and (4.41) we get

$$k = \frac{c - w}{r - g}. \tag{4.42}$$

Note that equation (4.42) determines k only if $r \neq g$. However, making use of Hôpital's Rule, we obtain that

$$\lim_{r \to g} k = -\frac{dw}{dr},$$

which is equivalent to equation (4.11a) for $0 \leqslant r < R$ and to equation (4.13a) for $r = R$.

Figure 4.2 illustrates some national income accounting concepts in the case of steady-state growth. The curve HFEC represents the $w - r$ and $c - g$ relationships of a given technique. Obviously, w and c can be read off the same axis since they are measured in terms of the same unit, the consumption unit, while both r and g are pure numbers. The straight lines in the figure are drawn on the assumption that the going rate of growth equals $\overline{OA}$ and the going rate of profit equals $\overline{OB}$. It follows that consumption per capita equals $\overline{OI}$ and the wage rate equals $\overline{OL}$. GD is the straight line going through points F and E. Because of equation (4.42) $\tan \alpha$ gives capital per head, k. Segment $\overline{LG}$ ($\overline{IG}$) gives profits per head (investment per head); this follows from $\overline{LG} = \overline{LE} \tan \alpha$ $(\overline{IG} = \overline{IF} \tan \alpha)$. Hence $\overline{OG}$ gives net income per head, y. Since $\overline{OG} = y = \overline{OD} \tan \alpha$, $\overline{OD}$ gives the net output-capital ratio, y/k.

In order to figure out the share of wages in net income, w/y, and the share of consumption, c/y, the straight line going through point G and point $P \equiv (-1, 0)$ has been drawn. Clearly, the share of wages is given by the segment $\overline{PN}$ and the consumption share by the segment $\overline{PM}$.

4.2. Labor commanded

A standard of value or numeraire which played an important role in the history of economic analysis was labor or, more precisely, "labor commanded." This standard was proposed by Adam Smith who also coined the name; it was adopted by, among others, T. R. Malthus. In more recent times J. M. Keynes had recourse to it under the name of the "wage-unit." Assuming for simplicity that there are only basic commodities and expressing all prices in terms of quantities of labor commanded implies setting

$$w = 1,$$

that is, adopting the nominal wage rate as numeraire. Hence the system of price equations becomes

$$\hat{\mathbf{p}} = (1 + r)\mathbf{A}\hat{\mathbf{p}} + \mathbf{l},$$

with $\hat{\mathbf{p}}$ as the vector of labor commanded prices. Solving for $\hat{\mathbf{p}}$ gives

$$\hat{\mathbf{p}} = [\mathbf{I} - (1 + r)\mathbf{A}]^{-1}\mathbf{l}.$$

Exercises 6.24 and 6.25 show that for $0 \leqslant r < R$ these prices are increasing and convex functions of the rate of profit r, and as r approaches R from below, $\hat{p}_j$ approaches $+\infty$; see Figure 4.3. (With $r > R$, the labor commanded prices would be negative and hence economically meaningless; as r approaches R from above, $\hat{p}_j$ approaches $-\infty$.) It goes without saying that the inverse of the labor commanded price $\hat{p}_j$ gives the wage rate in terms of the jth commodity.

4.3. The Standard commodity

Sraffa (1960, ch. IV) constructs a particular numeraire because of the useful properties it has. He normalizes prices by setting

$$\mathbf{d}^T \equiv \mathbf{x}^T(\mathbf{I} - \mathbf{A})$$

in equation (4.6b), where $\mathbf{x}$ is the left eigenvector of matrix $\mathbf{A}$ associated with the eigenvalue $1/(1 + R)$, which is the largest real eigenvalue of the

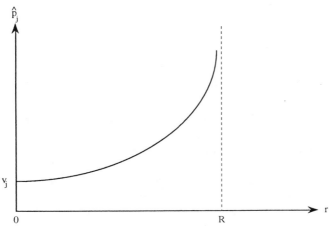

Figure 4.3

submatrix of basics normalized in such a way that $\mathbf{x}^T\mathbf{l} = 1$. Consequently,

$$\mathbf{x}^T = (1 + R)\mathbf{x}^T\mathbf{A}$$

$$\mathbf{x}^T\mathbf{l} = 1$$

$$\mathbf{x} \geqslant \mathbf{0}.$$

Sraffa uses this numeraire, which he calls "Standard commodity," to simplify the analysis of the mathematical properties of prices of production. More specifically, he uses it to show that

   (i) the rate of profit r reaches a finite and unique maximum, R, when the wage rate, w, equals zero, and the corresponding prices of basic commodities are positive;

  (ii) R is the lowest positive real number such that equation (4.6a) is satisfied with $w = 0$;

 (iii) for $0 \leqslant r \leqslant R$ the prices of basic commodities in general vary with r but remain positive and finite;

 (iv) prices can rise and fall as r changes, but none of the prices in terms of the Standard commodity can fall more rapidly than the wage rate; therefore, the relationship between the wage rate w and the rate of profit r is decreasing (for $w \geqslant 0$ and $r \geqslant 0$) irrespective of the numeraire chosen.

In order to demonstrate these statements, Sraffa also shows that

  (v) there is a Standard commodity provided that there is at least one basic commodity, and the former is unique;

(vi) if the Standard commodity is chosen as numeraire, then

$$w = \frac{R - r}{R};$$

(4.43)

(vii) non-basic products play no role in the construction of the Standard commodity.

It deserves mentioning that these results can also be obtained by using the Perron–Frobenius Theorem. In fact, Sraffa's demonstration of the existence and uniqueness of the Standard commodity can be considered a (not fully complete) proof of this theorem. Sraffa's presentation has the advantage of being easily accessible to the non-mathematical reader. Furthermore, he provides an economic rationale of the analytical tools he uses. Since his demonstration of the different statements is not complete, we did not find it convenient to follow his presentation. In order to complete his proofs a more complex mathematics than the one used here would be needed.

Statements (i)–(iv) have been proved in the first two sections of the chapter. Statement (v) is a direct consequence of the Perron–Frobenius Theorems. Statement (vii) follows directly from the arguments furnished in Subsection 2.3 with $G = R$. What remains to be done is to prove statement (vi). For the reader's convenience, we repeat all the relevant equations:

$$\mathbf{p} = (1 + r)\mathbf{A}\mathbf{p} + w\mathbf{l}$$

(4.44a)

$$\mathbf{x}^T(\mathbf{I} - \mathbf{A})\mathbf{p} = 1$$

(4.44b)

$$\mathbf{x}^T = (1 + R)\mathbf{x}^T\mathbf{A}$$

(4.44c)

$$\mathbf{x}^T\mathbf{l} = 1.$$

(4.44d)

Multiplying both sides of equation (4.44a) by $\mathbf{x}^T$ and rearranging terms gives

$$\mathbf{x}^T(\mathbf{I} - \mathbf{A})\mathbf{p} = r\mathbf{x}^T\mathbf{A}\mathbf{p} + w\mathbf{x}^T\mathbf{l},$$

and, taking into account equations (4.44b) and (4.44d),

$$1 = r\mathbf{x}^T\mathbf{A}\mathbf{p} + w.$$

(4.45)

Similarly, multiplying both sides of equations (4.44c) by $\mathbf{p}$ and rearranging terms gives

$$\mathbf{x}^T(\mathbf{I} - \mathbf{A})\mathbf{p} = R\mathbf{x}^T\mathbf{A}\mathbf{p},$$

and, because of equation (4.44b),

$$\mathbf{x}^T\mathbf{A}\mathbf{p} = \frac{1}{R}.$$

(4.46)

Finally, substituting (4.46) in (4.45) yields

$$1 = \frac{r}{R} + w,$$

which, solved for w, gives equation (4.43).

Statement (vi) is useful also because we do not need to calculate the Standard commodity in order to adopt it as numeraire. In fact, statements (v) and (vi) imply that

> (viii) there is a (composite) commodity such that if it is chosen as numeraire, then equation (4.43) holds.

Statement (viii) allows us to substitute equation (4.43) for equation (4.6b). When this is done the Standard commodity is chosen as numeraire even if we do not know in what proportions basic commodities enter into it.

It must be added, however, that the Standard commodity does not need to be the unique (composite) commodity which has the property mentioned in statement (viii). This point will be clarified in the historical notes in Chapter 6.

5. Historical notes

5.1. Systems with basic and non-basic commodities have been studied by Sraffa (1960). The first mathematical treatment of some of the propositions contained therein was provided by Newman (1962); see also Bharadwaj (1970), Schefold (1971), Pasinetti (1977, 1981a), Kurz (1977), Abraham-Frois and Berrebi (1979), Lippi (1979), Mainwaring (1984), Salvadori (1987a), and Bidard (1991), and the collection of essays in Steedman (1988a). The analysis presented in Subsection 1.1 follows Salvadori (1987a). See also the historical notes in Chapter 3.

5.2. The finding that changes in the rate of profit, given the technique in use, will generally be reflected in changes in relative (normal) prices can be traced back to the classical economists and particularly to Ricardo; see chapter I, "On Value," in the *Principles* (especially *Works* I, pp. 30–43) and the complete draft and an unfinished later version of his paper "Absolute Value and Exchangeable Value" (cf. *Works* IV). The dependence of prices on income distribution is explained by Ricardo in terms of the "variety of circumstances under which commodities are actually produced" (*Works* IV, p. 368), whereby he means the different proportions of (direct) labor to means of production of various kinds in the different industries. This in conjunction with the fact that "profits [are] increasing at a compound rate...makes a great part of the difficulty" (*Works* IX, p. 387; similarly IV, p. 388). The problem was also dealt with, for example, by Marx in vol. III of *Capital* ([1894] 1959, ch. XI). Joan Robinson (1953,

p. 95) discussed the phenomenon under the heading "price Wicksell effects," a term that was widely adopted in the so-called Cambridge controversies in the theory of capital; see Chapter 14 (see also exercises 6.18 and 6.19).

5.3. Marx clearly saw that prices of production are not proportional to labor values except in the case in which there is equal "organic composition of capital" across sectors. In terms of the concepts introduced in Section 3, this condition, which is equivalent to each of the statements (i)–(ix) in that section (see exercise 6.23), can be stated as follows:

$$\exists \varphi : \mathbf{A}\mathbf{v} = \varphi \mathbf{l}. \tag{4.47}$$

For a discussion of the role of the labor theory of value in the classical approach to the explanation of profits, see Sraffa (1951, xxxi–xxxiii) and Garegnani (1984). For a critique of Marx's labor value-based analysis of the rate of profit and prices of production, see Steedman (1977a). See also Roemer (1981).

5.4. The unit of consumption has generally been adopted as numeraire in steady state capital and growth theory; see, for example, Spaventa (1968), von Weizsäcker (1971) and Harris (1973). Yet the assumption that the unit of consumption is given and constant irrespective of the level of the rate of profit (and the level of the rate of growth) is difficult to sustain. The reason for this is clarified by Sraffa (1960, p. 33); see the summary statement of his argument in Subsection 9.1 of Chapter 13.

5.5. The labor commanded measure of value was given prominence by Adam Smith (*WN*, I.v). The relationship between the money wage rate and the money price of a particular good gives the product wage rate. The inverse gives the quantity of labor the proprietor of one unit of the good may "command" by selling the good in the respective market and hiring workers with the proceeds of the sale. Clearly, with the rate of profit equal to zero the quantities of labor "commanded" by the different commodities are equal to the quantities of labor "embodied" in them. With the rate of profit larger than zero the quantities of labor commanded generally exceed the quantities of labor embodied, a fact utilized by Smith in his approach to the explanation of shares of income other than wages.

In Keynes the "wage-unit" was introduced as a simplifying device: "It is my belief that much unnecessary perplexity can be avoided if we limit ourselves strictly to the two units, money and labour, when we are dealing with the behaviour of the economic system as a whole" (Keynes, *CW*, VII, p. 43).

5.6. The meaning of the Standard commodity and the role it plays in Sraffa's analysis (Sraffa, 1960) have met with several misunderstandings in the literature. In particular, the Standard commodity has been mistaken as a measure of "real wages" and as an attempt to resurrect the labor theory of value (see, for example, Burmeister, 1980a, 1980b, 1984, and Samuelson, 1987, p. 456). Moreover, there is some confusion about the relationship between the Standard commodity and Ricardo's search for an "invariable measure of value"; in fact, it is frequently maintained that the Standard commodity was meant to provide a solution to Ricardo's problem. For detailed attempts to clarify the different issues that are at stake, see Meldolesi (1966), Roncaglia (1978, ch. 4), and Kurz and Salvadori (1986, 1987, 1992, 1993a). In the latter contributions it is argued that (i) Sraffa saw only a single analytical purpose for the concept of the Standard commodity: it is conceived of as a useful, although not a necessary, tool of analysis; (ii) Sraffa relates the Standard commodity to Ricardo's search for an "invariable measure of value"; (iii) however, this is done only with regard to that aspect of Ricardo's search which is concerned with the impact of changes in distribution on relative prices within a *given* technique, whereas the other aspect of Ricardo's search, that is, the one related to interspatial and intertemporal comparisons and therefore *different* techniques, plays no role in the measuring device suggested by Sraffa. The understanding of this fact can perhaps be enhanced by observing that equation (4.43) cannot be graphed for different techniques in the same coordinate space.

6. Exercises

6.1. In order to prove some statements contained in Subsection 1.1 prove that the following statements are equivalent:

(i) there is a sequence of z indices $i_1, i_2, \ldots, i_z$ $(z \geqslant 1)$ such that

$$a_{ii_1} a_{i_1 i_2} \cdots a_{i_z j} > 0;$$

(ii) there is a natural number z such that

$$\mathbf{e}_i^T \mathbf{A}^{z+1} \mathbf{e}_j = \sum_{i_1=1}^{n} \sum_{i_2=1}^{n} \cdots \sum_{i_z=1}^{n} a_{ii_1} a_{i_1 i_2} \cdots a_{i_z j} > 0,$$

(iii) there is a natural number $z \leqslant n-1$ such that

$$\mathbf{e}_i^T \mathbf{A}^{z+1} \mathbf{e}_j = \sum_{i_1=1}^{n} \sum_{i_2=1}^{n} \cdots \sum_{i_z=1}^{n} a_{ii_1} a_{i_1 i_2} \cdots a_{i_z j} > 0,$$

(iv) $\mathbf{e}_i^T (\mathbf{A}^2 + \cdots + \mathbf{A}^n) \mathbf{e}_j > 0$.

[*Hint*: A product of nonnegative numbers is positive if and only if all of them are positive, whereas a sum of nonnegative numbers is positive if and only if at least one of them is positive. If there is a natural number z such that $\mathbf{e}_i^T \mathbf{A}^{z+1} \mathbf{e}_j > 0$, then there is a natural number $t \leqslant n-1$ such that $e_i^T A^{t+1} e_j > 0$ since if $z > n - 1$, at least two elements of the sequence $i, i_1, i_2, \ldots, i_z, j$ are equal.]

6.2. Prove that if the order of the square nonnegative matrix A is larger than 1, then the following statements are equivalent:

(i) the input matrix matrix A is indecomposable
(ii) $I + A + \cdots + A^{n-1} > 0$,
(iii) $A + A^2 + \cdots + A^n > 0$.

[*Hint*: Prove that (i) implies (ii) by using Theorem A.3.8 of the Mathematical Appendix; prove that (i) and (ii) imply (iii); then prove that if (i) does not hold, then also (ii) and (iii) do not.]

6.3. Show that a viable economy is able to produce a surplus if and only if it is not just viable.

6.4. If there is only one commodity, the input matrix $A = [a]$ is indecomposable irrespective of whether the element a is positive or nil. Does this fact imply that the only existing commodity is basic?

6.5. Determine which commodities are basics and which are not when the material input matrix A is one of the following (where "$+$" represents a positive element):

$$
\text{(i)} \begin{bmatrix} + & + & 0 & 0 \\ 0 & + & + & 0 \\ 0 & 0 & + & + \\ 0 & 0 & 0 & + \end{bmatrix}; \quad \text{(ii)} \begin{bmatrix} + & 0 & + \\ 0 & + & + \\ + & 0 & 0 \end{bmatrix}; \quad \text{(iii)} \begin{bmatrix} 0 & + & 0 & 0 \\ 0 & 0 & + & 0 \\ 0 & 0 & 0 & + \\ + & 0 & 0 & 0 \end{bmatrix}.
$$

[*Hint*: Find $A + A^2 + A^3 (+ A^4)$.]

6.6. Determine the prices and the wage rate at each rate of profit on the assumption that the technical conditions of production are given by

$$
A = \begin{bmatrix} 0 & \frac{2}{5} & \frac{1}{60} \\ \frac{2}{5} & 0 & \frac{1}{60} \\ \frac{1}{5} & \frac{1}{5} & \frac{13}{30} \end{bmatrix}, \quad l = \begin{bmatrix} 1 \\ 1 \\ 1 \end{bmatrix},
$$

and the numeraire consists of one unit of commodity 3. Then show that the wage rate is positive for $0 \leqslant r < 1 = R$, and for $r > 2$. However, some prices are negative for $r > 2$. [*Hint*: The wage rate is

$$
w = \frac{5}{6} \frac{30 - 13(1 + r) - 5(1 + r)^2 + 2(1 + r)^3}{25 + 15(1 + r) + 2(1 + r)^2},
$$

which is positive for $r < 1$ and $r > 2$, whereas the price of commodity 1 is negative for $r > \frac{120}{101}$.]

6.7. Prove equation (4.14). [*Hint*: The simplest way to prove that **B** is the inverse of **A** consists in showing that $\mathbf{AB} = \mathbf{I}$; however, you may also use the result of the next exercise.]

6.8. On the assumption that $\mathbf{b}^T\mathbf{a} \neq 1$ determine α in such a way that $(\mathbf{I} + \alpha\mathbf{ab}^T)$ is the inverse of matrix $(\mathbf{I} - \mathbf{ab}^T)$. What happens if $\mathbf{b}^T\mathbf{a} = 1$? [*Hint*: $\mathbf{ab}^T\mathbf{ab}^T = (\mathbf{b}^T\mathbf{a})\mathbf{ab}^T$.]

6.9. Prove that matrix $(\mathbf{I} - w\mathbf{ld}^T)^{-1}\mathbf{A}$, mentioned in Subsection 1.6, is indecomposable if **A** is indecomposable. [*Hint*: If **A** is indecomposable and **B** is nonnegative, then matrix $(\mathbf{A} + \mathbf{B})$ is indecomposable (why?).]

6.10. In Subsection 1.6 it has been shown that if there is a scalar r and a scalar $w, r > R$ and $0 \leqslant w \leqslant W$, such that equation (4.6) has a solution (matrix **A** being indecomposable), then at least one price has to be negative. Show that this is still true even if $w > W$. [*Hint*: Let w^s and $\mathbf{p}^s$ be the wage rate and the price vector, respectively, when the numeraire consists of the Standard commodity (see Subsection 4.3). Obviously, w^s and r are both positive if and only if $0 < r < R$ (why?). Since, by assumption,

$$w(r) = \frac{w^s(r)}{\mathbf{d}^T\mathbf{p}^s(r)} > 0,$$

for some $r > R$, $\mathbf{d}^T\mathbf{p}^s(r) < 0$ for that value of r. Hence....]

6.11. Prove the following statement: let **A** be a semipositive square matrix (not necessarily indecomposable); let λ_r be a real eigenvalue of **A** different from the largest, λ_m; and let **y** be a right (left) eigenvector associated with λ_r. Then **y** is not positive. [*Hint*: Read again the proof of Theorem A.3.6 in the Mathematical Appendix.]

6.12. Show that if there is a scalar r and a scalar $w, r > R^*$ and $0 \leqslant w \leqslant W$, such that equation (4.6) has a solution (matrix **A** being indecomposable or not), then vector **p** is not positive. [*Hint*: Use the result of the previous exercise; read Subsection 1.6 again.]

6.13. (Krause, 1981) A nonnegative decomposable matrix **S** has been called a "Sraffa matrix" if its canonical form **A** (see equation (A.24) of the Mathematical Appendix) satisfies the following properties:

(i) inequalities (4.22) hold;
(ii) the largest real eigenvalue of submatrix $\mathbf{A}_{11}$ is larger than the largest real eigenvalue of submatrix $\mathbf{A}_{ii}$ $(i = 2, 3, \ldots, s)$.

Prove that $\mathbf{Sy} = \lambda\mathbf{y}$ has a unique solution $\lambda \geqslant 0$, $\mathbf{y} > \mathbf{0}$ (up to a factor) if and only if **S** is a "Sraffa matrix." [*Hint*: Use the results contained in Subsection 2.5 and exercise 6.11.]

6.14. (Krause, 1981) Show that if matrix **A** is decomposable, then all the good properties of Section 1 hold if and only if **A** is a "Sraffa matrix" (see the previous exercise).

6.15. Choose a process to produce corn and a process to produce iron among those listed in Table 3.6 of the previous chapter and determine the k–r relationship and the y–r relationship on the assumption that $g = 0$ and only corn is consumed. Repeat the same exercise for each possible choice.

6.16. Perform the previous exercise on the assumption that $g = 0$ and only iron is consumed.

6.17. Perform the previous two exercises for $g = 0.1, g = 0.2$, and $g = 0.3$.

6.18. A negative price Wicksell effect is obtained when the k–r relationship relative to a given technique is increasing for some r. By exploring the solutions to the previous three exercises determine those cases which exhibit negative price Wicksell effects.

6.19. A negative real Wicksell effect is obtained when at a switch point the technique adopted at higher levels of the rate of profit has a value of capital per head higher than the technique adopted for lower levels of the rate of profit. By exploring the solutions to exercises 6.15–6.17 of this chapter and to exercise 8.14 of the previous chapter point out a number of examples of negative real Wicksell effects.

6.20. (Calculus)(Hosoda, 1990) There are two commodities; workers consume only commodity 1 and do not save, whereas capitalists consume only commodity 2 and save a proportion 0.1 of their income. The technical conditions of production are given by

$$\mathbf{A} = \begin{bmatrix} 0 & \frac{1}{2} \\ \frac{1}{8} & 0 \end{bmatrix}, \quad \mathbf{l} = \begin{bmatrix} 1 \\ 1 \end{bmatrix}.$$

Let the rate of profit r equal 10 g, where the growth rate g is considered the independent variable, and determine consumption per head (in value terms) as a function of the growth rate by using commodity 1 as numeraire. Show that this relationship is increasing.

6.21. (Calculus)(Hosoda, 1990) Perform the previous exercise by using commodity 2 as numeraire. Show that consumption per head (in value terms) as a function of the growth rate is first decreasing and then increasing.

6.22. (Steedman, 1988b) In Subsection 4.1, $k = \mathbf{q}^T \mathbf{A} \mathbf{p}$ is the value of capital per head in the economy as a whole on the assumption that commodities are consumed in proportion to vector **b**, when the growth rate equals g and the consumption unit serves also as the numeraire. On the other hand $h = (\mathbf{b}^T\mathbf{Ap}/\mathbf{b}^T\mathbf{l})$ is the value of capital per head in the production of the consumption unit. Draw a diagram analogous to Figure 4.2 and show how h is determined graphically. [*Hint*: Multiply equation (4.39a) by $\mathbf{b}^T$ and take account of equation (4.39b); then note that $w(-1) = (1/\mathbf{b}^T\mathbf{l})$.]

6.23. Prove that statement (4.47) is equivalent to each of the statements (i)–(ix) of Section 3. [*Hint*: Prove that statements (vi) and (vii) imply equation (4.47); show that $\varphi = (1 - \lambda)^{-1}\lambda$; then prove that statement (4.47) and equation (4.32) imply statement (vi).]

6.24. (Calculus) Prove that the derivatives of every degree of labor commanded prices (Subsection 4.2) as functions of the rate of profit are positive for $0 \leqslant r < R$. [*Hint*: Use the procedure adopted in Subsection 1.5.]

6.25. (Calculus) Prove that

$$\lim_{\substack{r \to R \\ r < R}} \hat{p}_h = +\infty$$

and

$$\lim_{\substack{r \to R \\ r > R}} \hat{p}_h = -\infty.$$

[*Hint*: $\hat{p}_h = p_h/w$.]

6.26. Choose a process to produce corn and a process to produce iron among those listed in Table 3.6 of Chapter 3. Determine the Standard commodity and the prices when the Standard commodity is used as numeraire. Repeat the same exercise for each possible choice.

6.27. Use the results of the previous exercise to comment on the opinion expressed by Blaug that a change in distribution "has no effect on relative prices measured in terms of the Standard commodity for the simple reason that the change alters the measuring rod in the same way as it alters the pattern of prices being measured" (Blaug, 1987, p. 436).

6.28. Determine the ratio between the quantity of labor "embodied" in one unit of the Standard commodity and the quantity of direct labor required to produce it.

6.29. An economy is said *profitable* if there is a price vector which gives rise to nonnegative profits on the assumption that the wage rate equals zero. In the model of this chapter the economy is profitable if and only if there exists a vector **p** such that

$$\mathbf{p} \geqslant \mathbf{Ap}.$$

Prove that the economic systems contemplated in Section 1 are profitable if and only if they are viable.

6.30. Derive the $w-r$ relationship if wages are paid *ante factum*. Is the price vector determined by equations (4.6) and the vector of labor commanded prices (see Subsection 4.2) affected by this change in the assumptions?

6.31. As in exercise 9.9 of Chapter 2, call *productive* the labor provided by workers directly involved in the production of corn and *unproductive* the labor provided by all other workers. Assume that each worker (productive or unproductive) consumes a basket of commodities described by vector **b**. Let $\mathbf{H} = (\mathbf{A} + \mathbf{lb}^T)$ and assume that the largest real eigenvalue of matrix **H** is less than unity. Determine the maximum number of unproductive workers per productive worker employed, given these conditions. [*Hint*: See hint to exercise 8.20 of Chapter 3.]

6.32. Discuss the condition on the largest real eigenvalue of matrix **H** mentioned in the previous exercise.

5

Choice of technique

In Chapter 4 it has been assumed that there is a single process for the production of each commodity. In this chapter it will be assumed that there are $v_i \geq 1$ processes to produce commodity i $(i = 1, 2, \ldots, n)$. As a consequence, the problem of the choice of technique arises. This problem has been analyzed in Chapters 2 and 3 with regard to the simple cases of a one-commodity and a two-commodity model, respectively. In the following discussion the reader will recognize that the substance of the results derived carries over to the more general case; however, some technicalities are necessary.

In obvious notation, each process is defined as

$$(\mathbf{a}^{(h)}, \mathbf{b}^{(h)}, l^{(h)}), \quad h = 1, 2, \ldots, \sum_{j=1}^{n} v_j,$$

where $\mathbf{a}^{(h)}$ is the commodity input vector, $\mathbf{b}^{(h)}$ is the output vector, and $l^{(h)}$ is the labor input. Since single production is assumed, $\mathbf{b}^{(h)}$ is a vector which has only one positive component, all other components being zero. Without a loss of generality we may assume that $\mathbf{b}^{(h)}$ is a unit vector. It is possible to arrange the processes in such a way that

$$\mathbf{b}^{(h)} = \mathbf{e}_i \quad \text{if } z_{i-1} < h \leq z_i, \quad \text{where } z_0 = 0$$

and

$$z_i = \sum_{j=1}^{i} v_j \ (i = 1, 2, \ldots, n).$$

If w, r, and $\mathbf{p}$ are the current wage rate, rate of profit, and price vector, respectively, then process $(\mathbf{a}^{(h)}, \mathbf{b}^{(h)}, l^{(h)})$ is not able to pay extra profits if

$$\mathbf{b}^{(h)T}\mathbf{p} \leq (1 + r)\mathbf{a}^{(h)T}\mathbf{p} + wl^{(h)}, \tag{5.1}$$

and it does not incur extra costs if

$$\mathbf{b}^{(h)T}\mathbf{p} \geqslant (1+r)\mathbf{a}^{(h)T}\mathbf{p} + wl^{(h)}.$$

In a *long-period position* no process can pay extra profits, and none of the operated processes incurs extra costs at the current rate of profit. In addition, the operated processes must be able to satisfy the requirements for use of the economy, that is, they must allow the production of the amounts of the different commodities in demand for consumption and investment purposes.

The argument of the present chapter develops in the following steps: Sections 1 and 2 will be concerned with the simplified case in which all commodities are required for use. In Section 3 a more general case will be studied: some commodities may not be required for use. All cases will be dealt with in terms of both procedures presented in Chapters 2 and 3, that is, the direct and the indirect approach, respectively. Sections 4 and 5 complete the argument: in the former a general framework of the analysis is presented, whereas the latter deals with the concept of the wage frontier.

1. A simplified case: All commodities are required for use

In the following discussion it will be assumed that all commodities are required for use. The choice of technique will be decided in terms of a given rate of profit, $r = r^*$. Let there be n processes, one for each commodity, which, if activated, at the going rate of profit r^* give rise to strictly positive prices. Then it will be proved that a long-period position exists. In Subsection 1.1 we shall make use of the indirect approach, in Subsection 1.2 of the direct one.

1.1. The indirect approach

A *technique* is defined as any n-tuple of processes consisting of one process for each commodity. For obvious reasons we are interested in viable techniques only which have a positive price vector for $r = r^*$. A technique is represented by the pair

$$(\mathbf{A}_h, \mathbf{l}_h) \quad h = 1, 2, \ldots, \prod_{i=1}^{n} v_i.$$

A technique is *cost-minimizing at the rate of profit* r^* if at the wage rate and the price vector corresponding to r^* no known process is able to pay extra profits. In other words, technique $(\mathbf{A}_k, \mathbf{l}_k)$ minimizes costs at the rate of profit r^*, if and only if

$$\mathbf{p}_k \leqslant (1 + r^*)\mathbf{A}_h\mathbf{p}_k + w_k\mathbf{l}_h, \quad h = 1, 2, \ldots, \prod_{i=1}^{n} v_i$$

where $\mathbf{p}_k$ and w_k are determined by the equations

$$\mathbf{p}_k = (1 + r^*)\mathbf{A}_k\mathbf{p}_k + w_k\mathbf{l}_k$$
$$\mathbf{d}^T\mathbf{p}_k = 1.$$

It is possible to prove that if there is a technique which has a positive price vector and a positive wage rate for $r = r^*$, then there is a cost-minimizing technique at rate of profit r^*. In order to do so, consider the following propositions which are the analogs of Propositions 3.1–3.3 in Subsection 5.2 of Chapter 3.

Proposition 5.1. If, at rate of profit r^*, process $(\mathbf{a}, \mathbf{b}, l)$ is able to pay extra profits at the positive prices and the positive wage rate of technique $(\mathbf{A}_h, \mathbf{l}_h)$, then there is a technique $(\mathbf{A}_k, \mathbf{l}_k)$ which can pay a wage rate larger than that paid by technique $(\mathbf{A}_h, \mathbf{l}_h)$, where the wage is measured in terms of a numeraire consisting of positive amounts of all commodities.

Proof. Let $(\mathbf{A}_k, \mathbf{l}_k)$ be the technique made up of process $(\mathbf{a}, \mathbf{b}, l)$ and the $n-1$ processes of technique $(\mathbf{A}_h, \mathbf{l}_h)$ producing commodities different from that produced by process $(\mathbf{a}, \mathbf{b}, l)$. Then,

$$\mathbf{p}_h \geqslant (1 + r^*)\mathbf{A}_k\mathbf{p}_h + w_h\mathbf{l}_k, \tag{5.2}$$

where $\mathbf{p}_h$ and w_h are such that

$$\mathbf{p}_h = (1 + r^*)\mathbf{A}_h\mathbf{p}_h + w_h\mathbf{l}_h$$
$$\mathbf{d}^T\mathbf{p}_h = 1,$$

where $\mathbf{d}$ is a given, positive vector. In order to simplify the proof we will assume that $\mathbf{l}_k > 0$; exercise 8.1 deals with the proof of Proposition 5.1 when $\mathbf{l}_k \geqslant 0$. Since inequality (5.2) holds,

$$[\mathbf{I} - (1 + r^*)\mathbf{A}_k]\mathbf{p}_h > 0.$$

Thus, matrix $[\mathbf{I} - (1 + r^*)\mathbf{A}_k]$ is invertible (see Theorem A.3.1 of the Mathematical Appendix) and

$$[\mathbf{I} - (1 + r^*)\mathbf{A}_k]^{-1} \geqslant 0,$$

which implies that the prices associated with technique $(\mathbf{A}_k, \mathbf{l}_k)$ at the rate of profit r^* are positive. Inequality (5.2) implies also that

$$\mathbf{p}_h \geqslant w_h[\mathbf{I} - (1 + r^*)\mathbf{A}_k]^{-1}\mathbf{l}_k, \tag{5.3}$$

that is,

$$1 = \mathbf{d}^T\mathbf{p}_h > w_h\mathbf{d}^T[\mathbf{I} - (1 + r^*)\mathbf{A}_k]^{-1}\mathbf{l}_k = \frac{w_h}{w_k}. \qquad \text{Q.E.D.}$$

The reader will recognize that if in the statement of Proposition 5.1 the wage were to be measured in terms of a numeraire consisting of positive amounts of some commodities only, then technique $(\mathbf{A}_k, \mathbf{l}_k)$ would pay a wage rate higher than *or equal* to the one paid by technique $(\mathbf{A}_h, \mathbf{l}_h)$. Proposition 5.1 is sufficient to show that if the numeraire consists of a positive amount of each commodity, then each technique which, at the given rate of profit r^*, is able to pay the highest possible wage rate is cost-minimizing at that rate of profit. The argument just presented implies that otherwise some techniques among those which are able to pay the highest possible wage rate might not be cost-minimizing.

The following Proposition 5.2 rules out the possibility that a technique which is not able to pay the highest possible wage rate can be a technique which minimizes costs.

Proposition 5.2. Let $(\mathbf{A}_h, \mathbf{l}_h)$ and $(\mathbf{A}_k, \mathbf{l}_k)$ be two techniques such that at rate of profit r^* $\mathbf{p}_h > \mathbf{0}, \mathbf{p}_k > \mathbf{0}$ and

$$w_k > w_h > 0. \qquad (5.4)$$

Then there is a process in technique $(\mathbf{A}_k, \mathbf{l}_k)$ which pays extra profits at the prices of technique $(\mathbf{A}_h, \mathbf{l}_h)$.

Proof. Assume the opposite. Then

$$[\mathbf{I} - (1 + r^*)\mathbf{A}_k]\mathbf{p}_h \leqslant w_h\mathbf{l}_k.$$

Since $\mathbf{d}^T[\mathbf{I} - (1 + r^*)\mathbf{A}_k]^{-1} \geqslant \mathbf{0}^T$, we obtain

$$1 = \mathbf{d}^T\mathbf{p}_h \leqslant w_h\mathbf{d}^T[\mathbf{I} - (1 + r^*)\mathbf{A}_k]^{-1}\mathbf{l}_k = \frac{w_h}{w_k}.$$

Hence the first of inequalities (5.4) is contradicted. Q.E.D.

If there is more than one cost-minimizing technique it is interesting to know whether they give rise to the same prices. This question is answered in the affirmative by Proposition 5.3.

Proposition 5.3. Let $(\mathbf{A}_h, \mathbf{l}_h)$ and $(\mathbf{A}_k, \mathbf{l}_k)$ be two techniques which are both cost-minimizing at rate of profit r^*, where $w_k > 0, w_h > 0, \mathbf{p}_k > \mathbf{0}, \mathbf{p}_h > \mathbf{0}$, then $w_k = w_h$ and $\mathbf{p}_k = \mathbf{p}_h$.

Proof. Obviously,

$$[\mathbf{I} - (1 + r^*)\mathbf{A}_k]\mathbf{p}_h \leqslant w_h\mathbf{l}_k \qquad (5.5a)$$

$$[\mathbf{I} - (1 + r^*)\mathbf{A}_h]\mathbf{p}_k \lessgtr w_k\mathbf{l}_h, \tag{5.5b}$$

where

$$[\mathbf{I} - (1 + r^*)\mathbf{A}_h]\mathbf{p}_h = w_h\mathbf{l}_h$$
$$[\mathbf{I} - (1 + r^*)\mathbf{A}_k]\mathbf{p}_k = w_k\mathbf{l}_k$$
$$\mathbf{d}^T\mathbf{p}_h = \mathbf{d}^T\mathbf{p}_k = 1.$$

It is an immediate consequence of Proposition 5.2 that

$$w_k = w_h.$$

Next, multiplying inequalities (5.5a) and (5.5b) by $[\mathbf{I} - (1 + r^*)\mathbf{A}_k]^{-1} \geqslant \mathbf{0}$ and $[\mathbf{I} - (1 + r^*)\mathbf{A}_h]^{-1} \geqslant \mathbf{0}$, respectively, we obtain

$$\mathbf{p}_h \lessgtr \mathbf{p}_k \lessgtr \mathbf{p}_h$$

and thus

$$\mathbf{p}_k = \mathbf{p}_h. \qquad \text{Q.E.D.}$$

Propositions 5.1–5.3 are important in themselves. In addition, they can be used to establish the following theorem, the proof of which is the same as the proof of Theorem 3.1.

Theorem 5.1.

  (a) If there is a technique which has a positive price vector and a positive wage rate for $r = r^*$, then there is a cost-minimizing technique at rate of profit r^*.[1]
  (b) A technique which gives rise to a vector of prices $\mathbf{p}^* \geqslant \mathbf{0}$ and a wage rate $w^* > 0$ for $r = r^*$ minimizes costs at rate of profit r^*, if and only if no other technique allows a wage rate higher than w^* for $r = r^*$, given a numeraire consisting of a positive amount of each commodity.
  (c) If there is more than one technique which minimizes costs at rate of profit r^*, and if these techniques pay a positive wage rate, then these techniques have the same wage rate and the same price vector at $r = r^*$.

Exercises 8.3–8.10 explore the analogs of Propositions 5.1–5.3 and Theorem 5.1 when the wage rate equals zero.

[1] If the number of processes is not finite, statement (a) is to be changed in the following way:

"If there is a technique which has a positive price vector and a positive wage rate for $r = r^*$ such that no technique can pay a wage rate larger than that paid by it, then there is a cost-minimizing technique at rate of profit r^*".

1.2. The direct approach

Let

$$A = \begin{bmatrix} \mathbf{a}^{(1)T} \\ \mathbf{a}^{(2)T} \\ \vdots \\ \mathbf{a}^{(m)T} \end{bmatrix}, \quad B = \begin{bmatrix} \mathbf{b}^{(1)T} \\ \mathbf{b}^{(2)T} \\ \vdots \\ \mathbf{b}^{(m)T} \end{bmatrix}, \quad \mathbf{l} = \begin{bmatrix} l^{(1)} \\ l^{(2)} \\ \vdots \\ l^{(m)} \end{bmatrix},$$

where $m = \sum_{j=1}^{n} v_j$. No process pays extra profits at wage rate w, rate of profit r, and price vector $\mathbf{p}$ if and only if

$$\mathbf{Bp} \leqslant (1+r)\mathbf{Ap} + w\mathbf{l}. \tag{5.6}$$

Prices are normalized by setting

$$\mathbf{d}^T \mathbf{p} = 1, \tag{5.7}$$

where $\mathbf{d}$ is a positive vector. A pair $(\mathbf{p}, w)$ is a long-period solution at the rate of profit r if

$$\mathbf{p} \geqslant \mathbf{0}, \quad w \geqslant 0, \tag{5.8}$$

equation (5.7) and inequality (5.6) are satisfied, and for each of the n commodities there is a process producing it such that it does not incur extra costs at prices $\mathbf{p}$, wage rate w, and rate of profit r. This last condition is satisfied if and only if there is a vector $\mathbf{x}$ such that

$$\mathbf{x} \geqslant \mathbf{0} \tag{5.9}$$
$$\mathbf{x}^T[\mathbf{B} - (1+r)\mathbf{A}]\mathbf{p} = w\mathbf{x}^T\mathbf{l} \tag{5.10}$$
$$\mathbf{x}^T\mathbf{B} > \mathbf{0}^T. \tag{5.11}$$

Equation (5.10), also because of inequalities (5.6) and (5.9), means that the ith element of vector $\mathbf{x}$ is nought if the process $(\mathbf{a}^{(i)}, \mathbf{b}^{(i)}, l^{(i)})$ incurs extra costs at prices $\mathbf{p}$, wage rate w, and rate of profit r. Inequality (5.11), then, asserts that for each commodity there is at least one process $(\mathbf{a}^{(j)}, \mathbf{b}^{(j)}, l^{(j)})$ producing it such that the jth element of vector $\mathbf{x}$ is positive. Hence, in order to determine the long-period prices corresponding to the rate of profit r, we just need to find vectors $\mathbf{p}$ and $\mathbf{x}$ and scalar w such that (5.6)–(5.11) are satisfied.

In order to simplify the exposition we are concerned here only with the case in which $w > 0$ and $\mathbf{l} > \mathbf{0}$. The cases in which either $w \geqslant 0$ or $\mathbf{l} \geqslant \mathbf{0}$ are addressed as exercises (see exercises 8.11–8.17). It is easily shown that the following holds:

Lemma 5.1. The system of inequalities (5.6)–(5.11) admits a solution with a positive w if and only if the following system of inequalities admits a solution:

$$[\mathbf{B} - (1 + r)\mathbf{A}]\mathbf{y} \leqslant \mathbf{l}, \tag{5.12a}$$

$$\mathbf{z}^T[\mathbf{B} - (1 + r)\mathbf{A}]\mathbf{y} = \mathbf{z}^T\mathbf{l}, \tag{5.12b}$$

$$\mathbf{z}^T[\mathbf{B} - (1 + r)\mathbf{A}] \geqslant \mathbf{d}^T, \tag{5.12c}$$

$$\mathbf{z}^T[\mathbf{B} - (1 + r)\mathbf{A}]\mathbf{y} = \mathbf{d}^T\mathbf{y}, \tag{5.12d}$$

$$\mathbf{y} \geqslant \mathbf{0}, \quad \mathbf{z} \geqslant \mathbf{0}. \tag{5.12e}$$

Proof. Let $(\mathbf{p}^*, w^*, \mathbf{x}^*)$ be a solution of system (5.6)–(5.11), then there is at least one process for each commodity such that the corresponding entry of vector $\mathbf{x}^*$ is positive. Let us pick one of these processes for each commodity and obtain a set of n processes which can be represented as $(\mathbf{C}, \mathbf{m})$ where $\mathbf{C}$ is the material input matrix, $\mathbf{m}$ is the labor input vector, the output matrix being the identity matrix by appropriate order of the rows of matrix $\mathbf{C}$ and vector $\mathbf{m}$. Since

$$[\mathbf{I} - (1 + r)\mathbf{C}]\mathbf{p}^* = w^*\mathbf{m},$$

and $w^*\mathbf{m} > \mathbf{0}$, matrix $[\mathbf{I} - (1 + r)\mathbf{C}]$ is invertible and its inverse is semipositive because of Theorem A.3.1 of the Mathematical Appendix. Therefore, there is a semipositive vector $\mathbf{u}$ such that

$$\mathbf{u}^T[\mathbf{I} - (1 + r)\mathbf{C}] = \mathbf{d}^T.$$

As a consequence there is a vector $\mathbf{z}$ such that

$$\mathbf{z}^T[\mathbf{B} - (1 + r)\mathbf{A}] = \mathbf{d}^T,$$

$$\mathbf{z}^T[\mathbf{B} - (1 + r)\mathbf{A}]\mathbf{y} = \mathbf{z}^T\mathbf{l},$$

$$\mathbf{z} \geqslant \mathbf{0},$$

where $\mathbf{y} = (1/w^*)\mathbf{p}^*$. This is enough to prove that system (5.12) admits a solution if system (5.6)–(5.11) admits a solution. Similarly, let $(\mathbf{y}^*, \mathbf{z}^*)$ be a solution of system (5.12), then

$$\mathbf{z}^{*T}\mathbf{B} \geqslant (1 + r)\mathbf{z}^{*T}\mathbf{A} + \mathbf{d}^T > \mathbf{0}^T.$$

Therefore, vectors $\mathbf{x}^* = \mathbf{z}^*, \mathbf{p}^* = (1/\mathbf{d}^T\mathbf{y}^*)\mathbf{y}^*$ and $w^* = 1/\mathbf{d}^T\mathbf{y}^*$ constitute a solution to system (5.6)–(5.11). This is enough to complete the proof.

Q.E.D.

Lemma 5.2. System (5.12) has a solution if and only if there is a nonnegative vector $\mathbf{v}$ such that

$$\mathbf{v}^T[\mathbf{B} - (1 + r)\mathbf{A}] > \mathbf{0}^T. \tag{5.13}$$

Proof. The "only if" part of the Lemma is trivial. In order to prove the "if" part, let us state that by the Equilibrium Theorem of Linear Programming (see Theorem A.4.3) we obtain that system (5.12) is equivalent to each of the following linear programming problems, which are dual to each other:

	(primal)		(dual)
Min	$z^T 1$	Max	$d^T y$
s. to	$z^T[B - (1 + r)A] \geqslant d^T$	s. to	$[B - (1 + r)A]y \leqslant 1$
	$z \geqslant 0,$		$y \geqslant 0.$

Since the zero vector is a feasible solution to the dual and since the primal has a feasible solution by hypothesis, both problems have optimal solutions because of the Duality Theorem of Linear Programming (see Theorem A.4.2).   Q.E.D.

Theorem 5.2. For a given rate of profit r,

(a) if and only if there is a nonnegative vector v such that inequality (5.13) holds, there is a price vector $p^* \geqslant 0$ and a wage rate $w^* > 0$ such that no process pays extra profits and at least one process for each commodity does not incur extra costs;

(b) the long-period wage rate w^* is the minimum w for which there is a vector p such that inequalities (5.6)–(5.8) are satisfied;

(c) if there is a long-period price vector $p^* > 0$ and a long-period wage rate $w^* > 0$, then they are unique.

Proof. Statement (a) is a direct consequence of Lemmas 5.1 and 5.2. By exploring the proofs of Lemmas 5.1 and 5.2 we obtain that $w^* = 1/d^T y^*$ and $p^* = w^* y^*$, where y^* is a solution to the dual problem in the proof of Lemma 5.2. The proof of statement (c) is left as an exercise since the procedure to prove it is analogous to that used in the proof of Proposition 5.3 of the previous subsection.   Q.E.D.

2. A special case: All commodities are basic in all systems

Let us take the indirect approach first. If all commodities are basic in a system, then all commodities have to be produced – that is, they are required for *use* – even if not all of them are required for *consumption*. As a consequence, if all commodities are basic in all systems, all are required for use whatever commodities are consumed. Thus, the analysis presented in Subsection 1.1 holds.

In the language of the direct approach, the condition that all commodities are basics in all systems reads:

$$\{x \geqslant 0, x^T[B - A] \geqslant 0^T\} \Rightarrow x^T B > 0^T. \tag{5.14}$$

Table 5.1

Processes	material inputs			labor		outputs		
	corn	iron	aluminium			corn	iron	aluminium
(1)	1	0	8	1	→	0	0	10
(2)	4	2	0	1	→	0	10	0
(3)	0	0	1	1	→	10	0	0
(4)	0	4	0	1	→	10	0	0

A pair $(\mathbf{p}, w)$ is a long-period solution at the rate of profit r if and only if equation (5.7) and inequalities (5.6) and (5.8) are satisfied and if for each of the commodities required for use there is a process producing it such that it does not incur extra costs at prices $\mathbf{p}$, wage rate w, and rate of profit r. This last condition is obtained if there is a vector $\mathbf{x}$ such that inequality (5.9) and equation (5.10) are satisfied and

$$\mathbf{x}^T[\mathbf{B} - \mathbf{A}] \geqslant \mathbf{c}^T, \tag{5.15}$$

where $\mathbf{c}$ is a nonnegative vector with positive entries corresponding to commodities required for *consumption*. In fact, since inequality (5.9) holds the positive entries of vector $\mathbf{x}$ correspond to commodities required for *use*. But because of implication (5.14), inequality (5.15) can be substituted by inequality (5.11). As a consequence, the analysis presented in Subsection 1.2 holds.

3. A more general case: Some commodities are not required for use

3.1. An example

It is perhaps best to analyze an example first. Let corn, iron, and aluminium be produced as in Table 5.1.

It is easily recognized that

(i) if $r^* \leqslant 10\sqrt{17}-41$, then both techniques made up of processes $(1, 2, 3)$ and of processes $(1, 2, 4)$, respectively, have positive prices;

(ii) if $10\sqrt{17} - 41 < r^* < \frac{1}{4}$, then the technique made up of processes $(1, 2, 4)$ has positive prices, whereas the technique made up of processes $(1, 2, 3)$ has not;

(iii) there is $\bar{r} = (5\sqrt{177} - 63)/38 < \frac{1}{4}$ such that if $0 \leqslant r \leqslant \bar{r}$, then the technique made up of processes $(1, 2, 3)$ is cost-minimizing, whereas if $\bar{r} \leqslant r \leqslant \frac{1}{4}$, then the technique made up of processes $(1, 2, 4)$ is cost-minimizing;

(iv) if $r^* \geqslant \frac{1}{4}$, then neither the technique made up of processes $(1, 2, 3)$ nor the one made up of processes $(1, 2, 4)$ has positive prices;

(v) there is a nonnegative vector **v** such that inequality (5.13) holds if and only if $r^* < \frac{1}{4}$.

Therefore, if all commodities are required for use, then the rate of profit cannot exceed $\frac{1}{4}$. However, if only corn is consumed and iron and aluminium are not, then the rate of profit can be larger than $\frac{1}{4}$ but must be lower than $(5\sqrt{17} - 13)/8$: it is enough that only processes (2) and (4) are operated, and the price of aluminium is set so high that process (3) is not able to pay extra profits.

There is a further difference if only corn is consumed. With $0 \leqslant r \leqslant \bar{r}$ only processes (1) and (3) need to be operated and the price of iron does not need to be determined by process (2); only a lower and an upper limit are determined: the price of iron must be so high that process (4) does not pay extra profits and so low that process (2) does not pay extra profits. Similarly, with $\bar{r} \leqslant r < \frac{1}{4}$, only processes (2) and (4) need to be operated and the price of aluminium does not need to be determined by process (1); once again only a lower and an upper limit are determined: the price of aluminium must be so high that process (3) does not pay extra profits and so low that process (1) does not pay extra profits. The reader should have recognized that the example given here is similar to the one presented in Section 6 of Chapter 3.

3.2. The direct approach

Once again a pair $(\mathbf{p}, w)$ is a long-period solution at the rate of profit r if and only if equations (5.7) and (5.10) and inequalities (5.6), (5.8), and (5.15) are satisfied. Moreover, in order to choose a numeraire constituted by commodities which are certainly produced, it is convenient to replace equation (5.7) with the following equation

$$\mathbf{c}^T\mathbf{p} = 1, \tag{5.16}$$

where **c** is, as in Section 2, a nonnegative vector with positive entries corresponding to commodities required for *consumption*. Hence, in order to determine the long-period prices corresponding to the rate of profit r we just need to find vectors **p** and **x** and scalar w such that

$$[\mathbf{B} - (1+r)\mathbf{A}]\mathbf{p} \leqslant w\mathbf{l}, \tag{5.17a}$$

$$\mathbf{x}^T[\mathbf{B} - (1+r)\mathbf{A}]\mathbf{p} = w\mathbf{x}^T\mathbf{l}, \tag{5.17b}$$

$$\mathbf{x}^T[\mathbf{B} - \mathbf{A}] \geqslant \mathbf{c}^T, \tag{5.17c}$$

$$\mathbf{p} \geqslant \mathbf{0}, \quad \mathbf{x} \geqslant \mathbf{0}, \quad w \geqslant 0, \quad \mathbf{c}^T\mathbf{p} = 1. \tag{5.17d}$$

Once again the exposition is simplified by assuming that $w > 0$ and $\mathbf{l} > \mathbf{0}$. The cases in which either $w \geqslant 0$ or $\mathbf{l} \geqslant \mathbf{0}$ will be dealt with as exercise 8.20. It is easily shown that the following holds.

Lemma 5.3. The system of inequalities (5.17) admits a solution with a positive w if and only if the following system of equations and inequalities admits a solution:

$$[\mathbf{B} - (1+r)\mathbf{A}]\mathbf{y} \leqslant \mathbf{l}, \tag{5.18a}$$

$$\mathbf{z}^T[\mathbf{B} - (1+r)\mathbf{A}]\mathbf{y} = \mathbf{z}^T\mathbf{l}, \tag{5.18b}$$

$$\mathbf{z}^T[\mathbf{B} - (1+r)\mathbf{A}] \geqslant \mathbf{c}^T, \tag{5.18c}$$

$$\mathbf{z}^T[\mathbf{B} - (1+r)\mathbf{A}]\mathbf{y} = \mathbf{c}^T\mathbf{y}, \tag{5.18d}$$

$$\mathbf{y} \geqslant \mathbf{0}, \mathbf{z} \geqslant \mathbf{0}. \tag{5.18e}$$

Proof. Let $(\mathbf{p}^*, w^*, \mathbf{x}^*)$ be a solution to system (5.17). Pick all processes corresponding to positive entries of vector $\mathbf{x}^*$. If more than one of these processes produces the same commodity pick only one of them. In this way we obtain a set of s, $s \leqslant n$, processes which can be represented as $(\mathbf{C}, \mathbf{D}, \mathbf{m})$, where $\mathbf{C}$ is the material input matrix, $\mathbf{D}$ is the output matrix, and $\mathbf{m}$ is the labor input vector. If $s = n$, the proof is similar to the proof of Lemma 5.1. If $s < n$, the matrix $(\mathbf{D} - \mathbf{C})$ has $n - s$ zero columns. Delete these columns in order to obtain the square matrices $\hat{\mathbf{C}}$ and $\hat{\mathbf{D}}$. Let $\hat{\mathbf{D}}$ be equal to the identity matrix by appropriate order of the rows of matrix $\mathbf{C}$ and vector $\mathbf{m}$. Finally, let $\hat{\mathbf{p}}^*$ and $\hat{\mathbf{c}}$ be obtained from $\mathbf{p}^*$ and $\mathbf{c}$, respectively, by deleting the entries corresponding to the columns of $\mathbf{C}$ deleted in order to obtain $\hat{\mathbf{C}}$. Since

$$[\mathbf{I} - (1+r)\hat{\mathbf{C}}]\hat{\mathbf{p}}^* = w^*\mathbf{m},$$

and $w^*\mathbf{m} > 0$, matrix $[\mathbf{I} - (1+r)\hat{\mathbf{C}}]$ is invertible and its inverse is semipositive because of Theorem A.3.1 of the Mathematical Appendix. Therefore, there is a semipositive vector $\mathbf{u}$ such that

$$\mathbf{u}^T[\mathbf{I} - (1+r)\hat{\mathbf{C}}] = \hat{\mathbf{c}}^T.$$

As a consequence there is a vector $\mathbf{z}$ such that

$$\mathbf{z}^T[\mathbf{B} - (1+r)\mathbf{A}] = \mathbf{c}^T$$
$$\mathbf{z}^T[\mathbf{B} - (1+r)\mathbf{A}]\mathbf{y} = \mathbf{z}^T\mathbf{l}$$
$$\mathbf{z} \geqslant \mathbf{0},$$

where $\mathbf{y} = (1/w^*)\mathbf{p}^*$. This is enough to prove that system (5.18) admits a solution if system (5.17) admits a solution. Similarly, let $(\mathbf{y}^*, \mathbf{z}^*)$ be a solution of system (5.18), then

$$\mathbf{z}^{*T}(\mathbf{B} - \mathbf{A}) \geqslant r\mathbf{z}^{*T}\mathbf{A} + \mathbf{c}^T \geqslant \mathbf{c}^T.$$

Therefore, vectors $\mathbf{x}^* = \mathbf{z}^*$, $\mathbf{p}^* = (1/\mathbf{c}^T\mathbf{y}^*)\mathbf{y}^*$ and scalar $w^* = 1/\mathbf{c}^T\mathbf{y}^*$ constitute a solution to system (5.17). This is enough to complete the proof.
Q.E.D.

Lemma 5.4. System (5.18) has a solution if and only if there is a nonnegative vector **v** such that

$$\mathbf{v}^T[\mathbf{B} - (1 + r)\mathbf{A}] \geqslant \mathbf{c}^T. \tag{5.19}$$

Proof. It is analogous to the proof of Lemma 5.2. The pair of dual linear programming problems each of which is equivalent to system (5.18) is the following:

	(primal)		(dual)
Min	$\mathbf{z}^T\mathbf{1}$	Max	$\mathbf{c}^T\mathbf{y}$
s. to	$\mathbf{z}^T[\mathbf{B} - (1+r)\mathbf{A}] \geqslant \mathbf{c}^T$	s. to	$[\mathbf{B} - (1+r)\mathbf{A}]\mathbf{y} \leqslant \mathbf{1}$
	$\mathbf{z} \geqslant \mathbf{0},$		$\mathbf{y} \geqslant \mathbf{0}.$

Q.E.D.

Theorem 5.3. For a given rate of profit r,

(a) if and only if there is a nonnegative vector **v** such that inequality (5.19) holds, there is a price vector $\mathbf{p}^* \geqslant \mathbf{0}$ and wage rate $w^* > 0$ such that no process pays extra profits and at least one process for each commodity required for use does not incur extra costs;

(b) the long-period wage rate w^* is the minimum w for which there is a vector **p** such that inequalities (5.6), (5.8), and (5.16) are satisfied;

(c) if there are two long-period price vectors and wage rates, $(\mathbf{p}^*, w^*)$ and $(\mathbf{p}^\circ, w^\circ)$, then the processes which are operated with one solution do not incur extra costs at the prices and wage rate of the other solution; moreover, the linear combination of price vectors and wage rates

$$(\lambda\mathbf{p}^* + (1 - \lambda)\mathbf{p}^\circ, \lambda w^* + (1 - \lambda)w^\circ)$$

with $0 \leqslant \lambda \leqslant 1$ is also a long-period price vector and wage rate;

(d) if there are two long-period price vectors and wage rates, $(\mathbf{p}^*, w^*)$ and $(\mathbf{p}^\circ, w^\circ)$, with $w^* > 0$ and $w^\circ > 0$, and if the numeraire consists of commodities which are produced in both solutions, then $w^* = w^\circ$ and the entries of vectors $\mathbf{p}^*$ and $\mathbf{p}^\circ$ corresponding to commodities which are produced in at least one of the solutions are equal.

Proof. The proof of statements (a) and (b) is analogous to the proof of statements (a) and (b) of Theorem 5.2. In order to prove statement (c), let $(\mathbf{y}^*, \mathbf{z}^*)$ and $(\mathbf{y}^\circ, \mathbf{z}^\circ)$ be two solutions to system (5.18). Then $\mathbf{z}^*$ and $\mathbf{z}^\circ$ are two solutions to the primal linear programming problem mentioned in the proof of Lemma 5.4, and $\mathbf{y}^*$ and $\mathbf{y}^\circ$ are two solutions to the dual.

Therefore

$$z^{*T}[B - (1 + r)A]y^\circ = z^{*T}l$$
$$z^{\circ T}[B - (1 + r)A]y^* = z^{\circ T}l,$$

because of the Equilibrium Theorem of Linear Programming (see Theorem A.4.3). This is enough to prove the first part of statement (c). The proof of the second part is trivial.

In order to prove statement (d), let (p^*, w^*, x^*) and $(p^\circ, w^\circ, x^\circ)$ be two solutions to system (5.17). Pick one process for each produced commodity among the processes corresponding to positive entries of vector x^*. In this way obtain a set of $s^*, s^* \leqslant n$, processes which can be represented as (C^*, D^*, m^*), where C^* is the material input matrix, D^* is the output matrix, and m^* is the labor input vector. In an analogous way we obtain $(C^\circ, D^\circ, m^\circ)$. If some of the processes $(C^\circ, D^\circ, m^\circ)$ produce commodities not produced by processes (C^*, D^*, m^*), add these processes to (C^*, D^*, m^*) in order to obtain $(\bar{C}^*, \bar{D}^*, \bar{m}^*)$. In an analogous way obtain $(\bar{C}^\circ, \bar{D}^\circ, \bar{m}^\circ)$. The processes $(\bar{C}^\circ, \bar{D}^\circ, \bar{m}^\circ)$ produce the same commodities as the processes $(\bar{C}^*, \bar{D}^*, \bar{m}^*)$. If the matrix $(\bar{D}^* - \bar{C}^*)$ has zero columns, delete these columns in order to obtain the square matrices $\hat{C}^*$ and $\hat{D}^*$. Let $\hat{D}^*$ be equal to the identity matrix by appropriate order of the rows of matrices $\bar{C}^*$ and $\bar{D}^*$ and vector $\bar{m}^*$. In an analogous way obtain $\hat{C}^\circ$ and $\hat{D}^\circ = I$. Finally let $\hat{p}^*, \hat{p}^\circ$, and $\hat{c}$ be obtained from p^*, p°, and c, respectively, by deleting the entries corresponding to the columns of $\bar{C}^*$ deleted in order to obtain $\hat{C}^*$. It is immediately obtained, because of the first part of statement (c), that

$$[I - (1 + r^*)\hat{C}^\circ]\hat{p}^\circ = w^*\bar{m}^\circ \tag{5.20a}$$
$$[I - (1 + r^*)\hat{C}^*]\hat{p}^* = w^\circ\bar{m}^* \tag{5.20b}$$
$$\hat{c}^T\hat{p}^* = \hat{c}^T\hat{p}^\circ = 1 \tag{5.20c}$$
$$[I - (1 + r^*)\hat{C}^\circ]\hat{p}^* = w^*\bar{m}^\circ \tag{5.20d}$$
$$[I - (1 + r^*)\hat{C}^*]\hat{p}^\circ = w^\circ\bar{m}^*. \tag{5.20d}$$

Statement (d) is proved if matrices $[I - (1 + r^*)\hat{C}^*]$ and $[I - (1 + r^*)\hat{C}^\circ]$ are invertible. The proof is trivial if $w^*\bar{m}^\circ > 0$ and $w^\circ\bar{m}^* > 0$. The general case is dealt with in exercise 8.19.   Q.E.D.

3.3. The indirect approach

The direct approach requires a knowledge of linear programming. But once linear programming is known it is simpler than the indirect approach. The reader may wonder why we would want to investigate the indirect approach in addition to the direct one, even though the former will basically yield the same results. A first reason is the following. In order to use linear programming the direct approach requires that the number of available processes is finite. No such requirement is needed if the indirect approach is used.[2] Further on, the indirect approach can manage even the case where the number of commodities is not finite if (i) the number of commodities consumed is finite, and (ii) in each *technique* the number of commodities required directly or indirectly to produce the consumed commodities is finite and we are not interested in determining the prices of unproduced commodities. In the previous sentence the word "technique" has been italicized since it needs to be redefined in a way that allows us to consider these cases.

Assume that the first s commodities, $s < n$, are consumed, while the others are not. Let **c** be a vector whose first s components are positive, all the others being nought. Let $(\mathbf{a}_i, \mathbf{b}_i, l_i)$, $i = 1, 2, \ldots, t$, be t processes, $s \leqslant t \leqslant n$. Then the triplet $(\mathbf{A}, \mathbf{B}, \mathbf{l})$, where

$$\mathbf{A} = \begin{bmatrix} \mathbf{a}_1^T \\ \mathbf{a}_2^T \\ \vdots \\ \mathbf{a}_t^T \end{bmatrix}, \quad \mathbf{B} = \begin{bmatrix} \mathbf{b}_1^T \\ \mathbf{b}_2^T \\ \vdots \\ \mathbf{b}_t^T \end{bmatrix}, \quad \mathbf{l} = \begin{bmatrix} l_1 \\ l_2 \\ \vdots \\ l_t \end{bmatrix},$$

will be called a *technique* (or a *system of production*) if there is a unique positive vector **x** such that

$$\mathbf{x}^T[\mathbf{B} - \mathbf{A}] = \mathbf{c}^T.$$

The existence condition requires that the number of processes in technique $(\mathbf{A}, \mathbf{B}, \mathbf{l})$ is greater than or equal to the number of commodities involved, whereas the uniqueness condition requires that the rows of matrix $[\mathbf{B} - \mathbf{A}]$ are linearly independent so that the number of processes is not larger than the number of commodities involved. That is, the number of processes in technique $(\mathbf{A}, \mathbf{B}, \mathbf{l})$ must be equal to the number of commodities involved.

A *cost-minimizing technique* is then defined as a technique at the prices of which no set of known processes can be operated in order to obtain extra profits. Therefore the technique $(\mathbf{A}_k, \mathbf{B}_k, \mathbf{l}_k)$ is *cost-minimizing at rate of profit r* if and only if

$$[\mathbf{B}_j - (1 + r)\mathbf{A}_j]\mathbf{p}_{kj} \leqslant w_k \mathbf{l}_j \quad \text{each } (\mathbf{A}_j, \mathbf{B}_j, \mathbf{l}_j) \in J,$$

where J is the set of all existing techniques and $(\mathbf{p}_{kj}, w_k)$ are determined by the following equations:

---

[2] See footnote 1.

$$[\mathbf{B}_{kj} - (1+r)\mathbf{A}_{kj}]\mathbf{p}_{kj} = w_k\mathbf{l}_{kj}$$
$$\mathbf{c}^T\mathbf{p}_{kj} = 1,$$

where $(\mathbf{A}_{kj}, \mathbf{B}_{kj}, \mathbf{l}_{kj})$ is the union of the set of processes in $(\mathbf{A}_k, \mathbf{B}_k, \mathbf{l}_k)$ and the set of those processes in $(\mathbf{A}_j, \mathbf{B}_j, \mathbf{l}_j)$ producing commodities not produced by processes in $(\mathbf{A}_k, \mathbf{B}_k, \mathbf{l}_k)$. It goes without saying that w_k does not depend on the latter processes. It is also useful to define vector $\mathbf{x}_{kj}$:

$$\mathbf{x}_{kj}^T[\mathbf{B}_{kj} - (1+r)\mathbf{A}_{kj}] = \mathbf{c}^T.$$

Since

$$1 = \mathbf{c}^T\mathbf{p}_{kj} = \mathbf{x}_{kj}^T[\mathbf{B}_{kj} - (1+r)\mathbf{A}_{kj}]\mathbf{p}_{kj} = w_k\mathbf{x}_{kj}^T\mathbf{l}_{kj}$$

we have

$$w_k = \frac{1}{\mathbf{x}_{kj}^T\mathbf{l}_{kj}}.$$

Going back to the example of Subsection 3.1, if $0 \leqslant r \leqslant \bar{r}$, the technique made up of processes (1, 3) is cost-minimizing; if $\bar{r} \leqslant r \leqslant (5\sqrt{17} - 13)/8$, then the technique made up of processes (2, 4) is cost-minimizing.

Proposition 5.4. Let $(\mathbf{A}_h, \mathbf{B}_h, \mathbf{l}_h)$ be a technique and let $(\mathbf{a}_i, \mathbf{e}_i, l_i)$ be a process in technique $(\mathbf{A}_j, \mathbf{B}_j, \mathbf{l}_j)$ such that $\mathbf{p}_{hj} \geqslant \mathbf{0}$ and

$$[\mathbf{e}_i - (1+r)\mathbf{a}_i]^T\mathbf{p}_{hj} > w_h l_i.$$

Then there is a technique $(\mathbf{A}_k, \mathbf{B}_k, \mathbf{l}_k)$ such that $w_k > w_h$.

Proof. Let $(\mathbf{C}, \mathbf{D}, \mathbf{q})$ be a set of processes obtained from the set of processes $(\mathbf{A}_{hj}, \mathbf{B}_{hj}, \mathbf{l}_{hj})$ by substituting the process producing commodity i by process $(\mathbf{a}_i, \mathbf{e}_i, l_i)$. Obviously,

$$[\mathbf{D} - (1+r)\mathbf{C}]\mathbf{p}_{hj} \geqslant w_h\mathbf{q}.$$

If the matrix $[\mathbf{D} - (1+r)\mathbf{C}]$ has zero columns, delete these columns in order to obtain the square matrices $\hat{\mathbf{C}}$ and $\hat{\mathbf{D}}$, respectively. Let $\hat{\mathbf{D}}$ be equal to the identity matrix by appropriate order of the rows of matrices $\mathbf{C}$ and $\mathbf{D}$ and vector $\mathbf{q}$. Moreover, let $\hat{\mathbf{p}}$ and $\hat{\mathbf{c}}$ be obtained by $\mathbf{p}_{hj}$ and $\mathbf{c}$, respectively, by deleting the entries corresponding to the columns of $\mathbf{C}$ deleted in order to obtain $\hat{\mathbf{C}}$. Hence

$$[\mathbf{I} - (1+r)\hat{\mathbf{C}}]\hat{\mathbf{p}} \geqslant w_h\mathbf{q}. \tag{5.21}$$

In order to simplify the proof assume, as in the proof of Proposition 5.1, that $w_h > 0$ and $\mathbf{q} > \mathbf{0}$. Since inequality (5.21) holds,

$$[\mathbf{I} - (1+r)\hat{\mathbf{C}}]\hat{\mathbf{p}} > \mathbf{0};$$

then matrix $[\mathbf{I} - (1+r)\hat{\mathbf{C}}]$ is invertible and its inverse is semipositive. Inequality (5.21) implies also that

$$1 = \hat{\mathbf{c}}^T \hat{\mathbf{p}} > w_h \hat{\mathbf{c}}^T [\mathbf{I} - (1+r)\hat{\mathbf{C}}]^{-1} \mathbf{q} = \frac{w_h}{w_k},$$

where w_k is the wage rate of technique $(\mathbf{A}_k, \mathbf{B}_k, \mathbf{l}_k)$ obtained from the set of processes $(\mathbf{C}, \mathbf{D}, \mathbf{q})$ by eliminating the processes producing those commodities which do not enter directly or indirectly into the production of the first s commodities. And this proves the proposition.   Q.E.D.

Proposition 5.5. Let $(\mathbf{A}_h, \mathbf{B}_h, \mathbf{l}_h)$ and $(\mathbf{A}_k, \mathbf{B}_k, \mathbf{l}_k)$ be two techniques such that $\mathbf{p}_{hk} \geqslant \mathbf{0}, \mathbf{p}_{kh} \geqslant \mathbf{0}$, and

$$0 < w_h < w_k.$$

Then there is a process in technique $(\mathbf{A}_k, \mathbf{B}_k, \mathbf{l}_k)$ which pays extra profits at prices $(\mathbf{p}_{hk}, w_h)$.

Proof. Assume that the proposition does not hold. Then

$$[\mathbf{B}_{kh} - (1+r)\mathbf{A}_{kh}]\mathbf{p}_{hk} \leqslant w_h \mathbf{l}_{kh},$$

therefore,

$$1 = \mathbf{c}^T \mathbf{p}_h = \mathbf{x}_{kh}[\mathbf{B}_{kh} - (1+r)\mathbf{A}_{kh}]\mathbf{p}_{hk} \leqslant w_h \mathbf{x}_{kh} \mathbf{l}_{kh} = \frac{w_h}{w_k}.$$

Hence a contradiction.   Q.E.D.

Proposition 5.6. Let $(\mathbf{A}_h, \mathbf{B}_h, \mathbf{l}_h)$ and $(\mathbf{A}_k, \mathbf{B}_k, \mathbf{l}_k)$ be two techniques which are both cost-minimizing at rate of profit r, where $\mathbf{p}_{hk} \geqslant \mathbf{0}, \mathbf{p}_{kh} \geqslant \mathbf{0}, w_h > 0$, and $w_k > 0$, then $w_k = w_h$ and $\mathbf{p}_{kh} = \mathbf{p}_{hk}$.

Proof. Obviously,

$$[\mathbf{B}_{hk} - (1+r)\mathbf{A}_{hk}]\mathbf{p}_{hk} = w_h \mathbf{l}_{hk} \qquad (5.22a)$$

$$[\mathbf{B}_{kh} - (1+r)\mathbf{A}_{kh}]\mathbf{p}_{kh} = w_h \mathbf{l}_{kh} \qquad (5.22b)$$

$$\mathbf{c}^T \mathbf{p}_{hk} = \mathbf{c}^T \mathbf{p}_{kh} = 1 \qquad (5.22c)$$

$$[\mathbf{B}_{kh} - (1+r)\mathbf{A}_{kh}]\mathbf{p}_{hk} \leqslant w_h \mathbf{l}_{kh} \qquad (5.22d)$$

$$[\mathbf{B}_{hk} - (1+r)\mathbf{A}_{hk}]\mathbf{p}_{kh} \leqslant w_k \mathbf{l}_{hk}. \qquad (5.22e)$$

It is an immediate consequence of Proposition 5.5 that

$$w_k = w_h.$$

Next, in order to follow the procedure used to prove Proposition 5.3 we need to prove that matrices obtained by deleting zero columns in matrices

$[\mathbf{B}_{kh} - (1 + r)\mathbf{A}_{kh}]$ and $[\mathbf{B}_{hk} - (1 + r)\mathbf{A}_{hk}]$ are invertible and their inverses are nonnegative.

Q.E.D.

Theorem 5.4.

(a) If there is a technique which has a positive price vector and a positive wage rate for $r = r^*$, then there is a cost-minimizing technique at rate of profit r^*.

(b) A technique is cost-minimizing at $r = r^*$ if and only if it is able to pay the largest wage rate among the techniques with nonnegative prices at r^* when the numeraire consists of a positive amount of each consumed commodity.

(c) If more than one cost-minimizing technique at rate of profit r^* exists, they all share the same wage rate and the same prices of commodities which are produced in at least one of them.

Proof. The proof is similar to the proof of Theorem 3.1.[3]

3.4. The indirect approach: An alternative framework

The indirect approach as presented in the previous subsection has the advantage that it can deal with some cases in which the number of existing commodities is infinite. However, it cannot determine the prices of non-produced commodities. If the number of existing commodities is finite, an alternative framework can be provided which is able to determine the prices of non-produced commodities: we can refer to a technique as a set of n processes which can be operated in order to satisfy the requirements for use, n being the number of existing commodities. If in the example of Subsection 3.1 only corn is consumed, the sets of processes $(1, 2, 3)$, $(1, 3, 4)$, $(1, 2, 4)$, $(2, 3, 4)$ will be the techniques. In techniques $(1, 2, 3)$ and $(1, 3, 4)$ the processes (2) and (4) would not be operated and they would be inserted in these techniques only in order to determine the price of iron. Similarly in techniques $(1, 2, 4)$ and $(2, 3, 4)$ the processes (1) and (3) would not be operated and they would be inserted in these techniques only in order to determine the price of aluminium. In techniques $(1, 3, 4)$ and $(2, 3, 4)$ there are two processes to produce corn, but this does not matter since only one of them can be operated; nevertheless we cannot avoid considering these techniques, otherwise we would delete the technique utilized when $\frac{1}{4} < r \leqslant (5\sqrt{17} - 13)/8$. In this subsection a formalization of this alternative indirect approach will be elaborated.

---

[3] If the number of processes is not finite, statement (a) is to be changed as is indicated in footnote 1.

Let us still assume that the first s commodities, $s < n$, are consumed, whereas the others are not (they are produced only if they enter directly or indirectly in the production of the first s commodities). Let $\mathbf{c}$ be a vector whose first s components are positive, all the others being nil. Let $(\mathbf{a}_i, \mathbf{b}_i, l_i)$, $i = 1, 2, \ldots, n$, be n processes. Then the triplet $(\mathbf{A}, \mathbf{B}, \mathbf{l})$, where

$$
\mathbf{A} = \begin{bmatrix} \mathbf{a}_1^T \\ \mathbf{a}_2^T \\ \vdots \\ \mathbf{a}_n^T \end{bmatrix}, \quad \mathbf{B} = \begin{bmatrix} \mathbf{b}_1^T \\ \mathbf{b}_2^T \\ \vdots \\ \mathbf{b}_n^T \end{bmatrix}, \quad \mathbf{l} = \begin{bmatrix} l_1 \\ l_2 \\ \vdots \\ l_n \end{bmatrix},
$$

will be called a *technique* (or a *system of production*) if there is a unique vector $\mathbf{x}$ such that:

$$\mathbf{x}^T[\mathbf{B} - \mathbf{A}] = \mathbf{c}^T, \tag{5.23}$$

and $\mathbf{x}$ is semipositive. The existence of a semipositive vector $\mathbf{x}$ requires that for each of the first s commodities and for each of the commodities required directly or indirectly to produce them in technique $(\mathbf{A}, \mathbf{B}, \mathbf{l})$ there is, in the same technique $(\mathbf{A}, \mathbf{B}, \mathbf{l})$, a process producing such a commodity; the uniqueness of vector $\mathbf{x}$ requires that the rows of matrix $[\mathbf{B} - \mathbf{A}]$ are linearly independent so that the number of processes is not larger than the number of commodities involved. That is, in each technique and for each commodity there is at least one process either producing or utilizing such a commodity.

The price vector $\mathbf{p}$ and the wage rate w of technique $(\mathbf{A}, \mathbf{B}, \mathbf{l})$ are determined by the equations

$$\mathbf{B}\mathbf{p} = (1 + r)\mathbf{A}\mathbf{p} + w\mathbf{l}$$

$$\mathbf{c}^T\mathbf{p} = 1,$$

where the numeraire has been chosen in such a way as to contain only commodities which are certainly produced.

A *cost-minimizing technique at rate of profit* r is defined as a technique at the prices of which at rate of profit r no known process can pay extra profits. Therefore the technique $(\mathbf{A}_k, \mathbf{B}_k, \mathbf{l}_k)$ is *cost-minimizing at rate of profit* r if and only if

$$[\mathbf{B}_j - (1 + r)\mathbf{A}_j]\mathbf{p}_k \leqslant w_k\mathbf{l}_j \quad \text{each } (\mathbf{A}_j, \mathbf{B}_j, \mathbf{l}_j) \in J,$$

where J is the set of all existing techniques and $(\mathbf{p}_k, w_k)$ are determined by the following equations:

$$[\mathbf{B}_k - (1 + r)\mathbf{A}_k]\mathbf{p}_k = w_k\mathbf{l}_k$$

$$\mathbf{c}^T\mathbf{p}_k = 1.$$

We are of course interested only in techniques which determine non-negative price vectors. With respect to produced commodities we know from Section 2 of Chapter 4 that their prices are nonnegative at rate of profit r and the wage rate is positive if and only if there is a nonnegative vector $\mathbf{x}$ such that

$$\mathbf{x}^T[\mathbf{B} - (1 + r)\mathbf{A}] = \mathbf{c}^T. \tag{5.24}$$

Moreover, if there is a nonnegative vector $\mathbf{x}$ satisfying equation (5.24) for $r = r^*$, then there is a nonnegative vector satisfying the same relation for each $-1 \leqslant r \leqslant r^*$. Therefore, in dealing with the problem of the choice of technique at rate of profit r we substitute equation (5.24) for equation (5.23) in the definition of a technique. In doing this, no problem arises except in the case in which equation (5.23) has a unique solution which is semipositive, whereas equation (5.24) either has no solution or has a solution which is not nonnegative. Following this procedure we only eliminate techniques which do not have nonnegative price vectors at rate of profit r and techniques with a zero wage rate.

With respect to unproduced commodities a kind of "free disposal rule" can be introduced. This can be done by assuming that for each process producing one of the first s commodities which does not utilize commodity $j, s < j \leqslant n$, there is another process with the same outputs and the same inputs except for some amount of commodity j included among its inputs. This second process would involve extra costs (extra profits) if the first process were utilized and the price of commodity j were negative (positive); furthermore, it will determine a zero price for commodity j when the two processes are in the same technique. Hence by inserting all these processes within the set of existing processes none of the last $n-s$ prices can be negative in a cost-minimizing technique.

Going back to the example of Subsection 3.1, if $0 \leqslant r \leqslant \bar{r}$, then techniques made up of processes $(1, 2, 3)$ and $(1, 3, 4)$, respectively, are both cost-minimizing; if $\bar{r} \leqslant r \leqslant \frac{1}{4}$, then techniques made up of processes $(1, 2, 4)$ and $(2, 3, 4)$, respectively, are both cost-minimizing; if $\frac{1}{4} \leqslant r \leqslant (5\sqrt{17} - 13)/8$, then techniques made up of processes $(2, 3, 4)$ and $(2, 4, 4^*)$ are cost-minimizing, where the process (4^*) has the same outputs and the same inputs as process (4) except for some amount of aluminium included among the inputs.

Within this framework the following Theorem can be stated, but we refrain from providing details of the proof.

Theorem 5.5.

(a) If there is a technique which has a positive price vector and a positive wage rate for $r = r^*$, then there is a cost-minimizing technique at rate of profit r^*.[4]

(b) A technique is cost-minimizing at $r = r^*$ only if it is able to pay the largest wage rate among the techniques with nonnegative prices at r^* when the numeraire consists of a positive amount of each consumed commodity.

(c) If more than one cost-minimizing technique at rate of profit r^* exists, they all share the same wage rate and the same prices of commodities which are produced in at least one of them, whereas the prices of commodities which are not produced in all of them are in a set which can be determined.

4. A general framework of the analysis

Let $1, 2, \ldots, s$ be the commodities which may be consumed; the other commodities, in finite or infinite number, being used only as means of production. Let R_i be the supremum of the set of rates of profit which are feasible when only commodity i is consumed. By using the language of the direct approach (in this case the number of commodities and the number of processes need to be finite),

$$R_i = \sup \{ r \in \mathbb{R} \mid \exists \mathbf{v} \in \mathbb{R}^m : \mathbf{v} \geqslant \mathbf{0}, \mathbf{v}^T [\mathbf{B} - (1 + r)\mathbf{A}] \geqslant \mathbf{e}_i^T \}$$

$$i = 1, 2, \ldots, s;$$

whereas by using the indirect approach,

$$R_i = \sup T_i \quad i = 1, 2, \ldots, s,$$

where T_i is the set of real numbers r such that, on the assumption that only commodity i is consumed, there is a technique which, at rate of profit r, has positive prices for (produced) commodities.

Let us rename the first s commodities in such a way that

$$R_1 \geqslant R_2 \geqslant \cdots \geqslant R_s.$$

It is an obvious consequence of the analysis presented in the previous section that if $R_i > r \geqslant R_{i+1}$, then there are cost-minimizing prices and a wage rate at the rate of profit r if and only if commodities $i+1, i+2, \ldots, s$ are not consumed.

If the set of consumed commodities depends on prices – in the sense that if the price of a commodity is large enough (relatively to the others), then that commodity is not consumed – then it is possible to prove that

---

[4] If the number of processes is not finite, statement (a) is to be changed in an analogous way as is indicated in footnote 1.

if $r < R_1$, there are long-period prices and wage rate at the rate of profit r. In this case if $R_i > r \geqslant R_{i+1}$, it is enough to determine prices on the assumption that only commodities $1, 2, \ldots, i$ are consumed, and then to increase the prices of commodities $i+1, i+2, \ldots, s$ in such a way that these commodities turn out to be non-consumed commodities. We refrain from providing a formal presentation of this assertion.

5. The wage–profit frontier

In this chapter it has been shown that if it is possible to produce the commodities which are requested for consumption at a growth rate equal to the rate of profit, then

(i) there is a price vector and wage rate such that, if they hold, no process is able to pay extra profits; and
(ii) there is a set of processes which do not incur extra costs and are able to (re)produce the consumption commodities in arbitrary proportions at a growth rate not larger than the rate of profit.

Two procedures to obtain this result have been provided. The direct approach and the indirect approach. The *direct* approach is based on linear programming. It allows the price vector and wage rate to be determined by solving the programme:

$$\text{Max} \qquad \mathbf{c}^T \mathbf{u}$$

$$\text{s. to} \quad [\mathbf{B} - (1+r)\mathbf{A}]\mathbf{u} \leqslant \mathbf{1}$$

$$\mathbf{u} \geqslant \mathbf{0},$$

where $\mathbf{c}$ is any vector whose positive entries refer to commodities requested for consumption, all the others being zero. Then the prices and the wage rate are determined by the equations

$$\mathbf{p} = \frac{1}{\mathbf{c}^T \mathbf{u}} \mathbf{u}$$

$$w = \frac{1}{\mathbf{c}^T \mathbf{u}},$$

where the numeraire has been chosen in such a way as to include only commodities which are certainly produced.

The *indirect* approach consists first in defining techniques as sets of processes which can be operated in order to satisfy the requirements for use and are able to determine uniquely the prices involved. Then the cost-minimizing technique(s) at the ruling rate of profit is (are) determined and it is proved that each of them is a technique which is able to pay the

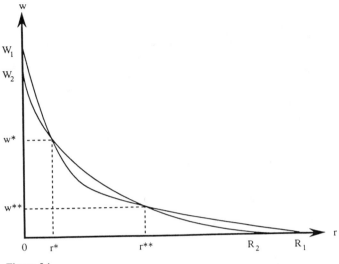

Figure 5.1

largest wage rate for the given rate of profit. The results obtained in terms of the two procedures are, of course, identical.

By means of both procedures it can be shown that the relationship between the wage rate and the rate of profit for the technology as a whole, which will be called the *wage–profit* frontier, is continuous and decreasing. Following the indirect approach we can use the fact that each $w–r$ relationship relative to a single technique is decreasing. If all these $w–r$ relationships relative to the different techniques are drawn in the same diagram (see Figure 5.1), the wage–profit frontier coincides with the outer envelope: an envelope of continuous and decreasing functions is of course continuous and decreasing. As has already been stated in Chapter 3, the points on the wage–profit frontier at which two techniques are cost-minimizing are called *switch points*. Moreover, if a technique is cost-minimizing at two disconnected ranges of the rate of profit and not so in between these ranges, we say that there is a *reswitching* of technique.

Prices of consumption commodities are continuous functions of the rate of profit, but prices of commodities which are not produced do not need to be uniquely determined and, as a consequence, the relationship between each of them and the rate of profit can be represented only as a correspondence.

In this reasoning the rate of profit has been used as the independent variable. From a purely mathematical point of view this has the advantage that the problem under consideration is linear. If, on the contrary, the wage rate were to be given, the problem would *not* be linear. However, there is another reason which speaks in favor of taking the rate of profit as the independent variable: the rate of profit is a pure number the meaning of which is independent of any normalization. The wage rate, on the other hand, depends on the chosen numeraire.

Yet there is no technical difficulty in considering the wage rate as the independent variable. If this is done, we can assert that for a given wage rate cost-minimizing techniques are techniques which can pay the largest rate of profit. This can be proved directly. It can also be shown by making use of the fact that the $w-r$ relationships are decreasing. Because of this a technique which, at wage rate w, pays a rate of profit r' lower than the highest possible one at w is also a technique which, at rate of profit r', pays a wage rate lower than the highest wage rate obtained by a technique at r'. Conversely, a technique which, at wage rate w, pays a rate of profit r'' equal to the highest possible one at w is also a technique which, at rate of profit r'', pays a wage rate equal to the highest possible one at r''.

6. **An extension: The small open economy**

Until now we have considered a closed economy, that is, an economy that does not trade with other economies. The pure theory of trade essentially constitutes an application of the theory of production, value and distribution. While a proper treatment of the pure theory of trade is beyond the scope of this book, an application to a typical case dealt within trade theory could illustrate the analytical power of the material developed in this book. The case under consideration is that of a "small open economy," that is, an economy that trades, but is so "small" that it has no influence on international prices and thus must take them as given. In order to be able to deal with this case a single and simple modification is required: some of the available processes from which producers can choose have to be interpreted as import–export processes.

Let commodities $1, 2, \ldots, m$ be tradeable and let $P_1, P_2, \ldots, P_m$ be their international prices, respectively. If $m < n$, then commodities $m + 1$, $m + 2, \ldots, n$ are not tradeable, either because the technology does not allow transportation (for example, buildings) or because of legal restrictions. Let $(\mathbf{a}, \mathbf{e}_j, l)$ be a process domestically producing commodity j, and assume that there are neither transportation costs to export commodity j nor to import commodity i and that no time is required. Then the process $[(P_i/P_j)\mathbf{a}, \mathbf{e}_i, (P_i/P_j)l]$ can be interpreted as a process producing commodity i by means of the domestic production of commodity j and its exportation in exchange for the imported commodity i. For each process domestically producing a tradeable commodity we have an additional $m - 1$ processes producing the other $m - 1$ tradeable commodities via international trade. Once these processes are included in the set of available processes, then the choice of technique will determine which commodities will be produced domestically and which will be imported in exchange for commodities produced domestically.[5]

If the import–export activity requires time (which, for simplicity is assumed to be equal to the time required in the production of any other commodity) and if there are transportation costs, then the formulation is similar but different. Let $\mathbf{a}_{ij}$ and l_{ij} be the vector of material inputs and the amount of labor, respectively, required to import one unit of commodity i and export P_i/P_j units of commodity j (which is the amount that the international market requires for one unit of commodity i). Then the relative import–export process is $[(P_i/P_j)\mathbf{e}_j + \mathbf{a}_{ij}, \mathbf{e}_i, l_{ij})$.

The same framework can also be used to deal with tariffs and bounties. In the case in which time and transportation costs matter, if t_i is the import tariff levied on commodity i and s_j is the bounty on the export of commodity j, both conceived of as rates proportional to the ruling international prices, then the relative import–export process is

$$\left(\frac{(1 + t_i)P_i}{(1 + s_j)P_j} \, \mathbf{e}_j + \mathbf{a}_{ij}, \mathbf{e}_i, l_{ij} \right).$$

To conclude, it deserves to be stressed that moving from a closed to an open economy has the same effect as introducing additional processes of production, and can thus be compared with technical progress which also involves the introduction of new processes.

7. Historical notes

7.1. The problem of the choice of technique has been discussed ever since the inception of systematic economic analysis in classical political economy. In early contributions to the problem, such as Ricardo's *Principles*, emphasis was generally on the technological dynamism of the modern economy and the effects technological change has on income distribution, employment and the growth performance of the system as a whole. There is a clear perception in the writings of the old authors that new methods of production would be introduced only insofar as they allowed the innovator to reduce unit costs and thus, other things being equal in the short run, pocket extra profits. In the course of the generalization of the new methods these extra profits were envisaged to be eliminated and a

---

[5] It goes without saying that balanced trade is assumed in the above argument, i.e. we set aside (net) capital exports or imports.

new general rate of profit was seen to emerge. See, for example, Ricardo (*Works* I, p. 387) and Marx ([1894] 1959, p. 264). See also the discussion in Section 2 of Chapter 1.

Since in the classical authors the argument was generally cast in terms of the quantity of labor directly and indirectly needed in the production of a particular commodity, cost minimization was taken to imply the minimization of the amount of labor "embodied" in the commodity.

7.2. Early formal treatments of the problem of the choice of technique subject to the criterion of cost minimization in terms of *in*equalities were provided by Whewell (1831), Tozer (1938), and von Bortkiewicz (1906–7); see Subsection 5.1 of Chapter 13. A fuller analysis of the problem was then put forward by von Neumann in a path breaking essay (see von Neumann, [1937] 1945). Von Neumann's contribution is discussed in Section 6 of Chapter 13. His approach has been generalized by Kemeny, Morgenstern, and Thompson (1956), Morishima (1960, 1964, 1969) and others. For a survey of these developments, see Morgenstern and Thompson (1976). Sraffa (1960) deals with the problem of the choice of technique in Part III of his book. The possibility of the reswitching of techniques is clearly stated by him. For a brief overview of Sraffa's approach to the problem of the choice of technique and a comparison with von Neumann's, see Sections 8 and 9 in Chapter 13.

7.3. Theorem 5.1 was proved by Morishima (1964, ch. 4), Garegnani (1973), and Łos and Łos (1976). Garegnani's proof was carried out in terms of the set of three propositions utilized here in the indirect approach. This procedure was then followed, with different proofs, by Salvadori (1982) and Bidard (1984a, 1990, 1991) with reference to joint production. A proof of Proposition 5.1 was also provided by Levhari (1965). In most of these analyses all commodities have been assumed to be basic. The problem of non-basics is for the first time systematically explored here.

7.4. The indirect approach has been analyzed using linear programming by Burmeister and Kuga (1970) and Fujimoto (1975). Other authors have used other tools like game theory; see, for example, Morishima (1969) and Morgenstern and Thompson (1976). When the indirect approach was adopted, single production was generally not assumed. When single production was assumed this was done in order to prove a "Non-Substitution Theorem" (cf. Bliss, 1975, ch. 11). A *Non-Substitution Theorem* is generally presented as a *uniqueness* theorem asserting that under certain specified conditions an economy will have one particular price structure for each admissible value of the rate of profit (see Subsection 4.3 in Chapter 1). However, the conventional presentation of the Theorem is somewhat misleading, since there are cases in which the independence of prices from final demand holds, while the uniqueness property does not need to hold. (See the numerical example in exercise 8.7 below which shows that prices need not be unique even if each industry produces only a single commodity as in the original formulation of the Theorem.) Therefore, the Non-Substitution Theorem should be presented as a theorem stating the independence of relative prices from demand rather than as a theorem stating the uniqueness of the price vector. See also the historical notes in Chapter 9.

7.5. The idea that the opening of foreign trade bears a close resemblance to technical progress, in that in both cases additional processes of production are made available to the economy, is clearly expressed in Ricardo's *Principles* in the chapter "On Foreign Trade" (Ricardo, *Works* I, ch. VII). Ricardo in fact compares the extension of trade to improvements in machinery, and, taking the real wage rate as given, investigates whether trade or improved machinery will have an impact on the general rate of profit. He concludes that if "by the extension of foreign trade, or by improvements in machinery, the food and necessaries of the labourer can be brought to market at a reduced price, profits will rise," whereas "if the commodities obtained at a cheaper rate ... be exclusively the commodities consumed by the rich, no alteration will take place in the rate of profits" (ibid., p. 132).

7.6. In recent years the pure theory of trade has been reformulated, using a "classical" approach to the theory of value and distribution and paying special attention to the fact that capital consists of produced means of production. A start was made by Parrinello (1970), followed by several contributions by Steedman, Metcalfe and Steedman, and Mainwaring; see in particular the collection of essays in Steedman (1979b), Steedman (1979a, 1987a) and Mainwaring (1991); see also Samuelson (1975). It was shown that several of the traditional trade theorems, derived within the Heckscher–Ohlin–Samuelson model, do not carry over to a framework with a positive rate of profit (interest) and produced inputs (capital goods). (As is well known, the Heckscher–Ohlin–Samuelson model of international trade assumes two countries producing the same two commodities by means of the same constant returns to scale technology, using the same two primary inputs, each of which is taken to be homogeneous between countries.) With a positive rate of interest that is uniform across countries some, though not all, of the standard theorems are undermined (including the "factor price equalization theorem"), while with different rates of interest in different countries all standard theorems except the Rybczynski theorem turn out to be untenable. The "gains" from trade for the single small open economy need not be positive. When in the Heckscher–Ohlin–Samuelson theory one of the two primary factors (land) is replaced by a factor called "capital," the "quantity" of which is represented in terms of a given total *value* of capital, then the theory is deprived of its logical coherence. For a summary statement of the critique of the conventional pure theory of trade, see Steedman (1987a).

8. Exercises

8.1. (Calculus) Prove Proposition 5.1 on the assumption that $l_h \geqslant 0, l \geqslant 0$, and

$$(\mathbf{u}^T(\mathbf{I} - \mathbf{A}_h) + \alpha(\mathbf{b} - \mathbf{a})^T \geqslant \mathbf{0}^T, \quad \mathbf{u} \geqslant \mathbf{0}, \quad \alpha \geqslant 0) \Rightarrow \mathbf{u}^T \mathbf{l}_h + \alpha l > 0,$$

but not necessarily $\mathbf{l}_h > \mathbf{0}$ and $l > 0$. [*Hint*: Let $\mathbf{y} = (1/w_h)\mathbf{p}_h$, then

$$\mathbf{y} \geqslant (1 + r^*)\mathbf{A}_k \mathbf{y} + \mathbf{l}_k$$

because of inequality (5.2). Then prove

$$\mathbf{y} \geqslant \mathbf{l}_k + (1 + r^*)\mathbf{A}_k \mathbf{l}_k + \cdots + (1 + r^*)^t \mathbf{A}_k^t \mathbf{l}_k + \cdots.$$

The above series is increasing and bounded, hence it is convergent. As a consequence

$$\lim_{t \to \infty} [(1 + r^*)\mathbf{A}_k]^t \mathbf{l}_k = \mathbf{0}. \tag{5.25}$$

If vector $\mathbf{l}_k$ were positive, then equality (5.25) would imply that

$$\lim_{t \to \infty} [(1 + r^*)\mathbf{A}_k]^t = \mathbf{0}. \tag{5.26}$$

Since (prove)

$$(\mathbf{u}^T(\mathbf{I} - \mathbf{A}_k) \geqslant \mathbf{0}^T, \mathbf{u} \geqslant \mathbf{0}) \Rightarrow \mathbf{u}^T \mathbf{l}_k > 0,$$

the next exercise allows us to assert that there is a natural number $z \leqslant n - 1$ such that

$$\mathbf{l}_k + \mathbf{A}_k \mathbf{l}_k + \mathbf{A}_k^2 \mathbf{l}_k + \cdots + \mathbf{A}_k^z \mathbf{l}_k > 0.$$

Hence (prove):

$$\mathbf{l}_k + (1 + r^*)\mathbf{A}_k \mathbf{l}_k + (1 + r^*)^2 \mathbf{A}_k^2 \mathbf{l}_k + \cdots + (1 + r^*)^z \mathbf{A}_k^z \mathbf{l}_k > 0.$$

Then, obtain from equality (5.25) that

$$\lim_{t \to \infty} [(1 + r^*)\mathbf{A}_k]^t \{\mathbf{l}_k + (1 + r^*)\mathbf{A}_k \mathbf{l}_k + (1 + r^*)^2 \mathbf{A}_k^2 \mathbf{l}_k + \cdots$$

$$+ (1 + r^*)^z \mathbf{A}_k^z \mathbf{l}_k\} = (z + 1) \lim_{t \to \infty} [(1 + r^*)\mathbf{A}_k]^t \mathbf{l}_k = \mathbf{0},$$

which implies equality (5.26). Finally (prove)

$$I + (1 + r^*)A_k + \cdots + (1 + r^*)^t A_k^t + \cdots = [I - (1 + r^*)A_k]^{-1} \geq 0.$$

Then $\cdots$]

8.2. Let the nonnegative $n \times n$ matrix $\mathbf{A}$ and the nonnegative n-vector $\mathbf{l}$ be such that

$$(\mathbf{u}^T(\mathbf{I} - \mathbf{A}) \geq \mathbf{0}^T, \mathbf{u} \geq \mathbf{0}) \Rightarrow \mathbf{u}^T \mathbf{l} > 0.$$

Then, prove that there is a natural number $z \leq n - 1$ such that

$$\mathbf{l} + \mathbf{A}\mathbf{l} + \mathbf{A}^2\mathbf{l} + \cdots + \mathbf{A}^z\mathbf{l} > \mathbf{0}.$$

Hint: If $\mathbf{l}$ is semipositive but not positive, let $\mathbf{l} = [\mathbf{y}^T, \mathbf{0}^T]^T$ by appropriate interchange of rows (applied also to both rows and columns of $\mathbf{A}$), where $\mathbf{y} > \mathbf{0}$. Since

$$\left(\begin{bmatrix} \mathbf{u}_1 \\ \mathbf{u}_2 \end{bmatrix}^T \geq \mathbf{0}, \begin{bmatrix} \mathbf{u}_1 \\ \mathbf{u}_2 \end{bmatrix}^T \begin{bmatrix} \mathbf{I} - \mathbf{A}_{11} & -\mathbf{A}_{12} \\ -\mathbf{A}_{21} & \mathbf{I} - \mathbf{A}_{22} \end{bmatrix} \geq \mathbf{0} \right) \Rightarrow \mathbf{u}_1^T \mathbf{y} > 0,$$

$\mathbf{u}_1^T \geq \mathbf{0}$ and $\mathbf{A}_{21} \geq \mathbf{0}$. Hence $\mathbf{l} + \mathbf{A}\mathbf{l}$ has a number of positive elements larger than $\mathbf{l}$. Since it is still true that

$$(\mathbf{u}^T(\mathbf{I} - \mathbf{A}) \geq \mathbf{0}^T, \mathbf{u} \geq \mathbf{0}) \Rightarrow \mathbf{u}^T(\mathbf{l} + \mathbf{A}\mathbf{l}) > 0,$$

the same procedure can be iterated. Then,...]

8.3. Prove the following proposition as a complement to Proposition 5.1.

Let $(\mathbf{A}_h, \mathbf{l}_h)$ be a technique such that $w_h = 0$ and $\mathbf{p}_h > \mathbf{0}$ at $r = r^*$ and let $(\mathbf{a}, \mathbf{b}, l)$ be a process not in $(\mathbf{A}_h, \mathbf{l}_h)$ which produces a commodity which is basic in technique $(\mathbf{A}_h, \mathbf{l}_h)$. If, at $r = r^*$, process $(\mathbf{a}, \mathbf{b}, l)$ is able to pay extra profits at the prices and the wage rate of technique $(\mathbf{A}_h, \mathbf{l}_h)$, then there is a technique $(\mathbf{A}_k, \mathbf{l}_k)$ which can pay a positive wage rate. [*Hint*: Let $(\mathbf{A}_k, \mathbf{l}_k)$ be the technique made up of process $(\mathbf{a}, \mathbf{b}, l)$ and the $n - 1$ processes of technique $(\mathbf{A}_h, \mathbf{l}_h)$ producing commodities different from that produced by process $(\mathbf{a}, \mathbf{b}, l)$. Then,

$$\mathbf{p}_h \geq (1 + r^*)\mathbf{A}_k \mathbf{p}_h.$$

Then prove that the commodity produced by process $(\mathbf{a}, \mathbf{b}, l)$ is basic in technique $(\mathbf{A}_k, \mathbf{l}_k)$. Finally, let $\mathbf{F}, \mathbf{m}$, and $\mathbf{y}$ be obtained by $\mathbf{A}_k, \mathbf{l}_k$, and $\mathbf{p}_h$ by deleting all entries related to non-basic commodities and to processes producing non-basic commodities. Then

$$\mathbf{y} \geq (1 + r^*)\mathbf{F}\mathbf{y},$$

where $\mathbf{F}$ is an indecomposable nonnegative square matrix (prove). Hence by statement (d) of Theorem A.3.5....]

8.4. Prove the following proposition as a complement to Proposition 5.1.

Let $(\mathbf{A}_h, \mathbf{l}_h)$ be a technique such that $w_h = 0$ and $\mathbf{p}_h > \mathbf{0}$ at $r = r^*$ and let $(\mathbf{a}, \mathbf{b}, l)$ be a process not in $(\mathbf{A}_h, \mathbf{l}_h)$ which produces a commodity which is non-basic in technique $(\mathbf{A}_h, \mathbf{l}_h)$. If, at $r = r^*$, process $(\mathbf{a}, \mathbf{b}, l)$ is able to pay extra profits at the prices and the wage rate of technique $(\mathbf{A}_h, \mathbf{l}_h)$, then there is a technique $(\mathbf{A}_k, \mathbf{l}_k)$ such that $w_k = 0$ and $\mathbf{p}_k \leqslant \mathbf{p}_h$, when the numeraire consists only of commodities which are basic in technique $(\mathbf{A}_h, \mathbf{l}_h)$. [*Hint*: Let $(\mathbf{A}_k, \mathbf{l}_k)$ be the technique made up of process $(\mathbf{a}, \mathbf{b}, l)$ and the $n - 1$ processes of technique $(\mathbf{A}_h, \mathbf{l}_h)$ producing commodities different from that produced by process $(\mathbf{a}, \mathbf{b}, l)$. Prove that if there are basics in technique $(\mathbf{A}_k, \mathbf{l}_k)$, then they are exactly the same commodities which are basic in technique $(\mathbf{A}_h, \mathbf{l}_h)$. Show that the wage rate and the prices of basics are the same in techniques $(\mathbf{A}_k, \mathbf{l}_k)$ and $(\mathbf{A}_h, \mathbf{l}_h)$. Then let

$$\mathbf{A}_k = \begin{bmatrix} \mathbf{F}_{11} & \mathbf{0} \\ \mathbf{F}_{21} & \mathbf{F}_{22} \end{bmatrix}, \quad \mathbf{p}_h = \begin{bmatrix} \mathbf{y}_1 \\ \mathbf{y}_2 \end{bmatrix},$$

where $\mathbf{F}_{11}$ and $\mathbf{y}_1$ refer to basics. Hence

$$\mathbf{y}_2 \geqslant (1 + r^*)\mathbf{F}_{22}\mathbf{y}_2 + (1 + r^*)\mathbf{F}_{21}\mathbf{y}_1.$$

Finally, prove that $[\mathbf{I} - (1 + r^*)\mathbf{F}_{22}]$ is invertible and its inverse is semi-positive (if $\mathbf{F}_{21}\mathbf{y}_1$ is not positive, apply the procedure of exercise 8.1, otherwise...) and that the price vector of non-basics in technique $(\mathbf{A}_k, \mathbf{l}_k)$ is

$$(1 + r^*)[\mathbf{I} - (1 + r^*)\mathbf{F}_{22}]^{-1}\mathbf{F}_{21}\mathbf{y}_1.$$

Hence....]

8.5. Provide comments on the relationship between the statements of the two previous exercises and of Proposition 5.1.

8.6. Prove the following proposition as a complement to Proposition 5.2.

Let $(\mathbf{A}_h, \mathbf{l}_h)$ and $(\mathbf{A}_k, \mathbf{l}_k)$ be two techniques such that at rate of profit r^*

$$\mathbf{p}_h > \mathbf{0}, \quad \mathbf{p}_k > \mathbf{0} \quad \text{and} \quad w_k > w_h = 0.$$

Then there is a process which pays extra profits at the prices of technique $(\mathbf{A}_h, \mathbf{l}_h)$. [*Hint*: Follow the procedure of the proof of Proposition 5.2 to obtain the contradiction $1 \leqslant 0$.]

8.7. (Kurz and Salvadori, 1994a) By using the example in Table 5.2 show that Proposition 5.3 cannot be generalized to the case in which $w_k \geqslant 0$, $w_h = 0$. [*Hint*: Prove that if $r = 1$, then techniques made up of processes $(1, 2)$, $(1, 4)$, and $(3, 4)$ are cost-minimizing with wage rates equal to zero. Then show that if corn is chosen as numeraire, the price of iron equals $\frac{3}{2}$ in the first technique, 1 in the third technique, and can assume any value between

Table 5.2

	material inputs		labor		outputs	
	corn	iron			corn	iron
(1)	$\frac{1}{2}$	—	1	→	1	—
(2)	$\frac{1}{4}$	$\frac{1}{3}$	2	→	—	1
(3)	$\frac{1}{3}$	$\frac{1}{6}$	1	→	1	—
(4)	—	$\frac{1}{2}$	1	→	—	1

1 and $\frac{3}{2}$ in the second technique. Finally show that the technique made up of processes (2, 3) has a maximum rate of profit lower than 1.]

8.8. Illustrate the case dealt with in exercise 8.7 by means of the diagrammatic device presented in Section 5 of Chapter 3.

8.9. Prove the following proposition as a complement to Proposition 5.3.

Let $(\mathbf{A}_h, \mathbf{l}_h)$ and $(\mathbf{A}_k, \mathbf{l}_k)$ be two techniques which are both cost-minimizing at rate of profit r^* and $w_k \geqslant 0$, $w_h = 0$, $\mathbf{p}_k > 0$, $\mathbf{p}_h > 0$; moreover commodity j is basic in both techniques. Then $w_k = w_h$ and $\mathbf{p}_k = \mathbf{p}_h$. [*Hint*: With no loss of generality assume $j = 1$, take the numeraire to consist of commodity 1 only, and introduce the following partitions

$$\mathbf{A}_h = \begin{bmatrix} B_h & \mathbf{C}_h \\ \mathbf{D}_h & \mathbf{F}_h \end{bmatrix}, \quad \mathbf{A}_k = \begin{bmatrix} B_k & \mathbf{C}_k \\ \mathbf{D}_k & \mathbf{F}_k \end{bmatrix}, \quad \mathbf{p}_h = \begin{bmatrix} 1 \\ \mathbf{y}_h \end{bmatrix}, \quad \mathbf{p}_k = \begin{bmatrix} 1 \\ \mathbf{y}_k \end{bmatrix},$$

where the B's are scalars, the $\mathbf{C}$'s are row vectors, and the $\mathbf{D}$'s are column vectors. Then,

$$[\mathbf{I} - (1 + r^*)\mathbf{F}_k]\mathbf{y}_h \leqslant (1 + r^*)\mathbf{D}_k$$
$$[\mathbf{I} - (1 + r^*)\mathbf{F}_h]\mathbf{y}_k \leqslant (1 + r^*)\mathbf{D}_h,$$

where

$$[\mathbf{I} - (1 + r^*)\mathbf{F}_h]\mathbf{y}_h = (1 + r^*)\mathbf{D}_h$$
$$[\mathbf{I} - (1 + r^*)\mathbf{F}_k]\mathbf{y}_k = (1 + r^*)\mathbf{D}_k.$$

Finally, apply the same procedure as in exercise 8.1 to prove that matrices $[\mathbf{I} - (1 + r^*)\mathbf{F}_h]$ and $[\mathbf{I} - (1 + r^*)\mathbf{F}_k]$ are invertible and their inverses are semipositive. Then ....]

8.10. Use the results of the previous exercises to prove the following statements.

(a) If there is a technique which has a positive price vector and a nonnegative wage rate for $r = r^*$, then there is a cost-minimizing technique at rate of profit r^*.[6]

(b) A technique which gives rise to a vector of prices $\mathbf{p}^* > 0$ and a wage rate $w^* \geqslant 0$ for $r = r^*$ minimizes costs at rate of profit r^* only if no other technique allows a wage rate higher than w^* for $r = r^*$, given a numeraire consisting of a positive amount of each commodity.

(c) If there is a commodity which is basic in all techniques, then a technique which gives rise to a vector of prices $\mathbf{p}^* > 0$ and a wage rate $w^* \geqslant 0$ for $r = r^*$ minimizes costs at rate of profit r^* if and only if no other technique allows a wage rate higher than w^* for $r = r^*$ and no technique among those which can pay the same wage rate has a lower price for some commodities, given a numeraire consisting only of commodities which are basic in all techniques.

(d) If there is more than one technique which minimizes costs at rate of profit r^*, then these techniques have the same wage rate. If this wage rate is positive, or if there is a commodity which is basic in all cost-minimizing techniques, then all cost-minimizing techniques at rate of profit r^* have the same price vector at $r = r^*$.

8.11. (Calculus) Prove Lemma 5.1 on the assumption that $\mathbf{l} \geqslant 0$ such that

$$(\mathbf{u}^T(\mathbf{B} - \mathbf{A}) \geqslant \mathbf{0}^T, \mathbf{u} \geqslant 0) \Rightarrow \mathbf{u}^T\mathbf{l} > 0,$$

but not necessarily $\mathbf{l} > 0$. [*Hint*: Note the similarity to exercise 8.1.]

8.12. Prove the following statement, as an alternative to Lemma 5.1.

The system of inequalities (5.6)–(5.11) admits a solution with a nonnegative w if and only if the following system of inequalities admits a solution:

$$\begin{bmatrix} \mathbf{B} - (1+r)\mathbf{A} & -\mathbf{l} \\ -\mathbf{d}^T & 0 \\ \mathbf{d}^T & 0 \end{bmatrix} \begin{bmatrix} \mathbf{y} \\ \alpha \end{bmatrix} \leqq \begin{bmatrix} \mathbf{0} \\ -1 \\ 1 \end{bmatrix},$$

$$\begin{bmatrix} \mathbf{z} \\ \beta \\ \gamma \end{bmatrix}^T \begin{bmatrix} \mathbf{B} - (1+r)\mathbf{A} & -\mathbf{l} \\ -\mathbf{d}^T & 0 \\ \mathbf{d}^T & 0 \end{bmatrix} \begin{bmatrix} \mathbf{y} \\ \alpha \end{bmatrix} = \gamma - \beta,$$

---

[6] If the number of processes is not finite, statement (a) is to be changed in the following way:

"If there is a technique which has a positive price vector and a nonnegative wage rate for $r = r^*$ such that no technique can pay a wage rate larger than that paid by it, then there is a cost-minimizing technique at rate of profit r^*."

$$\begin{bmatrix} \mathbf{z} \\ \beta \\ \gamma \end{bmatrix}^T \begin{bmatrix} \mathbf{B}-(1+r)\mathbf{A} & -\mathbf{l} \\ -\mathbf{d}^T & 0 \\ \mathbf{d}^T & 0 \end{bmatrix} \geqq \begin{bmatrix} \mathbf{0} \\ -1 \end{bmatrix}^T,$$

$$\begin{bmatrix} \mathbf{z} \\ \beta \\ \gamma \end{bmatrix}^T \begin{bmatrix} \mathbf{B}-(1+r)\mathbf{A} & -\mathbf{l} \\ -\mathbf{d}^T & 0 \\ \mathbf{d}^T & 0 \end{bmatrix} \begin{bmatrix} \mathbf{y} \\ \alpha \end{bmatrix} = -\alpha,$$

$$\begin{bmatrix} \mathbf{z} \\ \beta \\ \gamma \end{bmatrix} \geqq \mathbf{0}, \quad \begin{bmatrix} \mathbf{y} \\ \alpha \end{bmatrix} \geqq \mathbf{0}.$$

8.13. Prove the following statement, as an alternative to Lemma 5.2.

Let $\mathbf{l} > \mathbf{0}$. Then the system of inequalities in exercise 8.12 has a solution if and only if there is a semipositive vector $\mathbf{v}$ such that

$$\mathbf{v}^T[\mathbf{B}-(1+r)\mathbf{A}] \geqq \mathbf{0}^T.$$

8.14. Prove that the statement of exercise 8.13 is still valid for $\mathbf{l} \geqq \mathbf{0}$ such that

$$(\mathbf{u}^T(\mathbf{B}-\mathbf{A}) \geqq \mathbf{0}^T, \mathbf{u} \geqq \mathbf{0}) \Rightarrow \mathbf{u}^T\mathbf{l} > 0.$$

8.15. Show that the condition relating to the labor vector in exercises 8.1, 8.11, and 8.14 means that labor is necessary in the reproduction of commodities.

8.16. Use the results of previous exercises to prove the following statements:

(a) If and only if there is a nonnegative vector $\mathbf{v}$ such that the inequality in exercise 8.13 holds, then there is a price vector $\mathbf{p}^* \geqq \mathbf{0}$ and a wage rate $w^* \geqq 0$ such that no process pays extra profits and at least one process for each commodity does not incur extra costs.

(b) The long-period wage rate w^* is the minimum w for which there is a vector $\mathbf{p}$ such that

$$\begin{bmatrix} \mathbf{B}-(1+r)\mathbf{A} & -\mathbf{l} \\ -\mathbf{d}^T & 0 \\ \mathbf{d}^T & 0 \end{bmatrix} \begin{bmatrix} \mathbf{p} \\ w \end{bmatrix} \leqq \begin{bmatrix} \mathbf{0} \\ -1 \\ 1 \end{bmatrix},$$

$$\mathbf{p} \geqq \mathbf{0}, \quad w \geqq 0.$$

(c) If there are two long-period price vectors and wage rates, $(\mathbf{p}^*, w^*)$ and $(\mathbf{p}^\circ, w^\circ)$, then the processes which are operated with one solution do not incur extra costs at the prices and wage rate of the other solution; moreover, the linear combination of price vectors and wage rates

$$(\lambda\mathbf{p}^* + (1 - \lambda)\mathbf{p}^\circ, \lambda w^* + (1 - \lambda)w^\circ)$$

with $0 \leqslant \lambda \leqslant 1$ is also a long-period price vector and wage rate.

(d) If there are two long-period price vectors and wage rates, $(\mathbf{p}^*, w^*)$ and $(\mathbf{p}^\circ, \mathbf{w}^\circ)$, then $w^* = w^\circ$. If, moreover, either $w^* = w^\circ > 0$ or there is j such that

$$(\mathbf{u}^T(\mathbf{B} - \mathbf{A}) \geqslant \mathbf{0}^T, \mathbf{u} \geqslant \mathbf{0}) \Rightarrow \mathbf{u}^T\mathbf{B}\mathbf{e}_j > 0,$$

then $\mathbf{p}^* = \mathbf{p}^\circ$.

[*Hint*: For statement (b) look at the solution of exercise 8.12; for statement (c) look at proof of statement (c) of Theorem 5.4; for statement (d) look at the solution of exercise 8.9.]

8.17. Provide an economic interpretation of the condition given in statement (d) of the preceding exercise.

8.18. Prove statements (i)–(v) of Subsection 3.1

8.19. Prove statement (d) of Theorem 5.3 on the assumption that $w^*\bar{\mathbf{m}}^\circ \geqslant \mathbf{0}$ and $w^\circ\bar{\mathbf{m}}^* \geqslant \mathbf{0}$. [*Hint*: It is enough to prove that there are nonnegative vectors $\mathbf{z}^*$ and $\mathbf{z}^\circ$ such that $\mathbf{z}^{*T}[\mathbf{I} - (1 + r^*)\hat{\mathbf{C}}^*] > \mathbf{0}^T$ and $\mathbf{z}^{\circ T}[\mathbf{I} - (1 + r^*)\hat{\mathbf{C}}^\circ] > \mathbf{0}^T$. Let $\mathbf{z}_1^*$ be a nonnegative vector with the zero entries corresponding to processes $(\mathbf{C}^*, \mathbf{D}^*, \mathbf{m}^*)$ and the positive entries equal to the corresponding entries of vector $\mathbf{x}^\circ$. Let $\mathbf{z}_2^*$ be a nonnegative vector with the positive entries corresponding to those of the processes $(\mathbf{C}^*, \mathbf{D}^*, \mathbf{m}^*)$ which produce commodities not required for consumption. These positive entries are equal to the corresponding entries of vector $\mathbf{x}^*$. Let $\mathbf{z}_3^*$ be a nonnegative vector with the positive entries corresponding to all processes $(\mathbf{C}^*, \mathbf{D}^*, \mathbf{m}^*)$ and equal to the corresponding entries of vector $\mathbf{x}^*$. Show that there are scalars α and β such that

$$(\mathbf{z}_1^* + \alpha\mathbf{z}_2^* + \beta\mathbf{z}_3^*)^T[\mathbf{I} - (1 + r^*)\hat{\mathbf{C}}^*] > \mathbf{0}^T.]$$

8.20. Using the results of exercises 8.11–8.16 and 8.19 provide statements and proofs concerning the generalization of the results of Subsection 3.2 to the case of a zero wage rate and to the case of a semipositive labor vector if labor is directly or indirectly required in the reproduction of commodities.

8.21. (Robinson and Naqvi, 1967) Consider the technology described in Table 5.3 and prove that there are three switch points between the $w–r$ relationships of the two possible techniques. [*Hint*: The switch points are obtained at $r = 0.05$, $r = 0.1$, and $r = 0.2$.]

Table 5.3

Processes	material inputs			labor		outputs		
	corn	iron	aluminium			corn	iron	aluminium
(1)	35	50	0	18	→	75	0	0
(2)	35	50	0	9	→	0	150	0
(3)	16221	0	16221	16221	→	68200	0	0
(4)	55934	0	76336	51773	→	0	0	124500

Table 5.4

	material inputs		labor		outputs	
	corn	u-commodity			corn	u-commodity
(u)	0	$\dfrac{x}{6+y}$	$5+y-\dfrac{x}{6+y}$	→	1	0
(2u)	0	$\dfrac{5+y}{6+y}$	$\dfrac{1}{6+y}$	→	0	1

8.22. Investigate the technology of the preceding exercise by utilizing the framework of Subsection 3.3 on the assumption that only corn is consumed. Does this example contradict the result of exercise 8.17 of Chapter 3? Why not?

8.23. (Calculus) (Garegnani, 1970) Let $U = \{u \in \mathbb{R} \mid 0 \leqslant u \leqslant 1.505\}$ be a set of indices. Let us assume that for each $u \in U$ there is a commodity, called u-commodity, which can be utilized either to produce itself or to produce a further commodity called corn. Corn is the only commodity required for consumption. Finally, for each u there are the processes defined by the Table 5.4, where $x = 27e^{-2u}$, $y = \sqrt[10]{u^{11}}$, and e is the base of natural logarithms. Explore this technology and show that

(i) this economy can be analyzed within the framework of Subsection 3.3, but it cannot be analyzed within the frameworks of Subsections 3.2 and 3.4;

(ii) as r rises from 0 to 0.13 the u-commodity which is utilized to produce corn will vary continuously from the 0-commodity to the 1.505-commodity;

(iii) as r rises from 0.13 to the maximum admissible level in the economy, 0.2, the u-commodity which is utilized to produce corn will vary continuously from the 1.505-commodity to the 0-commodity;

(iv) there is no switch point in the sense that for no level of the rate of profit two distinct techniques are cost-minimizing.

Table 5.5

	material inputs			outputs	
	corn	iron	labor	corn	iron
(u)	0	$\dfrac{x}{6+y}$	$5+y-\dfrac{x}{6+y}$ $\rightarrow$	1	0
(z)	0	$\dfrac{5+z}{6+z}$	$\dfrac{1}{6+z}$ $\rightarrow$	0	1

[*Hint*: For each u the w–r relationship is

$$w = \frac{1-(5+y)r}{(5+y)+[x-(5+y)^2]r};$$

the envelope is found by setting the derivative with respect to u equal to zero; in doing this it is convenient to recall that $x' = -2x$ and $y' = (11y/10u)$, where x' and y' are the derivatives of x and y with respect to u.]

8.24. (Calculus) There are two commodities, corn and iron. Only corn is required for consumption. Let $U = \{u \in \mathbb{R} \mid 0 \leqslant u \leqslant 1.505\}$ and $Z = \{z \in \mathbb{R} \mid 0 \leqslant z \leqslant 2\}$ be two sets of indices. Let us assume that for each $u \in U$ there is a process producing corn and for each $z \in Z$ there is a process producing iron defined in Table 5.5 where $x = 27e^{-2u}$ and $y = \sqrt[10]{u^{11}}$. Explore this technology and show that

(i) this economy can be analyzed within the framework of Subsections 3.3 and 3.4, but it cannot be analyzed within the framework of Subsection 3.2;

(ii) whatever value r takes in the interval $[0, 0.2]$, where $r = 0.2$ is the maximum admissible r, iron is produced with the process corresponding to $z = 0$;

(iii) there is a r^*, $0.15 < r^* < 0.16$, such that as r rises from 0 to r^* the process operated to produce corn will vary continuously from that corresponding to $u = 0$ to that corresponding to $u = 1.505$;

(iv) whatever value r takes in the interval $[r^*, 0.2]$, corn is produced with the process corresponding to $u = 1.505$;

(v) there is no switch point, in the sense that for no rate of profit are two distinct techniques cost-minimizing.

[*Hint*: Since iron is the unique basic in all techniques prove point (ii) by taking iron as the numeraire. The wage frontier is then

$$w = 1 - 5r.$$

Prove that the cost-minimizing technique is that which minimizes the

Table 5.6

	material inputs				outputs		
	corn	u-comm	v-good	labor	corn	u-comm	v-good
(u)	0	$\dfrac{1}{1+2u}$	0	$\dfrac{u^2}{1+2u}$ →	1	0	0
(2u)	0	$\dfrac{1}{1+2u}$	0	$\dfrac{u}{1+2u}$ →	0	1	0
(v)	0	0	$\dfrac{3v}{5(1+v)}$	$\dfrac{2u}{5}$ →	1	0	0
(2v)	0	0	$\dfrac{5+2v}{5(1+v)^2}$	$\dfrac{3v}{5(1+v)}$ →	0	0	1

price of corn in terms of iron. Show that the relation between u and r for $0 \leqslant r \leqslant r^*$ is the locus

$$r = \frac{11y(6+y)^2}{55y(6+y)^2 + 6(120u + 20uy + 11y)x},$$

which is increasing in the relevant range and such that when $u = 1.505$, $r = r^*$.]

8.25. Compare the results of exercises 8.23 and 8.24.

8.26. (Bellino, 1993) Let $U = \{u \in \mathbb{Q} \mid u \geqslant 0\}$ and $V = \{v \in \mathbb{R} \mid v > 0$, either $v = 1$ or $v \notin \mathbb{Q}\}$ be a set of indices. Let us assume that for each $u \in U$ there is a commodity, called u-comm, which can be utilized either to produce itself or to produce a further commodity called corn, and for each $v \in V$ there is a commodity, called v-good, which can also be utilized either to produce itself or to produce corn. Corn is the only commodity required for consumption. Finally for each u and for each v there are the processes defined by the Table 5.6. Explore this technology and show that

(i) this economy can be analyzed within the framework of Subsection 3.3, but it cannot be analyzed within the frameworks of Subsections 3.2 and 3.4;
(ii) as r rises from 0 to infinity the wage–profit frontier is

$$w = \frac{1}{r};$$

(iii) if r is a rational number corn is produced with commodity r-comm;
(iv) if r is either 1 or an irrational number corn is produced with commodity r-good;
(v) there is only one switch point at $r = 1$.

[*Hint*: If u were varying in the whole range of nonnegative reals, then processes (u) and ($2u$) would determine the wage–profit frontier in (ii); analogously, if v were varying in the whole range of nonnegative reals, the processes (v) and ($2v$) would also determine the wage–profit frontier in (ii).]

6

Alternative descriptions of a technique

In this book production is conceived of as a circular process: commodities are produced by means of commodities. The present chapter is devoted to an investigation of three alternative ways to describe the technical conditions of production and a discussion of the relationships which exist between them and the description provided in the previous chapters. First, there is the view that production can be seen as a one-way avenue leading from the services of the "original" factors of production, labor and land, to the final product. Since in the following discussion we shall set aside the problem of land services, the product will be considered as obtained by a stream of labor inputs only. This approach to the theory of production is known as the "Austrian" approach, since it has been advocated by the founders of the Austrian tradition in economic thought, Menger, von Wieser, and von Böhm–Bawerk, and authors working in that tradition, most notably Wicksell and, more recently, Hicks. Second, there is the description of the conditions of production in terms of the concept of "vertical integration." The latter consists of a generalization of the concept of the "sub-system" introduced in Chapter 3 for the two-commodity case. According to the third alternative the price vectors generated by a technique at a number of different levels of the rate of profit can be used to describe that technique.

Throughout this chapter we will be concerned with a single "technique" as defined in the previous chapter and not with the whole set of existing processes. In Chapter 5 a technique is fully described by the pair $(\mathbf{A}, \mathbf{l})$, where $\mathbf{A}$ is the material input matrix and $\mathbf{l}$ is the labor input vector; in the present chapter alternative descriptions of a *technique* will be provided. The Austrian approach will be dealt with in Section 1, which is devoted to a discussion of the so-called "reduction to dated quantities of labor." In Section 2 the concept of vertical integration will be investigated.

164

Section 3 demonstrates how one can determine the material input matrix and the labor input vector from price vectors associated with a number of different levels of the rate of profit. In this context it turns out to be necessary to explore the distinction between "regular" and "irregular" techniques introduced in Section 1, utilized in Section 3, and further investigated in Section 4. Section 5 summarizes the issue, and Sections 6 and 7 provide the usual historical notes and exercises, respectively.

1. Reduction to dated quantities of labor

Let us start from equation (4.6a) which is reproduced here for convenience:

$$\mathbf{p} = w\mathbf{l} + (1 + r)\mathbf{A}\mathbf{p}. \tag{6.1}$$

Replacing $\mathbf{p}$ on the right-hand side of the equation by the right-hand side itself gives

$$\mathbf{p} = w\mathbf{l} + (1 + r)\mathbf{A}\left[w\mathbf{l} + (1 + r)\mathbf{A}\mathbf{p}\right] = w\mathbf{l} + w(1 + r)\mathbf{A}\mathbf{l} + (1 + r)^2\mathbf{A}^2\mathbf{p}.$$

Performing the same substitution again,

$$\mathbf{p} = w\mathbf{l} + w(1 + r)\mathbf{A}\mathbf{l} + (1 + r)^2\mathbf{A}^2\left[w\mathbf{l} + w(1 + r)\mathbf{A}\mathbf{l} + (1 + r)^2\mathbf{A}^2\mathbf{p}\right]$$
$$= w[\mathbf{l} + (1 + r)\mathbf{A}\mathbf{l} + (1 + r)^2\mathbf{A}^2\mathbf{l}] + (1 + r)^3\mathbf{A}^3\mathbf{l}] + (1 + r)^4\mathbf{A}^4\mathbf{p}.$$

By iterating this procedure one obtains[1]

$$\mathbf{p} = w[\mathbf{l} + (1 + r)\mathbf{A}\mathbf{l} + (1 + r)^2\mathbf{A}^2\mathbf{l} + \cdots + (1 + r)^t\mathbf{A}^t\mathbf{l} + \cdots] \tag{6.2}$$

This formula is known as the *reduction to dated quantities of labor*. In order to understand this interpretation note that

$\mathbf{l}$ is the vector of the quantities of labor directly needed to produce the final products;

$\mathbf{A}\mathbf{l}$ is the vector of the quantities of labor directly needed in the production of the means of production needed to produce the final products;

$\mathbf{A}^2\mathbf{l}$ is the vector of the quantities of labor directly needed in the

---

[1] From statement (b) of Theorem A3.3 of the Mathematical Appendix, it follows that if $-1 \leqslant r < R$, then

$$\mathbf{I} + (1 + r)\mathbf{A} + (1 + r)^2\mathbf{A}^2 + \cdots + (1 + r)^t\mathbf{A}^t + \cdots = [\mathbf{I} - (1 + r)\mathbf{A}]^{-1}.$$

On the contrary, with $r \geqslant R$ the series on the right-hand side of (6.2) does not converge.

production of the means of production needed to produce the means of production needed to produce the final products;

and so on.

It follows that the production which has been represented at the beginning of Chapter 4 as

$$\mathbf{A} \oplus \mathbf{l} \to \mathbf{I} \tag{6.3}$$

can also be represented as

$$\cdots \oplus \mathbf{l}_t \oplus \cdots \oplus \mathbf{l}_2 \oplus \mathbf{l}_1 \oplus \mathbf{l}_0 \to \mathbf{I}, \tag{6.4}$$

where $\mathbf{l}_t = \mathbf{A}^t \mathbf{l}$. In this way the amounts of commodity inputs disappear and in their place we find a stream of dated quantities of labor.

It has been shown how the description of the production process according to (6.3) can be transformed into the description according to (6.4). We may now ask whether it is also possible to perform the reverse translation, that is, to start from description (6.4) and arrive at description (6.3). The description of technique (6.3) involves $n^2 + n$ numbers, where n is the number of commodities, whereas the description of technique (6.4) seems to involve an infinite number of numbers. Therefore some special conditions among these numbers should hold in order for an equivalent description of type (6.3) to exist.

Let the s vectors $\mathbf{l}_0, \mathbf{l}_1, \mathbf{l}_2, \ldots, \mathbf{l}_{s-1}$ be linearly independent and let $\mathbf{l}_s = \mathbf{Kb}$, where

$$\mathbf{K} = [\mathbf{l}_0, \mathbf{l}_1, \mathbf{l}_2, \ldots, \mathbf{l}_{s-1}].$$

Moreover let $\mathbf{B} = [\mathbf{e}_2, \mathbf{e}_3, \ldots, \mathbf{e}_s, \mathbf{b}]$, where $\mathbf{e}_i$ is the ith unit vector. Then the following proposition holds.

Proposition 6.1. There is a matrix $\mathbf{A}$ such that $\mathbf{l}_t = \mathbf{A}^t \mathbf{l}_0$ for each t if and only if $\mathbf{l}_t = \mathbf{KB}^{t-s} \mathbf{b}$ for each $t \geqslant s$.

Proof. Let us assume that $\mathbf{l}_{t-1} = \mathbf{KB}^{t-1-s} \mathbf{b}$ and let us prove that if there is a matrix $\mathbf{A}$ such that $\mathbf{l}_t = \mathbf{A}^t \mathbf{l}_0$ for each t, then $\mathbf{l}_t = \mathbf{KB}^{t-s} \mathbf{b}$. This proves the "only if" part of the Proposition since $\mathbf{l}_s = \mathbf{Kb}$. It is immediately obtained that

$$\mathbf{AK} = \mathbf{KB} \tag{6.5}$$

since

$$\mathbf{A}[\mathbf{l}_0, \mathbf{l}_1, \ldots, \mathbf{l}_{s-1}] = [\mathbf{l}_1, \mathbf{l}_2, \ldots, \mathbf{l}_s] = \mathbf{K}[\mathbf{e}_2, \mathbf{e}_3, \ldots, \mathbf{e}_s, \mathbf{b}].$$

Therefore

$$\mathbf{l}_t = \mathbf{A}\mathbf{l}_{t-1} = \mathbf{AKB}^{t-1-s} \mathbf{b} = \mathbf{KB}^{t-s} \mathbf{b}.$$

Let $\mathbf{A}$ be a matrix satisfying equation (6.5). If $s = n$, then $\mathbf{A} = \mathbf{KBK}^{-1}$; if $s < n$, equation (6.5) has a solution for $\mathbf{A}$ since the rank of the $n \times s$ matrix $\mathbf{K}$ is s and therefore

$$\text{rank} \begin{bmatrix} \mathbf{K} \\ \mathbf{e}_i^T \mathbf{KB} \end{bmatrix} = s = \text{rank } \mathbf{K}$$

(cf. Subsection A.1.8 of the Mathematical Appendix). Then

$$\mathbf{l}_t = \mathbf{A}^t \mathbf{l}_0$$

for $0 \leqslant t \leqslant s$. In order to complete the proof of the "if" part, let $\mathbf{l}_t = \mathbf{KB}^{t-s}\mathbf{b}$ for each $t \geqslant s$. Hence, if $t \geqslant s$,

$$\mathbf{l}_t = \mathbf{KB}^{t-s}\mathbf{b} = \mathbf{A}^{t-s}\mathbf{Kb} = \mathbf{A}^{t-s}\mathbf{l}_s = \mathbf{A}^t\mathbf{l}_0. \qquad \text{Q.E.D.}$$

If $s = n$, then matrix $\mathbf{A}$ is uniquely determined by equation (6.5) once matrices $\mathbf{K}$ and $\mathbf{B}$ are given. In this case we say that the technique is *regular*. If $s < n$, matrix $\mathbf{A}$ is not uniquely determined. However, the following proposition can be proved.

Proposition 6.2. The sequence of dated quantities of labor of two techniques $(\mathbf{A}, \mathbf{l})$ and $(\mathbf{F}, \mathbf{m})$ with n commodities and n processes coincide for each time period, that is,

$$\mathbf{A}^t\mathbf{l} = \mathbf{F}^t\mathbf{m}, \quad \text{each } t \in \mathbb{N}_0$$

if and only if $\mathbf{F} = \mathbf{A} + \mathbf{Y}$ and $\mathbf{m} = \mathbf{l}$, where $\mathbf{Y}$ is a matrix such that $\mathbf{Y}[\mathbf{l}, \mathbf{Al}, \ldots, \mathbf{A}^n\mathbf{l}] = \mathbf{0}$. Furthermore, if one technique is regular, then both are and $\mathbf{F} = \mathbf{A}$.

Proof. The "if" part is trivial. As regards the "only if" part, by assumption

$$\mathbf{A}^0\mathbf{l} = \mathbf{F}^0\mathbf{m}.$$

Then $\mathbf{m} = \mathbf{l}$. By setting $\mathbf{Y} = \mathbf{F} - \mathbf{A}$ we obtain

$$\mathbf{A}^{t+1}\mathbf{l} = \mathbf{F}^{t+1}\mathbf{l} = \mathbf{AF}^t\mathbf{l} + \mathbf{YF}^t\mathbf{l} = \mathbf{A}^{t+1}\mathbf{l} + \mathbf{YA}^t\mathbf{l} \quad \text{each } t \in \mathbb{N}_0.$$

Hence

$$\mathbf{YA}^t\mathbf{l} = \mathbf{0} \quad \text{each } t \in \mathbb{N}_0. \qquad \text{Q.E.D.}$$

In Proposition 6.1 it was not assumed that matrix $\mathbf{A}$ is nonnegative. The fact that matrix $\mathbf{A}$ is nonnegative introduces further restrictions on matrices $\mathbf{K}$ and $\mathbf{B}$, and therefore on the sequence $\mathbf{l}_0, \mathbf{l}_1, \ldots, \mathbf{l}_t, \ldots$. In fact, because of Farkas's Lemma (see Theorem A.2.2 in the Mathematical Appendix) equation (6.5) has a nonnegative solution for $\mathbf{A}$ if and only if

$$(\mathbf{y} \in \mathbb{R}^s, \mathbf{Ky} \geqslant \mathbf{0}) \Rightarrow \mathbf{KBy} \geqslant \mathbf{0}.$$

This remark jointly with previous propositions proves the following theorem, which summarizes previous results. (Further elements of the analysis of regular and irregular techniques will be provided in Sections 3 and 4 below.)

Theorem 6.1. There is a semipositive matrix $\mathbf{A}$ such that $\mathbf{l}_t = \mathbf{A}^t \mathbf{l}_0$ for each t if and only if

(i) $\mathbf{l}_t = \mathbf{K}\mathbf{B}^{t-s}\mathbf{b}$ for each $t \geqslant s$,
(ii) $(\mathbf{y} \in \mathbb{R}^s, \mathbf{K}\mathbf{y} \geqslant \mathbf{0}) \Rightarrow \mathbf{K}\mathbf{B}\mathbf{y} \geqslant \mathbf{0}$.

If and only if $s = n$, matrix $\mathbf{A}$ is uniquely determined. If $s < n$ and matrices $\mathbf{A}$ and $\mathbf{F}$ are such that $\mathbf{l}_t = \mathbf{A}^t \mathbf{l}_0 = \mathbf{F}^t \mathbf{l}_0$, each t, then $\mathbf{F} = \mathbf{A} + \mathbf{Y}$, where $\mathbf{Y}$ is a matrix such that $\mathbf{Y}\mathbf{l}_t = \mathbf{0}$ for each t.

To conclude this section, it should be noted that by following a route similar to that leading to equation (6.2), one gets from equation (4.32)

$$\mathbf{v} = \mathbf{l} + \mathbf{A}\mathbf{l} + \mathbf{A}^2\mathbf{l} + \cdots + \mathbf{A}^t\mathbf{l} + \cdots,$$

where $\mathbf{v}$ is the vector of direct and indirect quantities of labor "embodied" in the different commodities.

2. Vertically integrated technical coefficients

In this section another representation of equation (6.1) will be introduced. The description under consideration is obtained as a generalization of the concept of the "subsystem" introduced in Chapter 3 for the two-commodity case.

Let vector $\mathbf{y}$ be any semipositive net output vector and vector $\mathbf{x}$ be the corresponding intensity vector. Hence

$$\mathbf{x}^T = \mathbf{x}^T\mathbf{A} + \mathbf{y}^T,$$

or, solving for $\mathbf{x}$,

$$\mathbf{x}^T = \mathbf{y}^T[\mathbf{I} - \mathbf{A}]^{-1}. \tag{6.6}$$

Let $\mathbf{k}$ designate the vector of capital stocks necessary to support the production of $\mathbf{y}$, where $\mathbf{k}^T = \mathbf{x}^T\mathbf{A}$. Because of (6.6) we have

$$\mathbf{k}^T = \mathbf{y}^T[\mathbf{I} - \mathbf{A}]^{-1}\mathbf{A}. \tag{6.7}$$

Hence, $[\mathbf{I} - \mathbf{A}]^{-1}\mathbf{A}$ is the matrix linking the quantities of the produced means of production, $\mathbf{k}$, to net outputs, $\mathbf{y}$. Define matrix $\mathbf{H}$ as

$$\mathbf{H} \equiv [\mathbf{I} - \mathbf{A}]^{-1}\mathbf{A}. \tag{6.8}$$

Equation (6.7) can then be written as

$$\mathbf{k}^T = \mathbf{y}^T\mathbf{H}. \tag{6.7'}$$

If $\mathbf{y} = \mathbf{e}_i$, where $\mathbf{e}_i$ is the ith unit vector, then $\mathbf{k}^T = \mathbf{e}_i^T \mathbf{H}$. That is, the ith row of matrix $\mathbf{H}$ is the vector of commodities required directly or indirectly to produce one (net) unit of commodity i, or the vector of commodities which enter into the subsystem producing commodity i. This subsystem is also called the "vertically integrated industry producing commodity i," and matrix $\mathbf{H}$ is called the *vertically integrated technical coefficients matrix*. The total quantity of labor employed will be given by

$$\mathbf{x}^T \mathbf{l} = \mathbf{y}^T [\mathbf{I} - \mathbf{A}]^{-1} \mathbf{l}.$$

Hence the vector

$$\mathbf{v} \equiv [\mathbf{I} - \mathbf{A}]^{-1} \mathbf{l} \tag{6.9}$$

dealt with in Section 3 of Chapter 4 is the vector of direct and indirect labor requirements per unit of net output of the different commodities.

The "vertically integrated" technical coefficients $(\mathbf{H}, \mathbf{v})$ are often a useful replacement for the "direct" coefficients $(\mathbf{A}, \mathbf{l})$. For example, equation (6.1) may be rewritten in terms of $(\mathbf{H}, \mathbf{v})$ as

$$\mathbf{p} = w\mathbf{v} + r\mathbf{H}\mathbf{p}. \tag{6.10}$$

According to equation (6.10) the price of each commodity can be seen as consisting of two "components": the total of direct and indirect wage payments incurred in the production of that commodity plus the profits on the value of the capital stocks required both directly and indirectly.

The identities (6.8) and (6.9) reveal the connection between vertically integrated coefficients $(\mathbf{H}, \mathbf{v})$ and direct coefficients $(\mathbf{A}, \mathbf{l})$. In order to get from the former to the latter, note that the following equation holds,

$$[\mathbf{I} - \mathbf{A}][\mathbf{I} + \mathbf{H}] = \mathbf{I} - \mathbf{A} + [\mathbf{I} - \mathbf{A}][\mathbf{I} - \mathbf{A}]^{-1} \mathbf{A} = \mathbf{I}.$$

Hence

$$[\mathbf{I} - \mathbf{A}] \equiv [\mathbf{I} + \mathbf{H}]^{-1}.$$

Taking this into account we obtain from identities (6.8) and (6.9), respectively,

$$\mathbf{A} \equiv [\mathbf{I} + \mathbf{H}]^{-1} \mathbf{H},$$

and

$$\mathbf{l} \equiv [\mathbf{I} + \mathbf{H}]^{-1} \mathbf{v}.$$

3. Techniques defined by price vectors

Given a technique $(\mathbf{A}, \mathbf{l})$, at each rate of profit r prices and the wage rate satisfying equations (4.6) of Chapter 4 can be determined. In this section it will be shown that starting from a number of price vectors and wage rates corresponding to different levels of the rate of profit, where this number is larger than the number of commodities, a technique $(\mathbf{A}^*, \mathbf{l})$ can be determined. If the original technique is regular, then the constructed technique is identical to the original one: $\mathbf{A}^* = \mathbf{A}$. If not, the prices and wage rate satisfying equations (4.6) for the *constructed* technique coincide with prices and wage rates satisfying equations (4.6) for the *original* technique at each rate of profit r such that $-1 \leqslant r < R$. This result can be summarized with the following *principle of duality between prices and techniques*: the price vectors and the wage rates generated by a technique at a number of rates of profit larger than the number of commodities summarize all the economically relevant aspects of the technique which has generated them.

From equation (6.2) we obtain that the price vector $\mathbf{p}$ is a linear combination of the vectors of dated quantities of labor. Furthermore, only the first s of these vectors are linearly independent ($s = n$ if technique $(\mathbf{A}, \mathbf{l})$ is regular, and $s < n$ if technique $(\mathbf{A}, \mathbf{l})$ is irregular). As a consequence at any $s + 1$ values r_i ($i = 0, 1, \ldots, s$) such that $-1 \leqslant r_i < R$, vectors $\mathbf{p}(r_i)$ are linearly dependent. Conversely:

Proposition 6.3. Let $\mathbf{p}_0, \mathbf{p}_1, \ldots, \mathbf{p}_s$ be the price vectors relative to the (different) rates of profit $r_0, r_1, \ldots, r_s$ ($-1 < r_i < R$), and let $w_0, w_1, \ldots, w_s$ ($w_i > 0$) be the corresponding wage rates. Then

  (i) the s vectors $\mathbf{p}_i$ ($i = 1, \ldots, s$) are linearly independent;
  (ii) the $s+1$ vectors $[w_i, (1+r_i)\mathbf{p}_i^T]^T$ ($i = 0, 1, \ldots, s$) are linearly independent.

Proof. Let t be the largest number of linearly independent vectors among $\mathbf{p}_0, \mathbf{p}_1, \ldots, \mathbf{p}_s$, and let us redefine indices in such a way that $\mathbf{p}_0, \mathbf{p}_1, \ldots, \mathbf{p}_{t-1}$ are linearly independent, whereas $\mathbf{p}_t$ is a linear combination of them. Statement (i) is equivalent to $t = s$. Since $t \leqslant s$, let us prove that $s \leqslant t$. Let $\mathbf{P} = [\mathbf{p}_0, \mathbf{p}_1, \ldots, \mathbf{p}_t]$, $\mathbf{w}^T = (w_0, w_1, \ldots, w_t)$, and $\mathbf{S}$ be the diagonal matrix having $1 + r_0, 1 + r_1, \ldots, 1 + r_t$ on the main diagonal. Since $\mathbf{p}_i, w_i$, and r_i ($i = 1, 2, \ldots, t + 1$) satisfy equation (6.1),

$$\mathbf{P} = \mathbf{APS} + \mathbf{lw}^T. \tag{6.11}$$

The choice of vectors $\mathbf{p}_0, \mathbf{p}_1, \ldots, \mathbf{p}_t$ implies that there is a unique (up to a factor) vector $\mathbf{z}$ such that

$$\mathbf{PSz} = \mathbf{0}. \tag{6.12}$$

By multiplying equation (6.11) by $\mathbf{z}$, we obtain

$$\mathbf{Pz} = \mathbf{APSz} + \mathbf{lw}^T\mathbf{z}. \tag{6.13}$$

If $\mathbf{l}\mathbf{w}^T\mathbf{z} = 0$, then $\mathbf{P}\mathbf{z} = \mathbf{0}$ and $\mathbf{S}^{-1}\mathbf{z}$ is a solution to equation (6.11). Hence a contradiction, since $\mathbf{S}^{-1}\mathbf{z}$ is not proportional to $\mathbf{z}$ (cf. the definition of matrix $\mathbf{S}$). Thus $\mathbf{l}\mathbf{w}^T\mathbf{z} \neq \mathbf{0}$. Then normalize $\mathbf{z}$ such that $\mathbf{w}^T\mathbf{z} = 1$. Let us now prove by induction that

$$\mathbf{P}\mathbf{T}^m\mathbf{z} = \sum_{j=0}^{m} (\mathbf{w}^T\mathbf{T}^{m-j}\mathbf{z})\mathbf{A}^j\mathbf{l}, \tag{6.14.m}$$

where $\mathbf{T} = \mathbf{S}^{-1}$. We first obtain from (6.13) that

$$\mathbf{P}\mathbf{z} = \mathbf{l}. \tag{6.14.0}$$

Then, we obtain from (6.14.m) that

$$\mathbf{A}\mathbf{P}\mathbf{T}^m\mathbf{z} = \sum_{j=0}^{m} (\mathbf{w}^T\mathbf{T}^{m-j}\mathbf{z})\mathbf{A}^{j+1}\mathbf{l} = \sum_{j=1}^{m+1} (\mathbf{w}^T\mathbf{T}^{m+1-j}\mathbf{z})\mathbf{A}^j\mathbf{l},$$

from which (6.14.m + 1) follows since

$$\mathbf{A}\mathbf{P} = \mathbf{P}\mathbf{T} - \mathbf{l}\mathbf{w}^T\mathbf{T}, \tag{6.15}$$

because of equality (6.11), and therefore

$$\mathbf{P}\mathbf{T}^{m+1}\mathbf{z} - (\mathbf{w}^T\mathbf{T}^{m+1}\mathbf{z})\mathbf{l} = \sum_{j=1}^{m+1} (\mathbf{w}^T\mathbf{T}^{m+1-j}\mathbf{z})\mathbf{A}^j\mathbf{l}.$$

Let us arrange equalities (6.14.0)–(6.14.m) as

$$\mathbf{P}[\mathbf{z}, \mathbf{T}\mathbf{z}, \ldots, \mathbf{T}^m\mathbf{z}] = \left[\mathbf{l}, (\mathbf{w}^T\mathbf{T}\mathbf{z})\mathbf{l} + \mathbf{A}\mathbf{l}, \ldots, \sum_{j=0}^{m} (\mathbf{w}^T\mathbf{T}^{m-j}\mathbf{z})\mathbf{A}^j\mathbf{l}\right].$$

Since $[\mathbf{l}, (\mathbf{w}^T\mathbf{T}\mathbf{z})\mathbf{l} + \mathbf{A}\mathbf{l}, \ldots, \sum_{j=0}^{m}(\mathbf{w}^T\mathbf{T}^{m-j}\mathbf{z})\mathbf{A}^j\mathbf{l}] = [\mathbf{l}, \mathbf{A}\mathbf{l}, \ldots, \mathbf{A}^m\mathbf{l}]\mathbf{V}_m$, where

$$\mathbf{V}_m := \begin{bmatrix} 1 & \mathbf{w}^T\mathbf{T}\mathbf{z} & \mathbf{w}^T\mathbf{T}^2\mathbf{z} & \cdots & \mathbf{w}^T\mathbf{T}^m\mathbf{z} \\ 0 & 1 & \mathbf{w}^T\mathbf{T}\mathbf{z} & \cdots & \mathbf{w}^T\mathbf{T}^{m-1}\mathbf{z} \\ \vdots & \vdots & \vdots & \vdots & \vdots \\ 0 & 0 & 0 & \cdots & 1 \end{bmatrix}$$

is square and invertible (it is upper triangular with elements on the main diagonal all different from zero), it follows that

$$\mathbf{P}[\mathbf{z}, \mathbf{T}\mathbf{z}, \ldots, \mathbf{T}^m\mathbf{z}]\mathbf{V}_m^{-1} = [\mathbf{l}, \mathbf{A}\mathbf{l}, \ldots, \mathbf{A}^m\mathbf{l}] \quad \text{each } m \in \mathbb{N}.$$

This proves that vectors $\mathbf{l}, \mathbf{A}\mathbf{l}, \ldots, \mathbf{A}^m\mathbf{l}$ are linear combinations of vectors $\mathbf{p}_1, \mathbf{p}_2, \ldots, \mathbf{p}_t$, that is, $t \geq s$, and statement (i) is proved. Since for $t = s$ equality (6.12) implies $\mathbf{w}^T\mathbf{z} \neq 0$, vectors $[w_i, (1 + r_i)\mathbf{p}_i^T]^T$ $(i = 0, 1, \ldots, s)$ are linearly independent. Hence statement (ii) holds. Q.E.D.

Exercises 7.14–7.19 and 7.21 prove the following propositions.

Proposition 6.4. Let price vectors $\mathbf{p}_1, \mathbf{p}_2, \ldots, \mathbf{p}_{s+1}$ and corresponding wage rates $w_1, w, \ldots, w_{s+1}$ be generated by the same technique $(\mathbf{A}, \mathbf{l})$ at rates of profit $r_1, r_2, \ldots, r_{s+1}$ $(r_i \neq r_j)$, respectively. If rank $[\mathbf{p}_1, \mathbf{p}_2, \ldots, \mathbf{p}_{s+1}] = s$, then all vectors $\mathbf{A}^h \mathbf{l}$ $(h = 0, 1, \ldots)$ and price vectors and wage rates at each rate of profit r, $-1 < r < R$, are determined.

Proposition 6.5. Let $(\mathbf{A}, \mathbf{l})$ and $(\mathbf{F}, \mathbf{m})$ be two techniques with n commodities and n processes and let

$$s = \min\{\text{rank } [\mathbf{l}, \mathbf{Al}, \ldots, \mathbf{A}^n \mathbf{l}], \text{ rank } [\mathbf{m}, \mathbf{Fm}, \ldots, \mathbf{F}^n \mathbf{m}]\}. \qquad (6.16)$$

The following statements are equivalent:

  (i) prices and wage rates of techniques $(\mathbf{A}, \mathbf{l})$ and $(\mathbf{F}, \mathbf{m})$ coincide at $s + 1$ different rates of profit $r_1, r_2, \ldots, r_{s+1}$ $(-1 < r_i < \min\{R_A, R_F\})$;
  (ii) prices and wage rates of techniques $(\mathbf{A}, \mathbf{l})$ and $(\mathbf{F}, \mathbf{m})$ coincide at each rate of profit r, $-1 \leqslant r < R_A = R_F$, and

$$s = \text{rank } [\mathbf{I}, \mathbf{Al}, \ldots, \mathbf{A}^n \mathbf{l}] = \text{rank } [\mathbf{m}, \mathbf{Fm}, \ldots, \mathbf{F}^n \mathbf{m}];$$

  (iii) $\mathbf{F} = \mathbf{A} + \mathbf{Y}$ and $\mathbf{m} = \mathbf{l}$, where $\mathbf{Y}$ is any matrix such that $\mathbf{Y}[\mathbf{l}, \mathbf{Al}, \ldots, \mathbf{A}^n \mathbf{l}] = \mathbf{0}$.

Moreover, if $s = n$, then $\mathbf{F} = \mathbf{A}$.

Proposition 6.6. Let vectors $\mathbf{p}_1, \mathbf{p}_2, \ldots, \mathbf{p}_{s+1}$ be linearly dependent and let each s of them be linearly independent. Let $r_1, r_2, \ldots, r_{s+1}, w_1, w_2, \ldots, w_{s+1}$ be scalars such that $r_i > -1$, $w_i > 0$, $r_i \neq r_j$ for $i \neq j$. Let $\mathbf{P} = [\mathbf{p}_1, \mathbf{p}_2, \ldots, \mathbf{p}_{s+1}]$, $\mathbf{w}^T = (w_1, w_2, \ldots, w_{s+1})$, and $\mathbf{S}$ be a diagonal matrix with $1 + r_1$, $1 + r_2, \ldots, 1 + r_{s+1}$ on the main diagonal.

  (i) Then there is a nonnegative matrix $\mathbf{A}$ and a semipositive vector $\mathbf{l}$ such that technique $(\mathbf{A}, \mathbf{l})$ generates price vectors $\mathbf{p}_1, \mathbf{p}_2, \ldots, \mathbf{p}_{s+1}$ associated with rates of profit $r_1, r_2, \ldots, r_{s+1}$ and wage rates $w_1, w_2, \ldots, w_{s+1}$, respectively, if and only if

$$\left(\mathbf{y} \in \mathbb{R}^{s+1}, \begin{bmatrix} \mathbf{w}^T \\ \mathbf{PS} \end{bmatrix} \mathbf{y} \geqslant \mathbf{0} \right) \Rightarrow \mathbf{Py} \geqslant \mathbf{0}. \qquad (6.17)$$

If there is a nonnegative matrix $\mathbf{A}$ and a semipositive vector $\mathbf{l}$ as defined in statement (i), then

  (ii) vectors $[w_i, (1 + r_i)\mathbf{p}_i^T]^T$ are linearly independent $(i = 1, 2, \ldots, s + 1)$;
  (iii) the vector space spanned by $\mathbf{p}_1, \mathbf{p}_2, \ldots, \mathbf{p}_{s+1}$ coincides with the vector space spanned by $\mathbf{l}, \mathbf{Al}, \mathbf{A}^2 \mathbf{l}, \ldots, \mathbf{A}^t \mathbf{l}, \ldots$;

(iv) vector $\mathbf{l}$ is uniquely determined and the set of solutions for $\mathbf{A}$ (not all nonnegative) is given by $\mathbf{A} = \mathbf{F} + \mathbf{Y}$, where $\mathbf{Y}$ is any $n \times n$ matrix such that $\mathbf{YP} = \mathbf{0}$ and $\mathbf{F}$ is any particular solution;

(v) if $s > 1$, then matrix $\mathbf{A}$ is semipositive;

(vi) if $s = n$, then technique $(\mathbf{A}, \mathbf{l})$ is uniquely determined and is regular.

Proposition 6.7. Under the assumptions of Proposition 6.6, scalar w_0 and vector $\mathbf{p}_0$ are the wage rate and the price vector generated by a technique defined by vectors $\mathbf{p}_1, \mathbf{p}_2, \ldots, \mathbf{p}_{s+1}$ and scalars $r_1, r_2, \ldots, r_{s+1}, w_1, w_2, \ldots, w_{s+1}$ at r_0 if and only if

$$\mathbf{p}_0 = [\mathbf{P}, \mathbf{0}] \left[\begin{bmatrix} \mathbf{w}^T \\ \mathbf{PS} \end{bmatrix}, \mathbf{e}_{s+2}, \mathbf{e}_{s+3}, \ldots, \mathbf{e}_{n+1} \right]^{-1} \begin{bmatrix} w_0 \\ (1 + r_0)\mathbf{p}_0 \end{bmatrix},$$

where $\mathbf{e}_j$ is the jth unit vector in $\mathbb{R}^{n+1}$, $\mathbf{0}$ is the $n \times (n-s)$ zero matrix, and $\mathbf{P}, \mathbf{w}$, and $\mathbf{S}$ are defined as in Proposition 6.6.

The main purpose of this section is to provide a complete characterization of any set of price vectors and the corresponding set of wage rates generated by a given technique. This goal is finally realized in the next proposition.

Proposition 6.8. Let J be a set of indices which includes $\{1, 2, \ldots, n+1\}$ and does not need to be finite or even countable. Let a set of positive vectors $\mathbf{p}_j$ $(j \in J)$, a set of scalars $r_j > -1$ $(r_h \neq r_k; j, h, k \in J)$ and another set of scalars $w_j > 0$ $(j \in J)$ be given. Let s $(\leqslant n)$ be the dimension of the vector space spanned by all vectors $\mathbf{p}_j$ $(j \in J)$. Then

(i) there is a nonnegative matrix $\mathbf{A}$ and a semipositive vector $\mathbf{l}$ such that technique $(\mathbf{A}, \mathbf{l})$ generates price vectors $\mathbf{p}_j$ associated with rates of profit r_j and wage rates w_j $(j \in J)$ and $r_j > R_\mathbf{A}$, where $R_\mathbf{A}$ is the maximum rate of profit defined by matrix $\mathbf{A}$;

(ii) any $s + 1$ vectors $[w_i, (1 + r_i)\mathbf{p}_i^T]^T$ $(j \in J)$ are linearly independent;

(iii) the vector space spanned by vectors $\mathbf{p}_j$ $(j \in J)$ coincides with the vector space spanned by $\mathbf{l}, \mathbf{Al}, \mathbf{A}^2\mathbf{l}, \ldots, \mathbf{A}^t\mathbf{l}, \ldots$;

(iv) vector $\mathbf{l}$ is uniquely determined and the set of solutions for $\mathbf{A}$ (not all nonnegative) is given by $\mathbf{A} = \mathbf{F} + \mathbf{Y}$, where $\mathbf{Y}$ is any $n \times n$ matrix such that $\mathbf{Yp}_j = \mathbf{0}$ $(j \in J)$ and $\mathbf{F}$ is any particular solution;

(v) if $s > 1$, matrix $\mathbf{A}$ is semipositive;

(vi) if $s = n$, technique $(\mathbf{A}, \mathbf{l})$ is uniquely determined and is regular if and only if

(a) any s vectors $\mathbf{p}_j$ $(j \in J)$ are linearly independent;

(b) for each $j \in J$, $\mathbf{p}_j = [[\mathbf{P}, \mathbf{0}] [\mathbf{w}, (\mathbf{PS})^T]^T, \mathbf{e}_{s+2}, \mathbf{e}_{s+3}, \ldots, \mathbf{e}_{n+1}]^{-1}$ $[w_j, (1 + r_j)\mathbf{p}_j^T]^T$, where $\mathbf{P} = [\mathbf{p}_1, \mathbf{p}_2, \ldots, \mathbf{p}_{s+1}]$, $\mathbf{w}^T = (w_1, w_2, \ldots,$

w_{s+1}), **S** is a diagonal matrix with $1 + r_1, 1 + r_2, \ldots, 1 + r_{s+1}$ on the main diagonal, and **0** is the $n \times (n-t)$ zero matrix;

(c) $(\mathbf{y} \in \mathbb{R}^{s+1}, [\mathbf{w}, (\mathbf{PS})^T]^T \mathbf{y} \geqslant \mathbf{0}) \Rightarrow \mathbf{Py} \geqslant \mathbf{0}$.

Proof. Let statements (a) and (c) hold. Vectors $\mathbf{p}_j$ and scalars r_j and w_j ($j = 1, 2, \ldots, s + 1$) satisfy the "if" part of Proposition 6.6. If also statement (b) holds, each triplet $(\mathbf{p}_j, r_j, w_j)$ ($j \in J$) satisfies the assumptions of Proposition 6.7. Then there are a nonnegative matrix **A** and a semipositive vector **l** such that technique $(\mathbf{A}, \mathbf{l})$ generates price vectors $\mathbf{p}_j$ associated with rates of profit r_j and wage rates w_j ($j \in J$), and statements (ii)–(vi) hold. Since $\mathbf{p}_j > \mathbf{0}$, each $j \in J$, then $r_j < R_A$ (see exercise 6.12 in Chapter 4) and the "if" part of the proposition is proved. Conversely, if vectors $\mathbf{p}_j$ and scalars r_j and w_j ($j \in J$) are the price vectors, the rates of profit and the wage rates generated by technique $(\mathbf{A}, \mathbf{l})$, respectively, and $-1 < r_j < R_A$ for each $j \in J$, then statement (a) (see Proposition 6.3), statement (b) (see Proposition 6.7), and statement (c) (because of Farkas's Lemma) hold.   Q.E.D.

The characterization of any set of price vectors and the corresponding set of wage rates generated by a given technique provided in Proposition 6.8 is complete since a technique which generates such prices and wage rates can be obtained. This technique is exactly the one originally utilized to determine those prices and wage rates if it is regular. If not, all techniques which can be determined from the given price vectors and wage rates share the same price vector and the same wage rate at each rate of profit in the range which is relevant from an economic point of view: $0 \leqslant r < R$.

4. Further remarks on regular and irregular techniques

In Section 1 the distinction between regular and irregular techniques was introduced. The relevance of this distinction has been illustrated in Sections 1 and 3. This section is devoted to a further investigation of the concept of regularity of a technique. Suppose that technique $(\mathbf{A}, \mathbf{l})$ is irregular, then matrix

$$\mathbf{K}^* = (\mathbf{l}, \mathbf{Al}, \mathbf{A}^2\mathbf{l}, \mathbf{A}^3\mathbf{l}, \ldots, \mathbf{A}^{n-1}\mathbf{l})$$

is singular and therefore there is a vector **z** such that $\mathbf{z}^T \mathbf{K}^* = \mathbf{0}^T$. Then $\mathbf{z}^T \mathbf{A}^t \mathbf{l} = 0$ for each integer number t, and, as a consequence of equation (6.2),

$$\mathbf{z}^T \mathbf{p} = w\mathbf{z}^T [\mathbf{l} + (1 + r)\mathbf{Al} + \cdots + (1 + r)^t \mathbf{A}^t \mathbf{l} + \cdots] = 0.$$

A change in numeraire, replacing

$$\mathbf{d}^T \mathbf{p} = 1$$

by

$$(\mathbf{d} + \tau\mathbf{z})^T\mathbf{p} = 1,$$

where τ is a given scalar, thus has no effect on prices and the wage rate.

Exercises 7.28 and 7.29 prove the following propositions which connect regularity to properties of eigenvectors of matrix $\mathbf{A}$.

Proposition 6.9. Technique $(\mathbf{A}, \mathbf{l})$ is regular if and only if $\mathbf{l}$ is not orthogonal to any (real or complex) left eigenvector of $\mathbf{A}$.

Proposition 6.10. If the dimension of an eigenspace associated to an eigenvalue of matrix $\mathbf{A}$ is larger than 1, then technique $(\mathbf{A}, \mathbf{l})$ is irregular whatever vector $\mathbf{l}$ is.

5. Concluding remarks

Let us summarize the four alternative but equivalent descriptions of a technique which have been provided. The reader should be able to go from any one to any other.

   (a) $(\mathbf{A}, \mathbf{l})$;
   (b) $(\mathbf{l}_0, \mathbf{l}_1, \ldots, \mathbf{l}_n)$;
   (c) $(\mathbf{H}, \mathbf{v})$;
   (d) $(\mathbf{p}(r_1), \mathbf{p}(r_2), \ldots, \mathbf{p}(r_{n+1}))$,

where prices are expressed in terms of the wage rate. It is a remarkable, yet obvious, fact that in all these alternatives exactly $n^2 + n$ magnitudes are needed to describe a regular technique with n commodities. These, of course, are not the only possible descriptions of a given technique. One can, for instance, apply to equation (6.10) the same procedure applied in Section 1 to equation (6.1) in order to obtain equation (6.2). The result will be

$$\mathbf{p} = w[\mathbf{v} + r\mathbf{H}\mathbf{v} + r^2\mathbf{H}^2\mathbf{v} + \cdots + r^t\mathbf{H}^t\mathbf{v} + \cdots].$$

This formula could be called "reduction to dated quantities of *embodied* labour." A further description of a technique emerges by defining vectors

$$\mathbf{v}_j = \mathbf{H}^j\mathbf{v} \quad \text{each} \quad j \in \mathbb{N}_0.$$

In fact it is possible to prove that vectors

$$(\mathbf{v}_0, \mathbf{v}_1, \ldots, \mathbf{v}_n)$$

describe a given technique as well as vectors $(\mathbf{l}_0, \mathbf{l}_1, \ldots, \mathbf{l}_n)$ do.

6. Historical notes

6.1. The principle of the reduction to dated quantities of labor can be traced far back in the history of our subject. It was clearly spelled out by

Adam Smith in chapter VI of book I of *The Wealth of Nations*, "Of the Component Parts of the Price of Commodities." There Smith argues that in an advanced state of society the price of a commodity can be conceived of as being made up of four components, the first three of which are wages, rents, and profits paid in the production of the commodity. With reference to corn production he added: "A fourth part, it may perhaps be thought, is necessary for replacing the stock of the farmer, or for compensating the wear and tear of his labouring cattle, and other instruments of husbandry. But it must be considered that the price of any instrument of husbandry... is itself made up of the same three parts [i.e., wages, rents, and profits]." Smith concluded: "Though the price of corn...may pay the price as well as the maintenance of the horse, the whole price still resolves itself either immediately or ultimately into the same three parts of rent, labour, and profit" (*WN*, I.vi.11).

Simple examples of production processes in which a finite series of dated labor inputs yields a final output were used by Ricardo especially in the chapter "On Value" of the *Principles* to illustrate the impact of changes in the rate of profit on relative prices (*Works* I, chap. I); see also Edelberg (1933).

6.2. Starting from Ricardo's approach to the theory of value and distribution, the reduction to dated quantities of labor was given an algebraic expression by Dmitriev in an essay published in Russian in 1898. The essay together with two others, one on Cournot's theory of competition, the other on marginal utility theory, was reprinted in 1904. A French translation of the three essays was published in 1968 (Dmitriev, 1968), and an English translation in 1974 (Dmitriev, [1898] 1974). Dmitriev investigated first what is meant by the total amount of labor expended in the production of a commodity and how this amount can be ascertained. In particular, are we in need of "historical digressions" in order to determine the indirect labor, that is, the one contained in the capital goods used and thus transferred to the commodity in the course of its production? Dmitriev disposed of this misconception by showing that it is from a knowledge of the current conditions of production of the different commodities alone that one can determine the quantities of labor embodied: "without any digressions into the prehistoric times of the first inception of technical capital, we can always find the total sum of the labour directly and indirectly expended on the production of any product *under present day production conditions*, both of this product itself and of those capital goods involved in its production" (Dmitriev, [1898] 1974, p. 44). Dmitriev represented production processes in terms of finite series of dated quantities of labor, that is, adopted what has been called an "Austrian" perspective, and since in the single-products case contemplated by him there are as many series of dated quantities of labor as there are products, he concluded that there are as many equations as unknowns.

Next Dmitriev turned to an analysis of the rate of profit and "natural" prices. He praised Ricardo who had clearly specified the factors determining the general rate of profit, that is, (i) the real wage rate and (ii) the technical conditions of production in the wage goods industries: "Ricardo's immortal contribution was his brilliant solution of this seemingly insoluble problem" (ibid., p. 58). Prices are explained in terms of a reduction to (a finite stream of) dated quantities of labor. Dmitriev also confirmed Ricardo's finding that relative prices are proportional to relative quantities of labor embodied in two special cases only: (i) when the reduction series are linearly dependent pairwise (see also Section 3 of Chapter 4); and (ii) when the rate·of profit is zero. Ricardo's concept of the inverse relationship between the general rate of profit and the real wage rate, given the technical conditions of production, that is, the "wage–profit relationship," was given a precise expression in Dmitriev's flow input–point output framework (see also Subsection 1.4 of Chapter 4). Dmitriev deserves the credit for having demonstrated that starting from the data of Ricardo's approach, relative prices and the rate of profit can be determined simultaneously. The system is complete and all objections of the kind put forward by Walras ([1874] 1954, Lesson 38), among others, that Ricardo's cost of production explanation of prices is circular since it defines prices from prices, are untenable. (See also Subsection 2.1 of Chapter 13, which deals with the contribution by von Bortkiewicz who based his own analysis on Dmitriev's.)

6.3. In the "Austrian" approach production is seen as a time-consuming process in which a series of the services of the original factors of production, labor and land, result in a final output. In the simplest case possible a single labor input in one period yields one unit of output of a particular product several periods later; this case is known as the *point* input–*point* output case. Familiar examples are the planting of a tree or the ageing of wine in a cellar. With several labor inputs in consecutive periods yielding a final output at a single date we have the *flow* input–*point* output case. The conception of the production process under consideration figured prominently in Carl Menger's ranking of goods in accordance with their relationship to want satisfaction: consumer goods are called "goods of the first order," while goods which (directly or indirectly) serve as instruments of production in the production of consumer goods are called "goods of a higher order" (cf. Menger, [1871] 1981). It played an important role in Eugen von Böhm-Bawerk's theory of capital and interest (von Böhm-Bawerk, [1889] 1959) and in Knut Wicksell's elaboration on the latter (Wicksell, [1893] 1954 and [1901] 1934). It was used by von Hayek (1941) and has recently been revived by Hicks (1970, 1973), Bernholz (1971), and

Faber (1979). See also Dorfman (1959), Orosel (1987), and Ritschl (1989, ch. 1). In most contributions to the Austrian theory it is assumed that the series of dated labor inputs is finite. This implies that there are no basic commodities (cf. Hagemann and Kurz, 1976, p. 685). For a discussion of contemporary Austrian capital theory in relationship to the contributions by Menger, von Böhm-Bawerk, Wicksell, Lindahl, and von Hayek, see Kurz (1992a, 1994b). See also Section 2 of Chapter 14.

6.4. The method of the reduction to dated quantities of labor is carefully investigated by Sraffa (1960, ch. 6). Sraffa also shows how it can be used to demonstrate that it is generally impossible "to find in the 'period of production' an independent measure of the quantity of capital which could be used, without arguing in a circle, for the determination of prices and of the shares in distribution" (p. 38). Hence one of the major concepts of the traditional "Austrian" theory of capital and interest is shown to be defective; for an investigation of this aspect, see Sections 2 and 3 of Chapter 14.

6.5. The concept of vertical integration is closely related to the concept of surplus around which the classical approach to the theory of value and distribution revolved (see Sections 1 and 2 of Chapter 1). In fact, in earlier authors the key to an explanation of shares of income other than wages was generally sought in the difference between two magnitudes, one of which involves vertical integration: on the one hand total employment of (productive) laborers producing a given gross output, and on the other hand the quantity of labor needed directly and indirectly to reproduce the means of production used up in the course of production and the means of subsistence in the support of those laborers, given real wages and the length of the working day. The difference between these two quantities of labor was envisaged to be the source of the surplus product. It is characteristic of early classical political economy that the concept of surplus was first applied to an explanation of the rent of land. (Because of their predominant concern with the problem of rent, some authors, such as Cantillon, alternatively suggested a land-based approach and conceived of the rents of land as essentially to be explained in terms of the difference between the total amount of land actually cultivated and the amount of land needed directly and indirectly to enable the laborers to subsist and to replace the various kinds of advances used up during the annual cycle of production.)

For a discussion of the concept of vertical integration and its historical roots, see Pasinetti (1965, 1973, 1986, 1988a), Kurz (1976), Walsh and Gram (1980, ch. 1), Scazzieri (1990), and Landesmann and Scazzieri (1993).

6.6. Matrix **H** was introduced by Pasinetti (1973) and constitutes a generalization of the concept of the sub-system developed by Sraffa (1960, appendix A). Pasinetti (1973) also introduced matrix $\mathbf{G} = \mathbf{A}[\mathbf{I} - \mathbf{A}]^{-1}$. With single production $\mathbf{G} = \mathbf{H}$ (see exercise 7.8; see also exercise 7.9). Pasinetti (1973) and Steedman (1989) studied matrix **G** when joint production holds and output matrix **B** cannot be reduced to a diagonal matrix. In this case

$$\mathbf{H} = [\mathbf{B} - \mathbf{A}]^{-1}\mathbf{A} \neq \mathbf{A}[\mathbf{B} - \mathbf{A}]^{-1} = \mathbf{G}.$$

6.7. Burno, Burmeister, and Sheshinski (1966; see also Bharadwaj, 1970) proved that the maximum number of switches between two techniques involving the same n commodities cannot exceed n. Corollary 6.3 gives a more precise answer to this question. As a consequence of Proposition 6.5 we have that if technique $(\mathbf{A}, \mathbf{l})$ and $(\mathbf{F}, \mathbf{m})$ are distinct, they cannot have a number of switches larger than s as defined by equation (6.16).

6.8. The concept of regular technique has been introduced by Schefold (1971, 1976a; see also 1976b) and used also by Raneda and Reus (1985). Section 3 follows closely Bidard and Salvadori (1993). They called the property developed in Section 3 "duality between a technique and the price vectors generated by it." In order to clarify what is meant by "duality," they refer to the fact that cost and production functions are dual to each other in the sense that either of them can describe the technology of the firm equally well: a number of properties of cost functions are established and duality proves that any other property is a consequence of them.

The derivation of a cost function from a production function, assuming cost-minimizing behavior on the part of producers, has been familiar since the beginning of the neoclassical theory of prices and distribution; see Shephard (1970) for an advanced treatment of the subject. More recently it has been shown that from any well-defined cost function exhibiting the usual properties it is possible to derive a unique notional production function, that is, a production function which would generate the given cost function as the result of the usual cost minimization procedure. Moreover, it has been shown that this notional production function is exactly the same as the actual production function whenever the latter is convex. If this convexity condition is not met, only those sections of the notional and the actual production function which do coincide are relevant to the derivation of the cost function. It follows that all the relevant information about the technical conditions of production are embodied equally well in either a production or a cost function, each being derivable from the other. A useful survey of duality approaches to microeconomics, including a discussion of the historical development of the subject, is provided by Diewert (1982). Important contributions to the duality theory are contained in Fuss and McFadden (1978); see also the discussion in Varian (1984).

6.9. The fact that if technique $(\mathbf{A}, \mathbf{l})$ is irregular, then there is a non-zero vector $\mathbf{z}$ such that a change of numeraire from any (composite) commodity $\mathbf{d}$ $(\mathbf{d}^T \mathbf{p} = 1)$ to commodity $\mathbf{d} + \tau \mathbf{z}$ $[(\mathbf{d} + \tau \mathbf{z})^T \mathbf{p} = 1]$, where τ is a given scalar, has no effect on prices or the wage rate is connected to a problem raised by Miyao (1977), who proved that the Standard commodity need not be the only (composite) commodity which has the property that if it is chosen as numeraire, then equation (4.43) of Chapter 4 holds. On this point see also Abraham-Frois and Berrebi (1978), Baldone (1980), and the postscriptum to Chapter 5 in Pasinetti (1981a).

7. Exercises

7.1. Determine a material input matrix $\mathbf{A}$ when $\mathbf{l}_0 = \mathbf{l}, \mathbf{l}_1 = \mathbf{A}\mathbf{l}$ and $\mathbf{l}_2 = \mathbf{A}^2\mathbf{l}$ are respectively given by:

(i) $\begin{bmatrix} 1 \\ 2 \end{bmatrix}$, $\begin{bmatrix} 1 \\ \frac{1}{2} \end{bmatrix}$, $\begin{bmatrix} \frac{1}{4} \\ \frac{1}{2} \end{bmatrix}$;   (ii) $\begin{bmatrix} 1 \\ 1 \end{bmatrix}$, $\begin{bmatrix} \frac{1}{2} \\ \frac{3}{4} \end{bmatrix}$, $\begin{bmatrix} \frac{3}{8} \\ \frac{7}{16} \end{bmatrix}$;

(iii) $\begin{bmatrix} 1 \\ 1 \end{bmatrix}$, $\begin{bmatrix} \frac{5}{8} \\ \frac{5}{6} \end{bmatrix}$, $\begin{bmatrix} \frac{95}{117} \\ \frac{85}{144} \end{bmatrix}$;   (iv) $\begin{bmatrix} 1 \\ 1 \end{bmatrix}$, $\begin{bmatrix} \frac{1}{2} \\ \frac{1}{2} \end{bmatrix}$, $\begin{bmatrix} \frac{1}{4} \\ \frac{1}{4} \end{bmatrix}$.

7.2. Determine the vector of direct and indirect quantities of labor "embodied" in the different commodities $\mathbf{v}$ relative to techniques (i)–(iv) of the previous exercise.

7.3. Show that if $\mathbf{A}\mathbf{l} = \lambda\mathbf{l}$, that is, if the labor theory of value holds, then

$$\mathbf{A}^h\mathbf{l} = \lambda^h\mathbf{l} \quad (h = 0, 1, 2, \ldots).$$

Then perform the reduction to dated quantities of labor taking account of the fact that $\lambda = 1/(1 + R)$.

7.4. Call

$$w[\mathbf{d}^T\mathbf{l} + (1 + r)\mathbf{d}^T\mathbf{A}\mathbf{l} + (1 + r)^2\mathbf{d}^T\mathbf{A}^2\mathbf{l} + \cdots + (1 + r)^t\mathbf{d}^T\mathbf{A}^t\mathbf{l} + \cdots]$$

the reduction to dated quantities of labor of a composite commodity consisting of d_1 units of commodity $1, d_2$ units of commodity $2, \ldots$, and d_n units of commodity n. Determine the reduction to dated quantities of labor of the Standard commodity.

7.5. Comment on the results of the previous two exercises.

7.6. Derive equation (6.10) from equation (6.1). [*Hint*: $(\mathbf{I}-\mathbf{A})\mathbf{p}=w\mathbf{l}+r\mathbf{A}\mathbf{p}$.]

7.7. (Steedman, 1977b) Prove that if matrix $\mathbf{A}$ is (in)decomposable, then matrix $\mathbf{H}$ is (in)decomposable. Can the distinction between basics and non-basics be conceived in terms of matrix $\mathbf{H}$? [*Hint*: If

$$\mathbf{A}=\begin{bmatrix}\mathbf{A}_{11} & \mathbf{0}\\ \mathbf{A}_{21} & \mathbf{A}_{22}\end{bmatrix},$$

then $\mathbf{H}$ is ....]

7.8. Prove that $[\mathbf{I}-\mathbf{A}]^{-1}\mathbf{A}=\mathbf{A}[\mathbf{I}-\mathbf{A}]^{-1}$. [*Hint*: It is enough to prove (why?) that $\mathbf{A}=[\mathbf{I}-\mathbf{A}]\mathbf{A}[\mathbf{I}-\mathbf{A}]^{-1}$.]

7.9. (Steedman, 1989) Let $\mathbf{G}\equiv\mathbf{A}[\mathbf{I}-\mathbf{A}]^{-1}$ and let $\mathbf{z}$ be the vector of values added per unit activity level, that is, $\mathbf{z}=(\mathbf{I}-\mathbf{A})\mathbf{p}=w\mathbf{l}+r\mathbf{A}\mathbf{p}$. Show that

$$\mathbf{z}=w\mathbf{l}+r\mathbf{G}\mathbf{z}.$$

7.10. Determine matrix $\mathbf{H}$ for the techniques of exercise 7.1.

7.11. Determine vector $\mathbf{v}$ and matrix $\mathbf{H}$ for the techniques of exercise 8.6 of Chapter 3.

7.12. (Raneda and Reus, 1985; Bidard and Salvadori, 1993) Let $s=\text{rank}(\mathbf{l},\mathbf{A}\mathbf{l},\ldots,\mathbf{A}^{n-1}\mathbf{l})$, then show that the vector space spanned by any s distinct $\mathbf{p}(r_i)$ ($i=1,2,\ldots,s$) is the vector space spanned by $\mathbf{l},\mathbf{A}\mathbf{l},\ldots,\mathbf{A}^{s-1}\mathbf{l}$. [*Hint*: This is a consequence of Proposition 6.3.]

7.13. (Bidard and Salvadori, 1993) Let $s=\text{rank}(\mathbf{l},\mathbf{A}\mathbf{l},\ldots,\mathbf{A}^{n-1}\mathbf{l})$, then show that the curve of normalized prices in $\mathbb{R}^n$

$$\mathbf{p}=\frac{1}{\mathbf{d}^T[\mathbf{I}-(1+r)\mathbf{A}]^{-1}\mathbf{l}}[\mathbf{I}-(1+r)\mathbf{A}]^{-1}\mathbf{l},$$

where $\mathbf{d}$ is any given semipositive vector for $-1<r<R$, is entirely contained in a subspace of dimension s and cuts any subspace of dimension t, $t<s$, in no more than t points. [*Hint*: This is a consequence of Proposition 6.3.]

7.14. (Bidard and Salvadori, 1993) Prove Proposition 6.4. [*Hint*: Explore the proof of Proposition 6.3 and show that vectors $\mathbf{A}^h\mathbf{l}$ ($h=0,1,\ldots$) are determined; then use the series (6.2).]

7.15. (Schefold, 1971, 1976a; Bidard and Salvadori, 1993) Prove Proposition 6.5. [*Hint*: It is a consequence of Propositions 6.4 and 6.2.]

7.16. (Bidard and Salvadori, 1993) Prove statements (i)–(iii) of Proposition

6.6. [*Hint*: Use Theorem A.2.2 of the Mathematical Appendix to prove that there exists a nonnegative matrix [l, A] such that:

$$\mathbf{P} = [\mathbf{l}, \mathbf{A}]\begin{bmatrix} \mathbf{w}^T \\ \mathbf{PS} \end{bmatrix}. \tag{6.18}$$

Since there exists a uniquely determined (up to a factor) vector $\mathbf{z}$ such that (6.12) holds, obtain that $\mathbf{l}\mathbf{w}^T\mathbf{z} \neq \mathbf{0}$ as in the proof of Proposition 6.3; hence $\mathbf{l} \geqslant \mathbf{0}$ and $\mathbf{w}^T\mathbf{z} \neq 0$. Since no entry of vector $\mathbf{z}$ is nought (show), obtain that

$$\mathbf{P}[\mathbf{z}, \mathbf{T}\mathbf{z}, \dots, \mathbf{T}^s\mathbf{z}] = \left[\mathbf{l}, (\mathbf{w}^T\mathbf{T}\mathbf{z})\mathbf{l} + A\mathbf{l}, \dots, \sum_{j=0}^{s}(\mathbf{w}^T\mathbf{T}^{s-j}\mathbf{z})\mathbf{A}^j\mathbf{l}\right]$$

by following the procedure supplied in the proof of Proposition 6.3; show that matrix $[\mathbf{z}, \mathbf{T}\mathbf{z}, \dots, \mathbf{T}^s\mathbf{z}]$ can be stated as the product of matrices

$$\begin{bmatrix} z_1 & 0 & 0 & \cdots & 0 \\ 0 & z_2 & 0 & \cdots & 0 \\ \vdots & \vdots & \vdots & \vdots & \vdots \\ 0 & 0 & 0 & \cdots & z_{s+1} \end{bmatrix} \begin{bmatrix} 1 & \lambda_1 & \lambda_1^2 & \cdots & \lambda_1^s \\ 1 & \lambda_2 & \lambda_2^2 & \cdots & \lambda_2^s \\ \vdots & \vdots & \vdots & \vdots & \vdots \\ 1 & \lambda_{s+1} & \lambda_{s+1}^2 & \cdots & \lambda_{s+1}^s \end{bmatrix},$$

where z_i is the ith element of vector $\mathbf{z}$ and $\lambda_i = 1/(1 + r_i)$ $(i = 1, 2, \dots, s + 1)$. Show that the determinants of both matrices are different from zero (cf. exercise 7.20); then

$$\mathbf{P} = \left[\mathbf{l}, (\mathbf{w}^T\mathbf{T}\mathbf{z})\mathbf{l} + A\mathbf{l}, \dots, \sum_{j=0}^{s}(\mathbf{w}^T\mathbf{T}^{s-j}\mathbf{z})\mathbf{A}^j\mathbf{l}\right][\mathbf{z}, \mathbf{T}\mathbf{z}, \dots, \mathbf{T}^s\mathbf{z}]^{-1};$$

that is, each vector $\mathbf{p}_1, \mathbf{p}_2, \dots, \mathbf{p}_{s+1}$ is a linear combination of vectors $\mathbf{l}$, $A\mathbf{l}, \dots, A^s\mathbf{l}$.]

7.17. (Bidard and Salvadori, 1993) Prove statement (iv) of Proposition 6.6. [*Hint*: Show that if $[\mathbf{l}, \mathbf{F}]$ is a solution to equation (6.18), then $[\mathbf{l} + \mathbf{y}, \mathbf{F} + \mathbf{Y}]$ is also one, where $[\mathbf{y}, \mathbf{Y}]$ is a solution to the equation

$$[\mathbf{l}, \mathbf{A}]\begin{bmatrix} \mathbf{w}^T \\ \mathbf{PS} \end{bmatrix} = \mathbf{0};$$

show that if the jth element of vector $\mathbf{y}$ is different from zero, then statement (ii) is contradicted.]

7.18. (Bidard and Salvadori, 1993) Prove statements (v) of Proposition 6.6. [*Hint*: Show that if $A = 0$, then $\mathbf{P} = \mathbf{l}\mathbf{w}^T$ and the rank of matrix $[\mathbf{w}, S^T\mathbf{w}\mathbf{l}^T]^T$ is not larger than 2.]

7.19. (Bidard and Salvadori, 1993) Prove statements (vi) of Proposition 6.6. [*Hint*: It is a consequence of statements (iii) and (iv).]

7.20. (Theory of Polynomials) The determinant

$$V(x_1, x_2, \ldots, x_n) := \det \begin{bmatrix} 1 & x_1 & x_1^2 & \cdots & x_1^{n-1} \\ 1 & x_2 & x_2^2 & \cdots & x_2^{n-1} \\ \vdots & \vdots & \vdots & \vdots & \vdots \\ 1 & x_n & x_n^2 & \cdots & x_n^{n-1} \end{bmatrix}$$

is called *Vandermonde determinant*. Show that

$$V(x_1, x_2, \ldots, x_n) = \prod_{1 \leqslant h < k \leqslant n} (x_k - x_h).$$

[*Hint*: Show that if we expand determinant $V(x_1, x_2, \ldots, x_n)$ by cofactors by the last row, we get a polynomial of degree $n-1$ in the variable x_n, the coefficient of x_n^{n-1} being equal to $V(x_1, x_2, \ldots, x_{n-1})$. If $x_n = x_i$ ($i = 1, 2, \ldots, n-1$), then $V(x_1, x_2, \ldots, x_n) = 0$. Hence (show)

$$V(x_1, x_2, \ldots, x_n) = V(x_1, x_2, \ldots, x_{n-1}) \prod_{i=1}^{n-1} (x_n - x_i).$$

Complete the proof by induction.]

7.21. (Bidard and Salvadori, 1993) Prove Proposition 6.7. [*Hint*: If $s < n$, show that

$$[\mathbf{P}, \mathbf{0}] \left[\begin{bmatrix} \mathbf{w}^T \\ \mathbf{PS} \end{bmatrix}, \mathbf{e}_{s+2}, \mathbf{e}_{s+3}, \ldots, \mathbf{e}_{n+1} \right]^{-1}$$

is the solution (not necessarily nonnegative) to equation (6.18) in which the last $n - s$ columns are zero vectors.]

7.22. (Miyao, 1977) Show that the following technique is irregular:

$$\mathbf{A} = \begin{bmatrix} 0.1 & 0.2 & 0.2 \\ 0.2 & 0.1 & 0.2 \\ 0.2 & 0.2 & 0.1 \end{bmatrix}, \quad \mathbf{l} = \begin{bmatrix} 1 \\ 2 \\ 3 \end{bmatrix}.$$

Determine a numeraire different from the Standard commodity such that the w–r relationship is a straight line.

7.23. (Baldone, 1980) Show that the following technique is irregular:

$$\mathbf{A} = \begin{bmatrix} 0 & 0.4 & 0 \\ 0.5 & 0 & 0 \\ 0.1 & 0.2 & 0.2 \end{bmatrix}, \quad \mathbf{l} = \begin{bmatrix} 1 \\ 1 \\ 1.25 \end{bmatrix}.$$

Table 6.1

r	p_1	p_2
0	$\frac{8}{3}$	$\frac{10}{3}$
$\frac{1}{5}$	$\frac{55}{16}$	$\frac{65}{16}$
$\frac{1}{2}$	$\frac{40}{7}$	$\frac{44}{7}$

Determine a numeraire consisting of a basic commodity and a non-basic commodity such that the w–r relationship is a straight line. [*Hint*: The first two commodities are basic, the third is non-basic; the numeraire to be found consists of $(5\sqrt{20} - 22)$ units of commodity 2 and $(20 - 4\sqrt{20})$ units of commodity 3.]

7.24. Determine the technique whose prices in terms of the wage rate corresponding to rates of profit $0, \frac{1}{5}$, and $\frac{1}{2}$ are given by Table 6.1.

7.25. Determine the technique whose prices in terms of the wage rate are given by the following functions of the rate of profit r:

$$p_1 = \frac{11 + r}{8 - 3r - r^2}$$

$$p_2 = \frac{3 + r}{8 - 3r - r^2}.$$

7.26. Let $\mathbf{B} = [\mathbf{e}_2, \mathbf{e}_3, \ldots, \mathbf{e}_s, \mathbf{b}]$, then prove that

(i) $\det(\lambda\mathbf{I} - \mathbf{B}) \equiv \lambda^s - b_1 - b_2\lambda - \cdots - b_s\lambda^{s-1}$;

(ii) the dimension of left and right eigenspaces associated with the eigenvalues of matrix $\mathbf{B}$ equals 1;

(iii) if $\mathbf{v}$ is a left eigenvector of matrix $\mathbf{B}$, then $v_1 \neq 0$; if $\mathbf{y}$ is a right eigenvector of matrix $\mathbf{B}$, then $y_s \neq 0$.

[*Hint*: If $\mathbf{v}$ is a left eigenvector of matrix $\mathbf{B}$ corresponding to eigenvalue λ, then $\lambda v_i = v_{i+1}$ $(i = 1, 2, \ldots, s-1)$ and $\lambda v_s = \mathbf{v}^T\mathbf{b}$; if $\mathbf{y}$ is a right eigenvector of matrix $\mathbf{B}$ corresponding to eigenvalue λ, then $\lambda y_1 = b_1 y_s$ and $\lambda y_i = y_{i-1} + b_i y_s$ $(i = 2, \ldots, s)$.]

7.27. Let matrix $\mathbf{B}$ be defined as in Section 1 and let E be the vector space spanned by vectors $\mathbf{l}, \mathbf{Al}, \ldots, \mathbf{A}^{s-1}\mathbf{l}$. Then

(i) there is an $(n-s) \times (n-s)$ matrix $\mathbf{C}$ such that

$$\det(\lambda\mathbf{I} - \mathbf{A}) = \det(\lambda\mathbf{I} - \mathbf{B})\det(\lambda\mathbf{I} - \mathbf{C});$$

(ii) any zero of polynomial det $(\lambda \mathbf{I} - \mathbf{C})$ which is not a zero of polynomial det $(\lambda \mathbf{I} - \mathbf{B})$ is an eigenvalue of matrix $\mathbf{A}$ such that all associated left eigenvectors are orthogonal to the labor vector $\mathbf{l}$ and no associated right eigenvector belongs to E;

(iii) any zero of polynomial det $(\lambda \mathbf{I} - \mathbf{B})$ which is not a zero of polynomial det $(\lambda \mathbf{I} - \mathbf{C})$ is an eigenvalue of matrix $\mathbf{A}$ whose dimension of left and right eigenspaces is one, the left eigenvectors are not orthogonal to labor vector $\mathbf{l}$, and the right eigenvectors belong to E;

(iv) any zero of both polynomials det $(\lambda \mathbf{I} - \mathbf{B})$ and det $(\lambda \mathbf{I} - \mathbf{C})$ is an eigenvalue of matrix $\mathbf{A}$ such that there are associated left eigenvectors which are orthogonal to the labor vector $\mathbf{l}$ and associated right eigenvectors which belong to E;

[*Hint*: If $\mathbf{K} = [\mathbf{K}_1^T, \mathbf{K}_2^T]^T$ where submatrix $\mathbf{K}_1$ is square and, with no loss of generality, invertible, then

$$\begin{bmatrix} \mathbf{K}_1 & \mathbf{0} \\ \mathbf{K}_2 & \mathbf{I} \end{bmatrix}^{-1} \mathbf{A} \begin{bmatrix} \mathbf{K}_1 & \mathbf{0} \\ \mathbf{K}_2 & \mathbf{I} \end{bmatrix} = \begin{bmatrix} \mathbf{B} & \mathbf{D} \\ \mathbf{0} & \mathbf{C} \end{bmatrix} \equiv \mathbf{F},$$

where $\mathbf{C} = -\mathbf{K}_2 \mathbf{K}_1^{-1} \mathbf{A}_{12} + \mathbf{A}_{22}, \mathbf{D} = \mathbf{K}_1^{-1} \mathbf{A}_{12}$; hence matrices $\mathbf{A}$ and $\mathbf{F}$ are similar; then use the result introduced in the previous exercise.]

7.28. Prove Proposition 6.9. [*Hint*: Use the results introduced in the previous exercise.]

7.29. Prove Proposition 6.10. [*Hint*: Use the results introduced in exercise 7.26.]

7.30. In Section 5 an additional description of a technique was introduced: $(\mathbf{v}_0, \mathbf{v}_1, \ldots, \mathbf{v}_n)$. Starting from this description of a technique determine the description of the technique in terms of vertically integrated technical coefficients $(\mathbf{H}, \mathbf{v})$.

7.31. (Calculus) In Section 5 a description of a technique was introduced: $(\mathbf{v}_0, \mathbf{v}_1, \ldots, \mathbf{v}_n)$. Show that

$$\mathbf{v}_t = \sum_{i=t}^{\infty} \binom{i}{t} \mathbf{l}_i,$$

$$\mathbf{l}_t = \sum_{i=t}^{\infty} \binom{i}{t} (-1)^{1-t} \mathbf{v}_i,$$

where $\mathbf{v}_t$ and $\mathbf{l}_t$ are as defined in Sections 5 and 1, respectively. [*Hint*: Consider the Taylor series with starting point 0 and starting point -1 of the function $\mathbf{p}(r) = [\mathbf{I} - (1+r)\mathbf{A}]^{-1} \mathbf{l}$, respectively.]

7

Fixed capital

Up to now it has been assumed that each process produces one and only one commodity, that is, single production has been assumed. Let us now introduce some models which admit joint production, but only in a special way. These models are highly interesting in themselves since they deal with the presence of means of production which last more than one period, that is, fixed capital. But they will also be a useful way to introduce joint production. While at this stage general fixed capital models cannot yet be introduced (see Chapter 9), it deserves mention that the class of fixed capital models dealt with in this chapter is large: it covers all cases in which there is no joint utilization of old machines. In all models of fixed capital presented in this book it is assumed, however, that old machines cannot be transferred between sectors. (The interested reader will find at the end of the Section 2 of Chapter 9 a list of results which hold when machines are not utilized jointly and do not need to hold when they are.)

The structure of the chapter is as follows. Section 1 presents the assumptions underlying the following analysis. In Section 2 the properties of a given technique utilizing durable capital goods are studied. Section 3 introduces the useful concept of the "core processes." Section 4 turns to a general discussion of the choice of technique problem and the determination of the cost-minimizing technique(s). Section 5 contains some remarks on the positivity of prices of finished goods and the assumption of "free disposal" of old items of durable capital goods. The problem of depreciation and of the annual charge to be paid on account of a fixed capital good exhibiting constant, decreasing or increasing efficiency in the course of its productive life will be dealt with in Section 6. The problem of the choice of technique is then illustrated in Section 7 in terms of the choice of the pattern of utilization of machinery. Section 8 comments on

186

the concept of the "plant" within the framework of the simplifying analysis of the present chapter. Sections 9 and 10 contain historical notes and exercises, respectively.

1. Basic definitions

In order to render the discussion less cryptic, let us first divide the commodities into two groups: commodities in the first group will be called *finished goods* and commodities in the second group will be called *old machines*. Let m be the number of finished goods and $(n - m)$ the number of old machines. The following axioms hold:

(i) Old machines are never requested for consumption, that is, they are requested only in order to be used as means of production.

(ii) Each process is assumed to produce one and only one finished good and, perhaps, an amount of one old machine.

(iii) Each process is also assumed to utilize as inputs only finished goods and, perhaps, an amount of one old machine.

(iv) No old machine can be utilized in the production of a finished good different from that alongside which it is produced. That is, old machines cannot be transferred among sectors; a *sector* being constituted by all the processes engaged in the production of a given finished good.

(v) All the processes in a sector can be divided in first degree processes, second degree processes, third degree processes, and so on. A *first degree process* is a process which exclusively uses finished goods as inputs. A *second degree process* is a process which uses finished goods and an amount of one old machine produced by a first degree process as inputs. A *third degree process* is a process which uses finished goods and an amount of one old machine produced by a second degree process as inputs, and so on. A machine produced by a first degree process and utilized by a second degree process is said to be "one year old." A machine produced by a second degree process and utilized by a third degree process is said to be "two years old," and so on. Each process in sector $i, i = 1, 2, \ldots, m$, produces an amount of the finished good i and may or may not produce an amount of an old machine.

(vi) Any machine can at any time be worn out at a zero scrap value. This is obtained by assuming that for each process producing an old machine there is another process with the same inputs and the same outputs except for the old machine which is not produced. In other words, old machines can be disposed of freely.

If these assumptions hold, we say that the technology is a *fixed capital technology*. All the elements needed to understand this interpretation of the previous axioms have been provided except one. In axioms (i)–(vi) each old machine is a commodity in itself, whereas in common language we speak of a machine at different ages as the *same* machine at different points in time. In order to avoid confusion, the expression *type of machine* will be used in the following sense. Two old machines one of which is among the inputs of a process and the other is among the outputs of the same process are (old) machines of the same *type*. More generally speaking, if there is a sequence of processes each of which (except the first one) uses as an input an old machine which has been produced as an output by the preceding process, then all machines involved constitute vintages of the same *type of machine*.

It will be assumed that there are $v_i, v_i \geqslant 1$, processes to produce finished good i $(i = 1, 2, \ldots, m)$. In obvious notation, each process is referred to as

$$(\mathbf{a}^{(h)}, \mathbf{b}^{(h)}, l^{(h)}), \quad h = 1, 2, \ldots, \sum_{j=1}^{m} v_j$$

where $\mathbf{a}^{(h)}$ is the commodity input vector, $\mathbf{b}^{(h)}$ is the output vector, and $l^{(h)}$ is the direct labor input. Vectors $\mathbf{a}^{(h)}$ and $\mathbf{b}^{(h)}$ can be partitioned in the following way:

$$\mathbf{a}^{(h)} = \begin{bmatrix} \mathbf{a}_0^{(h)} \\ \mathbf{a}_1^{(h)} \\ \vdots \\ \mathbf{a}_m^{(h)} \end{bmatrix}, \quad \mathbf{b}^{(h)} = \begin{bmatrix} \mathbf{b}_0^{(h)} \\ \mathbf{b}_1^{(h)} \\ \vdots \\ \mathbf{b}_m^{(h)} \end{bmatrix},$$

where subvectors $\mathbf{a}_0^{(h)}$ and $\mathbf{b}_0^{(h)}$ refer to finished goods and, obviously, have size m; subvectors $\mathbf{a}_i^{(h)}$ and $\mathbf{b}_i^{(h)}$ $(i = 1, 2, \ldots, m)$ refer to old machines utilized in the production of finished good i and, obviously, have size $t_{i1} + t_{i2} + \cdots + t_{is_i}$, where s_i is the number of types of old machines existing in sector i and t_{ij} is the maximum life of the jth type of old machines existing in sector i. (The first element of subvectors $\mathbf{a}_i^{(h)}$ and $\mathbf{b}_i^{(h)}$ refers to the one year old machine of type 1, the second element refers to the two year old machine of type 1, and so on until the t_{i1}th element; the $(t_{i1} + 1)$th element refers to the one year old machine of type 2, and so on.)

Let us number processes in such a way that the first v_1 processes produce finished good 1, the following v_2 processes produce finished good 2, . . . , the last v_m processes produce finished good m. Therefore if $z_{i-1} < h \leqslant z_i$, where $z_0 = 0$ and

$$z_i = \sum_{j=1}^{i} v_j, \quad (i = 1, 2, \ldots, m),$$

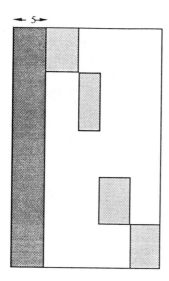

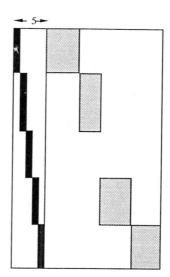

Figure 7.1a   Figure 7.1b

then $\mathbf{b}_0^{(h)} = \mathbf{e}_i$ (because of axiom (ii)); $\mathbf{a}_j^{(h)} = \mathbf{b}_j^{(h)} = \mathbf{0}$, $j \neq i$ (because of axiom (iv)); $\mathbf{e}_s^T \mathbf{b}_i^{(h)} > \mathbf{0}$ if either $\mathbf{e}_{s-1}^T \mathbf{a}_i^{(h)} > 0$ or $\mathbf{a}_i^{(h)} = \mathbf{0}$ and the sth element of the subvectors $\mathbf{a}_i^{(h)}$ and $\mathbf{b}_i^{(h)}$ refers to a one year old machine (because of axiom (v)); only one element of subvectors $\mathbf{a}_i^{(h)}$ and $\mathbf{b}_i^{(h)}$ may be positive, all the others being nought (because of axioms (ii) and (iii)).

Figures 7.1a and 7.1b represent the material input matrix and the output matrix whereby it is assumed that the existing processes are arranged in the following way: the first five commodities are finished goods, all other commodities are old machines, and all finished goods except commodity 3 are produced by using old machines. Grey areas represent nonnegative elements, white areas represent zero elements, and black areas represent positive elements. Moreover, the row vectors in the light grey areas are either zero vectors or vectors with one positive element (all others being nought): if the positive element in a row vector in the material input matrix is in the jth column, then the corresponding vector in the output matrix either has the positive element in the $(j + 1)$th column or has no positive element; if a row vector in the material input matrix is zero, then the corresponding vector in the output matrix is either a zero vector, or a vector with one positive element in a column referring to a one year old machine.

In this chapter we will not try to determine the prices of old machines which are not produced. This allows us to follow a generalization of the analysis presented in Subsection 3.3 of Chapter 5. Moreover, we will assume that all finished goods are consumed.[1] Of course, the prices of non-produced commodities vary within a set which can be determined in a way similar to that stated for single production in Subsection 3.4 of Chapter 5.

Let c be a vector whose first m components are positive, all the others being nought. Let $(\mathbf{a}_i, \mathbf{b}_i, l_i)$, $i = 1, 2, \ldots, s$, be s processes, $m \leqslant s \leqslant n$. Then the triplet $(\mathbf{A}, \mathbf{B}, \mathbf{l})$, where

$$\mathbf{A} = \begin{bmatrix} \mathbf{a}_1^T \\ \mathbf{a}_2^T \\ \vdots \\ \mathbf{a}_s^T \end{bmatrix}, \quad \mathbf{B} = \begin{bmatrix} \mathbf{b}_1^T \\ \mathbf{b}_2^T \\ \vdots \\ \mathbf{b}_s^T \end{bmatrix}, \quad \mathbf{l} = \begin{bmatrix} l_1 \\ l_1 \\ \vdots \\ l_s \end{bmatrix},$$

will be called a *technique* (or a *system of production*) if there is a nonnegative scalar r and a positive vector $\mathbf{x}$ (which is unique with respect to r) such that

$$\mathbf{x}^T[\mathbf{B} - (1 + r)\mathbf{A}] = \mathbf{c}^T.$$

The existence condition requires that the number of processes in technique $(\mathbf{A}, \mathbf{B}, \mathbf{l})$ is larger than or equal to the number of commodities involved: in technique $(\mathbf{A}, \mathbf{B}, \mathbf{l})$ for each process producing a machine there must be another process using that machine as an input; that is, for each type of machine j used in the production of finished good i there must be at least $1 + t_j$ processes producing finished good i in technique $(\mathbf{A}, \mathbf{B}, \mathbf{l})$, where t_j is the maximal age of the type of machine j in technique $(\mathbf{A}, \mathbf{B}, \mathbf{l})(t_j \geqslant 0)$. The uniqueness condition requires that the rows of matrix $[\mathbf{B} - (1 + r)\mathbf{A}]$ are linearly independent so that the number of processes is not larger than the number of commodities involved; as a consequence no more than one type of old machine can be used in each sector in that technique. It will be proved later (Theorem 7.2) that the magnitudes of the positive entries of vector $\mathbf{c}$ do not play any role in the definition of a technique.

The price vector $\mathbf{p}$ and the wage rate w of technique $(\mathbf{A}, \mathbf{B}, \mathbf{l})$ are defined by the equations

$$\mathbf{Bp} = (1 + r)\mathbf{Ap} + w\mathbf{l}$$

---

[1] Since finished goods include new machines, the assumption that all finished goods are consumed and no old machine is consumed in very restrictive. For an analysis that drops this assumption, see Kurz and Salvadori (1994b).

$$\mathbf{c}^T \mathbf{p} = 1,$$

where the numeraire has been set in such a way as to contain only commodities which are certainly produced. Note that prices of non-produced commodities are not determined. (Since all finished goods are consumed, the set of non-produced commodities contains only old machines.)

A *cost-minimizing technique* at rate of profit r is then defined as a technique at whose prices no set of known processes can be operated in order to obtain extra profits. Therefore, the technique $(\mathbf{A}_k, \mathbf{B}_k, \mathbf{l}_k)$ is *cost-minimizing at rate of profit r* if and only if

$$[\mathbf{B}_j - (1 + r)\mathbf{A}_j]\mathbf{p}_{kj} \leqslant w_k \mathbf{l}_j, \quad \text{each } (\mathbf{A}_j, \mathbf{B}_j, \mathbf{l}_j) \in J$$

where J is the set of all existing techniques and $(\mathbf{p}_{kj}, w_k)$ are determined by the following equations:

$$[\mathbf{B}_{kj} - (1 + r)\mathbf{A}_{kj}]\mathbf{p}_{kj} = w_k \mathbf{l}_{kj}$$

$$\mathbf{c}^T \mathbf{p}_{kj} = 1,$$

where $(\mathbf{A}_{kj}, \mathbf{B}_{kj}, \mathbf{l}_{kj})$ is the set of processes made up by all the processes in $(\mathbf{A}_k, \mathbf{B}_k, \mathbf{l}_k)$ and by those processes in $(\mathbf{A}_j, \mathbf{B}_j, \mathbf{l}_j)$ producing commodities not produced by processes in $(\mathbf{A}_k, \mathbf{B}_k, \mathbf{l}_k)$. Note that a process in technique $(\mathbf{A}_j, \mathbf{B}_j, \mathbf{l}_j)$ producing only a finished good enters into the set of processes $(\mathbf{A}_{kj}, \mathbf{B}_{kj}, \mathbf{l}_{kj})$ only if it is in technique $(\mathbf{A}_k, \mathbf{B}_k, \mathbf{l}_k)$.

2. A single technique

Let $(\mathbf{A}, \mathbf{B}, \mathbf{l})$ be a technique. We begin by first analyzing the properties of a technique and then the properties of cost-minimizing techniques. Matrices $\mathbf{A}$ and $\mathbf{B}$ are $s \times n$ matrices with $s \leqslant n$. If $s < n$, then there are $n - s$ columns which are nought in both matrices $\mathbf{A}$ and $\mathbf{B}$. Let us delete these columns to obtain matrices $\mathbf{C}$ and $\mathbf{D}$, respectively. In the following, we will refer to the triplet $(\mathbf{C}, \mathbf{D}, \mathbf{l})$ as a technique. This abuse of language must not confuse the reader. By appropriate reordering of commodities and processes, matrices $\mathbf{C}$ and $\mathbf{D}$ can be partitioned in the following way:

$$\mathbf{C} = \begin{bmatrix} \mathbf{C}_{11} & \mathbf{C}_{12} & \mathbf{0} & \mathbf{0} & \cdots & \mathbf{0} \\ \mathbf{C}_{21} & \mathbf{0} & \mathbf{C}_{23} & \mathbf{0} & \cdots & \mathbf{0} \\ \mathbf{C}_{31} & \mathbf{0} & \mathbf{0} & \mathbf{C}_{34} & \cdots & \mathbf{0} \\ \cdot & \cdot & \cdot & \cdot & \cdots & \cdot \\ \cdot & \cdot & \cdot & \cdot & \cdots & \cdot \\ \mathbf{C}_{m1} & \mathbf{0} & \mathbf{0} & \mathbf{0} & \cdots & \mathbf{C}_{mm+1} \end{bmatrix},$$

$$\mathbf{D} = \begin{bmatrix} \mathbf{D}_{11} & \mathbf{D}_{12} & 0 & 0 & \cdots & 0 \\ \mathbf{D}_{21} & 0 & \mathbf{D}_{23} & 0 & \cdots & 0 \\ \mathbf{D}_{31} & 0 & 0 & \mathbf{D}_{34} & \cdots & 0 \\ \cdot & \cdot & \cdot & \cdot & \cdots & \cdot \\ \cdot & \cdot & \cdot & \cdot & \cdots & \cdot \\ \cdot & \cdot & \cdot & \cdot & \cdots & \cdot \\ \mathbf{D}_{m1} & 0 & 0 & 0 & \cdots & \mathbf{D}_{mm+1} \end{bmatrix},$$

where each row of the $s_i \times m$ matrix $\mathbf{C}_{i1}$ is semipositive, the ith column of the $s_i \times m$ matrix $\mathbf{D}_{i1}$ equals the sum vector, the other columns being nought, the $s_i \times (s_i - 1)$ matrix $\mathbf{D}_{ii+1}$ has the form $[\mathbf{S}, \mathbf{0}]^T$, the $s_i \times (s_i - 1)$ matrix $\mathbf{C}_{ii+1}$ has the form $[\mathbf{0}, \mathbf{T}]^T$, sub-matrices $\mathbf{S}$ and $\mathbf{T}$ are diagonal with a strictly positive main diagonal, and $\mathbf{0}$ is a zero vector; $\sum_{i=1}^s s_i = s$.

The interpretation is the following. The first s_1 ($\geqslant 1$) processes produce the finished good 1 using, if $s_1 > 1$, a type of old machine which in technique $(\mathbf{A}, \mathbf{B}, \mathbf{l})$ lasts $s_1 - 1$ years; the next s_2 ($\geqslant 1$) processes produce the finished good 2 using, if $s_2 > 1$, a type of old machine which in technique $(\mathbf{A}, \mathbf{B}, \mathbf{l})$ lasts $s_2 - 1$ years; and so on.

Let $(\mathbf{A}, \mathbf{B}, \mathbf{l})$ be a fixed capital technique and let

$$\mathbb{R}^*_{(\mathbf{A},\mathbf{B},\mathbf{l})} = \{\rho \in \mathbb{R} | \rho \geqslant 0, \exists \mathbf{x} > 0 : \mathbf{x}^T[\mathbf{B} - (1 + r)\mathbf{A}] = \mathbf{c}^T\}.$$

The set $\mathbb{R}^*_{(\mathbf{A},\mathbf{B},\mathbf{l})}$ is not empty because of the definition of a technique. The following theorem explores some properties of this set.

Theorem 7.1. For each $r \in \mathbb{R}^*_{(\mathbf{A},\mathbf{B},\mathbf{l})}$

    (i) matrix $[\mathbf{D} - (1 + r)\mathbf{C}]$ is invertible and the first m rows of $[\mathbf{D} - (1 + r)\mathbf{C}]^{-1}$ are semipositive;
    (ii) prices of finished goods are nonnegative.

Lemma 7.1. If $r > -1$, $(\mathbf{u}^T[\mathbf{D} - (1 + r)\mathbf{C}] = (\mathbf{z}^T, \mathbf{0}^T)$, $\mathbf{z} \in \mathbb{R}^m$, $\mathbf{z} > 0, \mathbf{u} \geqslant 0) \Rightarrow \mathbf{u} > 0$.

Proof. It is immediately obtained that

$$\mathbf{u}_i^T[\mathbf{D}_{ii+1} - (1 + r)\mathbf{C}_{ii+1}] = \mathbf{0}^T \tag{7.1.i}$$

$$\mathbf{u}_1^T\mathbf{D}_{11} + \mathbf{u}_2^T\mathbf{D}_{21} + \cdots + \mathbf{u}_m^T\mathbf{D}_{m1} > \mathbf{0}^T, \tag{7.2}$$

where $(\mathbf{u}_1^T, \mathbf{u}_2^T, \ldots, \mathbf{u}_m^T) = \mathbf{u}^T$. Because of the form of matrices $\mathbf{D}_{ii+1}$ and $\mathbf{C}_{ii+1}$ ($i = 1, 2, \ldots, m$), equation (7.1.i) has non-trivial solutions for each r, and each non-trivial solution to it for $r > -1$ is either a positive vector or a negative one.[2] Then, because of the form of matrices $\mathbf{D}_{i1}$, equations (7.1.1)–(7.1.m) and inequality (7.2) have a solution only if $\mathbf{u}_i > \mathbf{0}$ each $i = 1, 2, \ldots, m$. Q.E.D.

Lemma 7.2. Let $\mathbf{a}$ be a nonnegative vector whose last $n - m$ entries are all nought and let $r > -1$. Then if there is a positive vector $\mathbf{q}$ such that

$$\mathbf{q}^T[\mathbf{D} - (1 + r)\mathbf{C}] = \mathbf{c}^T,$$

any vector $\mathbf{v}$ such that

$$\mathbf{v}^T[\mathbf{D} - (1 + r)\mathbf{C}] = \mathbf{a}^T$$

is nonnegative.

Proof. Assume that there exists a vector $\mathbf{v}$ with at least one negative element such that

$$\mathbf{v}^T[\mathbf{D} - (1 + r)\mathbf{C}] = \mathbf{a}^T.$$

Let i be such that

$$0 > \frac{\mathbf{v}^T\mathbf{e}_i}{\mathbf{q}^T\mathbf{e}_i} \leqslant \frac{\mathbf{v}^T\mathbf{e}_h}{\mathbf{q}^T\mathbf{e}_h} \quad \text{each } h.$$

Then

$$\mathbf{w} := \left[\mathbf{v} - \frac{\mathbf{v}^T\mathbf{e}_i}{\mathbf{q}^T\mathbf{e}_i}\mathbf{q}\right] \geqslant \mathbf{0}$$

and

$$\mathbf{w}^T[\mathbf{D} - (1 + r)\mathbf{C}] = \mathbf{a}^T - \frac{\mathbf{v}^T\mathbf{e}_i}{\mathbf{q}^T\mathbf{e}_i}\mathbf{c}^T := \mathbf{b}^T,$$

where $\mathbf{b}$ is a vector whose first m entries are all positive and the last $n - m$ are all nought. Then Lemma 7.1 applies and $\mathbf{w} > \mathbf{0}$. Hence we have a

---

[2] Let

$$\mathbf{v}^T\left\{\begin{bmatrix}\mathbf{S}\\\mathbf{0}\end{bmatrix} - (1 + r)\begin{bmatrix}\mathbf{0}\\\mathbf{T}\end{bmatrix}\right\} = \mathbf{0}^T,$$

where sub-matrices $\mathbf{S}$ and $\mathbf{T}$ are diagonal with a strictly positive main diagonal and $\mathbf{0}$ is a zero row vector. Then, for $r \neq -1$,

$$v_i s_i = v_{i+1}(1 + r)t_i,$$

that is,

$$v_{i+1} = (1 + r)^{-1}\frac{s_i}{t_i}v_i = v_1(1 + r)^{-i}\prod_{h=1}^{i}\frac{s_h}{t_h}.$$

contradiction, since the ith element of vector $\mathbf{w}$ cannot be positive. And this proves the Lemma.   Q.E.D.

Lemma 7.3. If there is a positive vector $\mathbf{q}$ such that

$$\mathbf{q}^T[\mathbf{D} - (1 + r)\mathbf{C}] = \mathbf{c}^T,$$

then matrix $[\mathbf{D} - (1 + r)\mathbf{C}]$ is invertible and the first m rows of $[\mathbf{D} - (1 + r)\mathbf{C}]^{-1}$ are semipositive.

Proof. If $\mathbf{y}$ is a solution to the equation

$$\mathbf{y}^T[\mathbf{D} - (1 + r)\mathbf{C}] = \mathbf{0}^T,$$

then also $-\mathbf{y}$ is one, and, by Lemma 7.2, both $\mathbf{y}$ and $-\mathbf{y}$ are nonnegative. Therefore $\mathbf{y} = \mathbf{0}$ and $\det([\mathbf{D} - (1 + r)\mathbf{C}]) \neq 0$. As a consequence there are semipositive vectors $\mathbf{z}_i$ such that $\mathbf{z}_i^T[\mathbf{D} - (1 + r)\mathbf{C}] = \mathbf{e}_i^T$ $(i = 1, 2, \ldots, m)$. Thus the first m rows of the matrix $[\mathbf{D} - (1 + r)\mathbf{C}]^{-1}$ are semipositive. And this proves the Lemma.   Q.E.D.

A corollary to Lemma 7.3 is the following

Theorem 7.2. The magnitudes of the positive entries of vector $\mathbf{c}$ play no role in the definition of a technique.

Proof of Theorem 7.1. Statement (i) is a direct consequence of Lemma 7.3. Statement (ii) is a direct consequence of statement (i) since the vector of prices of produced commodities, $\hat{\mathbf{p}}$, is determined by the equation

$$\hat{\mathbf{p}} = w[\mathbf{D} - (1 + r)\mathbf{C}]^{-1}\mathbf{l}.$$ Q.E.D.

In this section it has been proved that for each technique there is a set of values for the rate of profit such that if the going rate of profit is in that set, then the prices of finished goods are nonnegative. Section 4 is devoted to a discussion of the choice of techniques. It will be proved that if there is a technique $(\mathbf{A}, \mathbf{B}, \mathbf{l})$ such that $r^* \in \mathbb{R}^*_{(\mathbf{A}, \mathbf{B}, \mathbf{l})}$, then there is a cost-minimizing technique at the rate of profit r, where $0 \leqslant r \leqslant r^*$. Moreover, all prices will be nonnegative in cost-minimizing techniques. Before studying the choice of techniques a useful device–the "core processes"–will be examined in Section 3. This device allows us to grasp the single product nature of the fixed capital models investigated in this chapter.

3. A useful device: The core processes
Let $(\mathbf{C}, \mathbf{D}, \mathbf{l})$ be a technique. Let matrices $\mathbf{C}$ and $\mathbf{D}$ be partitioned as in the previous section. Let $\mathbf{x}_i^T(r)$ be a positive vector such that

$$\mathbf{x}_i^T(r)[\mathbf{D}_{ii+1} - (1 + r)\mathbf{C}_{ii+1}] = \mathbf{0}^T$$

$$\mathbf{x}_i^T(r)\mathbf{D}_{i1} = \mathbf{e}_i^T.$$

Vector $\mathbf{x}_i^T(r)$ exists for each $r > -1$ and each i (see footnote 1). Let us call the triplet

$$(\mathbf{x}_i^T(r)\mathbf{C}_{i1}, \mathbf{e}_i, \mathbf{x}_i^T(r)\mathbf{l}_i)$$

a *core-process of finished good i*. A core-process looks like a single product process with material and labor inputs as a function of r. The core processes of technique $(\mathbf{C}, \mathbf{D}, \mathbf{l})$ determine the prices of finished goods independently of the prices of old machines. This can easily be seen. Let the $m \times s$ matrix $\mathbf{X}(r)$ be defined as

$$\mathbf{X}(r) = \begin{bmatrix} \mathbf{x}_1^T(r) & \mathbf{0} & \mathbf{0} & \cdots & \mathbf{0} \\ \mathbf{0} & \mathbf{x}_2^T(r) & \mathbf{0} & \cdots & \mathbf{0} \\ \mathbf{0} & \mathbf{0} & \mathbf{x}_3^T(r) & \cdots & \mathbf{0} \\ \cdot & \cdot & \cdot & \cdots & \cdot \\ \cdot & \cdot & \cdot & \cdots & \cdot \\ \mathbf{0} & \mathbf{0} & \mathbf{0} & \cdots & \mathbf{x}_m^T(r) \end{bmatrix},$$

then the $m + 1$ equations

$$\mathbf{X}(r)\mathbf{D}\mathbf{p} = (1 + r)\mathbf{X}(r)\mathbf{C}\mathbf{p} + w\mathbf{X}(r)\mathbf{l}$$

$$\mathbf{c}^T\mathbf{p} = 1$$

determine the wage rate and the prices of the finished goods since the columns of matrix $\mathbf{X}(r)[\mathbf{D} - (1 + r)\mathbf{C}]$ relating to old machines have vanished. Moreover, by deleting all these zero columns, that is, all the columns referring to old machines, and corresponding elements of vectors $\mathbf{p}$ and $\mathbf{c}$ we obtain a single product technique with material and labor inputs as function of r, the output matrix being the usual matrix $\mathbf{I}$. Such a "single product technique" will be denoted as $(\mathbf{F}(r), \mathbf{X}(r)\mathbf{l})$, where $\mathbf{F}(r)$ is a square matrix obtained by the first m columns of matrix $\mathbf{X}(r)\mathbf{A}$. We will refer to the pair $(\mathbf{F}(r), \mathbf{X}(r)\mathbf{l})$ as the core-format of technique $(\mathbf{A}, \mathbf{B}, \mathbf{l})$.

Once the prices of finished goods have been ascertained, the prices of produced old machines can be determined from equation

$$\hat{\mathbf{D}}\mathbf{p} = (1 + r)\hat{\mathbf{C}}\mathbf{p} + w\hat{\mathbf{l}}, \tag{7.3}$$

where $\hat{\mathbf{D}}, \hat{\mathbf{C}},$ and $\hat{\mathbf{l}}$ are obtained from $\mathbf{D}, \mathbf{C},$ and $\mathbf{l}$, respectively, by deleting the m rows corresponding to processes not producing old machines. Equation (7.3) can be stated as

$$[\hat{\mathbf{D}}_2 - (1 + r)\hat{\mathbf{C}}_2]\mathbf{p}_2 = w\hat{\mathbf{l}} - [\hat{\mathbf{D}}_1 - (1 + r)\hat{\mathbf{C}}_1]\mathbf{p}_1, \tag{7.4}$$

where $\hat{\mathbf{D}} = [\hat{\mathbf{D}}_1, \hat{\mathbf{D}}_2]$, $\hat{\mathbf{C}} = [\hat{\mathbf{C}}_1, \hat{\mathbf{C}}_2]$, $\mathbf{p}^T = [\mathbf{p}_1^T, \mathbf{p}_2^T]$, and

$$\hat{\mathbf{C}}_2 = \begin{bmatrix} \hat{\mathbf{C}}_{12} & 0 & \cdots & 0 \\ 0 & \hat{\mathbf{C}}_{23} & \cdots & 0 \\ \cdot & \cdot & \cdots & \cdot \\ \cdot & \cdot & \cdots & \cdot \\ \cdot & \cdot & \cdots & \cdot \\ 0 & 0 & \cdots & \hat{\mathbf{C}}_{mm+1} \end{bmatrix},$$

$$\hat{\mathbf{D}}_2 = \begin{bmatrix} \hat{\mathbf{D}}_{12} & 0 & \cdots & 0 \\ 0 & \hat{\mathbf{D}}_{23} & \cdots & 0 \\ \cdot & \cdot & \cdots & \cdot \\ \cdot & \cdot & \cdots & \cdot \\ \cdot & \cdot & \cdots & \cdot \\ 0 & 0 & \cdots & \hat{\mathbf{D}}_{mm+1} \end{bmatrix},$$

where $\hat{\mathbf{C}}_{ii+1}$ and $\hat{\mathbf{D}}_{ii+1}$ are obtained from $\mathbf{C}_{ii+1}$ and $\mathbf{D}_{ii+1}$ by deleting the last row. Hence $\hat{\mathbf{C}}_{ii+1}$ is a nonnegative square matrix with positive elements only on the diagonal just below the main diagonal, and $\hat{\mathbf{D}}_{ii+1}$ is a square diagonal matrix with elements on the main diagonal all positive. Thus, matrix $[\hat{\mathbf{D}}_2 - (1+r)\hat{\mathbf{C}}_2]$ is a square matrix with elements on the main diagonal all positive and some negative elements on the diagonal below the main one, all other elements being nought. This is enough to assert that matrix $[\hat{\mathbf{D}}_2 - (1+r)\hat{\mathbf{C}}_2]$ is invertible and its inverse is semipositive (see exercise 10.1). This does not imply that prices of old machines are nonnegative, since the vector on the right-hand side of equation (7.4) may have negative elements.

We conclude this section with a further application of "core processes." Exercise 10.2 shows that $\mathbb{R}^*_{(\mathbf{A}, \mathbf{B}, \mathbf{l})}$ can consist of a number of disconnected segments. Let us prove that if this were the case, only the segment containing the zero may be relevant from an economic point of view since if r is in any of the other segments, then prices of old machines are not all nonnegative. This result is an obvious consequence of the following theorem, which is proved on the assumption that $\mathbf{l} > \mathbf{0}$. The case in which labor enters directly or indirectly into the production of finished goods is dealt with in exercise 10.3.

Theorem 7.3. Let $(\mathbf{A}, \mathbf{B}, \mathbf{l})$ be a fixed capital technique. If there is a nonnegative vector $\mathbf{p}$ such that

$$[\mathbf{B} - (1+r)\mathbf{A}]\mathbf{p} = \mathbf{l},$$

then there is a positive vector $\mathbf{z}$ such that

$$\mathbf{z}^T[\mathbf{B}-(1+g)\mathbf{A}]=\mathbf{c}^T,$$

where $0 \leqslant g \leqslant r$ and $\mathbf{c}$ is any vector whose first m entries are positive, the others being nought.

Proof. In order to simplify the proof it will be further assumed that $\mathbf{l} > \mathbf{0}$ (but see exercise 10.3). Since

$$[\mathbf{B}-(1+g)\mathbf{A}]\mathbf{p} = \mathbf{l} + (r-g)\mathbf{A}\mathbf{p} > \mathbf{0},$$

$$[[\mathbf{I}-(1+g)\mathbf{F}(g)],\mathbf{0}]\mathbf{p} = \mathbf{X}(g)[\mathbf{B}-(1+g)\mathbf{A}]\mathbf{p} > \mathbf{0},$$

where $\mathbf{F}(g)$ is the square matrix consisting of the first m columns of matrix $\mathbf{X}(g)\mathbf{A}$. Hence matrix $[\mathbf{I}-(1+g)\mathbf{F}(g)]$ is invertible and its inverse is semipositive because of Theorem A.3.1 of the Mathematical Appendix. Finally, let $\hat{\mathbf{c}} \in \mathbb{R}^m$ be the vector consisting of the first m elements of vector $\mathbf{c}$. Then

$$\hat{\mathbf{c}}^T[\mathbf{I}-(1+g)\mathbf{F}(g)]^{-1}\mathbf{X}(g)[\mathbf{B}-(1+g)\mathbf{A}]=\mathbf{c}^T,$$

which proves the Theorem since

$$\hat{\mathbf{c}}^T[\mathbf{I}-(1+g)\mathbf{F}(g)]^{-1}\mathbf{X}(g) > \mathbf{0}^T. \qquad\qquad \text{Q.E.D.}$$

4. The choice of technique

In this section the problem of the choice of technique in models with fixed capital but no joint utilization of old machines will be dealt with in highly abstract terms. In Section 7 some practically important illustrations will be given: these concern various aspects of the choice of the pattern of utilization of machines. With all final goods assumed to be consumed, we do not need to distinguish between basic and non-basic commodities. Since we are not interested in determining the prices of machines which are not produced, the complications analyzed in Subsection 3.4 of Chapter 5 need not be considered here. The reader may extend the analysis to cover the more general cases.

Proposition 7.1. Let $(\mathbf{A}_h, \mathbf{B}_h, \mathbf{l}_h)$ be a technique, let $r \in \mathbb{R}^*_{(\mathbf{A},\mathbf{B},\mathbf{l})}$, let $w_h > 0$ at rate of profit r, and let $(\mathbf{a},\mathbf{b},l)$ be a process producing the finished good i in technique $(\mathbf{A}_j, \mathbf{B}_j, \mathbf{l}_j)$ such that at rate of profit r $\mathbf{p}_{hj} \geqslant \mathbf{0}$ and

$$[\mathbf{b}-(1+r)\mathbf{a}]^T\mathbf{p}_{hj} > w_h l.$$

Then there is a technique $(\mathbf{A}_k, \mathbf{B}_k, \mathbf{l}_k)$ such that $r \in \mathbb{R}^*_{(\mathbf{A}_k,\mathbf{B}_k,\mathbf{l}_k)}$ and $w_k > w_h$ at the same rate of profit r.

Proof. Let $(\mathbf{M}, \mathbf{N}, \mathbf{q})$ be a set of processes obtained from the set of processes $(\mathbf{A}_{hj}, \mathbf{B}_{hj}, \mathbf{l}_{hj})$ by substituting the process producing finished good i of the same degree as process $(\mathbf{a}, \mathbf{b}, l)$ with process $(\mathbf{a}, \mathbf{b}, l)$ itself. Obviously,

$$[\mathbf{M} - (1 + r)\mathbf{N}]\mathbf{p}_{hj} \geqslant w_h\mathbf{q}.$$

The processes not producing finished good i in the set of processes $(\mathbf{M}, \mathbf{N}, \mathbf{q})$ are obviously able to determine the corresponding core processes. With respect to the processes producing finished good i we need to distinguish three cases. *Case 1*: Finished good i is produced within the two techniques $(\mathbf{A}_h, \mathbf{B}_h, \mathbf{l}_h)$ and $(\mathbf{A}_j, \mathbf{B}_j, \mathbf{l}_j)$ either with different types of machines or without utilizing old machines in at least one of the two techniques. *Case 2*: Commodity i is produced with the same type of machine in the two techniques and either process $(\mathbf{a}, \mathbf{b}, l)$ or the process of the same degree in technique $(\mathbf{A}_h, \mathbf{B}_h, \mathbf{l}_h)$ does not produce an old machine. *Case 3*: Commodity i is produced with the same type of machine in the two techniques and process $(\mathbf{a}, \mathbf{b}, l)$ produces the same old machine produced by the process of the same degree in technique $(\mathbf{A}_h, \mathbf{B}_h, \mathbf{l}_h)$. In case 1, the set of processes $(\mathbf{M}, \mathbf{N}, \mathbf{q})$ includes all processes of technique $(\mathbf{A}_j, \mathbf{B}_j, \mathbf{l}_j)$ producing finished good i. In case 2 the set of processes $(\mathbf{M}, \mathbf{N}, \mathbf{q})$ includes the processes of technique $(\mathbf{A}_h, \mathbf{B}_h, \mathbf{l}_h)$ producing finished good i which are of a degree lower than that of process $(\mathbf{a}, \mathbf{b}, l)$, and the processes producing finished good i in technique $(\mathbf{A}_j, \mathbf{B}_j, \mathbf{l}_j)$ which are of a degree larger than or equal to that of process $(\mathbf{a}, \mathbf{b}, l)$. In case 3, the set of processes $(\mathbf{M}, \mathbf{N}, \mathbf{q})$ includes process $(\mathbf{a}, \mathbf{b}, l)$ and all processes of technique $(\mathbf{A}_h, \mathbf{B}_h, \mathbf{l}_h)$ except that producing finished good i which is of the same degree as process $(\mathbf{a}, \mathbf{b}, l)$. In all the three cases, the mentioned processes producing finished good i in the set of processes $(\mathbf{M}, \mathbf{N}, \mathbf{q})$ are able to determine a core process. Let $(\mathbf{F}(r), \mathbf{X}(r)\mathbf{q})$ be the set of core processes derived from the set of processes $(\mathbf{M}, \mathbf{N}, \mathbf{q})$, as indicated above. Moreover, let $\hat{\mathbf{p}}$ and $\hat{\mathbf{c}}$ be obtained from $\mathbf{p}_{hj}$ and $\mathbf{c}$, respectively, by deleting the entries corresponding to the columns of $\mathbf{X}(r)\mathbf{M}$ deleted in order to obtain $\mathbf{F}(r)$. Hence

$$[\mathbf{I} - (1 + r)\mathbf{F}(r)]\hat{\mathbf{p}} \geqslant w_h\mathbf{X}(r)\mathbf{q}. \tag{7.5}$$

In order to simplify the proof we will assume that $\mathbf{X}(r)\mathbf{q} > \mathbf{0}$ (cf. exercise 10.4). Then

$$[\mathbf{I} - (1 + r)\mathbf{F}(r)]\hat{\mathbf{p}} > \mathbf{0}.$$

Hence

$$\hat{\mathbf{c}}^T[\mathbf{I} - (1 + r)\mathbf{F}(r)]^{-1} \geqslant \mathbf{0}^T.$$

By taking those processes of the set of processes $(\mathbf{M}, \mathbf{N}, \mathbf{q})$ corresponding to positive elements of vector

$$\hat{\mathbf{c}}^T[\mathbf{I} - (1 + r)\mathbf{F}(r)]^{-1}\hat{\mathbf{X}}(r)[\mathbf{B}_k - (1 + r)\mathbf{A}_k] = \mathbf{c}^T,$$

we obtain the set of processes $(\mathbf{A}_k, \mathbf{B}_k, \mathbf{l}_k)$, which is a technique since

$$\hat{\mathbf{c}}^T[\mathbf{I} - (1 + r)\mathbf{F}(r)]^{-1}\hat{\mathbf{X}}(r) > \mathbf{0}^T,$$

where $\hat{\mathbf{X}}(r)$ is obtained from $\mathbf{X}(r)$ by substituting the row vectors corresponding to zero elements of vector $\hat{\mathbf{c}}^T[\mathbf{I} - (1 + r)\mathbf{F}(r)]^{-1}$ with zero row vectors and then deleting all columns consisting only of zeros. Inequality (7.5) also implies that

$$1 = \hat{\mathbf{c}}^T\hat{\mathbf{p}} > w_h\hat{\mathbf{c}}^T[\mathbf{I} - (1 + r)\mathbf{F}(r)]^{-1}\mathbf{X}(r)\mathbf{q} = \frac{w_h}{w_k},$$

where w_k is the wage rate of technique $(\mathbf{A}_k, \mathbf{B}_k, \mathbf{l}_k)$. And this proves the Proposition.   Q.E.D.

Proposition 7.2. Let $(\mathbf{A}_h, \mathbf{B}_h, \mathbf{l}_h)$ and $(\mathbf{A}_k, \mathbf{B}_k, \mathbf{l}_k)$ be two techniques such that at rate of profit r $\mathbf{p}_{hk} \geqslant \mathbf{0}$, $\mathbf{p}_{kh} \geqslant \mathbf{0}$, and

$$0 < w_h < w_k.$$

Then there is a process in technique $(\mathbf{A}_k, \mathbf{B}_k, \mathbf{l}_k)$ which pays extra profits at rate of profit r, prices $\mathbf{p}_{hk}$, and wage rate w_h.

Proof. Assume that the Proposition does not hold. Then

$$[\mathbf{B}_{kh} - (1 + r)\mathbf{A}_{kh}]\mathbf{p}_{hk} \leqslant w_h\mathbf{l}_{kh}.$$

Therefore,

$$1 = \mathbf{c}^T\mathbf{p}_{hk} = \mathbf{x}_{kh}^T[\mathbf{B}_{kh} - (1 + r)\mathbf{A}_{kh}]\mathbf{p}_{hk} \leqslant w_h\mathbf{x}_{kh}^T\mathbf{l}_{kh} = \frac{w_h}{w_k}, \qquad (7.6)$$

where $\mathbf{x}_{kh}$ is defined by the equation

$$\mathbf{x}_{kh}^T[\mathbf{B}_{kh} - (1 + r)\mathbf{A}_{kh}] = \mathbf{c}^T.$$

The last equation in (7.6) is obtained as follows. Since

$$1 = \mathbf{c}^T\mathbf{p}_{kh} = \mathbf{x}_{kh}^T[\mathbf{B}_{kh} - (1 + r)\mathbf{A}_{kh}]\mathbf{p}_{kh} = w_k\mathbf{x}_{kh}^T\mathbf{l}_{kh},$$

$$w_k = \frac{1}{\mathbf{x}_{kh}^T\mathbf{l}_{kh}}.$$

Equations and inequalities (7.6) imply a contradiction.   Q.E.D.

Proposition 7.3. Let $(\mathbf{A}_h, \mathbf{B}_h, \mathbf{l}_h)$ and $(\mathbf{A}_k, \mathbf{B}_k, \mathbf{l}_k)$ be two techniques which are both cost-minimizing at rate of profit r where $\mathbf{p}_{hk} \geqslant \mathbf{0}$, $\mathbf{p}_{kh} \geqslant \mathbf{0}$, $w_k > 0$, and $w_h > 0$, then $w_k = w_h$ and $\mathbf{p}_{kh} = \mathbf{p}_{hk}$.

Proof. It is an immediate consequence of Proposition 7.2 that $w_k = w_h$ $(=w)$. Let us first prove that prices of finished goods are the same in both techniques. By using the core-formats of techniques $(\mathbf{A}_h, \mathbf{B}_h, \mathbf{l}_h)$ and $(\mathbf{A}_k, \mathbf{B}_k, \mathbf{l}_k)$, as introduced in Section 3, we immediately obtain

$$[\mathbf{I} - (1 + r)\mathbf{F}_h(r)]\hat{\mathbf{p}}_h = w\mathbf{X}_h(r)\mathbf{l}_h$$

$$[\mathbf{I} - (1 + r)\mathbf{F}_k(r)]\hat{\mathbf{p}}_k = w\mathbf{X}_k(r)\mathbf{l}_k$$

$$\hat{\mathbf{c}}^T\hat{\mathbf{p}}_{hk} = \hat{\mathbf{c}}^T\hat{\mathbf{p}}_{kh} = 1$$

$$[\mathbf{I} - (1 + r)\mathbf{F}_k(r)]\hat{\mathbf{p}}_h \leqslant w\mathbf{X}_k(r)\mathbf{l}_k$$

$$[\mathbf{I} - (1 + r)\mathbf{F}_h(r)]\hat{\mathbf{p}}_k \leqslant w\mathbf{X}_h(r)\mathbf{l}_h,$$

where $\mathbf{F}_j(r)$ is the $m \times m$ matrix obtained by the first m columns of matrix $\mathbf{X}_j(r)\mathbf{A}_j$, and $\hat{\mathbf{p}}_j$ and $\hat{\mathbf{c}}$ are vectors obtained by the first m elements of vectors $\mathbf{p}_j$ and $\mathbf{c}$ ($j = h, k$). Then the prices of finished goods are proved to be the same in both techniques by following the same procedure adopted in Chapter 5. In order also to prove that the prices of old machines which are produced in at least one of the two techniques are equal, let us first obtain in an obvious way that

$$[\hat{\mathbf{D}}_{hk2} - (1 + r)\hat{\mathbf{C}}_{hk2}]\bar{\mathbf{p}}_{hk} = w\hat{\mathbf{l}}_{hk} - [\hat{\mathbf{D}}_{hk1} - (1 + r)\hat{\mathbf{C}}_{hk1}]\hat{\mathbf{p}}_h \qquad (7.7a)$$

$$[\hat{\mathbf{D}}_{kh2} - (1 + r)\hat{\mathbf{C}}_{kh2}]\bar{\mathbf{p}}_{kh} = w\hat{\mathbf{l}}_{kh} - [\hat{\mathbf{D}}_{kh1} - (1 + r)\hat{\mathbf{C}}_{kh1}]\hat{\mathbf{p}}_k \qquad (7.7b)$$

$$[\hat{\mathbf{D}}_{kh2} - (1 + r)\hat{\mathbf{C}}_{kh2}]\bar{\mathbf{p}}_{hk} \leqslant w\hat{\mathbf{l}}_{kh} - [\hat{\mathbf{D}}_{kh1} - (1 + r)\hat{\mathbf{C}}_{kh1}]\hat{\mathbf{p}}_h \qquad (7.7c)$$

$$[\hat{\mathbf{D}}_{hk2} - (1 + r)\hat{\mathbf{C}}_{hk2}]\bar{\mathbf{p}}_{kh} \leqslant w\hat{\mathbf{l}}_{hk} - [\hat{\mathbf{D}}_{hk1} - (1 + r)\hat{\mathbf{C}}_{hk1}]\hat{\mathbf{p}}_k, \qquad (7.7d)$$

where $\bar{\mathbf{p}}_{hk}$ and $\bar{\mathbf{p}}_{kh}$ are obtained from $\mathbf{p}_{hk}$ and $\mathbf{p}_{kh}$ by eliminating the prices of finished goods and the prices of old machines which are not produced in both techniques, the other terms obviously being obtained in the same way as in Section 3. Finally, keeping in mind that $\hat{\mathbf{p}}_h = \hat{\mathbf{p}}_k$, we obtain from (7.7) that

$$[\hat{\mathbf{D}}_{kh2} - (1 + r)\hat{\mathbf{C}}_{kh2}]\bar{\mathbf{p}}_{hk} \leqslant [\hat{\mathbf{D}}_{kh2} - (1 + r)\hat{\mathbf{C}}_{kh2}]\bar{\mathbf{p}}_{kh},$$

$$[\hat{\mathbf{D}}_{hk2} - (1 + r)\hat{\mathbf{C}}_{hk2}]\bar{\mathbf{p}}_{kh} \leqslant [\hat{\mathbf{D}}_{hk2} - (1 + r)\hat{\mathbf{C}}_{hk2}]\bar{\mathbf{p}}_{hk},$$

and since $[\hat{\mathbf{D}}_{kh2} - (1 + r)\hat{\mathbf{C}}_{kh2}]$ and $[\hat{\mathbf{D}}_{hk2} - (1 + r)\hat{\mathbf{C}}_{hk2}]$ are invertible with nonnegative inverses (compare Section 3 and exercise 10.1),

$$\bar{\mathbf{p}}_{hk} \leqslant \bar{\mathbf{p}}_{kh} \leqslant \bar{\mathbf{p}}_{hk}. \qquad \text{Q.E.D.}$$

Theorem 7.4.

(a) If there is a technique $(\mathbf{A}, \mathbf{B}, \mathbf{l})$ such that $r^* \in \mathbb{R}^*_{(\mathbf{A},\mathbf{B},\mathbf{l})}$, then there is a cost-minimizing technique at rate of profit r, where $0 \leqslant r \leqslant r^*$.

(b) If there is a technique $(\mathbf{A}, \mathbf{B}, \mathbf{l})$ such that $r^* \in \mathbb{R}^*_{(\mathbf{A},\mathbf{B},\mathbf{l})}$, then there is a cost-minimizing technique at rate of profit r^*.

(c) A technique with a semipositive price vector at $r = r^*$ is cost-minimizing at $r = r^*$ if and only if it is able to pay the largest wage rate at $r = r^*$ when the numeraire consists of a positive amount of each consumed commodity.

(d) If there is more than one cost-minimizing technique at rate of profit r^*, then they share the same wage rate and the same prices of commodities which are produced in at least one of them.

(e) Price vectors of cost-minimizing techniques are semipositive.

(f) If only finished goods enter into the numeraire, then the $w - r$ relationship of a technique which is cost-minimizing at rate of profit r^* is decreasing at r^*.

Proof. The "only if" part of statement (c) is a direct consequence of Proposition 7.2. The "if" part is a consequence of Proposition 7.1: if there is a process able to pay extra profits, then there is a technique which can pay a larger wage rate; hence a contradiction. Statement (d) is equivalent to Proposition 7.3. Statement (b) is a direct consequence of statement (c) since the number of processes is finite.[3] If the price of old machine j is negative for technique $(\mathbf{A}_k, \mathbf{B}_k, \mathbf{l}_k)$, then there is a process paying extra profits at prices of technique $(\mathbf{A}_k, \mathbf{B}_k, \mathbf{l}_k)$ since Axiom (vi) of Section 1 holds. This proves statement (e). Statement (a) is a consequence of statements (b) and (e) because of Theorem 7.3. By differentiating totally with respect to r the equations defining the price vector $\mathbf{p}_k$ and the wage rate w_k of technique $(\mathbf{A}_k, \mathbf{B}_k, \mathbf{l}_k)$, which is cost-minimizing at the rate of profit r^*, we obtain

$$\mathbf{D}_k \dot{\mathbf{p}}_k = \mathbf{C}_k \mathbf{p}_k + (1 + r^*) \mathbf{C}_k \dot{\mathbf{p}}_k + \dot{w}_k \mathbf{l}_k \tag{7.8a}$$

$$\mathbf{c}^T \dot{\mathbf{p}}_k = 0, \tag{7.8b}$$

were $\dot{\mathbf{p}}_k$ and $\dot{w}_k$ are the vector of derivatives of prices of produced commodities with respect to r and the derivative of the wage rate with respect to r, respectively. From (7.8a) we obtain

$$[\mathbf{D}_k - (1 + r^*) \mathbf{C}_k] \dot{\mathbf{p}}_k = \mathbf{C}_k \mathbf{p}_k + \dot{w}_k \mathbf{l}_k,$$

that is,

$$\dot{\mathbf{p}}_k = [\mathbf{D}_k - (1 + r^*) \mathbf{C}_k]^{-1} \mathbf{C}_k \mathbf{p}_k + \dot{w}_k [\mathbf{D}_k - (1 + r^*) \mathbf{C}_k]^{-1} \mathbf{l}_k.$$

---

[3] If the number of processes is not finite, statement (b) is to be changed in the following way: "If there is a technique $(\mathbf{A}, \mathbf{B}, \mathbf{l})$ such that $r^* \in \mathbb{R}^*_{(\mathbf{A}, \mathbf{B}, \mathbf{l})}$ and no technique can pay a wage rate larger than that paid by technique $(\mathbf{A}, \mathbf{B}, \mathbf{l})$ at rate of profit r^*, then there is a cost-minimizing technique at rate of profit r^*." If the number of processes is not finite, statement (a) does not need to hold.

Then, because of equation (7.8b),

$$0 = \mathbf{c}^T \dot{\mathbf{p}}_k = \mathbf{c}^T [\mathbf{D}_k - (1 + r^*)\mathbf{C}_k]^{-1} \mathbf{C}_k \mathbf{p}_k$$
$$+ \dot{w}_k \mathbf{c}^T [\mathbf{D}_k - (1 + r^*)\mathbf{C}_k]^{-1} \mathbf{l}_k,$$

that is,

$$\dot{w}_k = - \frac{\mathbf{c}^T [\mathbf{D}_k - (1 + r^*)\mathbf{C}_k]^{-1} \mathbf{C}_k \mathbf{p}_k}{\mathbf{c}^T [\mathbf{D}_k - (1 + r^*)\mathbf{C}_k]^{-1} \mathbf{l}_k},$$

which is negative since $\mathbf{c}^T [\mathbf{D}_k - (1 + r^*)\mathbf{C}_k]^{-1} \geqslant \mathbf{0}^T$, because the last $n - m$ elements of vector $\mathbf{c}$ are nought, and $\mathbf{p}_k \geqslant \mathbf{0}$ because of statement (e) since technique $(\mathbf{A}_k, \mathbf{B}_k, \mathbf{l}_k)$ is cost-minimizing at rate of profit r^*. And this proves statement (f).   Q.E.D.

5. On the positivity of prices

Prices of finished goods are positive in each technique; prices of old machines are nonnegative in cost-minimizing techniques since free disposal of old machines has been assumed. But to assume free disposal for even one product is, strictly speaking, to deny a fundamental principle of Thermodynamics: the principle of the conservation of mass.[4] Free disposal has also been introduced in Subsection 3.4 of Chapter 5. But there it was only a *Hilfskonstruktion* since the commodity to be disposed of was in fact not produced. In this chapter, on the contrary, it would be an artificial solution to assume that the commodity to be disposed of is not produced. In the "real world" disposal is never really free. It may seem so because of the complete absence of property rights (for example, smoke in the air, radioactive waste at the bottom of the ocean) or because of complex questions of externalities in the presence of partially defined property rights (for example, creation of waste disposal sites). Nevertheless many theories assume "free disposal." This is perhaps because negative prices appear to be strongly unrealistic. But the price of a commodity which *must* be disposed of must be *negative* if nobody is interested in taking it for free.

An alternative to the assumption of free disposal of old machines could be the following. Assume that for each process producing an old machine $(\mathbf{a}, \mathbf{b}, l)$ there is another process $(\mathbf{a}', \mathbf{b}', l')$ with the same outputs except that the old machine is not produced and $\mathbf{a}' = \mathbf{a} + \mathbf{z}$ and $l' = l + t$, where $(\mathbf{z}, t)$ are the material and the labor inputs necessary to dispose of the old machine which appears as not produced. If this is done old machines may

---

[4] The free disposal assumption may of course be considered admissible if there are disposals from a "small" level of economic activity in a "large" environment.

have negative prices in cost-minimizing techniques, but the price of no old machine can be lower than $-(\mathbf{z}^T\mathbf{p} + tw)$. Obviously, if a machine can be discarded at no cost, then $\mathbf{z} = \mathbf{0}$ and $t = 0$ and the free disposal assumption is restored.

6. Depreciation, annual charge, and efficiency

Up to now no definition of a "new machine" has been provided. There is, however, no reason for not considering an input of a process of first degree, necessarily a finished good, as the "new machine." This can be regarded just as a convention and it does not change in any way the model built up so far.[5] The introduction of a "new machine" allows us to deal with depreciation. In fact, the change in the price of a type of machine over one production period is, by definition, the *economic depreciation* of that type of machine for that period. Of course, the depreciation per period will in general depend on the rate of profit. Even for a given rate of profit it depends on the age of the machine and is in general not equal to a constant fraction of the value of the machine at the beginning of its productive life.

Let $p_0(r), p_1(r), \ldots, p_t(r)$ be the prices of machines of the same type which are $0, 1, \ldots, t$ years old, respectively. (A machine of age 0 is, of course, a new machine.) In a given technique the type of machine under consideration is assumed to have an economic life of t years $(p_{t+1}(r) \equiv 0)$. Then the *depreciation of the i year old machine* is

$$M_i(r) = p_i(r) - p_{i+1}(r) \quad (i = 0, 1, \ldots, t-1)$$

$$M_t(r) = p_t(r).$$

The *annual charge on the i year old machine* is

$$Y_i(r) = (1 + r)p_i(r) - p_{i+1}(r) \quad (i = 0, 1, \ldots, t-1)$$

$$Y_t(r) = (1 + r)p_t(r).$$

Obviously,

$$p_i(r) = \frac{Y_i(r) + p_{i+1}(r)}{(1 + r)} = \sum_{h=i}^{t} \frac{Y_h(r)}{(1 + r)^{h-i+1}}; \quad (i = 0, 1, \ldots, t)$$

that is, the price of a machine is equal to the actual value of the flow of future annual charges.

The *efficiency* of an i year old machine can be defined as *constant*,

---

[5] Up to new also the physical units of measurement have not been discussed. In this section the physical units cannot be arbitrary: they need to be consistent for all machines, old and new, of the same type.

increasing or *decreasing* if the annual charge of that machine is equal, lower or higher than the annual charge of the $i+1$ year old machine of the same type. If the efficiency of a type of machine is constant whatever the age of the machine, then

$$p_i(r) = \sum_{h=i}^{t} \frac{Y(r)}{(1+r)^{h-i+1}} = Y(r) \frac{(1+r)^{t+1-i} - 1}{r(1+r)^{t-i+1}}.$$

Therefore,

$$p_0(r) = Y(r) \frac{(1+r)^{t+1} - 1}{r(1+r)^{t+1}},$$

and, as a consequence,

$$Y(r) = p_0(r) \frac{r(1+r)^{t+1}}{(1+r)^{t+1} - 1},$$

$$p_i(r) = p_0(r) \frac{(1+r)^{t+1} - (1+r)^i}{(1+r)^{t+1} - 1}, \quad (i = 0, 1, \ldots, t)$$

$$M_i(r) = p_0(r) \frac{r(1+r)^i}{(1+r)^{t+1} - 1}, \quad (i = 0, 1, \ldots, t)$$

which are the usual capitalization formulas.

7. The problem of capital utilization

With fixed capital there is always a problem of the choice of technique to be solved. This concerns both the choice of the *pattern of utilization* of a durable capital good and the choice of the *economic lifetime* of such a good. The utilization aspect in turn exhibits both an *extensive* and an *intensive* dimension. The former relates to the number of time units within a given time period (day, week) during which a durable capital good is actually operated, for example, whether a single-, a double-, or a treble-shift scheme is adopted; the latter relates to the intensity of operation per unit of active time (hour) of the item, for example, the speed at which a machine is run. The economic lifetime of a fixed capital good and the pattern of its operation are, of course, closely connected. In this section the problem of the choice of technique in the case of fixed capital (but no jointly utilized old machines) will be illustrated in terms of the utilization aspect which is obviously of great practical importance: when a producer plans to provide a certain productive capacity, this involves some decision as to the desired pattern of utilization of the type of machine he employs. Otherwise it would not be possible to decide the number of machines to install in order to provide that capacity.

John Stuart Mill expressed the opinion that keeping machines working through the twenty-four hours "is evidently the only economical mode of employing them" ([1848] 1965, p. 131). Yet what we actually observe is that most production units schedule the work process intermittently, shutting down regularly despite the increased fixed capital charge that incurs per unit of output. Despite the interest of the proprietors in utilizing the capital stock for the maximum possible time per period, under any given historical circumstances the intended "full" utilization is prevented by a variety of customary, institutional, technological, and economic factors. Our concern is exclusively with the latter two, that is, we take the customary and institutional framework as given.

Two things are to be noted. First, the physical characteristics of a process of production that uses a certain type of machine is generally not independent of the time during the twenty-four hours of the day during which the machine is operated. For example, it makes a difference whether the machine is worked at night or during the day: this difference can concern both the wear and tear of the machine, the pattern of maintenance and repair activities, and the quantities of complementary inputs, including labor, per unit of vendible output. Second, the prices of the different inputs into the production process behave differently over time. While some prices are time-invariant, others are time-specific. As regards the latter, an important example is the wage rate, a characteristic feature of which is that it often varies regularly by time of day (or day or week). Thus, in order to utilize plant and equipment outside of "ordinary working hours," which is an institutional datum, by scheduling work at night or at weekends or holidays, firms must generally pay higher wages to workers: they must pay what may be called the going "basic wage rate" and a wage premium or differential to compensate workers for their work during abnormal hours (or days). (See also Subsection 1.2 of Chapter 11 below.)

We may illustrate the principle of the choice of the cost-minimizing system of operation of machinery in terms of a simple example: the case under consideration is *shift work*. Suppose that a producer has the choice of operating a machine under a day or a night shift or under a double shift. Suppose for simplicity that under the night shift the amount of direct labor and the quantities of the means of production used up per unit of output are the same as under the day shift. Hence, under the double-shift system the same yearly output could be produced by working half of the machinery twice as long each day as under any one of the two single-shift systems. In addition assume that the machine's lifetime lasts two years under each one of the two single- and one year under the double-shift system, respectively. The technical alternatives from which the producer can choose are summarized in Table 7.1. The vector **a** denotes

Table 7.1

	material inputs					outputs	
	finished goods	old machine	day labor	night labor		finished goods	old machine
$(z+1)$	$\mathbf{a} + \mathbf{e}_h$	0	1	0	$\rightarrow$	$\mathbf{e}_i$	1
$(z+2)$	$\mathbf{a}$	1	1	0	$\rightarrow$	$\mathbf{e}_i$	0
$(z+3)$	$\mathbf{a} + \frac{1}{2}\mathbf{e}_h$	0	$\frac{1}{2}$	$\frac{1}{2}$	$\rightarrow$	$\mathbf{e}_i$	0

the vector of finished goods used as inputs per unit of output and $\mathbf{e}_h$ the hth unit vector, where commodity h represents the new machine; $\mathbf{e}_i$ denotes the ith unit vector where commodity i is the commodity produced. Process $(z+1)$ relates to the single-shift system when the new machine is utilized, whereas process $(z+2)$ relates to the single-shift system when the one year old machine is utilized. Only the day-shift alternative of the single-shift system is given, since under the premises of the present example the night-shift alternative turns out to be more costly for any positive level of the rate of profit and will therefore not be adopted. Process $(z+3)$ refers to the double-shift system.

Obviously, the producer can compare the cheapness of the three alternatives for each rate of profit and the corresponding prices and wage rate plus a wage premium to be paid for work performed at night. Let w be the going wage rate paid per unit of labor employed during the day shift, and $w(1+\alpha)$ the wage rate paid during the night shift, with $w, \alpha > 0$. Under the conditions specified, the question whether it would be profitable to schedule work regularly at night instead of at day is easily decided. All that matters is how the day-shift and night-shift wage bills compare. By adopting the latter the producer could economize on his machinery by one half per unit of output. On the other hand he would incur a larger wages bill. These two choices are represented by techniques $(\mathbf{A}_s, \mathbf{B}_s, \mathbf{l}_s)$ and $(\mathbf{A}_d, \mathbf{B}_d, \mathbf{l}_d)$, respectively ($s$ is for "single shift" and d is for "double shift"). With $\mathbf{p}$ as the price vector of finished goods, r as the rate of profit and π as the price of the one year old machine, the two alternatives are

$$(1+r)(\mathbf{a} + \mathbf{e}_h)^T\mathbf{p}_s + w_s = \mathbf{e}_i^T\mathbf{p}_s + \pi_s \tag{7.9a}$$

$$(1+r)(\mathbf{a}^T\mathbf{p}_s + \pi_s) + w_s = \mathbf{e}_i^T\mathbf{p}_s \tag{7.9b}$$

and

$$(1+r)(\mathbf{a} + \tfrac{1}{2}\mathbf{e}_h)^T\mathbf{p}_d + w_d + \tfrac{1}{2}\alpha w_d = \mathbf{e}_i^T\mathbf{p}_d, \tag{7.10}$$

respectively, where subscripts refer to the operated techniques. Equations (7.9) imply

$$(1 + r)\mathbf{a}^T\mathbf{p}_s + \frac{(1+r)^2}{2+r}\,\mathbf{e}_h^T\mathbf{p}_s + w_s = \mathbf{e}_i^T\mathbf{p}_s. \tag{7.11}$$

The single-shift technique is cost-minimizing and $w_s \geq w_d$ if and only if process $(z + 3)$ is not able to pay extra profits at the prices and wage rate of the single-shift technique. By using equation (7.11) this condition can be stated as

$$(1 + r)\mathbf{a}^T\mathbf{p}_s + \frac{(1+r)^2}{2+r}\,\mathbf{e}_h^T\mathbf{p}_s + w_s \leq (1 + r)(\mathbf{a} + \tfrac{1}{2}\mathbf{e}_h)^T\mathbf{p}_s + w_s + \tfrac{1}{2}\alpha w_s,$$

that is,

$$\frac{r(1 + r)}{2 + r}\,\mathbf{e}_h^T\mathbf{p}_s \leq \alpha w_s.$$

Moreover, Proposition 7.1 ensures that

$$\left(\frac{r(1 + r)}{2 + r}\,\mathbf{e}_h^T\mathbf{p}_s \leq \alpha w_s\right) \Leftrightarrow \left(\frac{r(1 + r)}{2 + r}\,\mathbf{e}_h^T\mathbf{p}_d \leq \alpha w_d\right).$$

Hence, whether the double-shift system proves superior depends on the price of the new machine, the wage premium, the wage rate, and the rate of profit. Moreover, it is irrelevant whether the comparison is made by using the prices and the wage rate of the single-shift or those of the double-shift technique.

While the example given may suffice to illustrate the aspect of the problem of the choice of technique at issue and to explain why rhythmic labor costs can induce firms optimally to schedule the work process intermittently, it of course hides many of the complications involved. However, it should not be difficult for the reader to reformulate specific aspects of the problem within the framework of the present analysis.

8. The plant

In this chapter it has been assumed that machines are not utilized jointly. The case of jointly utilized *old* machines must await Chapter 9, whereas the case in which *new* machines are utilized jointly can be developed within the analytical framework of the present chapter. One could, indeed, with regard to a process of the first degree (which by definition uses finished goods only), take more than one input as representing "new machines." These inputs could then be assembled to constitute a *plant*, so that even if there is only *one old machine*, it does, in fact, consist of more than one "machine" (quotation marks are required since common language rather than the technical language of the rest of the chapter is used).

This assumption, of course, is a strong one, since the cost-minimizing management of the fixed capital stock might well involve separating previously jointly utilized machines and reassembling them differently. There may indeed be cases in which the costs of separating and reassembling components of a plant are sufficiently large as to ensure that the cost-minimizing solution will not involve any such dismantling and reassembling. Further remarks on this issue will be added in Section 6 of Chapter 9.

9. **Historical notes**

9.1. The distinction between fixed and circulating capital is already present, in one way or another, in the contributions of the early economists. In the Physiocrats, Quesnay in particular, we encounter it in terms of the distinction between *avances annuelles*, *avances primitives*, and *avances foncières*: the "annual advances" are circulating capital, the "original advances" are fixed capital of medium longevity (tools and equipment), and the "ground advances" are the capital incorporated in the ground in terms of land melioration, irrigation etc., that is, what Marx called *la terre-capital*. The distinction between fixed and circulating capital is also to be found in Adam Smith (see, in particular, book II of *WN*) who, however, attempted to apply it at the same time to the sphere of production and the sphere of circulation and thus reckoned the money needed for circulating and distributing commodities among the circulating capital.

The earlier authors also saw that fixed capital introduces a complication into the theory of value: while the circulating part of the capital advances contributes entirely to the annual output, that is, "disappears" from the scene, so to speak, the contribution of the durable part is less obvious and can only be imputed in correspondence with what may be considered the wear and tear of fixed capital items. However, the earlier authors had little to offer about how this wear and tear and the related concept of depreciation are to be determined (see Kurz, 1977, ch. V.B). It was not until Ricardo's *Principles* (cf. *Works* I) that the problem of fixed capital began to be dealt with in a way which is more satisfactory analytically.

9.2. As Sraffa pointed out, the method of treating fixed capital as a joint product "fits easily into the classical picture." He added: "It was only after Ricardo had brought to light the complications which the use of fixed capital in various proportions brings to the determination of values that the plan in question was resorted to. It was first introduced by Torrens in the course of a criticism of Ricardo's doctrine. . . . Thereafter the method was generally adopted, even by the opponents of Torrens's theory: first by Ricardo in the next [i.e. third] edition of his *Principles*, then by Malthus in the *Measure of Value* and later by Marx, but afterwards it seems to have fallen into oblivion" (1960, pp. 94–5). In his criticism of Ricardo, referred to by Sraffa, Torrens expounds: "When capitals equal in amount, but of different degrees of durability, are employed, the articles produced, together with the residue of capital, in one occupation will be equal to the things produced, and the residue of capital in another occupation" (1818, p. 337). And in his *Essay on the Production of Wealth*, published in 1821,Torrens illustrates his concept in terms of the following example: "If a woollen and a silk manufacturer were each to employ a capital of 2,000 *l.*; and if the former were to employ 1,500 *l.* in durable machines, and 500 *l.* in wages and materials; while the latter employed only 500 *l.* in durable machines, and 1,500 *l.* in wages and materials; then the results of these equal capitals would, from the law of competition, be of equal exchangeable value; that is, the woollens, with the residue of the fixed capitals employed in preparing them, would be worth the same sum as the silks, with the residue of the fixed capital employed in their manufacture" (1821, p. 28).

9.3. While Ricardo, like Torrens, recognized the possibility of treating fixed capital in terms of the joint production method (see, for example, *Works* I, p. 33), he did not develop it. He rather advocated an approach according to which fixed capital in the course of its utilization gradually "transfers" its value to the commodities produced by means of it. As numerical examples in the first edition of the *Principles* indicate, Ricardo knew the annuity formula

$$Y(r) = p_0(r) \frac{r(1+r)^{t+1}}{(1+r)^{t+1} - 1},$$

which gives the correct annual charge to be paid for interest and depreciation in the special case of a machine operating with constant efficiency throughout its lifetime of $t + 1$ years (cf. *Works* I, pp. 54–62). (It would, of course, have been most surprising had a highly successful stock jobber, like Ricardo, not known this result.) Ricardo was thus also aware of the fact that the pattern of depreciation cannot be ascertained independently of income distribution, that is, the level of the rate of profit.

An early formalization of Ricardo's analysis of fixed capital was provided by Whewell (1831). The most important results of his algebraic treatment of durable instruments of production are (i) the elaboration of a procedure for the reduction of fixed capital to dated quantities of labor; and (ii) the derivation of the annuity formula. Taking Whewell's contribution as a starting point, a somewhat more sophisticated formalization was then provided by Tozer (1838). On the contribution of Whewell and the group of mathematical economists around him, see Campanelli (1982) and Henderson (1985); see also the discussion in Subsection 5.1 of Chapter 13 below.

The problem of fixed capital was also dealt with, and as far as we know quite independently of Whewell and Tozer, by Dmitriev ([1898] 1974) and von Bortkiewicz (1906–7 II, pp. 29–33) who rediscovered the results of their precursors and added some new results. On this tradition of dealing with the problem, see Kurz (1977, ch.V.B) and Sections 2 and 5 of Chapter 13. On von Bortkiewicz's elaboration of Ricardo's "transfer of value" approach, see also Casarosa (1977) and Perri (1990).

9.4. Marx dealt with the problem of fixed capital at length in part II of volume II of *Capital*, "The Turnover of Capital," and also in his analysis of simple and extended reproduction in part III of the same volume (see Marx, [1885] 1956). While his discussion contains several interesting observations, it is essentially limited to the case in which the pure labor theory of value holds. The second part of Marx's contention that the problem of wear and tear "offers peculiar difficulties and has hitherto not been treated at all by the political economists" (ibid., p. 459) cannot, of course, be sustained.

9.5. The opinion that fixed capital poses particular analytical difficulties was not shared by all economists. For example, Walras in Lesson 23 of his *Eléments* stressed with regard to the problem of the wear and tear of capital goods: "Nothing could be simpler than to take [this circumstance] into account mathematically" ([1874] 1954, p. 268). In his view "we need only suppose that whatever sum is necessary for maintaining the capital good intact or for replacing it when it is worn out is deducted from its annual [gross] income and reckoned as proportional to the price of the capital good. This is called the *depreciation* ('*amortissement*') of capital. The amount set aside for this purpose, that is, the *depreciation charge*, will vary with different capital goods; but once this charge has been levied, all capital goods become rigorously identical with respect to impairment through use, since they all become, as it were, permanent" (ibid., p. 268). With P as the price of a new capital good and μ as its annual depreciation, μP is the depreciation charge; μ equals $1/t$, where t is the lifetime of the capital good.

While there is no doubt that this treatment of fixed capital is mathematically simple, from an economic point of view it is unacceptable. In particular, it does not take into account the interest accruing on the depreciation charge from the time when the capital good is first put to productive use to the time when it has to be replaced.

9.6. In Leontief's early input–output model (see Leontief, 1941) the emphasis was on circulating capital; the presence of fixed capital was taken into account via depreciation quotas which were assumed to be included in the coefficients of the (square) input–output matrix **A**. In a later formulation Leontief explicitly considered the stocks of durable instruments of production needed in the production of the different commodities. In addition to the circulating capital matrix **A** he introduced a second (square) matrix **B**, which gives the amount of commodity *j* required as a stock to produce one unit of commodity *i* (see Leontief, 1953). As regards depreciation it is again assumed that it is given exogenously in terms of either a fixed percentage rate of decay of the capital stock in existence or as a fixed share of the initial stock. The former treatment implies "depreciation by evaporation," the latter implies linear depreciation. While for practical reasons these *ad hoc* rules may be the best choices available to the applied economist, they are unsatisfactory from a theoretical point of view. For a detailed exposition of the concept of "depreciation by evaporation," see Section 4 of Chapter 9 and the Historical notes of the same chapter.

9.7. The appropriateness of a joint production framework for an analysis of fixed capital was stressed by von Neumann ([1937] 1945). On von Neumann's model, see Sections 6, 7, and 9 of Chapter 13. Von Neumann's approach to fixed capital was utilized by Morishima in various contributions; see, in particular, Morishima (1969, pp. 89–91, and 1973, ch. 13).

9.8. Sraffa's investigation of fixed capital is contained in Chapter X of Part II of his book. Part II comprises altogether five chapters and deals with "Multiple-Product Industries and Fixed Capital." As Sraffa makes clear, his interest in joint production is predominantly motivated by "its being the genus of which Fixed Capital is the leading species" (1960, p. 63) since he follows the old classical idea of treating old machines left at the end of each period as economically different goods from the machines which entered production at the beginning of the period. His analysis develops in terms of the simplifying assumptions that each process utilizes no more than one old machine, the efficiency of each type of machine being constant. For a discussion of Sraffa's approach and a comparison of it with earlier approaches to fixed capital, see Roncaglia (1971, 1978) and Kurz (1977, ch. V.C).

9.9. Sraffa's model has been generalized by Schefold (1971, 1976c, 1978a, 1980b, 1989), Baldone (1974), and Varri (1974) to cover the case in which the efficiency of the machines is not constant (see also Sraffa, 1960, p. 66), whilst the premise that no process employs more than one old machine has been retained. These authors generally start from a given technique and the "truncations" which can be obtained from it. In the language of the present chapter this means that they consider as existing only the processes of the given technique plus the processes which need to exist because of axiom (vi) of Section 1. The techniques which include these further processes are the *truncations* of the originally given technique. In this way the choice of technique is reduced to the determination of the optimal economic lifetime of machines (see exercises 10.5 and 10.6 for an example).

The possibility of a machine becoming economically obsolete before the end of its technical lifetime is obviously ruled out in cases of constant or increasing efficiency. With decreasing or changing efficiency, however, a problem of the choice of technique, that is, of the *optimal truncation date*, arises. Premature truncation is advantageous as soon as the price (book value) of a partly worn out instrument of production becomes negative. Since the price of a machine (either new or "aged") is equal to the capital value one gets by discounting all future net receipts that may be obtained by further use of it, where the going rate of profit is taken as the discount rate, negative prices would indicate "losses" and would thus contradict the assumption of a fully settled competitive position of the economy. A change in the rate of profit could generally lead to changes in the optimal economic lifetimes of durable instruments of production. More particularly, it is possible that with a complex pattern of the time profile of efficiency the same length of economic life of an instrument is optimal at disconnected intervals of values of the rate of profit, while different lengths are advantageous in between. Here we encounter a variant of the reswitching phenomenon, that is, *the return of the same truncation period* (cf. exercises 10.5 and 10.6). Moreover, it should be clear that concepts such as "keeping the capital stock intact" and hence the notion of "reinvestment" cannot be defined independently of distribution. The model which underlies our above analysis, which is more general than the others, is a simplified version of the model investigated in Kurz and Salvadori (1994b). Important contributions to the theory of fixed capital, taking Sraffa's analysis as their starting point, are collected in Pasinetti (1980), Steedman (1988a, vol. II), and Salvadori and Steedman (1990).

9.10. The pattern of capital utilization was discussed by several earlier authors. See, for example, Marx's following statement which refers to a problem that bears a close resemblance to the one investigated in Section 7: "A prolongation of the working day does not entail any fresh expenditures in this, the most expensive portion of constant capital. Furthermore, the value of the fixed capital is thereby reproduced in a smaller number of turnover periods, so that the time for which it must be advanced to make a certain profit is abbreviated. A prolongation of the working-day therefore increases the profit, even if overtime is paid, or even if, up to a certain point, it is better paid than the normal hours of labour" (Marx, [1894] 1959, p. 77).

For an explicit discussion of the choice of the *system of operation of plant and equipment*, that is, the choice of the pattern of *utilization* of fixed capital, in a Sraffian framework, see Kurz (1986a, 1990c). In this context another variant of the reswitching of techniques can be shown to exist: the *return of the same system of operation of plant and equipment*. On the problem of capital utilization see also the study by Marris (1964), and the neoclassical contributions by Betancourt and Clague (1981) and Winston (1982).

9.11. A serious shortcoming of Böhm–Bawerk's approach to the theory of capital and interest was its limitation to circulating capital only. Various authors working in the Austrian tradition tried to overcome this limitation and to extend the analysis to the case of fixed capital. In doing so, Åkerman (1923–4), who was a student of Wicksell's, attempted to replace Böhm–Bawerk's concept of the "average period of production" with the technical lifetime of a fixed capital item as a measure of capital intensity, where this lifetime itself was considered variable. Wicksell, who in his earlier works (see in particular Wicksell, [1893] 1954 and [1901] 1934) had treated fixed capital in a cavalier way, elaborated on Åkerman's approach (see Wicksell, 1923). For a treatment of the problem of the value of a "balanced plant and equipment" as a proportion of replacement cost, starting from Wicksell's approach, see Champernowne and Kahn (1953–4), reprinted in Robinson (1956); see also Robinson (1959). For a critical account of the contributions by Wicksell and Åkerman, see Swan (1956), Huth (1989), and Garegnani (1990a). Important contributions to the problem of depreciation and the concept of keeping capital intact are collected in Parker and Harcourt (1969).

9.12. In von Hayek's view, capital theory holds the key to an explanation of industrial fluctuations (see von Hayek, 1931 and 1941). In his attempt to reformulate the Austrian approach to the theory of capital and interest, von Hayek was particularly concerned with tackling the problem of fixed capital, a characteristic feature of which consists in the fact that "the investment made at a moment of time gives rise to a *joint supply* of services over a period of time" (von Hayek, 1941, p. 67). While earlier authors belonging to the Austrian tradition were of the opinion that the heterogeneous collection of tools and materials actually in use could be reduced to a scalar quantity in terms of an average lapse of time between productive activities and their consumable result, von Hayek dispensed with this idea, which he considered fallacious. He replaced the traditional concept of the "average period of production" with what he called the "input function" and the "output function," respectively, and which were meant to adequately describe the complexities of the time-structure of production. However, von Hayek's contribution had little impact on the capital theoretic discussions even within circles of Austrian economists, and the analytical instruments he suggested did not make their way into the tool box generally used by economists. On von Hayek's 1941 approach to capital theory, see the contributions by Steedman (1994b) and Meacci (1994).

9.13. Next it was Hicks (1970, 1973), and then Nuti (1973), who studied the problem of fixed capital within an Austrian framework of the analysis; Hicks called his approach "neo-Austrian," According to Hicks fixed capital goods are "durable-*use*-goods" giving rise to intertemporal joint production of a final output at different dates: "their essential characteristic is that they contribute, not just to one unit of output, at one date, but to a sequence of units of output, at a sequence of dates" (Hicks, 1973, p. 8). As Hicks pointed out, taking into account fixed capital implied that some characteristic features of the old Austrian theory had to be abandoned. For example, while with the point input–point output assumption under-lying some of the traditional Austrian doctrine the notion of the degree of "roundaboutness" of a production process could be used as a measure of capital intensity, with flow input–flow output "the whole notion collapses" (ibid., p. 9).[6] With a process going on forever, the notion cannot even be given a clear meaning, whereas in other cases it cannot be presumed that the degree of roundaboutness and the rate of interest are inversely related (see exercise 10.6). Hicks thus dispensed with those Austrian concepts that he considered obsolete and tried to revive those that could be given a logically consistent formulation. He was particularly concerned with establishing, in terms of his "Fundamental Theorem" (1973, pp. 19–26) which is about the optimal truncation of production processes, the uni-queness of the rate of interest, given the wage rate and the technical alternatives of production. Interestingly, he was of the opinion that the uniqueness implies an economic lifetime of a fixed capital good which is inversely related to the rate of interest (see also Nuti, 1973, p. 490), that is, a result which, if it were true, could be seen as reflecting an old Austrian idea in a somewhat "diluted" form. However, as has been shown by Hagemann and Kurz (1976), this opinion is unfounded: the possibility of the return of the same truncation period cannot generally be ruled out even within the neo-Austrian scheme of production (cf. exercise 10.5). This

---

[6] As we have seen in Chapter 6, the notion collapses already in the case of flow input–point output.

finding seems to be sufficient to dispel the idea that a general economic theory can be constructed in "neo-Austrian" terms. On Hicks's approach to fixed capital, see also Burmeister (1974; 1980a, pp. 144–54), Howard (1980), and Kurz (1992a).

10. Exercises

10.1. In order to prove a property stated in Section 3 and utilized in the proof of Proposition 7.3 prove that if D is an $n \times n$ diagonal matrix with elements on the main diagonal all positive, and C is a nonnegative $n \times n$ matrix with positive elements only below the main diagonal, then matrix $(D - C)$ is invertible and its inverse is semipositive. [*Hint*: Apply statement (d) of Theorem A.3.2 of the Mathematical Appendix to the nonnegative matrix $D^{-1}C$. Note that $\det([\lambda I - D^{-1}C]) = \det([\lambda I]) = \lambda^n$: that is, all eigenvalues of matrix $D^{-1}C$ equal zero.]

10.2. (Kurz and Salvadori, 1994b) Let

$$A = \begin{bmatrix} 1 & 0 & 0 & 0 \\ 0 & 1 & 0 & 0 \\ 0 & 0 & 1 & 0 \\ 212 & 0 & 0 & 1 \end{bmatrix}, \quad B = \begin{bmatrix} 0 & 1 & 0 & 0 \\ 55 & 0 & 1 & 0 \\ 2 & 0 & 0 & 1 \\ 216 & 0 & 0 & 0 \end{bmatrix}, \quad l = \begin{bmatrix} 10 \\ 10 \\ 0.1 \\ 0.1 \end{bmatrix}.$$

Show that $\mathbb{R}^*_{(A,B,l)} = \{\rho \in \mathbb{R} \,|\, \text{either } 0 \leqslant \rho \leqslant 1 \text{ or } 2 \leqslant \rho \leqslant 3\}$.

10.3. (Calculus) Prove Theorem 7.3 on the assumption that $l \geqslant 0$ and such that

$$(u^T(B - A) \geqslant 0^T, u \geqslant 0) \Rightarrow u^T l > 0.$$

[*Hint*: See hint to exercise 8.1 of Chapter 5.]

10.4. (Calculus) Prove Proposition 7.1 on the assumption that $l_h \geqslant 0, l_j \geqslant 0$, and such that

$$(u^T(B_h - A_h) + v^T(B_j - A_j) \geqslant 0^T, u \geqslant 0, v \geqslant 0, u^T B_h + v^T B_j \geqslant 0^T)$$
$$\Rightarrow u^T l_h + v^T l_j > 0,$$

but not necessarily $l_h > 0$ and $l_j > 0$. [*Hint*: See hint to exercise 8.1 of Chapter 5.]

10.5. (Hagemann and Kurz, 1976) Show that in an economy with two finished goods (corn and a new tractor) and two old machines (1 and 2 year old tractors) whose processes are given by Table 7.2, the cost-minimizing technique is

(i) the technique made up by processes $(1, 2, 3, 4)$ if $0 \leqslant r \leqslant 0.47$,
(ii) the technique made up by processes $(1, 2, 6)$ if $0.6575 \leqslant r \leqslant 1.215$,

Table 7.2

Pro- ces- ses	material inputs				labor		outputs			
	corn	tractors of age					corn	tractors of age		
		0	1	2				0	1	2
(1)	1	—	—	—	1	→	—	1	—	—
(2)	6	1	—	—	2	→	20	—	1	—
(3)	8.45	—	1	—	3	→	20	—	—	1
(4)	9.850	—	—	1	2	→	20	—	—	—
(5)	6	1	—	—	2	→	20	—	—	—
(6)	8.45	—	1	—	3	→	20	—	—	—

Table 7.3

Processes	material inputs			labor		outputs		
	corn	tractors of age				corn	tractors of age	
		0	1				0	1
(1)	0.5	—	—	1	→	1	—	—
(2)	$\frac{31}{504}$	—	—	$\frac{3}{140}$	→	—	1	—
(3)	0.25	1	—	1	→	0.5	—	1
(4)	$\frac{2}{315}$	—	1	$\frac{1}{3}$	→	0.5	—	—
(5)	0.25	1	—	1	→	0.5	—	—

(iii) the technique made up by processes $(1, 5)$ if $0.47 \leqslant r \leqslant 0.6575$ or $1.215 \leqslant r \leqslant R$, where $R \cong 1.385$.

10.6. (Schefold, 1976c) Show that in the economy with two finished goods (corn and a new tractor) and one old machine (1 year old tractor) whose processes are depicted in Table 7.3 the cost-minimizing technique is

(i) the technique made up by processes $(2, 3, 4)$ if $0 \leqslant r \leqslant 0.25$ or $0.5 \leqslant r \leqslant 0.75$,

(ii) the technique made up by process (1) if $0.25 \leqslant r \leqslant 0.5$ or $0.75 \leqslant r \leqslant 1$.

The production of corn with the technique made up by processes $(2, 3, 4)$ can be considered more "roundabout" than the production of corn with the technique consisting of process (1). What does this example imply with regard to the view expressed in traditional Austrian capital theory that the rate of profit (the rate of interest) and the roundaboutness of techniques chosen are inversely related?

10.7. Let the processes producing commodity i in technique $(\mathbf{A}, \mathbf{B}, \mathbf{l})$ be as described in Table 7.4. Determine the core process of commodity i. Assume that the finished good h is the "new machine" of the type utilized

Table 7.4

Proces-	material inputs		labor		outputs	
ses	finished goods	old machines			finished goods	old machines
$(z+1)$	$a + e_h$	0	1	$\rightarrow$	e_i	e_{k+1}
$(z+2)$	a	e_{k+1}	1	$\rightarrow$	e_i	e_{k+2}
$(\dots)$	$\dots$	$\dots$	$\dots$	$\rightarrow$	$\dots$	$\dots$
$(z+j)$	a	e_{k+j-1}	1	$\rightarrow$	e_i	e_{k+j}
$(\dots)$	$\dots$	$\dots$	$\dots$	$\rightarrow$	$\dots$	$\dots$
$(z+s_i)$	a	e_{k+s_i-1}	1	$\rightarrow$	e_i	0

in the production of commodity i. Then show that such a machine has a constant efficiency whatever is the age of the machine and whatever is the rate of profit. Provide an economic interpretation of the "coefficients" of the core process.

10.8. Consider a fixed capital technology where each type of machine operates with constant efficiency whatever the age of the machine and whatever the rate of profit (as in the previous exercise). Determine the form of the core-format for a typical technique.

10.9. Let

$$A = mI, \quad B = \begin{bmatrix} qe & mI \\ q & 0^T \end{bmatrix}, \quad l = e,$$

where matrices A and B are $n \times n$, vector l is $n \times 1$, q and m are positive scalars, the identity matrix I and the sum vector e have the appropriate size. Only commodity 1 is consumed. Show that axioms (i)–(v) of Section 1 hold, commodity 1 is a finished good, and commodities $2, 3, \dots, n$ are old machines. Then show that if commodity 1 is at the same time the new machine, then the efficiency of the machine is constant. Finally, if commodity 1 is the numeraire, then

$$w = q - ma(r),$$

where

$$a(r) = \frac{r(1+r)^n}{(1+r)^n - 1}.$$

10.10. Argue that the assumptions of the previous exercise can be interpreted as follows: there is only one commodity (in the ordinary sense) which can either be consumed or used as a produced input; in the latter case, the efficiency of the capital input is constant during the n years.

10.11. (Calculus) Show that on the assumptions of exercise 10.9, if $qn \geqslant m$, then $\mathbb{R}^*_{(A,B,l)} \neq \varnothing$. Prove that the equation

$$\frac{q}{m} = a(R)$$

has a unique positive solution and show that this solution is the maximum rate of profit R.

10.12. On the assumptions of exercise 10.9, let k be the capital per capita and let y be the income per capita. Show that

$$k = m\frac{a(r) - a(g)}{r - g},$$

$$y = q - m\frac{ra(g) - ga(r)}{r - g}.$$

10.13. (Steedman, 1994a) Assume that there are several techniques of the type defined in exercise 10.9 with $n = 10, 4.903 \leqslant m \leqslant 5.202$, and

$$q = 45.613594\sqrt{m} - 10m - 50.5.$$

Then show that the wage frontier is

$$w = \frac{5.05[0.3 - a(r)]}{10 + a(r)},$$

and the k–r relationship is

$$k = \frac{10403}{20[10 + a(r)]^2}\frac{a(r) - a(g)}{r - g}.$$

Finally, show that if $g = 0$, then the y–k relationship is increasing, but if $g = 0.04$, then the y–k relationship is decreasing.

8

Joint production

Much of economic analysis has concentrated on single-product processes of production. This preoccupation with single production seems to be based on either or both of the following premises. First, single production is empirically far more important than joint production. Since from this point of view joint production is a *curiosum*, its study implies a search for generality for its own sake. Second, the results derived within a single-product framework essentially carry over to the joint products case. Hence the analysis of joint production systems is unrewarding since it does not substantially improve our understanding of economic phenomena.

While empirical investigations have undermined the first premise, theoretical analysis has raised doubts about the correctness of the second. The view that these cases of joint production, far from being "some peculiar cases," as John Stuart Mill tended to assume, "form the general rule, to which it is difficult to point out any clear or important exception" had been already advocated a century ago by William Stanley Jevons ([1871] 1965, p. 198); see also Steedman (1984a). However, from the point of view of economic theory, whether or not joint production is predominant in the "real world" does not appear to be that important. This follows from the fact that the presence of even one multiple-product process of production in an otherwise single-product system can qualitatively alter some of the characteristic features of the system as a whole (cf. exercises 8.10 and 8.11). Hence the simple fact that joint production exists at all, and is very common indeed, should suffice to make economists investigate it carefully.

The structure of the present chapter is as follows. In Section 1 a few numerical examples are discussed to illustrate the fact that certain properties of single product systems of production need not hold in the case of joint production; emphasis is on the impact of the requirements for use, or "demand," on relative prices. Section 2 introduces the direct and the indirect approaches, respectively. Section 3 is devoted to an analysis of the case in which the uniform rate of growth is equal to the rate of profit, whereas Section 4 deals with the case in which the growth rate may be smaller than the rate of profit. Section 5 draws the reader's attention to more general models. While Sections 3–5 deal only with the direct approach, Section 6 is concerned with elements of the indirect one. Sections 7 and 8 contain historical notes and exercises, respectively.

1. **Joint production and demand: Some examples**

In single product models analyzed in Chapters 2–6, if s commodities are involved in production, then at least s processes must be operated. As a consequence, if the rate of profit is uniform, in each technique prices of produced commodities are uniquely determined: a number of processes equal to the number of involved commodities means a number of equations equal to the unknowns to be ascertained. Moreover, a cost-minimizing technique is determined independently of the amounts of commodities required for use. These properties, as well as some others, do not hold when joint product processes are introduced into the picture. Some simple examples can clarify this point.

Example 8.1. Let us consider a two commodity world where there are three processes which are specified as in Table 8.1. The growth rate is taken to be equal to zero, the rate of profit to 1; capitalists are assumed to spend their entire income on silk only and workers on corn only.

Let x_j be the intensity of operation of process j ($j = 1, 2, 3$); let p_c and p_s be the prices of corn and silk, respectively; and let w be the wage rate. Then the following equations and inequalities need to be satisfied:

$$2(x_1 + x_2)p_c = w(x_1 + x_2 + x_3), \tag{8.1a}$$

$$2(x_1 + x_3)p_s = (x_1 + x_2 + x_3)(p_c + p_s), \tag{8.1b}$$

$$3(p_c + p_s) \leqslant w + 2(p_c + p_s), \tag{8.1c}$$

$$3p_c \leqslant w + 2(p_c + p_s), \tag{8.1d}$$

$$3p_s \leqslant w + 2(p_c + p_s), \tag{8.1e}$$

$$3(p_c + p_s)x_1 = [w + 2(p_c + p_s)]x_1, \tag{8.1f}$$

$$3p_c x_2 = [w + 2(p_c + p_s)]x_2, \tag{8.1g}$$

$$3p_s x_3 = [w + 2(p_c + p_s)]x_3, \tag{8.1h}$$

$$x_1 \geqslant 0, \quad x_2 \geqslant 0, \quad x_3 \geqslant 0, \quad x_1 + x_2 + x_3 > 0, \tag{8.1i}$$

Table 8.1

processes	inputs				outputs	
	corn	silk	labor		corn	silk
(1)	1	1	1	→	3	3
(2)	1	1	1	→	3	0
(3)	1	1	1	→	0	3

$$p_c + p_s = 1. \tag{8.1j}$$

Equations (8.1a) and (8.1b) imply that the requirements for use are satisfied. Inequalities (8.1c)–(8.1e) imply that no process is able to pay extra profits. Equations (8.1f)–(8.1h) imply, also because of inequalities (8.1i), that if a process is not able to pay the rate of profit $r = 1$, it is not operated. Inequalities (8.1i) imply that no process can be operated at a negative level and at least one process is operated. Equation (8.1j) fixes the numeraire.

It is immediately obtained that x_1 cannot vanish. In fact, if $x_1 = 0$ and either $x_2 = 0$ or $x_3 = 0$, then either equation (8.1a) and inequality (8.1c) or equations (8.1b) and (8.1j) are contradicted, respectively. If, moreover, $x_1 = 0$ and x_2 and x_3 are both positive, then equations (8.1g), (8.1h), and (8.1j) determine

$$p_c = p_s = \tfrac{1}{2}, \quad w = -\tfrac{1}{2},$$

which contradict inequality (8.1d). If $x_1 > 0$, neither x_2 nor x_3 can be positive. If $x_2 > 0$, then $p_s = 0$, $w = p_c = 1$, because of equations (8.1f), (8.1g), and (8.1j), which contradict equation (8.1b). If $x_3 > 0$, then $p_c = 0$, $w = p_s = 1$, because of equations (8.1f), (8.1h), and (8.1j), which contradict equation (8.1a). If $x_1 > 0$, $x_2 = x_3 = 0$, then equations (8.1a), (8.1b), and (8.1f) are not linearly independent and the following solutions are immediately obtained:

$$w = 2p_c = 2p_s,$$

which also satisfy the weak inequalities (8.1c)–(8.1e). Hence, because of equation (8.1j):

$$w = 1, \quad p_c = p_s = \tfrac{1}{2}.$$

If the demand by capitalists were 5 units of silk for each unit of corn consumed, and the demand by workers were 5 units of corn for each unit of silk consumed, then equations (8.1a) and (8.1b) would have to be replaced by the following equations

$$2(x_1 + x_2) = \frac{5w(x_1 + x_2 + x_3)}{5p_c + p_s} + \frac{(x_1 + x_2 + x_3)(p_c + p_s)}{p_c + 5p_s} \qquad (8.2a)$$

$$2(x_1 + x_3) = \frac{w(x_1 + x_2 + x_3)}{5p_c + p_s} + \frac{5(x_1 + x_2 + x_3)(p_c + p_s)}{p_c + 5p_s}, \qquad (8.2b)$$

with the other equations and inequalities still holding. Once again x_2 and x_3 cannot be positive. If $x_1 > 0$, $x_2 = x_3 = 0$, then equations (8.2a), (8.2b), and (8.1f) are not linearly independent and the following solutions are immediately obtained

$$15w = 40p_s = 24p_c,$$

which satisfy also the weak inequalities (8.1c)–(8.1e). Hence, because of equation (8.1j):

$$w = 1, p_c = \tfrac{5}{8}, p_s = \tfrac{3}{8}.$$

Prices are changed "merely" because of a change in "demand." But this is a very special example. The trick consists in the fact that workers consume more corn than silk and capitalists consume more silk than corn: gross profit and gross wages adapt themselves in order to guarantee that neither corn nor silk, which are produced by process (1) in the proportion 1:1, are overproduced: this gives rise to an equation which jointly with the equation due to the operation of process (1) determines prices. This example shows that with joint production "demand" may play an important role in determining prices, and that a technique cannot be defined simply with reference to consumed commodities. What matters is not only whether a commodity is consumed or not, but also the way it is consumed: the proportion in which it is consumed relative to other commodities, whether these proportions depend on prices and/or incomes, etc.

The reader must not think that "demand" can matter only when the number of operated processes is smaller than the number of commodities involved. While with the number of processes equal to the number of commodities involved small changes in demand will generally not affect prices, this need not always be true. Another simple example can clarify this point.

Example 8.2. Let us consider a pair of two commodity worlds. In both worlds there are three processes which are specified in Table 8.2. The growth rate is set equal to zero, the rate of profit is set equal to 1. In the first world corn and silk are consumed in the proportion 2:1, whereas in the second world they are consumed in the proportion 1:2.

Table 8.2

processes	inputs				outputs	
	corn	silk	labor		corn	silk
(1)	1	1	1	→	3	3
(2)	1	1	1	→	5	0
(3)	1	1	1	→	0	5

Let x_j be the intensity of operation of process j ($j = 1, 2, 3$); let p_c and p_s be the prices of corn and silk, respectively; let r be the rate of profit; and let w be the wage rate. Then in the first world the following equations and inequalities need to be satisfied:

$$2x_1 + 4x_2 - x_3 = 2\alpha, \tag{8.3a}$$

$$2x_1 - x_2 + 4x_3 = \alpha, \tag{8.3b}$$

$$3(p_c + p_s) \leqslant w + 2r(p_c + p_s), \tag{8.3c}$$

$$5p_c \leqslant w + 2r(p_c + p_s), \tag{8.3d}$$

$$5p_s \leqslant w + 2r(p_c + p_s), \tag{8.3e}$$

$$3(p_c + p_s)x_1 = [w + 2r(p_c + p_s)]x_1, \tag{8.3f}$$

$$5p_c x_2 = [w + 2r(p_c + p_s)]x_2, \tag{8.3g}$$

$$5p_s x_3 = [w + 2r(p_c + p_s)]x_3, \tag{8.3h}$$

$$x_1 \geqslant 0, \quad x_2 \geqslant 0, \quad x_3 \geqslant 0, \quad x_1 + x_2 + x_3 > 0, \tag{8.3i}$$

$$p_c + p_s = 1. \tag{8.3j}$$

Equations (8.3a) and (8.3b) imply that the requirements for use are satisfied, $\alpha > 0$ being a variable related to the size of the economy which, however, is not determined within this model. Inequalities (8.3c), (8.3d), and (8.3e) imply that no process is able to pay extra profits. Equations (8.3e), (8.3f), and (8.3g) imply, also because of inequalities (8.3i), that if a process is not able to pay the rate of profit $r = 1$, it will not be operated. Inequalities (8.3i) imply that no process can be operated at a negative level and at least one process is operated. Equation (8.3j) fixes the numeraire.

At least one of the x's must be zero because of equations (8.3f)–(8.3h). If $x_1 = 0$, then $x_2 > 0$ and $x_3 > 0$ because of equations (8.3a) and (8.3b). Then equations (8.3g), (8.3h), and (8.3j) determine

$$w = p_c = p_s = \tfrac{1}{2},$$

which contradict inequality (8.3c). Hence $x_1 > 0$. If $x_2 = 0$, then $x_3 < 0$ because of equations (8.3a) and (8.3b). Then one of the inequalities (8.3i) is contradicted. Hence $x_2 > 0$. If $x_3 = 0$, then $x_1 > 0$ and $x_2 > 0$ because of equations (8.3a) and (8.3b). Then equations (8.3f), (8.3g), and (8.3j) determine

$$w = 1, \quad p_c = \tfrac{3}{5}, \quad p_s = \tfrac{2}{5},$$

which also satisfy inequality (8.3e). In the second world the following equations should hold instead of equations (8.1a) and (8.1b):

$$2x_1 + 4x_2 - x_3 = \alpha \tag{8.4a}$$

$$2x_1 - x_2 + 4x_3 = 2\alpha, \tag{8.4b}$$

the other equations and inequalities still holding. The same procedure will determine

$$x_1 > 0, \quad x_2 = 0, \quad x_3 > 0$$

and

$$w = 1, \quad p_c = \tfrac{2}{5}, \quad p_s = \tfrac{3}{5}.$$

A change in "demand" may have some impact on which processes will and which will not be operated, and via this route may exert some influence on the determination of prices. The interested reader is invited to check that if more than one unit of corn is consumed per unit of silk, then the relevant prices will be that of the first world; whereas if more than one unit of silk is consumed per unit of corn, then the relevant prices will be that of the second world. Hence prices change spasmodically even though demand is assumed to change continuously. But what happens if the proportion in which corn and silk are consumed equals 1:1? It is easily checked that

$$x_1 > 0, \quad x_2 = 0, \quad x_3 = 0$$

and

$$w = 1, \quad \tfrac{2}{5} \leqslant p_c \leqslant \tfrac{3}{5}, \quad p_s = 1 - p_c.$$

This result will not surprise the reader of Chapter 5 of this book. Something similar has been encountered in Subsection 3.4 of that chapter with regard to *non-produced* commodities. The difference is that in the present context prices of *produced* commodities may not be uniquely determined: what is determined is a range within which they can assume any value (see also exercise 8.4).

It is perhaps useful to study yet another example to illustrate the results derived from the previous two examples.

Example 8.3. Consider a two commodity world where there are three processes which are defined by Table 8.2; the growth rate equals zero; capitalists consume only silk and workers consume only corn.

Equations (8.3c)–(8.3j) hold jointly with equations

$$(2x_1 + 4x_2 - x_3)p_c = w(x_1 + x_2 + x_3) \tag{8.5a}$$

$$(2x_1 - x_2 + 4x_3)p_s = r(x_1 + x_2 + x_3)(p_c + p_s). \tag{8.5b}$$

The reader will recognize easily that if $0 \leqslant r \leqslant \frac{4}{5}$, then

$$x_1 > 0, \quad x_2 = \frac{4 - 5r}{2 + 5r}x_1, \quad x_3 = 0$$

and

$$w = 2 - r, \quad p_c = \tfrac{3}{5}, \quad p_s = \tfrac{2}{5}.$$

However, if $\frac{4}{5} \leqslant r \leqslant \frac{6}{5}$, then

$$x_1 > 0, \quad x_2 = 0, \quad x_3 = 0$$

and

$$w = 2 - r, \quad p_c = \frac{2 - r}{2}, \quad p_s = \frac{r}{2}.$$

Finally, if $\frac{6}{5} \leqslant r \leqslant 2$, then

$$x_1 > 0, \quad x_2 = 0, \quad x_3 = \frac{5r - 6}{12 - 5r}x_1$$

and

$$w = 2 - r, \quad p_c = \tfrac{2}{5}, \quad p_s = \tfrac{3}{5}.$$

If the rate of profit is high or low small changes in demand will not affect prices, but if the rate of profit is between $\frac{4}{5}$ and $\frac{6}{5}$, then even infinitesimal changes in demand will affect prices. As a sort of compensation, correspondences are not needed to describe the relationships between prices and distribution: functions will do.

2. Joint production and demand: The direct and the indirect approach

Let there be a finite number of commodities (say n) and a number of processes. A *process* is defined by a triplet $(\mathbf{a}, \mathbf{b}, l)$, where $\mathbf{a}$ is a vector whose elements $a_1, a_2, \ldots, a_n$ are the amounts of commodities $1, 2, \ldots, n$ which, jointly with the amount of labor l, produce the amounts of commodities $b_1, b_2, \ldots, b_n$, which are the elements of the vector $\mathbf{b}$. It will be assumed that

(i) $\mathbf{a} \geqslant 0$, $\mathbf{b} \geqslant 0$, $l \geqslant 0$;
(ii) for each commodity there is at least one process by means of which it can be produced;

(iii) it is not possible to produce a nonnegative net product without employing a positive amount of labor.

When dealing with single production it was quite natural to study first a situation where the number of processes was just sufficient to determine both prices and produced quantities once the rate of profit on the one hand and demand on the other were taken as given. This procedure has been confirmed for simple fixed capital models in Chapter 7. But can we follow the same procedure in the case of joint production? Certainly we could, but is it convenient? The examples of the previous section should have clarified that (i) demand is a determinant of the operated processes, and (ii) once the processes that are to be operated are ascertained demand can still play some role in the determination of prices. Hence it appears to be appropriate to explore a different procedure.

A "technique" and a "cost-minimizing technique at rate of profit r" could be defined in the following way.

Definition 8.1. Let the nonnegative vector $\mathbf{d} \in \mathbb{R}^n$ define requirements for use, and let $(\mathbf{a}_i, \mathbf{b}_i, l_i)$, $i = 1, 2, \ldots, s$, be s processes, $1 \leqslant s \leqslant n$. Then the triplet $(\mathbf{A}, \mathbf{B}, \mathbf{l})$, where

$$
\mathbf{A} = \begin{bmatrix} \mathbf{a}_1^T \\ \mathbf{a}_2^T \\ \vdots \\ \mathbf{a}_s^T \end{bmatrix}, \quad
\mathbf{B} = \begin{bmatrix} \mathbf{b}_1^T \\ \mathbf{b}_2^T \\ \vdots \\ \mathbf{b}_s^T \end{bmatrix}, \quad
\mathbf{l} = \begin{bmatrix} l_1 \\ l_2 \\ \vdots \\ l_s \end{bmatrix},
$$

will be called a *technique* (or a *system of production*) if each semipositive vector $\mathbf{x}$ such that

$$
\mathbf{x}^T[\mathbf{B} - \mathbf{A}] = \mathbf{d}^T \tag{8.6}
$$

is actually positive and there is at least one such vector. It should be stressed that vector $\mathbf{d}$, mentioned in Definition 8.1, need not be constant; it could, for example, be thought of as a function of the rate of profit, the wage rate, the price vector, the intensity vector, the labor input vector, the input matrix, and the output matrix.

The prices of production for each system of production are defined by the following equations (jointly with equation (8.6) if $\mathbf{d}$ is a function of $\mathbf{p}$):

$$
\mathbf{B}\mathbf{p} = (1 + r)\mathbf{A}\mathbf{p} + w\mathbf{l} \tag{8.7a}
$$

$$
\mathbf{q}^T\mathbf{p} = 1, \tag{8.7b}
$$

where $\mathbf{p}$ is the price vector, r is the rate of profit, and w is the wage rate. Vector $\mathbf{d}$ cannot be used to define the numeraire since it is a variable vector, but any semipositive vector $\mathbf{q}$ whose positive elements refer to commodities which are certainly produced can perform this task. A cost-minimizing technique is then defined as a technique at whose prices no set of known processes can be operated in order to obtain extra profits.

Definition 8.2. The technique $(\mathbf{A}_k, \mathbf{B}_k, \mathbf{l}_k)$ is *cost-minimizing* at rate of profit r if and only if

$$[\mathbf{B}_j - (1 + r)\mathbf{A}_j]\mathbf{p}_{kj} \lessgtr w_k \mathbf{l}_j, \quad \text{each}(\mathbf{A}_j, \mathbf{B}_j, \mathbf{l}_j) \in J$$

where J is the set of all existing techniques and $(\mathbf{p}_{kj}, w_k)$ are determined by the following equations (jointly with the analog of equation (8.6) if $\mathbf{d}$ is a function of $\mathbf{p}$):

$$[\mathbf{B}_{kj} - (1 + r)\mathbf{A}_{kj}]\mathbf{p}_{kj} = w_k \mathbf{l}_{kj}$$
$$\mathbf{q}^T \mathbf{p}_{kj} = 1,$$

where $(\mathbf{A}_{kj}, \mathbf{B}_{kj}, \mathbf{l}_{kj})$ is the set of processes made up of all the processes in $(\mathbf{A}_k, \mathbf{B}_k, \mathbf{l}_k)$ and a number of processes in $(\mathbf{A}_j, \mathbf{B}_j, \mathbf{l}_j)$ equal to the number of commodities produced by processes in $(\mathbf{A}_j, \mathbf{B}_j, \mathbf{l}_j)$ and not produced by processes in $(\mathbf{A}_k, \mathbf{B}_k, \mathbf{l}_k)$, and involving all these commodities either as inputs or outputs.

The approach just sketched is what in previous chapters has been called the *indirect* approach. But there is also the *direct* approach which consists of determining vectors $\mathbf{p}$ and $\mathbf{x}$ and scalar w such that

$$[\mathbf{B} - (1 + r)\mathbf{A}]\mathbf{p} \lessgtr w\mathbf{l}, \tag{8.8a}$$

$$\mathbf{x}^T[\mathbf{B} - (1 + r)\mathbf{A}]\mathbf{p} = w\mathbf{x}^T \mathbf{l}, \tag{8.8b}$$

$$\mathbf{x}^T[\mathbf{B} - \mathbf{A}] = \mathbf{d}^T, \tag{8.8c}$$

$$\mathbf{x} \geqslant \mathbf{0}, \quad w \geqslant 0, \quad \mathbf{q}^T\mathbf{p} = 1, \tag{8.8d}$$

where $(\mathbf{A}, \mathbf{B}, \mathbf{l})$ represents the set of all available processes. Vector $\mathbf{p}$ is referred to as the price vector, vector $\mathbf{x}$ as the intensity vector, and scalar w as the wage rate. If $(\mathbf{p}^*, \mathbf{x}^*, w^*)$ is a solution of the system of equations and inequalities (8.8), then we say that there is a cost-minimizing technique, and $\mathbf{p}^*$ $(\mathbf{x}^*, w^*)$ is referred to as the *long-period price vector* (*intensity vector, wage rate*).

In accordance with what has been stated at the beginning of this section, matrices $\mathbf{A}$ and $\mathbf{B}$ and vector $\mathbf{l}$ satisfy the following assumptions:

Assumption 8.1. It is not possible to produce something without using some material inputs, that is,

$$\mathbf{e}_j^T \mathbf{A} \geqslant \mathbf{0}. \quad j = 1, 2, \ldots, m$$

Assumption 8.2. All commodities are producible, that is,

$$\mathbf{B}\mathbf{e}_j \geqslant \mathbf{0}. \quad j = 1, 2, \ldots, n$$

Assumption 8.3. Labor is indispensable for the reproduction of commodities, that is,

$$(\mathbf{x} \geqq \mathbf{0}, \mathbf{x}^T(\mathbf{B} - \mathbf{A}) \geqq \mathbf{0}) \Rightarrow \mathbf{x}^T\mathbf{l} > 0.$$

It has not been required that

$$\mathbf{p} \geqq \mathbf{0},$$

since prices do not need to be nonnegative in general if there is no free disposal of all commodities. Despite its problematic character we shall, in the following discussion, assume free disposal.

Assumption 8.4 (free disposal). For each process producing commodity i jointly with commodity j $(i \neq j)$ there is another process with the same outputs and the same inputs except that commodity i is not produced $(i, j = 1, 2, \ldots, n)$.[1]

The reader who, for perfectly good reasons, is unwilling to follow us in this regard may instead have recourse to an alternative which is analogous to the one presented in Section 5 of Chapter 7. In this case prices do not need to be nonnegative, but a minimum negative level for each long-period price is obtained. Exercise 8.6 shows that an existence theorem which holds when there is free disposal need not hold in the absence of it.

3. A uniform growth rate equal to the rate of profit

In Chapters 2–3 and 5 two approaches to the problem of the choice of technique have been suggested and explored. In Chapter 7 a special case of a joint production model has been analyzed: a used machine is produced jointly with a finished good with no other element of joint production involved. However, in Chapter 7 only the indirect approach has been used. In this chapter, on the contrary, only the direct approach will be considered. The reader should have understood from the previous two sections that when general joint production is allowed for, the indirect approach is markedly more difficult to handle than the direct approach. Moreover, the indirect approach finds its *raison d'être* in the separation of price formation from the choice of technique, that is, in the possibility of splitting a complex issue in two simpler issues. Therefore, in dealing with joint production, it seems quite natural to abandon the indirect approach and focus attention on the direct approach only. (However, we

---

[1] The reader will notice that in example 8.1 of Section 1 above processes (2) and (3) relative to process (1) satisfy the assumption of free disposal with respect to silk and corn, respectively.

shall see in Section 6 that a combined use of both the direct and the indirect approach prove to be helpful in some cases.)

In the previous two sections we have seen that "demand" matters in determining prices: we need to know not only which commodities are consumed and which are not, as in the case of single production with non-basics and in the case of fixed capital models; in addition we need to know the exact proportions in which the commodities are consumed and in which they are required for investment purposes. The simplest case to be studied is the case in which commodities are always consumed in the same proportions and net investment is undertaken such that the growth rate equals the rate of profit. The present section will be devoted to an analysis of this constellation. The following section will deal with the case in which commodities are still consumed in given proportions, but the growth rate is lower than the rate of profit. A more general case will be referred to in the next but one section.

If commodities are always consumed in proportion to vector $\mathbf{c}$ and investment is undertaken such that the growth rate equals the rate of profit r, then the vector $\mathbf{d}$ of equation (8.8c) is given by

$$\mathbf{d}^T = r\mathbf{x}^T\mathbf{A} + \alpha\mathbf{c}^T,$$

where $\alpha \geqslant 0$ is determined by the size of the economy and is considered here as given. Under these circumstances it is convenient to fix the numeraire in such a way that $\mathbf{q} = \mathbf{c}$ in equation (8.8d), which implies that the numeraire is defined in terms of commodities which will certainly be produced. Finally, the analysis is greatly simplified by neglecting the case in which $w = 0$ and/or $\alpha = 0$. In this case system (8.8) can be written:

$$[\mathbf{B} - (1+r)\mathbf{A}]\mathbf{p} \leqslant w\mathbf{l}, \tag{8.9a}$$

$$\mathbf{x}^T[\mathbf{B} - (1+r)\mathbf{A}]\mathbf{p} = w\mathbf{x}^T\mathbf{l}, \tag{8.9b}$$

$$\mathbf{x}^T[\mathbf{B} - (1+r)\mathbf{A}] = \alpha\mathbf{c}^T, \tag{8.9c}$$

$$\mathbf{x} \geqslant \mathbf{0}, w > 0, \alpha > 0, \mathbf{c}^T\mathbf{p} = 1. \tag{8.9d}$$

Lemma 8.1. The system of inequalities (8.9) admits a solution if and only if the following system of inequalities admits a solution:

$$[\mathbf{B} - (1+r)\mathbf{A}]\mathbf{y} \leqslant \mathbf{l}, \tag{8.10a}$$

$$\mathbf{z}^T[\mathbf{B} - (1+r)\mathbf{A}]\mathbf{y} = \mathbf{z}^T\mathbf{l}, \tag{8.10b}$$

$$\mathbf{z}^T[\mathbf{B} - (1+r)\mathbf{A}] \geqslant \mathbf{c}^T, \tag{8.10c}$$

$$\mathbf{z}^T[\mathbf{B} - (1+r)\mathbf{A}]\mathbf{y} = \mathbf{c}^T\mathbf{y}, \tag{8.10d}$$

$$\mathbf{y} \geqslant \mathbf{0}, \quad \mathbf{z} \geqslant \mathbf{0}. \tag{8.10e}$$

230 Theory of production

Proof. If $(\mathbf{p}^*, w^*, \mathbf{x}^*)$ is a solution to system (8.9), then $(\mathbf{y}^*, \mathbf{z}^*)$, where

$$\mathbf{y}^* = \frac{1}{w^*}\mathbf{p}^*, \quad \mathbf{z}^* = \frac{1}{\alpha}\mathbf{x}^*,$$

is a solution to system (8.10). Let $(\mathbf{y}^*, \mathbf{z}^*)$ be a solution of system (8.10), then

$$\mathbf{z}^{*T}[\mathbf{B} - (1 + r)\mathbf{A}] \geqslant \mathbf{c}^T.$$

If

$$\mathbf{z}^{*T}[\mathbf{B} - (1 + r)\mathbf{A}]\mathbf{e}_i > \mathbf{c}^T\mathbf{e}_i,$$

then $\mathbf{e}_i^T\mathbf{y}^* = 0$, as a consequence of equation (8.10d). Then, because of the free disposal assumption, there is another solution to system (8.10), $(\mathbf{y}^*, \mathbf{z}^{**})$, such that

$$\mathbf{z}^{**T}[\mathbf{B} - (1 + r)\mathbf{A}] = \mathbf{c}^T.$$

Therefore vectors $\mathbf{x}^* = \alpha\mathbf{z}^{**}$, $\mathbf{p}^* = (1/\mathbf{d}^T\mathbf{y}^*)\mathbf{y}^*$ and $w^* = (1/\mathbf{d}^T\mathbf{y}^*)$ constitute a solution to system (8.9). This completes the proof. Q.E.D.

Lemma 8.2. System (8.10) has a solution if and only if there is a nonnegative vector $\mathbf{v}$ such that

$$\mathbf{v}^T[\mathbf{B} - (1 + r)\mathbf{A}] \geqslant \mathbf{c}^T. \tag{8.11}$$

Proof. The "only if" part of the Lemma is trivial. In order to prove the "if" part, let us remark that by the Equilibrium Theorem of Linear Programming (cf. Theorem A.4.3 of the Mathematical Appendix) we obtain that system (8.10) is equivalent to each of the following Linear Programming Problems, which are dual to each other.

	(primal)		(dual)
Min	$\mathbf{z}^T\mathbf{l}$	Max	$\mathbf{c}^T\mathbf{y}$
s. to	$\mathbf{z}^T[\mathbf{B} - (1 + r)\mathbf{A}] \geqslant \mathbf{c}^T$	s. to	$[\mathbf{B} - (1 + r)\mathbf{A}]\mathbf{y} \leqslant \mathbf{l}$
	$\mathbf{z} \geqslant \mathbf{0}$,		$\mathbf{y} \geqslant \mathbf{0}$.

Since the zero vector is a feasible solution to the dual and since the primal has a feasible solution by hypothesis, both problems have optimal solutions because of the Duality Theorem of Linear Programming. Q.E.D.

Theorem 8.1. If commodities are consumed in proportion to vector $\mathbf{c}$ and a uniform growth rate equal to the rate of profit holds, then at the rate of profit r

- (a) there is a cost-minimizing technique if and only if there is a nonnegative vector $\mathbf{v}$ such that inequality (8.11) holds;
- (b) the long-period wage rate w^* is the minimum w for which there is a vector $\mathbf{p}$ such that inequalities (8.9a) and (8.9d) are satisfied.

Proof. Statement (a) is a direct consequence of Lemmas 8.1 and 8.2. By exploring the proofs of Lemmas 8.1 and 8.2 we obtain that $w^* = (1/\mathbf{d}^T\mathbf{y}^*)$ and $\mathbf{p}^* = w^*\mathbf{y}^*$, where $\mathbf{y}^*$ is a solution to the dual problem in the proof of Lemma 8.2.   Q.E.D.

The results obtained in this case are not that much different from those obtained in Chapter 5. The reason for this is that it was possible to use linear programming. In Chapter 5 it could be shown that if the growth rate is lower than the rate of profit and/or commodities are consumed in different proportions, then a solution with unchanged prices could be found by just varying the intensity vector $\mathbf{x}$. It is this fact which is not necessarily true when joint production is allowed for. Solutions have to be found in a different way.

4. A uniform growth rate lower than the rate of profit

If commodities are always consumed in proportion to vector $\mathbf{c}$ and investment is undertaken such that a uniform growth rate g lower than the rate of profit r obtains, then the vector $\mathbf{d}$ of equation (8.8c) is

$$\mathbf{d}^T = g\mathbf{x}^T\mathbf{A} + \alpha\mathbf{c}^T,$$

where $g < r$ is given and $\alpha \geqslant 0$ is determined by the size of the economy and is considered here as given. Under these circumstances it is still convenient to fix the numeraire in such a way that $\mathbf{q} = \mathbf{c}$ in equation (8.8d), which implies that the numeraire is defined in terms of commodities which will certainly be produced. Once again, the analysis is strongly simplified by neglecting the case in which $w = 0$ and/or $\alpha = 0$. Thus system (8.10) can be written:

$$[\mathbf{B} - (1 + r)\mathbf{A}]\mathbf{p} \leqslant w\mathbf{l}, \tag{8.12a}$$

$$\mathbf{x}^T[\mathbf{B} - (1 + r)\mathbf{A}]\mathbf{p} = w\mathbf{x}^T\mathbf{l}, \tag{8.12b}$$

$$\mathbf{x}^T[\mathbf{B} - (1 + g)\mathbf{A}] = \alpha\mathbf{c}^T, \tag{8.12c}$$

$$\mathbf{x} \geqslant \mathbf{0}, \quad w > 0, \quad \alpha > 0, \quad \mathbf{c}^T\mathbf{p} = 1. \tag{8.12d}$$

In a similar way as in Lemma 8.1 it is possible to show that system (8.12) admits a solution if and only if the following system (8.13) admits a solution. But since $g < r$, system (8.13) is not equivalent to a pair of dual linear programming problems.

$$[\mathbf{B} - (1 + r)\mathbf{A}]\mathbf{y} \leqslant \mathbf{l}, \tag{8.13a}$$

$$\mathbf{z}^T[\mathbf{B} - (1 + r)\mathbf{A}]\mathbf{y} = \mathbf{z}^T\mathbf{l}, \tag{8.13b}$$

$$\mathbf{z}^T[\mathbf{B} - (1 + g)\mathbf{A}] \geqslant \mathbf{c}^T, \tag{8.13c}$$

$$z^T[B - (1 + g)A]y = c^Ty, \tag{8.13d}$$

$$y \geqslant 0, \quad z \geqslant 0. \tag{8.13e}$$

There are at least two ways of showing that system (8.13) has a solution if there is a nonnegative vector v satisfying inequality (8.11). Both ways, however, require a knowledge of mathematical issues which are beyond those utilized in this book. In this book, in fact, only linear algebra and the theory of linear programming have been utilized. It is beyond the scope of this book to provide the elements of topology required to solve system (8.13) and the more complicated system presented in the following section. Yet it is possible to provide an algorithm using only linear algebra by means of which system (8.13) can be solved. However, proving that this algorithm really converges requires knowledge of computational methods which have actually been avoided even in dealing with linear programming problems. In the following only a sketch of the proof of the following Theorem 8.2 will be provided.

Theorem 8.2. If commodities are consumed in proportion to vector c and a uniform growth rate g lower than the rate of profit r holds, then at the rate of profit r and at the growth rate $g < r$ there is a cost-minimizing technique if and only if there is a nonnegative vector v such that inequality (8.11) holds.

Sketch of the proof. Consider the following system (8.14).

$$[B - (1 + r)A]y \leqslant 1, \tag{8.14a}$$

$$z^T[B - (1 + r)A]y = z^T1, \tag{8.14b}$$

$$z^T[B - (1 + r)A] \geqslant c^T - (r - g)u^TA, \tag{8.14c}$$

$$z^T[B - (1 + r)A]y = c^Ty - (r - g)u^TAy, \tag{8.14d}$$

$$y \geqslant 0, \quad z \geqslant 0, \tag{8.14e}$$

where u is a given vector. System (8.14) is equivalent to each of the following linear programming problems, which are dual to each other.

	(primal)		(dual)
Min	z^T1	Max	$[c^T - (r - g)u^TA]y$
s. to	$z^T[B - (1 + r)A] \geqslant c^T - (r - g)u^TA$	s. to	$[B - (1 + r)A]y \leqslant 1$
	$z \geqslant 0,$		$y \geqslant 0.$

Since the zero vector is a feasible solution to the dual and since the primal has a feasible solution by hypothesis, both problems have optimal solutions because of the Duality Theorem of Linear Programming. On the other hand if $(\mathbf{y}^*, \mathbf{z}^*)$ is a solution to system (8.14) such that $\mathbf{z}^* = \mathbf{u}$, then $(\mathbf{y}^*, \mathbf{z}^*)$ is also a solution to system (8.13). Thus the difficulty consists of proving that given the assumptions of the theorem there is a vector $\mathbf{u}^*$ such that a solution $\mathbf{z}^*$ to the primal is equal to $\mathbf{u}^*$. The interested reader is invited to consider the hint given for exercise 8.2. Q.E.D.

A completely different proof can be obtained by transforming system (8.13) in a *Linear Complementarity Problem*. The Linear Complementarity Problem is the following: For a given $n \times n$ matrix $\mathbf{M}$ and a given vector $\mathbf{q} \in \mathbb{R}^n$, find a solution to the system

$$\mathbf{w} = \mathbf{M}\mathbf{u} + \mathbf{q}, \tag{8.15a}$$

$$\mathbf{w} \geqslant 0, \quad \mathbf{u} \geqslant 0, \tag{8.15b}$$

$$\mathbf{w}^T \mathbf{u} = 0. \tag{8.15c}$$

Dantzig and Manne (1974) have proved that if $\mathbf{M}$ and $\mathbf{q}$ are such that

$$\mathbf{M} = \begin{bmatrix} 0 & -\mathbf{C} \\ \mathbf{C}^T + \mathbf{D}^T & 0 \end{bmatrix}, \quad \mathbf{q} = \begin{bmatrix} -\mathbf{l} \\ \mathbf{c} \end{bmatrix}, \tag{8.16}$$

with $\mathbf{D} \geqslant 0$, and if the following linear programming problems, (P) and (D^*),

	(P)		(D^*)
Min	$\mathbf{x}^T \mathbf{l}$	Max	$\mathbf{c}^T \mathbf{p}$
s. to	$\mathbf{x}^T(\mathbf{C} + \mathbf{D}) \geqslant \mathbf{c}^T$	s. to	$\mathbf{C}\mathbf{p} \leqslant \mathbf{l}$
	$\mathbf{x} \geqslant 0,$		$\mathbf{p} \geqslant 0,$

have optimal solutions, then there is an algorithm (referred to in the mathematical literature as the *Lemke complementarity pivot algorithm*) which will construct a solution to system (8.15).

If the reader is ready to accept this result, then the following proof of Theorem 8.2 can be provided. An advantage of this proof consists of the fact that $\mathbf{l} > 0$ is not assumed, as it is in the proof by Lippi sketched in the hint given for exercise 8.2.

Proof of Theorem 8.2. Let us put

$$\mathbf{C} = \mathbf{B} - (1 + r)\mathbf{A}$$
$$\mathbf{D} = (r - g)\mathbf{A} \geqslant 0$$

in equalities (8.16). Inequalities (8.13a), (8.13c), and (8.13e) can be stated as

$$\mathbf{M}\mathbf{u} + \mathbf{q} \geqslant 0 \tag{8.17a}$$

$$\mathbf{u} \geqslant 0; \tag{8.17b}$$

where $\mathbf{u} = [\mathbf{z}^T, \mathbf{y}^T]^T$. Similarly, equations (8.13b) and (8.13d) can be stated as

$$\mathbf{u}^T \mathbf{M} \mathbf{u} + \mathbf{q}^T \mathbf{u} = 0. \tag{8.17c}$$

Systems (8.15) and (8.17) are obviously equivalent. Hence system (8.13) is recognized as being a Linear Complementarity Problem of the type studied by Dantzig and Manne (1974). Thus it is sufficient to prove that the Linear Programming Problems (P) and (D^*) have optimal solutions. This is immediately obtained since the zero vector is a feasible solution to the dual of Problem (P), Problem (D), and to Problem (D^*), whereas Problem (P) and the dual of Problem (D^*), Problem (P^*), have feasible solutions by assumption. Since all four problems (P), (D), (P^*), and (D^*) have feasible solutions, both pairs of dual problems have optimal solutions because of the Duality Theorem of Linear Programming.   Q.E.D.

It is worth mentioning that in the previous chapters the proof of the existence of a cost-minimizing technique was associated with the proof of uniqueness of those elements of the long-period price vector referring to commodities actually produced. This is not true anymore when joint production is involved. Exercises 8.3–8.4 provide examples of non-uniqueness with respect to all elements of long-period price vectors. It is also to be stressed that the assumption of free disposal has an important role in obtaining Theorem 8.2. Exercise 8.6 shows that if there is no free disposal, the theorem does not hold. In previous chapters, a long-period position (or a cost-minimizing technique) was associated with the largest real wage rate that could be paid for a given rate of profit. This does not need to be true when joint production is involved. Exercise 8.8 provides an example showing this. (See also exercise 8.9 for an analogous case in which the real wage rate rather than the rate of profit is given.)

5. Toward more general models

Sections 3 and 4 have clarified the fact that a solution to system (8.16) may depend on the properties of function $\mathbf{d}$, which describes consumption and investment paths. If people do not always consume commodities in the same proportions, then the source of saving, which, in equilibrium equals investment, is also required (cf. Subsection 1.7 of Chapter 4 and Subsections 2.2 and 2.3 of Chapter 15). Some interesting models dealing with these problems have been developed by Morishima (1969), Bidard and Hosoda (1985), and Bidard and Franke (1987). Since the mathematical tools utilized in their analyses include topology, we refrain from discussing these models in any detail. We only want to add some remarks concerning the case in which workers consume commodities in proportion to vector $\mathbf{b}_w$ and capitalists consume them in proportion to vector $\mathbf{b}_c$. Moreover, vector $\mathbf{b}_w$ is assumed as given whereas vector $\mathbf{b}_c$ can be a function of prices.

If workers and capitalists consume commodities in different proportions, vector $\mathbf{d}$ of equation (8.8c) is given by

$$\mathbf{d}^T = g\mathbf{x}^T\mathbf{A} + \frac{[W + (r-g)K_w]}{\mathbf{b}_w^T\mathbf{p}}\mathbf{b}_w^T + \frac{(r-g)K_c}{\mathbf{b}_c^T\mathbf{p}}\mathbf{b}_c^T, \qquad (8.18)$$

where, as in Subsection 1.7 of Chapter 4, $W = w\mathbf{x}^T\mathbf{l}$, K_w is the capital owned by workers (since they save) and is assumed to equal $\theta w\mathbf{x}^T\mathbf{l}$ (where θ depends on r, g, and workers' consumption habits: a formal expression for θ will be provided in Chapter 15), and $K_c = \mathbf{x}^T\mathbf{A}\mathbf{p} - \theta w\mathbf{x}^T\mathbf{l}$ is the capitalists' own capital. In fact $[W + (r-g)K_w]/\mathbf{b}_w^T\mathbf{p}$ is the number of workers' consumption units which workers can afford, whereas $(r-g)K_c/\mathbf{b}_c^T\mathbf{p}$ is the number of capitalists' consumption units which capitalists can afford. Of course we are interested only in the cases in which $K_c = \mathbf{x}^T\mathbf{A}\mathbf{p} - \theta w\mathbf{x}^T\mathbf{l} > 0$ and $r > g$. Therefore, equation (8.8c) becomes

$$\mathbf{x}^T[\mathbf{B} - (1+g)\mathbf{A}]$$
$$= \mathbf{x}^T\left\{[1 + (r-g)\theta]\frac{w}{\mathbf{b}_w^T\mathbf{p}}\mathbf{l}\mathbf{b}_w^T + \frac{(r-g)}{\mathbf{b}_c^T\mathbf{p}}\mathbf{A}\mathbf{p}\mathbf{b}_c^T - (r-g)\theta\frac{w}{\mathbf{b}_c^T\mathbf{p}}\mathbf{l}\mathbf{b}_c^T\right\}.$$

Let us assume that there is a nonnegative vector $\mathbf{v}$ such that

$$\mathbf{v}^T[\mathbf{B} - (1+r)\mathbf{A}] \geqslant \mathbf{b}_w^T.$$

Then there is a solution to system (8.8) for

$$\mathbf{d}^T = g\mathbf{x}^T\mathbf{A} + \mathbf{b}_w^T,$$

because of Theorem 8.2. Let $(\mathbf{p}^*, w^*, \mathbf{z})$ be one of those solutions and let $(\mathbf{A}^*, \mathbf{B}^*, \mathbf{l}^*)$ be the processes corresponding to positive entries of vector $\mathbf{z}$. Then there is a vector $\mathbf{y}$ such that $(\mathbf{p}^*, w^*, \mathbf{y})$ is a solution to system (8.8) for

$$\mathbf{d}^T = g\mathbf{x}^T\mathbf{A} + \mathbf{b}_c^T$$

if

$$\mathbf{b}_c \in B := \{\mathbf{b} \in \mathbb{R}^n \mid \mathbf{b} \geqslant 0, \exists \mathbf{q} \geqslant 0 : \mathbf{q}^T[\mathbf{B}^* - (1+g)\mathbf{A}^*] = \mathbf{b}^T\}.$$

(Obviously, $\mathbf{b}_w \in B$.) Then we can prove the following theorem.

Theorem 8.3. If

    (i) $\mathbf{b}_c \in B$, and

    (ii) capitalists' capital is not negative when commodities are consumed in proportion to vector $\mathbf{b}_w$, that is,

$$(\mathbf{z}^T\mathbf{A}\mathbf{p} - \theta w\mathbf{z}^T\mathbf{l}) \geqslant 0,$$

then there is a solution to system (8.8) for **d** as defined in equation (8.18). In this solution **p** = **p*** and $w = w^*$.

Proof. $(\mathbf{p}^*, w^*, \alpha\mathbf{z} + \beta\mathbf{y})$ is a solution to system (8.8) for **d** as defined in equation (8.18) if and only if

$$\alpha\mathbf{b}_w^T\mathbf{p}^* = [1 + (r - g)\theta]w(\alpha\mathbf{z}^T\mathbf{l} + \beta\mathbf{y}^T\mathbf{l}) \tag{8.19a}$$

$$\beta\mathbf{b}_c^T\mathbf{p}^* = (r - g)[\alpha\mathbf{z}^T\mathbf{A}\mathbf{p}^* + \beta\mathbf{y}^T\mathbf{A}\mathbf{p}^* - \theta w(\alpha\mathbf{z}^T\mathbf{l} + \beta\mathbf{y}^T\mathbf{l})]. \tag{8.19b}$$

System (8.19) is homogeneous, so that only the ratio β/α can be determined. By the definition of **z** and **y** we obtain

$$\mathbf{z}^T[\mathbf{B} - (1 + g)\mathbf{A}]\mathbf{p}^* = \mathbf{b}_w^T\mathbf{p}^*$$
$$\mathbf{y}^T[\mathbf{B} - (1 + g)\mathbf{A}]\mathbf{p}^* = \mathbf{b}_c^T\mathbf{p}^*$$
$$\mathbf{z}^T[\mathbf{B} - (1 + r)\mathbf{A}]\mathbf{p}^* = w^*\mathbf{z}^T\mathbf{l}$$
$$\mathbf{y}^T[\mathbf{B} - (1 + r)\mathbf{A}]\mathbf{p}^* = w^*\mathbf{x}^T\mathbf{l},$$

which imply that

$$(r - g)\mathbf{z}^T\mathbf{A}\mathbf{p}^* = \mathbf{b}_w^T\mathbf{p}^* - w^*\mathbf{z}^T\mathbf{l} \tag{8.20a}$$

$$(r - g)\mathbf{y}^T\mathbf{A}\mathbf{p}^* = \mathbf{b}_c^T\mathbf{p}^* - w^*\mathbf{y}^T\mathbf{l}. \tag{8.20b}$$

By using equations (8.20) we obtain from each of the equations (8.19) that

$$\frac{\beta}{\alpha} = \frac{(r - g)[\mathbf{z}^T\mathbf{A}\mathbf{p} - \theta w\mathbf{z}^T\mathbf{l}]}{[1 + (r - g)\theta]w\mathbf{x}^T\mathbf{l}}. \tag{8.21}$$

Thus, the homogeneous linear system (8.19) is consistent. Moreover, $\beta/\alpha \geqslant 0$ since the numerator of the fraction on the right-hand side of equation (8.21) is not negative because of statement (ii).   Q.E.D.

Theorem 8.3 is a generalization of a result presented in Subsection 1.7 of Chapter 4 since if single production prevails, then the set B coincides with the nonnegative orthant. The result is particularly useful when fixed capital models are considered. As we have seen in Chapter 7, and as we will see in Chapter 9, in this case the set B coincides with the set $\{\mathbf{b} \in \mathbb{R}^n | \mathbf{b}^T = (\mathbf{b}_1^T, \mathbf{b}_2^T), \mathbf{b}_1 \geqslant 0, \mathbf{b}_2 = 0\}$, where $\mathbf{b}_1$ refers to final goods and $\mathbf{b}_2$ to old machines.

6. Elements of the indirect approach

In Section 2 the basic definitions of the indirect and the direct approach have been provided. At the beginning of Section 3 it has been argued that the direct approach is simpler than the indirect one and therefore only the direct approach has been analyzed in this chapter. But there are some elements of the indirect approach which can be useful anyway. Suppose, for instance, that a solution to system (8.9) with $\mathbf{c} > \mathbf{0}$ is such that only single product processes are operated. Then these processes can be operated in order to satisfy any consumption path and any investment path (provided that the growth rate is not too high): a solution to the general problem (8.8) has been found. This is so just because although there is joint production, the cost-minimizing technique happens to be one in which there is single production only.

We may now ask: Does the cost-minimizing technique of necessity have to be a single product one in order to find a solution of this type? Or does some less restrictive condition work as well? In this section we will first show that as far as system (8.12) is concerned – that is, provided that all people are assumed to consume commodities in the same proportions and a uniform growth rate not larger than the rate of profit holds – then there is a cost-minimizing technique which consists of exactly n processes. When this holds we say that the cost-minimizing technique is square, a *square technique* being a technique with a number of processes equal to the number of commodities involved. We will then analyze some special square techniques. The special square techniques which will be considered have the property that their processes can be operated in order to satisfy any consumption basket with a growth rate not larger than the rate of profit.

Theorem 8.4. Let $(\mathbf{y}^*, \mathbf{z}^*)$ be a solution to system (8.13). Then there is a square cost-minimizing technique, that is, there are n processes $(\mathbf{A}^*, \mathbf{B}^*, \mathbf{l}^*)$ and a solution to system (8.13), $(\mathbf{y}^{**}, \mathbf{z}^{**})$, such that the equations

$$[\mathbf{B}^* - (1 + r)\mathbf{A}^*]\mathbf{y}^{**} = \mathbf{l}^*$$
$$\bar{\mathbf{z}}^{**T}[\mathbf{B}^* - (1 + g)\mathbf{A}^*] = \mathbf{c}^T$$

are satisfied, where $\mathbf{z}^{**}$ is the vector $\bar{\mathbf{z}}^{**}$ augmented with zeros.

The proof of Theorem 8.4 is trivial after the following two Lemmata have been proved.

Lemma 8.3. Let $(\mathbf{y}^*, \mathbf{z}^*)$ be a solution to system (8.13). Then there is a solution $(\mathbf{y}^*, \mathbf{z}^{**})$ to the same system such that the number of operated processes is less than or equal to n.

Proof. Let $(\mathbf{y}^*, \mathbf{z}^{**})$ be a solution to system (8.13) with as few positive elements of vector $\mathbf{z}^{**}$ as possible. Then it is sufficient to prove that the rows of matrix $[\mathbf{B} - (1 + g)\mathbf{A}]$ corresponding to positive elements of vector $\mathbf{z}^{**}$ are linearly independent. Let $[\bar{\mathbf{B}} - (1 + g)\bar{\mathbf{A}}]$ be a matrix arranged with these rows and assume that there is $\bar{\mathbf{u}} \neq \mathbf{0}$ such that

$$\bar{\mathbf{u}}^T[\bar{\mathbf{B}} - (1 + g)\bar{\mathbf{A}}] = \mathbf{0}.$$

Then $(\mathbf{y}^*, \mathbf{z}^{**} + \lambda\mathbf{u})$ is still a solution to system (8.13) for $\lambda \neq 0$ but close enough to zero, where $\mathbf{u}$ is a vector obtained by augmenting $\bar{\mathbf{u}}$ with zeros. As a consequence it is possible to find λ^* such that $(\mathbf{z}^{**} + \lambda^*\mathbf{u})$ is still semi-positive, but has one zero element more than $\mathbf{z}^{**}$. Hence a contradiction.

Q.E.D.

Lemma 8.4. Let $(\mathbf{y}^*, \mathbf{z}^{**})$ be a solution to system (8.13). Then there is a solution $(\mathbf{y}^{**}, \mathbf{z}^{**})$ to the same system such that the number of weak inequalities which are satisfied as equations in (8.13a) is greater than or equal to n.

Proof. Let the weak inequalities which are satisfied as equations in (8.13a) when the solution $(\mathbf{y}^*, \mathbf{z}^{**})$ is adopted be

$$[\mathbf{B}^\circ - (1 + r)\mathbf{A}^\circ]\mathbf{y}^* = \mathbf{l}^\circ.$$

If the rank of matrix $[\mathbf{B}^\circ - (1 + r)\mathbf{A}^\circ]$ equals n, then $\mathbf{y}^{**} = \mathbf{y}^*$. If the rank of matrix $[\mathbf{B}^\circ - (1 + r)\mathbf{A}^\circ]$ is lower than n, then there is a vector $\mathbf{v} \neq \mathbf{0}$ such that

$$[\mathbf{B}^\circ - (1 + r)\mathbf{A}^\circ]\mathbf{v} = \mathbf{0}.$$

Since the free disposal assumption holds, if $\mathbf{e}_i^T\mathbf{y}^* = 0$, then $\mathbf{e}_i^T\mathbf{v} = 0$. As a consequence, $(\mathbf{y}^* + \lambda\mathbf{v})$ is still a solution to system (8.13) for $\lambda \neq 0$ and close enough to zero. Hence it is possible to find λ^* such that $(\mathbf{y}^* + \lambda^*\mathbf{v})$ is still semipositive and such that either (i) it has one zero element more than $\mathbf{y}^*$, or (ii) a further weak inequality in (8.13a) is satisfied as an equation; statement (i) being a special case of (ii) because of the free disposal assumption. This algorithm can be repeated until the number of weak inequalities which are satisfied as equations in (8.13a) reaches n.

Q.E.D.

Theorem 8.4 ensures that if system (8.13) has a solution, then there is a square cost-minimizing technique. As a consequence, if system (8.13) has a *unique* solution, then there is a unique cost-minimizing technique which is square. Therefore, a small change in the pattern of demand will not affect prices since the new pattern can be satisfied by a change in the intensity vector only. This is not necessarily true, of course, if more than one solution to system (8.13) exists.

In the remaining part of this section we will refer to $(\mathbf{A}, \mathbf{B}, \mathbf{l})$ as a square (cost-minimizing) technique. In technique $(\mathbf{A}, \mathbf{B}, \mathbf{l})$ a commodity is said to be *separately producible* if it is possible to produce a net output consisting of a unit of that commodity alone with a nonnegative intensity vector. That is, commodity j is separately producible if and only if there is a nonnegative vector $\mathbf{x}_j$ such that

$$\mathbf{x}_j^T[\mathbf{B} - \mathbf{A}] = \mathbf{e}_j^T,$$

where $\mathbf{e}_j$ is the jth unit vector. A technique is called *all-productive* if all commodities are separately producible in it, that is, if for each semipositive vector $\mathbf{y}$ there is a nonnegative vector $\mathbf{x}$ such that

$$\mathbf{x}^T[\mathbf{B} - \mathbf{A}] = \mathbf{y}^T.$$

If $(\mathbf{A}, \mathbf{B}, \mathbf{l})$ is all-productive, then $[\mathbf{B} - \mathbf{A}]^{-1} \geqslant 0$. In fact

$$(\mathbf{x}_1, \mathbf{x}_2, \ldots, \mathbf{x}_n)^T[\mathbf{B} - \mathbf{A}] = (\mathbf{e}_1, \mathbf{e}_2, \ldots, \mathbf{e}_n)^T = \mathbf{I}.$$

Thus, $[\mathbf{B} - \mathbf{A}]^{-1} = (\mathbf{x}_1, \mathbf{x}_2, \ldots, \mathbf{x}_n)^T \geqslant 0$. This is important since equation (8.7a) can be written as

$$[\mathbf{B} - \mathbf{A}]\mathbf{p} = r\mathbf{A}\mathbf{p} + w\mathbf{l},$$

that is,

$$\mathbf{p} = r[\mathbf{B} - \mathbf{A}]^{-1}\mathbf{A}\mathbf{p} + w[\mathbf{B} - \mathbf{A}]^{-1}\mathbf{l}.$$

Hence all the properties of single product techniques with respect to the *price* system hold, since the Perron–Frobenius Theorem can be applied to the nonnegative matrix $[\mathbf{B} - \mathbf{A}]^{-1}\mathbf{A} = \mathbf{H}$, and vector $[\mathbf{B} - \mathbf{A}]^{-1}\mathbf{l}$ is nonnegative.

Similarly, if a uniform growth rate g holds, equation

$$\mathbf{x}^T[\mathbf{B} - (1 + g)\mathbf{A}] = \mathbf{c}^T$$

can be written

$$\mathbf{x}^T[\mathbf{B} - \mathbf{A}] = g\mathbf{x}^T\mathbf{A} + \mathbf{c}^T,$$

that is,

$$\mathbf{x}^T = g\mathbf{x}^T\mathbf{A}[\mathbf{B} - \mathbf{A}]^{-1} + \mathbf{c}^T[\mathbf{B} - \mathbf{A}]^{-1}.$$

Hence all the properties of single product techniques with respect to the *quantity* system hold, since the Perron–Frobenius Theorem can be applied to the nonnegative matrix $\mathbf{A}[\mathbf{B} - \mathbf{A}]^{-1} = \mathbf{G}$, and $\mathbf{c}^T[\mathbf{B} - \mathbf{A}]^{-1}$ is nonnegative.

A process is *indispensable* within a technique if it has to be activated whatever net output is to be produced, that is, process $(\mathbf{e}_j^T\mathbf{A}, \mathbf{e}_j^T\mathbf{B}, \mathbf{e}_j^T\mathbf{l})$ is *not* indispensable within technique $(\mathbf{A}, \mathbf{B}, \mathbf{l})$ if and only if there is a net output vector $\mathbf{y} \geqslant 0$ and a nonnegative intensity vector $\mathbf{x}$ such that $\mathbf{x}^T[\mathbf{B} - \mathbf{A}] = \mathbf{y}^T$ and $\mathbf{e}_j^T\mathbf{x} = 0$. An all-productive technique whose processes are all indispensable is called *all-engaging*. Obviously, if $(\mathbf{A}, \mathbf{B}, \mathbf{l})$ is all-engaging, then $[\mathbf{B} - \mathbf{A}]^{-1} > 0$.

Technique $(\mathbf{A}, \mathbf{B}, \mathbf{l})$ is called r_0-*all-productive* (r_0-*all-engaging*) if the technique $((1 + r_0)\mathbf{A}, \mathbf{B}, \mathbf{l})$ is all-productive (all-engaging). Thus, if $(\mathbf{A}, \mathbf{B}, \mathbf{l})$ is r_0-all-productive then

$$\mathbf{p} = (r - r_0)[\mathbf{B} - (1 + r_0)\mathbf{A}]^{-1}\mathbf{A}\mathbf{p} + w[\mathbf{B} - (1 + r_0)\mathbf{A}]^{-1}\mathbf{l}$$

and

$$\mathbf{x}^T = (g - r_0)\mathbf{x}^T\mathbf{A}[\mathbf{B} - (1 + r_0)\mathbf{A}]^{-1} + \mathbf{c}^T[\mathbf{B} - (1 + r_0)\mathbf{A}]^{-1},$$

that is, an r_0-all-productive technique has all the simple properties of single product techniques for all $r \geqslant r_0$ and all $g \geqslant r_0$.

This section has clarified that in some cases there is an advantage in using both the direct and the indirect approach jointly. With the direct approach we determine the operated processes corresponding to an appropriate "fictitious" demand, then we consider only the cost-minimizing technique and explore the possibility of determining the equilibrium corresponding to the actual demand by just changing the intensity vector, the price vector remaining unchanged. This procedure will be utilized in dealing with general fixed capital models in the next chapter.

7. Historical notes

7.1. Joint production is obviously of great empirical importance; see the early account given by Simmonds (1873) and Steedman (1984a). Therefore it is hardly surprising that the phenomenon was taken notice of from the beginning of economic analysis. Cases of joint production and joint costs are in fact mentioned by major mercantilists and physiocrats. The main object of their analyses, that is, the sectors of primary production such as agriculture, mining and fishing, is in fact characterized by universal joint production. However, it was not until Adam Smith's *The Wealth of Nations* that an attempt was made to transcend the purely descriptive treatment of the problem and to begin to deal with it in analytical terms. Smith was well aware of the possibility that with joint production the proportions in which the products are produced need not coincide with those in which they are wanted. He concluded, with reference to the hunting nations of North America, that in this case the overproduced amount(s) of the products would be "thrown away as things of no value" (*WN*, I.xi.c.4). Here we encounter, possibly for the first time in the history of economic thought, the "Rule of Free Goods." Yet apart from this Smith did not feel obliged to modify his cost of production approach to the explanation of (relative) prices developed in chapter 6 of book I of *The Wealth of Nations*. In particular, it seems clear that he considered prices as being determined independently of anything resembling demand schedules (see Kurz, 1986b, 1990a, and 1992b). A fundamental weakness involved in his approach (and the contributions by several authors after him) consists of the fact that he appeared to think that the cost of production and thus the total price of the composite output can be ascertained independently of and prior to the manner, in which "this price is to be divided upon the different parts" of the produce (*W N*, I.xi.m.12).

7.2. Interestingly, joint products were later referred to by major marginalist authors, in particular Jevons ([1871] 1965), as phenomena which, they asserted, cannot be analyzed within a theory of value of a "classical" orientation. For, the argument reads, with joint production the number of processes of production operated will generally fall short of the number of products whose prices have to be ascertained. Hence there is a problem of underdeterminacy: in the case of only one process producing two products, the work-horse of all earlier contributions to the problem under consideration, there is one equation too few. It is concluded that the very basis of classical analysis, the labor theory of value, breaks down, since "it is impossible to divide up the labour and say that so much is expended on producing X, and so much on Y" (Jevons, [1871] 1965, p. 200). Essentially the same point is made by Knut Wicksell with respect to durable capital goods, used for different purposes, that is, intertemporal joint production. He argues that it is "just as absurd to ask how much labour is invested in either one or the other annual use as it is to try to find out what part of pasture goes into wool and what part into mutton" (Wicksell, [1901] 1934, vol. I, p. 260). A way out of this impasse was seen as consisting of the introduction of the principle of substitution in consumption, which in turn was given a choice theoretical foundation centered around the notion of marginal utility. It was not until Marshall ([1890] 1977) that the principle of substitution was extended to the sphere of production, assuming, within limits, the flexibility of net output proportions in joint production processes.

It deserves to be stressed that with continuous substitution in production the number of processes operated will generally fall short of the number of commodities produced. Hence both in the case in which there are "too few" processes (early marginalism) and in the case in which there are "too many" (mature marginalism), demand schedules are assumed to bridge the gap, that is, to satisfy the condition "that our theory has as many equations as it has unknowns, neither more nor less" (Marshall, [1890] 1977, Mathematical Appendix, note XXI, p. 703).

7.3. The objection that with joint production the classical cost of production approach to an explanation of value can no longer be sustained was not generally accepted. In a critical discussion of Gustav Cassel's simplified representation of the Walrasian general equilibrium system Frederik

Zeuthen entered into an investigation of joint production: "It is sometimes emphasized that here the principle of cost is annulled. This may be correct in the sense that the distribution of costs between products is not determined by technical relations alone, e.g., how a part of the price of coal is apportioned to coke, gas, and tar. However, on the assumed free mobility... there will be a complete and automatic determination of prices." Zeuthen continues: "This can be imagined as follows. In the example of cattle-breeding there may exist two forms of business, one predominantly concerned with dairy products and requiring a lot of labor, the other predominantly concerned with the production of meat and thus requiring a larger live stock. ... It follows that for each new method of production for a commodity there will be... a new cost equation which contributes to the solution of the system" (Zeuthen, 1933, p. 15).

Zeuthen's implicit reference is, of course, to John Stuart Mill, who in chapter 16 of book III of his *Principles*, "Of Some Peculiar Cases of Value," had maintained that in the case of joint production "cost of production can have nothing to do with deciding the value of the associated commodities relatively to each other. It only decides their joint value. ... A principle is wanting to apportion the expenses of production between the two. Since cost of production here fails us, we must revert to a law of value anterior to cost of production, and more fundamental, the law of demand and supply" (Mill, [1848] 1965, p. 583). (The example of coke and coal-gas is also Mill's.) Apparently, Zeuthen was not convinced by Mill's reasoning and thought that an equality between the number of commodities and the number of methods of production operated would be secured even in the case of joint production, so that a determinate solution of prices would obtain. Essentially the same supposition is to be found in Sraffa's treatment of joint production (1960, p. 43; see also below, note 7.5)

7.4. A most important contribution to the theory of joint production was provided by John von Neumann ([1937] 1945). Von Neumann's approach will be dealt with in some detail in Sections 6, 7, and 9 of Chapter 13. Here we mention only that subsequent authors taking the von Neumann model as a starting point were concerned with weakening some of the overly restrictive premises underlying its original formulation. Kemeny, Morgenstern, and Thompson (1956) replaced the assumption that every process requires as an input or produces as an output some positive amount of every good, which, from an empirical point of view, appears to be especially unsatisfactory, with Assumptions 8.1–8.3 (cf. Section 3) and added the requirement that the value of the total product is positive. With this change they were able to show that all of von Neumann's original results hold true with the exception that the expansion factor is no longer unique: there is rather a finite number of expansion factors.

Morishima in several contributions (see Morishima, 1960, 1964, 1969) was concerned with overcoming the restrictive assumptions about consumption and saving behavior. (Von Neumann had assumed that all wages are consumed and all interest incomes are saved and invested.) He introduced consumer choice and more general saving functions into the model. In his most general formulation he started from the premise that workers, like capitalists, save a constant fraction of their income and consume the rest so that their demand for each good depends on relative prices and their income.

For an assessment of the von Neumann model and further developments in economic theory taking it as a starting point, see Morgenstern and Thompson (1976), Bruckmann and Weber (1971), Łos, Łos, and Wieczorek (1976) and Dore, Chakravarty, and Goodwin (1989).

7.5. Sraffa's analysis of pure joint production is contained in chapters VII–IX of Part II of his book, which is dedicated to "Multiple-Product Industries and Fixed Capital" (Sraffa, 1960, pp. 43–62). The three chapters are introduced by him as "in the main a preliminary to the discussion of Fixed Capital and Land" (p. 43, n. 1). He begins the first section of Part II (§50) with an explicit reference to the problem of underdeterminacy in the familiar case in which two products are produced by a single process and states: "The conditions would no longer be sufficient to determine the prices. There would be more prices to be ascertained than there are processes, and therefore equations to determine them" (p. 43). "In these circumstances," Sraffa continues, "there will be room" either "for a second, parallel process which will produce the two commodities by a different method and [...] in different proportions" or for the production of "a third commodity by two distinct processes" which use the two jointly produced commodities "as means of production in different proportions." Such further processes "will not only be possible – [they] will be necessary if the number of processes is to be brought to equality with the number of commodities so that the prices may be determined" (p. 43). Sraffa concludes §50 by assuming that "the number of processes should be equal to the number of commodities" (p. 44), that is, presupposes *square* systems of production. This assumption is also retained in the closing section of the third and final part of his book, "Switch in Methods of Production" (§96, pp. 86–7), which is devoted to a discussion of the problem of the choice of technique in the presence of joint production. (The argument in this section cannot be sustained, as has been shown by Bidard, 1984a, and Salvadori, 1979b, 1979c, 1982, 1984, 1985.)

In §50 Sraffa also puts forward the concept of "the proportions in which... commodities... are required for use" (p. 43, n. 2). There are clear indications that he was aware of the fact that, even though the operable processes are equal in number to the commodities involved, they may not be able to match whatever "requirements for use" there may be (cf. p. 47). However, in defining the system of production (pp. 44–5) he does not mention this problem. Being concerned with *one* viable system only, it may be conjectured that Sraffa implicitly assumed that the proportions in which the commodities are wanted can in fact be met by those in which they are produced. Yet, as Salvadori (1979c, 1982, 1985) has stressed, a system of production can be defined only with respect to given requirements for use.

7.6. Following Sraffa's lead, much of the literature on joint production, taking his contribution as the starting point, was concerned with square systems. The first attempt at formalizing some of his propositions was Manara (1968). The analysis of square systems of joint production was substantially enhanced by several contributions by Schefold (1971, 1976a, 1976b, 1978b, 1988, 1989): the concepts of "all-productive techniques" and "all-engaging techniques" have all been introduced and fully investigated by him. A rich taxonomy of special cases of square systems is to be found in Giorgi and Magnani (1978).

Some justification for Sraffa's assumption asserting that each system contains exactly as many processes as commodities has been provided by Steedman (1976) and Schefold (1978c, 1980a) in the special case in which the economy is taken as growing steadily at a rate equal to the rate of profit and the consumption pattern is independent of prices and incomes (see also Bidard 1986). In this case such an equality can actually be proved if free disposal is assumed (see also Saucier, 1984a). The proof presented here for the case of a growth rate not larger than the rate of profit is obtained following a procedure utilized by Salvadori (1988a) for the general fixed capital models dealt with in the next chapter. An alternative proof has been provided by Schefold (1988). However, in the general case it cannot be presumed that the number of processes operated is equal to the number of commodities. Moreover, it has been shown by several authors that such an assumption may even preclude the existence of "cost-minimizing systems" (see Bidard, 1984a; Duménil and Lévy, 1984; Lévy, 1984; Salvadori, 1979b, 1979c, 1982, 1984, 1985).

The main issue addressed in the above mentioned papers by Steedman (1976) and Schefold (1978c, 1980a) is the relationship between Sraffa's analysis and that of von Neumann. The "von Neumann model" considered for the comparison was the system of inequalities (8.13), which however is *not* the original von Neumann model. Thus, Steedman and Schefold were able to take the rate of profit rather than the wage rate, as in the original von Neumann model, as given. Salvadori (1980) related system (8.13) to a model presented by Morishima (1969). Morishima's proof of existence required the continuity of some consumption functions, and this continuity assumption implies that all commodities, including furnaces and pig-iron, will be consumed provided their prices are sufficiently low. This proof is applicable to system (8.13) only if vector **c** is positive. Salvadori's (1980) proof used Linear Complementarity as in Section 4. Bidard and Hosoda (1985) and Bidard and Franke (1987) generalized his analysis using different analytical tools. Lippi (1979) used system (8.13) as a reference system with respect to a square technique *à la* Sraffa. The prices of the square technique are positive if and only if all processes are operated in the reference system. This argument was intended to show that negative prices in square techniques *à la* Sraffa are associated with inefficient processes whose operation is required in order to dispose of some products. A similar intention underlies the contributions by C. Filippini (1977) and by C. Filippini and L. Filippini (1982) who used the concept of "dominance"; the latter was then developed by Lévy (1984) and Duménil and Lévy (1984).

The definition of "technique" used above, which can take care of both square and non-square systems, follows closely the one provided by Salvadori (1985, pp. 174–5). (See also Craven, 1979, for another definition, not related to Sraffa's analysis.) It deserves to be stressed that by this token the Sraffa approach is transformed in such a way that the result bears a close resemblance to the von Neumann approach as transformed by Morishima (1960, 1964, 1969).

For a survey of joint production analysis in a Sraffian framework see Salvadori and Steedman (1988). Important contributions to the theory of joint production, taking Sraffa's analysis as their starting point, are collected in Pasinetti (1980), Steedman (1988a, vol. II) and Salvadori and Steedman (1990).

8. Exercises

8.1. Generalize Lemmata 8.11–8.15 and Theorem 8.1 as in exercises 7.11–7.15 of Chapter 5.

8.2. (Topology) (Lippi, 1979) Complete the sketch of the proof of Theorem 8.2. [Hint: Let $F(\mathbf{u})$ be the set of the solutions to the primal for a given $\mathbf{u}$. You need to prove that there is $\mathbf{u}^*$ such that $\mathbf{u}^* \in F(\mathbf{u}^*)$. Prove that $F(\mathbf{u})$ is a convex set for each given $\mathbf{u}$ and that correspondence $F(\mathbf{u})$ is upper-semicontinuous. In order to apply the Kakutani Theorem, you then need to find a convex compact set K such that if $\mathbf{u} \in K$, then $F(\mathbf{u}) \in K$. Let $\mathbf{q}^* \in F(\mathbf{0})$,

Table 8.3

	commodity inputs					outputs		
	1	2	3	labor		1	2	3
(1)	$\frac{1}{10}$	$\frac{2}{5}$	$\frac{1}{10}$	$\frac{1}{8}$	$\rightarrow$	$\frac{1}{5}$	$\frac{3}{5}$	—
(2)	—	$\frac{2}{5}$	$\frac{1}{10}$	$\frac{7}{6}$		$\frac{1}{6}$	$\frac{1}{2}$	—
(3)	$\frac{3}{10}$	$\frac{3}{10}$	—	$\frac{1}{10}$	$\rightarrow$	—	—	$\frac{5}{2}$
(4)	$\frac{1}{10}$	$\frac{1}{10}$	—	3	$\rightarrow$	—	—	1

Table 8.4

	commodity inputs				outputs	
	1	2	labor		1	2
(1)	1	2	1	$\rightarrow$	5	7
(2)	2	1	1	$\rightarrow$	7	5
(3)	1	2	1	$\rightarrow$	5	—
(4)	1	2	1	$\rightarrow$	—	7
(5)	2	1	1	$\rightarrow$	7	—
(6)	2	1	1	$\rightarrow$	—	5

and let

$$K = \{\mathbf{u} | \mathbf{u} \geqslant \mathbf{0}, \mathbf{u}^T \mathbf{l} \leqslant \mathbf{q}^{*T} \mathbf{l}\}.$$

Prove that $\mathbf{u} \in K$ implies that $F(\mathbf{u}) \in K$.]

8.3. (D'Agata, 1985) There are three commodities and the four processes of Table 8.3 plus the processes needed in order to satisfy the free disposal assumption. The growth rate equals zero, commodities are consumed in the proportion one to one, and the rate of profit equals 0.5. Show that there are two cost-minimizing techniques: one of them consists of processes $(1, 2, 3)$, another consists of processes $(1, 2, 4)$. Show that if prices are normalized by setting $\mathbf{e}^T \mathbf{p} = 1$, then the price vector and the wage rate of the first cost-minimizing technique are $(\frac{601}{1120}, \frac{347}{1120}, \frac{172}{1120})^T$ and $\frac{17}{560}$, respectively, whereas the price vector and the wage rate of the second one are $(\frac{545}{1240}, \frac{615}{1240}, \frac{170}{1240})^T$ and $\frac{1}{620}$, respectively.

8.4. (Franke, 1986) There are two commodities and the six processes of Table 8.4. The growth rate equals zero, commodities are consumed in proportion of ten units of commodity 1 to eleven units of commodity 2. Show that if $0 \leqslant r < 1$, then one and only one cost-minimizing technique exists: it consists of processes $(1, 2)$. Show that if $1 < r \leqslant 3$, then there are three cost-minimizing techniques: one of them consists of processes $(1, 2)$,

Table 8.5

	commodity inputs				outputs	
	1	2	labor		1	2
(1)	2	—	1	→	5	1
(2)	—	1	1	→	1	3
(3)	1	—	1	→	1	3

another one consists of processes $(1, 3)$, the third one consists of processes $(2, 6)$. Show that if prices are normalized by setting $e^T \mathbf{p} = 1$, then the price vector and the wage rate of the first cost-minimizing technique are $(\frac{1}{2}, \frac{1}{2})^T$ and $(9 - 3r)/2$, respectively, the price vector and the wage rate of the second one are $(1, 0)^T$ and $(4 - r)$, respectively, and the price vector and the wage rate of the third one are $(0, 1)^T$ and $(4 - r)$, respectively. Show that if $r = 1$, then there are the same three cost-minimizing techniques, but if both processes (1) and (2) are operated any vector (p_1, p_2) such that $p_1 = 1 - p_2, 0 \leqslant p_2 \leqslant 1$, is a long-period price vector. Show that if $3 < r \leqslant 4$, then there are two cost-minimizing techniques: one consists of processes $(1, 3)$, the other one consists of processes $(2, 6)$.

8.5. Show that the last four processes of Table 8.4 exist as a consequence of the free disposal assumption since the first two processes exist. Then find the processes which need to exist as a consequence of the free disposal assumption when the processes of Table 8.3 exist.

8.6. (Salvadori, 1979b, 1979c, 1985) Assume that the free disposal assumption does not hold. There are two commodities and the three processes of Table 8.5. The growth rate equals zero, commodities are consumed in the proportion one to one. Show that if $0 \leqslant r \leqslant 1$, then there is a cost-minimizing technique. Show that if $1 < r < \frac{9}{5}$, then there is no cost-minimizing technique, but if processes (2) and (3) are deleted, a cost-minimizing technique would be obtained from the remaining processes. Comment on this result.

8.7. (d'Autume, 1988, 1990; Schefold, 1988) Show that if in exercise 8.6 the free disposal assumption is introduced again, that is, if, in the language of this chapter, the processes of Table 8.5 exist jointly with the processes of Table 8.6, then a cost-minimizing technique exists for $1 < r < \frac{9}{5}$ and consists of processes $(2, 6)$. Why does this not come as a surprise?

8.8. (Salvadori, 1979b, 1979c, 1985) There are two commodities and the three processes of Table 8.7 plus the processes needed in order to satisfy the free disposal assumption. The growth rate equals zero, workers consume only commodity 2 and capitalists consume only commodity 1.

Table 8.6

	commodity inputs				outputs	
	1	2	labor		1	2
(4)	2	—	1	→	5	—
(5)	2	—	1	→	—	1
(6)	—	1	1	→	1	—
(7)	—	1	1	→	—	3
(8)	1	—	1	→	1	—
(9)	1	—	1	→	—	3

Table 8.7

	commodity inputs				outputs	
	1	2	labor		1	2
(1)	1	1	2	→	2	4
(2)	—	3	1	→	3	—
(3)	—	1	2	→	2	—

Show that if $(\sqrt{33}-3)/4 < r < 1$, then the long-period real wage rate is lower than that which can be paid by operating some other pair of processes, except for $r = (4\sqrt{5}-5)/5$. [*Hint*: In order to calculate the *real* wage rate, let the numeraire consist of commodity 2 only. If $(\sqrt{41}-5)/2 \leqslant r < (4\sqrt{5}-5)/5$, then the long-period real wage rate is obtained by operating processes $(1,2)$, but a higher real wage rate can be obtained by operating processes $(1,3)$. If $(4\sqrt{5}-5)/5 < r < 1$, then the long-period real wage rate is obtained by operating processes $(1,3)$, but a higher real wage rate can be obtained by operating processes $(1,2)$. What happens if $(\sqrt{33}-3)/4 < r \leqslant (\sqrt{41}-5)/2$?]

8.9. (Salvadori, 1981) There are two commodities, the processes (1) and (3) of Table 8.7, and the processes needed in order to satisfy the free disposal assumption. The growth rate equals zero, workers consume only commodity 2 and capitalists consume commodities in the proportion one to one. The real wage rate consists of one unit of commodity 2. Determine the "long-period rate of profit." Then introduce process (2) and determine once again the long-period rate of profit. Compare the two rates of profit; comment on these results with reference to Marx's notion of the "falling rate of profit."

8.10. (Salvadori and Steedman, 1988) Let $(\mathbf{A}, \mathbf{B}, \mathbf{l})$ be a square technique and let $\mathbf{B} = \mathbf{I} + b\mathbf{e}_1\mathbf{e}_2^T$. Show that if $\mathbf{e}_i^T \mathbf{L}\mathbf{l}\mathbf{e}_2^T \mathbf{L}\mathbf{e}_1 < \mathbf{e}_2^T \mathbf{L}\mathbf{l}\mathbf{e}_i^T \mathbf{L}\mathbf{e}_1$, where $\mathbf{L} =$

$[\mathbf{I} - (1+r)\mathbf{A}]^{-1}$, then there is a value for b so large that $\mathbf{e}_i^T \mathbf{p}$ is negative. [*Hint*: Show that

$$\mathbf{p} = w\mathbf{Ll} - b\mathbf{Le}_1 \mathbf{e}_2^T \mathbf{p},$$

and therefore (see exercise 6.8 of Chapter 4)

$$\mathbf{p} = w\left[\mathbf{I} - \frac{b}{1 + b\mathbf{e}_2^T \mathbf{Le}_1} \mathbf{Le}_1 \mathbf{e}_2^T\right]\mathbf{Ll} = w\mathbf{Ll} - \frac{bw\mathbf{e}_2^T \mathbf{Ll}}{1 + b\mathbf{e}_2^T \mathbf{Le}_1} \mathbf{Le}_1.$$

Then, . . .]

8.11. There are n commodities and the n processes of the previous exercise plus the processes which need to exist because of the free disposal assumption. Show that if $\mathbf{e}_i^T \mathbf{Lle}_2^T \mathbf{Le}_1 < \mathbf{e}_2^T \mathbf{Lle}_i^T \mathbf{Le}_1$, where $\mathbf{L} = [\mathbf{I} - (1+r)\mathbf{A}]^{-1}$, then there is a value for b so large that one of the first two elements of the long-period price vector is nought. [*Hint*: Solve previous exercise.]

9

Jointly utilized machines

In Chapter 7 fixed capital has been introduced as a special form of joint production which has been investigated even before introducing general joint production models. In that chapter, however, only a special form of fixed capital was dealt with: only a single old machine was allowed for in each process and these machines were assumed as being ordered in the sense that each has an unambiguous age. It has also been shown that this form of fixed capital is compatible with the joint utilization of *new* machines. The present chapter is devoted to an analysis of more general fixed capital models. Specifically, old machines will be allowed to be used jointly. Only one assumption still needs to hold: machines cannot be transferred from one sector to another, that is, an oven once utilized to produce bread cannot be used during its lifetime to produce biscuits. On this assumption a number of "desirable" properties will be shown to hold. Among these properties there is the fact that consumption patterns do not matter at all in determining prices or operated processes, whereas the growth rate can play a role in determining the cost-minimizing technique and, therefore, prices.

From a formal point of view, the chapter provides some axiomatic definitions of fixed capital technologies and some theorems exploring these concepts. Definitions are introduced by assuming the possibility of partitioning the set of commodities and the set of processes in order to satisfy certain properties. Granting this possibility, the subsets of commodities defined by these properties can be interpreted as "the old machine set"and "the finished good set," respectively. This procedure allows us to avoid, in defining fixed capital models, the use of words like "machine," which have not yet been defined. Other than in Chapter 7, in the analysis of the problem of the choice of technique, the direct approach rather than the indirect approach is followed.

250

Several sets of assumptions will be investigated. To begin with, only the premise of the non-transferability of old machines among sectors with no joint production of finished goods will be formalized. Some theorems show that in this general case prices are independent of consumption patterns even if they may not be independent of the growth rate and do not need to be unique unless the rate of profit equals the growth rate. Another set of assumptions deals with the situation already studied in Chapter 7. For the sake of completeness the main results of Chapter 7 are easily obtained now by means of the direct approach. Two other sets of assumptions extend the previous models to cover the case of scrap which is fully utilized. The previous results are restated for these cases. A further assumption allows for the ageing of machines and therefore an analysis of depreciation and efficiency.

The structure of the chapter is as follows. Section 1 will define the concept of a fixed capital technology. Section 2 will present the main results derived within the framework of the present chapter. The problem of depreciation is dealt with in Section 3, while Section 4 is devoted to a critical discussion of the concept of "depreciation by evaporation" or "depreciation by radioactive decay." Section 5 investigates the problem of scrap. Section 6 turns once again to the notion of the plant introduced in Section 8 of Chapter 7. Section 7 provides historical notes and Section 8 exercises.

1. Fixed capital technology

It is assumed that there are m processes and n commodities. Each process of production i $(i = 1, 2, \ldots, m)$ is defined by the triplet $(\mathbf{a}_i, \mathbf{b}_i, l_i)$, where $\mathbf{a}_i = (a_{i1}, a_{i2}, \ldots, a_{in})^T$ is the nonnegative material input vector, $\mathbf{b}_i = (b_{i1}, b_{i2}, \ldots, b_{in})^T$ is the nonnegative output vector, and l_i, a scalar, is the nonnegative labor input. Thus, the whole technology is defined by the triplet $(\mathbf{A}, \mathbf{B}, \mathbf{l})$, where

$$\mathbf{A} = \begin{bmatrix} \mathbf{a}_1^T \\ \mathbf{a}_2^T \\ \vdots \\ \mathbf{a}_m^T \end{bmatrix}, \quad \mathbf{B} = \begin{bmatrix} \mathbf{b}_1^T \\ \mathbf{b}_2^T \\ \vdots \\ \mathbf{b}_m^T \end{bmatrix}, \quad \mathbf{l} = \begin{bmatrix} l_1 \\ l_2 \\ \vdots \\ l_m \end{bmatrix}.$$

Assumptions 8.1–8.3 of Chapter 8 hold. The assumption regarding the *non-transferability of fixed capital* reads as follows:

Assumption 9.1. There are two subsets, S and T, of the set of commodities N such that

(A.1.1) $S \cap T = \varnothing, \quad S \cup T = N;$

(A.1.2) commodities in T are never consumed;

(A.1.3) each process produces one and only one commodity in S;

(A.1.4) if commodity $i \in T$ is produced by process j producing commodity $h \in S$, then there is no process producing a commodity $k \in S, k \neq h$, such that it either produces i or utilizes i as an input;

(A.1.5) for each process producing commodity $j \in T$ there is a process with the same inputs and the same outputs except that commodity j is not produced.

It is immediately recognized that if and only if single production holds, Assumption 9.1 is satisfied with $S = N$ and $T = \emptyset$. On the contrary, if Assumption 9.1 holds with $S \neq N$ and $T \neq \emptyset$, then, for the sake of simplicity, we can refer to the commodities in T as "old machines" and to the commodities in S as "finished goods." The rationale for the above axioms can now be stated as follows. Axiom (A.1.1) implies that a commodity is either an old machine or a finished good, but never both. Axiom (A.1.2) implies that old machines are never consumed. Axiom (A.1.3) rules out joint production proper. Axiom (A.1.4) states that old machines cannot be transferred among sectors. Axiom (A.1.5) implies that old machines can be disposed of at no cost (leaving no scrap behind).

If Assumption 9.1 holds, we may reorder commodities and processes in the following way: the first s commodities are in S, the next t_1 commodities are in T and are produced jointly with commodity 1, the next t_2 commodities are in T and are produced jointly with commodity 2,..., the next t_s commodities are in T and are produced jointly with commodity s, some t_i may be equal to zero, $t_1 + t_2 + \cdots + t_s = t, s + t = n$; the first m_1 processes produce commodity 1, the next m_2 processes produce commodity 2,..., the next m_s processes produce commodity s, $m_1 + m_2 + \cdots + m_s = m$. In order to simplify the notation, let us also introduce $t_0 = 0$ and $m_0 = 0$.

Therefore Axiom A.1.4, that is, old machines cannot be transferred among sectors, is equivalent to the following properties of matrices $\mathbf{A}$ and $\mathbf{B}$:

(i) if $k \in S$, $b_{hk} > 0$ if and only if $\sum_{j=0}^{k-1} m_j < h \leqslant \sum_{j=0}^{k} m_j$;

(ii) if $k \in S$ and $s + \sum_{j=0}^{k-1} t_j < i \leqslant s + \sum_{j=0}^{k} t_j$, then $b_{hi} > 0$ or $a_{hi} > 0$ only if $\sum_{j=0}^{k-1} m_j < h \leqslant \sum_{j=0}^{k} m_j$.

In Figures 9.1a and 9.1b matrices $\mathbf{A}$ and $\mathbf{B}$, respectively, are represented on the assumption that $s = 5$ and that all commodities but commodity 3 are produced by using old machines: grey areas represent nonnegative elements, white areas represent zero elements, and black areas represent positive elements. (Comparing Figures 9.1 and 7.1 shows that the grey

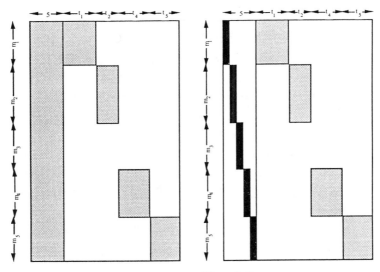

Figure 9.1a   Figure 9.1b

areas in the former correspond to the grey and the light grey areas in the latter.)

The special case in which there is only a *single non-transferable machine* is characterized as follows:

Assumption 9.2. Assumption 9.1 holds and

(A.2.1) each process produces not more than one commodity in T;
(A.2.2) each process utilizes not more than one commodity in T as an input;
(A.2.3) there is a natural number z such that the set of old machines T can be partitioned in z subsets $T_1, T_2, \ldots, T_z$ in such a way that old machines in T_1 are produced without utilizing old machines, and each old machine in T_i $(i = 2, 3, \ldots, z)$ is produced utilizing an old machine in T_{i-1}, with $T_i \cap T_j = \varnothing$ $(i \neq j)$, and $\bigcup_{i=1}^{z} T_i = T$.

For simplicity, the commodities in T_i can be called *i year old machines*. The reader will recognize that Assumption 9.2 summarizes the axioms stated in Chapter 7. The following examples are intended to illustrate the power of the definitions adopted.

Example 9.1. There are two commodities whose processes are represented by Table 9.1 (" + " represents a positive number); only commodity 1 is consumed.

Table 9.1

	commodity inputs				outputs	
	1	2	labor		1	2
(1)	+	+	+	→	+	+
(2)	+	+	+	→	+	+

Table 9.2

	commodity inputs						outputs			
	1	2	3	4	labor		1	2	3	4
(1)	+	+	0	y_1	+	→	+	0	0	y_3
(2)	+	+	0	y_2	+	→	0	+	0	y_4
(3)	+	0	0	z_1	+	→	0	0	+	+
(4)	0	+	0	z_2	+	→	0	0	+	+
(5)	0	0	0	+	+	→	0	0	+	z_3

It is easily recognized that Assumption 9.1, except Axiom (A.1.5), holds. In order for Axiom (A.1.5) to hold we just need to add processes (3) and (4), where process (3) is identical to process (1) except that commodity 2 is not produced, and process (4) is identical to process (2) except that commodity 2 is not produced. When this is done, commodity 1 can be interpreted as a finished good and commodity 2 as an old machine. It is also easily recognized that if both commodities were to be consumed, then the technology would be of the wool–mutton type of joint production with free disposal either of wool or of mutton. The reader should note that examples with such a paradoxical character are possible only if there is not more than one finished good.

Example 9.2. There are four commodities whose processes are represented by Table 9.2; only commodity 3 is consumed.

It is easily recognized that if $y_i = z_j = 0$, each i, each j, then Assumption 9.2 except Axiom (A.1.5) holds. Once the appropriate processes needed in order to satisfy Axiom (A.1.5) are introduced, commodities 1, 2, and 3 can be interpreted as finished goods and commodity 4 as a one year old machine. Nevertheless, it is unclear if there is a new machine: in Assumption 9.2

there is, in fact, no need for the concept of a "new machine." Further, if $y_i = 0$, each i, and $z_j > 0$, some j, then Assumption 9.1 holds once the appropriate processes needed to satisfy Axiom (A.1.5) have been introduced, but Assumption 9.2 does not. Finally, if $y_i > 0$, some i, then Assumption 9.1 does not hold.

As in Chapter 8 a technique is defined as a set of n processes of production that satisfy requirements for use, that is, as a triplet $(\hat{\mathbf{A}}, \hat{\mathbf{B}}, \hat{\mathbf{l}})$ such that there is a nonnegative vector $\mathbf{x}$ satisfying the equation

$$\mathbf{x}^T(\hat{\mathbf{B}} - \hat{\mathbf{A}}) = \mathbf{d}^T, \tag{9.1}$$

where

$$\hat{\mathbf{A}} = \begin{bmatrix} \mathbf{a}_{i_1} \\ \mathbf{a}_{i_2} \\ \vdots \\ \mathbf{a}_{i_n} \end{bmatrix}, \quad \hat{\mathbf{B}} = \begin{bmatrix} \mathbf{b}_{i_1} \\ \mathbf{b}_{i_2} \\ \vdots \\ \mathbf{b}_{i_n} \end{bmatrix}, \quad \hat{\mathbf{l}} = \begin{bmatrix} l_{i_1} \\ l_{i_2} \\ \vdots \\ l_{i_n} \end{bmatrix},$$

and $\mathbf{d}$ are the requirements for use; $\mathbf{d}$ does not need to be constant and can be a function of process intensities, prices, the wage rate and the rate of profit, matrices $\hat{\mathbf{A}}$ and $\hat{\mathbf{B}}$ and vector $\hat{\mathbf{l}}$.

The price vector $\mathbf{p}$ and the wage rate w of technique $(\hat{\mathbf{A}}, \hat{\mathbf{B}}, \hat{\mathbf{l}})$ are defined, for a given rate of profit r, by equations

$$\hat{\mathbf{B}}\mathbf{p} = (1 + r)\hat{\mathbf{A}}\mathbf{p} + w\hat{\mathbf{l}} \tag{9.2}$$

$$\mathbf{e}^T\mathbf{p} = 1. \tag{9.3}$$

A *cost-minimizing technique* is a technique whose prices are such that no existing process is able to pay extra profits, that is, $(\hat{\mathbf{A}}, \hat{\mathbf{B}}, \hat{\mathbf{l}})$ is a cost-minimizing technique at the rate of profit r if

$$\mathbf{B}\mathbf{p} \leqslant (1 + r)\mathbf{A}\mathbf{p} + w\mathbf{l}, \tag{9.4}$$

where $\mathbf{p}$ and w satisfy equations (9.2) and (9.3).

It will be assumed throughout this chapter that the requirements for consumption are represented by a given vector. This additional assumption will not change the results obtained since it will be shown that the pattern of consumption, or consumers' demand, does not play any role in determining prices: in other words, a Non-Substitution Theorem holds. Hence $\mathbf{d}$ in equation (9.1) is defined as

$$\mathbf{d}^T = g\mathbf{x}^T\hat{\mathbf{A}} + \mathbf{c}^T, \tag{9.5}$$

where g is the growth rate and $\mathbf{c}$ is a given vector whose first s entries are nonnegative and the last t entries equal zero because of Axiom (A.1.2).

2. **Main results**

Before stating the conditions for the existence and uniqueness of a cost-minimizing technique some Lemmata will be introduced. The following Lemma 9.1 summarizes Theorem 8.2 and the statement (a) of Theorem 8.1 of the previous chapter. It is reported here only for the sake of simplifying references.

Lemma 9.1. If the following Assumption 9.3 holds, and if $g \leqslant r$, then the following system of equations and inequalities has a solution:

$$[\mathbf{B} - (1 + r)\mathbf{A}]\mathbf{y} \leqslant \mathbf{l}, \tag{9.6a}$$

$$\mathbf{q}^T[\mathbf{B} - (1 + g)\mathbf{A}] \geqslant \mathbf{a}^T, \tag{9.6b}$$

$$\mathbf{q}^T[\mathbf{B} - (1 + r)\mathbf{A}]\mathbf{y} = \mathbf{q}^T\mathbf{l}, \tag{9.6c}$$

$$\mathbf{q}^T[\mathbf{B} - (1 + g)\mathbf{A}]\mathbf{y} = \mathbf{a}^T\mathbf{y}, \tag{9.6d}$$

$$\mathbf{q} \geqslant \mathbf{0}, \quad \mathbf{y} \geqslant \mathbf{0}, \tag{9.6e}$$

where $\mathbf{a}$ is a given semipositive vector.

Assumption 9.3. There is a vector $\mathbf{z}$ such that

$$\mathbf{z} \geqslant \mathbf{0}, \quad \mathbf{z}^T[\mathbf{B} - (1 + r)\mathbf{A}] \geqslant \mathbf{a}^T.$$

The following two Lemmata introduce the procedure which will be followed to derive the consequences of Assumption 9.1. This procedure resembles the one followed in Chapter 7, but is different in some respects. This is so since when old machines are not utilized jointly, a machine is overproduced (with a zero price) when it is not utilized in production at all. On the contrary, when old machines are utilized jointly, a machine may be overproduced (with a zero price) even if it is utilized in production. As a consequence the relative intensities of operation of processes producing the same finished good matter in determining whether a used machine is overproduced or not. Since the growth rate contributes to the determination of the relative intensities of operation of processes producing the same finished good, it also contributes to the determination of which of the used machines will be overproduced and, as a consequence, to the determination of prices. In order to avoid the difficulties we encountered in Section 3 of Chapter 5, we will consider only those values of the rate of profit at which all finished goods can be produced. The generalization is obvious.

Lemma 9.2. Let Assumptions 9.1 and 9.3 hold, let $g \leqslant r$, and let $(\mathbf{q}^*, \mathbf{y}^*)$ be a solution to system (9.6) for $\mathbf{a} = \hat{\mathbf{a}}$, where $\hat{\mathbf{a}}$ is a vector with each of the first s elements being equal to 1, and each of the others being equal to 0. Then there is a vector $\mathbf{q}^{**}$ such that $(\mathbf{q}^{**}, \mathbf{y}^*)$ is a solution to system (9.6) for $\mathbf{a} = \mathbf{c}$, where $\mathbf{c}$ is a semipositive vector whose last $(n-s)$ entries are nought.

Proof. Let $\mathbf{Q} = [q_{hk}]$ be an $s \times m$ matrix such that

$$
q_{hk} = \begin{cases} \mathbf{e}_h^T \mathbf{q}^* & \text{if} \quad \sum_{i=0}^{k-1} m_i < h \leq \sum_{i=0}^{k} m_i \\ 0 & \text{otherwise.} \end{cases}
$$

Let us define the matrices $\mathbf{D}_0, \mathbf{C}_0, \mathbf{D}_1, \mathbf{C}_1$, obtained by the following division of matrices $\mathbf{QA}$ and $\mathbf{QB}$: $(\mathbf{D}_0, \mathbf{D}_1) = \mathbf{QB}$, $(\mathbf{C}_0, \mathbf{C}_1) = \mathbf{QA}$, $\mathbf{C}_0$ and $\mathbf{D}_0$ being square. Since Assumption 9.1 holds and since the first s entries of $\hat{\mathbf{a}}$ are positive, all the others being equal to zero,

$$\mathbf{D}_0, \mathbf{C}_0, \mathbf{D}_1, \mathbf{C}_1 \text{ are nonnegative,} \quad \mathbf{D}_0 \text{ is diagonal,} \quad \text{diag } \mathbf{D}_0 > 0,$$
(9.7)

$$[\mathbf{D}_0 - (1+r)\mathbf{C}_0]\mathbf{y}_s^* + [\mathbf{D}_1 - (1+r)\mathbf{C}_1]\mathbf{y}_t^* = \mathbf{Ql},$$ (9.8)

$$[\mathbf{D}_1 - (1+g)\mathbf{C}_1] \geqslant 0, \quad [\mathbf{D}_1 - (1+g)\mathbf{C}_1]\mathbf{y}_t^* = 0,$$ (9.9)

$$\mathbf{e}^T[\mathbf{D}_0 - (1+r)\mathbf{C}_0] \geqslant \mathbf{e}^T,$$ (9.10)

where $(\mathbf{y}_s^{*T}, \mathbf{y}_t^{*T}) = \mathbf{y}^{*T}$. It is immediately recognized, because of (9.9), that if there is a nonnegative solution $\mathbf{v}^*$ to the equation

$$\mathbf{v}^T[\mathbf{D}_0 - (1+r)\mathbf{C}_0] = \mathbf{c}_s^T,$$

where $(\mathbf{c}_s^T, \mathbf{0}^T) = \mathbf{c}^T$, then vector $\mathbf{q}^{**} = \mathbf{Q}^T\mathbf{v}^*$ satisfies the Lemma. To prove that $\mathbf{v}^*$ exists it is enough to apply Theorem A.3.1 of the Mathematical Appendix to the square nonnegative matrix $\mathbf{C}_0\mathbf{D}_0^{-1}$ to show, because of inequality (9.10) and since $\mathbf{e} > 0$, that matrix $[\mathbf{D}_0 - (1+g)\mathbf{C}_0]$ is invertible and

$$[\mathbf{D}_0 - (1+r)\mathbf{C}_0]^{-1} \geqslant 0.$$ (9.11)

Q.E.D.

Lemma 9.3. Let Assumptions 9.1 and 9.3 hold and let $\mathbf{y}^* = (\mathbf{y}_s^{*T}, \mathbf{y}_t^{*T})^T$ be defined as in Lemma 9.2, then $\mathbf{y}_s^* > 0$ and the weak inequality (9.10) is satisfied as an equation.

Proof. Let $(\mathbf{q}_1^{**}, \mathbf{y}^*)$ be a solution to system (9.6) for $\mathbf{a} = \mathbf{e}_i, i \in \{1, 2, \ldots, s\}$. Thus,

$$\mathbf{q}_1^{**T}[\mathbf{B} - (1+g)\mathbf{A}]\mathbf{y}^* = \mathbf{e}_i^T\mathbf{y}^*$$

$$\mathbf{q}_1^{**T}[\mathbf{B} - (1+r)\mathbf{A}]\mathbf{y}^* = \mathbf{q}_1^{**T}\mathbf{l},$$

that is,

$$\mathbf{e}_i^T \mathbf{y}^* = \mathbf{q}_1^{**T}\mathbf{l} + (r - g)\mathbf{q}_1^{**T}\mathbf{A}\mathbf{y}^*.$$

Then, the first part of the Lemma is obtained since $(r - g) \geqslant 0$ and $\mathbf{q}_i^{**T}\mathbf{l} > 0$ because of Assumption 9.3. The second part of the Lemma is an immediate consequence of the first part.   Q.E.D.

Now the main theorems concerning existence, uniqueness, and the decreasing wage property can be proved.

Theorem 9.1. If Assumption 9.1 holds and $g \leqslant r$, then Assumption 9.3 is sufficient for the existence of a cost-minimizing technique. The choice of cost-minimizing techniques is independent of vector $\mathbf{c}$ provided that $\mathbf{c} = (\mathbf{c}_s^T, \mathbf{0}^T)^T$ and $\mathbf{c}_s \geqslant \mathbf{0}$.

Proof. Because of Lemma 9.2 and Axiom (A.1.5) the following system has a solution:

$$[\mathbf{B} - (1 + r)\mathbf{A}]\mathbf{y} \leqslant \mathbf{l}, \tag{9.12a}$$

$$\mathbf{q}^T[\mathbf{B} - (1 + g)\mathbf{A}] = \mathbf{c}^T, \tag{9.12b}$$

$$\mathbf{q}^T[\mathbf{B} - (1 + r)\mathbf{A}]\mathbf{y} = \mathbf{q}^T\mathbf{l}, \tag{9.12c}$$

$$\mathbf{q} \geqslant \mathbf{0}, \quad \mathbf{y} \geqslant \mathbf{0}. \tag{9.12d}$$

Then, since Theorem 8.3 of the previous chapter holds, we can select n processes in order to make up the technique $(\hat{\mathbf{A}}, \hat{\mathbf{B}}, \hat{\mathbf{l}})$ such that equations (9.1), (9.2), (9.3), (9.5), and inequality (9.4) are satisfied.   Q.E.D.

If the assumption of non-transferability of old machines were to be removed, that is, if Axiom A.1.4 did not hold, Lemma 9.2 and, therefore, Theorem 9.1 could not be established because matrices $\mathbf{A}$ and $\mathbf{B}$ would not have the required properties.

Theorem 9.2. If on the assumptions of Theorem 9.1 the rate of growth is taken to equal the rate of profit, that is, $g = r$, then the prices in terms of the wage rate of finished goods actually produced are uniquely determined, even if more than one cost-minimizing technique exists.

Proof. We will prove the Theorem under the assumption that all finished goods are produced. The generalization is trivial. Assume that there are two pairs of vectors $(\mathbf{y}^*, \mathbf{q}^*)$ and $(\bar{\mathbf{y}}^*, \bar{\mathbf{q}}^*)$ satisfying system (9.6) for $g = r$ and $\mathbf{a} = \hat{\mathbf{a}}$, where $\hat{\mathbf{a}}$ is defined as in Lemma 9.2, then we obtain from the following Lemma 9.4 that

$$\mathbf{y}_s^{*T} \leqslant \bar{\mathbf{y}}_s^{*T} \leqslant \mathbf{y}_s^{*T}.$$

                                                              Q.E.D.

Lemma 9.4. On the assumptions of Theorem 9.2, if **u** is any vector such that

$$\mathbf{u} \geqslant \mathbf{0}, \quad [\mathbf{B} - (1 + r)\mathbf{A}]\mathbf{u} \leqslant \mathbf{l},$$

then $\mathbf{u}_s \leqslant \mathbf{y}_s^*$, where $(\mathbf{u}_s^T, \mathbf{u}_t^T)^T = \mathbf{u}$ and $(\mathbf{y}_s^{*T}, \mathbf{y}_t^{*T})^T = \mathbf{y}^*$.

Proof. Since

$$[\mathbf{D}_0 - (1 + r)\mathbf{C}_0]\mathbf{u}_s + [\mathbf{D}_1 - (1 + r)\mathbf{C}_1]\mathbf{u}_t \leqslant \mathbf{Q}\mathbf{l},$$

we obtain, also because of inequality (9.9), that

$$[\mathbf{D}_0 - (1 + r)\mathbf{C}_0]\mathbf{u}_s \leqslant \mathbf{Q}\mathbf{l}.$$

Then the Lemma is proved because equations (9.8), (9.9), and inequality (9.11) hold. Q.E.D.

The following theorem restates the main results of Chapter 7 by using the direct approach.

Theorem 9.3. If in addition to the assumptions of Theorem 9.1 Assumption 9.2 holds, then

(a) the choice of cost-minimizing techniques is independent of the growth rate;
(b) prices of actually produced finished goods in terms of the wage rate are increasing functions of the rate of profit and are uniquely determined even if more than one cost-minimizing technique exists.

Proof. Let $\mathbf{q}^{**}$ and $\mathbf{y}^*$ be solutions of the following Linear Programming Problem and of its dual, respectively:

$$\text{Min} \quad \mathbf{q}^T \mathbf{l}$$
$$\text{s. to} \quad \mathbf{q}^T[\mathbf{B} - (1 + r)\mathbf{A}] \geqslant \hat{\mathbf{a}}^T$$
$$\mathbf{q} \geqslant \mathbf{0},$$

where $\hat{\mathbf{a}}$ is defined as in Lemma 9.2. With no loss of generality (see Lemma 8.4) let the number of weak inequalities

$$[\mathbf{B} - (1 + r)\mathbf{A}]\mathbf{y}^* \leqslant \mathbf{l}$$

which are satisfied as equations be greater than or equal to n. Statement (a) is proved by showing that there is a vector $\mathbf{q}^* \geqslant \mathbf{0}$ with positive elements only in correspondence with the just mentioned equations and such that

$$\mathbf{q}^{*T}[\mathbf{B} - (1 + g)\mathbf{A}] = \hat{\mathbf{a}}^T.$$

Since Assumption 9.2 holds and $\mathbf{y}^* \geqslant \mathbf{0}$, the proof of statement (a) follows as in Theorem 7.3 of Chapter 7. Statement (b) is an immediate consequence of statement (a), Theorem 9.2, and the fact that $\mathbf{y}^*$ is a solution to the linear programming problem

$$\text{Max} \qquad \mathbf{c}^T\mathbf{y}$$
$$\text{s. to} \quad [\mathbf{B} - (1 + r)\mathbf{A}]\mathbf{y} \leqslant \mathbf{1}$$
$$\mathbf{y} \geqslant \mathbf{0},$$

where $\mathbf{c}$ is any semipositive vector with the last t elements equal to zero.

Q.E.D.

Exercises 8.5–8.8 show that if Assumption 9.1 holds and Assumption 9.2 does not, then

(a) Assumption 9.3 is not necessary for the existence of a cost-minimizing technique;

(b) the choice of cost-minimizing techniques may depend on the growth rate;

(c) if more than one cost-minimizing technique exists, then
  (i) if $g < r$, uniqueness of prices, in terms of the wage rate, of both finished goods and old machines may not obtain,
  (ii) uniqueness of prices, in terms of the wage rate, of old machines may not obtain even if $g = r$;

(d) if $g > r$, a price in terms of the wage rate may be a decreasing function of the rate of profit.

3. Depreciation

Up to now no definition of a "new machine" has been provided nor has the ageing of machines been defined (except when Assumption 9.2 holds), nor have the physical units of machines been considered in order to be consistent among machines of the same "type," a concept which has also not been introduced. However, in order to say something about depreciation we need all these things since depreciation of a "type of machine" for one production period (year) is nothing else than the change in the price of that "type of machine" over that period. In this section a further assumption will be introduced. If the following assumption holds, then all previously mentioned concepts are well defined and this will allow us to deal with depreciation.

Assumption 9.4. Assumption 9.1 holds and it is possible to normalize the physical units of commodities in T in such a way that there are two natural numbers u and v such that the set T can be partitioned both in u subsets $T_{1*}, T_{2*}, \ldots, T_{u*}$ and in v subsets $T_{*1}, T_{*2}, \ldots, T_{*v}$ with the following properties.

(A.4.1) $T_{h*} \cap T_{k*} = \varnothing \, (h \neq k); \quad \bigcup_{i=1}^{u} T_{i*} = T;$

$T_{*h} \cap T_{*k} = \varnothing \, (h \neq k); \quad \bigcup_{i=1}^{v} T_{*i} = T;$

(A.4.2) the set $T_{ij} := T_{i*} \cap T_{*j}$ is either empty or consists of one commodity;

(A.4.3) $T_{ij} = \varnothing$ implies $T_{i,j+1} = \varnothing$;

(A.4.4) for each set T_{i*} there is a commodity s_i in S such that if a process has α units of the commodity in T_{i1} among its outputs, then it has α units of commodity s_i among its inputs;

(A.4.5) let $T_{ij} \neq \varnothing$ with $j \geqslant 2$, then if a process has α units of the commodity in T_{ij} among its outputs, then it has α units of the commodity in $T_{i,j-1}$ among its inputs.

If Assumption 9.4 holds, then it is possible to interpret the commodity in $T_{ij} \, (T_{ij} \neq \varnothing)$ as the j year old machine of type i. Commodity s_i mentioned in Axiom (A.4.4) can be interpreted as the new machine generating the old machine of type i. Let us remark that s_h may equal s_k, that is, machines of type h and machines of type k may be generated by the same new machine. When this interpretation is adopted, Axiom (A.4.3) means that if no machine of type i can be j years old, then no machine of type i can be $j + 1$ years old. Similarly, Axioms (A.4.4) and (A.4.5) mean that if α machines of type i of age j are produced with a process, then that process utilizes α machines of type i of age $j - 1$.

As was done in Chapter 7, let $p_0(r), p_1(r), \ldots, p_t(r)$ be the prices of machines of the same type which are $0, 1, \ldots, t$ years old, respectively. (A machine which is 0 years old is, of course, a new machine.) In a given cost-minimizing technique the type of machine under consideration is assumed as having an economic life of t years $(p_{t+1}(r) \equiv 0)$. Then the *depreciation of the i year old machine* is

$$M_i(r) = p_i(r) - p_{i+1}(r) \quad (i = 0, 1, \ldots, t-1)$$

$$M_t(r) = p_t(r).$$

The *annual charge relative to the i year old machine* is

$$Y_i(r) = (1+r)p_i(r) - p_{i+1}(r) \quad (i = 0, 1, \ldots, t-1)$$

$$Y_t(r) = (1+r)p_t(r).$$

As in Chapter 7, the *efficiency* of an i year old machine can be defined as *constant, increasing* or *decreasing* if the annual charge of that machine is equal to, lower or higher than the annual charge of the $i + 1$ year old machine of the same type. If the efficiency of a type of machine is constant whatever the age of the machine, then usual capitalization formulas are obtained as in Chapter 7:

$$Y(r) = p_0(r) \frac{r(1+r)^{t+1}}{(1+r)^{t+1} - 1},$$

$$p_i(r) = p_0(r) \frac{(1+r)^{t+1} - (1+r)^i}{(1+r)^{t+1} - 1}, \quad (i = 0, 1, \ldots, t)$$

$$M_i(r) = p_0(r) \frac{r(1+r)^i}{(1+r)^{t+1} - 1}. \quad (i = 0, 1, \ldots, t)$$

4. "Depreciation by evaporation"

In the literature one frequently encounters the concept of "depreciation by evaporation," or "depreciation by radioactive decay." This is obtained by assuming that the annual charge of the "new machine" equals $(d+r)p_0(r)$, where d is a constant real number and $0 < d < 1$; d is called "rate of depreciation." If one wants to use the framework provided in this chapter in order to formalize the concept of "depreciation by evaporation," then this can be done in the following three ways.

(i) Consider the two processes depicted in Table 9.3. These processes determine the following two equations:

$$(1+r)(\mathbf{a} + \mathbf{e}_h)^T \mathbf{p}_s + lw = \mathbf{e}_i^T \mathbf{p}_s + \mathbf{e}_k^T \mathbf{p}_t \tag{9.15a}$$

$$(1+r)[(1-d)\mathbf{a}^T \mathbf{p}_s + \mathbf{e}_k^T \mathbf{p}_t] + (1-d)lw = (1-d)\mathbf{e}_i^T \mathbf{p}_s + (1-d)\mathbf{e}_k^T \mathbf{p}_t. \tag{9.15b}$$

Then by multiplying equation (9.15a) by $(d+r)/(1+r)$ and equation (9.15b) by $(1/1+r)$ and adding them one obtains

$$(1+r)\mathbf{a}^T \mathbf{p}_s + (d+r)\mathbf{e}_h^T \mathbf{p}_s + lw = \mathbf{e}_i^T \mathbf{p}_s. \tag{9.16}$$

Process $(z+2)$ of Table 9.3 does not satisfy Assumption 9.4.

(ii) An alternative way to use the framework provided in this chapter in order to formalize the concept of "depreciation by evaporation" consists of taking into account the u processes depicted in Table 9.4. In fact these processes determine the following u equations:

$$(1+r)(\mathbf{a} + \mathbf{e}_h)^T \mathbf{p}_s + lw = \mathbf{e}_i^T \mathbf{p}_s + \mathbf{e}_k^T \mathbf{p}_t \tag{9.17.1}$$

$$\cdots\cdots\cdots\cdots\cdots$$

$$(1+r)[(1-d)^{j-1}\mathbf{a}^T \mathbf{p}_s + \mathbf{e}_{k+j-2}^T \mathbf{p}_t] + (1-d)^{j-1}lw$$
$$= (1-d)^{j-1}\mathbf{e}_i^T \mathbf{p}_s + \mathbf{e}_{k+j-1}^T \mathbf{p}_t \tag{9.17.j}$$

Table 9.3

	material inputs		labor		outputs	
	finished goods	old machines			finished goods	old machines
$(z+1)$	$\mathbf{a}+\mathbf{e}_h$	$\mathbf{0}$	1	$\rightarrow$	$\mathbf{e}_i$	$\mathbf{e}_k$
$(z+2)$	$(1-d)\mathbf{a}$	$\mathbf{e}_k$	$(1-d)1$	$\rightarrow$	$(1-d)\mathbf{e}_i$	$(1-d)\mathbf{e}_k$

Table 9.4

	material inputs		labor		outputs	
	finished goods	old machines			finished goods	old machines
$(z+1)$	$\mathbf{a}+\mathbf{e}_h$	$\mathbf{0}$	1	$\rightarrow$	$\mathbf{e}_i$	$\mathbf{e}_k$
$(z+2)$	$(1-d)\mathbf{a}$	$\mathbf{e}_k$	$(1-d)1$	$\rightarrow$	$(1-d)\mathbf{e}_i$	$\mathbf{e}_{k+1}$
$(\ldots)$	$\ldots$	$\ldots$	$\ldots$	$\rightarrow$	$\ldots$	$\ldots$
$(z+j)$	$(1-d)^{j-1}\mathbf{a}$	$\mathbf{e}_{k+j-2}$	$(1-d)^{j-1}1$	$\rightarrow$	$(1-d)^{j-1}\mathbf{e}_i$	$\mathbf{e}_{k+j-1}$
$(\ldots)$	$\ldots$	$\ldots$	$\ldots$	$\rightarrow$	$\ldots$	$\ldots$
$(z+u-1)$	$(1-d)^{u-2}\mathbf{a}$	$\mathbf{e}_{k+u-3}$	$(1-d)^{u-2}1$	$\rightarrow$	$(1-d)^{u-2}\mathbf{e}_i$	$\mathbf{e}_{k+u-2}$
$(z+u)$	$(1-d)^{u-1}\mathbf{a}$	$\mathbf{e}_{k+u-2}$	$(1-d)^{u-1}1$	$\rightarrow$	$(1-d)^{u-1}\mathbf{e}_i$	$(1-d)\mathbf{e}_{k+u-2}$

. . . .

$$(1+r)[(1-d)^{u-1}\mathbf{a}^T\mathbf{p}_s + \mathbf{e}_{k+u-2}^T\mathbf{p}_t] + (1-d)^{u-1}lw$$
$$= (1-d)^{u-1}\mathbf{e}_i^T\mathbf{p}_s + (1-d)\mathbf{e}_{k+u-2}^T\mathbf{p}_t, \qquad (9.17.u)$$

where $j = 2, 3, \ldots, u-1$. Then by multiplying equation (9.17.u) by $1/(1+r)^{u-1}$ and equation (9.17.j) by $(d+r)/(1+r)^j$, $j = 1, 2, \ldots, u-1$, and adding them one once again obtains equation (9.16) (cf. exercise 8.11). All processes *but the last one* of Table 9.4 satisfy Assumption 9.4.

(iii) Finally, if the reader is ready to consider a model with an infinite number of commodities and an infinite number of operated processes, then it is possible to consider the processes of Table 9.5.[1] In fact these processes determine the following infinite number of equations:

$$(1+r)(\mathbf{a}+\mathbf{e}_h)^T\mathbf{p}_s + lw = \mathbf{e}_i^T\mathbf{p}_s + \mathbf{e}_k^T\mathbf{p}_t \qquad (9.18.1)$$

. . . .

$$(1+r)[(1-d)^{j-1}\mathbf{a}^T\mathbf{p}_s + \mathbf{e}_{k+j-2}^T\mathbf{p}_t] + (1-d)^{j-1}lw$$
$$= (1-d)^{j-1}\mathbf{e}_i^T\mathbf{p}_s + \mathbf{e}_{k+j-1}^T\mathbf{p}_t \qquad (9.18.j)$$

. . . .

[1] This analysis requires a more general definition of vector space than that provided in the Mathematical Appendix.

Table 9.5

	material inputs		labor		outputs	
	finished goods	old machines			finished goods	old machines
$(z+1)$	$\mathbf{a} + \mathbf{e_h}$	$\mathbf{0}$	1	$\rightarrow$	$\mathbf{e_i}$	$\mathbf{e_k}$
$(z+2)$	$(1-d)\mathbf{a}$	$\mathbf{e_k}$	$(1-d)l$	$\rightarrow$	$(1-d)\mathbf{e_i}$	$\mathbf{e_{k+1}}$
$(...)$	...	...	...	$\rightarrow$	...	...
$(z+j)$	$(1-d)^{j-1}\mathbf{a}$	$\mathbf{e_{k+j-2}}$	$(1-d)^{j-1}l$	$\rightarrow$	$(1-d)^{j-1}\mathbf{e_i}$	$\mathbf{e_{k+j-1}}$
$(...)$	...	...	...	$\rightarrow$	...	...

where $j = 2, 3, \ldots$. Then by multiplying equation (9.18.j) by $(d+r)/(1+r)^j$, $j = 1, 2, \ldots$, and adding them one once again obtains equation (9.16) (cf. exercise 8.12). All processes of Table 9.5 satisfy Assumption 9.4.

The analysis just elaborated has made it clear that the assumption of "depreciation by evaporation" can be expressed in terms of the model provided in this chapter by using a finite number of processes and a finite number of commodities: however, in this case the age of machines cannot be defined; hence the concept of *depreciation* remains somewhat vague. Alternatively, the concept can be formalized by using an infinite number of processes and an infinite number of commodities: in this case the presentation corresponds with the idea of a "machine" becoming older every year, but it requires the premise that the "machine" has an infinite lifetime. Therefore, we may conclude that the concept of "depreciation by evaporation" is highly implausible.

A limiting case of "depreciation by evaporation" is obtained when $d = 0$. This is typically the case of a machine lasting forever with a constant efficiency. Machines with an infinite lifetime and constant efficiency or "depreciation by evaporation" have been often assumed in the literature, since they can be dealt with very simply: in fact, only new machines with their annual charges need to be taken into account. The framework provided in this chapter is also able to take into account other cases of machines with an infinite lifetime: exercise 8.13 investigates the case of a perennial machine whose efficiency exhibits a cyclical pattern over time.

5. The problem of scrap

Up to now free disposal of old machines has been assumed. An interesting variant could be the introduction of a different assumption asserting that the entire amount of scrapped machines are required, directly or indirectly, in the reproduction of the finished goods they are produced with. This variant will be formalized in this section.

Assumption 9.5. It is possible to mark outputs in such a way that two subsets, S and T, of the set of commodities N can be distinguished so that

(A.5.1) $S \cap T = \varnothing, S \cup T = N$;

(A.5.2) commodities in T are never consumed;

(A.5.3) commodities in T are never produced as marked outputs;

(A.5.4) each process produces one and only one commodity in S as a marked output;

(A.5.5) if commodity $i \in T$ is produced by process j producing commodity $h \in S$ as a marked output, then there is no process producing a commodity $k \in S$ as a marked output, $k \neq h$, such that either it produces i or it utilizes i as an input;

(A.5.6) for each process producing commodity $j \in T$ there is a process with the same inputs and the same outputs except that commodity j is not produced and some other commodities in S are produced as non marked outputs;

(A.5.7) commodities in S which are produced as non-marked outputs are fully utilized, directly or indirectly, in the reproduction of the marked outputs they are produced with, that is, let $\mathbf{B}_1, \mathbf{B}_2$, and $\mathbf{B}_3$ ($\mathbf{B}_1 + \mathbf{B}_2 + \mathbf{B}_3 = \mathbf{B}$) be $m \times n$ nonnegative matrices such that the positive entries of $\mathbf{B}_1$ are the marked outputs, the positive entries of $\mathbf{B}_2$ are the non marked outputs of commodities in S, and the positive entries in $\mathbf{B}_3$ are the outputs of commodities in T, then

$$(\mathbf{x} \geqslant \mathbf{0}, \ \mathbf{x}^T(\mathbf{B} - \mathbf{A}) \geqslant \mathbf{0}) \Rightarrow \mathbf{x}^T(\mathbf{B}_2 - \mathbf{A}) \leqslant \mathbf{0}.$$

It is immediately recognized that if and only if Assumption 9.1 holds Assumption 9.5 is satisfied with all commodities in S produced as marked outputs. On the contrary, if Assumption 9.5 holds and Assumption 9.1 does not, then we can, for simplicity, refer to the commodities in T as *old machines*, the commodities in S as *finished goods*, and the non marked outputs of finished goods as *scrapped machines*.

Assumption 9.6. Assumption 9.5 and Axioms (A.2.1), (A.2.2), and (A.2.3) hold.

Theorem 9.4. In Theorems 9.1 and 9.2 Assumption 9.1 can be substituted by Assumption 9.5; in Theorem 9.3 Assumption 9.2 can be substituted by Assumption 9.6.

Proof. To prove the Theorem we just need the following Lemma 9.5.

Q.E.D.

Lemma 9.5. Let $\mathbf{A}, \mathbf{C}, \mathbf{D}$ be square matrices of the same dimension such that

(i) $\mathbf{D}$ is diagonal and diag $\mathbf{D} > \mathbf{0}$,

(ii) $(\mathbf{x} \geqslant \mathbf{0}, \ \mathbf{x}^T(\mathbf{D} + \mathbf{C} - \mathbf{A}) \geqslant \mathbf{0}) \Rightarrow \mathbf{x}^T(\mathbf{C} - \mathbf{A}) \leqslant \mathbf{0}$,

(iii) $\exists \mathbf{q}: \mathbf{q} \geqslant \mathbf{0}, \ \mathbf{q}^T(\mathbf{D} + \mathbf{C} - \mathbf{A}) > \mathbf{0}$.

Then the matrix $(\mathbf{D} + \mathbf{C} - \mathbf{A})$ is non-singular and $(\mathbf{D} + \mathbf{C} - \mathbf{A})^{-1} \geqslant 0$.

Proof. It is sufficient to remark that

$$(\mathbf{x} \geqslant 0, \mathbf{x}^T(\mathbf{D} + \mathbf{C} - \mathbf{A}) > 0) \Rightarrow \mathbf{x} > 0;$$

then the proof follows the proofs of Lemma A.3.1 and Theorem A.3.1 in the Mathematical Appendix.   Q.E.D.

6. On the plant once again

In Chapter 7 it has been argued that the framework provided there can well be used to deal with jointly utilized *new* machines if the costs of separating and reassembling components of a plant are sufficiently large. This assertion was quite vague, but it can now be rendered clear in terms of the following example.

Example 9.3. There are seven commodities whose processes are represented by Table 9.6 ($\beta \leqslant 5$); only commodity 1 is consumed.

It is immediately recognized that Assumption 9.1 holds: commodities 1 and 2 are finished goods, whereas commodities 3–7 are old machines. Processes (12)–(23) are introduced in order to satisfy Axiom (A.1.5) with respect to processes (2)–(11); hence we concentrate on processes (1)–(11). Process (2) produces two old machines (commodities 3 and 5), whereas process (8) produces only one old machine (commodity 6); moreover, process (2) has larger costs in terms of commodity 1 and labor. These costs can be interpreted as costs of separating the two components (commodities 3 and 5) of a plant (commodity 6). Analogously, process (3) utilizes two old machines (commodities 3 and 5), whereas process (9) utilizes only one old machine (commodity 6); moreover, process (3) has larger costs in terms of commodity 1 and labor. These costs can be interpreted as costs of reassembling the two components (commodities 3 and 5) of a plant (commodity 6). Similar arguments apply for processes (6) and (10) and processes (7) and (11).

It is easily recognized that if $\beta = 1$, then it is never convenient to separate and reassemble the components of the plant (cf. exercise 8.16). If this is so we can put to one side processes (2), (3), (6), (7), (12)–(15), and (18)–(20): all the other processes include the only operable processes. Moreover, these last processes taken in isolation satisfy Assumption 9.2, that is, the assumptions of Chapter 7. This is the case in which "the costs of separating and reassembling the components of a plant are sufficiently large." On the contrary, if $\beta = 3$, processes (8)–(11) and (21)–(23) are never operated, that is, it is always convenient to separate and reassemble the components of a plant (cf. exercise 8.18). Finally, if $\beta = 2$, all processes (1)–(23) need to

Table 9.6

	commodity inputs								outputs						
	1	2	3	4	5	6	7	labor		1	2	3	4	5	6	7
(1)	5	0	0	0	0	0	0	1	→	0	1	0	0	0	0	0
(2)	5	2	0	0	0	0	0	1	→	20	0	1	0	1	0	0
(3)	5	0	1	0	1	0	0	1	→	30	0	0	1	0	0	0
(4)	5	1	0	1	0	0	0	1	→	30	0	0	0	1	0	0
(5)	5	1	0	0	1	0	0	1	→	30	0	1	0	0	0	0
(6)	5	1	1	0	0	0	0	1	→	30	0	0	1	1	0	0
(7)	5	0	0	1	1	0	0	1	→	20	0	0	0	0	0	0
(8)	β	2	0	0	0	0	0	$\frac{4}{5}$	→	20	0	0	0	0	1	0
(9)	β	0	0	0	0	1	0	$\frac{4}{5}$	→	30	0	0	1	0	0	0
(10)	β	1	1	0	0	0	1	$\frac{4}{5}$	→	30	0	0	0	0	0	1
(11)	β	0	0	0	0	0	1	$\frac{4}{5}$	→	20	0	0	0	0	0	0
(12)	5	2	0	0	0	0	0	1	→	20	0	0	0	1	0	0
(13)	5	2	0	0	0	0	0	1	→	20	0	1	0	0	0	0
(14)	5	2	0	0	0	0	0	1	→	20	0	0	0	0	0	0
(15)	5	0	1	0	1	0	0	1	→	30	0	0	0	0	0	0
(16)	5	1	0	1	0	0	0	1	→	30	0	0	0	0	0	0
(17)	5	1	0	0	1	0	0	1	→	30	0	0	0	0	0	0
(18)	5	1	1	0	0	0	0	1	→	30	0	0	0	1	0	0
(19)	5	1	1	0	0	0	0	1	→	30	0	0	1	0	0	0
(20)	5	1	1	0	0	0	0	1	→	30	0	0	0	0	0	0
(21)	β	2	0	0	0	0	0	$\frac{4}{5}$	→	20	0	0	0	0	0	0
(22)	β	0	0	0	0	1	0	$\frac{4}{5}$	→	30	0	0	0	0	0	0
(23)	β	1	1	0	0	0	1	$\frac{4}{5}$	→	30	0	0	0	0	0	0

be considered in order to determine cost-minimizing techniques (cf. exercise 8.17).

The analysis of this example should have clarified that there are cases in which the complication of models with jointly utilized machines can be put to one side by using the device of the "plant." But in order to analyze when this can be done we need a complete model which includes not only the processes in which the plant is not dismantled and reassembled, but all processes. As a consequence, this analysis cannot avoid dealing with the complications connected with models which allow for jointly utilized (old) machines.

7. **Historical notes**

7.1. The fact that modern production processes are increasingly characterized by the joint utilization of durable means of production has been
noted by many authors since the time of the classical economists. It was
especially emphasized in contributions to the genre of industrial-technological literature, which boomed at the beginning of the 19th century and
which of course was an offspring of the Industrial Revolution. Important
works in this direction include Charles Babbage's *On the Economy of
Machinery and Manufactures* ([1832] 1986) and Andrew Ure's *Philosophy
of Manufactures* (1835). Babbage was fascinated with contemporary industrial technology and its application in the factory system. He provided an
analysis of machine functions and studied the emerging forms of industrial
organization with its sophisticated division of labor and division of skills.
He wrote: "There exists a natural, although, in point of number, a very
unequal division amongst machines: they may be classed as; *1st. Those
which are employed to produce power*; and as, *2dly. Those which are intended
merely to transmit force and execute work.* The first of these divisions is
of great importance, and is very limited in the variety of its species,
although some of those species consist in numerous individuals" (1986,
p. 16). One of the main tasks of the organization of the labor process
consists of judiciously combining elements of these two types of machinery.

The significance of the industrial-technological literature to political
economy was not always properly appreciated. Exceptions were John
Stuart Mill ([1848] 1965) and Karl Marx. Elaborating on the works of
Babbage, Ure, and others, Marx, in chapter XV (in the German original:
Chapter 13), "Machinery and Modern Industry," of volume I of *Capital*,
dealt in detail with what he called "systems of machinery." He wrote,
reflecting the above passage quoted from Babbage: "A fully developed
machinery consists of three essentially different parts, the motor mechanism,
the transmitting mechanism, and finally the tool or working machine"
([1867] 1954, p. 352). The simultaneous use of several machines in a given
line of production is well expressed in the following passages: "Each detail
machine supplies raw material to the machine next in order; and since
they are all working at the same time, the product is always going through
the various stages of its fabrication. ... A system of machinery, whether it
reposes on the mere co-operation of similar machines, as in weaving, or
on a combination of different machines, as in spinning, constitutes in itself
a huge automaton, whenever it is driven by a self-acting prime mover.
... An organised system of machines, to which motion is communicated
by the transmitting mechanism from a central automaton, is the most
developed form of production by machinery. Here we have, in the place

of the isolated machine, a mechanical monster whose body fills whole factories, and whose demon power, at first veiled under the slow and measured motions of his giant limbs, at length breaks out into the fast and furious whirl of his countless working organs" (ibid., pp. 359–61).

While these discussions contain interesting observations, many of a philosophical nature, on the socio-technological revolutions that were taking place, they do not really lead to an adequate treatment of the jointness of utilization of durable capital goods in the theory of value and distribution: the analytical approaches put forward in this field remain essentially confined to the case of a single type of fixed capital good, or rather a "representative machine," in each sector of the economy, despite the overwhelming empirical importance of the joint utilization of different kinds of machines.

7.2. The problem of machines that are utilized jointly is, of course, mentioned in the literature on capital utilization. In Robin Marris's classic study *The Economics of Capital Utilisation* (1964), it is stressed: "The fixed capital employed in a typical manufacturing establishment consists of a wide variety of inter-connected equipment, all collaborating in final output. But although the various items are usually essential to one another, i.e. are inter-dependent in the general production process, it is by no means essential that all be operated at identical rates of utilisation. ... It would appear that for each type of equipment there should exist an 'optimum rate of utilisation' which maximises the type's contribution to the general rate of profit." Marris then points out the difficulty of the problem under consideration: "If this optimum rate of utilisation for each type of equipment could be determined independently of the factors influencing the optimum rates of the other types, the problem would be simple. We would find each type's independently determined optimum rate and then compute the number of units required, by dividing in each case the required output by the product of the hourly rate of output of that type of equipment and the optimum rate of utilisation expressed in machine-hours per annum. Unfortunately, this solution is rarely available. Because intermediate outputs are usually required in virtually fixed proportions, the optimum rate of utilisation on any one type of equipment is inevitably affected by the operating conditions of the other types, and these in turn depend on what has been decided about the first type. *The solution is therefore inevitably simultaneous and inevitably complex*" (1964, pp. 28–9; emphasis added). It is emphasized that changes in the pattern of operation of plant and equipment generally necessitate the decomposition and reassembling of at least some parts of the capital stock. See also the studies by Betancourt and Clague (1981), and Winston (1982), which are cast in a neoclassical framework and use production functions. The book by Scherer et al. (1975) is predominantly concerned with the size of plants operated by firms and the question of returns to scale. While these studies are rich in terms of the empirical material they present, being essentially restricted analytically to a *partial* framework, they cannot provide the required "simultaneous and complex solution." Moreover, in the few cases in which there is more than a passing reference to the joint utilization of machines only very special cases are dealt with.

7.3. While the original formulations of the Non-Substitution Theorem assumed single production and therefore circulating capital only (see the historical notes to Chapter 5), later formulations allowed for the existence of fixed capital (see Samuelson, 1961, Mirrlees, 1969, Stiglitz, 1970, and Krause, 1986). The case of jointly utilized machines is dealt with by Stiglitz (1970) under a number of restrictive conditions. Exercise 8.5 below shows a case in which the theorem interpreted as a uniqueness theorem does not hold (see the historical notes to Chapter 5).

7.4. Sraffa's analysis of fixed capital (1960, ch. X) is limited to the special case in which each sector uses a single type of durable capital good only. Interestingly, most of the contributions to the problem of fixed capital in the Sraffian tradition are restricted to this case. The analysis was extended to cover special cases of the joint utilization of different types of machines by Schefold (1971, 1989), with no analysis of the choice of technique. Roncaglia (1971) discussed the case in which the efficiency of machines is constant throughout their lifetime, still with no analysis of the choice of technique. The problem of "scrap" was also dealt with by Varri (1981). The concept of the "plant" was at the center of a debate among Baldone (1987), Roncaglia (1976), Salvadori (1977, 1979a, 1986a, 1987b), and Varri (1976, 1979, 1987). The present chapter follows rather closely Salvadori (1986a, 1987b, 1988a).

7.5. The concept of "depreciation by evaporation" is still widely used in both theoretical and applied economics. It does, for example, underlie much of the work in input–output analysis; Leontief himself made use of it (cf. Leontief, 1953; see also the historical note 9.4 of Chapter 7). Meade adopted it in his neoclassical model of economic growth (cf. Meade, 1961). Hicks used it in *Capital and Growth* (1965); yet interestingly he entertained the opinion: "I do not think that this statement [i.e. the assumption that a fixed proportion of a durable capital good is used up per period] implies a confusion between depreciation in value terms and physical using-up; or that it involves us in a concept of 'evaporation,' in the manner of Professor Meade. What it does imply is an absence of indivisibilities, so that in each period a part of the stock of each capital good is actually discarded" (1965, pp. 161–2, fn. 3).

In the so-called Cambridge controversy in the theory of capital (for a summary statement, see Chapter 14), in the majority of contributions in which fixed capital was taken into account at all, "depreciation by evaporation" was assumed. Samuelson introduced it in the following terms: "To keep [the capital] good homogeneous independently of age, one has to assume a force of mortality independent of age (or an exponential life table). This means that physical depreciation is always directly proportional to the physical stock" (Samuelson, 1962, p. 197); see also Solow (1963), Spaventa (1968) and Harris (1973). The concept was explicitly criticized by Morishima (1969, p. 89, and 1973, ch. 13) and Garegnani (1970, p. 409, fn. 3): while the former's point of reference is the von Neumann model, the latter's is Sraffa's analysis.

8. Exercises

8.1. Show that if and only if Assumption 9.2 holds the axioms stated in Chapter 7 hold.

8.2. Provide details of the proof of the second part of Lemma 9.3.

8.3. Prove Theorem 9.2 on the assumption that not all finished goods are produced.

8.4. Provide details of the proof of Theorem 9.3.

8.5. (Salvadori, 1986a, 1988a) There are five commodities whose processes are represented by Table 9.7; only commodity 1 is consumed. Show that Assumption 9.1 holds: commodities 1, 2, and 3 are finished goods; commodities 4 and 5 are old machines. Then determine prices and the wage rate for each feasible rate of profit. Show that

(i) if $0 \leqslant r \leqslant \alpha$ and $0 \leqslant g \leqslant (\sqrt{2} - 1)$, where α is the positive real solution of the equation

$$15 - 17r - 36r^2 - 16r^3 - 2r^4 = 0,$$

then the technique made up of processes (1, 2, 4, 5, 10) is cost-minimizing;

(ii) if still $0 \leqslant r \leqslant \alpha$, but $(\sqrt{2} - 1) \leqslant g \leqslant \beta$, where β is the positive real solution of the equation

$$12 - 7r - 28r^2 - 17r^3 - 3r^4 = 0,$$

then the technique made up of processes (1, 2, 3, 4, 5) is cost-minimizing;

Table 9.7

	commodity inputs							outputs				
	1	2	3	4	5	labor		1	2	3	4	5
(1)	1	0	0	0	0	1	→	0	1	0	0	0
(2)	2	0	0	0	0	1	→	0	0	1	0	0
(3)	0	1	0	0	0	2	→	5	0	0	1	1
(4)	0	0	0	1	0	0	→	5	0	0	0	2
(5)	0	1	0	0	1	2	→	5	0	0	1	0
(6)	0	1	0	0	0	2	→	5	0	0	0	1
(7)	0	1	0	0	0	2	→	5	0	0	1	0
(8)	0	1	0	0	0	2	→	5	0	0	0	0
(9)	0	0	0	1	0	0	→	5	0	0	0	0
(10)	0	1	0	0	1	2	→	5	0	0	0	0

(iii) if $g = (\sqrt{2} - 1)(< \alpha)$ and $0 \leqslant r \leqslant \alpha$, then the previously mentioned two techniques are both cost-minimizing, and

(a) if $(\sqrt{2} - 1) < r < \alpha$, then the prices of all commodities are different;

(b) if $r = (\sqrt{2} - 1)$, then the prices of finished goods are the same in both techniques, but the prices of old machines are not.

8.6. (Salvadori, 1988a) There are two commodities whose processes are represented by Table 9.8; only commodity 1 is consumed. Show that Assumption 9.1 holds: commodity 1 is a finished good; commodity 2 is an old machine. Then determine prices and the wage rate for each feasible rate of profit. Show that

(i) Assumption 9.3 holds only if $r < \alpha$, where α is the positive real solution of the equation

$$r^2 - 3r - 39 = 0,$$

whereas the technique made up of processes (2, 5) is cost-minimizing if $g = 0$ and $(61/24) \leqslant r \leqslant 39$;

(ii) if $0 \leqslant r \leqslant \beta$ and $0 \leqslant g \leqslant 1.5$, where β is the positive real solution of the equation

$$309r^2 + 6073r - 11701 = 0,$$

then the technique made up of processes (1, 4) is cost-minimizing;

Table 9.8

	commodity inputs				outputs	
	1	2	labor		1	2
(1)	25	10	1	→	125	25
(2)	1	1	1	→	40	1
(3)	1	0	20	→	5	1
(4)	25	10	1	→	125	0
(5)	1	1	1	→	40	0
(6)	1	0	20	→	5	0

Table 9.9

	commodity inputs					outputs		
	1	2	3	labor		1	2	3
(1)	1	0	0	1	→	0	1	0
(2)	0	3	2	0	→	14	0	3
(3)	0	5	2	0	→	18	0	5
(4)	0	3	2	0	→	14	0	0
(5)	0	5	2	0	→	18	0	0

(iii) if $0 \leqslant r \leqslant \beta$ and $1.5 \leqslant g \leqslant 4$, then the technique made up of processes $(1, 3)$ is cost-minimizing;

(iv) if $0 < g < 1.5$ and $\beta < r < (61/24)$, then the techniques made up of processes $(1, 2)$, $(1, 4)$, and $(2, 3)$, respectively, are all cost-minimizing with three different price vectors;

(v) if the technique made up of processes $(1, 2)$ is adopted, the price of commodity 1 in terms of the wage rate is a decreasing function of the rate of profit.

8.7. (Salvadori, 1986a) There are three commodities whose processes are represented by Table 9.9; only commodity 1 is consumed. Show that Assumption 9.1 holds: commodities $1, 2$ are finished goods; commodity 3 is an old machine. Then determine prices and the wage rate for each feasible rate of profit. Then show that

(i) if $0 \leqslant r \leqslant (\sqrt{13/3} - 1)$ and $0 \leqslant g \leqslant \frac{1}{2}$, then the technique made up of processes $(1, 2, 4)$ is cost-minimizing;

Table 9.10

	commodity inputs				labor		outputs			
	1	2	3	4	labor		1	2	3	4
(1)	1	0	0	0	1	→	2	0	0	0
(2)	1	0	0	0	1	→	0	1	1	0
(3)	0	0	1	0	1	→	0	1	0	1
(4)	0	0	0	1	1	→	0	1	2	0
(5)	0	0	1	0	1	→	0	1	0	0
(6)	0	0	0	1	1	→	0	1	0	0

(ii) if $0 \leqslant r \leqslant 1$ and $\frac{1}{2} \leqslant g \leqslant 1$, then the technique made up of processes (1, 2, 3) is cost-minimizing;

(iii) if $g = \frac{1}{2}$ and $0 \leqslant r \leqslant 1$, then the previously mentioned two techniques are both cost-minimizing, and the price vectors are different.

8.8. (Salvadori, 1986a) There are four commodities whose processes are represented by Table 9.10; only commodity 2 is consumed. Show that Assumption 9.1 holds: commodities 1 and 2 are finished goods; commodities 3 and 4 are old machines. Then determine prices and the wage rate for each feasible rate of profit. Show that

(i) if $0 \leqslant r \leqslant 1$ and $0 \leqslant g \leqslant (\sqrt{2} - 1)$, then the technique consisting of processes (3, 4, 5) and (3, 4, 6) are both cost-minimizing, commodity 1 is not produced, and commodities 3 and 4 both have a zero price in both cost-minimizing techniques;

(ii) if still $0 \leqslant r \leqslant 1$ but $(\sqrt{2} - 1) \leqslant g \leqslant 1$, then the technique consisting of processes (1, 2, 3, 4) is cost-minimizing.

If $g = (\sqrt{2} - 1)$ and $0 \leqslant r \leqslant 1$, then the previously mentioned three techniques are all cost-minimizing. Find out whether or not the prices of commodities are equal in the different techniques.

8.9. Can you show that Axiom (A.2.3) is necessary in order to obtain Theorem 9.3? [*Hint*: Use the results of the previous three exercises.]

8.10. Show that the technologies given in exercises 8.5–8.7 satisfy Assumption 9.4 whereas the one given in exercise 8.8 does not.

8.11. Show that equations (9.17) imply equation (9.16). [*Hint*: Follow the procedure suggested in the text. You also need to prove that

$$(d+r)\sum_{j=1}^{u-1}\frac{(1-d)^{j-1}}{(1+r)^j} + \left(\frac{1-d}{1+r}\right)^{u-1} = 1.$$

Since $d + r = (1 + r) - (1 - d)$, the left-hand side above can be stated as

$$\sum_{j=1}^{u-1}\left(\frac{1-d}{1+r}\right)^{j-1} - \sum_{j=1}^{u-1}\left(\frac{1-d}{1+r}\right)^{j} + \left(\frac{1-d}{1+r}\right)^{u-1},$$

which equals

$$\left(\frac{1-d}{1+r}\right)^{0} - \left(\frac{1-d}{1+r}\right)^{u-1} + \left(\frac{1-d}{1+r}\right)^{u-1}$$

which equals 1.]

8.12. (Calculus) Show that equations (9.18) imply equation (9.16). [*Hint*: Follow the procedure suggested in the text. You also need to prove that

$$(d + r) \lim_{u \to \infty} \sum_{j=1}^{u} \frac{(1-d)^{j-1}}{(1+r)^{j}} = 1.$$

Follow a procedure similar to that suggested in the hint of the previous exercise in order to show that the left-hand side above equals

$$\left(\frac{1-d}{1+r}\right)^{0} - \lim_{u \to \infty}\left(\frac{1-d}{1+r}\right)^{u},$$

then, ...]

8.13. Follow the procedure used in Section 4 in order to show that (i) the technology described in exercise 8.8 can represent that of a machine lasting forever, and (ii) the price of commodity 3 equals the price of a machine which is an odd number of years old, whereas the price of commodity 4 equals the price of a machine which is an even number of years old. Show that in this case Assumption 9.4 holds with commodity 1 interpreted as the new machine. Then show that if $0 \leqslant r \leqslant 1$ and $(\sqrt{2} - 1) \leqslant g \leqslant 1$, then the new machine and the machines which are an even number of years old exhibit an increasing efficiency, whereas machines which are an odd number of years old exhibit a decreasing efficiency.

8.14. Provide details of the proof of Theorem 9.4.

8.15. Provide details of the proof of Lemma 9.2.

8.16. Take the data of example 9.3 and assume that $\beta = 1$. Show that Assumption 9.1 holds: commodities 1 and 2 are finished goods; commodities 3–7 are old machines. Then determine prices and wage rate for each feasible rate of profit. Finally, show that processes (2), (3), (6), (7), (12)–(15), and (18)–(20) are never operated.

8.17. Take the data of example 9.3 and assume that $\beta = 2$. Show that

Assumption 9.1 holds: commodities 1 and 2 are finished goods; commodities 3–7 are old machines. Then determine prices and the wage rate for each feasible rate of profit.

8.18. Take the data of example 9.3 and assume that $\beta = 3$. Show that Assumption 9.1 holds: commodities 1 and 2 are finished goods; commodities 3–7 are old machines. Then determine prices and the wage rate for each feasible rate of profit. Finally, show that processes (2)–(11), and (21)–(23) are never operated.

10

Land

In the previous chapters it was assumed that commodities are produced by means of commodities with (homogeneous) labor as the only "visible" original factor of production. This does not mean, of course, that natural resources were taken to be entirely absent: it means only that they were assumed to be *non-scarce*. The fish in the sea is not a commodity, it is rather an animal living freely in the water: a "spontaneous rude produce of water," in the words of Adam Smith. Fish caught and brought to the market however is a commodity. The inputs required to obtain it consist of ships, boats, fuel, fishing-nets, and so on; yet they do not include living fish. But if the catch of today has an effect on tomorrow's catch, or if someone's fishing has an effect on someone else's fishing, then natural resources have explicitly to be taken into account in the analysis. This means that natural resources need to be investigated when they are in short supply, that is, when they are *scarce*. Whether a particular natural resource will be scarce depends, of course, on the net amounts of the different commodities to be produced, that is, the "requirements for use," given the quantities of the various natural resources available for capitalist productive purposes and the technological alternatives from which producers can choose. The scarcity of a natural resource is thus not something that should be *assumed* at the outset: it should rather emerge as a result of the analysis, given the data of the problem under consideration. Hence with regard to natural resources and their utilization "demand" matters throughout.

Historically, the natural resource whose role has first been analyzed in some detail in the theory of production and distribution is *land*, the natural resource which is typically associated with agriculture. The present chapter will be devoted to a discussion of land. Following a long-standing tradition in economic analysis, it will be assumed throughout that the use of land does not involve a change in the land itself: in Ricardo's terms, land is possessed of "indestructible powers." If land were to change its quality in the course of its productive use, then it would have to be treated as an exhaustible or, possibly, as a renewable resource (cf. crop rotation, three-fallowing, etc.); simple cases of exhaustible and renewable resources will be analyzed in Chapter 12.

In Section 1 three special models will be investigated. These models are designed to formalize some ideas concerning the origin of rent introduced into economic analysis by some classical economists. In Section 2 a more general model will be presented and a general statement on the existence of long-period positions will be put forward and proved. In these two sections the net product of the economy is regarded as given. Section 3 introduces models which are even more general and in which the net product can vary with prices and distribution. Section 4 introduces the wage frontier for technologies using land. Section 5 introduces relationships between prices and outputs and rent rates and outputs, respectively. Historical notes and Exercises are provided by Sections 6 and 7, respectively.

Throughout the entire chapter the growth rate is assumed as being equal to zero. This is an important assumption. In fact, if the economy is taken as growing at a positive rate and if land saving forms of technical progress are set aside, then the intensity with which the scarcity of land will be felt increases over time, and prices and distribution are bound to change. As a consequence, we cannot consider a single period of time only, since the prices of inputs at the beginning of a period of production need not be the same as the prices of outputs at its end.

A remark about the terminology used is in place. In the literature it is rather common to refer to commodities whose production requires land as *agricultural commodities*, and to commodities whose production does *not* require land as *industrial commodities*. These locutions are, of course, potentially misleading. We will nevertheless use them for the sake of brevity: the reader is therefore warned not to interpret these notions *verbatim*. It should be noted, however, that the analytics of the case in which there is a multiplicity of agricultural products also covers the case in which in the production of "industrial commodities" land is needed, for example as a site.

1. **Models of extensive and intensive rent**

In this section we will consider systems of production in which there is only one agricultural commodity, say "corn"; that is, only corn is produced by using land. Land need not be uniform in quality. It will be assumed that each quality of land is available in a given (finite) amount.

Landlords are assumed to have no use for their land other than renting it out to corn producers. (If, on the contrary, landlords were to use their land for other purposes also, such as hunting, recreation, etc., then some other good(s) would be produced by means of land.) An important implication of the premise that there is no alternative use for land is that the "reservation price" of the land service, that is, that price at which the landlord will choose to retain some positive amount of his land, is zero. In other words, if a particular quality of land is not fully employed in the cultivation of corn, then it cannot yield a rent because of competition among landlords. Hence, what may be dubbed "absolute rent" (a term with several connotations in the history of rent theory, which, however, need not interest us here) cannot be considered in this section.

While agricultural production is generally characterized by joint production proper (for example, wheat and straw, or wool and mutton), each process is, for reasons of simplicity, taken to produce a single product only. Hence pure joint production is ruled out. Requirements for use are defined in terms of a given vector of net products. Moreover, in order to avoid complications of the sort encountered in Chapter 5, the given vector of net products is assumed to be strictly positive. Finally, it will be assumed, in turn, that two of the following three assumptions hold.

(a) There is one process for the production of each commodity other than corn.
(b) There is one process for the production of corn on each quality of land.
(c) There is one quality of land.

It will be shown that when assumptions (a, b) hold, then rent arises as a consequence of the extension of cultivation to "less fertile" qualities of land: this is the familiar case of *extensive rent*. When assumptions (a, c) hold, then rent is due to the intensification of cultivation on the only extant quality of land: this is the familiar case of *intensive rent proper*. When assumptions (b, c) hold, then rent is due to economizing in the use of corn as a means of production in industry: this is the case of *external differential rent*. The common element of the last two cases, of course, is that only a single quality of land is utilized, whose scarcity is reflected in the duality of methods using the land or its product.

This section is mainly devoted to a clarification of some heuristic aspects concerning the origin of rent, that is, the scarcity of land. However, in Subsection 1.1 a proposition will be proved which refers to the existence of long-period positions. This result, connected with the concept of extensive rent, will be illustrated in terms of an example in Subsection 1.2. Subsection 1.3 will discuss the order of fertility and that of rentability, respectively, into which the different qualities of land can be brought. Subsections 1.4 and 1.5 will deal with intensive rent proper and external differential rent, respectively. However, in accordance with the aim of the section as a whole, only a simplified exposition of intensive rent will be given and no attempt will be made to prove the existence of long-period positions. It is only in the following sections that general results concerning the existence of such positions will be provided.

1.1. Extensive rent

Let $\mathbf{d}$ be the given vector of net products. Let n be the number of commodities: commodities $1, 2, \ldots, n-1$, are industrial commodities; commodity n is corn. There is one process $(\mathbf{a}_i, \mathbf{e}_i, \mathbf{0}, l_i)$ to produce industrial commodity i $(i = 1, 2, \ldots, n-1)$, where $\mathbf{a}_i \in \mathbb{R}^n$ is the commodity input vector, $\mathbf{e}_i \in \mathbb{R}^n$ is the output vector, $\mathbf{0} \in \mathbb{R}^m$ is the land input vector, and l_i is the labor input. Let m be the number of the different qualities of land, and let t_j be the existing amount of land of quality j $(j = 1, 2, \ldots, m)$. There is one process $(\mathbf{a}_{n-1+j}, \mathbf{e}_n, c_{n-1+j,j}\mathbf{e}_j, l_{n-1+j})(j = 1, 2, \ldots, m)$ to produce corn on each available quality of land, where $c_{n-1+j,j}$ designates the amount of land of quality j needed to produce one unit (bushel) of corn, that is, the respective land input coefficient.

Let us define

$$A = \begin{bmatrix} \mathbf{a}_1^T \\ \mathbf{a}_2^T \\ \vdots \\ \mathbf{a}_{n+m-1}^T \end{bmatrix}, \quad B = \begin{bmatrix} \mathbf{b}_1^T \\ \mathbf{b}_2^T \\ \vdots \\ \mathbf{b}_{n+m-1}^T \end{bmatrix}, \quad C = \begin{bmatrix} \mathbf{c}_1^T \\ \mathbf{c}_2^T \\ \vdots \\ \mathbf{c}_{n+m-1}^T \end{bmatrix},$$

$$\mathbf{l} = \begin{bmatrix} l_1 \\ l_2 \\ \vdots \\ l_{n+m-1} \end{bmatrix}, \quad \mathbf{t} = \begin{bmatrix} t_1 \\ t_2 \\ \vdots \\ t_m \end{bmatrix}, \tag{10.1}$$

where $\mathbf{b}_i = \mathbf{e}_i \in \mathbb{R}^n$ and $\mathbf{c}_i = \mathbf{0} \in \mathbb{R}^m$ if $i = 1, 2, \ldots, n-1$, and $\mathbf{b}_i = \mathbf{e}_n \in \mathbb{R}^n$ and $\mathbf{c}_i = c_{i,i-n+1}\mathbf{e}_{i-n+1} \in \mathbb{R}^m$ if $i = n, n+1, \ldots, n+m-1$. Moreover, let $\mathbf{x} \in \mathbb{R}^{n+m-1}$ be the vector of the intensities of operation of the processes, $\mathbf{p} \in \mathbb{R}^n$ the price vector, w the wage rate, $\mathbf{q} \in \mathbb{R}^m$ the vector of rent rates, and r the rate of profit. The rate of profit is taken to be given from outside the system. Obviously, in a long-period position

$$\mathbf{x} \geqslant \mathbf{0}, \quad \mathbf{p} \geqslant \mathbf{0}, \quad w \geqslant 0, \quad \mathbf{q} \geqslant \mathbf{0}. \tag{10.2a}$$

Moreover,

$$\mathbf{x}^T(\mathbf{B} - \mathbf{A}) = \mathbf{d}^T, \tag{10.2b}$$

since **d** is the given vector of net products,

$$\mathbf{x}^T\mathbf{C} \leqslant \mathbf{t}^T, \tag{10.2c}$$

since t_i is the existing amount of land of quality i,

$$\mathbf{x}^T\mathbf{Cq} = \mathbf{t}^T\mathbf{q}, \tag{10.2d}$$

since the rent of land of quality j equals zero if land of this quality is not fully employed,

$$\mathbf{Bp} \leqslant (1 + r)\mathbf{Ap} + \mathbf{Cq} + w\mathbf{l}, \tag{10.2e}$$

since no process can pay extra profits,

$$\mathbf{x}^T\mathbf{Bp} = \mathbf{x}^T[(1 + r)\mathbf{Ap} + \mathbf{Cq} + w\mathbf{l}], \tag{10.2f}$$

since processes incurring extra costs cannot be operated. Finally, let us normalize prices by setting

$$\mathbf{u}^T\mathbf{p} = 1, \tag{10.2g}$$

where **u** is a given semipositive vector.

In order to simplify the exposition, let us bring the different processes producing corn into a ranking according to the level of the wage rate they are able to pay when they are combined with the $n - 1$ industrial processes and rent rates equal zero. That is, the "technique," as defined in Chapter 5, made up of the first $n - 1$ processes and process $i (i = n, n + 1, \ldots, n + m - 1)$ when land is neglected, is able to pay a higher wage rate than that paid by the "technique" made up by the first $n - 1$ processes and process $i + 1$ when land is neglected. This orders the processes defined in (10.1) and the corresponding qualities of land, an order that depends on the level of the rate of profit: if r changes, the order can be expected to change. (The reason why this is so has been expounded in Chapter 5.)

It is possible that not all the single product "techniques" just mentioned are able to pay a nonnegative wage rate. If none of them is able to pay a nonnegative wage, then the system of inequalities (10.2) has no solution, given r, even if vector **q** and inequality (10.2c) are neglected. Assume then that the first s "techniques," $1 \leqslant s \leqslant m$, are able to pay a nonnegative wage, whereas the last $m - s$ are not. Finally, it is possible that some of the single product "techniques" mentioned above pay the same nonnegative wage rate. This is a complication which will be dealt with later; for the moment assume that they are all different.

Let us define the sets

$$D_i = \left\{ \mathbf{d} \in \mathbb{R}^n \,|\, \mathbf{d} \geqslant \mathbf{0}, \exists \mathbf{x} \geqslant \mathbf{0} : \mathbf{x}^T(\mathbf{B} - \mathbf{A}) = \mathbf{d}^T, \mathbf{x}^T \mathbf{C} \leqslant \sum_{j=1}^{i} t_j \mathbf{e}_j^T \right\}$$

$$(i = 1, 2, \ldots, s).$$

Obviously,

$$D_1 \subset D_2 \subset \cdots \subset D_s.$$

If $n = 3$ and corn enters directly or indirectly into the production of all commodities, then each of the D-sets has the shape shown in Figure 10.1 (see exercise 7.1). In the remainder of this subsection it will be shown that if the given vector of net products $\mathbf{d}$ is in D_s, then there are vectors $\mathbf{x}^*, \mathbf{p}^*$, and $\mathbf{q}^*$ and scalar w^* which are a solution to system (10.2). The converse is obvious.

Suppose first that the given vector of net products $\mathbf{d}$ is so small that $\mathbf{d}$ is in D_1. Then, if no rent is paid so that the use of land can be neglected, the usual theory of the choice of technique for single product techniques (see Chapter 5) can be applied and it is possible to prove that the technique made up by the first n processes is cost-minimizing. Thus all farmer-capitalists want to rent land 1. Since land 1 is not scarce with respect to the given vector of net products, competition among landlords prevents a positive rent.

Assume now that the given vector of net products $\mathbf{d}$ has larger entries so that corn cannot be produced by using land 1 alone, that is, land 1 is in short supply ($\mathbf{d} \notin D_1$). If $\mathbf{d} \in D_2$, then demand can be satisfied if both qualities of land 1 and 2 are cultivated to some extent. If both processes n and $n + 1$ are to be operated, the cost of producing corn with either one of them must be the same – where "costs" are here taken to include wages, the value of the produced means of production used up, profits at the going rate, and rents – so that neither one of them is more profitable than the other. Therefore, if $\mathbf{d} \notin D_1$ and $\mathbf{d} \in D_2$, the owners of land 1 are able to get a positive rent because of competition among the farmer-capitalists. As a consequence, land 1 must be fully cultivated, otherwise the competition among their owners will reduce the rent of land 1 to zero. If land 2 is not fully cultivated, its owners cannot obtain a positive rent. Therefore, if the requirements for use can be satisfied by utilizing the whole of land 1 and a part of land 2 (that is, $\mathbf{d} \notin D_1$ and $\mathbf{d} \in D_2$), competition leads to a zero rent for land 2 and a positive rent for land 1 such that neither process n nor process $n + 1$ is more profitable than the other.

In general, let the given vector of net products $\mathbf{d}$ be such that $\mathbf{d} \notin D_{i-1}$ and $\mathbf{d} \in D_i$, some $i \leqslant s$. Then there is a vector $\mathbf{x}^*$ such that

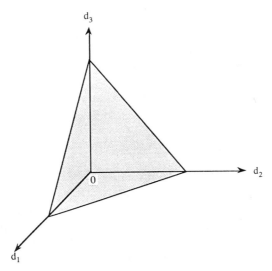

Figure 10.1

$$x^{*T}(\mathbf{B} - \mathbf{A}) = \mathbf{d}^T$$

$$x^{*T}\mathbf{C}\mathbf{e}_j = t_j \quad j = 1, 2, \dots, i - 1$$

$$x^{*T}\mathbf{C}\mathbf{e}_i \leqslant t_i$$

$$x^{*T}\mathbf{C}\mathbf{e}_j = 0. \quad j = i + 1, i + 2, \dots, m$$

Let the vector $\mathbf{p}^*$ and scalar w^* be the price vector and wage rate of the "technique," as defined in Chapter 5, made up of the first $n - 1$ processes and process i neglecting the use of land. Let them be normalized in such a way that $\mathbf{u}^T\mathbf{p}^* = 1$. Since $i \leqslant s, \mathbf{p}^* \geqslant 0$, and $w^* \geqslant 0$. Finally, there is a non-negative vector $\mathbf{q}^*$ such that

$$\mathbf{B}_i\mathbf{p}^* = (1 + r)\mathbf{A}_i\mathbf{p}^* + \mathbf{C}_i\mathbf{q}^* + w^*\mathbf{l}_i \tag{10.3}$$

$$\mathbf{q}^*\mathbf{e}_j = 0, \quad j = i, i + 1, \dots, m$$

where $\mathbf{B}_i, \mathbf{A}_i, \mathbf{C}_i$, and $\mathbf{l}_i$ are obtained from $\mathbf{B}, \mathbf{A}, \mathbf{C}$, and $\mathbf{l}$, respectively, by deleting the last $m - i$ rows. In fact, the first $n - 1$ equations and the last one in (10.3) are satisfied because of the definition of $\mathbf{p}^*$ and w^*, and in each of the other equations (10.3) there is only one entry of vector $\mathbf{q}^*$ to be determined; and this entry must be positive because if rents were neglected the process relative to that equation would pay extra profits at prices $\mathbf{p}^*$ and wage rate w^*. Hence vectors $\mathbf{x}^*, \mathbf{p}^*$, and $\mathbf{q}^*$ and scalar w^*

constitute a solution to system (10.2). In this solution processes $1, 2, \ldots, n + i$ are operated; lands $1, 2, \ldots, i$ are fully employed and land $i + 1$ is partially employed; the rent of land $i + 1$ equals zero and the rents of the other cultivated lands are such that none of processes $n, n + 1, \ldots, n + s$ either incurs a loss or yields extra profits; moreover, non-operated processes are not able to pay extra profits.

The above model formalizes the concept of *extensive rent* as it was used, for example, by Ricardo. That quality or type of land which, though cultivated, is not fully employed is commonly called *marginal land*, while those qualities or types of land which are fully employed are called *intra-marginal*.

Two special cases remain to be analyzed.

(i) Two or more lands are marginal. This case refers to a constellation where some of the single product "techniques" mentioned above pay the same wage rate. In order to simplify the exposition, let the single product "techniques" made up of the $n - 1$ industrial processes and either process $n + i - 1$ or process $n + i$ pay the same wage rate. This wage rate is both lower than that paid by "techniques" made up by the $n - 1$ industrial processes and any one of processes $n, n + 1, \ldots, n + i - 2$ and higher than that paid by "techniques" made up by the $n - 1$ industrial processes and any one of processes $n + i + 1, n + i + 2, \ldots, n + s - 1$. In this case, if the given vector of net products $\mathbf{d}$ is not in D_{i-1} but is in

$$D_i = D_{i+1} = \left\{ \mathbf{d} \in \mathbb{R}^n \mid \mathbf{d} \geqslant \mathbf{0}, \exists \mathbf{x} \geqslant \mathbf{0} : \mathbf{x}^T(\mathbf{B} - \mathbf{A}) = \mathbf{d}^T, \mathbf{x}^T \mathbf{C} \leqslant \sum_{j=1}^{i+1} t_j \mathbf{e}_j^T \right\},$$

then the previous analysis applies. However, in the present case vector $\mathbf{x}^*$ is no longer uniquely determined since it needs to satisfy the following constraints:

$$\mathbf{x}^{*T}(\mathbf{B} - \mathbf{A}) = \mathbf{d}^T$$

$$\mathbf{x}^{*T}\mathbf{Ce}_j = t_j \quad j = 1, 2, \ldots, i - 1$$

$$\mathbf{x}^{*T}\mathbf{Ce}_i \leqslant t_i$$

$$\mathbf{x}^{*T}\mathbf{Ce}_{i+1} \leqslant t_{i+1}$$

$$\mathbf{x}^{*T}\mathbf{Ce}_j = 0. \quad j = i + 2, i + 3, \ldots, m$$

In particular the entries of vector $\mathbf{x}^*$ relative to processes $n + i - 1$ and $n + i$ are not uniquely determined. However, since the single product "techniques" made up of the $n - 1$ industrial processes and either process $n + i - 1$ or process $n + i$ have the same price vectors (see Chapter 5), no other element of the analysis is to be changed. The case under consideration is, of course, the one in which two lands are simultaneously marginal.

(ii) The marginal land is fully utilized. The other special case is that in which for the given vector of net products **d** there is a nonnegative vector **x** such that $\mathbf{x}^T(\mathbf{B} - \mathbf{A}) = \mathbf{d}^T$ and $\mathbf{x}^T\mathbf{C} = \sum_{j=1}^{i} t_j\mathbf{e}_j^T$. This is the case in which the marginal land is fully employed. In this case the competition among landlords need not be enough to bring the respective rent rate to zero. It is possible (see exercise 7.3) that the marginal land yields its proprietors a positive rent (though this is not necessarily the case). As a consequence the number of processes operated may *fall short* of the number of commodities and qualities of land paying rent: thus prices, rents, and wage rate cannot fully be determined and they may assume any level within a closed and bounded range. To the reader of this book findings of this kind should no longer come as a surprise.

The two special cases just mentioned show that the uniqueness of solutions to system (10.2) cannot be proved. However, it is possible to show that if qualities of land $i, i + 1, \ldots, k$ are marginal, then the given vector of net products **d** is in D_k and is not in D_{i-1}. (If there is only one marginal land, $k = i$.) In fact, equations

$$\mathbf{Bp} = (1 + r)\mathbf{Ap} + \mathbf{Cq} + w\mathbf{l},$$

$$\mathbf{e}_i^T\mathbf{q} = 0, \quad \mathbf{e}_{i+1}^T\mathbf{q} = 0, \ldots, \quad \mathbf{e}_k^T\mathbf{q} = 0, \quad \mathbf{u}^T\mathbf{q} = 1$$

have one and only one solution and in this solution $\mathbf{e}_j^T\mathbf{q} > 0$ if $j < i$ and $\mathbf{e}_j^T\mathbf{q} < 0$ if $j > k$. Therefore, if $(\mathbf{x}_1, \mathbf{p}_1, w_1, \mathbf{q}_1)$ and $(\mathbf{x}_2, \mathbf{p}_2, w_2, \mathbf{q}_2)$ are solutions to system (10.2) with marginal land(s) not fully cultivated, then $\mathbf{p}_1 = \mathbf{p}_2$, $w_1 = w_2$, $\mathbf{q}_1 = \mathbf{q}_2$ and $(\lambda\mathbf{x}_1 + (1 - \lambda)\mathbf{x}_2, \mathbf{p}_1, w_1, \mathbf{q}_1)$, with $0 \leqslant \lambda \leqslant 1$, is also a solution to system (10.2).

We may summarize the results arrived at in this subsection as follows. If the given rate of profit r is nonnegative and lower than

$$\text{Sup}\,\{\rho \in \mathbb{R} \mid \exists \mathbf{v} \in \mathbb{R}^m : \mathbf{v} \geqslant \mathbf{0}, \quad \mathbf{v}^T[\mathbf{B} - (1 + \rho)\mathbf{A}] > \mathbf{0}^T\},$$

then it is possible to order the qualities of land and define sets $D_1 \subset D_2 \subset \cdots \subset D_s$ as above, and if the given vector of net products **d** is in D_s, then system (10.2) has a solution.

1.2. An example

It is perhaps useful to illustrate the above argument in terms of a numerical example. Let the technology be defined by the processes described in Table 10.1. Moreover, assume that altogether 10 units of land of quality 1 and 2 units of land of quality 2 are available. Exercise 8.15 of Chapter 3 has shown that if land inputs are neglected, processes (1) and (2) are operated if $0 \leqslant r \leqslant 0.1$ or $0.2 \leqslant r \leqslant R$, whereas processes (1) and (3) are operated if $0.1 \leqslant r \leqslant 0.2$, with $R \cong 0.387$. If land inputs cannot be

Table 10.1

	commodity inputs		land inputs			outputs	
	iron	corn	1	2	labor	iron	corn
(1)	—	$\frac{379}{423}$	—	—	$\frac{89}{10}$ →	1	—
(2)	$\frac{1}{2}$	$\frac{1}{10}$	1	—	$\frac{9}{50}$ →	—	1
(3)	$\frac{1}{4}$	$\frac{5}{12}$	—	1	$\frac{3}{2}$ →	—	1

neglected, we need to analyze several ranges within which the (exogenously given) rate of profit can assume values.

If $0 \leqslant r < 0.1$ or $0.2 < r \leqslant R' \cong 0.378$, where R' is the maximum rate of profit when processes (1) and (3) are operated, and land uses are set aside, then

$$D_1 = \left\{ \mathbf{d} \in \mathbb{R}^2 \mid 0 \leqslant d_2 \leqslant \frac{1912}{423} - \frac{379}{423} d_1, 0 \leqslant d_1 \leqslant \frac{1912}{379} \right\}$$

$$D_2 = \left\{ \mathbf{d} \in \mathbb{R}^2 \mid 0 \leqslant d_2 \leqslant \frac{2216}{423} - \frac{379}{423} d_1, 0 \leqslant d_1 \leqslant \frac{2216}{379} \right\}.$$

If $\mathbf{d} \in D_1$, only land of quality 1 is cultivated and no type of land yields a rent; if $\mathbf{d} \notin D_1$, $\mathbf{d} \in D_2$, then land of quality 1 is fully cultivated and land of quality 2 is marginal.

On the contrary, if $0.1 < r < 0.2$, then

$$D_1 = \left\{ \mathbf{d} \in \mathbb{R}^2 \mid 0 \leqslant d_2 \leqslant \frac{304}{423} - \frac{379}{423} d_1, 0 \leqslant d_1 \leqslant \frac{304}{379} \right\}$$

$$D_2 = \left\{ \mathbf{d} \in \mathbb{R}^2 \mid 0 \leqslant d_2 \leqslant \frac{2216}{423} - \frac{379}{423} d_1, 0 \leqslant d_1 \leqslant \frac{2216}{379} \right\}.$$

If $\mathbf{d} \in D_1$, only land of quality 2 is cultivated and no type of land yields a rent; if $\mathbf{d} \notin D_1$, $\mathbf{d} \in D_2$, then land of quality 2 is fully cultivated and land of quality 1 is marginal.

Moreover, if $R' < r \leqslant R$, then

$$D_1 = \left\{ \mathbf{d} \in \mathbb{R}^2 \mid 0 \leqslant d_2 \leqslant \frac{1912}{423} - \frac{379}{423} d_1, 0 \leqslant d_1 \leqslant \frac{1912}{379} \right\},$$

and if $\mathbf{d} \notin D_1$, then no long-period position exists.

Finally, if $r = 0.1$ or $r = 0.2$, then there can be no rent since

$$D_1 = D_2 = \left\{ \mathbf{d} \in \mathbb{R}^2 \mid 0 \leqslant d_2 \leqslant \frac{2216}{423} - \frac{379}{423} d_1, 0 \leqslant d_1 \leqslant \frac{2216}{379} \right\}.$$

If $\mathbf{d} \notin D_1 = D_2$, then no long-period position exists.

We can summarize the results of this example as follows. A long-period position exists if and only if $0 \leqslant r \leqslant R$, and

$$\mathbf{d} \in \left\{ \mathbf{d} \in \mathbb{R}^2 \,|\, 0 \leqslant d_2 \leqslant \frac{2216}{423} - \frac{379}{423} d_1, 0 \leqslant d_1 \leqslant \frac{2216}{379} \right\}$$

when $0 \leqslant r \leqslant R'$ or

$$\mathbf{d} \in \left\{ \mathbf{d} \in \mathbb{R}^2 \,|\, 0 \leqslant d_2 \leqslant \frac{1912}{423} - \frac{379}{423} d_1, 0 \leqslant d_1 \leqslant \frac{1912}{379} \right\}.$$

when $R' < r \leqslant R$.

1.3. Order of fertility and order according to rent per acre (order of rentability)

In Subsection 1.1 an existence condition for an extensive rent model has been expounded. It has also been shown that the different qualities of land can be ranked according to the order in which they are taken into cultivation. This order will be called the *order of fertility*. It has been stressed that the order of fertility generally depends on distribution: a change in the level of the rate of profit may involve a change in the order of fertility.

The different qualities of land can also be ranked according to the rent they yield per acre, that is, the rate of rent; we may also talk of the *order of rentability*. In early contributions to rent theory it has commonly been assumed that the order of fertility and that of rentability coincide. This is certainly true in the following particular cases: (i) rent due to different distances of the plots of homogeneous land on which corn is grown from the location, for example, the "town," where most of the net output of corn is consumed, provided freight costs are proportionate to distance; (ii) the case in which all methods of production available to cultivate the different plots of land exhibit the same number of acres (of the different qualities of land) per unit of output and can be ordered in such a way that for each pair of them the one which uses a larger amount of at least one commodity input does not use less of any other commodity input. However, the traditional view cannot be sustained in general; this subsection shows why.

Obviously, all fully cultivated types of land yield a higher rent per acre than those types which are not fully utilized. Therefore the order of fertility has some influence on the order of rentability. However, even though land of quality i will be taken into cultivation prior to land of quality j, it is possible that the rent per acre of land i is smaller than the rent per acre of land j when land of quality k, $k > j$, is marginal. In this subsection we will clarify this point by means of a graphical tool. The same tool will also be used in the following two subsections.

Let $(\hat{\mathbf{A}}_i, \hat{\mathbf{l}}_i, \hat{\mathbf{c}}_i)$ be a set of processes made up by the $n - 1$ industrial processes and process $n + i - 1$, producing corn. The first $n - 1$ elements of vector $\hat{\mathbf{c}}_i$ are zeros, whereas the nth element equals $c_{n-1+i,i}$. If processes $(\hat{\mathbf{A}}_i, \hat{\mathbf{l}}_i, \hat{\mathbf{c}}_i)$ are operated, then $\mathbf{p}$, w, and q_i, the ith element of vector $\mathbf{q}$, need to satisfy the following equations:

$$\mathbf{p} = (1 + r)\hat{\mathbf{A}}_i \mathbf{p} + q_i \hat{\mathbf{c}}_i + w\hat{\mathbf{l}}_i \tag{10.4a}$$

$$\mathbf{u}^T \mathbf{p} = 1. \tag{10.4b}$$

Hence w and q_i need to satisfy the following equation:

$$1 = q_i \mathbf{u}^T [\mathbf{I} - (1 + r)\hat{\mathbf{A}}_i]^{-1} \hat{\mathbf{c}}_i + w\mathbf{u}^T [\mathbf{I} - (1 + r)\hat{\mathbf{A}}_i]^{-1} \hat{\mathbf{l}}_i. \tag{10.5}$$

Equation (10.5) represents a straight line in the (q_i, w) plane. This straight line will be called the q_i–w relationship. In a similar way the relationships between rent per acre and wage rate can be ascertained for each $i = 1, 2, \ldots, s$. These q_i–w relationships $(i = 1, 2, \ldots, s)$ may even be drawn in the same diagram, keeping in mind that q_i is the rent *per acre* of land of quality i. Hence the intersection of the q_i–w relationship and the q_j–w relationship $(i \neq j)$ can sensibly be interpreted only in the following way: at the corresponding wage rate land of quality i and land of quality j yield the same rent *per acre*. This being said, the s straight lines (10.5) can be drawn as in Figure 10.2, where $s = 3$.

From Figure 10.2 it follows that if $\mathbf{d} \notin D_1$ and $\mathbf{d} \in D_2$, then the rate of rent obtained by an owner of land of quality 1 equals $q' > 0$, whereas no other quality of land is able to yield a positive rent. But if $\mathbf{d} \notin D_2$ and $\mathbf{d} \in D_3$, then the rate of rent yielded by land of quality 1 is $q'' < q'''$, where q''' is the rate of rent associated with land of quality 2. This is a consequence of the fact that in the example depicted the q_1–w relationship cuts the q_2–w relationship at a wage rate lower than w_3.

1.4. Intensive rent proper: Intensification of the use of land

Let $\mathbf{d}$ be the given vector of net products. As in the previous subsections the number of commodities is n: commodities $1, \ldots, n - 1$ are industrial commodities, that is, they are not produced by utilizing land, while commodity n is corn. Land is now assumed to be of uniform quality and available in an amount which totals t units (acres). There is one process $(\mathbf{a}_i, \mathbf{e}_i, 0, l_i)$ to produce industrial commodity i $(i = 1, 2, \ldots, n - 1)$, where $\mathbf{a}_i \in \mathbb{R}^n$ is the commodity input vector, $\mathbf{e}_i \in \mathbb{R}^n$ is the output vector, 0 is the quantity of land needed (directly) per unit of the respective output, and l_i is the corresponding labor input. There are m processes $(\mathbf{a}_j, \mathbf{e}_n, c_j, l_j)$ $(j = n, n + 1, \ldots, n + m - 1)$ to produce corn.

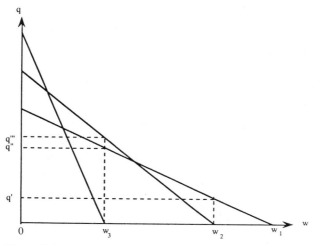

Figure 10.2

Let us define matrices

$$
A = \begin{bmatrix} \mathbf{a}_1^T \\ \mathbf{a}_2^T \\ \vdots \\ \mathbf{a}_{n+m-1}^T \end{bmatrix}, \quad
B = \begin{bmatrix} \mathbf{b}_1^T \\ \mathbf{b}_2^T \\ \vdots \\ \mathbf{b}_{n+m-1}^T \end{bmatrix}, \quad
\mathbf{c} = \begin{bmatrix} c_1 \\ c_2 \\ \vdots \\ c_{n+m-1} \end{bmatrix}, \quad
\mathbf{l} = \begin{bmatrix} l_1 \\ l_2 \\ \vdots \\ l_{n+m-1} \end{bmatrix},
$$

where $\mathbf{b}_i = \mathbf{e}_i \in \mathbb{R}^n$ and $c_i = 0$ if $i = 1, 2, \ldots, n - 1$, and $\mathbf{b}_i = \mathbf{e}_n \in \mathbb{R}^n$ and $c_i > 0$ if $i = n, n + 1, \ldots, n + m - 1$. Moreover, let $\mathbf{x} \in \mathbb{R}^{n+m-1}$ be the vector of the intensities of operation of the different processes, $\mathbf{p} \in \mathbb{R}^n$ the price vector, w the wage rate, q the rate of rent, and r the rate of profit. Obviously, in a long-period position, for a given r,

$$\mathbf{x}^T(\mathbf{B} - \mathbf{A}) = \mathbf{d}^T, \tag{10.6a}$$

$$\mathbf{x}^T \mathbf{c} \leqslant t, \tag{10.6b}$$

$$\mathbf{x}^T \mathbf{c} q = tq, \tag{10.6c}$$

$$\mathbf{B}\mathbf{p} \leqslant (1 + r)\mathbf{A}\mathbf{p} + q\mathbf{c} + w\mathbf{l}, \tag{10.6d}$$

$$\mathbf{x}^T \mathbf{B}\mathbf{p} = \mathbf{x}^T[(1 + r)\mathbf{A}\mathbf{p} + q\mathbf{c} + w\mathbf{l}], \tag{10.6e}$$

$$\mathbf{x} \geqslant \mathbf{0}, \quad \mathbf{p} \geqslant \mathbf{0}, \quad w \geqslant 0, \quad q \geqslant 0, \quad \mathbf{u}^T \mathbf{p} = 1, \tag{10.6f}$$

where $\mathbf{u}$ is a given semipositive vector. The exposition can again be simplified by ordering the different processes producing corn in accordance with the level of the wage rate they are able to pay when they are combined with the $n - 1$ industrial processes, and the rent rate is equal to zero. Hence the "technique," as defined in Chapter 5, made up of the first $n - 1$ processes and process i $(i = n, n + 1, \ldots, m - 1)$ when land is neglected, is able to pay a higher wage rate than the "technique" made up by the first $n - 1$ processes and process $i + 1$ when land is neglected. As was pointed out in the previous subsection, this order generally depends on the level of the rate of profit: if r changes, the order can be expected to change too. It is also possible, as in Subsection 1.1, that not all single product "techniques" just mentioned are able to pay a nonnegative wage rate. If none of them is able to do so, then system (10.6) has no solution even if the variable q and inequality (10.6b) are left out of consideration. Assume then that the first s, $1 \leqslant s \leqslant m$, are able to pay a nonnegative wage rate, whereas the last $m-s$ are not. Finally, it is possible that at the given rate of profit some of the single product "techniques" mentioned above pay the same nonnegative wage rate. This is a complication which will be dealt with in exercise 7.4; here it will be assumed that the wage rates are all different. Then let us define the sets

$$D_i = \{\mathbf{d} \in \mathbb{R}^n \,|\, \mathbf{d} \geqslant \mathbf{0}, \exists \mathbf{x} \geqslant \mathbf{0} : \mathbf{x}^T(\mathbf{B} - \mathbf{A}) = \mathbf{d}^T, \mathbf{x}^T \mathbf{c} \leqslant t, \mathbf{x}^T \mathbf{e}_{j+n-1} = 0,$$
$$j \neq i \quad \text{and} \quad j \leqslant m\} \quad (i = 1, 2, \ldots, s).$$

Let the entries of the given vector of net products $\mathbf{d}$ be so small that $\mathbf{d}$ is in $D_1 \cap D_2 \cap \cdots \cap D_s$. Then, if no rent is paid so that the use of land can be neglected, the usual theory of the choice of technique for single product techniques (see Chapter 5) can be applied; and it is possible to prove that the technique made up by the first n processes is cost-minimizing. Since land is not scarce, given the vector of net products, competition among landlords rules out a positive rent. In this subsection no effort is made to prove a precise statement. Rather we continue the exposition by using Figure 10.3, which gives the $q-w$ relationships in a case in which $s = 3$. It deserves to be noted that in the case of intensive rent proper the qualification added in the previous subsection regarding the possibility of drawing the $q-w$ relationships in the same diagram is not necessary, since now q is the rent rate relative to the *same* quality of land. Because of the chosen order of processes the $q-w$ relationship which cuts the horizontal axis at the highest w is *related to* the $q-w$ relationship relative to process n; the $q-w$ relationship which cuts the horizontal axis at the lowest w is *related to* the $q-w$ relationship relative to process $n + 2$; the remaining $q-w$ relationship is *related to* the $q-w$ relationship relative to process $n + 1$.

We may now distinguish between several cases (where the case $\mathbf{d} \in \bigcap_{i=1}^{3} D_i$ is for obvious reasons left out of consideration).

Case 1: $\mathbf{d} \notin D_1$, $\mathbf{d} \in D_2$, and $\mathbf{d} \in D_3$.

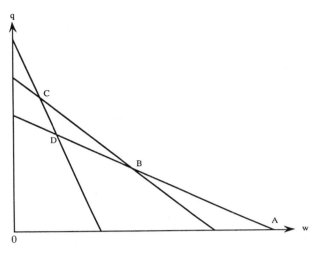

Figure 10.3

In this case equation (10.6a) and inequality (10.6b) can be satisfied by operating the first $n - 1$ processes and, alternatively,

(i) process $n + 1$,
(ii) process $n + 2$,
(iii) processes n and $n + 1$,
(iv) processes n and $n + 2$,
(v) processes $n + 1$ and $n + 2$,
(vi) all processes.

In the alternatives (i), (ii), and (v) the land would not be fully employed, and therefore the rate of rent q would be zero. As a consequence process n would yield extra profits, that is, inequality (10.6d) could not hold. In alternative (vi) the weak inequality (10.6d) should be an equation because of equation (10.6e) and inequalities (10.6f). This would be the case if and only if the three $q–w$ relationships were to meet in a point, which they do not (in Figure 10.3). In alternative (iv), if processes n and $n + 2$ are operated in such a way that the land is fully cultivated, then the wage rate and the rent rate are determined by the intersection of the $q–w$ relationships relative to these two processes (point D in Figure 10.3) in order to satisfy equation (10.6e). But since this intersection is below the $q–w$ relationship of process $n + 1$, process $n + 1$ would yield extra profits: once again inequality (10.6d) cannot hold. Finally, in alternative (iii), if processes n and $n + 1$ are operated in such a way that the land is fully employed, then the wage rate and the rent rate are determined by the intersection of the q–w relationships relative to these two processes (point B in Figure 10.3) in order to satisfy equation (10.6e). Moreover, since the other q–w relationship passes below point B, inequality (10.6d) is satisfied. Hence system (10.6) has one and only one solution.

Case 2: $\mathbf{d} \notin D_1$, $\mathbf{d} \notin D_2$,   and $\mathbf{d} \in D_3$.

Here, too, a unique solution can be found by operating the $n-1$ industrial processes and processes $n+1$ and $n+2$ in such a way that land is fully employed. Then the wage rate w and the rent rate q are determined by point C, the intersection of the q–w relationships relative to the operated processes.

The above model can be interpreted as a formalization of the concept of intensive rent proper as it was used by Ricardo, among others. When $\mathbf{d} \in \bigcap_{i=1}^{3} D_i$, the net amount of corn produced can be increased through the gradual extension of process n. As soon as the whole area is cultivated, the net production of corn can be increased ($\mathbf{d} \notin D_1$ and $\mathbf{d} \in D_2$) through the gradual extension of process $n+1$ at the expense of process n: this requires that the rent rate rises to the point where processes n and $n+1$ can both be operated. As soon as process $n+1$ is used to cultivate the whole area the net production of corn can be increased ($\mathbf{d} \notin D_1, \mathbf{d} \notin D_2$, and $\mathbf{d} \in D_3$) only if the rent rises to the point where processes $n+1$ and $n+2$ can both be operated. Then, once again the net amount of corn produced can be increased through the gradual extension of process $n+2$ at the expense of process $n+1$.

However, the exposition is not yet complete. The definition of the D-sets does *not* imply:

$$D_1 \subset D_2 \subset \cdots \subset D_s.$$

Hence we need to consider a few additional cases which can be represented with the help of Figure 10.3. They are the following:

Case 3: $\mathbf{d} \in D_1$, $\mathbf{d} \notin D_2$,   and $\mathbf{d} \notin D_3$,
Case 4: $\mathbf{d} \notin D_1$, $\mathbf{d} \in D_2$,   and $\mathbf{d} \notin D_3$,
Case 5: $\mathbf{d} \in D_1$, $\mathbf{d} \in D_2$,   and $\mathbf{d} \notin D_3$,
Case 6: $\mathbf{d} \in D_1$, $\mathbf{d} \notin D_2$,   and $\mathbf{d} \in D_3$.

It is possible to show that in each of the cases 3–6 there is more than one solution to system (10.6). In case 3 one solution is given by point A, and land is not fully employed; the other solution is given by point B: processes n and $n+1$ are operated in such a way that land is fully utilized. In case 4 the two solutions are given by points B and C, whereas in case 5 they are given by points A and C. In case 6 there are three solutions represented

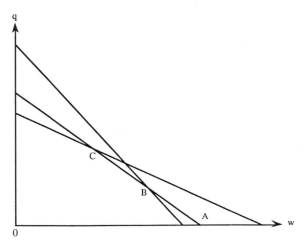

Figure 10.4

by points *A*, *B*, and *C*, respectively. Exercise 7.6 provides a numerical example for this case (see also exercise 7.7).

In the model of intensive rent proper considered here, multiple solutions are possible, but can we assert that if there is an i such that $\mathbf{d} \in D_i$, then there is a solution to system (10.6)? We have seen that if the q–w relationships are located as depicted in Figure 10.3, then this can be asserted. However, if they are located as in Figure 10.4, then this cannot be done. In this case, if $\mathbf{d} \notin D_1$, $\mathbf{d} \in D_2$, and $\mathbf{d} \notin D_3$, then no solution to system (10.6) can be found. In fact the vector of net product $\mathbf{d}$ can be obtained only in points *A*, *B*, *C*. In point *A* no rent is paid but process n pays extra profits. In points *B* and *C* land is fully employed and a rent is paid, but in both cases there is a process paying extra profits. Exercise 7.8 provides a numerical example for this case.

To intensify the cultivation of land (of uniform quality) is not the only possible way of increasing the net output of the agricultural product. An alternative to the intensification of the use of land is economy in the use of the product of land in industry. With the total output of corn given, the net output of corn can be increased by gradually replacing a method in industry which uses relatively more corn as an input with a method which uses relatively little. Hence, in this case the scarcity of land would not be reflected by the duality of methods in cultivating land, but rather by the duality of methods using the product of land – corn – in producing one of the industrial commodities. This is the case of external differential rent, "external" because it is outside agriculture that different methods of production are employed to produce the same commodity: the difference in the methods concerns the different intensity with which corn is used as a means of production. As will be seen below, analytically this case bears a close resemblance to the case of intensive rent proper. Hence, both cases may be considered variants of intensive rent.

1.5. External differential rent: Economy in the use of the product of land

Let $\mathbf{d}$ be the given vector of net products. Let n be the number of commodities: commodities $1, 2, \ldots, n-1$, are industrial commodities; commodity n is corn. Land is taken to be of uniform quality; let t be the available amount. There are m processes $(\mathbf{a}_i, \mathbf{e}_1, 0, l_i)$ $(i = 1, 2, \ldots, m)$ to produce industrial commodity 1, which is called "iron," where $\mathbf{a}_i \in \mathbb{R}^n$ is the commodity input vector, $\mathbf{e}_1 \in \mathbb{R}^n$ is the output vector, 0 is the land input, and l_i is the labor input. There is one process $(\mathbf{a}_{m+j-1}, \mathbf{e}_j, 0, l_{m+j-1})$ to produce industrial commodity j $(j = 2, \ldots, n-1)$, where $\mathbf{a}_{m+j-1} \in \mathbb{R}^n$ is the commodity input vector, $\mathbf{e}_j \in \mathbb{R}^n$ is the output vector, 0 is the land input, and l_{m+j-1} is the labor input. Finally, there is one process $(\mathbf{a}_{n+m-1}, \mathbf{e}_n, c, l_{m+n-1})$ to produce corn, where $\mathbf{a}_{n+m-1} \in \mathbb{R}^n$ is the commodity input vector, $\mathbf{e}_n \in \mathbb{R}^n$ is the output vector, c is the land input, and l_{m+n-1} is the labor input.

Let us define

$$
\mathbf{A} = \begin{bmatrix} \mathbf{a}_1^T \\ \mathbf{a}_2^T \\ \vdots \\ \mathbf{a}_{n+m-1}^T \end{bmatrix}, \quad
\mathbf{B} = \begin{bmatrix} \mathbf{b}_1^T \\ \mathbf{b}_2^T \\ \vdots \\ \mathbf{b}_{n+m-1}^T \end{bmatrix}, \quad
\mathbf{c} = \begin{bmatrix} 0 \\ 0 \\ \vdots \\ 0 \\ c \end{bmatrix}, \quad
\mathbf{l} = \begin{bmatrix} l_1 \\ l_2 \\ \vdots \\ l_{n+m-1} \end{bmatrix},
$$

where $\mathbf{b}_i = \mathbf{e}_1 \in \mathbb{R}^n$ if $i = 1, 2, \ldots m$, and $\mathbf{b}_i = \mathbf{e}_{i-m+1} \in \mathbb{R}^n$ if $i = m+1$, $m+2, \ldots, m+n-1$. Moreover, let $\mathbf{x} \in \mathbb{R}^{n+m-1}$ be the intensity vector of operation of the different processes, $\mathbf{p} \in \mathbb{R}^n$ the price vector, w the wage rate, q the rate of rent, and r the rate of profit. Obviously, in a long-period position, for a given r,

$$\mathbf{x}^T(\mathbf{B} - \mathbf{A}) = \mathbf{d}^T, \tag{10.7a}$$

$$\mathbf{x}^T \mathbf{c} \leqslant t, \tag{10.7b}$$

$$\mathbf{x}^T \mathbf{c} q = tq, \tag{10.7c}$$

$$\mathbf{B}\mathbf{p} \leqslant (1 + r)\mathbf{A}\mathbf{p} + q\mathbf{c} + w\mathbf{l}, \tag{10.7d}$$

$$\mathbf{x}^T \mathbf{B}\mathbf{p} = \mathbf{x}^T[(1 + r)\mathbf{A}\mathbf{p} + q\mathbf{c} + w\mathbf{l}], \tag{10.7e}$$

$$\mathbf{x} \geqslant 0, \quad \mathbf{p} \geqslant 0, \quad w \geqslant 0, \quad q \geqslant 0, \quad \mathbf{u}^T\mathbf{p} = 1, \tag{10.7f}$$

where **u** is a given semipositive vector. The exposition can be simplified by ordering the different processes producing iron in accordance with the level of the wage rate they are able to pay when they are combined with the last $n-1$ processes, and the rent rate equals zero. Hence the "technique," as defined in Chapter 5, made up of the last $n-1$ processes and process i $(i = 1, 2, \ldots, m-1)$ when land is neglected, is able to pay a higher wage rate than the "technique" made up of the last $n-1$ processes and process $i+1$ when land is neglected. As was pointed out in the previous subsections this order generally depends on the level of the rate of profit: if r changes, the order can be expected to change. It is also possible, as in previous subsections, that not all single product "techniques" just mentioned are able to pay a nonnegative wage rate. If none of them is able to pay a nonnegative wage, then the system of inequalities (10.7) has no solution even if the variable q and inequality (10.7b) are neglected. Assume then that the first s, $1 \leqslant s \leqslant m$, are able to pay a nonnegative wage rate, whereas the last $m-s$ are not. Finally, it is possible that some of the single product "techniques" mentioned above pay the same nonnegative wage rate. This is a complication which is similar to that which will be dealt with in exercise 7.4; in the following discussion we shall for simplicity assume that the wage rates are all different. Then let us define the sets

$$D_i = \{ \mathbf{d} \in \mathbb{R}^n | \mathbf{d} \geqq \mathbf{0}, \exists \mathbf{x} \geqq \mathbf{0} : \mathbf{x}^T(\mathbf{B}-\mathbf{A}) = \mathbf{d}^T, \mathbf{x}^T\mathbf{c} \leqslant t, \mathbf{x}^T\mathbf{e}_j = 0,$$
$$j \neq i \text{ and } j \leqslant m \} \quad (i = 1, 2, \ldots, s).$$

On the premises stated, the exposition of external differential rent can follow exactly the discussion of intensive rent proper presented in Subsection 1.4. In the preceding subsection we referred to exercises 7.6 and 7.7 as dealing with a case with multiple solutions to system (10.6), and to exercise 7.8 as dealing with a case in which system (10.6) has no solution despite the fact that the given vector of net products can be matched with the existing land. With respect to external differential rent, comparable examples are provided by exercises 7.10 and 7.11.

2. Given net products and land: The general model

The previous section was devoted to some heuristic considerations concerning the two variants of intensive rent and the elaboration of a general result concerning a model of pure extensive rent. In the present section a general existence theorem for a long-period position will be provided. This theorem will state a condition which is sufficient but not necessary. However, before turning to an investigation of the general framework suggested in this section, we shall analyze the robustness of the general results arrived at.

2.1. On the robustness of some previous results

The results derived in Subsection 1.1 are subject to two sets of assumptions. The first set concerns assumptions (a) and (b) stated at the beginning of Section 1, which rule out the possibility that extensive and intensive rent can arise in the same model. The second set concerns the assumptions of single production, the existence of only one agricultural commodity, and a given vector of net products. In the following discussion the assumption of a given vector of net products will be retained, while the remaining two assumptions of the second set will be removed. We thus ask whether the results presented in Subsection 1.1 are robust, that is, carry over to the case in which there is joint production and/or more than one agricultural commodity. In order not to mix the two aspects, we shall assume that joint production is limited to the production of industrial commodities.

Consider the following example. There are three commodities, two qualities of land, and the four processes described in Table 10.2. The rate of profit equals 50 per cent ($r = 0.5$). From exercise 8.3 of Chapter 8 we know that if land inputs are neglected, then if processes (1, 2, 3) are operated process (4) incurs extra costs, whereas if processes (1, 2, 4) are operated process (3) incurs extra costs. Hence if land is not neglected, but the net products are such that processes (1, 2, 3) are able to produce them without cultivating the whole of land 1, then there is a solution in which rent rates are zero. Similarly, if the net products are such that processes (1, 2, 4) are able to produce them without cultivating the whole of land 2, then there is *another* solution in which rent rates are zero. Yet lands 1 and 2 cannot both be cultivated: if land 1 (2) is wholly cultivated and land 2 (1) is partially cultivated so that the rent rate of land 2 (1) equals zero, then the rent rate of land 1 (2) would have to be negative! Thus, even if it were possible to prove that commodities 1, 2, and 3 can be produced if and only if their net products d_1, d_2, and d_3 are such that

$$6d_1 - 8d_2 + 7d_3 \leqslant 32t_1 + 13t_2,$$

system (10.2) (appropriately modified) has a solution if and only if

$$6d_1 - 8d_2 + 7d_3 \leqslant \max\{32t_1, 13t_2\},$$

and has two distinct solutions if and only if

$$6d_1 - 8d_2 + 7d_3 \leqslant \min\{32t_1, 13t_2\}.$$

Hence if joint production is introduced into the picture, the results of Subsection 1.1 need not hold.

Exercises 7.13–7.16 analyze examples in which single production holds, but there is more than one agricultural commodity. In exercise 7.13 the

Table 10.2

	commodity inputs			land inputs		labor		outputs		
	1	2	3	1	2	labor		1	2	3
(1)	$\frac{1}{10}$	$\frac{2}{5}$	$\frac{1}{10}$	—	—	$\frac{1}{8}$	$\rightarrow$	$\frac{1}{5}$	$\frac{3}{5}$	—
(2)	—	$\frac{2}{5}$	$\frac{1}{10}$	—	—	$\frac{7}{6}$		$\frac{1}{6}$	$\frac{1}{2}$	—
(3)	$\frac{3}{10}$	$\frac{3}{10}$	—	1	—	$\frac{1}{10}$	$\rightarrow$	—	—	$\frac{5}{2}$
(4)	$\frac{1}{10}$	$\frac{1}{10}$	—	—	1	3	$\rightarrow$	—	—	1

analog of system (10.2) has no solution, even if it is possible to produce the net product with processes that are able to pay nonnegative prices, wage rate, and rent rates. In exercises 7.14–7.16 more than one solution exists. Hence in this case too the results of Subsection 1.1 do not hold. In exercises 7.13–7.15 two agricultural commodities can be produced on the same qualities of land. On the contrary, in exercise 7.16 each quality of land is specific to a given product.

2.2. The model

Assume that there are n commodities and s qualities of land. A process or a method of production is defined by a quadruplet $(\mathbf{a}, \mathbf{b}, \mathbf{c}, l)$ where $\mathbf{a} \in \mathbb{R}^n$ is the commodity input vector, $\mathbf{b} \in \mathbb{R}^n$ is the output vector, $\mathbf{c} \in \mathbb{R}^s$ is the land input vector, and l is the labor input, a scalar; of course $\mathbf{a} \geqslant 0, \mathbf{b} \geqslant 0, \mathbf{c} \geqslant 0, l \geqslant 0$. Since joint production is allowed for in this subsection more than one element of $\mathbf{b}$ can be positive. Vector $\mathbf{c}$ can also have more than one positive element. This is the case, for example, when the farmer-capitalist has to pay a rent for the use of a source of water in addition to the rent he pays for the use of the land he cultivates. (In Chapter 11 it will also be taken into account that some qualities of labor may be scarce; the analysis presented in this section is thus of wider applicability as may seem at first sight.)

Assume that there are m processes. They are defined by quadruplets

$$(\mathbf{a}_j, \mathbf{b}_j, \mathbf{c}_j, l_j). \quad j = 1, 2, \ldots, m$$

Then define matrices $\mathbf{A}$, $\mathbf{B}$, $\mathbf{C}$ and vector $\mathbf{l}$ as follows:

$$\mathbf{A} = \begin{bmatrix} \mathbf{a}_1^T \\ \mathbf{a}_2^T \\ \vdots \\ \mathbf{a}_m^T \end{bmatrix}, \quad \mathbf{B} = \begin{bmatrix} \mathbf{b}_1^T \\ \mathbf{b}_2^T \\ \vdots \\ \mathbf{b}_m^T \end{bmatrix}, \quad \mathbf{C} = \begin{bmatrix} \mathbf{c}_1^T \\ \mathbf{c}_2^T \\ \vdots \\ \mathbf{c}_m^T \end{bmatrix}, \quad \mathbf{l} = \begin{bmatrix} l_1 \\ l_2 \\ \vdots \\ l_m \end{bmatrix}.$$

Let **d** be the vector of net products and **t** the vector of the existing amounts of the different qualities of land. In this section vector **d** is considered a constant vector. The next section deals with the cases in which the net products are functions of profits, wages, rents, and prices. It should be stressed, however, that for the purpose of the present analysis **d** must be taken as constant throughout with respect to time. If it were not so, prices would change over time. Therefore a complete analysis would have to consider the whole time path of prices and produced quantities (cf. the analysis presented in Chapter 12).

Let $x \in \mathbb{R}^m$ be the vector of intensities with which the different processes are operated, $p \in \mathbb{R}^n$ the price vector, w the wage rate, $q \in \mathbb{R}^s$ the vector of rent rates, and r the rate of profit. Take the rate of profit r as given. Since joint production is not ruled out, in order to guarantee that prices are nonnegative we will assume free disposal. The reader is asked to recall the warnings expressed in Section 2 of Chapter 8. In a long-period position

$$x^T(B - A) \geqq d^T, \tag{10.8a}$$

$$x^T(B - A)p = d^Tp, \tag{10.8b}$$

$$x^TC \leqq t^T, \tag{10.8c}$$

$$x^TCq = t^Tq, \tag{10.8d}$$

$$Bp \leqq (1 + r)Ap + Cq + wl, \tag{10.8e}$$

$$x^TBp = x^T[(1 + r)Ap + Cq + wl], \tag{10.8f}$$

$$x \geqq 0, \quad p \geqq 0, \quad w \geqq 0, \quad q \geqq 0, \quad u^Tp = 1, \tag{10.8g}$$

where **u** is a given semipositive vector. If $w > 0$, labor can be used as numeraire. In this case system (10.8) can be written as

$$x^T(B - A) \geqq d^T, \tag{10.9a}$$

$$x^T(B - A)p = d^Tp, \tag{10.9b}$$

$$x^TC \leqq t^T, \tag{10.9c}$$

$$x^TCq = t^Tq, \tag{10.9d}$$

$$Bp \leqq (1 + r)Ap + Cq + l, \tag{10.9e}$$

$$x^TBp = x^T[(1 + r)Ap + Cq + l], \tag{10.9f}$$

$$x \geqq 0, \quad p \geqq 0, \quad q \geqq 0. \tag{10.9g}$$

System (10.9) can easily be transformed in such a way that it becomes identical with system (8.13) and, therefore, can be dealt with in the same way as was the latter in Section 3 of Chapter 8. Indeed, if we introduce matrices

$$\bar{\mathbf{B}} = [\mathbf{B}, -\mathbf{C}], \quad \bar{\mathbf{A}} = [\mathbf{A}, \mathbf{0}], \quad \bar{\mathbf{d}} = \begin{bmatrix} \mathbf{d} \\ -\mathbf{t} \end{bmatrix}, \quad \bar{\mathbf{p}} = \begin{bmatrix} \mathbf{p} \\ \mathbf{q} \end{bmatrix},$$

then system (10.9) can be written as

$$\mathbf{x}^T(\bar{\mathbf{B}} - \bar{\mathbf{A}}) \geqslant \bar{\mathbf{d}}^T, \tag{10.10a}$$

$$\mathbf{x}^T(\bar{\mathbf{B}} - \bar{\mathbf{A}})\bar{\mathbf{p}} = \bar{\mathbf{d}}^T\bar{\mathbf{p}}, \tag{10.10b}$$

$$\bar{\mathbf{B}}\bar{\mathbf{p}} \leqslant (1 + r)\bar{\mathbf{A}}\bar{\mathbf{p}} + \mathbf{l}, \tag{10.10e}$$

$$\mathbf{x}^T\bar{\mathbf{B}}\bar{\mathbf{p}} = \mathbf{x}^T[(1 + r)\bar{\mathbf{A}}\bar{\mathbf{p}} + \mathbf{l}], \tag{10.10f}$$

$$\mathbf{x} \geqslant \mathbf{0}, \quad \bar{\mathbf{p}} \geqslant \mathbf{0}. \tag{10.10g}$$

System (10.10) is identical with system (8.13). In Chapter 8 we have seen that system (8.13) has a solution if there is a nonnegative vector $\mathbf{v}$ satisfying inequality (8.11). Hence system (10.10) has a solution if there is a nonnegative vector $\mathbf{v}$ satisfying the following inequality:

$$\mathbf{v}^T[\bar{\mathbf{B}} - (1 + r)\bar{\mathbf{A}}] \geqslant \bar{\mathbf{d}}^T.$$

This allows us to state the following Theorem.

Theorem 10.1. System (10.8) has a solution with a positive w if there is a nonnegative vector $\mathbf{v}$ such that

$$\mathbf{v}^T[\mathbf{B} - (1 + r)\mathbf{A})] \geqslant \mathbf{d}^T$$

$$\mathbf{v}^T\mathbf{C} \leqslant \mathbf{t}^T.$$

The condition mentioned in Theorem 10.1 could be considered as a generalization of the usual condition of viability for single product systems to systems with land. Yet the usual condition of viability is a necessary and sufficient condition for the existence of positive prices for single product systems. On the contrary, the condition just mentioned is only sufficient. Indeed, for the example given in Subsection 1.2, Theorem 10.1 ensures that there is a solution if

$$0 \leqslant d_1 \leqslant \frac{10152 - 1551(1 + r) - 4169(1 + r)^2}{758(1 + r)} \tag{10.11a}$$

$$0 \leqslant d_2 \leqslant \frac{10152 - 1551(1 + r) - 4169(1 + r)^2}{846} - \frac{379(1 + r)}{423}d_1. \tag{10.11b}$$

However, toward the end of Subsection 1.2 we saw that a solution for much larger ranges of variations of variables exists. In particular, if $r = 0.1$

the ratio between the area defined by inequalities (10.11) and the area of the set of points in which there is a solution is about 54%. This ratio decreases to about 22 percent if $r = 0.2$; it is lower than 1% if $r = R'$; it tends to 0 as r tends to R.

3. Toward more general models

In Section 5 of Chapter 8 we have mentioned some models which consider net products as functions of incomes and prices. These models are not fully investigated in this book since they require the use of mathematical tools which go well beyond linear algebra and linear programming. As an example, consider the model in which workers consume commodities in proportion to vector $\mathbf{b}_w$, capitalists consume commodities in proportion to vector $\mathbf{b}_c$, and landowners consume commodities in proportion to vector $\mathbf{b}_l$. In this case system (10.8) would be changed by replacing inequality (10.8a) and equation (10.8b) with

$$\mathbf{x}^T(\mathbf{B} - \mathbf{A}) \geqslant w \frac{\mathbf{x}^T\mathbf{l}}{\mathbf{b}_w^T\mathbf{p}}\mathbf{b}_w^T + r\frac{\mathbf{x}^T\mathbf{Ap}}{\mathbf{b}_c^T\mathbf{p}}\mathbf{b}_c^T + \frac{\mathbf{x}^T\mathbf{Cq}}{\mathbf{b}_l^T\mathbf{p}}\mathbf{b}_l^T \tag{10.12a}$$

$$\mathbf{x}^T(\mathbf{B} - \mathbf{A})\mathbf{p} = w\mathbf{x}^T\mathbf{l} + r\mathbf{x}^T\mathbf{Ap} + \mathbf{x}^T\mathbf{Cq}, \tag{10.12b}$$

the other equations and inequalities being unchanged and referred to in the following as (10.12c)–(10.12g). Since system (10.12a)–(10.12g) is not able to determine the size of the economy, a further condition is required. It could, for example, be

$$\mathbf{x}^T\mathbf{l} = L, \tag{10.12h}$$

where L is the total amount of labor employed. This does not mean that labor is taken as being fully employed.

No attempt will be made here to prove that a solution to system (10.12) exists. We just want to show that if net products are functions of incomes and prices, then a further origin of rent and hence an additional concept of rent has to be introduced: rent is determined by the conditions of production jointly with the pattern of consumption as a function of incomes and prices. This variety of rent has been called "singular rent" since it appears when all qualities of land involved are fully employed and the number of processes involved is smaller than the number of commodities produced plus the number of qualities of land used.

Singular rent will be introduced here under very special assumptions, as extensive and intensive rent were in Section 1, in order to isolate this concept from other varieties of rent discussed in Section 1. In particular, we will assume that each process produces a single commodity and that all the assumptions (a), (b), and (c) mentioned in Section 1 hold. With these assumptions system (10.12) can be stated as (note that the output matrix **B** equals the identity matrix **I**):

$$\mathbf{x}^T = \mathbf{x}^T \mathbf{A} + w\frac{\mathbf{x}^T \mathbf{l}}{\mathbf{b}_w^T \mathbf{p}}\mathbf{b}_w^T + r\frac{\mathbf{x}^T \mathbf{A}\mathbf{p}}{\mathbf{b}_c^T \mathbf{p}}\mathbf{b}_c^T + q\frac{\mathbf{x}^T \mathbf{c}}{\mathbf{b}_l^T \mathbf{p}}\mathbf{b}_l^T, \tag{10.13a}$$

$$\mathbf{x}^T \mathbf{c} \leqslant t, \tag{10.13b}$$

$$q\mathbf{x}^T \mathbf{c} = qt, \tag{10.13c}$$

$$\mathbf{p} = (1 + r)\mathbf{A}\mathbf{p} + q\mathbf{c} + w\mathbf{l}, \tag{10.13d}$$

$$\mathbf{x} \geqslant 0, \quad \mathbf{p} \geqslant 0, \quad q \geqslant 0, \quad \mathbf{u}^T \mathbf{p} = 1, \quad \mathbf{x}^T \mathbf{l} = L. \tag{10.13e}$$

Vectors $\mathbf{b}_w, \mathbf{b}_c, \mathbf{b}_l$ are normalized by setting:

$$\mathbf{b}_w^T(\mathbf{I} - \mathbf{A})^{-1}\mathbf{l} = \mathbf{b}_c^T(\mathbf{I} - \mathbf{A})^{-1}\mathbf{l} = \mathbf{b}_l^T(\mathbf{I} - \mathbf{A})^{-1}\mathbf{l} = 1; \tag{10.14}$$

this also implies that $\mathbf{b}_w^T\mathbf{p}, \mathbf{b}_c^T\mathbf{p}, \mathbf{b}_l^T\mathbf{p} > w$ for $r > 0$.

By taking account of equalities (10.14), equation (10.13a) yields

$$\mathbf{x}^T\mathbf{l} = w\frac{\mathbf{x}^T\mathbf{l}}{\mathbf{b}_w^T\mathbf{p}} + r\frac{\mathbf{x}^T\mathbf{A}\mathbf{p}}{\mathbf{b}_c^T\mathbf{p}} + q\frac{\mathbf{x}^T\mathbf{c}}{\mathbf{b}_l^T\mathbf{p}},$$

$$\mathbf{x}^T\mathbf{c} = w\frac{\mathbf{x}^T\mathbf{l}}{\mathbf{b}_w^T\mathbf{p}}\mathbf{b}_w^T(\mathbf{I} - \mathbf{A})^{-1}\mathbf{c} + r\frac{\mathbf{x}^T\mathbf{A}\mathbf{p}}{\mathbf{b}_c^T\mathbf{p}}\mathbf{b}_c^T(\mathbf{I} - \mathbf{A})^{-1}\mathbf{c} + q\frac{\mathbf{x}^T\mathbf{c}}{\mathbf{b}_l^T\mathbf{p}}\mathbf{b}_l^T(\mathbf{I} - \mathbf{A})^{-1}\mathbf{c},$$

and by taking account of equations (10.13c) and (10.13e),

$$r\frac{\mathbf{x}^T\mathbf{A}\mathbf{p}}{\mathbf{b}_c^T\mathbf{p}} = L - \frac{wL}{\mathbf{b}_w^T\mathbf{p}} - \frac{qt}{\mathbf{b}_l^T\mathbf{p}},$$

$$\mathbf{x}^T\mathbf{c} = \frac{wL}{\mathbf{b}_w^T\mathbf{p}}\mathbf{b}_w^T(\mathbf{I} - \mathbf{A})^{-1}\mathbf{c} + r\frac{\mathbf{x}^T\mathbf{A}\mathbf{p}}{\mathbf{b}_c^T\mathbf{p}}\mathbf{b}_c^T(\mathbf{I} - \mathbf{A})^{-1}\mathbf{c} + \frac{qt}{\mathbf{b}_l^T\mathbf{p}}\mathbf{b}_l^T(\mathbf{I} - \mathbf{A})^{-1}\mathbf{c}.$$

Hence

$$\frac{\mathbf{x}^T\mathbf{c}}{L} = \mathbf{b}_c^T(\mathbf{I} - \mathbf{A})^{-1}\mathbf{c} + w\frac{(\mathbf{b}_w - \mathbf{b}_c)^T(\mathbf{I} - \mathbf{A})^{-1}\mathbf{c}}{\mathbf{b}_w^T\mathbf{p}}$$

$$+ \frac{qt}{L}\frac{(\mathbf{b}_l - \mathbf{b}_c)^T(\mathbf{I} - \mathbf{A})^{-1}\mathbf{c}}{\mathbf{b}_l^T\mathbf{c}}. \tag{10.15}$$

According to whether or not land is scarce and therefore the rent rate is positive or zero, we may discriminate between two groups of long-period positions.

(i) Consider first the case in which $q = 0$ and $t > \mathbf{x}^T\mathbf{c}$. From equation (10.15) we obtain

$$\frac{t}{L} > \frac{\mathbf{x}^T\mathbf{c}}{L} = \mathbf{b}_c^T(\mathbf{I} - \mathbf{A})^{-1}\mathbf{c} + w\frac{(\mathbf{b}_w - \mathbf{b}_c)^T(\mathbf{I} - \mathbf{A})^{-1}\mathbf{c}}{\mathbf{b}_w^T\mathbf{p}}.$$

Hence if

$$\frac{t}{L} > \mathbf{b}_c^T(\mathbf{I} - \mathbf{A})^{-1}\mathbf{c} + \frac{(\mathbf{b}_w - \mathbf{b}_c)^T(\mathbf{I} - \mathbf{A})^{-1}\mathbf{c}}{\mathbf{b}_w^T[\mathbf{I} - (1 + r)\mathbf{A}]^{-1}\mathbf{l}},$$

a solution to system (10.13) is given by

$$\mathbf{p} = w[\mathbf{I} - (1 + r)\mathbf{A}]^{-1}\mathbf{l} \tag{10.16a}$$

$$q = 0 \tag{10.16b}$$

$$\mathbf{x}^T = L\left[\mathbf{b}_c + \frac{1}{\mathbf{b}_w^T[\mathbf{I} - (1 + r)\mathbf{A}]^{-1}\mathbf{l}}(\mathbf{b}_w - \mathbf{b}_c)\right]^T(\mathbf{I} - \mathbf{A})^{-1}. \tag{10.16c}$$

(ii) Consider now the case in which $q > 0$ and $t = \mathbf{x}^T\mathbf{c}$. On the hypothesis, to be verified later, that $q > 0$, we obtain from equations (10.13c) and (10.15):

$$\frac{t}{L} = \mathbf{b}_c^T(\mathbf{I} - \mathbf{A})^{-1}\mathbf{c} + w\frac{(\mathbf{b}_w - \mathbf{b}_c)^T(\mathbf{I} - \mathbf{A})^{-1}\mathbf{c}}{\mathbf{b}_w^T\mathbf{p}}$$

$$+ \frac{qt}{L}\frac{(\mathbf{b}_l - \mathbf{b}_c)^T(\mathbf{I} - \mathbf{A})^{-1}\mathbf{c}}{\mathbf{b}_l^T\mathbf{p}}. \tag{10.17}$$

Any solution of system (10.13) with $q > 0$ needs to satisfy equation (10.17). From equation (10.13d) we obtain

$$\mathbf{p} = q[\mathbf{I} - (1 + r)\mathbf{A}]^{-1}\mathbf{c} + w[\mathbf{I} - (1 + r)\mathbf{A}]^{-1}\mathbf{l}.$$

And since $\mathbf{u}^T\mathbf{p} = 1$ because of (10.13e),

$$w = \frac{1 - q\mathbf{u}^T[\mathbf{I} - (1 + r)\mathbf{A}]^{-1}\mathbf{c}}{\mathbf{u}^T[\mathbf{I} - (1 + r)\mathbf{A}]^{-1}\mathbf{l}}.$$

Hence,

$$\mathbf{p} = q[\mathbf{I} - (1 + r)\mathbf{A}]^{-1}\mathbf{c} + \frac{1 - q\mathbf{u}^T[\mathbf{I} - (1 + r)\mathbf{A}]^{-1}\mathbf{c}}{\mathbf{u}^T[\mathbf{I} - (1 + r)\mathbf{A}]^{-1}\mathbf{l}}[\mathbf{I} - (1 + r)\mathbf{A}]^{-1}\mathbf{l}$$

and

$$\mathbf{b}_w^T\mathbf{p} = \frac{\mathbf{b}_w^T[\mathbf{I} - (1 + r)\mathbf{A}]^{-1}\mathbf{l}}{\mathbf{u}^T[\mathbf{I} - (1 + r)\mathbf{A}]^{-1}\mathbf{l}}$$

$$+ \left(\mathbf{b}_w^T[\mathbf{I} - (1+r)\mathbf{A}]^{-1}\mathbf{c} - \frac{\mathbf{b}_w^T[\mathbf{I} - (1+r)\mathbf{A}]^{-1}\mathbf{l}\mathbf{u}^T[\mathbf{I} - (1+r)\mathbf{A}]^{-1}\mathbf{c}}{\mathbf{u}^T[\mathbf{I} - (1+r)\mathbf{A}]^{-1}\mathbf{l}}\right)q,$$

$$\mathbf{b}_l^T\mathbf{p} = \frac{\mathbf{b}_l^T[\mathbf{I} - (1 + r)\mathbf{A}]^{-1}\mathbf{l}}{\mathbf{u}^T[\mathbf{I} - (1 + r)\mathbf{A}]^{-1}\mathbf{l}}$$

$$+ \left(\mathbf{b}_l^T[\mathbf{I} - (1+r)\mathbf{A}]^{-1}\mathbf{c} - \frac{\mathbf{b}_l^T[\mathbf{I} - (1+r)\mathbf{A}]^{-1}\mathbf{l}\mathbf{u}^T[\mathbf{I} - (1+r)\mathbf{A}]^{-1}\mathbf{c}}{\mathbf{u}^T[\mathbf{I} - (1+r)\mathbf{A}]^{-1}\mathbf{l}}\right)q.$$

That is, w, $\mathbf{b}_w^T \mathbf{p}$, and $\mathbf{b}_l^T \mathbf{p}$ are linear functions of q. By substituting these linear functions in equation (10.17) a second degree algebraic equation in q is obtained (since $\mathbf{b}_w^T \mathbf{p} \neq 0 \neq \mathbf{b}_l^T \mathbf{p}$). This equation collapses to a linear equation if $\mathbf{b}_w = \mathbf{b}_c \neq \mathbf{b}_l$, or $\mathbf{b}_w = \mathbf{b}_l \neq \mathbf{b}_c$, or $\mathbf{b}_w \neq \mathbf{b}_c = \mathbf{b}_l$. Moreover, if $\mathbf{b}_w = \mathbf{b}_c = \mathbf{b}_l$, then equality (10.17) is not an equation in q anymore: it can hold only by a fluke. Let q^* be a solution to the mentioned second degree equation; if $q^* > 0$, then $(q^*, w^*, \mathbf{p}^*, \mathbf{x}^*)$ is a solution of system (10.13), where:

$$w^* = \frac{1 - q^* \mathbf{u}^T [\mathbf{I} - (1+r)\mathbf{A}]^{-1} \mathbf{c}}{\mathbf{u}^T [\mathbf{I} - (1+r)\mathbf{A}]^{-1} \mathbf{l}},$$

$$\mathbf{p}^* = q^* [\mathbf{I} - (1+r)\mathbf{A}]^{-1} \mathbf{c} + w^* [\mathbf{I} - (1+r)\mathbf{A}]^{-1} \mathbf{l},$$

$$\mathbf{x}^{*T} = L \mathbf{b}_c^T (\mathbf{I} - \mathbf{A})^{-1} + \frac{w^* L}{\mathbf{b}_w^T \mathbf{p}^*} (\mathbf{b}_w - \mathbf{b}_c)^T (\mathbf{I} - \mathbf{A})^{-1}$$

$$+ \frac{q^* t}{\mathbf{b}_l^T \mathbf{p}^*} (\mathbf{b}_l - \mathbf{b}_c)^T (\mathbf{I} - \mathbf{A})^{-1}.$$

Let us call q^* the rate of *demand-led rent* or *singular rent*. Of course, one or two alternative rates of singular rent for each value of the rate of profit may exist, but there cannot be more than two. It is also obvious that if all social classes consume commodities in the same fixed proportions, that is, if $\mathbf{b}_w = \mathbf{b}_c = \mathbf{b}_l$, then this kind of rent cannot arise. Nor can it arise if vectors $\mathbf{l}$ and $\mathbf{c}$ are proportional (cf. exercise 7.20).

4. Wage–profit and rents–profit frontiers

In the previous sections of this chapter the rate of profit has been assumed to be given. Yet in earlier chapters of this book we have often studied the wage–profit frontier, that is, the wage rate as a function of the rate of profit. This analysis can obviously be carried out in the present case too. This means that the requirements for use are fixed by giving the net products either as a constant vector or as a function of prices and incomes, and the rate of profit is changed from zero to its maximum value. The wage–profit and the rents–profit frontiers are then determined. Generally we are interested in proving that the wage–profit frontier is decreasing. But this is not the case in the models analyzed in Sections 2 and 3. In particular exercises 7.24 and 7.25 provide examples of increasing wage–profit frontiers for both variants of intensive rent models presented in Subsections 1.3 and 1.4 and for the singular rent model presented in Section 3.

Only in the extensive rent model presented in Subsection 1.1 can we assert that the wage–profit frontier is decreasing. This is so since the wage–profit frontier is, in this case, obtained by joining segments of w–r relationships of single product techniques which were analyzed in Chapter 4.

Since each w–r relationship is decreasing the wage frontier is also decreasing. An example will suffice to clarify this point.

Consider the example of Subsection 1.2 and define the sets

$$D_0 = \left\{ \mathbf{d} \in \mathbb{R}^2 \mid 0 \leqslant d_2 \leqslant \frac{304}{423} - \frac{379}{423} d_1, 0 \leqslant d_1 \leqslant \frac{304}{379} \right\}$$

$$D_1 = \left\{ \mathbf{d} \in \mathbb{R}^2 \mid 0 \leqslant d_2 \leqslant \frac{1912}{423} - \frac{379}{423} d_1, 0 \leqslant d_1 \leqslant \frac{1912}{379} \right\}$$

$$D_2 = \left\{ \mathbf{d} \in \mathbb{R}^2 \mid 0 \leqslant d_2 \leqslant \frac{2216}{423} - \frac{379}{423} d_1, 0 \leqslant d_1 \leqslant \frac{2216}{379} \right\}.$$

If $\mathbf{d} \in D_0$, then the land services can be neglected and the wage–profit frontier is determined as in Chapter 5. If $\mathbf{d} \notin D_0$ and $\mathbf{d} \in D_1$, then the land services can be neglected only if $0 \leqslant r \leqslant 0.1$ or $0.2 \leqslant r \leqslant R$. In this case the wage–profit frontier is the w–r relationship of the "technique" made up by processes (1) and (2) when the services of land are neglected. Land 1 is always partially cultivated and its rent rate equals zero. Land 2 is not cultivated if $0 \leqslant r < 0.1$ or $0.2 < r \leqslant R$, but it is fully cultivated if $0.1 < r < 0.2$. Finally, if $\mathbf{d} \notin D_1$ and $\mathbf{d} \in D_2$, then the wage–profit frontier is the *inner* envelope of the w–r relationships relative to the "techniques" which can be defined when land services are neglected. The rent rate of land 1 is positive if and only if $0 \leqslant r < 0.1$ or $0.2 \leqslant r \leqslant R'$, whereas the rent rate of land 2 is positive if and only if $0.1 < r < 0.2$. For $R' < r \leqslant R$ there is no long-period position.

5. Price–output and rents–output relationships

In Subsection 4.4 of Chapter 1 the possibility of constructing a relationship between the price vector and the gross output quantity vector for a given technology, given the rate of profit, was mentioned. This relationship, it was emphasized, can be represented as a constant function if single production holds, returns to scale are constant, and all commodities are produced. In Chapter 5 we have seen that if not all commodities are produced, then the prices of non-produced commodities can vary in a *set* which can be determined. Hence in this case the relationship between price and gross output for a given rate of profit is a correspondence.[1] In this section we introduce the above-mentioned relationship, assuming that returns to scale are constant with regard to each particular quality of land, though, of course, not across different qualities of land. Obviously,

---

[1] However the set of possible price vectors for a given rate of profit (and a given vector of gross outputs if returns are not constant) is connected.

since rents are to be considered we have also to take into account the rents-output relationships. In the following discussion reference will be made to *net* outputs rather than to *gross* outputs.

From an analytical point of view there is not much to be discussed. We have just to calculate the solution(s) to system (10.8) for each vector **d** such that the same system (10.8) has a solution. In Subsection 1.2 all these solutions have been calculated for the numerical example under consideration. In particular, if the rate of profit r equals 0.3 and commodities are consumed in the proportion of one unit of corn to one unit of iron, and if the consumption of corn (iron) is between 0 and 956/401, then prices are determined by the operation of processes (1) and (2) of Table 10.1 and no land gets a rent; whereas if the consumption of corn (iron) is between 956/401 and 1108/401, then prices are determined by the operation of all processes of Table 10.1, rent on land 1 is positive, but rent on land 2 is zero.

In the example of Subsection 1.2 an increase in demand, that is, quantities required for use, can increase the rent rates and prices in terms of the wage rate, but it cannot decrease them. This is generally true when the assumptions of extensive rent expounded in Subsection 1.1 hold (see exercise 7.26). But it is not true in general (see exercise 7.27). Moreover, the existence of more than one solution to systems (10.6) and (10.7) considered in Subsections 1.4 and 1.5 implies that for a given vector of net product **d** more than one price vector and rent rate vector are determined. Thus, the relationships between prices and rents on one hand and the rate of profit and net outputs on the other are, again, correspondences rather than functions. And this is so even if all commodities are consumed. Moreover, the set of price vectors and rent rate vectors corresponding to a given rate of profit and a given vector of net products need not be connected (see exercises 7.28–7.30).

6. Historical notes

6.1. In early contributions to political economy there are essentially only two types of income contemplated: the wages of labor and the rent of land. It is only later, particularly in some of the writings of the physiocrats and in Adam Smith, that profits are separated from the two other kinds of income and are dealt with analytically. The overall view which emerges from the writings of Petty ([1662] 1986), Quesnay ([1759] 1972), and Smith (*WN*) is that of rent as a surplus over the cost of production on land, including (in the case of Smith) the income (profits) of farmers. The size of total rents is seen to depend on the fertility of the soil and on the methods by means of which it is cultivated. While the concept of rent due to *differential* costs of production in agriculture surfaces variously in the literature, rent is generally interpreted in the sense of *absolute* rent. According to Adam Smith "the rent of land...considered as the price paid for the use of the land, is naturally a monopoly price" (*WN*, I.xi.a.5). Smith also contended that the "natural" price of each commodity finally resolves itself into wages, profit and rent, that is, the rent of land is a component part of prices (see *WN*, I.vi), a doctrine which was first attacked by Anderson (1777b) and then by Ricardo ([1817] *Works* I).

It is worth mentioning, however, that Petty already introduced the principle of extensive (differential) rent in its simplest form: rent due to different distances of the plots of land on which corn is grown from the location, for example, the town, where most of the net output of corn is consumed: "if the Corn which feedeth London, or an Army, be brought forty miles thither, then the Corn growing within a mile of London, or the quarters of such Army, shall have added unto its natural price, so much as the charge of bringing it thirty nine miles doth amount unto" (Petty, [1662] 1986, p. 48). With a single price ruling in the market place of the town, the proprietors of the more favorably situated plots of land will be able to pocket the differences in transport cost as rent: they "will not onely yield more rent for these Reasons': the price of their land will be higher, that is, will yield "more years purchase then in remote places, by reason of the pleasure and honour extraordinary of having Lands there" (ibid., p. 49). Since the extent to which distant lands have to be cultivated depends on the total amount of corn needed in town, so does the amount of rent due to location. The larger the amount of corn to be produced, the larger is the amount of this kind of rent generated.

6.2. According to widespread opinion, David Ricardo deserves the credit for having developed what is known as the "classical" theory of rent. In the Preface to his *Principles*, Ricardo with his characteristic modesty and love of truth expressed a different opinion: "In 1815, Mr. Malthus...and a Fellow of University College, Oxford,... presented to the world, nearly at the same moment, the true doctrine of rent" (*Works* I, p. 5). The reference is to T. R. Malthus's *Inquiry into the Nature and Progress of Rent* (1815) and E. West's *Essay on the Application of Capital to Land* (1815). Yet Ricardo was both too modest and in one respect he was even wrong. He was too modest since he had already dealt with the problem of at least extensive rent in his "Notes on Bentham's 'Sur les Prix,'" written in 1810–11 but not published during his lifetime (see *Works* III, pp. 259–341, particularly p. 287); and in the same year, 1815, he had published his "Essay on the Influence of a low Price of Corn on the Profits of Stock" in the *Edinburgh Review*, in which he had laid out, in critical response to Malthus's doctrine and with extensive use of numerical examples, the principles of extensive and intensive rent (proper). And he was wrong in that at least the concept of extensive rent had already been elaborated by William Petty and James Anderson (1777a,b) (see also Schumpeter, 1954).

With these qualifications in mind, it is certainly appropriate to consider the chapter "On Rent" in Ricardo's *Principles* as the *locus classicus* of the classical theory of rent. Ricardo developed his argument in terms of the assumption of "free competition," that is, he set aside the problem of absolute rent. This becomes clear in his discussion of the cause(s) of rent: "If all land had the same properties, if it were unlimited in quantity, and uniform in quality, no charge would be made for its use, unless where it possessed peculiar advantages of situation. It is only, then, because land is not unlimited in quantity and uniform in quality, and because in the progress of population, land of an inferior quality, or less advantageously situated, is called into cultivation, that rent is ever paid for the use of it" (*Works* I, p. 70). Ricardo went on to expound the concept of extensive rent: "When in the progress of society, land of the second degree of fertility is taken into cultivation, rent immediately commences on that of the first quality, and the amount of that rent will depend on the difference in the quality of these two portions of land" (ibid.). Since in Ricardo's view "the value of corn is regulated by the quantity of labour bestowed on its production on that quality of land, or with that portion of capital, which pays no rent," the famous dictum follows: "Corn is not high because a rent is paid, but a rent is paid because corn is high" (ibid., p. 74). Hence, in the case of extensive diminishing returns rent is not a component part of the price of a commodity as Adam Smith had wrongly contended. Ricardo also expressed the view that the order of the different plots of land according to "fertility" corresponds to the order according to the associated rates of rent per acre, such that the "most fertile" land always yields the highest rent per acre, the second-best land the second highest, and so on (ibid., p. 70), a view shared by Marx ([1894] 1959, p. 665).

With land there is always a problem of the choice of technique to be solved. This is made clear by Ricardo when he addresses the problem of intensive rent proper: "It often, and, indeed, commonly happens, that before No. 2, 3, 4, or 5, or the inferior lands are cultivated, capital can be employed more productively on those lands which are already in cultivation. ... In such case, capital will be preferably employed on the old land, and will equally create a rent; for rent is always the difference between the produce obtained by the employment of two equal quantities of capital and labour" (ibid., p. 71).

6.3. An early attempt at formalizing certain aspects of Ricardo's approach to the theory of value and distribution, including his explanation of rent, was made by William Whewell (1829, 1831). The problem of rent was also dealt with by Vladimir K. Dmitriev in the fourth part of his 1898 essay on Ricardo's theory of value (Dmitriev, [1898] 1974). However, Dmitriev was not so much concerned with a reformulation of the Ricardian doctrine, as with fusing it and the theory of price put forward by Auspitz and Lieben (1889).

6.4. An important contribution to the theory of rent, location and spatial resource allocation was made by Johann Heinrich von Thünen in *Der isolirte Staat* (1826). Von Thünen's basic model assumes land as being differentiated only in terms of the distance of its location from a central town which is also the market place where the produce of land, for example, rye, is sold. With freight costs proportionate to distance and with output per acre depending on the amount of labor employed per acre, each producer chooses his method of production in such a way that the marginal net product of labor equals the given and uniform real wage in terms of rye. Von Thünen is able to show that land rent from rye production is a diminishing function of distance. Essentially the same argument is then applied to other agricultural products like milk and other dairy products, vegetables, or lumber. Comparing the rentability of the different uses to which land can be put at each distance, the proprietor of land then decides to raise the product promising the highest rent. This leads to von Thünen's famous scheme of concentric "rings" of specialization around the market place. It is shown that the lower the transportation costs and the more rapidly returns are diminishing, the larger will be the distance from the center at which a commodity is produced.

This model is then extended in various directions by von Thünen. Here it suffices to emphasize that von Thünen deserves the credit for having attempted to tackle the difficult problem of a multiplicity of agricultural products produced from a single quality of land and for having put into sharp relief the importance of joint products in agricultural production. Indeed, some of his results concerning the spacial location of certain productive activities derive precisely from his clear understanding of the importance of joint production in the primary sector of the economy (see Kurz, 1986b).

6.5. Léon Walras dealt with Ricardo's theory of rent in Lesson 39 of his *Eléments* ([1874] 1954, pp. 404–18). His main objection suggests that Ricardo and his followers failed to develop "a unified general theory to determine the prices of all productive services in the same way" (ibid., p. 416). Walras contended that such a theory, can be elaborated by generalizing the principle of scarcity, which the classical economists had limited to natural resources, to all factors of production, including "capital." However, as the subsequent discussion of the issue showed, it is doubtful that labor, capital, and land, and thus wages, profits, and rents, can be treated on a par. Reservations about this possibility were already expressed by Knut Wicksell in *Über Wert, Kapital und Rente* (1893), in which he boldly attempted to synthesize the marginal utility and marginal productivity approaches to the theory of value of Jevons and Menger with von Böhm–Bawerk's analysis of capital and interest within the framework of a Walrasian general equilibrium model. For a discussion of the problem of "capital" in neoclassical theory, see Sections 1–3 of Chapter 14.

Wicksell's reservations seem to have left little impression on the authors of some major twentieth-century contributions to the marginalist tradition. Moreover, once the idea had been accepted that a parallel could be drawn between profits and capital on the one hand and rent and homogeneous land on the other, the radical conclusion was close at hand that a separate consideration of natural resources was perhaps dispensable, that is, all factors of production except labor could be aggregated into a single magnitude called "capital." Thus, for example, in "neoclassical" growth theory, which boomed in the late 1950s and throughout the 1960s (cf. in particular Solow, 1956, 1970), the conditions of production were described in terms of a two-factor aggregate production function $Q = F(K, L)$. See, however, Meade (1961) who tried to preserve the canonical trinity formula in the theory of production according to which there are three factors, including "land" used as short-hand for natural resources in general.

6.6. In some interpretations the von Neumann model is said to abstract altogether from natural resources. This is a misrepresentation, since what von Neumann really assumes is "that the natural factors of production, including labour, can be expanded in unlimited quantities" (1945, p. 2). Hence natural factors are explicitly taken to be non-scarce. For a discussion of the von Neumann model and its "classical" features, see Sections 5 and 6 of Chapter 13.

6.7. Modern mathematical treatments of Ricardo's approach to rent theory were elaborated by Paul Samuelson (1959) and Luigi Pasinetti (1960). Both analyses are based on strongly simplifying assumptions. Pasinetti, and Samuelson for most of his paper, developed their arguments in terms of the following premises: (i) there is only one type of agricultural product, called "corn"; (ii) corn is the only wage-good and capital consists entirely of the wage-bill, that is, corn is produced by labor and land alone. It was argued that in these circumstances there is a simple aggregate production function for agriculture as a whole. This claim has recently been contested by Michio Morishima (1989; see in particular pp. 50–1).

According to Morishima, if land is diversified in quality a separate production function has to be constructed for each quality of land even on the extremely special premises mentioned above. However, as Kurz and Salvadori (1992) have demonstrated, Morishima's criticism cannot be sustained: taking Sraffa's chapter on "Land" (1960, ch. XI) as a starting point, an aggregate sectoral production function is shown to exist in the above case. It should also be clear that with more general assumptions no such function can be constructed.

6.8. The most important reformulation of the classical theory of rent was provided by Sraffa (1960, ch. XI). As Sraffa stresses, the scarcity of land is generally reflected in the co-existence of two or more processes producing the same commodity. In the pure case of *extensive* diminishing returns, in which there is only one process for the production of corn for each quality of land, different qualities of land will be used side by side in order to produce the amount of corn required (see Subsection 1.1 above). In the pure case of *intensive* diminishing returns, two methods of production will be employed concurrently in general and will allow the determination of the (uniform) rent of land and the price of corn. Output can be increased by gradually replacing the first method with the second one (see Subsection 1.4 above). For a summary statement of Sraffa's treatment of diminishing returns, see Subsection 8.1 of Chapter 13.

Sraffa remarks only briefly on "more complex cases" (ibid., p. 76), in particular the multiplicity of agricultural products. He writes: "What is required in any case is that the number of separate processes should be equal to the number of qualities of land plus the number of products concerned; and, moreover, that the links or overlaps between the various products and the various lands on which they are grown should be sufficient for the determination of the rents and of the prices" (ibid., p. 77). However, as we have seen above, the system cannot always be guaranteed to be "square." Sraffa also maintains that "in the case of a single quality of land, the multiplicity of agricultural products would not give rise to any complications" (ibid.), a proposition which, as we have seen, is difficult to sustain.

6.9. Sraffa's book has stimulated a new interest in the classical explanation of the rent of land and has triggered the publication of several works which generalized his approach, and amended it where necessary. Quadrio-Curzio (1967, 1980), Montani (1972, 1975), and Kurz (1976, 1978, 1979) provided detailed accounts of extensive and intensive rent. See also Guichard (1979, 1980). Abraham-Frois and Berrebi (1980) have written a useful summary statement of the early discussions of the theory of rent inspired by Sraffa's contribution; see also Quadrio-Curzio (1987).

Abraham-Frois and Berrebi (1980, ch. 4) and Saucier (1981, ch. X, 1984) have shown the possibility of external differential rent by operating one process producing corn and two processes producing an industrial commodity and utilizing corn in different proportions; Saucier (1981, p. 234) has called this variety of rent "external differential rent." The concept of "singular rent" was introduced by Salvadori (1983). The general framework of the analysis adopted here in Section 2 was first put forward and utilized by Salvadori (1979c, 1986b, 1987c). Some of the results derived within this framework have also been established by Denicolò (1982). D'Agata (1981–82, 1983a, 1983b, 1984, 1985) has provided a number of examples which show the non-existence and non-uniqueness of a long-period position when either intensive rent or joint production or more than one agricultural commodity are involved. See also Erreygers (1990). Bidard (1991, ch. XIX) has dealt with system (10.12). See also the collection of essays on the classical approach to the theory of rent edited by him (Bidard, 1987). Some additional papers on rent theory are contained in Steedman (1988a, vol. II).

6.10. Metcalfe and Steedman (1972), Montet (1979), and Steedman (1982) have looked at the presence of land from another standpoint: they studied the frontier among the wage rate, the rent rate and the rate of profit on the assumption that land is scarce without, however, taking the quantity system explicitly into account. The results have been utilized to criticize neoclassical analysis, especially the analysis of international trade (see, for instance, Metcalfe and Steedman, 1977, and some other papers contained in Steedman, 1979b).

7. Exercises

7.1. Show that if corn enters directly or indirectly into the production of all industrial commodities, then set D_i, as defined in Subsection 1.1, has the form

$$D_i = \{\mathbf{d} \in \mathbb{R}^n \,|\, \mathbf{d} \geqq \mathbf{0}, d_n \leqslant \alpha_i - \mathbf{d}_1^T \mathbf{b}\},$$

where d_n is the nth element of $\mathbf{d}$, $[\mathbf{d}_1^T, d_n^T]^T = \mathbf{d}$, α_i is a positive scalar, and $\mathbf{b}$ is a positive vector independent of i. [*Hint*: Let $\hat{\mathbf{A}}$ be obtained from $\mathbf{A}$ by deleting the last $m - i$ rows and let $\hat{\mathbf{C}}$ be obtained from $\mathbf{C}$ by deleting the last $m - i$ rows and columns. Then partition $\hat{\mathbf{A}}$ and $\hat{\mathbf{C}}$ in the following way:

$$\hat{\mathbf{A}} = \begin{bmatrix} \mathbf{A}_{11} & \mathbf{A}_{12} \\ \mathbf{A}_{21} & \mathbf{A}_{22} \end{bmatrix}, \quad \hat{\mathbf{C}} = \begin{bmatrix} \mathbf{C}_1 \\ \mathbf{C}_2 \end{bmatrix},$$

where $\mathbf{A}_{11}$ is $(n-1) \times (n-1)$ and $\mathbf{C}_2$ is $i \times i$ and diagonal, and obtain by appropriate partition of vector **x** that

$$\mathbf{d}_1^T = \mathbf{x}_1^T(\mathbf{I} - \mathbf{A}_{11}) - \mathbf{x}_2^T\mathbf{A}_{21}$$
$$d_n = \mathbf{x}_2^T(\mathbf{e} - \mathbf{A}_{22}) - \mathbf{x}_1^T\mathbf{A}_{12}$$
$$\mathbf{x}_2^T\mathbf{C}_2 \lessgtr \mathbf{t}^T.$$

Prove that

$$d_n = \mathbf{x}_2^T[\mathbf{e} - \mathbf{A}_{22} - \mathbf{A}_{21}(\mathbf{I} - \mathbf{A}_{11})^{-1}\mathbf{A}_{12}] - \mathbf{d}_1^T(\mathbf{I} - \mathbf{A}_{11})^{-1}\mathbf{A}_{12},$$
$$\mathbf{x}_2^T \leqslant \mathbf{t}^T\mathbf{C}_2^{-1}.$$

Finally, ...]

7.2. Draw a diagram analogous to Figure 10.1 when corn does not enter directly or indirectly into the production of all industrial commodities.

7.3. Show that if for the given vector of net products **d** there is a nonnegative vector **x*** such that $\mathbf{x}^{*T}(\mathbf{B} - \mathbf{A}) = \mathbf{d}^T$ and $\mathbf{x}^{*T}\mathbf{C} = \sum_{j=1}^{i} t_j \mathbf{e}_j^T$, then $(\mathbf{x}^*, \mathbf{p}^*, w, \mathbf{q}^*)$ is a solution to system (10.2), where $\mathbf{p}^*, w^*, \mathbf{q}^*$ are determined by equations (10.3) and

$$\mathbf{q}^*\mathbf{e}_j = 0 \quad j = i+1, i+2, \ldots, m$$
$$0 \leqslant \mathbf{q}^*\mathbf{e}_i \leqslant \alpha,$$

where α is a positive scalar to be determined in order to satisfy inequality (10.2e). [*Hint:* Let **p*** and w^* be determined as functions of $\mathbf{q}^*\mathbf{e}_i = q_i$ by equations (10.4) and let the other element of vector **q** be determined by equation (10.3). Then....]

7.4. Draw the analog of Figure 10.3 when two of the single product "techniques" built up in Subsection 1.3 by neglecting the use of land pay the same nonnegative wage rate at the given rate of profit. Then again present the argument of that subsection with the obvious changes required by this condition.

7.5. Assume that there are m qualities of land and m processes; for land of quality j there is a process producing one unit of corn by means of l_j units of labor and c_j units of land j ($j = 1, 2, \ldots, m$). On the assumption that there are altogether t_j units of land j, show that it is possible to build up a non-increasing relationship between the wage rate and the quantity of labor employed. [*Hint:* With no lack of generality assume that $l_1 \leqslant l_2 \leqslant \cdots \leqslant l_m$ and let L be the quantity of labor employed. Show that if

$$\sum_{h=1}^{i-1} \frac{l_h t_h}{c_h} < L < \sum_{h=1}^{i} \frac{l_h t_h}{c_h},$$

then $w = 1/l_i$.]

Table 10.3

	commodity inputs						outputs		
	1	2	3	land	labor		1	2	3
(1)	0	0	0.1	0	1	→	1	0	0
(2)	0	0	0.6	0	1	→	0	1	0
(3)	0.1	0.4	0.1	i	1	→	0	0	1
(4)	0.5	0.2	0.2	1	1	→	0	0	1
(5)	0.3	0.3	0.1	1	3	→	0	0	1

Table 10.4

	corn	land	labor		corn
(1)	$\frac{7}{10}$	$\frac{1}{5}$	$\frac{2}{5}$	→	1
(2)	$\frac{7}{24}$	$\frac{1}{2}$	2	→	1
(3)	$\frac{21}{32}$	$\frac{1}{7}$	1	→	1

7.6. (D'Agata, 1983a) There are three commodities whose production processes are represented by Table 10.3. Consumption consists of 90 units of commodity 1, 60 units of commodity 2, and 19 units of commodity 3. There are 100 units of homogeneous land. Determine prices, wage rate, and the rate of rent for each feasible rate of profit. Then show that if $\frac{1}{3} < r < (\sqrt{1105} - 23)/18$, three long-period positions exist, made up of processes $(1, 2, 3)$, $(1, 2, 3, 4)$, and $(1, 2, 4, 5)$, respectively.

7.7 (Freni, 1991) There is one commodity, say corn, whose production processes are represented by Table 10.4. Consumption consists of 35 units of corn and there are 24 units of homogeneous land. Determine prices, wage rate, and the rate of rent for each feasible rate of profit. Then show that if $r = 1/7$, then three long-period positions exist and are made up of processes (1), $(1, 2)$, $(2, 3)$, respectively. Then determine the range of values of the rate of profit in which more than one solution exists.

7.8. (D'Agata, 1983a) There are three commodities whose production processes are represented by Table 10.5. Consumption consists of 90 units of commodity 1, 60 units of commodity 2, and 19 units of commodity 3. There are 100 units of homogeneous land. Determine prices, wage rate, and the rate of rent for each feasible rate of profit. Then show that

(i) if $1/9 \leqslant r < 19/41$, then two long-period positions exist, made up of processes $(1, 2, 3, 4)$ and $(1, 2, 3, 5)$, respectively;

Table 10.5

	commodity inputs						outputs		
	1	2	3	land	labor		1	2	3
(1)	0	0	0.1	0	1	→	1	0	0
(2)	0	0	0.6	0	1	→	0	1	0
(3)	0.1	0.4	0.1	1	1	→	0	0	1
(4)	0.1	0.1	0.3	1	2.2	→	0	0	1
(5)	0.1	0.1	0.4	1	1	→	0	0	1

(ii) if $0 \leqslant r \leqslant 19/41$, then at least one solution exists, whereas no solution exists if $r > 19/41$;

(iii) if processes (4) and (5) did not exist, then one solution would exist for $0 \leqslant r \leqslant (\sqrt{101} - 6)/5(> 19/41)$.

Then calculate what will happen if either only process (4) or only process (5) were missing.

7.9. Assume that land is uniform in quality and that there are m processes producing corn; each process j produces one unit of corn by means of l_j units of labor and c_j units of land ($j = 1, 2, \ldots, m$). On the assumption that there are altogether t units of land, show that it is possible to build up a non-increasing relationship between the wage rate and the quantity of labor employed. [*Hint*: Draw the analog of Figure 10.3; let s be the number of processes which are on the upper envelope of the q–w relationships; since the other processes are never utilized, eliminate them and renumber the s non-dominated processes from 1 to s; then $l_1 \leqslant l_2 \leqslant \cdots \leqslant l_s$, $c_1 \geqslant c_2 \geqslant \cdots \geqslant c_s$; let L be the quantity of labor employed and t the amount of existing land. Show that if

$$\frac{l_i}{c_i} < \frac{L}{t} < \frac{l_{i+1}}{c_{i+1}},$$

then $w = (c_i - c_{i+1})/(c_i l_{i+1} - c_{i+1} l_i)$.]

7.10. (D'Agata, 1983b) There are three commodities whose production processes are represented by Table 10.6. Consumption consists of 10 units of commodity 1, 10 units of commodity 2, and 78 units of commodity 3. There are 100 units of homogeneous land. Determine prices, wage rate, and the rate of rent for each feasible rate of profit. Then show that there is a range of values for the rate of profit in which three long-period

Table 10.6

	commodity inputs						outputs		
	1	2	3	land	labor		1	2	3
(1)	0	0.1	0	0	1	→	1	0	0
(2)	0.3	0.3	0.4	0	1	→	0	1	0
(3)	0.4	0.4	0.3	0	0.1	→	0	1	0
(4)	0.1	0.1	0.2	0	5.5	→	0	1	0
(5)	0.1	0.1	0.1	1	1	→	0	0	1

Table 10.7

	commodity inputs						outputs		
	1	2	3	land	labor		1	2	3
(1)	0	0.1	0	0	1	→	1	0	0
(2)	0.1	0.1	0.6	0	0.2	→	0	1	0
(3)	0.1	0.1	0.5	0	1.8	→	0	1	0
(4)	0.5	0.3	0.3	0	0.1	→	0	1	0
(5)	0.1	0.1	0.1	1	1	→	0	0	1

positions exist, made up of processes $(1,3,5)$, $(1,2,3,5)$, and $(1,2,4,5)$, respectively.

7.11. (D'Agata, 1983b) There are three commodities whose production processes are represented by Table 10.7. Consumption consists of 10 units of commodity 1, 10 units of commodity 2, and 79 units of commodity 3. There are 100 units of homogeneous land. Determine prices, wage rate, and the rate of rent for each feasible rate of profit. Then show that

(i) there is a range of values of the rate of profit in which two long-period positions exist, made up of processes $(1,2,4,5)$ and $(1,3,4,5)$, respectively;
(ii) if processes (2) and (3) did not exist, then at least one solution would exist for a larger range of values of the rate of profit.

Then calculate what will happen if either only process (2) or only process (3) were missing.

7.12. (D'Agata, 1985) Provide details of the proof of the assertion in Subsection 2.1 with regard to an economy whose technology is given in Table 10.2.

Table 10.8

	commodity inputs			land inputs			outputs	
	1	2	labor	I	II		1	2
(1)	0.3	0.1	1	1	0	→	1	0
(2)	0.1	0.3	1.5	0	5	→	1	0
(3)	0.1	0.2	0.1	2	0	→	0	1
(4)	0.2	0.1	0.5	0	1	→	0	1

Table 10.9

	commodity inputs			land inputs			outputs	
	1	2	labor	I	II		1	2
(1)	0.2	0.1	1	10	0	→	1	0
(2)	0.4	0.3	1	0	10	→	1	0
(3)	0.1	0.2	1.1	1.1	0	→	0	1
(4)	0.2	0.1	1	0	1	→	0	1

7.13. (D'Agata, 1984) There are two commodities whose production processes are represented by Table 10.8. Consumption consists of 15 units of commodity 1 and 35 units of commodity 2. There are 100 units of land of quality I and 100 units of land of quality II. Determine prices, wage rate, and the rate of rent for each feasible rate of profit. Then show that there is a range of values of the rate of profit in which no long-period position exists, but there should exist at least one such position if processes (2) and (3) were not available.

7.14. (D'Agata, 1984) There are two commodities whose production processes are represented by Table 10.9. Consumption consists of 34 units of commodity 2. There are 100 units of land of quality I and 250 units of land of quality II. Determine prices, wage rate, and the rate of rent for each feasible rate of profit. Then show that there is a range of values of the rate of profit in which there are three long-period positions.

7.15. (D'Agata, 1984) There are two commodities whose production processes are represented by Table 10.10. Consumption consists of 20 units of commodity 1 and 120 units of commodity 2. There are 100 units of land of quality I and 300 units of land of quality II. Determine prices, wage rate, and the rate of rent for each feasible rate profit. Then show that there is a range of values of the rate of profit in which two long-period positions exist.

Table 10.10

	commodity inputs			land inputs			outputs	
	1	2	labor	I	II		1	2
(1)	0.1	0.1	10	1	0	→	1	0
(2)	0.5	0.3	0.1	0	1	→	1	0
(3)	0.1	0.1	0.1	0.5	0	→	0	1
(4)	0.3	0.2	0.5	0	1	→	0	1

Table 10.11

	commodity inputs				land inputs				outputs		
	1	2	3	labor	I	II	III	IV	1	2	3
(1)	2	2	0	10	1	0	0	0	→	6	0	0
(2)	2	2	2	4	0	1	0	0	→	12	0	0
(3)	4	2	0	36	0	0	1	0	→	0	18	0
(4)	0	2	2	4	0	0	0	1	→	0	10	0
(5)	1	1	1	5	0	0	0	0	→	0	0	3

7.16. (Erreygers, 1990) There are three commodities whose production processes are represented by Table 10.11. Consumption consists of 7 units of commodity 1 and 7 units of commodity 2. There is 1 unit of each quality of land. Assume that the rate of profit is 0.3 and show that three long-period positions exist. [*Hint*: It is possible to operate in a long-period position either processes $(2, 3, 4, 5)$ or processes $(1, 2, 3, 5)$; moreover, if processes $(2, 3, 4, 5)$ are operated, either land of quality II or land of quality IV are fully employed, but not both.]

7.17. Show that if there is a nonnegative vector **v** such that

$$\mathbf{v}^T[\mathbf{B} - (1 + r)\mathbf{A}] > \mathbf{0}^T,$$

then there is a non-empty subset Ω such that if $\mathbf{d} \in \Omega$, then system (10.8) has a solution with a positive w. [*Hint*: Use Theorem 10.1.]

7.18. Show that if there is a nonnegative vector **v** such that

$$\mathbf{v}^T[\mathbf{B} - \mathbf{A}] \geqq \mathbf{d}^T$$

$$\mathbf{v}^T\mathbf{C} < \mathbf{t}^T,$$

then there is a real number $R > 0$ such that if $r \in [0, R)$, then system (10.8) has a solution with a positive w. [*Hint*: Use Theorem 10.1.]

Table 10.12

	commodity inputs			land inputs			outputs	
	1	2	labor	I	II		1	2
(1)	—	$\frac{1}{2}$	1	1	—	$\rightarrow$	1	—
(2)	$\frac{1}{2}$	—	1	—	—	$\rightarrow$	—	1
(3)	—	$\frac{2}{3}$	1	—	1	$\rightarrow$	1	—

7.19. Comment on the results stated in the previous two exercises.

7.20. Prove that the singular rent analyzed in Section 3 cannot arise if vectors **c** and **l** are proportional. [*Hint*: Consider equalities (10.14).]

7.21. (Salvadori, 1983) There are two commodities whose production processes are processes (1) and (2) in Table 10.12. There exist 4 units of land, and 7 units of labor are employed. Determine prices, wage rate, and the rate of rent for each feasible rate of profit when either

  (i) workers consume only corn and both capitalists and landlords consume only iron; or
 (ii) both workers and landlords consume only corn and capitalists consume only iron; or
(iii) workers consume only iron and both capitalists and landlords consume only corn; or
 (iv) both workers and capitalists consume only iron and landlords consume only corn.

7.22. Perform exercise 7.21 on the assumption that the three processes of Table 10.12 exist. Compare the results obtained with those of the previous four exercises. Comment on your findings.

7.23. (D'Agata, 1984) There are two commodities whose production processes are represented by Table 10.10. There are 100 units of land of quality I and 300 units of land of quality II. Let the rate of profit be 0.5. Show that if consumption consists either of 20 units of commodity 1 and 119 units of commodity 2 or of 20 units of commodity 1 and 120 units of commodity 2, then a long-period position is obtained when processes (1, 2, 3) are operated and land of quality I is fully cultivated. Then show that a higher consumption can be associated with a lower employment of labor. (Hence, in this case the "employment multiplier" of additional consumption would be negative.)

Table 10.13

	commodity inputs		labor	land inputs		outputs	
	1	2				1	2
(1)	0.2	0.6	0.6	1	$\rightarrow$	1	0
(2)	0.4	0.2	1	1	$\rightarrow$	1	0
(3)	0.3	0.2	0.2	0	$\rightarrow$	0	1

7.24. (Erreygers, 1990) There are two commodities whose production processes are represented by Table 10.13. Consumption is such that land is fully utilized and the three processes are all operated. Let the numeraire consist of one unit of commodity 1 and one unit of commodity 2. Show that the prices p_1 and p_2, the wage rate w and the rent rate q are nonnegative only if $1/4 \leqslant r \leqslant 3/7$. Furthermore, show that the $w-r$ relationship is increasing.

7.25. Draw the wage–profit frontiers and the rent(s)–profit frontiers defined by the numerical examples in exercises 7.6–7.11, 7.13–7.15, and 7.21–7.22, respectively.

7.26. Prove that the price–output and rent–output relationships are nondecreasing functions when the assumptions underlying the analysis of extensive rent hold, all commodities are consumed, and labor is the numeraire. [*Hint*: Take into account Theorem 5.1 of Chapter 5.]

7.27. (Saucier, 1984b) There are three commodities whose production is represented by Table 10.14. There is 1 unit of land I, 1 unit of land II, 50 units of land III, and 300 units of land IV. Assume that the rate of profit is zero and that only commodity 3 is consumed. Determine the prices and rents as functions of the net output of commodity 3 when labor is the numeraire. Show that the rent of land III as a function of net output of corn is not nondecreasing. [*Hint*: Determine five intervals of variation of the net product of commodity 3. In the first interval, processes $(1, 2, 4)$ are operated and no rent is paid. In the second, processes $(1, 2, 4, 5)$ are operated and land III gets a positive rent. In the third, the same processes $(1, 2, 4, 5)$ are operated, but the rent is paid on land I and not on land III. In the fourth, processes $(1, 2, 3, 5)$ are operated and land I gets a positive rent. In the fifth, all processes are operated and lands I and IV get positive rents.]

7.28. There are three commodities whose processes are represented by Table 10.3. There are 100 units of homogeneous land. The rate of profit is 1/2. Determine prices, wage rate, and the rate of rent corresponding to

Table 10.14

	commodity inputs				land inputs					outputs		
	1	2	3	labor	I	II	III	IV		1	2	3
(1)	$\frac{1}{3}$	$\frac{1}{3}$	$\frac{1}{6}$	6	0	0	0	0	$\rightarrow$	1	0	0
(2)	$\frac{1}{12}$	$\frac{1}{3}$	$\frac{1}{12}$	8	$\frac{3}{5000}$	0	0	0	$\rightarrow$	0	1	0
(3)	$\frac{1}{12}$	$\frac{1}{3}$	$\frac{1}{12}$	16	0	$\frac{1}{5000}$	0	0	$\rightarrow$	0	1	0
(4)	$\frac{13}{24}$	$\frac{23}{60}$	$\frac{8}{15}$	3	0	0	$\frac{1}{20}$	0	$\rightarrow$	0	0	1
(5)	$\frac{1}{2}$	$\frac{1}{3}$	$\frac{1}{2}$	11	0	0	0	$\frac{1}{10}$	$\rightarrow$	0	0	1

all feasible net products of commodity 3 on the assumption that the net product of commodity 1 consists of 90 units and the net product of commodity 2 consists of 60 units. [*Hint*: First solve exercise 7.6.]

7.29. There is a commodity, say corn, whose processes are represented by Table 10.4. There are 24 units of homogeneous land. Determine prices, wage rate, and the rate of rent for each feasible net product of corn when the rate of profit is $1/7$. [*Hint*: First solve exercise 7.7.]

7.30. There are three commodities whose processes are represented by Table 10.11. Consumption consists of 7 units of commodity 1 and 7 units of commodity 2. There is one unit of each quality of land. Assume that the rate of profit is 0.3 and determine prices, wage rate, and rates of rent corresponding to all feasible net products of commodity 1 on the assumption that the net product of commodity 2 consists of 7 units and the net product of commodity 3 is nought. [*Hint*: First solve exercise 7.16.]

11

Persistent wage and profit rate differentials

The long-period analysis presented up to now has been subject to a set of simplifying assumptions, two of which will be weakened in the present chapter. This concerns, first, the assumption that labor is homogeneous and, second, the hypothesis that there is a uniform rate of profit throughout the economy. This second concept was motivated in Chapter 1 in terms of a tendency toward an equalization of the rates of return in different employments of capital in conditions of free competition due to the cost-minimizing behavior of producers. In that chapter it was also pointed out that the classical economists saw factors at work that accounted for *persistent* inequalities in wage and profit rates. In this chapter we will follow them and take into consideration different qualities of labor and different employments of the same quality of labor as well as different employments of capital, where the differences in quality or employment generally give rise to differences in the ordinary wage rates and rates of profit of the different labors and capitals. Hence, a major concern in this chapter will be with discussing some of the main factors determining wage and profit rate differentials in a long-period position.

The classical authors and in particular Adam Smith took pains to provide theoretical reasons why such differentials do exist: Smith's analysis "Of Wages and Profit in the different Employments of Labour and Stock" in chapter X of book I of *The Wealth of Nations* contains a careful account of the different factors affecting the remuneration of different qualities of labor and the profitability of different employments of capital.

The structure of the chapter is as follows. In Section 1 we shall deal with heterogeneous labor. We shall first, in Subsection 1.1, investigate how the classical authors tried to cope with heterogeneous labor in the theory of value and distribution. The procedure commonly followed by these authors was to aggregate concrete labors using weights proportional to the wage rates of those concrete labors. Next, in Subsection 1.2, we investigate the reasons given by Smith and others to explain persistent wage differentials. Section 2 will be devoted to an analysis of different characteristics defining the employment of capital as far as these characteristics will be reflected in profit rate differentials. Emphasis will be on different risks of capital employment. Section 3 contains a few additional historical remark.

1. Heterogeneous labor

Thus far it has been assumed that only one quality of labor is used in each process of production and, in addition, that all processes use the same quality of labor. The use of different qualities of labor in different processes or the use of different combinations of various qualities of labor in different processes have not been taken into consideration. The entire analysis was based on the assumption that labor is homogeneous. This allowed us to describe the labor inputs in the different processes of production available in terms of a vector, l. With a given working time per week (month, year) per worker it would also be easy to get from a given amount of labor needed to the number of people to be employed. More important, the assumption of homogeneous labor allowed us to develop the argument in terms of a single wage rate, w. For, with free competition among workers any differences in pay within and across industries would lead to movements of some workers seeking to benefit from the more favorable conditions elsewhere. These movements would tend to abolish any wage differentials that may exist at a given moment of time. In long-period analysis the premise of homogeneous labor entails necessarily a uniform wage rate.

It goes without saying that labor is not homogeneous: in fact there is an impressive diversity of concrete labors. This fact did not, of course, escape the attention of the classical authors and those authors contributing to the tradition of economic analysis initiated by them. Nevertheless, most of the respective analyses proceed from the assumption that labor can be treated as if it were uniform. Our first concern will therefore be with how these authors thought it possible to "neutralize" the irrevocable heterogeneity of concrete labors in the theory of value and distribution. A second question will be whether the heterogeneity of labor is reflected in relative wages, and how the wage differentials can be explained.

1.1. The aggregation of different kinds of labor

As to the question of the commensurability of hours of qualitatively different labor, the answer to be found in the writings of the classical economists is (almost) unanimous: quantities of different kinds of concrete labor are aggregated via the relative wage rates of those different kinds of labor. The *locus classicus* of this approach to the problem of "reduction" of different kinds of labor to a single kind of labor is Adam Smith's *The Wealth of Nations* (*WN*, I.v–vi, viii, x).[1] The problem is stated as follows: "It is often difficult to ascertain the proportion between two different quantities of labour. The time spent in two different sorts of work will not always alone determine this proportion. The different degrees of hardship endured, and of ingenuity exercised, must likewise be taken into account. There may be more labour in an hour's hard work than in two hours' easy business" (*WN*, I.v.4). Smith continues that "it is difficult to find any accurate measure of hardship and ingenuity," but that in practice a sufficiently accurate allowance is made for these aspects in the market exchange of the products of different labors. With the exchange values of the products approximately reflecting these differences it seems to follow that the same can be said of the wage rates of the different kinds of labor. While Smith does not explicitly say this here, there are other passages which support the interpretation given. In his explanation of the rule governing the exchange relationship between commodities in the "early and rude state of society" he states: "If the one species of labour should be more severe than the other, some allowance will naturally be made for this superior hardship; and the produce of one hour's labour in the one way may frequently exchange for that of two hours labour in the other" (*WN*, I.vi.2). And in the following paragraph he stresses: "In the advanced state of society, allowances of this kind, for superior hardship and superior skill, *are commonly made in the wages of labour*; and something of the same kind must probably have taken place in its earliest and rudest period" (*WN*, I.vi.3; emphasis added). Whenever Smith refers to the "quantity" of labor in discussing the exchange relationships between commodities in the "advanced state of society" he can thus safely be assumed to refer to a wage-rate-aggregated quantity of labor.

David Ricardo was even more explicit in this regard. In all three editions of the *Principles* he makes it clear that the concept of the "quantity of labour" used by him presupposes the aggregation of different kinds of labor via given wage rates. In the third edition this is particularly emphasized by the subdivision of what was section I of the chapter "On Value" in the previous editions; the new section II bears the title: "Labour of different qualities differently rewarded. This no cause of variation in the relative value of commodities" (*Works* I, p. 20). Ricardo introduces the section in

---

[1] In much of what he said on the subject, Smith was anticipated by authors such as Cantillon, Mandeville and Anderson; see the notes of the editors of the Glasgow edition to *The Wealth of Nations* on the subject.

the following terms: "In speaking, however, of labour, as being the foundation of all value, and the relative quantity of labour as almost exclusively determining the relative value of commodities, I must not be supposed to be inattentive to the different qualities of labour, and the difficulty of comparing an hour's or a day's labour, in one employment, with the same duration of labour in another." Ricardo approvingly quotes Smith's view on the matter and stresses that he is measuring the "quantity" of labor embodied in a commodity not simply by counting hours of labor needed in the production of the respective commodity, but by counting hours of different kinds of labor which are weighted by their relative wage rates: "The estimation in which different qualities of labour are held, comes soon to be adjusted in the market with *sufficient precision for all practical purposes*, and depends much on the comparative skill of the labourer, and intensity of the labour performed" (ibid.).

Karl Marx can be said to have adopted essentially the same approach to the problem of the heterogeneity of labor. The widespread tendency among some interpreters of Marx's theory to attribute various meanings to his concept of "abstract labour" notwithstanding, it can be shown to be but a different expression of the received classical conception of a "quantity of labour": the different kinds of labor are to be aggregated via the (gold) money wage rates (see Steedman, 1985).

The classical conception is also to be found in Sraffa (1960). After having removed the premise that wages consist only of the necessary subsistence of the workers and thus enter "the system on the same footing as the fuel for the engines or the feed for the cattle, ... the quantity of labour employed in each industry has now to be represented explicitly, taking the place of the corresponding quantities of subsistence." Sraffa adds: "We suppose labour to be uniform in quality or, what amounts to the same thing, we assume differences in quality to have been previously reduced to equivalent differences in quantity so that each unit of labour receives the same wage" (ibid., pp. 9–10). Obviously, this is possible only, if wages are used as weights, or multipliers, to "reduce" different concrete labors to some "common" labor.

We may now provide some formalization of the classical conception of the "quantity of labour." We shall for simplicity consider a single system of production only and assume single-product processes of production. Let the number of commodities produced be n and the number of different kinds of labor used be s. The production of one unit of commodity j can then be represented by the triplet $(\mathbf{a}_j, \mathbf{e}_j, \mathbf{l}_j)$, where $\mathbf{e}_j$ is the output vector, $\mathbf{a}_j$ is the n-vector of material inputs, and $\mathbf{l}_j = (l_{j1}, l_{j2}, \ldots, l_{js})^T$ is the s-vector of labor inputs per unit of output. The material and labor inputs needed in the production, per unit of output, of the n different commodities can be summarized in the $n \times n$-matrix $\mathbf{A}$ and the $n \times s$-matrix $\mathbf{L}$, respectively; the output matrix being, as usual, the identity matrix $\mathbf{I}$. With the wage rate for each quality of labor i, w_i $(i = 1, 2, \ldots, s)$, taken as given, and expressing all value magnitudes in terms of a commodity bundle $\mathbf{d}, \mathbf{d} \geqslant 0$, we have the following system of prices

$$\mathbf{p} = (1 + r)\mathbf{A}\mathbf{p} + \mathbf{L}\mathbf{w}$$
$$\mathbf{d}^T\mathbf{p} = 1,$$

with $\mathbf{w}$ as the vector of wage rates. We may now reduce the differences in quality to equivalent differences in quantity so that each unit of labor receives the same wage. To this effect we first have to specify in terms of which unit we want to measure the "quantity" of labour. The obvious candidates for this purpose are either a particular kind of labor or a given bundle of labors, similar to the commodity bundle used to express prices. In the following discussion we shall assume that the unit of measurement is one hour of labor of quality k. Hence, after the reduction all labor will receive the same wage which equals the wage paid per unit of labor of quality k, w_k. This implies that the labor input coefficients, l_{ji}, of matrix $\mathbf{L}$ are multiplied by w_i/w_k and then added across all i's, $i = 1, 2, \ldots, s$. Hence we get back to the old formulation of the system of prices,

$$\mathbf{p} = (1 + r)\mathbf{A}\mathbf{p} + w\mathbf{l},$$

where $w = w_k, \mathbf{l} = \mathbf{L}\hat{\mathbf{w}}$, and $\hat{\mathbf{w}}^T = (w_1/w_k, w_2/w_k, \ldots, w_s/w_k)$ is the vector of relative wages in terms of w_k.

This aggregation of different labors via wage rates is a purely formal procedure. It can be carried out at any moment of time irrespective of whether the wages structure is relatively stable or not. However, in order to be consistent with the long-period method, relative wages ought not to change with changes in the level of the rate of profit or changes in the methods of production used. It was, in fact, a major concern of the classical economists to provide arguments in support of the view that relative wages change very little over time. If this were to be true then changes in the relative "quantities of labor" needed to produce commodities could safely be assumed not to reflect changes in relative wages, but changes in quantities of different labors used. Hence we have to turn to how the classical economists explained wage differentials and their relative constancy over time.

1.2. Wage differentials

Both Smith and Ricardo expressed the view that relative wages are comparatively stable over long periods of time. In Smith we read:

> The proportion between the different rates both of wages and profit in the different employments of labor and stock, seems not to be much affected... by the riches or poverty, the advancing, stationary, or declining state of the society. Such revolutions in the publick welfare, though they affect the general rates both of wages and profit, must in the end affect them equally in all different employments. The proportion between them, therefore, must remain the same, and cannot well be altered, at least for any considerable time, by any such revolutions. (*WN*, I.x.c.63; see also I.vii.36).

Similarly Ricardo, who maintained: "The scale, when once formed, is liable to little variation. If a day's labour of a working jeweller be more valuable than a day's labour of a common labourer, it has long ago been adjusted, and placed in its proper position in the scale of value" (*Works* I, pp. 20–1). He adds that whatever inequality there might originally have been in the different kinds of human labor, "it continues nearly the same from one generation to another; or at least, that the variation is very inconsiderable from year to year, and therefore, can have little effect, for short periods, on the relative value of commodities" (ibid., p. 22).

The arguments put forward by the classical authors to assert the relative constancy of relative wages are, in the last instance, arguments concerning the constancy of the factors which in these authors' view are to a large extent responsible for relative wages being what they are. Therefore, the explanation of wage differentials given by these authors holds the key to their assertion of the stability of the differentials over time. Smith discusses these problems in chapter X of book I of the *The Wealth of Nations*. He groups the factors affecting relative wages in two principal ones: (i) inequalities arising from the nature of the employments themselves; and (ii) inequalities occasioned by political interventions. Here we are concerned with the first group only. Smith expounds:

> The five following are the principal circumstances which, so far as I have been able to observe, make up for a small pecuniary gain in some employments, and counter-balance a great one in others: first, the agreeableness or disagreeableness of the employments themselves; secondly, the easiness and cheapness, or the difficulty and expence of learning them; thirdly, the constancy or inconstancy of employment in them; fourthly, the small or great trust which must be reposed in those who exercise them; and, fifthly, the probability or improbability of success in them" (*WN*, I.x.b.1).

The five circumstances mentioned involve economic aspects and social norms and conventions. In the following discussion attention will focus on the economic factors accounting for wage differentials: (i) differences in the costs of production of different skills; (ii) the scarcity of particular talents; (iii) differences in the degree to which the laborers' capacity to work can be utilized in different employments; (iv) differences in the trust that must be reposed in the workers; and (v) different risks involved in becoming qualified for the employment to which one is educated. In an attempt to provide a more precise expression than the one given by Smith of the role of the various circumstances in determining wage differentials, some of the propositions contained in previous chapters of the present book prove useful.[2]

(i) Human capital. We begin with the second circumstance mentioned by Smith. He draws a strict analogy between an item of fixed capital and skilled labor power and thus can be said to have anticipated the concept of "human capital" (see also Spengler, 1977). He writes:

> When any expensive machine is erected, the extraordinary work to be performed by it before it is worn out, it must be expected, will replace the capital laid out upon it, with at least the ordinary profits. A man educated at the expence of much labour and time to any of those employments which require extraordinary dexterity and skill, may be compared to one of those expensive machines. The work which he learns to perform, it must be expected, over and above the usual wages of common labour, will replace to him the whole expence of his education, with at least the ordinary profits of an equally valuable capital. It must do this too in a reasonable time, regard being had to the very uncertain duration of human life, in the same manner as to the more certain duration of the machine" (*WN*, I.x.b.6).[3]

---

[2] It should be noted that in Section 7 of Chapter 7 we have already come across a particular case in which a wage premium is to be paid in order to compensate workers for the extra "hardship" or "disagreeableness" of their employment, that is, the first circumstance mentioned by Smith: reference is to work scheduled at night or during weekends. In this case the equalizing effect of free competition is reflected in the inequality of remuneration that is necessary to render different employments equally attractive.

[3] Smith estimates the productive life of a man, after completing his apprenticeship, at 10 to 12 years' purchase; see Smith (*LJ* (A) vi.60 and *LJ* (B) 225). Apparently Smith has taken these figures from Cantillon (1755, p. 19).

Smith concludes: "The difference between the wages of skilled labour and those of common labour, is founded upon this principle" (*WN*, I.x.b.7).[4]

There are, in principle, two problems involved here, that is, *education* and *experience*. The first concerns the acquisition of certain skills outside the process of production of commodities, that is, learning in what may be called the "education sector" of the economy.[5] The second concerns the acquisition of skills in the course of producing commodities, that is, learning on the job or "learning by doing." With respect to the problem of education we can consider some "education processes." For example, different labors, including the labor of the student himself, and material inputs are required in order to "produce" a one year old elementary student. This one year old elementary student is among the inputs (including further labor by the student himself) required to "produce" a two year old elementary student, and so on. Suppose now that in order to educate a locomotive driver τ years (including elementary school) are required. This implies the existence of τ education processes, the last one of which "produces" the locomotive driver. All the inputs have been paid by the locomotive driver *in spe* (or by his parents) or are goods provided by the state. If provided by the state, the costs of these goods, though costs to the community as a whole, do not enter into the "price" of the locomotive driver.[6] That price is thus determined in the same way as the price of any other commodity discussed in Chapter 4. Suppose now that locomotive drivers have a professional life of T years. Then, analogously to what has been seen in Chapter 7 (or 9), T utilization processes are required. Each process includes among the inputs a locomotive driver of a given "vintage" and his labor, and produces a locomotive driver of a

---

[4] The treatment of the acquired skills of a population as a part of a nation's fixed capital is confirmed in chapter I of book II, "Of the Division of Stock." There Smith emphasizes that the fixed capital of a society consists also "of the aquired and useful abilities of all the inhabitants or members of the society. The acquisition of such talents, by the maintenance of the acquirer during his education, study, or apprenticeship, always costs a real expence, which is *a capital fixed and realized, as it were, in a person*." Smith continues: "The improved dexterity of a workman may be considered in the same light as a machine or instrument of trade which facilitates and abridges labour, and which, though it costs a certain expence, repays that expence with profit" (*WN*, II.i.17; emphasis added).

[5] Education works against the negative effects of the division of labor which Smith saw as threatening the system of natural liberty because they rendered the major part of the people incapable of fulfilling their private and public obligations (cf. *WN*, V.i.f).

[6] The problem of which inputs are to be provided by the state and are to be financed through taxation is beyond the scope of this book. We are assuming that the state has no property rights in the skills of the future locomotive driver.

one year older "vintage" jointly with the transportation of people and goods, with the only exception of the last process, which does not produce any locomotive driver. The pay received by the locomotive driver can now be conceived as consisting of two components, one is the wage for his current work, the other is the annual charge for the use of his skills, that is,

$$\omega_t = w + (1 + r)\pi_t - \pi_{t+1},$$

where ω_t is the total payment received by a locomotive driver in the tth year of his professional career, π_t is the value of the human capital incorporated in the skills of a locomotive driver in the tth year of its utilization ($t = 1, 2, \ldots, T; \pi_{T+1} = 0$), and w is the ordinary wage rate for unskilled labor.

As we have seen in Section 6 of Chapter 7 (see also Section 3 of Chapter 9), the annual charge is independent of the age of the machine if efficiency is constant over time. Analogous is the case of human capital in which experience does not increase skills or age decrease efficiency. If, on the contrary, experience (or age) matters, then efficiency is increasing (decreasing) and, therefore, so is the annual charge from one year to the next. It cannot even be excluded that the annual charge is negative in the first years. This would be the case if some of the skills required in the profession under consideration can be obtained only as a result of some training on the job.[7]

If skilled labor is formalized in this way, what appears among the inputs is labor of an homogeneous quality. The differences in total payment received by the workers are to be ascribed to some other inputs supplied by the worker in the very same time in which he supplies unskilled labor.

[7] In the above exposition we have assumed that the locomotive driver has the property of all his own skills. A more sophisticated analysis could consider the use of the locomotive driver as a combination of *two jointly utilized machines* (see Chapter 9). The first machine is a property of the locomotive driver himself and includes the original skills of the locomotive driver plus *some* skills which are obtained by the experience within the firm. The second machine is a property of the firm and includes the *remaining* skills which are obtained as a result of the worker's experience within the firm. The annual charge of the latter machine is certainly negative in the first years of employment of the locomotive driver. There are many possible ways to divide the skills between the two machines and, as a consequence, to decide their annual charges. The choice of techniques determines the cost-minimizing division of the property rights regarding these skills between the locomotive driver and the firm. It is natural to presume that in the cost-minimizing technique the first machine encompasses those skills which are *utilizable* in other firms also, whereas the second machine encompasses those skills which are *not* utilizable in other firms, that is, are *not* transferable between firms.

(ii) Scarcity of talents. Besides cost of production, wage differentials may reflect relative scarcities of different labors. In a long-period setting scarcity can refer to natural talents only, since all the labors that do not presuppose particular talents that are in short supply can be produced and reproduced. However, the smaller the natural talent the higher are the costs of producing a certain quality of skilled work: in the extreme the costs become infinitely high, which means that endowed with his talent, the person under consideration cannot acquire the skill or capability he or she seeks.

These problems were also seen by Adam Smith. He emphasizes that there are "genius or superior talents" that "excel in any profession, in which but few arrive at mediocrity." It could be thought that the wages of those possessed of such rare talents are very high, indeed. However, this is generally not so, Smith observes, since a large part of the reward of these people is non-pecuniary and consists in "the reputation which attends upon superior excellence" and "the publick admiration which attends upon such distinguished abilities" (*WN*, I.x.b.23–4). By way of illustration Smith refers to artists, poets, and philosophers. Their "products" are unique, that is, they cannot generally be reproduced by others. Therefore, cost of production cannot explain the prices of these products. This view is confirmed by Ricardo who pointed out that the price these products fetch is largely, if not exclusively, determined by demand "and varies with the varying wealth and inclinations of those who are desirous to possess them" (*Works* I, p. 12). In the following discussion we shall set aside these products together with the exceptional natural talents giving rise to them.[8]

As regards the frequency distribution of the natural talents with which a given population is endowed, it cannot be excluded that given the quantities of commodities to be produced, some of these talents may turn out to be scarce. The scarcity of these talents is reflected in rents, that is, additions to the ordinary wage earned in the respective profession by the holders of these talents.[9] However, as far as the scarcity of natural talents does play a role in explaining wage differentials, the analysis of the rent

---

[8] To set aside commodities, "the value of which is determined by their scarcity alone" is motivated by Ricardo in terms of the assertion that "these commodities ... form a very small part of the mass of commodities daily exchanged in the market" (*Works* I, p. 12).

[9] There is also the possibility of overcoming the scarcity of certain talents by upgrading them through education. Smith was in fact of the opinion that "the difference of natural talents in different men is, in reality, much less than we are aware of; and the very different genius which appears to distinguish men of different professions, when grown up to maturity, is not upon many occasions so much the cause, as the effect of the division of labour. The difference between the most dissimilar characters, between a philosopher and a common street porter, for example, seems to arise not so much from nature, as from habit, custom, and education" (*WN*, I.ii.4; similarly I.x.b.25).

of land in Chapter 10 can be used. This can be illustrated in terms of the following argument. To this effect, the model (10.8) in Subsection 2.2 of Chapter 10 has to be interpreted in a slightly different way: not as referring to homogeneous labor and s different qualities of land, but rather to s different qualities of labor. Accordingly, the element c_{ij} of matrix $\mathbf{C}$ designates the amount of labor of quality j used in process i. As a consequence the following identity needs to hold

$$\mathbf{Ce} \equiv \mathbf{l}.$$

The pay received by a worker of quality j, ω_j, may now be considered as consisting of two components: the wage rate for his work, w, and the rate of rent for the use of his natural talents, q_j,

$$\omega_j = w + q_j.$$

Obviously, if a particular natural talent is not scarce, then the rent for its use is zero.

(iii) The utilization of labor. Smith points out that "employment is much more constant in some trades than in others" (*WN*, I.x.b.12). This is due to a variety of circumstances that account for the fact that certain works can be carried out only intermittently, such as seasonal variations in weather and climate which in certain periods prevent certain laborers from doing their work, or seasonal variations in demand for the product of labor. The general principle governing differential wages in these cases is, according to Smith: "What he [a worker] earns, therefore, while he is employed, must not only maintain him while he is idle, but make him some compensation for those anxious and desponding moments which the thought of so precarious a situation must sometimes occasion.... The high wages of those workmen, therefore, are not so much the recompence of their skill, as the compensation for the inconstancy of their employment" (*WN*, I.x.b.12).[10] This case is easily incorporated in the sort of models presented in this book. We have only to consider the entries of the labor input vector **l** not as the time *at work*, but as the time *actually paid*, which is obtained by multiplying the time at work by a number larger than unity and which is independent of distribution.[11]

---

[10] The most drastic example given by Smith of an employment that combines the greatest degree of dishonorableness and detestation with a high degree of inconstancy of employment is that of public executioner. This employment, Smith points out, "is in proportion to the quantity of work done, better paid than any common trade whatever" (*WN*, I.x.b.2).

[11] It goes without saying that there are cases in which a worker who would otherwise be idle for much of the time because of the inconstancy of his principal employment seeks a second or even third occupation.

(iv) Trust in workers. "The wages of labour," Smith contends, "vary according to the small or great trust which must be reposed in the workmen" (*WN*, I.x.b.17). The examples he gives concern the work performed, and the superior wages earned, by goldsmiths and jewellers and highly skilled professionals such as physicians, lawyers, and attorneys. There are several problems touched upon here, which, in modern parlance, concern aspects of moral hazard and thus asymmetric information. There is, on the one hand, the problem of supervising and monitoring the workers. Workers may shirk, they may take away property of the owner of the firm which they can use themselves, or they may sabotage production by destroying property which they cannot use, such as expensive machinery, etc. The solution suggested by Smith foreshadows the concept of "efficiency wages" (cf. Akerlof and Yellen, 1986). On the other hand, there is a problem clients typically face, that is, that of assessing the quality of the "product," common examples being special services such as a surgery or a car reparation. The lack of information on their part is a potential source of extra income on the part of the supplier of the service. In the following discussion we shall deal with the first category of problems only, which, as will be seen, are essentially problems of the choice of technique and can thus be tackled in terms of the analysis presented in Chapter 5.

In fact, the producer may provide incentives to workers in terms of extra benefits (pecuniary and other) to increase their work effort and refrain from sabotaging the production process, on the assumption that the effects of their efforts can be easily checked *ex post*. The problem of "efficiency wages" can now be stated as follows. Let us start with a simplified version. For each process in which workers are paid the normal wage rate there are other h processes with the same material inputs and the paid labor input multiplied by $\alpha_1, \alpha_2, \ldots, \alpha_h$, respectively ($1 < \alpha_1 < \alpha_2 < \cdots < \alpha_h$). The output per unit of labor is also increased: to a larger payment to labor corresponds a larger "effort" performed by workers and, therefore, a larger output. Obviously the determination of the appropriate α is a problem of the choice of techniques. While this version is able to illustrate the basic idea underlying the payment of wage premia as an incentive to increase workers' effort, it leaves out of consideration the fact that, in general, a change in effort is not only reflected in higher outputs, but also in different quantities of inputs worked. In other words, different levels of effort are generally associated with different processes of production. It goes without saying that in this more general framework the problem of the choice of technique cannot be reduced to a choice of α. A more general analysis can also take into account the material and labor inputs connected with the *post factum* check of the effects of the efforts.

(v) Risk. The final circumstance mentioned by Smith concerns the probability or improbability "that any person shall ever be qualified for the employment to which he is educated." This is essentially the problem of the risk of failure in different occupations, and thus a comparison to lotteries is close at hand: "In a perfectly fair lottery, those who draw the prizes ought to gain all that is lost by those who draw the blanks. In a profession where twenty fail for one that succeeds, that one ought to gain all that should have been gained by the unsuccessful twenty" (*WN*, I.x.b.22). This refers us back to the problem of human capital dealt with under point (i) above. There the labor input in an "education process" was assumed to be unskilled labor paid at the normal rate. In the presence of risk the following modification is necessary: we have to take into account not only the costs incurred by each laborer in order to obtain his own skill, but also the costs incurred by all those who attempted to obtain that skill, but, alas, failed.

Here we assume that the available processes reflecting the probability of success are given. A more complete analysis would require an investigation of the factors determining this probability, that is, the number of failures observed on average per success. Such an analysis would have to start from the premise that each individual is confronted with a set of alternative educational options from which he or she can choose, where any of these options, if carried out successfully, would result in the adoption of a particular profession. Hence, a choice of education-cum-profession problem would have to be solved. Among the factors affecting this choice the attitude to risk by individual actors can be assumed to play an important role. An analysis of this problem of choice is, however, beyond the scope of this book. Suffice it to say that Smith was of the opinion that young people in particular tend to exhibit a remarkable "contempt for risk and the presumptuous hope of success" (*WN*, I.x.b.29).

As we have seen, the analysis elaborated in this book can without difficulty be applied to the problems of human capital, scarcity of talents, utilization of labor power, and work effort. However, in order to effectuate this the original model(s) with homogeneous labor and a uniform wage rate had to be adapted in several respects. To conclude, we may ask whether it is possible to aggregate the different concrete labors via relative wages, as was suggested by the classical economists and Sraffa, in order to get back to the original model in terms of the "quantity of labour." Strictly speaking, this aggregation procedure requires that relative wages are unaffected by changes in the general rate of profit and in the techniques used. However, this requirement is not met. A single example suffices to show this. With a rise in the general rate of profit not only the values of physical capitals will generally be affected, but the values of human capitals also. With the relative values of different human capitals changing, relative wages will of necessity change too. Similarly, with a change in technique, given the rate of profit, the relative costs of production of different skills will generally change and *a fortiori* so will relative wages. However, this negative conclusion as regards the "quantity of labour" approach must not be mistaken for a negative conclusion on the classical theory as such. As the preceding analysis has shown, there is no need whatsoever to have recourse to the aggregation of different qualities of labor. The latter may be useful in some cases, but it is not an essential part of the classical approach to the theory of distribution and value.

Other factors accounting for wage differentials, such as the power of particular trade unions that manage to negotiate higher wages for the workers they represent, important as they undoubtedly are, need not detain us here, since the main concern of the present analysis is with free competition.

2. Different employments of capital

The factors which, according to Smith, affect wages, are, at least in principle, also susceptible to affecting profits in different employments of capital. Yet, Smith maintains, "of the five circumstances...two only affect the profits of stock; the agreeableness or disagreeableness of the business, and the risk or security with which it is attended." The first of the two circumstances, Smith adds, is however not very important, and as regards the second he observes that "the ordinary profit of stock, though it rises with the risk, does not always seem to rise in proportion to it." He concludes "that, in the same society or neighborhood, the average and ordinary rates of profit in the different employments of stock should be more nearly upon a level than the pecuniary wages of the different sorts of labour. They are so accordingly" (*WN*, I.x.b.34).

In both cases attitudes of investors play an important role. These attitudes can be said to express both socio-cultural values and norms and individual preferences. In regard to the second circumstance, it is particularly the attitude to risk that matters. Smith does not discuss how the actions of investors, expressing these attitudes, lead to the observation that "in all the different employments of stock, the ordinary rate of profit varies more or less with the certainty or uncertainty of the returns" (*WN*, I.x.b.33). He rather takes it for granted that the different sectors of the economy can be classified according to risk. The higher is the risk, the higher is the risk premium to be paid under ordinary circumstances, yet, as we have seen, in Smith's view the premium generally does not fully compensate the higher risk. This is expounded with reference to the "most hazardous of all trades," that of a smuggler: "To compensate it completely, the common returns ought, over and above the ordinary profits of stock, not only to make up for all occasional losses, but to afford a surplus profit to the adventurers of the same nature with the profit of the insurers. But if the common returns were sufficient for all this, bankruptcies would not be more frequent in these than in other trades" (*WN*, I.x.b.33). Another case in point, Smith adds, is the trade of speculation: "The speculative merchant exercises no one regular, established, or well-known branch of business. He is a corn merchant this year, and a wine merchant the next, and a sugar, tobacco, or tea merchant the year after.... His profits or losses, therefore, can bear no regular proportion to those of any one established and well-known branch of business" (*WN*, I.x.b.38). The problem of risk is, of course, also present in the less spectacular sectors of the eonomy, as Smith explains with regard to two sectors of primary production, agriculture and mining (cf. Smith, *LJ* (A) vi.68–9). In both cases the success of the business is uncertain: a farmer raising corn may lose the harvest due to bad weather; a proprietor of an ore mining for the precious metals may have worked a poor pit. The risk of failure of the farmers in some years and of the miners in some pits must be compensated in terms of an above normal rate of profit.

A closer analysis of the determination of profit rate differentials would require a proper treatment of the problem of risk, which, however, is beyond the scope of this book.

3. Historical notes

3.1. Not all authors writing in the first half of the nineteenth century were happy with the device suggested by Smith and adopted by Ricardo of reducing differences in quality of labor to equivalent differences in quantity by means of the given wage structure. A notable exception was Samuel Bailey who in his *Critical Dissertation on the Nature, Measure and Causes of Value*, published in 1825, criticized Ricardo and James Mill on the ground that the existence of considerable wage differentials destroys "the integrity of the rule" of ascertaining the value of commodities in terms of "quantities" of labor: "It must be altogether incorrect to designate *quantity* of labour the sole cause [of value] when quality of labour is so steady in its effects. ... However inconsiderable its effects may be, they cannot be consistently either denied or overlooked" (Bailey, 1825, pp. 210 and 213).

3.2. John Stuart Mill in chapter IV of book III of his *Principles* makes it abundantly clear that relative wages affect the relative values of commodities: "Wages do enter into value. The *relative* wages of the labour necessary for producing different commodities, affect their value just as much as the relative quantities of labour. ... In considering, however, the causes of *variations* in value, quantity of labour is the thing of chief importance; for when that varies, it is generally in one or a few commodities at a time, but the variations of wages (except passing fluctuations) are usually general, and have no considerable effect on value" (Mill, [1848] 1968, vol. III, p. 481). See also Mill's "Summary of the Theory of Value" in chapter VI, especially propositions XIV–XV.

Chapter XIV of book II deals with the differences of wages in different employments and consists essentially in a critical investigation of Adam Smith's respective argument, "the best exposition yet given of this portion of the subject" (Mill, [1848] 1968, vol. II, p. 380). Mill finds fault with Smith's opinion that certain inequalities of remuneration are supposed to compensate for the disagreeable circumstances of particular employments. This "is altogether a false view of the state of facts," since: "The really exhausting and the really repulsive labours, instead of being better paid than others, are almost invariably paid the worst of all, because performed by those who have no choice. It would be otherwise in a favourable state of the general labour market. ... But when the supply of labour so far exceeds the demand that to find an employment at all is an uncertainty, and to be offered it on any terms a favour, the case is totally the reverse. ... The more revolting the occupation, the more certain it is to receive the minimum of remuneration, because it devolves on the most helpless and degraded, on those who from squalid poverty, or from want of skill and education, are rejected from all other employments" (ibid., p. 383).

The problem of scarce natural talents is discussed by Mill under the heading of "natural monopolies," and the respective wage paid is considered "a kind of monopoly price" (ibid., p. 385). Mill stresses that "there is a natural monopoly in favour of skilled labourers against the unskilled, which makes the difference of reward exceed, sometimes in a manifold proportion, what is sufficient merely to equalize their advantages" (ibid., p. 386). This is due to the fairly rigid stratification of society in different classes: "So complete, indeed, has hitherto been the separation, so strongly marked the line of demarcation, between the different grades of labourers, as to be almost equivalent to an hereditary distinction of caste; each employment being chiefly recruited from the children of those already employed in it, or in employments of the same rank with it in social estimation" (ibid., p. 387).

3.3. A major concept of Marx's entire analysis is that of "abstract labour." There has been some discussion about whether this concept is just another version of the classical concept of "quantity of labour," that is, based on wage rates taken as weights to aggregate quantities of concrete labors.

The uncertainty surrounding this question is first due to the fact that Marx is not sufficiently precise in defining the concept of abstract labor. Second, while in his early writings there is ample evidence that he followed the classical authors, in his later writings he is less explicit and refers to wage-rate aggregation "only elliptically at best" (Steedman, 1985, p. 560). However, these elliptic remarks appear to imply that the vector of abstract labor per unit of concrete labor is proportional to the wage-rate vector. For example, in volume III of *Capital* Marx assumed that "the rate of surplus value... is the same in all spheres of production" and stressed that differences "in the level of wages... in no way affect the degree of exploitation of labour"; he illustrated this in terms of the following example: "If the work of a goldsmith is paid at a higher rate than that of a day labourer, for example, the former's surplus labour also produces a correspondingly greater surplus-value than does that of the latter" (Marx, [1894] 1959, p. 264). The postulated uniformity of the rate of surplus value, however, requires the classical wage-rate aggregation of different kinds of labor.

For a discussion of Marx's concept of "abstract labour" and of the "reduction" of skilled labor to unskilled labor, see Rubin (1928), Roncaglia (1974b) and Rowthorn (1980a). For a discussion of heterogeneous labor and the Marxian theory of value, see Bródy (1970), Morishima (1973, pp. 190–4, 1978), Bowles and Gintis (1977, 1978), Krause (1980, 1981, 1982), Zalai (1980), Steedman (1985), and Schefold (1989, part II, ch. 20b, and part III, ch. 4a).

3.4. For a discussion of heterogeneous labor within a "classical" framework of the analysis, see Roncaglia (1974a), Steedman (1980), Filippini, Scanlon, and Tarantelli (1983), Erreygers (1994) and Parrinello (1994).

3.5. The concept of "human capital" essentially consists of an application of the principles of capital theory to human agents of production. The idea of comparing the acquired stock of skills and productive knowledge embodied in people to capital goods rendering specific services can be traced back far into history. For example, William Petty in his *Political Arithmetick* (1676) drew a parallel between the loss of armaments and other instruments of warfare and that of martial skills as a consequence of losses of human lives. Alfred Marshall dealt with the problem of human capital in some detail in chapter VI of book IV of his *Principles of Economics* ([1890] 1977), "Industrial Training." Emphasis is on the long-term nature of investment in human capital and the role of the family and the state in undertaking it. He also pointed out some additional benefits deriving from such investment: "the wisdom of expending public and private funds on education is not to be measured by its direct fruits alone. It will be profitable as a mere investment, to give the masses of the people much greater opportunities than they can generally avail themselves of. For by this means many, who would have died unknown, are enabled to get the start needed for bringing out their latent abilities. And the economic value of one great industrial genius is sufficient to cover the expenses of the education of a whole tow; for one new idea, such as Bessemer's chief invention, adds as much to England's productive power as the labour of a hundred thousand men" (Marshall, [1890] 1977, 1920, p. 179). The induced innovations triggered by improvements in society's stock of productive knowledge was considered by many authors, including Frank Knight (1944), as an effective means to counter the tendency of diminishing returns in a growing economy.

More recently, the theory of human capital, approached from a neoclassical perspective, has become a major field of research. It was particularly the publication of Gary Becker's *Human Capital* (1964) that triggered a large number of studies of the various aspects of the problem under consideration. According to Becker rational agents confronted with educational and professional choices base their decisions on a comparison of the rates of return on alternative investments, and the associated earning streams. Adopting a partial long-period framework, he derives the conventional optimality conditions for an individual agent in terms of marginal rates of return and opportunity costs of funds. Becker also distinguishes between human capital that is specific to the firm in which a worker is employed, and which is largely the result of training on the job, and human capital that is valuable across different employments. The concept of firm-specific human capital, which constitutes an important aspect of "asset specificity," plays a key role in theories of the firm and institutions dealt with in terms of the so-called transactions cost approach; see the overviews provided by Williamson (1979, 1981). (The problem of human capital plays also a crucial role in the literature on life insurance.)

12

On limits to the long-period method

The analysis presented so far has been exclusively concerned with the problem of the existence of long-period positions of the economic system characterized by "stationary" prices, with the price of a commodity obtained as an output at the end of the production period being the same as the price of that commodity used as an input at the beginning of that period. It has been indicated repeatedly, though, commencing with Chapter 1, that in order to exhibit this property, an economic system has to fulfill certain requirements. For example, technical innovation must be set aside and in the presence of nonconstant returns to scale the system must be stationary. Otherwise, relative prices would have to change.

The main object of this chapter is to introduce the reader to some important cases in which some or all prices will of necessity change over time. Section 1 takes as a starting point the analysis of self-reproducing non-basics in Sections 3 and 6 of Chapter 3 and in Section 4 of Chapter 5. The earlier analysis focused on the problem of the existence, or lack thereof, of a long-period position in the case in which some self-reproducing non-basic cannot be produced, given the level of the general rate of profit. In contradistinction, in this chapter emphasis will be on the determination of the short-period price of that non-basic, a given amount of which is taken to be available from previous periods of production, and on whether or not it will be produced in the short period. The determination of the price of the non-basic will be carried out on the assumption that all other commodities fetch their long-period prices, that is, a *partial* analysis is employed to discuss the problem under consideration.

The problem of obsolete used machines, dealt with in Section 2, is also framed in such a way that a partial analysis is possible. In the short period there generally are machines that have been in active use in the past, but have now been superseded. These obsolete machines may still be worth

340 Theory of production

employing for what they can get. Hence there is an element of scarcity involved with regard to them. It will be assumed that all prices except those of the obsolete machines are at their long-period levels.

Much of the conventional economic analysis, and with few exceptions the analysis contained in the preceding chapters of this book, too, is based on the twin assumptions of the free gifts of nature and the free disposal of wastes. Accordingly, the environment is envisaged as being simultaneously a horn of plenty and a bottomless sink. The discussion in the following two sections abandons, though in an elementary form only, the free gifts of nature assumption.

Section 3 contains a brief introduction to the theory of renewable resources. A resource is called "renewable" if it allows constant periodic removals from its stock without running that stock down: natural growth will make good the loss in biomass due to harvest. A renewable resource is either "depletable" or "nondepletable." A depletable resource is actually depleted if the levels of the periodic removals from its stock are unduly high and thus cannot be made good by the natural growth of the resource. Biological resources such as bird and fish populations and forests may be depleted by excess harvesting. (It goes without saying that their survival may also be endangered by external effects of the processes of human production and consumption, that is, the pollution of the environment in which they live.) Geothermal and solar energy are generally treated as nondepletable resources in economics. The case dealt with in some detail in Section 3 concerns a renewable resource such as blackberries or salmon. To simplify the analysis, it is assumed that the resource which can either be produced artificially or harvested in its natural habitat is a non-basic. This allows once again a treatment of the problem in terms of a partial analysis.

Section 4 introduces the problem of "exhaustible" resources. They are a borderline case of renewable resources in that they are either not naturally regenerated at all or regenerated on a time scale that is irrelevant to human exploitation. Typical cases are ores such as coal, oil, and metals: setting aside the possibility of recycling (which for obvious reasons cannot but be incomplete anyway), any removal reduces their stocks. Some exhaustible resources (coal, oil, gas) are used to produce energy which is an input in many, if not all, production processes. This precludes their investigation in terms of a partial analysis. The time path of the exhaustion of the former kind of resources is then analyzed in terms of a model based on a set of strong assumptions, perhaps the most important of which is that there is an ultimate "backstop technology," based on the use of solar energy. Setting aside technical progress and the discovery of new deposits of natural resources, the economy is to be expected to converge gradually to a system of production in which only solar energy will be employed since all the exhaustible resources have already been used up: this is the system's ultimate position. While this can be assumed to be the general rule, the analysis presented shows that there are exceptions to it. Sections 5 and 6 contain Historical notes and Exercises, respectively.

Before we enter into a discussion of our subject matter the reader's attention should be drawn to the following proviso. In all cases in which prices are bound to change over time and agents can be assumed as being aware of it, the question concerning the "expectations" of agents, and the formation of these expectations, cannot, in principle, be avoided. This raises formidable problems for economic theorizing. The assumption of perfect foresight, that is, perfect information on the part of agents on all future states of the world, entertained in the theory of intertemporal equilibrium (see Section 5 of Chapter 14), simply evades the issue. On the other hand, introducing expectations involves the danger of depriving the analysis of a solid basis: depending on the particular hypothesis about their formation and how they affect the actions of agents, "anything goes" appears to be the unavoidable conclusion.

Here we abstain from entering into a discussion of the problems associated with the indisputable uncertainty clouding the future. Hence the following analysis can be but a preliminary step toward a proper investigation of the subject. One (admittedly weak) rationalization of this neglect could be the following. Whereas it has to be admitted that the cases dealt with seem to indicate that there is hardly ever a constellation that gives rise to static prices and an invariant income distribution, it may be argued that in many cases the factors affecting relative prices and income distribution will change only slowly over time. Hence the long-period method employed throughout the preceding chapters of this book could be defended on the grounds that it is applicable, as a first approximation, to cases in which these changes are indeed sufficiently slow and gradual. Moreover, given the unsatisfactory state of economic theorizing in cases in which this premise is not met, the long-period method appears to be the only acceptable one available at present.

1. Self-reproducing non-basics

In the Historical notes of Chapter 3 it has been argued that the solution suggested in Section 6 of that chapter to the main problem associated with self-reproducing non-basics, that is, that they cannot be produced if the rate of profit is too high, is a long-period consequence of a short-period analysis. In fact, the "solution" we are speaking of simply asserts that in the circumstances in which some self-reproducing non-basics cannot be produced, given the level of the rate of profit, a long-period position can exist only if consumption patterns are such that these self-reproducing non-basics are not demanded.[1] The short-period problem is the following. Assume that the rate of profit is such that some self-reproducing non-basics cannot be produced in the long period, but some amounts of them are actually in existence (stemming from earlier rounds of production). In these circumstances the non-basics can be traded and, therefore, priced. The following questions arise: (i) Will these commodities be produced in the short run? (ii) How will their prices be determined, assuming that all other commodities fetch their long-period prices?

In order to simplify the analysis, consider a simple economy in which

(i) there are n commodities;
(ii) there is only one single-product process to produce each of the n commodities;
(iii) the first $n-1$ commodities are basic, the nth commodity is a self-reproducing non-basic which will be called "beans."

The material input matrix and the labor input vector are, respectively,

$$\mathbf{A} = \begin{bmatrix} \mathbf{A}_{11} & \mathbf{0} \\ \mathbf{A}_{21} & a_{nn} \end{bmatrix}, \quad \mathbf{l} = \begin{bmatrix} \mathbf{l}_1 \\ l_n \end{bmatrix},$$

where $\mathbf{A}_{11}$ is a semipositive irreducible $(n-1) \times (n-1)$ matrix, $\mathbf{0}$ and $\mathbf{l}_1$ are column vectors, $\mathbf{A}_{21}$ is a row vector, and a_{nn} and l_n are scalars.

Let r be the given rate of profit. On the assumption that the numeraire consists of basic commodities only, the wage rate w and the price vector of basic commodities $\mathbf{p}_1$ are determined by the equations

$$\mathbf{p}_1 = (1+r)\mathbf{A}_{11}\mathbf{p}_1 + w\mathbf{l}_1$$
$$\mathbf{c}_1^T \mathbf{p}_1 = 1.$$

As we have seen in Chapter 4, if beans are consumed and $(1+r)a_{nn} < 1$, then the price of beans p_n is determined by the equation

$$p_n = (1+r)(\mathbf{A}_{21}\mathbf{p}_1 + a_{nn}p_n) + wl_n.$$

Assume now that $(1+r)a_{nn} > 1$ and, in addition, that an amount $v > 0$ of beans is in existence. This is, of course, a short-period situation which could be the result of an unexpected change in, for example, the level of the rate of profit or the technical conditions of production. We are not interested

---

[1] The same problem is also considered in Section 2 of Chapter 4, and the "solution" is discussed in Section 4 of Chapter 5.

here in the cause that is responsible for the situation under discussion. What is relevant for the analysis is that these circumstances cannot prevail in the long period, but they are, of course, not exceptional in the short period.

In order to determine the price of beans in the short period, we have to deal with "demand." The most simple conceptualization of demand possible in the present context is perhaps that based on the following assumptions:

(iv) the economy is stationary, that is, the uniform rate of growth is equal to zero;

(v) people do not need to consume beans, and if they don't consume them, then the amounts of basic commodities consumed are given and constant; let $\mathbf{b}$ be the vector of commodities consumed when beans are not consumed: $\mathbf{b}^T \mathbf{e}_n = 0$;

(vi) in consumption beans and commodity 1 are perfect substitutes, that is, with an appropriate choice of the units in which commodities are measured the vector of the amounts of commodities consumed is $\mathbf{b}$, if $p_n > p_1$, $(\mathbf{b} - b_1 \mathbf{e}_1 + b_1 \mathbf{e}_n)$, if $p_n < p_1$, or any convex linear combination of these vectors, if $p_n = p_1$. (It goes without saying that commodity 1 and beans are not substitutes as means of production.)

Since the situation under consideration is not a long-period position, prices will change over time. Assume, however, that the prices of basic commodities and the wage rate are at their long-period levels. In order to simplify the notation, let π_t be the price per unit (kg) of beans at time t; let $k = (1 + r)\mathbf{A}_{21}\mathbf{p}_1 + wl_n$ be the cost of basic commodities per unit of beans (including profits) and labor; let x_t be the intensity of operation of the beans process at time t; let s_t be the amount of commodity 1 produced in order to be consumed at time t; let $a = a_{nn}$ and $b = b_1$; let p be the price of commodity 1, $p = \mathbf{e}_n^T \mathbf{p}_1$. If in each moment in time the production of beans yields the same rate of profit which can be obtained in the other sectors, then the following inequalities and equations are to be satisfied.

$$\pi_{t+1} \leqslant k + (1 + r)a\pi_t, \quad t \in \mathbb{N}_0 \tag{12.1a}$$

$$x_{t+1}\pi_{t+1} = x_{t+1}[k + (1 + r)a\pi_t], \quad t \in \mathbb{N}_0 \tag{12.1b}$$

$$x_t\pi_t \leqslant x_t p, \quad t \in \mathbb{N}_0 \tag{12.1c}$$

$$s_t\pi_t \geqslant s_t p, \quad t \in \mathbb{N}_0 \tag{12.1d}$$

$$x_t + s_t \geqslant ax_{t+1} + b, \quad t \in \mathbb{N} \tag{12.1e}$$

$$(x_t + s_t)\pi_t = (ax_{t+1} + b)\pi_t, \quad t \in \mathbb{N} \tag{12.1f}$$

$$v + s_0 \geqslant ax_1 + b, \tag{12.1g}$$

$$(v + s_0)\pi_0 = (ax_1 + b)\pi_0, \tag{12.1h}$$

$$\pi_t \geqslant 0, x_t \geqslant 0, s_t \geqslant 0. \quad t \in \mathbb{N}_0 \tag{12.1i}$$

Inequality (12.1a) means that nobody can obtain extra profits by producing beans available at time $t + 1$. Equation (12.1b) implies, because of inequalities (12.1a) and (12.1i), that beans will be available at time $t + 1$ only if their production is able to pay the ruling rate of profit. Inequality (12.1c) means that if beans are produced, then their price cannot be larger than that of the perfect substitute of beans. Inequality (12.1d) states that if the perfect substitute of beans is produced in order to be consumed, then its price cannot be larger than that of beans. Inequality (12.1e) (or (12.1g)) implies that the amount of beans produced plus the amount of the perfect substitute produced in order to be consumed is not lower than b, and equation (12.1f) (or (12.1h)) implies that if it is larger, then the price of beans is zero (the price of commodity 1 is p by definition). The meaning of inequalities (12.1i) is obvious.

There is a set of prices which, if adopted, ensure a uniform rate of profit along the whole path of the "exhaustion" of beans, if and only if system (12.1) is consistent. With different prices a uniform rate of profit is not possible in at least one period. A truly dynamical analysis would necessitate the proper modeling of the reactions of those producers who recognize this fact from the point in time onward in which they do so. This is beyond the scope of this book. The present chapter is devoted to a preliminary analysis of certain aspects of the problem under consideration only.

Let us first prove three propositions which lead to a relationship between x_t and π_t such as the one illustrated in Figure 12.1, which needs to hold if inequalities and equations (12.1) hold.

Proposition 12.1. If $0 < x_t < b$, then $\pi_t = p$.

Proof. Since $x_t < b, s_t > 0$, because of inequality (12.1e); then inequality (12.1d) implies that $\pi_t \geqslant p$. Since $x_t > 0, \pi_t \leqslant p$, because of inequality (12.1c).
                                                                    Q.E.D

Proposition 12.2. If $b \sum_{j=0}^{h} a^j < x_t < b \sum_{j=0}^{h+1} a^j$ and $\pi_t > 0$, then $\pi_t = p_{h+1}$, where

$$p_h = \frac{p - k \dfrac{[(1 + r)a]^h - 1}{(1 + r)a - 1}}{[(1 + r)a]^h} \quad h = 0, 1, \ldots, T$$

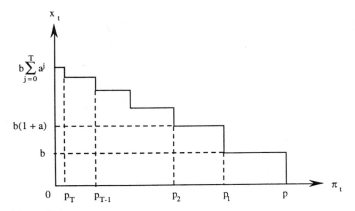

Figure 12.1

and

$$T = \max \left\{ t \in \mathbb{N} \mid \frac{[(1+r)a]^t - 1}{(1+r)a - 1} \leqslant \frac{p}{k} \right\}.$$

Proof. Since $x_t > b, x_{t+1} > 0$, because of equation (12.1f); then $\pi_t < \pi_{t+1} \leqslant p$, because of equation (12.1b) and inequality (12.1c); then $s_t = 0$, because of inequalities (12.1d) and (12.1i). Let us now prove that the proposition holds for $h = 0$. Since $x_t < b(1 + a)$, then $ax_{t+1} + b < b(1 + a)$, because of equation (12.1f). Therefore $0 < x_{t+1} < b$ and, as a consequence of Proposition 12.1, $\pi_{t+1} = p$. Finally, we obtain that

$$\pi_t = \frac{p - k}{(1+r)a} = p_1$$

from equation (12.1b). Now let us prove that if the proposition holds for $h = n$, then it holds for $h = n + 1$. Since $b \sum_{j=0}^{n+1} a^j < x_t < b \sum_{j=0}^{n+2} a^j$, then $b \sum_{j=0}^{n+1} a^j < ax_{t+1} + b < b \sum_{j=0}^{n+2} a^j$, because of equation (12.1f). Then $b \sum_{j=0}^{n} a^j < x_{t+1} < b \sum_{j=0}^{n+1} a^j$ and therefore $\pi_{t+1} = p_{n+1}$ since the proposition holds for $h = n$. From equation (12.1b) we obtain that

$$\pi_t = \frac{p_{n+1} - k}{(1+r)a} = p_{n+2}.$$

Finally, if $h > T$, then $p_h < 0$. Q.E.D

Proposition 12.3. If $x_t = b \sum_{j=0}^{h} a^j$ and $\pi_t > 0$, then $p_{h+1} \leqslant \pi_t \leqslant p_h$.

Proof. Let us first prove that the proposition holds for $h = 0$. Inequality (12.1c) implies that $\pi_t \leqslant p$. Since $x_t = b, s_t = ax_{t+1}$, because of equation

(12.1e); hence, s_t and x_{t+1} are either both positive or both zero; if both s_t and x_{t+1} are positive, then $p \leqslant \pi_t < \pi_{t+1} \leqslant p$ because of inequality (12.1d), equation (12.1b), and inequality (12.1c): hence a contradiction; therefore both s_t and x_{t+1} equal zero. Since $x_{t+1} = 0$, then $s_{t+1} > 0$, because of inequality (12.1e), and therefore

$$p \leqslant \pi_{t+1} \leqslant k + (1+r)a\pi_t,$$

because of inequalities (12.1d) and (12.1a). Hence $\pi_t \geqslant p_1$. This completes the proof of the proposition for $h = 0$. Next, let us prove that if the proposition holds for $h = n$, then it holds for $h = n + 1$. Since $x_t \geqslant b$, then $x_{t+1} > 0$ and $s_t = 0$ as in the proof of Proposition 12.2. Since $x_t = b \sum_{j=0}^{n+1} a^j$, then $b \sum_{j=0}^{n+1} a^j = ax_{t+1} + b$, because of equation (12.1f). Hence $x_{t+1} = b \sum_{j=0}^{n} a^j$ and therefore $p_{n+1} \leqslant \pi_{t+1} \leqslant p_n$, because the proposition holds for $h = n$. Then, as a consequence of equation (12.1b), $p_{n+1} \leqslant k + (1+r)a\pi_t \leqslant p_n$. That is,

$$p_{n+2} = \frac{p_{n+1} - k}{(1+r)a} \leqslant \pi_t \leqslant \frac{p_n - k}{(1+r)a} = p_{n+1},$$

which completes the proof.   Q.E.D

These results can be expressed in a relationship between x_t and π_t as in Figure 12.1, where it has been assumed that $p = 42$, $k = 5$, $a = 0.8$, $r = 0.5$, $b = 10$. Of course, $T = 5$.

   The ground is now prepared for studying the dynamics of the price and the quantity of beans produced. The relationship mentioned above between x_t and π_t depends only on technology and demand: it is independent of v, the amount of beans available at time 0. We need to distinguish between two cases.

Case (i). $0 < v \leqslant b \sum_{j=0}^{T} a^j$. In this case we can obtain the same propositions as above with v and π_0 instead of x_t and π_t by substituting inequality (12.1g) and equation (12.1h) for inequality (12.1e) and equation (12.1f) wherever the latter appear in the proofs. If there is a nonnegative integer number $h \leqslant T$ such that $v = b \sum_{j=0}^{h} a^j$, then π_0 is not uniquely determined but has to assume a value from a range $(p_{h+1} \leqslant \pi_0 \leqslant p_h,$ if $h < T$; $0 \leqslant \pi_0 \leqslant p_T$, if $h = T)$: any of these values can be chosen as a solution for π_0. Otherwise π_0 is uniquely determined. Once we have π_0, the dynamics of the beans price are determined by the difference equation (12.1b) for $t \leqslant T^*$, where T^* is to be determined as the higher value such that $x_{T^*} > 0$. Therefore,

$$\pi_t = \left[\pi_0 + \frac{k}{(1+r)a - 1} \right] [(1+r)a]^t - \frac{k}{(1+r)a - 1}, \quad t = 0, 1, \ldots, T^*$$

The dynamics of the quantity of beans produced are determined by the difference equation (12.1f) for $x_0 = v, s_t = 0$, and $t \leqslant T^*$. That is,

$$x_t = \left[\frac{v(1-a)-b}{1-a}\right]\left(\frac{1}{a}\right)^t + \frac{b}{1-a}. \quad t = 0, 1, \ldots, T^*$$

T^* can then be determined as the minimum value of x_t such that $x_t < b$, that is,

$$T^* = \min \{t \in \mathbb{N}_0 \mid [v(1-a)-b]a^{-t} + ab \leqslant 0\}.$$

Case (ii). $v > b \sum_{j=0}^{T} a^j$. The above procedure would require a negative π_0. This being impossible, some amount of beans has to be disposed of at time 0. This requires that π_0 equals 0. Then the amount of beans to be disposed of at time 0 is exactly $v - b \sum_{j=0}^{T} a^j$, if $p_T > 0$ (the special case in which $p_T = 0$ is dealt with as exercise 6.3). The dynamics of the price of beans are determined once again by the difference equation (12.1b) for $\pi_0 = 0$ and $t \leqslant T$. Therefore,

$$\pi_t = k\frac{[(1+r)a]^t - 1}{(1+r)a - 1}. \quad t = 0, 1, \ldots, T$$

The dynamics of the quantity of beans produced is determined by the difference equation (12.1f) for $x_0 = b \sum_{j=0}^{T} a^j$ and $t \leqslant T$. That is,

$$x_t = b \sum_{j=0}^{T} a^{j-t} + \frac{b}{1-a}(1 - a^{-t}).$$

Then, by taking into account that $\sum_{j=0}^{T} a^j = (1 - a^{T+1})/(1-a)$, one obtains that

$$x_t = b\frac{1 - a^{T+1-t}}{1-a}.$$

Note that $\pi_T = p$ and $x_T = b$.

The above analysis has shown that there are paths of the price of beans and of the quantity of beans produced, respectively, such that beans producers obtain the same rate of profit as all other producers. These paths would be adopted if there were perfect foresight. But what, if there is not? Suppose first that the actual (x_t, π_t) is above the relationship depicted in Figure 12.1. If producers happened to be totally myopic, with the price of beans approaching p some beans would be still available, but nobody would want them. The assumption of totally myopic behavior is, of course, as dubious as that of perfect foresight. A truly dynamic model would have to take into account the reaction of those producers who recognize the fact just mentioned from the point in time onward in which they do so.

Assume now that the actual (x_t, π_t) is below the relationship depicted in Figure 12.1. In the case of totally myopic behavior beans will be exhausted before the price of beans has had time to approach p. Again, a proper dynamic analysis would have to take into account the reactions of those who (first) recognize this fact. The above analysis has also shown that in the long run the price of beans is not lower than p: this is the result which has been obtained in Section 6 of Chapter 3 and generalized in Section 4 of Chapter 5.

2. Obsolete used machines

Next we deal with the case of machines of an obsolete type: they may still be worth employing for what they can get, and if they are in fact employed they will receive a nonnegative price. Sraffa mentioned obsolete machines in his book in the last section of the chapter devoted to land (see Sraffa, 1960, §91). These machines are indeed "similar to land in so far as they are employed as means of production, although not currently produced" (ibid., p. 78).

In this section a simple model with obsolete machines will be analyzed, in which all prices except those of the obsolete machines are taken to be at their long-period levels. In order to simplify the analysis, consider an economy in which

(i) there are n finished goods and m old machines;

(ii) to produce the $n + m$ commodities there are $n + m$ processes constituting a cost-minimizing technique (as defined in Chapters 7 and 9);

(iii) there are also u processes that produce finished good n, say corn, by means of some of the n finished goods and s old machines of an obsolete type, $u \geqslant s$.

The output matrix, the material input matrix and the labor input vector relative to the u processes mentioned in (iii) are, respectively, $\mathbf{B} = [\mathbf{B}_1, \mathbf{B}_2]$, $\mathbf{A} = [\mathbf{A}_1, \mathbf{A}_2]$ and $\mathbf{l}$, where $\mathbf{B}_1 = [\mathbf{0}, \mathbf{e}]$, where $\mathbf{0}$ is an $u \times (n-1)$ zero matrix and $\mathbf{e}$ is the summation vector, $\mathbf{B}_2$ is a $u \times s$ semipositive matrix, $\mathbf{A}_1$ is a $u \times n$ semipositive matrix, $\mathbf{A}_2$ is a $u \times s$ semipositive matrix each row of which has at least one positive element, and $\mathbf{l}$ is a semipositive vector.

Let r be the given rate of profit; the long-period levels of the wage rate w and the price vector of finished goods $\mathbf{p}_1$ are determined by the $n + m$ equations relative to the $n + m$ processes mentioned in (ii). Moreover, the s old machines of an obsolete type mentioned in (iii) are in short supply, that is, the existing amounts of them are not enough to produce the requested amount of corn with the processes mentioned in (iii) and, therefore, corn will also be produced by means of the non-obsolete machines. As a consequence, the price vector of finished goods equals $\mathbf{p}_1$ also in the short period. The price vector of the old machines of an obsolete type may be changing over time. Let $\mathbf{y}_t$ be the vector of prices of obsolete old machines; let $\mathbf{k} = [(1 + r)\mathbf{A}_1 - \mathbf{B}_1]\mathbf{p}_1 + w\mathbf{l}$ ($\mathbf{k}$ is a constant vector); let $\mathbf{x}_t$ be the intensity of operation, at time t, of the processes using the obsolete old machines; let $\mathbf{v}$ be the vector of the amounts of obsolete old machines existing at time 0; let t^* be the maximum age that any obsolete old machine can attain minus the minimum age of any machine in stock at time 0. Then the following inequalities and equations are to be satisfied for each $0 \leqslant t \leqslant t^*$.

$$\mathbf{B}_2\mathbf{y}_{t+1} \leqslant (1 + r)\mathbf{A}_2\mathbf{y}_t + \mathbf{k}, \tag{12.2a}$$

$$\mathbf{x}_{t+1}^T\mathbf{B}_2\mathbf{y}_{t+1} = \mathbf{x}_{t+1}^T[(1 + r)\mathbf{A}_2\mathbf{y}_t + \mathbf{k}], \tag{12.2b}$$

$$\mathbf{x}_{t+1}^T\mathbf{A}_2 \leqslant \mathbf{x}_t^T\mathbf{B}_2, \tag{12.2c}$$

$$\mathbf{x}_{t+1}^T\mathbf{A}_2\mathbf{y}_t = \mathbf{x}_t^T\mathbf{B}_2\mathbf{y}_t, \tag{12.2d}$$

$$\mathbf{x}_1^T\mathbf{A}_2 \leqslant \mathbf{v}^T, \tag{12.2e}$$

$$\mathbf{x}_1^T\mathbf{A}_2\mathbf{y}_0 = \mathbf{v}^T\mathbf{y}_0, \tag{12.2f}$$

$$\mathbf{y}_t \geqslant 0, \mathbf{x} \geqslant 0. \tag{12.2g}$$

Inequality (12.2a) means that nobody can obtain extra profits by producing corn available at time $t + 1$ with obsolete old machines. Equation (12.2b) implies, because of inequalities (12.2a) and (12.2g), that corn available at time $t + 1$ will be produced with obsolete old machines only if the ruling rate of profit will be obtained by this production activity. Inequalities (12.2c) and (12.2e) mean that the amounts of obsolete old machines operated at time $t + 1$ are not larger than the amounts of the same machines disposable at time t. Then equations (12.2d) and (12.2f) imply, also because of inequalities (12.2g), that if an obsolete old machine has been disposed of, then its price is zero. The meaning of inequalities (12.2g) is obvious.

In order to put system (12.2) into a more workable form, let us introduce the $ut^* \times s(t^* + 1)$ matrix $\mathbf{E}(r)$, the vector $\mathbf{y} \in \mathbb{R}^{s(t^*+1)}$, the vector $\mathbf{h} \in \mathbb{R}^{st^*}$, the vector $\mathbf{x} \in \mathbb{R}^{st^*}$, and the vector $\mathbf{w} \in \mathbb{R}^{s(t^*+1)}$:

$$\mathbf{E}(r) = \begin{bmatrix} -(1+r)\mathbf{A}_2 & \mathbf{B}_2 & 0 & \cdots & 0 & 0 \\ 0 & -(1+r)\mathbf{A}_2 & \mathbf{B}_2 & \cdots & 0 & 0 \\ \cdot & \cdot & \cdot & \cdots & \cdot & \cdot \\ \cdot & \cdot & \cdot & \cdots & \cdot & \cdot \\ 0 & 0 & 0 & \cdots & \mathbf{B}_2 & 0 \\ 0 & 0 & 0 & \cdots & -(1+r)\mathbf{A}_2 & \mathbf{B}_2 \end{bmatrix},$$

$$y = \begin{bmatrix} y_0 \\ y_1 \\ \vdots \\ y_{t^*} \end{bmatrix}, \quad h = \begin{bmatrix} k \\ k \\ \vdots \\ k \end{bmatrix}, \quad x = \begin{bmatrix} x_1 \\ x_2 \\ \vdots \\ x_{t^*} \end{bmatrix}, \quad w = \begin{bmatrix} -v \\ 0 \\ \vdots \\ 0 \end{bmatrix}.$$

Then system (12.2) can be stated as

$$E(r)y \leqslant h, \tag{12.3a}$$

$$x^T E(r)y = x^T h, \tag{12.3b}$$

$$x^T E(0) \geqslant w^T, \tag{12.3g}$$

$$x^T E(0)y = w^T y, \tag{12.3h}$$

$$y \geqslant 0, x \geqslant 0. \tag{12.3i}$$

System (12.3) has the same form as system (8.13) of Chapter 8 with $E(r)$ instead of $[B - (1 + r)A]$, $E(0)$ instead of $[B - (1 + g)A]$. It is important to note that $E(0) - E(r) \geqslant 0$ as well as $(r - g)A \geqslant 0$ in Chapter 8. Hence we can use the same procedure adopted in Chapter 8. Thus system (12.3) has a solution if there are a nonnegative vector f and a nonnegative vector g such that

$$f^T E(r) \geqslant w^T \tag{12.4a}$$

$$E(0)g \leqslant h. \tag{12.4b}$$

Finally, it is easily checked that the zero vector satisfies inequality (12.4a), whereas exercise 6.9 shows that inequality (12.4b) also has always a nonnegative solution. Hence system (12.3) has a solution, and therefore system (12.2) has also a solution.

Two cases are now to be distinguished: one is related to the analysis of fixed capital in Chapter 7, the other to that in Chapter 9. In the *first* case each process may produce either one machine or none and must utilize one machine. Moreover, for each old machine there is at least one process utilizing it and for each machine *older than one year* there is at least one process producing it. Exercise 6.10 shows that in the first case the prices of obsolete machines are independent of the time period and of v, provided that obsolete machines are in short supply: $y_0 = y_1 = \cdots = y_{t^*}$. Things are different in the *second* case: if two machines are always utilized jointly and one of the two is not available, then the price of the other one is obviously zero. Exercises 6.11–6.14 provide some examples in which the obsolete machines are *not* in short supply, that is, corn can be produced at time 0 without utilizing non-obsolete machines. In this case corn will be produced with obsolete machines only and therefore its price cannot be the long-period price; if corn entered directly or indirectly into the production of other commodities, then too the prices of these other commodities would change over time. This is the reason why in exercises 6.11–6.14 corn is not supposed to be a means of production of any commodity.

3. **Renewable resources**

Renewable resources are resources that are capable of regenerating themselves as long as the environment that nurtures them remains favorable. This environment can be natural or artificial. The beans mentioned in Section 1 as well as all agricultural, aquacultural, and zootechnical products are grown in an *artificial* environment. These products are as much commodities as all commodities dealt with in previous chapters (and in Section 1 of this chapter); we do not need to add anything on them here. Suffice it to say that the size of the artificial environment in which they live is enlarged or reduced in proportion to the harvest. This implies that the natural laws of the growth of these populations living in an artificial environment are described by a set of alternative processes and the choice of technique will also determine the size of the artificial environments utilized. On the contrary, the natural laws of the growth of the populations living in a natural environment cannot be controlled by men. Fish populations mentioned at the very beginning of Chapter 10 are a typical example of renewable resources grown in a *natural* environment. The costs connected with the use of these resources are typically the costs of their appropriation, for example, the costs of the catch in the case of fish, since these resources are assumed to grow naturally. In regard to such resources "free disposal" does not imply their destruction, but rather their "conservation."

The natural environment in which a renewable resource is nurtured is often not privately owned. Everyone can appropriate the resource, which thus becomes a private property only after the act of appropriation.[2] The costs of the appropriation of the resource are larger or smaller depending, *inter alia*, on the existing stock of the resource, which, in turn, depends on the previously appropriated amount as well as on the size of the natural environment in which the resource is nurtured.

It is beyond the scope of this book to provide a detailed analysis of renewable resources nurtured in a natural environment. This section will

---

[2] If a natural environment is privately owned, the catch is under the control of the owner of the environment and, therefore, a rent is generally to be paid in order to obtain the permission to catch. The determination of this rent is not analyzed here.

just provide a sketch of the problem involved on the assumption that the natural resource that is harvested is a commodity (say *salmon*) which does not enter into the production of any commodity. In particular, it does not enter into the production of salmon produced using an aquacultural method of production.[3] (An alternative would be to assume that commodities produced with wild salmon do not enter directly or indirectly into the production of wild salmon itself nor into the production of artficially grown salmon, but it may enter into the production of some non-basics like smoked salmon, salmon sandwiches, salmon specialities in restaurants, etc.) These assumptions are very strong; their only justification is that they render the problem susceptible to a partial analysis as in the preceding sections of this chapter. To simplify matters as much as possible, assume in addition that the demand for caught wild salmon is specified in the same way as that for beans in Section 1, that is, the demand for caught wild salmon equals b (0) if its price is lower (larger) than that of its substitute and can assume any value between 0 and b if the price of caught wild salmon equals that of its substitute. Let p be the price of the perfect substitute of caught wild salmon, that is, salmon produced "artificially." The only other elements we need for our analysis are: (i) the natural growth law of wild salmon and (ii) the harvest cost function per pound of wild salmon. To avoid an incompatibility in the units of account (number of salmon versus number of pounds of salmon), we shall assume that the "quantity" of salmon can always be expressed in terms of some measure of weight, that is, pounds.[4]

The usual assumption in bioeconomic models and in the fishery literature is that the growth of stock is a non-monotonic function simply of the size of the stock itself. With v_t salmon in existence at time t, and setting aside human harvesting, then at time $t + 1$ there will be v_{t+1} salmon, where

$$v_{t+1} = v_t + f(v_t);$$

---

[3] There is the problem that in order to produce salmon artificially one needs wild salmon first. Eventually, non-wild salmon can be produced either by means of non-wild or by means of wild salmon. This implies a further economic choice, that is, that concerning the timing of the catch of wild salmon which for some time may then be grown in a fish-pond just in order to reproduce themselves until they are finally brought to the market. This problem is analysed in exercises 6.15 and 6.16.

[4] Thus, we implicitly set aside the problem that salmon are heterogeneous, that is, differ from one another in several characteristics, for example weight, size, age etc. Otherwise we would have to take into account some jointness of production in fishery.

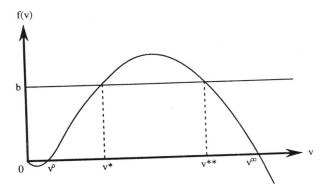

Figure 12.2

$f(v_t)$ is assumed to be negative for very low and very high values of $v_t > 0$, whereas in the range in which $f(v_t) \geqslant 0$, $[v^\circ, v^{\circ\circ}]$, $f(v_t)$ is first increasing and then decreasing. (Obviously, $f(v_t) \geqslant -v_t$ and $f(0) = 0$.) Figure 12.2 illustrates the assumed shape of $f(v_t)$. The idea is that if the population of salmon is very small, then procreation is difficult, and if it is getting very large, then the "carrying capacity" for the resource of the environment will eventually be met. The growth function depicted in Figure 12.2 has a threshold level of fish stock, v°, which is essential for the survival of the species. If the population falls below this threshold level, reproduction is less than natural mortality, and the species gradually dies out.

If wild salmon is caught then

$$v_{t+1} = v_t + f(v_t) - x_{t+1},$$

where x_{t+1} is the catch in period $t + 1$. Next we have to specify the harvest cost function. Let $(\mathbf{a}(v_t), l(v_t))$ be the material input vector and the labor input required per pound of salmon available at time $t + 1$, then the cost per pound available at time $t + 1$, $k(v_t)$, is

$$k(v_t) = (1 + r)\mathbf{a}(v_t)^T \mathbf{p} + wl(v_t).$$

Since caught wild salmon is a non-basic commodity which enters neither directly nor indirectly into the production of any commodity, we can consider vector $\mathbf{p}$ as determined independently of $k(v_t)$ (cf. Section 1). It is quite natural to assume that $k(v)$ is a decreasing function and that $k(v) > p$ for v sufficiently close to zero (see Figure 12.3).[5]

---

[5] There appears to be no harm in assuming $\lim_{v \to 0} k(v) = +\infty$.

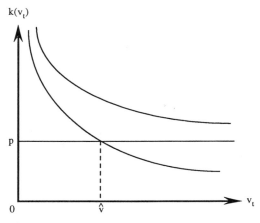

Figure 12.3

If $k(v_t)$ happens to be always greater than p whatever size v_t assumes (see the upper curve in Figure 12.3), then only artificially grown salmon will be brought to the market; wild salmon will instead be left to itself. A necessary condition for wild salmon to be caught by a specialized salmon fishing industry is that there is a $\hat{v}$ such that $k(\hat{v}) = p$ (see the lower curve in Figure 12.3).

Let π_t indicate the price of caught wild salmon available for consumption at time t, x_t the amount of wild salmon caught at time t, s_t the amount of salmon, available at time t, produced using an aquaculture method of production, whose price per unit, p, is given and constant. Then the following inequalities and equations need to be satisfied:

$$\pi_{t+1} \leqslant k(v_t), \quad t \in \mathbb{N}_0 \tag{12.5a}$$

$$x_{t+1}\pi_{t+1} = x_{t+1}k(v_t), \quad t \in \mathbb{N}_0 \tag{12.5b}$$

$$x_t\pi_t \leqslant x_t p, \quad t \in \mathbb{N} \tag{12.5c}$$

$$s_t\pi_t \geqslant s_t p, \quad t \in \mathbb{N} \tag{12.5d}$$

$$x_t + s_t \geqslant b, \quad t \in \mathbb{N} \tag{12.5e}$$

$$(x_t + s_t)\pi_t = b\pi_t, \quad t \in \mathbb{N} \tag{12.5f}$$

$$v_{t+1} = v_t + f(v_t) - x_{t+1}, \quad t \in \mathbb{N}_0 \tag{12.5g}$$

$$v_t \geqslant 0, \pi_t \geqslant 0, x_t \geqslant 0, s_t \geqslant 0. \quad t \in \mathbb{N} \tag{12.5h}$$

Inequality (12.5a) means that nobody can expect to obtain extra profits by catching wild salmon available at time $t + 1$. Equation (12.5b) implies,

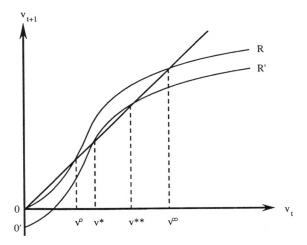

Figure 12.4

because of inequalities (12.5a) and (12.5h), that caught wild salmon will be available at time $t + 1$ only if their catch is able to pay the ruling rate of profit. Inequality (12.5c) means that if wild salmon is caught at time t, then its price cannot be larger than the price of the aquaculturally produced salmon. Inequality (12.5d) means that if salmon produced artificially is available at time t, then its price cannot be larger than the price of caught wild salmon. Inequality (12.5e) and equation (12.5f) imply that the amount of caught salmon (wild or not) available at time t is not lower than b, and if it is larger, then the price of caught wild salmon is zero (the price of salmon produced in aquaculture equals p by definition). Equation (12.5g) gives the natural growth law of wild salmon. Inequalities (12.5h) are obvious.

In this chapter we will not try to determine the path of the price of wild salmon nor that of the catch. We limit our analysis to the determination of the stationary points. These points are long-period solutions of the model. Obviously, a stationary point is characterized by the fact that $v_t = v_{t+1}$. Figure 12.4 plots v_{t+1} against v_t. The intersections with the 45° line give the stationary points. The line OR is the diagram of equation (12.5g) on the assumption that x_{t+1} equals zero, that is, there is no catch at time $t + 1$. The line $O'R'$ is the diagram of equation (12.5g) on the assumption that x_{t+1} equals b, that is, the catch at time $t + 1$ is the largest possible one given the conditions of demand. It has been assumed that there are v^* and v^{**} such that $v° < v^* \leqslant v^{**} < v°°$, and $f(v^*) = f(v^{**}) = b$. In order to determine the actual relation between v_t and v_{t+1}, we need a further element. If there is no v such that $k(v) < p$, then wild salmon can live happily in their environment: nobody will go after them and economists need not investigate the development of their population. OR gives the actual relationship between v_t and v_{t+1} in this case. Assume now that there is a v such that $k(v) \leqslant p$. Then, because of the assumptions entertained with regard to $k(v)$, there is $\hat{v} > 0$ such that $p = k(\hat{v})$ (see Figure 12.3). The actual relationship between v_t and v_{t+1} will coincide with the curve OR for $0 \leqslant v_t < \hat{v}$, with the curve $O'R'$ for $v_t > \hat{v}$, and with the whole segment connecting the two curves for $v = \hat{v}$. Then we can distinguish different cases according to where $\hat{v}$ is located.

(i) If $0 \leqslant \hat{v} < v^{\circ}$, then system (12.5) has a stationary point for $v = v^{**}$, $\pi = k(v^{**})$, $x = b$, $s = 0$, and another stationary point for $v = v^{*}$, $\pi = k(v^{*})$, $x = b$, $s = 0$; but the second one is not stable. A further stationary point is obtained when the population of wild salmon is doomed to death: $v = 0$, $\pi = k(0)$, $x = 0$, $s = b$.

(ii) If $v^{\circ} < \hat{v} < v^{*}$, then system (12.5) has the abovementioned stationary points and two further stationary points: one for $v = v^{\circ}$, $\pi = k(v^{\circ})$, $x = 0$, $s = b$, another for $v = \hat{v}$, $\pi = p$, $x = f(\hat{v})$, $s = b - x$.

(iii) If $v^{*} < \hat{v} < v^{**}$, then system (12.5) has the abovementioned stationary points except the point $v = v^{*}$, $\pi = k(v^{*})$, $x = b$, $s = 0$, and the point $v = \hat{v}$, $\pi = p$, $x = f(\hat{v})$, $s = b - x$.

(iv) If $v^{**} < \hat{v} < v^{\circ\circ}$, then system (12.5) has three of the abovementioned stationary points: one for $v = v^{\circ}$, $\pi = k(v^{\circ})$, $x = 0$, $s = b$, another one for $v = \hat{v}$, $\pi = p$, $x = f(\hat{v})$, $s = b - x$, finally one when the population of wild salmon is doomed: $v = 0$, $\pi = k(0)$, $x = 0$, $s = b$.

(v) If $\hat{v} > v^{\circ\circ}$, then system (12.5) has three stationary points, two of which were mentioned before: one for $v = v^{\circ}$, $\pi = k(v^{\circ})$, $x = 0$, $s = b$, another for $v = v^{\circ\circ}$, $\pi = k(v^{\circ\circ})$, $x = 0$, $s = b$, finally one when the population of wild salmon is doomed: $v = 0$, $\pi = k(0)$, $x = 0$, $s = b$. Therefore, if $\hat{v} > v^{\circ\circ}$, wild salmon are not fished for in the long period; they might, however, be pursued in the short period.

Figure 12.5 gives an example of case (ii). In this figure it is easily shown that if v_t is in a neighborhood of 0, then v_{t+1} will be closer to 0 than v_t. Hence the stationary point related to the case in which the population of wild salmon is doomed is a (locally) stable stationary point. A similar argument can show that the stationary points characterized by the existence of a population of v^{**} and $v^{\circ\circ}$ of wild salmon are also stable. On the contrary, v° and v^{*} are unstable stationary points: if v_t is in a neighborhood of v° (or v^{*}), then v_{t+1} is farther away from v° (v^{*}) than v_t. Figure 12.5 also shows that the dynamics around $\hat{v}$ are complex in cases (ii) and (iv): the path around this stationary point cannot easily be predicted.

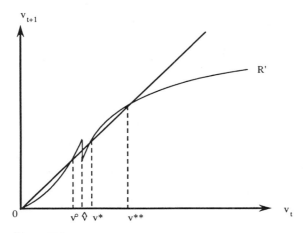

Figure 12.5

The analysis presented here arrives at the conclusion that in the case under consideration there are some significant long-period positions. We shall refrain from investigating model (12.5) any further (but see exercises 6.15 and 6.16). In the analysis presented in this section the natural environment and thus the "carrying capacity" for the resource were assumed to be unchanged over time. This is another strong assumption. Humans might be interested in operating in the environment for reasons not related to catching wild salmon. Moreover, the life of salmon can be affected by all kinds of human activities, productive and others, through their impact on the natural habitat of salmon. These issues, however, are beyond the scope of this book.

4. Exhaustible resources

A renewable resource can be exhausted in the sense that it can be used up completely (or destroyed via the destruction of its environment). However, when we speak of exhaustible resources we commonly refer to resources that are available in given stocks. These stocks can be depleted, and are indeed depleted each time parts of them are actually removed for productive (or consumptive) purposes; they cannot, however, be increased. A characteristic feature of exhaustible resources therefore is that their natural rate of growth is zero (or very close to zero). Typical examples of exhaustible resources are fossil fuels and oil.

In this section we shall first develop a model of production with exhaustible resources. It is obvious that crucial features of the models presented in previous chapters of this book do not carry over to the new analytical framework. This concerns, in particular, the stationarity of prices and the real wage rate, given the rate of profit, and of the proportions in which the commodities are produced. We shall, however, attempt to modify the original approach only to the extent to which it is indispensible, since otherwise the questions asked could not be answered. We shall then, in a second step, illustrate the "working" of the model in terms of a numerical example.

4.1. The model

If an exhaustible resource did not enter into the production of any commodity, we could study its pricing over time as in the model of Section 1 with $k = 0$ and $a = 1$ (see exercises 6.17 and 6.18). Yet several exhaustible resources are important sources of energy, which is needed as an input in all kinds of production processes. Therefore it cannot sensibly be assumed that exhaustible resources do not enter into the production of other commodities. Since it is beyond the scope of this book to provide a detailed analysis of exhaustible resources, we will restrict the following investigation to the introduction of some of the problems involved in dealing with these kind of resources. The argument is based on the following assumptions.

(i) There are s deposits of substances which can enter into the production of some commodity, but cannot be produced; the amounts of these substances which have been utilized cannot be re-utilized anymore (as, for example, land in Chapter 10). These substances will be called exhaustible resources. Each deposit contains one resource, and for each resource there is one deposit. (Therefore, s is also the number of resources: deposits of the same "resource" are dealt with as deposits of different exhaustible resources, and different grades of the same "resource" are also dealt with as different exhaustible resources.) Each resource is available in homogeneous quality and in a quantity which at time 0 is known with certainty. Hence, discoveries of new deposits (or resources) are excluded.

(ii) Innovations in extracting or using a resource are set aside.

(iii) All exhaustible resources are private property.

(iv) Each of these resources is assumed to provide directly or indirectly[6] the same service (thermal units of energy), which can, however, be also produced by solar energy whose energy source does not risk exhaustion in any relevant time frame.

---

[6] Assume, for instance, that electric energy can be produced from oil which is extracted from the ground. The unextracted oil is the resource, whereas the extracted oil is a commodity produced by means of that resource. Then we say that the resource *indirectly* produces energy.

(v) The commodities required annually for consumption are defined by a vector **d**, which, for simplicity, is assumed as given and constant over time, that is, independent of prices and quantities, including the quantities of the exhaustible resources left over. It is assumed that vector **d** is sufficiently small so that it can always be produced by using one of the available techniques. (In particular, it is possible to produce vector **d** without using the exhaustible resources.)

First of all it is necessary to explain why the owners of natural resources do not sell the whole amount they own at current prices in order to invest the proceeds in an industry where the normal rate of profit can be obtained. In other words, the storing of natural resources, which may be considered a "conservation industry," cannot be operated if it does not pay a "royalty" to the owner of the resource. In competitive conditions the size of this royalty must be such that the going rate of profit is earned in the business. As a consequence, natural resources have to be revalued over time, that is, their prices have to increase over time and, therefore, all prices will have to change over time. It goes without saying that in the present case a long-period position, narrowly defined, can be reached only after *all* exhaustible resources used in production *have actually been exhausted*. This would, however, restrict the concept of long period to a vanishing class of cases. In this context it suffices to draw the reader's attention to the fact that the advocates of the long-period method, whether of classical or of traditional neoclassical orientation, were, of course, aware that normal prices are bound to change over time, that is, did not assume stationary conditions of the economic system. However, on the assumption that these changes are sufficiently small between two consecutive periods they were considered negligible in a first step of the analysis. While this may be a useful procedure in many cases we shall, in the following discussion, abandon it and study the changes in prices and quantities over time.

The purpose of the model elaborated in this subsection is to determine the path the economy takes from time zero to time τ, when the quantities of commodities produced in the economy are in what may be called an *ultra*, or ultimate, long-period position and all exhaustible natural resources have indeed been entirely used up. The argument will be developed on the assumption that a uniform and constant rate of profit is obtained in each production activity (however, see, the warnings in Section 1).

Some further warnings concerning the explanatory power of the following model should be added. It hardly needs to be stressed that assumption (i) according to which the amounts of resources are known with certainty is very strong indeed. In everyday experience new deposits are continuously discovered. The opposite extreme would consist in assuming that for each exhausted deposit (resource) another one with the same characteristics is discovered and that the cost of the search (in terms of labor and commodities) is always the same. In this case the resources would not be *exhaustible* and each deposit could in fact be treated as if it were a machine (see Chapters 7 and 9): the price of the new machine equals the cost of the search and the price of an old machine of age *t* equals the value of the deposit after *t* periods of utilization. Since the "resources" would not be exhaustible anymore, their prices would be constant over time, as is commonly assumed in long-period analysis. The difficulty is due to the fact that "reality" is between the two extremes. An analysis of the "realistic" case, however, is beyond the scope of this book.

Assumption (iv) (together with the second part of assumption (v)) is necessary in order to avoid the "end of the world" scenario, on which there is nothing to be said. Although the "end of the world" has repeatedly been forecast (see, for example, the gloomy perspectives entertained by the Club of Rome), it has not yet become a part of the "plan of Providence," to use a term employed by Adam Smith (*TMS*, III.5.7). This is so because assumptions (i) and (ii) do not actually hold good. Seen from this perspective, assumption (iv) may be considered as a sort of simple corrective device to counterbalance assumptions (i) and (ii). It goes without saying that in our view the limitations of the following analysis do not imply that it is useless, but rather that it needs to be improved.

Assume that *n* different commodities are produced in the economy. A process or method of production is defined by a quadruple $(\mathbf{a}, \mathbf{b}, \mathbf{c}, l)$ where $\mathbf{a} \in \mathbb{R}^n$ is the commodity input vector, $\mathbf{b} \in \mathbb{R}^n$ is the output vector, $\mathbf{c} \in \mathbb{R}^s$ is the exhaustible resources input vector, and l is the labor input, a scalar; of course $\mathbf{a} \geqslant 0, \mathbf{b} \geqslant 0, \mathbf{c} \geqslant 0, l \geqslant 0$. It is important to remark that the inputs referred to in vector $\mathbf{c}$ are inputs of the resources *as they are provided by nature*, for example, extracted oil is *not* contained in $\mathbf{c}$, but in $\mathbf{b}$, if $(\mathbf{a}, \mathbf{b}, \mathbf{c}, l)$ is an extraction process, or in $\mathbf{a}$, if $(\mathbf{a}, \mathbf{b}, \mathbf{c}, l)$ is a process that uses it, unless the extraction costs equal zero.

Assume that there are *m* processes. They are defined by quadruplets

$$(\mathbf{a}_j, \mathbf{b}_j, \mathbf{c}_j, l_j). \quad i = 1, 2, \ldots, m$$

Then define matrices $\mathbf{A}$, $\mathbf{B}$, $\mathbf{C}$ and vector $\mathbf{l}$ as follows:

$$\mathbf{A} = \begin{bmatrix} \mathbf{a}_1^T \\ \mathbf{a}_2^T \\ \vdots \\ \mathbf{a}_m^T \end{bmatrix}, \quad \mathbf{B} = \begin{bmatrix} \mathbf{b}_1^T \\ \mathbf{b}_2^T \\ \vdots \\ \mathbf{b}_m^T \end{bmatrix}, \quad \mathbf{C} = \begin{bmatrix} \mathbf{c}_1^T \\ \mathbf{c}_2^T \\ \vdots \\ \mathbf{c}_m^T \end{bmatrix}, \quad \mathbf{l} = \begin{bmatrix} l_1 \\ l_2 \\ \vdots \\ l_m \end{bmatrix}.$$

Since the situation we are analyzing is not a long-period position, prices are changing over time. In order to simplify the notation, let $\mathbf{p}_t$ be the vector of the prices in terms of units of labor commanded available at time $t \in \mathbb{N}_0$, let $\mathbf{y}_t$ be the vector of prices (book values) in terms of units of labor commanded of exhaustible resources available at time $t \in \mathbb{N}_0$, let $\mathbf{x}_t$ be the intensity of operation of processes at time $t \in \mathbb{N}$, and let $\mathbf{z}_t$ be the vector of the amounts of exhaustible resources available at time $t \in \mathbb{N}_0$. In addition, assume the rate of profit to be given and constant. Then the following inequalities and equations are to be satisfied for each $t \in \mathbb{N}_0$:

$$\mathbf{B}\mathbf{p}_{t+1} \leqslant (1+r)(\mathbf{A}\mathbf{p}_t + \mathbf{C}\mathbf{y}_t) + w_{t+1}\mathbf{l}, \tag{12.6a}$$

$$\mathbf{x}_{t+1}^T \mathbf{B}\mathbf{p}_{t+1} = \mathbf{x}_{t+1}^T[(1+r)(\mathbf{A}\mathbf{p}_t + \mathbf{C}\mathbf{y}_t) + w_{t+1}\mathbf{l}], \tag{12.6b}$$

$$\mathbf{y}_{t+1} \leqslant (1+r)\mathbf{y}_t, \tag{12.6c}$$

$$\mathbf{z}_{t+1}^T \mathbf{y}_{t+1} = (1+r)\mathbf{z}_{t+1}^T \mathbf{y}_t, \tag{12.6d}$$

$$\mathbf{x}_t^T \mathbf{B} \geqslant \mathbf{x}_{t+1}^T \mathbf{A} + \mathbf{d}^T, \tag{12.6e}$$

$$\mathbf{x}_t^T \mathbf{B}\mathbf{p}_t = [\mathbf{x}_{t+1}^T \mathbf{A} + \mathbf{d}^T]\mathbf{p}_t, \tag{12.6f}$$

$$\mathbf{z}_t^T \geqslant \mathbf{x}_{t+1}^T \mathbf{C} + \mathbf{z}_{t+1}^T, \tag{12.6g}$$

$$\mathbf{z}_t^T \mathbf{y}_t = [\mathbf{x}_{t+1}^T \mathbf{C} + \mathbf{z}_{t+1}^T]\mathbf{y}_t, \tag{12.6h}$$

$$\mathbf{p}_t \geqslant 0, \mathbf{y}_t \geqslant 0, \mathbf{z}_t \geqslant 0, \mathbf{x}_t \geqslant 0. \tag{12.6i}$$

Inequality (12.6a) means that nobody can get extra profits by producing commodities available at time $t + 1$. Equation (12.6b) implies, because of inequalities (12.6a) and (12.6i), that commodities available at time $t + 1$ will be produced only if the ruling rate of profit is obtained. Inequality (12.6c) means that nobody can get extra profits by storing exhaustible resources from time t to time $t + 1$. Equation (12.6d) implies, because of inequalities (12.6c) and (12.6i), that exhaustible resources will be stored from time t to time $t + 1$ only if the ruling rate of profit will be obtained by this storage activity. Inequality (12.6e) implies that the amounts of commodities produced are not lower than the amounts of commodities required, and equation (12.6f) implies that if an amount is larger, then the price of that commodity is zero. Inequality (12.6g) implies that the amounts of exhaustible resources available at time t are not lower than the amounts of exhaustible resources available at time $t + 1$ plus the amounts of exhaustible resources utilized to produce commodities available at time $t + 1$, and equation (12.6h) implies that if an amount is larger, then the price of that exhaustible resource is zero. The meaning of inequalities (12.6i) is obvious. It has been assumed that the *nominal* wage rate is constant over time and serves as the numeraire, that is,

$$w_t = 1 \quad (t \in \mathbb{N}) \tag{12.6j}.$$

This implies, of course, that if prices are changing over time, then the real wage, that is, the amounts of commodities which a worker can afford, is also changing.[7]

Model (12.6) is not yet complete, since some initial conditions are needed. A first obvious initial condition is that the amounts of exhaustible resources available at time 0 are given, that is,

$$z_0 = \bar{z}. \tag{12.6k}$$

A second initial condition, which is perhaps less obvious, is that the amounts of commodities available at time 0 are given. This can be stated as

$$x_0 = v, \tag{12.6l}$$

where v is a given vector larger than d.

Assumptions (iv) and (v) imply that there are vectors $\bar{x}$ and $\bar{p}$ such that

$$\bar{x}^T(B - A) \geqq d^T,$$
$$\bar{x}^T(B - A)\bar{p} = d^T\bar{p},$$
$$\bar{x}^T C = 0^T,$$
$$B\bar{p} \leqq (1 + r)A\bar{p} + l,$$
$$\bar{x}^T B\bar{p} = \bar{x}^T[(1 + r)A\bar{p} + l],$$
$$\bar{x} \geqq 0, \bar{p} \geqq 0.$$

In the following discussion we will refer to the processes operated at the intensity vector $\bar{x}$ as the *long-period processes*, the other processes not being long-period.

There seem to be only three possible patterns of development of quantities in an economy that is subject to the above premises. First, it operates its long-period processes from the beginning. This would be the case if the system of production using solar energy happened to be the cost-minimizing system, given the rate of profit. Then none of the exhaustible natural resources would ever be used. This case has implicitly

---

[7] A more complex analysis could start from a constant *real* wage rate in terms of a given bundle of commodities h. If w_1 is still the numeraire, then

$$w_t = \frac{h^T p_t}{h^T p_1} \quad (t \in \mathbb{N}).$$

This, however, would require more sophisticated mathematical tools.

been dealt with in earlier chapters of this book, in particular in Chapter 5, which allowed for several alternative techniques, none of which used an exhaustible resource. Second, the system begins by gradually using up some of its exhaustible resources until the point comes at which the use of solar energy proves to be less costly than that of any one of the remaining resources. Finally, it is possible that this point is reached only after all exhaustible resources have already been depleted. However, as we shall see below, in terms of a numerical example, there are other possibilities to be taken into consideration in the present *general* framework.

Obviously, we cannot know in advance the time, call it τ, at which the quantities of commodities produced in the economy will be in their ultimate position. We may, however, conjecture that in period T this will be the case, that is, $T \geqslant \tau$. On this assumption we study the paths of prices and quantities from time 0 to time T. After having carried out the analysis we are in a position to assess whether or not the assumption that $T \geqslant \tau$ holds. Our conjecture is confirmed if there is no non–long-period process which, if operated with the resources available at time T, pays extra profits at prices $\mathbf{y}_T$, $\mathbf{p}_T$, $\mathbf{y}_{T+1}$, $\mathbf{p}_{T+1}$, where $\mathbf{y}_T$ and $\mathbf{p}_T$ are the going prices in period T as determined by the analysis, $\mathbf{y}_{T+1} = (1+r)\mathbf{y}_T$, $\hat{\mathbf{B}}\mathbf{p}_{T+1} = \hat{\mathbf{l}} + (1+r)\hat{\mathbf{A}}\mathbf{p}_T$, and $(\hat{\mathbf{A}}, \hat{\mathbf{B}}, \mathbf{0}, \hat{\mathbf{l}})$ are the long-period processes. If we discover that the conjecture is false, we simply perform the exercise for a larger T. No attempt will be made here to prove that this algorithm actually converges; an example must suffice (see Subsection 4.2). To prepare the ground for it, the following considerations are useful. On the assumption that $T \geqslant \tau$, system (12.6) can be written in the following way, where $0 \leqslant t \leqslant T$:

$$\mathbf{B}\mathbf{p}_{t+1} \leqslant (1+r)(\mathbf{A}\mathbf{p}_t + \mathbf{C}\mathbf{y}_t) + \mathbf{l}, \quad 0 \leqslant t \leqslant T-1 \tag{12.7a}$$

$$\mathbf{x}_{t+1}^T \mathbf{B}\mathbf{p}_{t+1} = \mathbf{x}_{t+1}^T [(1+r)(\mathbf{A}\mathbf{p}_t + \mathbf{C}\mathbf{y}_t) + \mathbf{l}], \quad 0 \leqslant t \leqslant T-1 \tag{12.7b}$$

$$\mathbf{y}_{t+1} \leqslant (1+r)\mathbf{y}_t, \quad 0 \leqslant t \leqslant T-1 \tag{12.7c}$$

$$\mathbf{z}_{t+1}^T \mathbf{y}_{t+1} = (1+r)\mathbf{z}_{t+1}^T \mathbf{y}_t, \quad 0 \leqslant t \leqslant T-1 \tag{12.7d}$$

$$\mathbf{v}^T \geqslant \mathbf{x}_1^T \mathbf{A} + \mathbf{d}^T, \tag{12.7e}$$

$$\mathbf{v}^T \mathbf{p}_0 = [\mathbf{x}_1^T \mathbf{A} + \mathbf{d}^T]\mathbf{p}_0, \tag{12.7f}$$

$$\mathbf{x}_t^T \mathbf{B} \geqslant \mathbf{x}_{t+1}^T \mathbf{A} + \mathbf{d}^T, \quad 1 \leqslant t \leqslant T-1 \tag{12.7g}$$

$$\mathbf{x}_t^T \mathbf{B}\mathbf{p}_t = [\mathbf{x}_{t+1}^T \mathbf{A} + \mathbf{d}^T]\mathbf{p}_t, \quad 1 \leqslant t \leqslant T-1 \tag{12.7h}$$

$$\mathbf{x}_T^T \mathbf{B} \geqslant \bar{\mathbf{x}}^T \mathbf{A} + \mathbf{d}^T, \tag{12.7i}$$

$$\mathbf{x}_T^T \mathbf{B}\mathbf{p}_T = [\bar{\mathbf{x}}^T \mathbf{A} + \mathbf{d}^T]\mathbf{p}_T, \tag{12.7j}$$

$$\bar{\mathbf{z}}^T \geqslant \mathbf{x}_1^T \mathbf{C} + \mathbf{z}_1^T, \tag{12.7k}$$

$$\bar{\mathbf{z}}^T \mathbf{y}_0 = [\mathbf{x}_1^T \mathbf{C} + \mathbf{z}_1^T]\mathbf{y}_0, \tag{12.7l}$$

$$\mathbf{z}_t^T \geqslant \mathbf{x}_{t+1}^T \mathbf{C} + \mathbf{z}_{t+1}^T, \quad 1 \leqslant t \leqslant T-1 \tag{12.7m}$$

$$\mathbf{z}_t^T \mathbf{y}_t = [\mathbf{x}_{t+1}^T \mathbf{C} + \mathbf{z}_{t+1}^T]\mathbf{y}_t, \quad 1 \leqslant t \leqslant T-1 \tag{12.7n}$$

$$\mathbf{p}_t \geqslant \mathbf{0}, \mathbf{y}_t \geqslant \mathbf{0}, \quad 0 \leqslant t \leqslant T \tag{12.7o}$$

$$\mathbf{z}_t \geqslant \mathbf{0}, \mathbf{x}_t \geqslant \mathbf{0}. \quad 1 \leqslant t \leqslant T \tag{12.7p}$$

The above system can be put in a more workable form by introducing the following matrices and vectors:

$$\mathbf{E}(r) = \begin{bmatrix} -(1+r)\mathbf{A} & \mathbf{B} & \mathbf{0} & \cdots & \mathbf{0} & \mathbf{0} \\ \mathbf{0} & -(1+r)\mathbf{A} & \mathbf{B} & \cdots & \mathbf{0} & \mathbf{0} \\ \cdot & \cdot & \cdot & \cdots & \cdot & \cdot \\ \cdot & \cdot & \cdot & \cdots & \cdot & \cdot \\ \mathbf{0} & \mathbf{0} & \mathbf{0} & \cdots & \mathbf{B} & \mathbf{0} \\ \mathbf{0} & \mathbf{0} & \mathbf{0} & \cdots & -(1+r)\mathbf{A} & \mathbf{B} \end{bmatrix},$$

$$\mathbf{G} = \begin{bmatrix} \mathbf{C} & \mathbf{0} & \cdots & \mathbf{0} & \mathbf{0} \\ \mathbf{0} & \mathbf{C} & \cdots & \mathbf{0} & \mathbf{0} \\ \cdot & \cdot & \cdots & \cdot & \cdot \\ \cdot & \cdot & \cdots & \cdot & \cdot \\ \mathbf{0} & \mathbf{0} & \cdots & \mathbf{C} & \mathbf{0} \end{bmatrix},$$

$$\mathbf{F}(r) = \begin{bmatrix} -(1+r)\mathbf{I} & \mathbf{I} & \mathbf{0} & \cdots & \mathbf{0} & \mathbf{0} \\ \mathbf{0} & -(1+r)\mathbf{I} & \mathbf{I} & \cdots & \mathbf{0} & \mathbf{0} \\ \cdot & \cdot & \cdot & \cdots & \cdot & \cdot \\ \cdot & \cdot & \cdot & \cdots & \cdot & \cdot \\ \mathbf{0} & \mathbf{0} & \mathbf{0} & \cdots & \mathbf{I} & \mathbf{0} \\ \mathbf{0} & \mathbf{0} & \mathbf{0} & \cdots & -(1+r)\mathbf{I} & \mathbf{I} \end{bmatrix},$$

$$\mathbf{p} = \begin{bmatrix} \mathbf{p}_0 \\ \mathbf{p}_1 \\ \vdots \\ \mathbf{p}_T \end{bmatrix}, \quad \mathbf{y} = \begin{bmatrix} \mathbf{y}_0 \\ \mathbf{y}_1 \\ \vdots \\ \mathbf{y}_T \end{bmatrix}, \quad \mathbf{h} = \begin{bmatrix} 1 \\ 1 \\ \vdots \\ 1 \end{bmatrix}, \quad \mathbf{z} = \begin{bmatrix} \mathbf{z}_1 \\ \mathbf{z}_2 \\ \vdots \\ \mathbf{z}_T \end{bmatrix},$$

$$\mathbf{x} = \begin{bmatrix} \mathbf{x}_1 \\ \mathbf{x}_2 \\ \vdots \\ \mathbf{x}_T \end{bmatrix}, \quad \mathbf{k} = \begin{bmatrix} \mathbf{d} - \mathbf{v} \\ \mathbf{d} \\ \vdots \\ \mathbf{d} \\ \mathbf{d} + \mathbf{A}^T \bar{\mathbf{x}} \end{bmatrix}, \quad \mathbf{w} = \begin{bmatrix} -\bar{\mathbf{z}} \\ \mathbf{0} \\ \vdots \\ \mathbf{0} \end{bmatrix}.$$

Then system (12.7) can be stated as follows:

$$E(r)\mathbf{p} - (1+r)\mathbf{Gy} \leqslant \mathbf{h}, \tag{12.8a}$$

$$\mathbf{x}^T[E(r)\mathbf{p} - (1+r)\mathbf{Gy}] = \mathbf{x}^T\mathbf{h}, \tag{12.8b}$$

$$F(r)\mathbf{y} \leqslant \mathbf{0}, \tag{12.8c}$$

$$\mathbf{z}^T F(r)\mathbf{y} = 0, \tag{12.8d}$$

$$\mathbf{x}^T E(0) \geqslant \mathbf{k}^T, \tag{12.8e}$$

$$[\mathbf{x}^T E(0)]\mathbf{p} = \mathbf{k}^T\mathbf{p}, \tag{12.8f}$$

$$\mathbf{z}^T F(0) + \mathbf{x}^T \mathbf{G} \geqslant \mathbf{w}^T, \tag{12.8g}$$

$$[\mathbf{z}^T F(0) + \mathbf{x}^T\mathbf{G}]\mathbf{y} = \mathbf{w}^T\mathbf{y}, \tag{12.8h}$$

$$\mathbf{p} \geqslant \mathbf{0}, \mathbf{y} \geqslant \mathbf{0}, \mathbf{x} \geqslant \mathbf{0}, \mathbf{z} \geqslant \mathbf{0}. \tag{12.8i}$$

System (12.8) can easily be transformed into a system similar to system (8.13) of Chapter 8. In order to do so, let us introduce matrix $\mathbf{M}(r)$ and vectors $\mathbf{u}, \mathbf{f}, \mathbf{s}, \mathbf{g}$:

$$\mathbf{M}(r) = \begin{bmatrix} E(r) & -(1+r)\mathbf{G} \\ 0 & F(r) \end{bmatrix}, \quad \mathbf{u} = \begin{bmatrix} \mathbf{p} \\ \mathbf{y} \end{bmatrix}, \quad \mathbf{f} = \begin{bmatrix} \mathbf{h} \\ 0 \end{bmatrix}, \quad \mathbf{s} = \begin{bmatrix} \mathbf{x} \\ \mathbf{z} \end{bmatrix}, \quad \mathbf{g} = \begin{bmatrix} \mathbf{k} \\ \mathbf{w} \end{bmatrix}.$$

Then system (12.8) can be stated as

$$\mathbf{M}(r)\mathbf{u} \leqslant \mathbf{f}, \tag{12.9a}$$

$$\mathbf{s}^T\mathbf{M}(r)\mathbf{u} = \mathbf{s}^T\mathbf{f}, \tag{12.9b}$$

$$\mathbf{s}^T\mathbf{M}(0) \geqslant \mathbf{g}^T, \tag{12.9c}$$

$$\mathbf{s}^T\mathbf{M}(0)\mathbf{u} = \mathbf{g}^T\mathbf{u}, \tag{12.9d}$$

$$\mathbf{u} \geqslant \mathbf{0}, \quad \mathbf{s} \geqslant \mathbf{0}. \tag{12.9e}$$

System (12.9) has the same form as system (8.13) of Chapter 8 (and as system (12.3) of Section 2). It is easily shown (see exercise 6.19) that if there is a nonnegative vector $\bar{\mathbf{x}}$ such that

$$\bar{\mathbf{x}}^T[\mathbf{B} - (1+r)\mathbf{A}] \geqslant \mathbf{d}^T, \quad \bar{\mathbf{x}}^T\mathbf{C} = \mathbf{0}^T, \quad \bar{\mathbf{x}}^T\mathbf{A} \leqslant (1+r)\bar{\mathbf{x}}^T\mathbf{A} \leqslant \mathbf{v}^T - \mathbf{d}^T, \tag{12.10}$$

then system (12.9) (and therefore system (12.7)) has a solution whatever T is.

Let us explore the model presented in this section with the help of a simple numerical example.

4.2. *A numerical example*

Let energy be the only basic commodity in an economy whose technology has only single-product processes of production. The amount of energy consumed plus the amount of energy required to produce all the other (non-basic) commodities is assumed to be equal to unity per year. That is, the economy requires one unit of energy every year (to satisfy "final demand") plus the energy required to produce energy itself. Energy can be produced by using oil, an exhaustible resource obtained at zero extraction cost, or by using solar energy, a non-exhaustible resource. The available processes to produce energy are described in Table 12.1. To rule out the problem of a choice of technique as regards the consumed non-basic products it will be assumed that there is only one process available for each of them. (There is no need to specify the processes producing non-basics.) The amount of oil available at time 0 equals $\frac{3}{4}$ units; the rate of profit is taken to be unity.

We may now distinguish between several cases according to the amount of energy available at time 0. In order to simplify the notation, let x_t be the amount of energy produced at time t by using oil, and let q_t be the amount of energy produced at time t without using oil. Moreover, let p_t be the price of energy available at time t and let y_t be the price of oil available at time t.

Case (i). Assume first that the amount of energy available at time 0 is larger than $\frac{1217}{990}$. It can easily be verified (see exercise 6.20) that if $T = 1$, then $p_0 = y_0 = y_1 = 0, p_1 = 1, x_1 = \frac{10}{9}, q_1 = 0$. Moreover, at prices $p_1 = 1$, $y_1 = y_2 = 0$ and $p_2 = \frac{51}{5}$ the non–long-period process pays extra profits. Therefore we try out a larger T. It can easily be verified (see exercise 6.20) that if $T = 2$, then $p_0 = 0, p_1 = 5, p_2 = 11, y_0 = 4, y_1 = 8, y_2 = 16, x_1 = \frac{227}{198}$, $x_2 = \frac{35}{99}, q_1 = 0, q_2 = \frac{75}{99}$. Moreover, at time 3 the non–long-period process cannot be operated since there is no oil. If we try out a larger T, we will find the following results: $p_0 = 0, p_1 = 5, p_t = \frac{25}{2} - \frac{75}{2}(\frac{1}{5})^t$ for $t \geqslant 2, y_t = 4(2^t)$ for $0 \leqslant t \leqslant 2$, there is no oil for $t \geqslant 3, x_1 = \frac{227}{198}, x_2 = \frac{35}{99}, x_t = 0$ for $t \geqslant 3$, $q_1 = 0, q_2 = \frac{75}{99}, q_t = \frac{10}{9}$ for $t \geqslant 3$. Note that whereas the long-period quantities are obtained in three periods, the long-period price of energy, $\frac{25}{2}$, is obtained for t tending to infinity only. A closer look at the model will reveal that p_0 needs to be zero since an amount of energy is wasted at time 0. This is so because energy cannot be saved, and in order to produce one unit of energy no more than two-tenth-units of energy are required. Note that the energy utilized in production at time 0 is $\frac{1}{5}x_1 = \frac{227}{990}$; since one unit of energy is used to produce the non-basics, at time 0 no more than $1 + \frac{227}{990} = \frac{1217}{990}$ can be required. Hence all available energy exceeding that amount at time 0 is wasted.

Table 12.1

	inputs		outputs
energy	oil	labor	energy
$\frac{1}{10}$	—	10 $\rightarrow$	1
$\frac{1}{5}$	$\frac{1}{2}$	1 $\rightarrow$	1

Case (ii). Let us now explore the model by analyzing the above example on the assumption that $\frac{209}{180} < v < \frac{1217}{990}$. Just to make things less difficult let us, for instance, fix $v = \frac{11}{9}$. It can easily be verified that if $T = 1$, then $p_0 = y_0 = y_1 = 0$, $p_1 = 1$, $x_1 = \frac{10}{9}$, $q_1 = 0$. Moreover, at prices $p_1 = 1$, $y_1 = y_2 = 0$ and $p_2 = \frac{51}{5}$ the non–long-period process pays extra profits. Therefore we try out a larger T. It can easily be verified that if $T = 2$, then $p_0 = \frac{275}{9}$, $p_1 = \frac{145}{9}$, $p_2 = \frac{119}{9}$, $y_0 = \frac{26}{9}$, $y_1 = \frac{52}{9}$, $y_2 = \frac{104}{9}$, $x_1 = \frac{173}{162}$, $x_2 = \frac{35}{81}$, $q_1 = \frac{7}{81}$ and $q_2 = \frac{55}{81}$. Moreover, at time 3 the non–long-period process cannot be operated since there is no oil.

If we try out a larger T, we will find the following results: $p_t = \frac{25}{2} - \frac{325}{18}(\frac{1}{5})^t$ for $t \geq 0$, $y_t = \frac{26}{9}(2^t)$ for $0 \leq t \leq 2$, there is no oil for $t \geq 3$, $x_1 = \frac{173}{162}$, $x_2 = \frac{35}{81}$, $x_t = 0$ for $t \geq 3$, $q_1 = \frac{7}{81}$, $q_2 = \frac{55}{81}$, $q_t = \frac{10}{9}$ for $t \geq 3$. Once again, whereas the long-period quantities are obtained in the third period, the long-period price of energy, $\frac{25}{2}$, is obtained only for t tending to infinity. A closer look at the model will reveal that energy is always produced with the process which does not use oil, and therefore p_t is determined by the difference equation

$$p_{t+1} = 10 + \tfrac{1}{5}p_t,$$

whose solution is

$$p_t = \tfrac{25}{2} + (p_0 - \tfrac{25}{2})(\tfrac{1}{5})^t,$$

where p_0 is a constant to be determined. At the same time the conservation of oil requires that

$$y_t = 2^t y_0,$$

where y_0 is also a constant to be determined. Then p_0 and y_0 are determined in such a way that the process producing energy with oil can be operated in order to produce energy available at time 1 and at time 2.

In view of what has been said so far the reader might suppose that the resource is of necessity exhausted in the first few periods and it is only thereafter that the long-period quantities obtain. However, this need not be so, as the following case shows.

Case (iii). If $\frac{10}{9} < v < \frac{209}{180}$, then energy will be produced for a few periods without utilizing oil, and only in a later period will energy production utilize oil and exhaust the resource. In the limiting case, in which $v = \frac{10}{9}$, the resource will never be used even though its price will always be positive. Assume first that $v = \frac{2001}{18000}$. Table 12.2 gives the prices and quantities for values of T going from 1 to 5. If T is higher, then the values of the last row are confirmed; moreover, oil is exhausted for $t \geq 6$, $p_t = \frac{25}{2} - \frac{14375}{6}(\frac{1}{5})^t$ for $t \geq 0$, $x_t = 0$ for $t \geq 6$, $q_t = \frac{10}{9}$ for $t \geq 6$. Hence, only energy available at times 4 and 5 is produced with oil, whereas energy available before (and afterward) is produced without utilizing oil.

Assume now that $v = \frac{10}{9}$. There is neither enough energy to produce energy with oil and to satisfy demand nor is it possible to increase the available amount of energy from period to period, as it was actually the case when v was taken to equal $\frac{20001}{18000}$. Whatever the T is for which the exercise is performed, we will find that $p_t = \frac{25}{2} + (p_0 - \frac{25}{2})(\frac{1}{5})^t$ for $t \geq 0$, $y_t = 2^t y_0$ for $t \geq 0$, $x_t = 0$ for $t \geq 0$, $q_t = \frac{10}{9}$ for $t \geq 0$, where p_0 and y_0 are not determined, but need to be such that

$$\frac{13}{2} < (p_0 - \frac{25}{2})(\frac{1}{5})^t + 2^t y_0 \quad \text{each } t \in \mathbb{N}_0$$
$$p_0 \geq 0, \text{ and } y_0 \geq 0.$$

A possible solution is $p_0 = \frac{25}{2}$ and $y_0 = 7$. In this case too the energy price, and not only the quantities, are in their long-period position.

It goes without saying that the different patterns of development the model displays, depending on the amount of energy available at time zero, could not have been derived starting from a partial framework, as many analyses in resource economics do, but presupposes a *general* framework. The present considerations thus demonstrate anew that the results derived in a partial setting should be regarded with skepticism and should not be accepted unless confirmed in a general setting.

5. Historical notes

5.1. For a treatment of the short-run behavior of the price of a self-reproducing non-basic, see Salvadori (1990) and Freni (1993).

5.2. Machines of an obsolete type that are still in use are referred to by Sraffa in his book, not in the chapter on fixed capital, but in the final paragraph of the chapter on land. He states: "The quasi-rent (if we may apply Marshall's term in a more restricted sense than he gave it) which is received for those fixed capital items ... is determined precisely in the same way as the rent of land" (Sraffa, 1960, p. 78). In Marshall's *Principles* the term quasi-rent is used "for the income derived from machines and

Table 12.2

T	y_0	y_1	y_2	y_3	y_4	y_5	P_0	P_1	P_2	P_3	P_4	P_5	x_1	x_2	x_3	x_4	x_5	q_1	q_2	q_3	q_4	q_5
1	0	0	–	–	–	–	45	19	–	–	–	–	$\frac{1}{1800}$	–	–	–	–	$\frac{1999}{1800}$	–	–	–	–
2	0	0	0	–	–	–	50	20	14	–	–	–	0	$\frac{1}{180}$	–	–	–	$\frac{667}{600}$	$\frac{199}{180}$	–	–	–
3	0	0	0	0	–	–	825	175	45	19	–	–	0	0	$-\frac{1}{18}$	–	–	$\frac{667}{600}$	$\frac{67}{60}$	$\frac{19}{18}$	–	–
4	0	0	0	0	0	–	4200	850	180	46	$\frac{96}{5}$	–	0	0	0	$\frac{10}{18}$	–	$\frac{667}{600}$	$\frac{67}{60}$	$\frac{7}{60}$	$\frac{10}{18}$	–
5	$\frac{43}{120}$	$\frac{43}{60}$	$\frac{43}{30}$	$\frac{43}{15}$	$\frac{86}{15}$	$\frac{172}{15}$	$\frac{7225}{3}$	$\frac{1475}{3}$	$\frac{325}{3}$	$\frac{95}{3}$	$\frac{49}{3}$	$\frac{199}{15}$	0	0	0	$\frac{73}{162}$	$\frac{85}{81}$	$\frac{667}{600}$	$\frac{67}{60}$	$\frac{7}{6}$	$\frac{62}{81}$	$\frac{5}{81}$

other appliances for production made by man" ([1890] 1977, p. 63). In §6 of chapter VIII of book V, quoting from the Preface to the first edition of the *Principles*, Marshall adds however the following qualification which seems to be more in line with Sraffa's use of the term: "That which is rightly regarded as interest on 'free' or 'floating' capital, or on new investments of capital, is more properly treated as a sort of rent – a *Quasi-rent* – on old investments of capital" (ibid., p. 341). Yet the importance of this qualification is played down again in the immediately following remark that "there is no sharp line of division between floating capital and that which has been 'sunk' for a special branch of production, nor between new and old investments of capital; each group shades into the other gradually." Marshall concludes that "even the rent of land is seen, not as a thing by itself, but as the leading species of a large genus" (ibid., pp. 341–2). On the factors affecting the magnitude of quasi-rents, see Marshall's discussion in chapter VIII of book VI (especially pp. 516–22). For a discussion of Sraffa's concept of quasi-rent, see Schefold (1989, pp. 172–8).

5.3. The existence of renewable and exhaustible resources that constrain human productive activity and the growth of the economy was recognized early in the literature. However, in classical political economy the emphasis was on the scarcity of land as the main barrier to economic growth. Moreover, the idea was widespread that land and other natural resources, whether exhaustible or not, could be dealt with in essentially the same way. This idea is present, for example, in Adam Smith, who in dealing with the problem of the rent of mines clearly invokes the principle of differential rent. In part II of chapter XI of book I of *The Wealth of Nations* he states: "Whether a coal-mine, for example, can afford any rent, depends partly upon its fertility, and partly upon its situation. A mine of any kind may be said to be either fertile or barren, according as the quantity of mineral which can be brought from it by a certain quantity of labour, is greater or less than what can be brought by an equal quantity from the greater part of other mines of the same kind.... There are some [coal-mines] of which the produce is barely sufficient to pay the labour, and replace, together with its ordinary profits, the stock employed in working them. They afford some profit to the undertaker of the work, but no rent to the landlord. They can be wrought advantageously by nobody but the landlord, who being himself the undertaker of the work, gets the ordinary profit of the capital which he employs in it. Many coal-mines in Scotland are wrought in this manner, and can be wrought in no other. The landlord will allow nobody else to work them without paying some rent, and nobody can afford to pay any" (*WN*, I.xi.c.10–13). Basically the same principle is seen at work with regard to renewable resources, such as forests (*WN*, I.xi.c.16).

In David Ricardo's *Principles* the chapter "On Rent" is followed by a chapter "On the Rent of Mines," of barely three pages length. After pointing out that mines, as well as land, generally pay a rent to their owners, Ricardo concludes: "Since this principle [of rent] is precisely the same as that which we have already laid down respecting land, it will not be necessary further to enlarge on it" (*Works* I, p. 85). In this chapter Ricardo also justifies the use of gold and silver as the general media in which the value of all other commodities is estimated, and *a fortiori* the use of the long-period method, in terms of the allegedly "slow and gradual" effects on the costs of production of gold and silver of the exhaustion of old mines, the discovery of new ones and the introduction of improved methods of mining.

Karl Marx in his treatment of rent in mining in the short chapter XLVI of vol. III of *Capital* essentially reiterates the position of the classical economists: "Wherever rent exists at all, differential rent appears at all times, and is governed by the same laws, as agricultural differential rent.... Mining rent proper is determined in the same way as agricultural rent" (Marx, [1894] 1959, pp. 773 and 775).

5.4. Ricardo's approach was also adopted by John Stuart Mill in chapter II of book IV, "Influence of the Progress of Industry and Population on Values and Prices," of his *Principles*. There it is stated: "The only products of industry, which, if population did not increase, would be liable to a real increase of cost of production, are those which, depending on a material which is not renewed, are either wholly or partially exhaustible; such as coal, and most if not all metals; for even iron, the most abundant as well as most useful of metallic products,... is susceptible of exhaustion so far as regards its richest and most tractable ores" (Mill, *Collected Works*, vol. III, [1848] 1965, p. 712). However, in Mill we encounter also, possibly for the first time in the history of economic thought, a glimpse of the idea of rent due to the inherent scarcity associated with a depletable stock such as a body of ore being mined, which became prominent in later discussions. In chapter V of book III Mill points out: "In some instances the owners [of mines] limit the quantity raised, in order not too rapidly to exhaust the mine: in others there are said to be combinations of owners to keep up a monopoly price by limiting the production" (ibid., p. 493). It is interesting to note that the concept of a decelerated exploitation of the body of ore is closely connected to the idea of a collusion among the owners of the different mines. (See also historical note 5.8 below.)

5.5. William Stanley Jevons in *The Coal Question* (1865) dealt at some length with the impact of the gradual exhaustion of Britain's coal mines on domestic economic prosperity and arrived at the pessimistic conclusion:

"While other countries mostly subsist upon the annual and ceaseless income of the harvest, we are drawing more and more upon a capital which yields no annual interest, but once turned to light and heat and motive power, is gone forever into space" (p. 412). As the quotation shows, Jevons drew a clear dividing line between arable land, according to him an inexhaustible natural resource, and stocks of ores beneath the soil. In the long run the wealth of a nation cannot be founded on the latter because of their exhaustibility. Jevons entertained the idea that the prices of the different kinds of coal would rise as the stocks were depleted. He did not discuss, however, how the movement of prices and royalties and the rate of the depletion of stocks are related. Nor did he ask the question how the scarcity value of a stock of useful ore in finite supply is determined.

Alfred Marshall in the *Principles*, taking issue with the treatment of exhaustible resources by the classical economists, stresses that "a royalty is *not* a rent, though often so called. For, except when mines, quarries, etc., are practically inexhaustible, the excess of their income over their direct outgoings has to be regarded, in part at least, as the price got by the sale of stored-up goods – stored up by nature indeed, but now treated as private property; and therefore the marginal supply price of minerals includes a royalty in addition to the marginal expenses of working the mine." He adds: "the royalty itself on a ton of coal, when accurately adjusted, represents that diminution in the value of the mine, regarded as a source of wealth in the future, which is caused by taking the ton out of nature's storehouse" (Marshall, [1890] 1977, p. 364).

5.6. The first author to address the problem of the "optimal" depletion of a deposit appears to have been J. L. Gray (1913, 1914). Gray assumed a given stock of homogeneous ore; mining costs are taken to increase more than proportionately with the amount mined. The maximization of the present value of net proceeds accruing in the course of the extraction of the ore resulted in an "optimal" time pattern of extractions. It also ascribed a maximum present value to the stock in existence at any point in time, and thus also to the stock in existence at the beginning of the initial period. By this token the rent earned by the proprietor of the mine can be determined.

5.7. In 1931 H. Hotelling published his paper "The economics of exhaustible resources" in which he presented what became known as "Hotelling's Rule" (Hotelling, 1931). It concerns the optimality condition regarding the net income maximizing rate of ore depletion for a homogeneous stock and requires that the marginal ton extracted in any period should yield the owner of the mine the same net income, in present value. If this condition is not met, economic agents will strive to exploit arbitrage opportunities: these adjustments result in the economy following what is called a resource-conserving Hotelling path.

5.8. Hotelling's contribution was the starting point of a rapidly growing literature on resource economics. As regards exhaustible resources, emphasis is on the time-path of exhaustion as a problem of intertemporal resource allocation with a given intertemporal utility function expressing time preference. Partial models, taking the prices of all goods other than that of the resource as given, predominate. The costs of extraction are frequently measured in terms of a single variable called "effort" which, *ex hypothesi*, can be ascertained independently of relative prices and income distribution. It is also a rather common feature of this literature that the rate of discount is taken as given and constant over the entire time horizon, which is either finite or infinite. Much of this literature explores the problem in terms of variants of multi-period Arrow–Debreu equilibrium analysis (for a brief summary of crucial features of the latter, see Subsection 5.4 of Chapter 14). The emphasis is mainly on the problem of efficiency rather than existence of equilibrium. Modern literature often suggests that a monopoly extraction path may be welfare superior to the competitive path. (See also the observation by John Stuart Mill reported in historical note 5.4.) For summary statements of the current state of the art and open questions: (i) on renewable resources, see, in particular, Clark (1976), Dasgupta and Heal (1979, ch. 5), A. C. Fisher (1981, ch. 3), Conrad and Clark (1987, ch. 2), and Neher (1990, part III); (ii) on exhaustible resources, see, in particular, Dasgupta and Heal (1979, chs. 6–7 and 10), A. C. Fisher (1981, ch. 2), Conrad and Clark (1987, ch. 3), and Neher (1990, part IV).

5.9. While, as we have seen, Ricardo devoted a separate chapter to exhaustible resources, Sraffa mentions them only in passing and renewable resources not at all: "Natural resources which are used in production, such as land and mineral deposits..." (Sraffa, 1960, p. 74) is the only reference to exhaustible resources to be found in his book.

Exhaustible resources were, however, dealt with by some authors working in the tradition of Sraffa's analysis. A start was made by Parrinello (1983), who questioned the appropriateness of the long-period method in the case under consideration. A more detailed discussion was provided by Schefold (1989, part II, ch. 19b). One of Schefold's concerns was with showing that the theory of exhaustible resources "is of practical relevance only under exceptional circumstances, so that the classicists may be excused for having ignored it by subsuming the incomes of mine owners to the general theory of rent" (ibid., p. 228). Schefold provided altogether four reasons in support of this defense of the approach of the classical authors and Sraffa: (i) the uncertainty concerning the future course of prices; (ii) the unpredictability of the impact of technical progress on the process of extraction; (iii) the relatively slow change of the royalty in any one mine; and (iv) the great importance of cost differentials between mines and thus differential rents in explaining the residual income of mine owners.

His own formalization of the problem is different from that utilized here. The present formulation derives from Salvadori (1987c). The difference consists mainly in the fact that Salvadori (1987c) assumes $\mathbf{p}_0 = \bar{\mathbf{p}}$ instead of equation (12.61). Other formulations have been provided by Gibson (1984), Roncaglia (1983, 1985b), Pegoretti (1986, 1990), and Quadrio Curzio (1983, 1986). See also Gehrke and Lager (1993).

5.10. Another approach to dealing with the problem of the interdependence of economic and environmental systems has been put forward by Nicholas Georgescu-Roegen (1971, 1976). According to him standard economic analysis is fundamentally flawed since it contradicts basic physical laws. In his view what is needed is the formulation of an economics that is in agreement with the laws of thermodynamics, in particular the "Entropy Law." To this effect Georgescu-Roegen developed, among other things, the "flow-fund" model of production as an alternative to both the activity analysis model and the conventional production function model, both of which are said to be unable to tackle the time aspect of production properly. See also the summary statements of Georgescu-Roegen's model in Tani (1986, ch. 7) and Zamagni (1987, section 6.4).

While Georgescu-Roegen was mainly concerned with the Second Law of thermodynamics, the argument of Perrings (1987) rests mainly on the First Law according to which the mass of the global system is fixed: matter can be neither destroyed nor created. All production, whether human or non-human, involves merely the transformation of this fixed mass following physical laws. An early version of this point of view is characteristic of the writings of some of the classical authors. As Marx, referring to Pietro Verri and William Petty, stated: "man can work only as Nature does, that is by changing the form of matter" (Marx, [1867] 1954, p. 50). Perrings considers his approach rooted in the classical tradition.

In more recent years the concept of the "sustainability" of economic activity has played an important role in some of the discussions. For an investigation of problems related to this concept, see, for example, O'Connor (1991).

6. Exercises

6.1. Show that if $(1 + r)a = 1$, then Propositions 12.1–12.3 still hold except that in Proposition 12.2

$$p_h = p - hk \quad h = 0, 1, \dots, T$$

and

$$T = \max \{t \in \mathbb{N} \mid tk \leqslant p\}.$$

6.2. Perform the same analysis of Section 1 on the assumption that $(1 + r)a = 1$. [*Hint*: See previous exercise; $\pi_t = \pi_0 + kt$.]

6.3. In the analysis of Section 1, assume that $v > b \sum_{j=0}^{T-1} a^j$ and $p_T = 0$. Show that the amount of beans to be disposed of at time 0 is not uniquely determined.

6.4. The assumptions of Section 1 hold. Moreover, there is a storage process, that is, a process whose inputs consist of one unit of beans and whose outputs consist of one unit of beans. Draw the analog of Figure 12.1 on the assumption that $p(1 + r)(1 - a) < k$. [*Hint*: Beans may be stored but never produced (why?); determine the analog of Propositions 12.1–12.3.]

6.5. The same as the previous exercise, except that now $p(1 + r)(1 - a) > k$. [*Hint*: Beans are stored for $0 \leqslant \pi_t < k/((1 + r)(1 - a))$, produced for $k/((1 + r)(1 - a)) < \pi_t < p$, and either stored or produced or both for $\pi_t = k/((1 + r)(1 - a))$ (why?); determine the analog of Propositions 12.1–12.3 for the two intervals.]

6.6. Perform the same analysis as the one in Section 1 on the assumptions of exercises 6.4 and 6.5. Show that beans will never be wasted.

6.7. Perform the previous three exercises on the assumption that not all beans can be saved, that is, the inputs of the storage process consist of one unit of beans but its outputs consist of d unit of beans, where $0 < d < 1$. Show that the role played in those exercises by $(1 - a)$ is played here by $(d^{-1} - a)$.

6.8. The assumptions of Section 1 hold. Moreover, there is another process to produce beans. The inputs consist of α units of beans plus basic commodities and labor whose value is κ (including the profit on the basic commodities), the output consists of one unit of beans. Draw the analog of Figure 12.1 on the assumption that $p(1 + r)(\alpha - a) > k - \kappa$. [*Hint*: Determine the analog of Propositions 12.1–12.3; it is better if you have first solved exercises 6.4–6.7.]

6.9. Show that inequality (12.4b) has always a nonnegative solution. [*Hint*: The difficulty consists of the fact that $\mathbf{h}$ is not necessarily nonnegative; use the form of matrix $\mathbf{E}(0)$ and the fact that each row of $\mathbf{A}_2$ has at least one positive element; let $\mathbf{g}_{t^*} = \mathbf{0}$, then let $\mathbf{g}_{t^*-1}$ be such that $(1 + r)\mathbf{A}_2\mathbf{g}_{t^*-1} + \mathbf{k} \geqslant \mathbf{0}, \ldots$, then let $\mathbf{g}_0$ be such that $(1 + r)\mathbf{A}_2\mathbf{g}_0 + \mathbf{k} - \mathbf{B}_2\mathbf{g}_1 \geqslant \mathbf{0}$.]

6.10. In the analysis of Section 2, show that if (i) each process utilizing obsolete machines may produce either one obsolete machine or none and must utilize one obsolete machine, (ii) for each obsolete machine there is at least one process utilizing it and for each obsolete machine *older than one year* there is at least one process producing it, then the prices of obsolete machines are independent of the time period and of **v**, provided that obsolete machines are in short supply. [*Hint*: The processes which

	obsolete machines inputs		other expenses (including profits)		outputs	
	m_3	m_4			corn	m_4
(1)	1	—	4	$\rightarrow$	1	1
(2)	—	2	6	$\rightarrow$	1	—
(3)	1	—	—	$\rightarrow$	—	1
(4)	1	—	—	$\rightarrow$	1	—
(5)	—	1	—	$\rightarrow$	—	1

Table 12.3

utilize t^* year old machines uniquely determine the price of a t^* year old machine; then, recursively....]

6.11. If corn, a non-basic non-utilized in production, is produced with non-obsolete machines, its price is 6.2 in terms of a numeraire consisting of basic commodities only. But there are 5 units of machine m_3 and 1 unit of machine m_4, which can also be utilized to produce corn: processes (1)–(2) of Table 12.3 are available and machines not utilized in production are (freely) disposed of. Corn is not utilized in production and four units of corn are required for consumption each year. Show that if the rate of profit is uniform and equal to 10 percent ($r = 0.1$), then over time machines m_3 and m_4 are exhausted and prices and produced quantities must satisfy the following inequalities and equations, where π_t is the price of corn at time t, p_{it} is the price of machine m_i at time t, x_{it} is the intensity of operation of the process utilizing machine m_i at time $t-1$, and s_t is the amount of corn produced with a non-obsolete machine at time t.

$$\pi_1 + p_{41} \leqslant 1.1 p_{30} + 4, \tag{12.11a}$$

$$x_{31}[\pi_1 + p_{41}] = x_{31}[1.1 p_{30} + 4], \tag{12.11b}$$

$$\pi_{t+1} \leqslant 2.2 p_{4t} + 6, \quad t = 0, 1 \tag{12.11c}$$

$$x_{4,t+1}\pi_{t+1} = x_{4,t+1}[2.2 p_{2t} + 6], \quad t = 0, 1 \tag{12.11d}$$

$$\pi_t \leqslant 6.2, \quad t = 1, 2 \tag{12.11e}$$

$$s_t \pi_t = 6.2 s_t, \quad t = 1, 2 \tag{12.11f}$$

$$x_{1t} + x_{2t} + s_t \geqslant 4, \quad t = 1, 2 \tag{12.11g}$$

$$(x_{1t} + x_{2t} + s_t)\pi_t = 4\pi_t, \quad t = 1, 2 \tag{12.11h}$$

$$x_{31} \leqslant 5, \tag{12.11i}$$

$$x_{31}p_{30} = 5p_{30}, \tag{12.11j}$$

$$x_{41} \leqslant 1, \tag{12.11k}$$

$$x_{41}p_{40} = p_{40}, \tag{12.11l}$$

$$x_{42} \leqslant 2x_{31}, \tag{12.11m}$$

$$x_{42}p_{41} = 2x_{31}p_{41}. \tag{12.11n}$$

6.12. Solve the inequalities and equations of the previous exercise; show that the annual charge of an obsolete machine can be negative and provide an economic interpretation of this.

6.13. Given the other assumptions of exercise 6.11 assume in addition that machines not utilized in production can be stored, but they become older anyway, that is, process (3) is also available. Determine the analog of system (12.11) and solve it. [*Hint*: The annual charges of obsolete machines cannot be negative.]

6.14. Given the other assumptions of exercise 6.11 assume in addition that machines not utilized in production can be stored with no effect on them, that is, processes (4) and (5) are also available. Determine the analog of system (12.11) and solve it. [*Hint*: More than two periods are needed; the annual charges of obsolete machines are positive.]

6.15. Introduce in the analysis of Section 3 two further processes producing salmon, one by means of wild salmon, the other by means of produced salmon. Show that if the rate of profit is uniform, then over time prices and produced quantities must satisfy the following inequalities and equations, where π_t is the price of wild salmon at time t, p_t is the price of produced salmon available at time t, x_t is the amount of wild salmon caught at time t, s_t is the amount of salmon produced at time t by means of produced salmon, y_t is the amount of salmon produced at time t by means of produced salmon. (What are a and b?)

$$\pi_{t+1} \leqslant k(v_t),$$

$$x_{t+1}\pi_{t+1} = x_{t+1}k(v_t),$$

$$p_{t+1} \leqslant (1+r)ap_t + b,$$

$$s_{t+1}p_{t+1} = s_{t+1}[(1+r)ap_t + b],$$

$$p_{t+1} \leqslant (1+r)a\pi_t + b,$$

$$y_{t+1}p_{t+1} = y_{t+1}[(1+r)a\pi_t + b],$$

$$x_t\pi_t \leqslant x_t p_t,$$

$$(s_t + y_t)\pi_t \geqslant (s_t + y_t)p_t,$$

$$x_t + s_t + y_t \geqslant b + a(s_{t+1} + y_{t+1}),$$
$$(x_t + s_t + y_t)\pi_t = [b + a(s_{t+1} + y_{t+1})]\pi_t,$$
$$(x_t + s_t + y_t)p_t = [b + a(s_{t+1} + y_{t+1})]p_t,$$
$$v_{t+1} = v_t + f(v_t) - x_{t+1},$$
$$v_t \geqslant 0, \quad \pi_t \geqslant 0, \quad x_t \geqslant 0, \quad s_t \geqslant 0, \quad y_t \geqslant 0.$$

6.16. In the model of the previous exercise, assume $r = 0$, $a = 0.25$, $b = 50$, $k(v) = 100 - v$, $v_0 = 61$, $f(v_t) = -0.5v_t$ if $0 \leqslant v_t \leqslant 20$, $f(v_t) = v_t - 30$ if $20 \leqslant v_t \leqslant 30$, $f(v_t) = 15 - 0.5v_t$ if $v_t \geqslant 30$. Show that a solution exists such that $y_2 > 0$, $y_t = 0$ each $t \neq 2$. Show that another solution exists such that $y_3 > 0$, $y_t = 0$ each $t \neq 3$. In the first solution $x_1 > 0$, $x_t = 0$ each $t \neq 1$, $s_t > 0$ each $t > 2$. In the second solution $x_t > 0$ each $t \leqslant 2$, $s_t > 0$ each $t \geqslant 3$. What happens to wild salmon in the two solutions?

6.17. Show that if $a = 1$ and $k = 0$, then Propositions 12.1–12.3 still hold except that in Propositions 12.2 and 12.3 $b \sum_{j=0}^{h} a^j = (h + 1)b$. What does this imply for T?

6.18. Perform the same analysis of Section 1 on the assumption that $a = 1$ [*Hint*: See the previous exercise; $x_t = v - bt$; $T^* = \min\{t \in \mathbb{N} \mid v \leqslant (t + 1)b\}$.]

6.19. Show that if there is a nonnegative vector $\bar{\mathbf{x}}$ such that inequalities (12.10) hold, then system (12.9) has a solution. [*Hint*: $\mathbf{M}(r)\mathbf{0} \leqslant \mathbf{f}$; $\mathbf{y}^T \mathbf{M} \geqslant \mathbf{g}^T$, where

$$\mathbf{y}^T = (\bar{\mathbf{x}}^T, \bar{\mathbf{x}}^T, \dots, \bar{\mathbf{x}}^T, \mathbf{0}^T, \mathbf{0}^T, \dots, \mathbf{0}^T).]$$

6.20. Work out the calculations relative to Case (i) of Subsection 4.2.

6.21. Work out the calculations relative to Case (ii) of Subsection 4.2.

6.22. Work out the calculations relative to Case (iii) of Subsection 4.2.

13

Production as a circular flow and the concept of surplus

In Chapter 1 and in the Historical Notes of the subsequent chapters an attempt was made to lay bare the origins of the concepts used in the present book and to provide a brief summary of the historical development of the ideas and arguments contained in the main text. While these notes may prove useful for a better understanding of some of the roots of the approach elaborated, they cannot, scattered and sparse as they are, replace a pointed discussion of the analytical tradition to which the present investigation belongs. This chapter is designed to make good that lacuna. The emphasis is on the conceptualization of production as a *circular* flow and the related concept of social *surplus*. In contradistinction, in Austrian and in much of neoclassical analysis, production is conceived of as a *linear* flow which leads from the services of the primary factors of production to final goods. The neoclassical theory of production and income distribution will be dealt with in Chapter 14.

A major concern will be with the two main intellectual sources of the present book: Piero Sraffa's *Production of Commodities by Means of Commodities* (1960) and John von Neumann's essay "Über ein ökonomisches Gleichungssytem und eine Verallgemeinerung des Brouwerschen Fixpunktsatzes" (1937) ["A Model of General Economic Equilibrium" (1945)], and the tradition in the history of economic thought to which these belong. As the reader will have noticed, the approach chosen in this book is essentially a "cross-breed" of the analyses of Sraffa and von Neumann. The discussion of the relationship between the contributions by Sraffa and von Neumann seems to be all the more necessary since they are frequently regarded as belonging to vastly different or even diametrically opposed traditions in economic thought.

The structure of the chapter is as follows. Section 1 deals with the origins and early formulations of the concept of production as a circular flow.

As will be shown, this concept provided both the basis for the theory of value and distribution and the theory of quantities (or sectoral proportions) and growth. Section 2 summarizes the further developments of this concept by Ladislaus von Bortkiewicz and Georg von Charasoff who took Marx's schemes of reproduction and his labor-value based theory of the rate of profit and prices of production as their starting point. Section 3 is devoted to Wassily Leontief's conceptualization of the economy as a circular flow and his contributions to the input–output analysis. In Section 4 Robert Remak's device of "superimposed prices" will be scrutinized; these prices, if adopted by the economic system, allow each sector of the economy to replace its used up means of production and the means of consumption in the support of the producers employed in the sector. Section 5 deals with two themes which at first sight might be regarded as falling somewhat outside the scope of the general argument in this chapter: (i) the Rule of Free Goods in alternative approaches to the theory of value and distribution; and (ii) the treatment of the problem of the choice of technique in earlier authors and the use of inequalities. However, the relevance of this discussion will become clear in Section 6 which is dedicated to an analysis of the von Neumann growth model. It will be argued that the latter belongs to the "classical" tradition of economic thought. This interpretation is confirmed in Section 7 in which it is shown, first, that the conventional "neoclassical" interpretation does not stand up to examination, and, second, that there are reasons to consider von Neumann's model as containing, among other things, an answer to his colleague Remak. Section 8 deals with Sraffa's contribution and the revival of the "classical" approach, while Section 9 contains a comparison of the analyses of Sraffa and von Neumann.

1. Origins of the concept of production as a circular flow

Before we deal with the origins of the concept of production as a circular flow, it is worth pointing out that this concept was explicitly adopted by von Neumann and Sraffa. The former stressed that it is a characteristic feature of his approach that "goods are produced not only from 'natural factors of production', but in the first place from each other," that is, the processes of production may be "circular" (von Neumann, 1945, p. 1). Similarly Sraffa, whose book is concerned with what its title says: the production of commodities by means of commodities. In appendix D, "References to the Literature," Sraffa emphasized that the view of the system of production and consumption as a "circular process" to be found in earlier authors "stands in striking contrast to the view presented by modern theory, of a one-way avenue that leads from 'Factors of production' to 'Consumption goods'" (Sraffa, 1960, p. 93).

1.1. Early contributions

The concept of production as a circular flow, and the related concept of the surplus product, can be traced back to the very beginnings of classical political economy (see also Gilibert, 1987, and Chapter 1). It is present as early as in the works of William Petty and Richard Cantillon and was given a clear two-sectoral expression in the *Tableau Economique* of François Quesnay. The concept surfaces in the writings of Adam Smith; it is put into sharp relief in David Ricardo's *Essay on the Influence of a Low Price of Corn on the Profits of Stock* published in 1815 (cf. Ricardo, *Works* VI), in Ricardo's *Principles* (cf. Ricardo, *Works* I) and in the second edition of Robert Torrens's *Essay on the External Corn Trade* (cf. Torrens, 1820). In these early formulations the two problems which were to absorb the energies of generations of economists are already clearly visible. First, there is the problem of *quantity* for which a structure of the levels of operations of processes is needed in order to guarantee the reproduction of the means of production employed in the course of production and the satisfaction of the needs and wants of the different classes of society (perhaps making allowance for the growth of the system). Secondly, there is the problem of *price* for which a structure of exchange values of the different commodities is needed in order to guarantee a distribution of income between the different classes of society consistent with the repetition of the productive process on a given (or an increasing) level in conditions of free competition.

A clear statement of the two problems is provided, for example, by Torrens.[1] He also makes it clear that the concept of surplus provides the key to an explanation of shares of income other than wages and the *rate* of profit. In the *Essay* he determines the agricultural rate of profit in physical terms and takes the exchange value of manufactured goods relatively to corn to be adjusted so that the same rate of profit obtains in manufacturing:

> If an agricultural capital consisting of fifty quarters of corn as seed, and fifty quarters as food, can raise a produce of one hundred and fifty quarters, then a manufacturing capital employed for the same period, and consisting of fifty quarters of corn as food, with

---

[1] On Torrens's contribution see also Schefold (1981, section 4) and de Vivo (1985, 1986).

fifty cwt of raw flax, equal in productive cost and therefore in value to fifty quarters, will fabricate a quantity of cloth equivalent to one hundred and fifty quarters of corn (Torrens, 1820, p. 361).

Torrens continues:

Hence it may be laid down as a *general principle*, that in whatever proportion the quantity of produce obtained from the soil exceeds the quantity employed in raising it, in that proportion the value of manufactured goods will exceed the values of the food and material expended in preparing them (ibid.; emphasis added).

Torrens acknowledges his indebtedness to Ricardo's "original and profound inquiry into the laws by which the rate of profits is determined" (Torrens, 1820, p. xix).[2]

1.2. More general models

It was, of course, clear to the older authors that the capital advanced in a sector is never homogeneous with the sector's product. As Malthus stresses in a letter to Ricardo: "In no case of production, is the produce exactly of the same nature as the capital advanced. Consequently we can never properly refer to a *material rate of produce*"; hence "it is not the particular profits or rate of produce upon the land which determines the general profits of stock" (cf. Ricardo, *Works* VI, pp. 117–18; emphasis added). Does Malthus's objection imply that far from being "general," the principle upon which Ricardo's and Torrens's approach to the explanation of profits rests is extremely special and breaks down as soon as more general cases are concerned?

The following argument shows that Malthus's objection can be taken care of, at least under conditions in which the different sectors of the economy exhibit the same input proportions. Therefore, the applicability of the principle is not limited to the case in which there is only one sector which is in the special position of not using the products of other sectors while all the others must use its product as capital. This is illustrated by Torrens in his *Essay on the Production of Wealth*, published in 1821, in terms of the following schema of the production of commodities by means of commodities:

Let us suppose that there exists a society consisting of one hundred cultivators, and one hundred manufacturers, and that the one

---

[2] Torrens's "general principle" is of course the same thing as the "basic principle" referred to by Sraffa in his discussion of Ricardo's early theory of profits (cf. Sraffa, 1951, p. xxxi). See the Historical notes of Chapter 3.

hundred cultivators expend one hundred quarters of corn and one hundred suits of clothing, in raising two hundred and twenty quarters of corn, while the one hundred manufacturers expend one hundred quarters of corn and one hundred suits of clothing, in preparing two hundred and twenty suits (Torrens, 1821, pp. 372–3).

Torrens concludes that the rate of profit is given in terms of the "surplus" left after the amounts of the used up means of production and the means of subsistence in the support of laborers have been deducted from the gross output. With the surplus and the social capital consisting of the same commodities in the same proportions, the rate of profit can be determined without having recourse to the system of relative prices. Torrens makes it clear that in the simple case under consideration, in which both sectors require the same amounts of both commodities per unit of output, the exchange ratio of the two commodities is 1:1, that is, it springs directly from the physical schema.

However, the physical schema is not only important for the determination of relative prices, it also provides the basis for assessing the potential for expansion of the economy. As Torrens stresses, "this surplus, or profit of ten per cent. they [that is, the cultivators and manufacturers] might employ either in setting additional labourers to work, or in purchasing luxuries for immediate enjoyment" (ibid., p. 373). If in each sector the entire surplus were to be used for accumulation purposes in the same sector, then the rates of expansion of the two sectors would be equal to one another and equal to the rate of profit. Champernowne (1945, p. 10) in his commentary on von Neumann's growth model was later to call a constellation of equi-proportionate growth a "quasi-stationary state."

According to Marx "the system of the physiocrats is the first systematic conception of capitalist production" (Marx, [1885] 1956, p. 364). The two basic aspects distinguished above, that of quantities and that of prices, are also present in Marx's analysis. Indeed, the notion of production as a circular flow is used by Marx both in his "schemes of reproduction" in volume II of *Capital* (ibid., part III) and in his discussion of the so-called transformation of values into prices of production in volume III (cf. Marx, [1894] 1959, part II). However, although Marx stresses the physical aspect of reproduction, his formulation of the system of production is in terms of labor-value magnitudes and not, as for example in Torrens, in terms of commodities or use values. In his treatment of the aspect of quantities Marx is concerned with studying under which conditions the system is capable of reproducing itself either on the same or an upward spiralling level, that is, the case of "simple" and that of "extended reproduction." He shows that an expansion of the economy at a given and constant rate of growth is possible, where this rate depends on the proportion of the surplus value accumulated, that is, ploughed back into the productive system to increase its scale of operation.

As is well known, Marx's labor-value based reasoning is logically flawed (see the brief discussion in Subsection 2.3 of Chapter 1). However, he is to be credited with having shown clearly that the classical theory of distribution and normal prices, and of growth and quantities, have a common origin in the concepts of social surplus and production as a circular flow. Torrens and Marx can indeed be said to have anticipated the essence of the duality relationship between the two sets of variables emphasized by later theorists and particularly by von Neumann. As Morishima stresses: "It is indeed a great surprise to find that many of von Neumann's novel ideas were clearly stated in *Capital*" (Morishima, 1973, p. 8).

2. **Further developments: Von Bortkiewicz and von Charasoff**

The concept of production as a circular flow and that of the surplus product where further developed by Ladislaus von Bortkiewicz, Georg von Charasoff, Wassily Leontief, and Robert Remak, to name but some of the most important authors. Several of these contributions came from authors of Russian origin and derived directly from a critical investigation of Marx's analysis. This is the case, for example, with regard to the contributions of von Bortkiewicz and von Charasoff which will be summarized in this section (see also Seraphim, 1925, and Gilibert, 1991).

2.1. *Ladislaus von Bortkiewicz*

Von Bortkiewicz was born in 1868 in St Petersburg into a family of Polish descent. From 1901 to the year of his death, 1931, he taught economics and statistics at the University of Berlin, the same university which in the late twenties also had Wassily Leontief, John von Neumann, and Robert Remak among its members. In 1906 von Bortkiewicz entered the stage with the first of his three-part treatise "Wertrechnung und Preisrechnung im Marxschen System"; the remaining two parts followed in the subsequent year (von Bortkiewicz, 1906–7 I, II, and III) [parts II and III were translated into English as "Value and Price in the Marxian System" (see von Bortkiewicz, 1952)]. In 1907 his paper "Zur Berichtigung der grundlegenden theoretischen Konstruktion von Marx im dritten Band des 'Kapital'" (von Bortkiewicz, 1907) ["On the Correction of Marx's Fundamental Theoretical Construction in the Third Volume of 'Capital'" (see von Bortkiewicz, 1952)] was published.

A major source of inspiration for von Bortkiewicz was the formalization of Ricardo's theory of distribution and "natural" prices provided by

Vladimir K. Dmitriev. Dmitriev was born near Smolensk in the same year as von Bortkiewicz and is considered the first Russian mathematical economist (see Nemchinov, 1964, and Nuti, 1987). In 1898 Dmitriev published an essay (in Russian) on the theory of value in Ricardo. (On Dmitriev's contribution see the Historical notes of Chapter 6.) Von Bortkiewicz elaborated on Dmitriev's formalization and used the tools forged by his precursor in his critique of Marx's theory of value and distribution.

The main objects of von Bortkiewicz's contributions can be summarized as follows. First, he wants to demonstrate that Marx's construction of necessity failed. Second, he is concerned with showing that value analysis is not an indispensable step on the way to a consistent theory of the rate of profit and prices of production. Third, and notwithstanding what has just been said, he wants to show that prices and the rate of profit can be related to value and surplus value magnitudes in a logically impeccable way. Fourth, this leads him to a rejection of the then dominant critique of Marx which erroneously took the value-based reasoning in itself rather than Marx's mistaken use of it as the source of various misconceptions: as the title of the second paper indicates, von Bortkiewicz aims at the "correction" rather than the refutation of Marx's construction. Finally, and perhaps most importantly, von Bortkiewicz attempts to show that Ricardo's doctrine is superior to Marx's in almost every respect. His treatise is indeed as much about Ricardo as it is about Marx. He accuses Marx of variously retrogressing to opinions which had already been shown to be defective by Ricardo. There is a single exception though: "If there is a point of general importance, in which Marx in a certain respect turns out to be superior to Ricardo, then it is the doctrine of the *origin of profits*" (1906–7 III, p. 472; von Bortkiewicz's emphasis).

Von Bortkiewicz points out that the *data* from which the classical approach to the theory of value and distribution starts are sufficient to determine the rate of profit and relative prices; no additional data are needed to determine these variables. (On the data, see Subsection 2.4 of Chapter 1.) He develops his argument both in terms of an approach in which it is assumed that commodities are obtained by a finite stream of labor inputs (von Bortkiewicz, 1906–7), and one in which production is circular (von Bortkiewicz, 1907). Following Dmitriev, whom he praises for his innovative work (cf. 1906–7 II, pp. 34–9), von Bortkiewicz casts his argument in algebraic form. Considering the set of price equations associated with a given system of production with n commodities, it is recognized that the number of unknowns exceeds the number of equations by two: there are $n + 2$ unknowns (n prices, the nominal wage rate, and the rate of profit) and n equations. With the real wage rate given from outside the system and fixing a standard of value or numeraire, one gets two additional equations (and no extra unknown) and the system can be solved for the rate of profit and prices in terms of the numeraire. Von Bortkiewicz then derives a number of results, some of which are already to be found in Dmitriev, while others are new. One of his concerns is with fixed capital; he derives the following results. (i) The annual charge of a fixed capital good which operates with constant efficiency is equal to a fixed annuity (1906–7 II, pp. 29–32). (ii) A formula for the reduction to dated quantities of labor can also be found in the case of fixed capital. (iii) Contrary to Marx's opinion and in agreement with Ricardo's, the rate of profit depends exclusively on the conditions of production in the wage goods industries and in those industries that directly or indirectly provide them with means of production.[3] (iv) According to the approach adopted by Marx, which von Bortkiewicz dubbs "successivist" (ibid., p. 38), the determination of the general rate of profit and prices of production proceeds in two steps. First, the general rate of profit is ascertained: it is here that the labor theory of value is taken to be indispensable, because it allows the determination of the rate of profit as the ratio between total surplus value and social capital, that is, magnitudes that are independent of the variables to be ascertained. In a second step this "value rate of profit" is then used to calculate prices, starting from labor values. However, as von Bortkiewicz demonstrates, Marx's "successivism" is generally untenable: it cannot be presumed that once the "transformation" of values into prices has been carried out, the "price rate of profit", that is, the one where both the surplus product and the social capital are evaluated in price terms, equals the value rate of profit. Hence there is a contradiction.[4] Confirming a finding by Dmitriev, von Bortkiewicz concludes that the rate of profit and prices of production must be determined *simultaneously* (1906–7 II, pp. 37–8; 1907).

As we have seen, von Bortkiewicz was predominantly concerned with the price and distribution aspect, while the quantity and growth aspect was given little attention by him. It was von Charasoff who pointed out a fundamental duality between the two.

---

[3] Ironically, as von Bortkiewicz stresses, the correct view fits much better with Marx's concept of the origin of profits: "If it is true that the level of the rate of profits in no way depends on the conditions of production of those commodities which do not enter wages, then it should be fairly clear that the origin of profits is to be sought in the wage relation and not in the positive impact of capital on productivity" (1906–7 III, p. 446).

[4] This was already pointed out by M. Tugan-Baranovsky (1905), who concluded that only the price rate of profit matters. Tugan-Baranovsky's contribution was approvingly referred to by von Bortkiewicz (1906–7 I, pp. 41 et seq.).

2.2. Georg von Charasoff

Georg von Charasoff was born in Tiflis in 1877. He wrote his Ph.D. thesis in mathematics at the University of Heidelberg and then appears to have lived the life of an independent scholar. He published two books in 1909 and 1910, respectively (see von Charasoff, 1909 and 1910), both in German, the second of which, *Das System des Marxismus: Darstellung und Kritik*, is of particular interest to us. In it von Charasoff anticipated several results of modern reformulations of the classical approach to the theories of value, distribution and growth. However, because of his highly condensed and abstract argument, which is essentially mathematical without making use of formal language, his contribution was largely ignored at the time of its publication and has only recently been rediscovered.[5]

Von Charasoff corroborates the main results obtained by von Bortkiewicz and puts forward several new ones. He develops his main argument within the framework of an interdependent model of (single) production, which exhibits all the properties of the later input–output model, and which is fully specified in terms of use values and labor needed per unit of output.

The central concept of his analysis is that of a "series of production" (*Produktionsreihe*): it consists of a sequence, starting with any (semipositive) net output vector (where net output is defined exclusive of wage goods), followed by the vector of the means of production and the means of subsistence in the support of workers needed to produce this net output vector, then the vector of the means of production and the means of subsistence needed to produce the previous vector of inputs, and so on. Von Charasoff calls the first input vector "capital of the first degree" (*Kapital erster Ordnung*), the second input vector "capital of the second degree" (*Kapital zweiter Ordnung*), etc. This series "has the remarkable property that each element of it is both the product of the following and the capital of the preceding element; its investigation is indispensable to the study of all the theoretical questions in political economy" (von Charasoff, 1910, p. 120).

The series under consideration is closely related to the expanded Leontief inverse (see Subsection 4.2). Let **y** denote the *n*-dimensional vector of net outputs and **A** the $n \times n$ matrix of the "augmented" input coefficients, that is, each coefficient represents the sum of the respective material and wage good input per unit of output, since von Charasoff, like the classical economists and Marx, reckoned wage payments among capital advances.[6]

---

[5] The credit goes to Egidi and Gilibert (1984); for a summary statement of von Charasoff's contribution, see Kurz (1989, pp. 44–6).

[6] If $(\mathbf{A}^*, \mathbf{l})$ is a technique as defined in Chapter 5 and **b** is the vector of commodities consumed per unit of labor employed, then $\mathbf{A} = \mathbf{A}^* + \mathbf{l}\mathbf{b}^T$.

Then the series is given by

$$\mathbf{y}^T, \mathbf{y}^T\mathbf{A}, \mathbf{y}^T\mathbf{A}^2, \ldots, \mathbf{y}^T\mathbf{A}^k, \ldots$$

With circular production this series is infinite. What else can be said about it? Tracing it backward: first, all commodities that are "luxury goods" disappear from the picture; next, all commodities that are specific means of production needed to produce the luxury goods disappear; then the specific means of production needed in the production of these means of production disappear, etc. On the implicit assumption that none of the commodities mentioned so far enters in its own production, "it is clear that from a certain finite point onward no further exclusions have to be made, and all the remaining elements of the series of production will always be made up of the selfsame means of production, which in the final instance, are indispensable in the production of all the different products and which therefore will be called *basic products* (*Grundprodukte*)." Von Charasoff adds: "The whole problem of price boils down...to the determination of the prices of these basic products. Once they are known, the prices of the means of production used in the production of luxuries and finally also the prices of the latter can be derived" (ibid., pp. 120–1). The analysis has therefore to focus primarily on the conditions of production of the basic products.

A further property of the "series of production" deserves to be stressed: the capital of the second degree $(\mathbf{y}^T\mathbf{A}^2)$ is obtained by multiplying the capital of the first degree $(\mathbf{y}^T\mathbf{A})$ by $\mathbf{A}$. "Yet since the physical composition of a sum of capitals is obviously always a medium between the physical compositions of the summands, it follows that capitals of the second degree deviate from one another to a smaller extent than is the case with capitals of the first degree" (ibid., p. 123). The farther one goes back in the "series of production," the more equal the compositions of the capitals become, that is, capitals of a sufficiently high degree "may practically be seen as different quantities of one and the same capital: the *original* or *prime capital* (*Urkapital*)." This finding is of the utmost importance for determining the rate of profit and the maximum rate of growth of the system. For it turns out that "this original type, to which all capitals of lower degree converge, possesses the property of growing in the course of the process of production without any qualitative change, and that the rate of its growth gives the general rate of profits" (ibid., p. 124).

The rate of profit can thus be ascertained in terms of a comparison of two quantities of the same composite commodity: the "original capital." Let $\mathbf{u}$ designate the n-dimensional vector of an elementary unit of the "original capital," $\mathbf{u} \geqslant \mathbf{0}$, then $\mathbf{u}^T\mathbf{A}$ is the (original) capital corresponding to $\mathbf{u}^T$, and we have

$$\mathbf{u}^T = (1 + r)\mathbf{u}^T\mathbf{A}, \qquad\qquad (13.1)$$

with r as the general rate of profit. Von Charasoff emphasizes: "The original capital expresses the idea of a surplus-value yielding, growing capital in its purest form, and the rate of its growth appears in fact as the general capitalist profit rate" (ibid., p. 112). And: "The original capital is nothing else than the basic production, whose branches are taken in particular dimensions. As regards these dimensions the requirement is decisive that gross profits of the basic production...are of the same type as its total capital" (ibid., p. 126). This finding can be said to generalize Torrens's "general principle" (or the "basic principle" referred to by Sraffa; see the historical notes of Chapter 3): it relies neither on the existence of a single sector whose capital is physically identical with its product and whose product is used by all sectors as an input nor on the special case in which all sectors exhibit the same input proportions.[7]

These considerations provide the key to a solution of the problem of price. For, if the various capitals can be conceived of "as different amounts of the selfsame capital...", then prices must be proportional to the dimensions of these, and the problem of price thus finds its solution in this relationship based on law" (ibid., p. 123). Let $\mathbf{p}$ designate the n-dimensional vector of prices, $\mathbf{p} \geqslant \mathbf{0}$, then we have the following system of price equations

$$\mathbf{p} = (1 + r)\mathbf{A}\mathbf{p}. \qquad\qquad (13.2)$$

Thus, while $\mathbf{u}$ equals the left-hand eigenvector of $\mathbf{A}$, $\mathbf{p}$ equals the right-hand eigenvector; $1/(1 + r)$ equals the dominant eigenvalue of matrix $\mathbf{A}$. The solution to the price problem can therefore be cast in a form, in which "the notion of labor is almost entirely by-passed" (ibid., p. 112). Implicit in this reasoning is the abandonment of the labor theory of value as a basis for the theory of relative prices and the rate of profit: taking the technical conditions of production and the real wage rate as given, prices both of basics and of non-basics and the general profit rate can be determined without having recourse to labor values.

With von Neumann ([1937] 1945), von Charasoff shares a concern with the potential for equi-proportionate expansion in the production of all

---

[7] Von Charasoff's construction also bears a close resemblance to Saraffa's device of the Standard system in which the rate of profit "appears as a ratio between quantities of commodities irrespective of their prices" (Sraffa, 1960, p. 22). See Subsection 4.3 of Chapter 4.

commodities. In the hypothetical case in which all profits are accumulated, the proportions of the different sectors equal the proportions of the original capital. In this case the actual rate of growth equals the rate of profit: the system expands along a von Neumann ray. Von Charasoff was perhaps the first author to note clearly what more than two decades later von Neumann was to call "the remarkable duality (symmetry) of the monetary variables (prices p_j, interest factor β) and the technical variables (intensities of production q_i, coefficient of expansion of the economy α)" (von Neumann, 1945, p. 1).

3. Wassily Leontief and input–output analysis

Leontief was born in 1906 in the same town as von Bortkiewicz, St Petersburg (cf. Dorfman, 1987). After his studies at the university of his home town, then Leningrad, he went to Berlin to work on his doctorate under the supervision of von Bortkiewicz. In 1928 he published a part of his thesis titled "Die Wirtschaft als Kreislauf."[8] In it Leontief put forward a two-sectoral input–output system which was designed to describe the production, distribution, and consumption aspects of an economy as a single process. In 1932 Leontief joined the faculty at Harvard University and began with the construction of the first input–output tables of the American economy. These tables together with the corresponding mathematical model were published in 1936 and 1937 (see Leontief, 1941; see also Leontief, 1987). In this section we shall deal first with Leontief's 1928 article and then provide a summary statement of the closed and open input–output model.

3.1. The economy as a circular flow

In his Ph.D. thesis Leontief advocates the view that economics should start from "the ground of what is objectively given (*dem Boden der objektiven Gegebenheit*)" (Leontief, 1928, p. 583); economic concepts are meaningless and potentially misleading unless they can be observed and measured. Leontief adopts what he called a "naturalistic" perspective (ibid., p. 622; the English translation [p. 211] speaks of a "material" perspective). The starting point of the then going marginalist approach, that is, the *homo oeconomicus*, is considered inappropriate because it gives too much room to imagination and too little to facts (ibid., pp. 619–20). Economic analysis should rather focus on the concept of circular flow

---

[8] An English translation titled "The Economy as a Circular Flow" which, however, omits certain passages, was published in 1991; see Leontief (1991). In the following discussion the English version will be used whenever this is possible. Page numbers in square brackets refer to the latter.

which expresses one of the fundamental "objective" features of economic life. The "technological" point of view need not contradict the "economic" one. On the contrary, a meticulous investigation of the "technological" aspect is an indispensable prerequisite to any economic reasoning, for it provides the basis on which a theoretical edifice can be erected.

Leontief distinguishes between "cost goods" and "revenue goods," that is, inputs and goods satisfying final demand. Throughout his investigation he implicitly assumes single production and constant returns to scale; scarce natural resources are mentioned only incidentally. That is, the argument is developed within the confines of what was to become known as the Nonsubstitution Theorem (see Subsection 4.3 of Chapter 1). In much of the analysis it is also assumed that the system of production (and consumption) is indecomposable. Leontief suggests (ibid., p. 585) that the process of production should be described in terms of three sets of "technical coefficients": (i) "cost coefficients," that is, the proportion in which two cost goods h and k participate in the production of good i (in our notation: a_{ih}/a_{ik}); (ii) "productivity coefficients," that is, the total quantity produced of good i in relation to the total quantity used up of the jth input (in our notation: $1/a_{ij}$); (iii) "distribution coefficients," that is, the proportion of the total output of a certain good allotted to a particular point in the scheme of circular flow; as is explained later in the paper, such a point may represent a particular group of property income receivers. A major concern of Leontief's is with a stationary system characterized by constant technical coefficients; in addition he discusses cases in which one or several coefficients change, thereby necessitating adjustments of the system as a whole. We shall set aside the second problem and focus attention on the "reproduction" aspect only.

Starting from a physically specified system of production-cum-distribution, Leontief sketches the concept of vertical integration (ibid., p. 589) and, referring back to Adam Smith, expounds the concept of the reduction to dated quantities of labor (ibid., pp. 596 and 621–2) (see also Sections 1 and 2 of Chapter 6). As regards the latter, he points out that because of the circular character of production "a complete elimination of a factor of production from the given system is in principle impossible. Of course, the size of the 'capital factor' can be reduced to any chosen level by referring back to even earlier periods of production" (ibid., p. 622 [p. 211]).[9] Leontief, like Dmitriev three decades earlier, emphasizes that this reduction has nothing to do with an historical regress: "the entire process must be carried out on the basis of the production scheme in force at any one moment" (ibid., p. 596, fn. 6 [p. 192 fn]).

[9] Interestingly, the formulation used by Sraffa (1960, p. 35) is similar to Leontief's.

Next Leontief addresses the problem of the exchange relationships. Emphasis is on "the general conditions which must be fulfilled within the framework of a circular flow" (ibid., p. 598 [p. 193]). Leontief expounds:

> The total output, i.e. the sum of the individual intermediate outputs from all stages of production within a single production period, is distributed over individual spheres of ownership (*Eigentumsbereiche*) in such a manner that further production cannot take place within individual stages of production. A redistribution must take place by means of specific acts of exchange: this will assemble into cost groups complying with the existing cost structure all those goods needed to continue the circular flow (*'produktionsfähige' Kostengruppen*). The question arises of which exchange proportion will enable this grouping to take place (ibid., p. 598 [p. 194]).

The concept of "value" adopted here is explicitly qualified as one which has nothing to do with any intrinsic property of goods; it rather refers to the "exchange relation deduced from all the relationships...analysed so far" (ibid.). Leontief then explains his concept in terms of a model with two goods. The "relations of reproduction" are tabulated as follows:

$$aA + bB \to A$$
$$(1 - a)A + (1 - b)B \to B,$$

where A and B give the total quantities produced of two, possibly composite, commodities, and a and b [$(1 - a)$ and $(1 - b)$] give the shares of those commodities used up as means of production and means of subsistence in the first (second) sector.

The model just presented is formally identical with the first system of production Sraffa discusses in his book (1960, p. 3). Incidentally, Sraffa calls these relations "the methods of production and productive consumption." However, the systems are interpreted differently by the two authors. While Sraffa contemplates a pure subsistence economy, Leontief refers to stationary conditions only. This difference in interpretation becomes clear when Leontief turns to the question of the distribution of the product implicit in the above relations.

Leontief in fact assumes that a part of the product of each sector is appropriated by a so-called ownership group. He expounds: "In the general circular flow scheme, income from ownership is of course considered alongside other cost items without the slightest direct reference to how it originates (the phenomenon of ownership). It is the task of interest theory to investigate these fundamental relationships" (ibid., p. 600 [p. 196]). His argument, which is not always easy to follow, results in setting up price equations which reflect the going rule that fixes the distribution of income.[10] Counting unknowns and equations, Leontief finds that the price system is indeterminate since the number of variables exceeds the number of equations by one. He concludes: "No clear resolution of this problem is possible. One may vary at will the exchange proportions and consequently the distribution relationships of the goods without affecting the circular flow of the economy in any way" (ibid., pp. 598–9 [p. 194]). In other words, the same quantity system is compatible with different price systems reflecting different distributions of income (similarly Sraffa, 1960, p. 11). Hypothetical variations of the latter are, of course, possible only to the extent to which they do not endanger the survival of the economic system; in a narrowly defined subsistence economy no such variation would be possible. Later in the paper Leontief makes it clear that the existence of property income presupposes a surplus product left after making allowance for the requirements of reproduction, which are defined inclusive of the necessary subsistence: "The sense of the surplus theory (*Ueberschußtheorie*) is represented by the classical school (e.g. even by Ricardo) and ... is best understood if one enquires into the use of this 'free' income. The answer is: it either accumulates or is used up unproductively" (Leontief, 1928, p. 619 [p. 209]).

Hence the exchange ratios of goods reflect not only "natural," that is, essentially technological, factors, but also "social causes." Given the rate of interest together with the system of production and productive consumption, prices can be determined and can be shown to equal total unit costs. "But this is the 'law of value' of the so-called objective value theory" (ibid., p. 601 [p. 196]), Leontief concludes.

3.2. Input–output analysis

While Leontief conceived of his early contribution as being firmly rooted in the classical tradition, he called his input–output method developed in the 1930s and 1940s "an adaptation of the neo-classical theory of general equilibrium to the empirical study of the quantitative inter-dependence between interrelated economic activities" (Leontief, 1966, p. 134). Scrutiny shows, however, that in his input–output analysis he preserved the concept of circular flow and did not, as is maintained by some interpreters, adopt the Walras–Cassel view of production.[11] In the second

---

[10] Von Bortkiewicz who was Leontief's supervisor was not entirely happy with the latter's argument. In a confidential appraisal of the Ph.D. thesis von Bortkiewicz called some of Leontief's theoretical constructs "very doubtful"; see Leontief's introductory note to the English version of his 1928 paper (Leontief, 1991, p. 179).

[11] For a characterization of the Walras–Cassel point of view, see Subsection 7.1.

edition of *The Structure of American Economy*, published in 1951, he explicitly rejected the view of production as a one-way avenue that leads from the services of the "original" factors of production: land, labor, and capital – the "venerable trinity" – to final goods (Leontief, 1951, p. 112). Unlike the theories of Walras and Cassel, in Leontief there are no given initial endowments of these factors. We shall refrain from speculating about the reasons for the change in Leontief's characterization of his own approach which seems to have occurred after Leontief's move from Europe to the United States.[12]

Input–output analysis is meant to provide a detailed, that is, disaggregated, quantitative description of the structural characteristics of all component parts of a given economic system.[13] The interdependence between the different sectors of a given system is described by a set of linear equations; the numerical magnitude of the coefficients of these equations reflect the system's structural properties. The coefficients are ascertained empirically; they are commonly derived from statistical input–output tables which describe the flow of goods and services between the different sectors of a national economy over a given period of time, usually a year. All entries in these tables are supposed, at least in principle, to represent quantities of specific goods or services. In static input–output analysis the input coefficients are generally assumed to be constant, that is, independent of the overall level and composition of final demand. The problem of the choice of technique, which plays an important role in classical and neoclassical analysis, is generally given only slight attention. It goes without saying that the main concern of input–output analysis is not with the elaboration of a coherent theoretical economics but with providing a useful tool for empirical research.

(i) The closed Leontief model. When all sales and purchases are taken to be endogenous, the input–output system is called "closed." In this case final demand is treated as if it were an ordinary industry: the row associated with it represents the "inputs" it receives from the various industries, and the corresponding column giving the value added in the various industries is assumed to represent its "output" allocated to these industries. With $\mathbf{A}$ as the nonnegative "structural matrix" of an economy giving both the material input requirements and final demand,[14] and $\mathbf{x}$ as the n vector of

---

[12] For a comparison of Leontief's approach and that of Walras, and the different traditions to which the two belong, see Gilibert (1981).

[13] For an overview of input–output analysis, see Leontief (1966, 1987), Miller and Blair (1985), and Pasinetti (1977, ch. 4).

[14] Leontief formulates his argument in terms of the transpose of matrix $\mathbf{A}$. We shall in the following discussion stick to the formulation adopted earlier in this book.

gross outputs, the closed input–output model is given by the linear homogeneous system

$$\mathbf{x}^T = \mathbf{x}^T\mathbf{A},$$

that is,

$$\mathbf{x}^T(\mathbf{I} - \mathbf{A}) = \mathbf{0}.$$

This model is discussed in Leontief (1941). As we have seen in Chapter 4, in order for the system of equations to have nonnegative solutions, the largest real eigenvalue of matrix $\mathbf{A}$ must be unity.[15] The price system which is dual to the above quantity system is

$$\mathbf{p} = \mathbf{A}\mathbf{p}, \tag{13.3}$$

that is,

$$(\mathbf{I} - \mathbf{A})\mathbf{p} = \mathbf{0}.$$

The problem of the existence of a (non-negative) solution of system (13.3) was first investigated by Remak (1929); his contribution will be dealt with in Section 4.

(ii) The open Leontief model. In the second edition of Leontief (1941), which was published a decade later, Leontief elaborated the "open" input–output model which treats the technological and the final demand aspects separately. Now $\mathbf{A}$ represents exclusively the matrix of interindustry coefficients and $\mathbf{y}$ the vector of final demand, which is given from outside the system. The matrix of input coefficients is then used to determine the sectoral gross outputs as well as the necessary intersectoral transactions that enable the system to meet final demand and reproduce all used up means of production. The equation describing the relationship between $\mathbf{x}$ and $\mathbf{y}$ is

$$\mathbf{x}^T\mathbf{A} = \mathbf{y}^T = \mathbf{x}^T,$$

that is,

$$\mathbf{x}^T(\mathbf{I} - \mathbf{A}) = \mathbf{y}^T.$$

---

[15] This does not mean that the economy is unable to produce a surplus. In fact, if $(\mathbf{A}^*, \mathbf{I})$ is a technique as defined in Chapter 5, then

$$\mathbf{A} = \begin{bmatrix} \mathbf{A}^* & \mathbf{I} \\ \mathbf{v}^T & h \end{bmatrix},$$

where $\mathbf{v}$ is the vector of values added per unit of output, and h is the input of labor in households per unit of labor employed. Therefore, if the largest eigenvalue of matrix $\mathbf{A}^*$ is not larger than 1, then the definitions of $\mathbf{v}$ and h imply that the largest eigenvalue of matrix $\mathbf{A}$ equals 1.

On the assumption that the inverse of matrix $(\mathbf{I} - \mathbf{A})$ exists, we get as the general solution of the open input–output model

$$\mathbf{x}^T = \mathbf{y}^T(\mathbf{I} - \mathbf{A})^{-1}.$$

The "Leontief inverse matrix" $(\mathbf{I} - \mathbf{A})^{-1}$ is semipositive if the largest real eigenvalue of matrix $\mathbf{A}$ is smaller than unity (cf. Chapter 4). With $\mathbf{l}$ as the vector of direct labor inputs, the corresponding total (that is, direct and indirect) labor requirement, L, equals

$$L = \mathbf{x}^T\mathbf{l} = \mathbf{y}^T(\mathbf{I} - \mathbf{A})^{-1}\mathbf{l}.$$

As to the determination of prices in the open input–output model, Leontief proposes a set of "value-added price equations." The price each productive sector is assumed to receive per unit of output equals the total outlays incurred in the course of its production. These outlays comprise the payments for material inputs purchased from the same or other productive sectors plus the *given* "value added." Assuming a closed economy without a government, the latter represents payments to the owners of productive factors: wages, rents, interest and profits. The price system which is dual to the above quantity system is given by

$$(\mathbf{I} - \mathbf{A})\mathbf{p} = \mathbf{v},$$

where $\mathbf{p}$ is the n vector of prices and $\mathbf{v}$ is the vector of values added per unit of output. Solving for $\mathbf{p}$ gives

$$\mathbf{p} = (\mathbf{I} - \mathbf{A})^{-1}\mathbf{v}.$$

The main problem with this approach is that the magnitudes of value added per unit of output in the different sectors cannot generally be determined prior to and independently of the system of prices. Another way of putting it is that in this formulation two things are lost sight of: the constraint binding changes in the distributive variables, and the dependence of relative prices on income distribution – facts stressed by Leontief in his 1928 paper.[16]

We now turn to the contribution of Robert Remak. As we have seen, Leontief's 1928 analysis was limited to the case with only two commodities. One year later Remak published a paper titled "Kann die Volkswirtschaftslehre eine exakte Wissenschaft werden?" ["Can Economics Become

---

[16] It should be noted, however, that the above price system played a not very important role in theoretical investigations and a negligible one in practical applications.

an Exact Science?"], generalizing the price system to the n commodity case, $n \geqslant 2$ (Remak, 1929).[17]

4. Remak on "superposed prices"

Robert Remak, born in 1888, studied mathematics with Georg Frobenius and H. A. Schwarz. In 1929 he acquired the *venia legendi* in mathematics at the University of Berlin and was a *Privatdozent* there until 1933. John von Neumann was a *Privatdozent* at the same university from 1927 to 1929 (see Ulam, 1958). Remak died in the concentration camp at Auschwitz.

According to the information gathered by Wittmann from some of Remak's former friends and colleagues, Remak was in all probability stimulated by a group of economists around von Bortkiewicz to study the problem of the conditions under which positive solutions of systems of linear equations obtain (cf. Wittmann, 1967, p. 401). His 1929 paper was a result of these studies.

4.1. Methodological issues

Remak begins his paper (Remak, 1929, p. 703) with a definition of what he means by an exact science which bears a close resemblance to Leontief's "naturalistic" point of view: an exact science regards as "exactly correct" only what can be ascertained by physical observation, counting or calculation. He then applies this definition to economics, which he tends to equate with Marshallian demand and supply analysis[18]; his concern is particularly with the demand side. He argues:

> All existing approaches in theoretical economics always start from these [demand] functions, which characterize the buyer's behavior at different prices. However, since this behavior can be neither experimentally nor theoretically ascertained quantitatively, there is no way to get from these theories to practical calculations. We will therefore take into consideration approaches which result in quantitative calculations that can also be carried out practically (ibid., pp. 711–12).

[17] Of Remak's paper only the greater part of the third section dealing with the existence problem of price equilibrium is available in English (cf. Baumol and Goldfeld, 1968, pp. 271–7). Hence the motivation of his paper and its economic reasoning are largely unknown in the English-speaking world. In Section 4 we shall summarize the main argument.

[18] Marshall's *Principles of Economics* is the only book referred to in the entire paper (cf. ibid., p. 709, fn.). Therefore, the foundation of the view conveyed by Baumol and Goldfeld (1968, p. 267) that Remak aimed at pointing out "a serious gap in Walras' argument" is unclear.

The alternative–Remak suggests – are what he calls "superposed price systems" (*superponierte Preissysteme*): "A superposed price system has nothing to do with values. It only satisfies the condition that each price covers the prices of the things required in production, and the consumption of the producer on the assumption that it is both just and feasible" (ibid., p. 712).[19] Its calculation obviously requires a detailed knowledge of the socio-technical relations of production, that is, the methods of production in use and the needs and wants of producers (ibid., pp. 712–13).

For most of the paper, and particularly in its third part which formalizes the argument, Remak assumes a stationary economy. Yet he makes it clear that this is but a first step toward an analysis of a dynamic economic system, that is, one evolving over time: while a stationary economy can be represented by a single point in what Remak calls the "economic phase space" made up of a finite number of economic coordinates, a developing economy involves "a moving point which in the phase space describes a curve" (ibid., p. 717).

4.2. "Superposed prices"

Remak then constructs "superposed prices" for an economic system in which there are as many single-product processes of production as there are products, and each process or product is represented by a different "person."[20] It would not affect the logic of the argument, if the term "person" were to be replaced by the term "industry" or "activity" (see also Wittmann, 1967, p. 404). The amounts of the different commodities acquired by a person over "a certain period of time, that is, a year," in exchange for its own product, are of course the amounts needed as means of production to produce this product, given the technical conditions of production, and the amounts of consumption goods in support of the person (and its family), given the levels of sustenance. With an appropriate choice of units, the resulting system of "superposed prices" can be written as

$$\mathbf{p} = \mathbf{A}\mathbf{p}, \tag{13.4}$$

---

[19] In an addendum to his paper published in 1933, Remak stresses: "A price does not emerge from supply and demand, it is rather a number which has to satisfy certain conditions. The price of a commodity must cover the prices of the expenses contained in it including the cost of living, which may be taken to be known, of the people participating in its production. This leads to the superposed price systems" (1933, p. 840). Remak also talks of " 'reasonable' prices" (*"vernünftige"* Preise).

[20] The somewhat unfortunate phrasing of the problem by Remak may have been the source of the misconception that his concern was with a pure exchange economy; for this interpretation, see Gale (1960, p. 290) and Newman (1962, p. 60).

where **A** is the augmented matrix of inputs (means of production and consumption) per unit of output, and **p** is the vector of exchange ratios. Remak then discusses system (13.4) and arrives at the conclusion that there is a solution to it which is semipositive and unique except for a scale factor.[21]

Model (13.4) refers to a kind of ideal economy with independent producers, no wage labor and hence no profits; it thus bears a close resemblance to Marx's concept of "simple commodity production." However, it could also be interpreted as reflecting a socialist economic system.[22] Indeed, as Remak stresses, "the *main task* of an exact economics would consist in deciding between these two views by means of exact instruments of calculation" (1929, p. 704; emphasis added): reference is to the socialist versus the capitalist point of view.

According to Remak there are two problems to be solved here. First, whether an appropriate price system for a socialist economy can be found. Without being able to demonstrate that a system of "'reasonable' prices" actually exists, the socialist alternative would be deprived of its rational basis: "These prices... represent a 'necessary' condition in the mathematical sense for an efficient economy exempt from unemployment and crises to exist" (Remak, 1933, p. 840). Remak takes pride in having shown with his concept of "superposed prices" that such a solution in fact exists and how it can be determined. The second and much more difficult problem concerns the comparative assessment of the economic efficiency of capitalism and socialism, respectively. In his view the problem boils down to the question of whether the modern capitalist economy is "extremal," that is, whether it fully uses its productive potential or forgoes production possibilities. In view of unemployment and idle plant and equipment Remak sees reason to conjecture that it fails on this account (1929, pp. 706, 721–2).

Although Remak's discussion is occasionally rather cloudy, two closely connected causes are singled out as being responsible for the malfunctioning of the capitalist economy: first, the role money plays in the system, and second, the distribution of income and thus purchasing power between capital owners and workers. Scrutiny shows that Remak advocates some kind of underconsumption-cum-miscalculation explanation of effective demand failures. He stresses repeatedly "that a wrong method of calculation gives rise to a lack of sales and thus prevents the realisation of a technically

---

[21] It should be mentioned that Remak does not make use of the mathematical tools provided by Perron and his own former teacher Frobenius.

[22] The view that system (13.4) is open to alternative interpretations is especially emphasized by Remak in his second paper (1933, p. 840).

feasible additional production" (ibid., p. 733–4). Hence, in Remak the investigation of alternative schemes of price formation serves the purpose of finding out whether "an economy which is perceived to be both just and efficient (*zweckmäßig*) can be brought about by appropriate directions regulating the formation of prices of all commodities" (ibid., p. 724). In his second article, which was written under the impact of the Great Depression, Remak concludes that it can be surmised "that the system of 'reasonable' prices would allow merchants to apply only much lower mark ups than the usual ones, which would lead in effect to putting a severe curb on profits" (1933, p. 841).

5. The problem of the choice of technique and the Rule of Free Goods

As has been argued in Chapter 1, in analyzing the problem of value and distribution the classical economists proceeded in two steps. They first investigated an economy using a *given* system of production. Then they addressed the problem – *which* system of production, or technique, will be adopted by cost-minimizing producers from a given set of alternatives. Our analysis of contributions to the concept of production as a circular flow was thus so far concerned with the first aspect only. In this section we deal with the second aspect. In addition, we shall attempt to trace the origin of the Rule of Free Goods in the history of economic thought. This section prepares the ground for an analysis of the von Neumann model, in Section 6, and a discussion of alternative interpretations of its character, in Section 7. In the course of the following argument we shall take the opportunity to question some received opinions regarding the originality of ideas.

5.1. The use of inequalities

The problem of the choice of technique can be divided into two sub-problems: (i) Which methods of production should be chosen from a given set of alternative methods? (ii) Should a newly available method of production be adopted? Problem (i) is investigated, for example, in chapter 2 of Ricardo's *Principles*, "On Rent." Emphasis is on which kinds of land (or methods of production) will be used in order to produce given outputs. With free competition the problem of the choice of technique consists of finding, given the real wage rate, a cost-minimizing system of production, including the cultivation of land, for which commodity prices, rents and the rate of profit are nonnegative and no process yields extra profits. Problem (ii) – in modern parlance, whether an invention will become an innovation – is investigated in chapter 31, "On Machinery." There Ricardo also provides, albeit in a rudimentary form, an analysis of the transition of the economy from one long-period position to another. Initially the capitalist "who made the discovery of the machine, or who first usefully applied it, [would make]...great profits for a time" (*Works* I, p. 387), that is, would pocket "extra" or "surplus" profits." Competition would then bring about a fall in prices to costs of production and force other capitalists to adopt the superior method of production. The adjustment process would eventually establish a new long-period position characterized by a new system of production and the associated new levels of the rate of profit, of real wages, and of prices (similarly Smith, *WN*, I.x.b.43). Ricardo was thus also concerned with investigating the logical generation of a long-period position of the economy.[23]

Only a few years after the publication of the third edition of Ricardo's *Principles* in 1821 a group around William Whewell at the University of Cambridge applied "symbolic language...to the solution of some problems in Political Economy" (Tozer, 1838, p. 507).[24] This included the treatment of the problem of the choice of technique in algebraic terms employing *in*equalities. Whewell in a paper published in 1831 investigates the case where a given amount of commodities can be produced either by direct labor alone, without the assistance of machinery, that is, what Ricardo called "unassisted labour," or by labor operating a machine that lasts for only a year and is itself the product of a series of labor inputs. He demonstrates that "the machine can be employed without loss" if (in Whewell's notation)

$$l + l' + l'' + \&c. < L$$

(Whewell, 1831, p. 20), where the left-hand side of the inequality gives the direct and indirect amount of labor needed to produce the given output by means of the machine, while the right-hand side gives the amount of unassisted labor required with the alternative method of production. Thus, Whewell adds, "when machinery is employed, it has always cost less labour than would obtain the same produce without machinery" (ibid.). John Edward Tozer, whose algebraic formulation is more sophisticated, follows Whewell in using inequalities in the discussion of the problem of the choice of technique. Summarizing his argument in terms of p and p_1, that is, the price of produce before and after the introduction of machinery, he writes:

[23] Therefore, it is misleading to characterize the classical approach as one which is exclusively concerned with "a fixed economic universe" and thus "cannot account for the generation of an equilibrium because it refers to an empirically unique observed economy" (Punzo, 1991, p. 15).

[24] On Whewell and the group of mathematical economists, see Campanelli (1982) and Henderson (1985).

"It may be observed that p_1 cannot be $> p$; if it were, more than the ordinary profit would arise from employing labour, and the machine would be superseded" (ibid., p. 512).

The classical approach to the problem of the choice of technique in terms of extra profits and extra costs was also adopted by Karl Marx. His discussion of the falling tendency of the rate of profit in Volume III of *Capital* starts from the premise: "No capitalist ever voluntarily introduces a new method of production, no matter how much more productive it may be,... so long as it reduces the rate of profit" (Marx, [1894] 1959, p. 264). Yet if no capitalist ever "voluntarily" does so, how is it then possible that the general rate of profit declines? Marx's answer reads as follows. While a capitalist who first employs a new method of production that allows him to produce at lower costs per unit of output will reap extra profits, competition will eventually lead to the general adoption of the new method and bring about a fall in prices. It is this fall in prices which, according to Marx, is the proximate reason why the general rate of profit is bound to fall in consequence of the gradual replacement of an old method of production by a new one.

Marx's analysis is of particular interest since it was the focus of a criticism elaborated by Ladislaus von Bortkiewicz in the final part of his three-part treatise "Wertrechnung und Preisrechnung im Marxschen System" (von Bortkiewicz, 1906–7), in which another formalization of the problem of the choice of technique in terms of inequalities is provided. Since we are not aware of any evidence showing that von Bortkiewicz was familiar with the writings of Whewell or Tozer, we may credit him with the independent introduction of a new tool in economic analysis. Compared with the discussions of his precursors, von Bortkiewicz's is more interesting from an economic point of view.

Von Bortkiewicz accuses Marx of having committed an elementary error by not taking into account that the price changes "affect the product in the same measure as the capitalist's advances" (1906–7 III, p. 458). He then demonstrates in terms of some simple models of production that the introduction and generalization of a new method of production can never reduce the rate of profit, given the real wage rate, and will raise it if the new method contributes directly or indirectly to a cheapening of wage goods (cf. ibid., pp. 454–68).[25] The comparison of two methods by means of which a commodity can be produced is carried out on the premise "that prices (and thus also the price expression of the commodity bundle constituting the real wage) are still the old ones" (ibid., p. 457). The criterion adopted is whether a method incurs extra costs or yields extra profits: if

---

[25] This finding anticipates the essence of the Okishio theorem (see Okishio, 1963).

it incurs extra costs it will not be adopted; if it yields extra profits it will be introduced and will gradually replace the old method.

5.2. *The Rule of Free Goods*

Next, we discuss the Rule of Free Goods in earlier authors. This rule is meant to cope with a special aspect of the problem of the choice of technique (see also the discussion in Section 5 of Chapter 7). A distinction has to be made between the application of this rule (i) to "original" factors of production, in particular different qualities of land on the one hand and (one or several qualities of) labor on the other, and (ii) to produced commodities.

The notion that in conditions of free competition the services of certain factors of production, such as some qualities of land, which are in excess supply assume a zero price, was a standard element in classical rent theory from James Anderson to David Ricardo. See, for example, the following statement by Ricardo in which reference is to land available in abundant quantity: "no rent could be paid for such land, for the reason stated why nothing is given for the use of air and water, or for any of the gifts of nature which exist in boundless quantity" (*Works* I, p. 69). It deserves to be stressed that in classical economics that rule was not applied to labor; see, for example, Ricardo's discussion of the labor displacing effects of the introduction of machinery: the presence of unemployed laborers is not assumed to drive the wage to zero (cf. *Works* I, ch. 31). Put differently, while the "reservation price" for all primary inputs other than labor is taken to be zero or very close to zero, for labor it is positive.

Obviously, with single production no produced commodity can be a free good, other than in the ultra-short period. Hence, if the Rule of Free Goods were to be applied to products at least some of the processes of production must be multiple-product processes. As was pointed out in the historical notes of Chapter 8, that rule was already invoked by Adam Smith in his discussion of value and distribution in the case of joint production.

To conclude, both kinds of application of the Rule of Free Goods were known to classical authors. Hence any claim to originality by later authors with regard to this rule appears to be unsubstantiated.

6. **The von Neumann growth model**

Jansci (John) von Neumann was born in Budapest in 1903. He studied mathematics with Erhard Schmidt in Berlin and with Hermann Weyl and George Polya in Zurich; he was also in close contact with David Hilbert in Göttingen. He completed his doctorate in mathematics from the University of Budapest in 1926 and in the following year assumed the position of a *Privatdozent* at the University of Berlin; in 1929 he transferred to the same position at the University of Hamburg. In 1930 he went to Princeton University as a visiting lecturer; in 1931 he was offered a professorship and in 1933 he was invited to join the Institute for Advanced Study in Princeton as a professor (see Ulam, 1958; Thompson, 1987). Von Neumann read his paper on the growth model for the first time in the winter of 1932 at the Mathematical Seminar of Princeton University (cf. von Neumann, 1945, p. 1). In 1936 he gave the paper in Karl Menger's famous Mathematical Colloquium at the University of Vienna; the paper was then for the first time published in the proceedings of the colloquium, *Ergebnisse eines mathematischen Kolloquiums* (von Neumann, 1937).

In his paper von Neumann assumes that there are n goods which can be produced by m constant returns to scale production processes. The problem is to establish which processes will actually be used and which not, being "unprofitable." Von Neumann takes the real wage rate, consisting of the "necessities of life," to be given and paid at the beginning of the (uniform) production period. In addition, he assumes "that all income in excess of necessities of life will be reinvested" (1945, p. 2). The characteristic features of the model include: (i) "Goods are produced not only from 'natural factors of production,' but in the first place from each other. These processes of production may be circular" (ibid., p. 1); (ii) the processes of production "can describe the special case where good G_j can be produced only jointly with certain others, viz. its permanent joint products" (ibid., p. 2); (iii) both circulating and fixed capital can be dealt with: "wear and tear of capital goods are to be described by introducing different stages of wear as different goods, using a separate P_i [process i] for each of these" (ibid., p. 2). These assumptions are coupled with the Rule of Free Goods: "if there is excess production of G_j, G_j becomes a free good and its price $[p_j] = 0$" (ibid., p. 3).

Von Neumann's approach can be summarized as follows. Let **A** and **B** be the $m \times n$ input and output matrices, respectively, where **A** includes the means of subsistence in the support of workers; and let **q** be the m-dimensional vector of activity levels and **p** the n-dimensional price vector. $\alpha = 1 + g$ is the expansion factor, where g is the expansion or growth rate; $\beta = 1 + r$ is the interest factor, where r is the rate of interest (or rate of profit). The model is subject to the following axioms.

$$\mathbf{q}^T\mathbf{B} \geqq \alpha\mathbf{q}^T\mathbf{A}, \tag{13.5a}$$

$$\mathbf{B}\mathbf{p} \leqq \beta\mathbf{A}\mathbf{p}, \tag{13.5b}$$

$$\mathbf{q}^T(\mathbf{B} - \alpha\mathbf{A})\mathbf{p} = 0, \tag{13.5c}$$

$$\mathbf{q}^T(\mathbf{B} - \beta\mathbf{A})\mathbf{p} = 0, \tag{13.5d}$$

$$\mathbf{q} \geqslant \mathbf{0}, \quad \mathbf{p} \geqslant \mathbf{0}. \tag{13.5e}$$

Axiom (13.5a) implies that α times the inputs for a given period are not larger than the outputs of the previous period. Axiom (13.5b) is the no extra profits condition. Axiom (13.5c) states the free disposal assumption. Axiom (13.5d) implies that processes which incur extra costs will not be operated. Finally, (13.5e) requires that both the intensity and the price vector are semipositive. In order to demonstrate that for any pair of nonnegative matrices $\mathbf{A}$ and $\mathbf{B}$ there are solutions for $\mathbf{q}$ and $\mathbf{p}$ and for $\alpha, \alpha \geqslant 0$, and $\beta, \beta \geqslant 0$, von Neumann assumes in addition:

$$\mathbf{A} + \mathbf{B} > \mathbf{0}, \tag{13.6}$$

which implies that every process requires as an input or produces as an output some positive amount of every good.

On the basis of these givens von Neumann demonstrates the existence of a solution. He determines (i) which processes will be operated; (ii) at what rate the economic system will grow; (iii) what prices will obtain; (iv) what the rate of interest will be; and (v) that, of necessity, $\alpha = \beta$, that is, the growth and the interest factor are equal.

The stimulation to publish an English version of the paper came from Nicholas Kaldor, then chairman of the editorial committee of *The Review of Economic Studies*. Kaldor also arranged for the translation of the paper and was concerned with rendering the mathematically demanding paper attractive to an audience of economists. A first step in the pursuit of this goal appears to have been the adaptation of the paper's title (cf. Kaldor, 1989, p. x), a literal translation of the original German version of which would have been "On an Economic System of Equations and a Generalization of Brouwer's Fixed Point Theorem." The second part of the title which reflects von Neumann's assessment that the main achievement of the paper consisted in the generalization of a mathematical theorem was dropped entirely, and the neutral term "economic system of equations" was replaced by the not-so-neutral term "model of general economic equilibrium."

The second step consisted in asking David Champernowne, "the most mathematically-minded economist I knew, to write an explanatory paper *ad usum delphini*, for the use of the semi-numerates, to appear alongside it in the *Review of Economic Studies*" (ibid., p. x).[26] In a footnote to the introduction of his paper, Champernowne thanks Nicholas Kaldor for help with economic ideas, and Piero Sraffa and a Mr. Crum for "instruction

---

[26] It is interesting to note that in the title of Champernowne's paper (see Champernowne, 1945) the title of the English version of von Neumann's paper is referred to incompletely: the adjective "general" is left out.

in subjects discussed in this article" (Champernowne, 1945, p. 10, n. 1). Interestingly, in Champernowne's interpretation von Neumann's model emerges as one characterized essentially by "classical" features. This interpretation is fully confirmed by our investigation of the classical economists from Adam Smith to David Ricardo and those authors working in the "classical" tradition prior to von Neumann. Indeed, there are striking similarities between the contributions of these economists and von Neumann. These concern: (i) the concept of production as a circular flow; (ii) the concept of the surplus product which forms the basis of an explanation of all shares of income other than wages; (iii) the notion of a uniformly expanding economy in which the rate of expansion is determined endogenously, that is, a "quasi-stationary system;" (iv) the concept of duality of the relationship between relative quantities and the rate of growth on the one hand and that between relative prices and the rate of interest (rate of profit) on the other; (v) the way in which the problem of the choice of technique is approached and the use of inequalities in it; and (vi) the way the Rule of Free Goods is applied to primary factors of production and to products, respectively. Von Neumann in fact applied that rule in the same way as the classical economists did. While he assumed "that the natural factors of production, including labour, can be expanded in unlimited quantities" (1945, p. 2), this did not make him treat all these factors alike. Rather, he singled labor out as the only factor that is exempt from that rule; all other primary factors, although needed in production, "disappear" from the scene because they are taken to be non-scarce.[27] Labor is assumed to receive an exogenously given wage bundle which is independent of the degree of employment.[28]

[27] Assuming that natural resources are non-scarce is of course not the same thing as assuming that there are no natural resources at all. Von Neumann's model is frequently misinterpreted in the latter sense. In this context it deserves to be noted that von Neumann does not define goods in the same way as Debreu (1959, p. 32): he does not consider a particular plot of land in a particular location as a special good. However, with the system growing forever, the point will surely come where some natural resource(s) will become scarce. Surprisingly, von Neumann does not seem to have seen this point. As Professor Samuelson has pointed out to us in private correspondence, "More by inadvertence than conscious intention, v.N. failed to emphasize the *basic classical* notion of land resources as unproducible or diminishable." The total neglect of the problem of scarce primary resources such as land distinguishes his analysis in fact both from the analyses of the classical and the neoclassical economists. For a possible explanation of this neglect, see Section 7 below.

[28] "At most, one could say that a 'Rule of Zero "Excess" Wages' is applied because labour is less than fully employed" (Steedman, 1987b, p. 419). The interpretation given by Dore of von Neumann's use (or rather non-use) of the Rule of Free

The contention that von Neumann's approach has been anticipated in all important aspects by authors working in the "classical" tradition is, of course, not meant to play down the importance of von Neumann's contribution. After all it was he who provided a comprehensive and general formulation of what other authors were able to put forward only partially and with respect to special cases, and it was he who was able to prove the existence of a solution.

7. On alternative interpretations of the von Neumann model

The "classical" interpretation suggested by Champernowne (1945) and others, including Kaldor (1961, p. 181), Morishima (1973, p. 3), and Goodwin (1986), is not generally shared by economists. The dominant view is expressed well by Kenneth Arrow: "Though von Neumann makes no reference..., it seems very clear that he took Cassel's work as a starting point" (Arrow, 1989, p. 17). This interpretation is shared by the editors of the volume in which Arrow's paper was published, who maintain that the Cassellian system "forms the backdrop to the model expounded in his 1937 paper" (Dore, Chakravarty and Goodwin, 1989, p. 2; see also Weintraub, 1985, p. 77, and Punzo, 1989). And Lionel McKenzie in his entry "General Equilibrium" in *The New Palgrave* contended that Cassel's model "was generalized to allow joint production in a special context by von Neumann" (1987, p. 500). The reference is to Gustav Cassel's *Theoretische Sozialökonomie* published in 1918, which contains a considerably simplified version of Walras's theory (see Cassel, 1918).[29] It is known as the "Walras-Cassel model," a name coined by Robert Dorfman, Paul Samuelson, and Robert Solow (1958, p. 346). In this section we shall first summarize the "Walras–Cassel model" and the modifications of it suggested by Karl Schlesinger and Abraham Wald in the mid 1930s in Karl Menger's famous *Kolloquium* in Vienna. We shall then point out the difficulties in the conventional "neoclassical" interpretation of the von Neumann model. The section concludes with a comparison of the analyses of von Neumann and Remak which suggests that von Neumann's model contains, among other things, an answer to his mathematical colleague.

Goods is difficult to sustain: according to Dore (1989, p. 83) in the von Neumann model "Cassel's 'principle of scarcity'... is given an extreme binary interpretation whereby a resource has either a positive economic value if it is fully utilized, or its value is zero. ... Unless every single man and woman is fully employed, the social value of labour is zero; this is indeed extreme. Why did von Neumann resort to this formulation?" The answer to this question is: he did not.

[29] Cassel's book was published in English as *The Theory of Social Economy* in 1923; a revised translation of the fifth German edition was published in 1932 (see Cassel, 1932).

7.1. The Walras–Cassel model

The proximate starting point of the development of modern neoclassical general equilibrium theory was the analysis put forward by Gustav Cassel in his *Theoretische Sozialökonomie*, published in 1918 (Cassel, [1918] 1932).[30] In chapter IV of book I of the treatise Cassel presented two models, one of a stationary economy, the other one of an economy growing along a steady-state path.

In his first model Cassel assumes, in our notation, that there are z (primary) factors of production, with Z_j the amount of services provided by the jth factor in existence, and n goods. Goods are produced by means of factor services with fixed technical coefficients of production: let a_{ij} designate the amount of factor j needed per unit of output of good i.[31] There are as many single-product processes of production as there are goods to be produced, that is, there is no choice of technique. With S_i representing the amount of good i produced, the equality of supply and demand for each factor service requires

$$\sum_{i=1}^{n} a_{ij}S_i = Z_j, \quad j = 1, 2, \ldots, z. \tag{13.7}$$

With free competition extra profits will be zero across processes. Let q_j be the price of factor service j and p_i the price of good i. Then we have

$$p_i = \sum_{j=1}^{z} a_{ij}q_j, \quad i = 1, 2, \ldots, n. \tag{13.8}$$

In addition, Cassel introduces the demand for each good as a function of the prices of all goods, that is,

$$D_i = F_i(p_1, p_2, \ldots, p_n), \quad i = 1, 2, \ldots, n. \tag{13.9}$$

"Now the demand for any particular commodity, given a state of equilibrium, must coincide with the supply of it, since the fixing of prices, in accordance with the principle of scarcity, must be such as to restrict demand so as to satisfy it with the available supply of commodities" (Cassel, 1932, p. 140). It follows that

$$D_i = S_i, \quad i = 1, 2, \ldots, n. \tag{13.10}$$

---

[30] Dorfman, Samuelson and Solow (1958, p. 349) aptly called Cassel a "popularizer of the Walrasian system." It should be noted, however, that in Cassel ([1918] 1932) Walras is never mentioned.

[31] Here production is conceived of as a unidirectional process that leads from the services of original factors of production to consumption goods. Later in his book Cassel also discusses production with produced means of production.

Equations (13.7)–(13.10) constitute an economic system which satisfies the then going criterion of completeness, that is, there are as many equations as there are unknowns to be ascertained.

Next, Cassel turns to the model of a uniformly progressing economy, which however is sketched only verbally. The model is introduced in the following terms: "We must now take into consideration the society which is progressing at a uniform rate. In it, the quantities of the factors of production which are available in each period, that is our $[Z_1 \cdots Z_z]$, are subject to a uniform increase. We shall represent by $[g]$ the fixed rate of this increase, and of the uniform progress of the society generally" (ibid. p. 152). In Cassel's view this generalization to the case of an economy growing at a given and constant rate does not cause substantial problems. The previous equations can easily be adapted appropriately, "so that the whole pricing problem is solved" (ibid., p. 153).

Cassel's first model was scrutinized by several authors, including Knut Wicksell ([1919] 1934), Hans Neisser (1932), Heinrich von Stackelberg (1933), and Frederick Zeuthen (1933). A recurrent criticism concerned the assumed positivity of the prices of factor services. In the words of Wicksell: "The 'simultaneous equations' are no guarantee that any 'variable' cannot assume the value of nil, even if we are discussing so important a social factor as wages, or so questionable – not to say odious – a social factor as the rent of land, site-rent, or certain monopoly revenue, etc." (Wicksell, 1934, p. 228). Zeuthen was presumably the first to argue that Cassel's quantity equations (13.7) ought to be written as inequalities, that is,

$$\sum_{i=1}^{n} a_{ij} S_i \lessgtr Z_j, \quad j = 1, 2, \ldots, z, \tag{13.7'}$$

since the demand for any factor service could fall short of or at most be equal to its supply, but can never exceed it. In case the demand for a factor service were smaller than its supply, then the factor service could not be considered scarce. The "principle of scarcity" according to which only productive resources which are in short supply have positive prices, could therefore not be applied to the factor under consideration: its price would be equal to zero. Hence, if in equation (13.7') the strict inequality holds, then $q_j = 0$ (cf. Zeuthen, 1933, p. 6).

Essentially the same modification was suggested by Karl Schlesinger (1935) and Abraham Wald (1935, 1936) in their contributions to Karl Menger's mathematical seminar at the University of Vienna.[32] This modification was considered necessary in order to rescue the Casellian

---

[32] There were other modifications introduced by Schlesinger and Wald which need not concern us here; see Weintraub (1985) and Arrow (1989).

general equilibrium approach to the determination of prices and rates of remuneration of factor services. As is well known, Wald's 1935 paper contains the first proof of the existence of a competitive equilibrium we know of.

We are now in a position to assess the claim that von Neumann's model should be seen as a contribution to the "Walras–Cassel model," or, more generally, to neoclassical long-period theory. For the following argument, see also Kurz and Salvadori (1993b).

7.2. *Some difficulties in the conventional interpretation*

It is a characteristic feature of the "Walras–Cassel model," as of neoclassical theory in general, that it attempts to explain all prices and quantities, including the prices of productive services and the employment levels of these services, in terms of demand and supply. As has been pointed out in Subsection 4.1 of Chapter 1, the data or independent variables from which the theory starts are the following. It takes as given

   (i) initial endowments of the economy and who owns them;
   (ii) preferences of consumers; and
   (iii) the set of available techniques.

On the basis of these data the theory tries to find an "equilibrium" price vector that simultaneously clears all markets for goods and services.

Those who claim that von Neumann's model can be given a neoclassical interpretation would have to demonstrate that the former starts from the same set of data (i)–(iii) and centers around the same theoretical concepts: "demand" and "supply." Such a demonstration is still lacking, and the following discussion shows why.

In von Neumann's model there are no initial endowments that could constrain productive activity and economic expansion: it is explicitly assumed that primary factors are available in abundance and that there is no historically given endowment of the economy with physical or value capital.[33] This observation leads to the following one. As expounded in Section 4 of Chapter 1, the neoclassical economists explain all distributive variables, including profits, symmetrically in terms of supply and demand in regard to the respective factors of production, including a factor called "capital." This *necessitates* that one starts from a given "quantity of

---

[33] This is one of the reasons why Koopmans considered von Neumann's paper "not very good economics" (Koopmans, 1974). Another reason for this harsh judgment was the treatment of the consumption of workers, which, in Champernowne's interpretation, reduced "the role of the worker–consumer to that of a farm animal" (Champernowne, 1945, p. 12).

capital," the "scarcity" of which is seen to be reflected in the level of the rate of profit, or rate of interest.[34] In contradistinction, and this concerns a crucial difference, in the von Neumann model we encounter exactly the same asymmetry in the theory of distribution that is characteristic of classical analysis: the real wage rate is given and profits are conceived of as a residual magnitude. As Kaldor stressed at the 1958 Corfu conference on the theory of capital, there is no reason to presume "that von Neumann's model was merely Wicksell, Marshall or the whole neo-classical school in a new disguise" (cf. Lutz and Hague, 1961, pp. 296–7).

Finally, it deserves to be mentioned that in the von Neumann model the (long-term) rate of growth is determined *endogenously* rather than exogenously, as in Cassel's neoclassical analysis which takes as given the rates of growth of all primary factors and assumes their continuous full employment. No such assumption is to be found in von Neumann.

In von Neumann's model preferences can at most be said to play a rather concealed role: the only route through which they could exert some influence on the equilibrium solution is via the so-called necessities of life which are taken into account in the (augmented) input matrix **A**. If the necessities of life reflect to some extent consumers' choice, as is argued by Samuelson (1989), it might be said that tastes play a role in the determination of relative prices and income distribution. For, with a different vector of wage goods reflecting workers' needs, even with available technical processes given, the process(es) chosen, the product(s) that have zero prices and the rate of interest may be different (see the numerical example in Steedman, 1977a, pp. 186–91). Samuelson is, of course, right in stressing that a change in the real wage rate may, and generally will, result in a change in the equilibrium solution of a von Neumann model. Yet in von Neumann's analysis the vector of goods constituting the means of subsistence of workers does not depend on relative prices. Hence, while it is perhaps an exaggeration to maintain that the von Neumann model is characterized by "a complete omission of final demand" (Arrow, 1989, p. 22), it is, of course, true that 'in contrast to Walras's formulae..., no direct marginalistic connection between prices and quantities is assumed" (Menger, 1973, p. 56).

As regards the assumption of a given set of alternative processes of production from which producers can choose, there is no material difference between the neoclassical (with the "Walras–Cassel model" as a

---

[34] Since "capital" is set aside in the formulations of Schlesinger and Wald, it is not surprising that the concept of the rate of interest (or rate of profit) makes no appearance.

special case) and the von Neumann model.[35] However, there are important differences in the way in which the latter and the "Walras–Cassel model" conceptualize production. While in the latter production is conceived of as the direct transformation of the services of the original factors of production into final goods, in the von Neumann model it is assumed that commodities are produced by means of commodities. While the "Walras–Cassel model" totally sets aside capital goods, the von Neumann model takes into account both circulating and fixed capital.

Hence salient features of any type of (long-period) neoclassical model, including the Walras–Cassel variant of it, are absent in von Neumann's formulation. We may therefore conclude that the conventional interpretation of the latter is in serious trouble. On the other hand there are no elements in the von Neumann model contradicting the "classical" interpretation put forward in preceding sections.

7.3. Von Neumann and Remak

Wittmann (1967, pp. 407–8) points out that Remak delivered his paper at a meeting of the Berlin Mathematical Society and that his ideas were discussed at the Institute of Mathematics in Berlin. He also conjectures that von Neumann was familiar with Remak's ideas. According to Wittmann's sources most of Remak's colleagues "derided" the conclusions of his paper.

It is possible that von Neumann was among those colleagues who took a critical position toward Remak's contribution. We may even consider the possibility that von Neumann's paper contains, *inter alia*, an implicit answer to his colleague. Since we do not know of any statement to this effect by von Neumann himself, the only evidence on which such an interpretation could possibly rest has to be derived from a careful textual comparison of the papers of the two authors (see Kurz and Salvadori, 1993b).

Both authors are concerned with the efficiency, or otherwise, of what von Neumann calls "the normal price mechanism" of a capitalist economy (von Neumann, 1945, p. 1). While Remak contended that the way prices are formed in a capitalist economy is partly responsible for the fact that the system is statically (and dynamically) non "extremal," that is, inefficient, a main result of von Neumann's paper reads: "the normal price mechanism brings about... the technically most efficient intensities of production"

---

[35] It should be noted, though, that the "Viennese" economists Schlesinger and Wald, following Cassel's basic model, assumed that there is only one fixed-coefficients method of production for each commodity, that is, there is no choice of technique.

(1945, p. 1).[36,37] The other factor mentioned by Remak as being potentially detrimental to efficiency, money, is also touched upon by von Neumann. The passage just quoted is followed by the adjunct: "This seems not unreasonable since we have eliminated monetary complications" (ibid., p. 1).

Remak in his paper is not at all concerned with scarce natural resources, such as land; he mentions the problem only in passing. He rather focuses attention on systems of production that are in a self-replacing state and in which there are at most three types of income: wages, interest, and profits. By implication, none of the natural resources utilized is scarce and therefore yields its owner a rent. In accordance with the capitalism versus socialism debate that Remak is interested in, the emphasis is on the conflict between workers and capital owners over the distribution of the product. Interestingly, the total neglect of the problem of scarcity is also a characteristic feature of von Neumann's model. If his concern had been with generalizing the "Walras–Cassel model," as is maintained by the conventional interpretation, this neglect would be totally incomprehensible, whereas it can easily be understood if one of his implicit aims was refuting Remak's view.

Just like Remak, von Neumann adopts a circular notion of production and considers the means of subsistence an integral part of the advances at the beginning of the uniform period of production. However, in every respect von Neumann's model is more general than Remak's. Repeatedly one gets the impression that where Remak drops an idea or poses a question that is beyond the scope of his own model, von Neumann offers a conceptualization and provides an answer. While Remak emphasizes that what is at stake is the question of the dynamic (in)efficiency of an economy, and then restricts his discussion essentially to the case of a stationary system, von Neumann adopts a dynamic framework of the analysis, albeit limited to the case of steady-state growth. While Remak is aware of the fact that an important aspect of the efficiency issue is how the problem of the choice of technique is decided, von Neumann tackles the problem head on. While Remak notes incidentally that production and consumption activities may generate "waste" which has to be disposed

---

[36] In the German original von Neumann uses the expression: "die rein technisch *zweckmäßigste* Verteilung der Produktionsintensitäten" (italics added). He thus uses the same terminology as Remak (1929, p. 724). More important, the concept of efficiency adopted by the two authors appears to be the same.

[37] Interestingly, Champernowne in his commentary on the von Neumann model remarks on the above passage: "This may immediately suggest an argument in favour of free enterprise in the real world" (Champernowne, 1945, p. 16).

of,[38] von Neumann starts directly from the assumption of general joint production coupled with the assumption of free disposal of all superfluous products. While Remak discusses markup pricing without addressing the problem of the mutual consistency of the markups, including the rate of interest, the given real wage rate(s) and the given technical conditions of production, von Neumann demonstrates that the rate of interest, that is, the general markup across all processes of production, is uniquely determined by the technical alternatives, given the real wage rate(s).

Circumstantial evidence and a detailed textual comparison seem to support the conjecture that von Neumann's model contained, among other things, an answer to his mathematical colleague. Compared with the widespread opinion that von Neumann's model was meant to provide a solution to a problem posed by Cassel, that of uniform growth, and not dealt with by Schlesinger and Wald, this interpretation appears to us to be more plausible. Indeed, in our view there are too many elements in the analyses of von Neumann and the "Viennese" economists Schlesinger and Wald that are difficult to reconcile, while we are not aware of any aspect contradicting our interpretation. It goes without saying that we cannot prove that we are right: *se non è vero, è ben trovato.*

8. Sraffa and the revival of the classical approach

Piero Sraffa was born in Turin in 1898. After graduation from the local university he went to the London School of Economics (1921–2) where he attended lectures by Cannan, Foxwell, and Gregory. During his first stay in England, Keynes asked him to contribute an article on the Italian banking system for the *Manchester Guardian*. The article was also published in Italian, and provoked fierce reactions by the Fascist government. In November 1923 Sraffa was appointed to a lectureship in Political Economy and Public Finance at the University of Perugia. The preparation of his lecture stimulated him to write "Sulle relazioni fra costo e quantità prodotta" (1925) which contains an analysis of the foundations of decreasing, constant, and increasing returns in Marshall's theory and a critical discussion of the latter's partial equilibrium approach. (Sraffa's criticism has been referred to in Subsection 4.4 of Chapter 1.) Not least due to this article Sraffa obtained a full professorship in Political Economy at the University of Cagliari, a post he held *in absentia* to the end of his life, donating his salary to the library. Edgeworth's high opinion of the article

---

[38] Remak even mentions the possibility of "negative prices" in this context (1929, p. 726) and points out that the negativity of the price of a substance that has to be removed corresponds with the positivity of the price of the respective disposal service.

led to an invitation to publish a version of it in the *Economic Journal* (cf. Sraffa, 1926). Moreover, Sraffa was offered a lectureship in Cambridge. In October 1927 Sraffa began his teaching in Cambridge, giving courses on the theory of value and on the relationships between banks and industry in continental Europe. He was to lecture for only three years, finding the very task increasingly difficult. In 1930 Sraffa was appointed to the position of the librarian of the Marshall Library and was also placed in charge of the Cambridge program of graduate studies in economics. He gave up lecturing for good.

Shortly after his arrival in Cambridge Sraffa showed Keynes the set of propositions which were to grow into *Production of Commodities by Means of Commodities*. But his work on the manuscript was somewhat overwhelmed both by the intense debate in Cambridge surrounding Keynes's *Treatise on Money*, and later, *The General Theory*, and by Sraffa's assuming the editorship of the Royal Economic Society's edition of *The Works and Correspondence of David Ricardo* in 1930. By the late forties, the publication of the Ricardo edition had long been delayed. (For the causes of this delay, see Pollit, 1990). The first volumes of *The Works and Correspondence of David Ricardo* were finally published in 1951. The edition, for which Sraffa was awarded the golden medal Söderstrom by the Swedish Royal Academy in 1961, is widely acknowledged to be a scholarly masterpiece. In the late 1950s Sraffa eventually found time to put together, revise and complete his notes on the classical approach to the theory of production which were eventually published as *Production of Commodities by Means of Commodities. Prelude to a Critique of Economic Theory* (Sraffa, 1960).

8.1. From partial to general analysis

In Chapter 1 we have analyzed briefly the criticism levelled by Sraffa (1925) at the analysis of variable cost industries within the framework of partial equilibrium. As we have seen there, the following cases can be distinguished: variable returns that are (i) internal to the firm; (ii) external to the firm but internal to the industry; and (iii) external to both the firm and the industry. Case (i) is incompatible with the assumption of perfect competition. Case (iii) is incompatible with the method of partial equilibrium since variable returns affect the production of more than one commodity in the same direct way, thus making it impossible to avoid a general equilibrium reasoning. Only variable returns of type (ii), whose empirical importance is dubious, are thus compatible with Marshall's analysis of the supply curve of an industry under perfect competition. From this Sraffa (1925) concluded that the assumption of constant returns is the most convenient one for the analysis of the supply curve of an industry under competitive conditions. The price would thus depend only on the cost of production of the industry under consideration. Yet this proposition could not leave Sraffa satisfied. He was confronted with two alternatives: either to abandon the assumption of perfect competition or to abandon partial equilibrium analysis. As is well known, Sraffa initially followed the first route, but soon switched to the second.

In his 1926 paper the second alternative is ruled out on the grounds that an examination of "the conditions of simultaneous equilibrium in numerous industries" is far too complex: "the present state of our knowledge... does not permit of even much simpler schema being applied to the study of real conditions" (1926, p. 541). The adoption of the first alternative instead was motivated in terms of two related arguments. First, the abandonment of the hypothesis of perfect competition is suggested by "everyday experience... that a very large number of undertakings – and the majority of those which produce manufactured consumers' goods – work under conditions of individual diminishing costs" (1926, p. 543). Secondly, it is argued that the "chief obstacle against which [businessmen] have to contend when they want gradually to increase their production does not lie in the cost of production... but in the difficulty of selling the larger quantity of goods without reducing the price, or without having to face increased marketing expenses. This... is only an aspect of the usual descending demand curve, with the difference that instead of concerning the whole of a commodity, whatever its origin, it relates only to the goods produced by a particular firm" (ibid.).

Sraffa's article of 1926 launched the analysis of imperfect competition; see Joan Robinson's *Economics of Imperfect Competition* (1933). Apart from his contribution to the *Economic Journal* symposium on increasing returns (cf. Sraffa, 1930), Sraffa did not participate further in the debate on the Marshallian theory of value. He rather focused attention on an analysis of "the process of diffusion of profits throughout the various stages of production and of the process of forming a normal level of profits throughout all the industries of a country... [a problem] beyond the scope of this article" (1926, p. 550; see also Eatwell and Panico, 1987). This problem constitutes the main topic of *Production of Commodities*.

8.2. Production of Commodities by Means of Commodities

In his book Sraffa was explicitly concerned with reviving the "standpoint... of the classical economists from Adam Smith to Ricardo" (Sraffa, 1960, p. v). The affiliation of his analysis with the theories of the old classical economists is stressed again in the following remark concerning the concept of "price" or "value" adopted in the book: "Such classical terms as 'necessary price,' 'natural price,' or 'price of production' would meet the case, but value and price have been preferred as being shorter and in the present context (which contains no reference to market prices) no more ambiguous" (ibid., p. 9). Finally, appendix D to the book provides additional "References to the Literature" concerning special ideas and concepts of classical derivation, "the source of which may not be obvious" (ibid., p. 93).

Scrutiny shows that Sraffa follows the classical authors not only in terms of the method adopted and the general approach chosen, but broadly in terms of the two-part structure of the argument that we also encountered in Subsection 2.4 of Chapter 1. In one part he is concerned with investigating *given* "systems of production." The relationship between relative prices, the general rate of profit and the wage rate implicit in the given system of production, or "technique," is analyzed partly in formal terms: it is systems of equations that prove to be appropriate in this context. Subsequently Sraffa turns to the problem of which system of production will be adopted from a set of alternative systems, that is, the problem of the choice of technique. Hence, what was initially taken as given is now an *unknown*. This is dealt with in chapter XII, "Switch in Methods of Production." Sraffa assumes that the choice between alternative techniques "will be exclusively grounded on cheapness" (ibid., p. 83). In other words, he is concerned with determining the *cost-minimizing* system(s) of production. In comparing different methods of production to produce the same commodity the phenomena of *extra costs* and *extra profits* make an appearance. Although Sraffa does not provide a formalization of his argument, it is clear that in this context inequalities rather than equations would be appropriate.

The basic premise that Sraffa starts from is that commodities are produced by means of commodities. This then leads to the concept of surplus, to the distinction between basic and non-basic products, and to the assumption that there is at least one basic commodity (chapters I and II, §§ 1–12). The main aim of chapter III (§§ 13–22) is to provide a "preliminary survey" (§ 20) of price movements consequent upon changes in distribution on the assumption that the methods of production remain unchanged. Sraffa concludes "this preliminary survey of the subject" by asserting that

> the relative price-movements of two products come to depend, not only on the 'proportions' of labour to means of production by which they are respectively produced, but also on the 'proportions' by which those means have themselves been produced, and also on the 'proportions' by which the means of production of those means of production have been produced, and so on. The result is that

the relative price of two products may move...in the opposite direction to what we might have expected on the basis of their respective 'proportions'; besides, the prices of their respective means of production may move in such a way as to reverse the order of the two products as to higher and lower proportions; *and further complications arise, which will be considered subsequently* (ibid., p. 15; emphasis added).

The complete analysis of price movements in the case of single production is provided in chapter VI (§§ 45–9). This chapter also contains the well known example of the "old wine" and the "oak chest" showing that the difference between the prices of two commodities can be positive or negative depending on income distribution. The analysis is significantly simplified by the use of the "Standard Commodity" (cf. Section 4.3 of Chapter 4 above) as numeraire. Chapters IV and V of Sraffa's book are in fact devoted to the introduction of this tool of analysis and to the study of its properties.

While Part I of Sraffa's book is devoted to single-product industries and circulating capital, Part II deals with joint production (chapters VII–IX), fixed capital (chapter X), and land (chapter XI). Concerning these issues, see the numerous references to Sraffa in the Historical notes to Chapters 8, 7 and 9, and 10, respectively. Additional elements will be added in the next section. Part III of Sraffa's book is devoted to the problem of the choice of technique, an issue dealt with in many places of the present book, especially in Chapter 5.

8.3. The question of no assumption on returns

In the Preface to *Production of Commodities* Sraffa stresses that he has not introduced any assumption on returns in the book since it is *not* concerned with changes either in the *scale of production* or in the *proportions* in which the "factors of production" are employed (ibid., p. v). The effects of these changes on the costs of production are central to his critique of Marshall's supply functions in the 1920s.[39,40] A comparison

---

[39] In the 1925 article it is stated that increasing returns are related to *changes in the scale of production* whereas diminishing returns are related to *changes in the proportions* in which "factors" are employed.

[40] There are three decades and a half between the publication of Sraffa's articles in the 1920s and that of his book. Sraffa himself in the Preface to *Production of Commodities* recalls "the disproportionate length of time over which so short a work has been in preparation." He adds however: "Whilst the central propositions had taken shape in the late 1920's, particular points, such as the Standard commodity, joint products and fixed capital, were worked out in the 'thirties and early 'forties. In the period since 1955, while these pages were being put together

of that critique with *Production of Commodities* shows that in both the reference is essentially to the same determinants of variable returns. That is, Sraffa's analysis of the relationship between quantities produced and prices is carried out in terms of basically the same factors. Panico and Salvadori (1994) have provided a detailed account of this fact. In the following discussion we refer only to the case of diminishing returns.

In Parts I and II of *Production of Commodities* Sraffa leaves no doubt that he takes as given the quantities produced of commodities and the processes operated. This is particularly clear in Chapter XI, devoted to "Land" and diminishing returns. The exposition of extensive rent (§ 86), of intensive rent (§ 87), and of the problem of a multiplicity of agricultural products (§ 89) is, in some sense, complicated by the fact that the quantities produced and the processes operated are to be considered as given. For the way in which the results are presented, risks are not being recognized as the outcome of a process of diminishing returns. Therefore, in § 88 it is explicitly stated that the results presented in §§ 86–7 (and 89) are indeed the outcome of such a process (of diminishing returns), and the connection that exists "between the employment of two methods of producing corn on land of a single quality and a process of 'intensive' diminishing returns" is fully explained. This connection is considered "less obvious" than the connection between the employment of n methods of producing corn on n different qualities of land and a process of "'extensive' diminishing returns," which is considered to be "readily recognized." The abovementioned connection is reported in the following two paragraphs:

> From this standpoint the existence side by side of two methods can be regarded as a phase in the course of a progressive increase of production on the land. The increase takes place through the gradual extension of the method that produces more corn at a higher unit cost, at the expense of the method that produces less. As soon as the former method has extended to the whole area,

out of a mass of old notes, little was added, apart from filling gaps which had become apparent in the process" (Sraffa, 1960, p. vi). In the same Preface Sraffa also states that "in 1928 Lord Keynes read a draft of the opening propositions of this [book]" (ibid.). Panico and Salvadori (1994) refer to a letter by Keynes to his wife, dated 28 November 1927, in which Keynes describes "a long talk with Sraffa about his work. It is very interesting and *original*" (Keynes's emphasis; see Unpublished writings of J. M. Keynes, copyright The Provost and Scholars of King's College, Cambridge 1993, King's College Library, Cambridge; the letter is also referred to in Potier, 1991, pp. 59–60). The "central propositions" of *Production of Commodities* were thus elaborated shortly after writing the article published in December 1926 in the *Economic Journal*.

the rent rises to the point where a third method which produces still more corn at a still higher cost can be introduced to take the place of the method that has just been superseded. Thus the stage is set for a new phase of increase of production through the gradual extension of the third method at the expense of the intermediate one. In this way the output may increase continuously, although the methods of production are changed spasmodically.

While the scarcity of land thus provides the background from which rent arises, the only evidence of this scarcity to be found in the process of production is the duality of methods: if there were no scarcity, only one method, the cheapest, would be used on the land and there could be no rent (ibid., p. 76).

These are the only paragraphs of the book where Sraffa is not actually considering gross output quantities as given. Changes in quantities, however, are not necessary for the argument, they are only introduced for "didactical" reasons, in order to let the reader recognize a connection between the *given* situation and a *process*. But, at the same time, the reader cannot avoid recognizing that:

(i) the process described is relating the changes in the quantity of a single output to changes in the methods of production producing that output;

(ii) the changes in the methods of production mentioned in (i) involve a change in prices[41] and eventually a change in other methods of production;

(iii) when an increase in the production using land takes place, all processes are assumed to be unchanged; that is, returns to scale would be constant if there were no scarcity of land;

(iv) in the process described the quantities produced of all other commodities using the "land of single quality" are assumed to be unchanged.

Observation (iii) implies that the process of diminishing returns described in § 88 is exactly the same as that presented in Sraffa's paper of 1925:

... diminishing returns must of necessity occur because it will be the producer himself who, for his own benefit, will arrange the doses of the factors and the methods of use in a decreasing order,

---

[41] In a footnote appended to the word "superseded" in the first paragraph quoted above, Sraffa adds: "The change in methods of production, if it concerns a basic product, involves of course a change of Standard system," which is an implicit reference to a change in *all* prices.

going from the most favourable ones to the most ineffective, and he will start production with the best combinations, resorting little by little, as these are exhausted, to the worst ones (Sraffa, 1925, p. 288; translation by J. Eatwell and A. Roncaglia, p. 11).

Moreover, both the analysis in 1925 and the analysis of § 88 of the book published in 1960 build up a relationship between quantities on the one side and prices on the other. The analysis of 1925 is a partial equilibrium analysis and therefore deals with only two variables, that is, the quantity produced of a single commodity and the price of that same commodity. In contradistinction, the analysis of 1960 takes into account changes in at least one quantity produced and changes in all prices. The above observation (iv) enables the reader to see a relationship between gross output quantities and prices (given the rate of profit), which is the relationship mentioned in Subsection 4.4 of Chapter 1.

9. Sraffa and von Neumann

We now come to the relationship between the contributions of Sraffa and von Neumann. It will be argued that the analyses of the two authors are not only compatible with one another but may mutually benefit from each other. This is why the approach chosen in the present book is essentially a "cross-breed" of the two. We shall first deal with what may be called the "Champernowne connection" between Sraffa's analysis in 1960 and that of von Neumann.

9.1. The "Champernowne connection"

In the course of his investigation Champernowne puts forward several concepts and raises a number of issues which we re-encounter in Sraffa (1960). Champernowne uses the notion of "system of production" (ibid., p. 14), which figures prominently in Sraffa's analysis. He notes that in the von Neumann model the role of the "worker–consumer" can be compared to that of a "farm animal," for example, a work horse, whose costs consist of his "fodder, stabling, etc." (ibid., p. 12), an analogy that recurs in Sraffa's formulation in chapter II of his book: "We have up to this point regarded wages as consisting of the necessary subsistence of the workers and thus entering the system on the same footing as the fuel for the engines or the feed for the cattle" (1960, p. 9). The rate of interest, Champernowne stresses, "depends on the technical processes of production which are available" (1945, p. 12); Sraffa, on the other hand, elaborates the Standard system with R as the "Standard ratio or Maximum rate of profits" representing a ratio between quantities of commodities (1960, p. 22). Champernowne raises the question of what would happen if the real wage were higher than originally assumed and concludes that "there will be a change in the equilibrium conditions... with a lower rate of interest and a lower rate of expansion" (ibid., p. 16); this foreshadows the inverse relationship between the rate of profit and the real wage rate analyzed by Sraffa.

Recently, Paul Samuelson, on the occasion of the fiftieth anniversary of the first publication of von Neumann's paper, has commented on Champernowne's paper. While he is full of praise for Champernowne's "brilliant interpretation for economists of the model's mathematics," he criticizes him for having fallen victim to "Kaldorian influences" and "Sraffian dogmas" (Samuelson, 1989, pp. 100 and 106). Samuelson's "Revisionist View of von Neumann's Growth Model" is intended to show that "this Anglian interpretation does not stand up to examination" (ibid., p. 100). Samuelson especially takes issue with Champernowne's observation that in the von Neumann model preferences play a "comparatively minor" role in the determination of equilibrium prices. Yet Samuelson argues, if the "necessities of life" reflect to some extent consumers' choice, then tastes do play a role in the determination of prices and the rate of interest. Samuelson concludes: "Sraffa's revisionist movement toward classical economics and away from neoclassical economics of the post-1870 mainstream gets no cogent *logical* support from von Neumann" (ibid., p. 106).

It has already been argued that the dependence of the equilibrium solution on the basket of wage goods cannot be considered sufficient reason to interpret the von Neumann model in the conventional neoclassical manner. Neither can it be taken to point toward a deficiency in Sraffa's analysis, as Samuelson appears to imply. To see this, let us take a closer look at Sraffa's argument. Sraffa, very much like von Neumann, begins his analysis by assuming that wages consist of the necessary subsistence of workers. Accordingly, *real* wages are given. He then observes that wages, besides the ever-present element of subsistence, may include a share of the surplus. This involves a complication; Sraffa expounds:

> The choice of the wage as the independent variable in the preliminary stages was due to its being there regarded as consisting of specified necessaries determined by physiological or social conditions *which are independent of prices or the rate of profits.* But as soon as the possibility of variations in the division of the product is admitted, *this consideration loses much of its force.* And when the wage is to be regarded as "given" in terms of a more or less abstract standard, and *does not acquire a definite meaning until the prices of commodities are determined*, the position is reversed. The rate of profits, as a ratio, has a significance which

is independent of any prices, and can well be "given" before the prices are fixed. ... In the following sections the rate of profits will therefore be treated as the independent variable (Sraffa, 1960, p. 33; emphases added).[42]

Hence Sraffa, unlike von Neumann who assumes subsistence wages throughout, does not exclude the possibility of relative prices having an impact on the vector of goods consumed by workers. However, as to how this dependence of workers' consumption on prices and distribution might be conceptualized, Sraffa offers nothing in his book.

Champernowne in his commentary put forward the idea of a "first" and a "second approximation" in the theory of prices.[43] Accordingly, factors like a shift in demand "may conveniently be considered as the 'special cases' of price-theory, to be introduced in the *second approximation*; and not, as is common in traditional economics, at the centre of the theory. For the basic influences determining equilibrium prices v. Neumann's model provides a novel approach; here, perhaps for the first time, is a self-contained theory of the determination of prices, ignoring the second approximation" (Champernowne, 1945, p. 17; emphasis in the original). As Champernowne emphasizes, von Neumann's "first approximation" approach is particularly powerful with regard to intermediary goods. In a footnote he adds: "And even in the case of final consumers' goods, the prices... are *largely* to be explained by the technical conditions of production, rather than 'marginal utility'"; then follows, in brackets, the interesting adjunct: "The exceptions being joint products, or commodities with largely increasing or decreasing cost" (ibid, p. 17, fn.).

9.2. Comparing the analyses of Sraffa and von Neumann

If we compare the analyses of von Neumann and Sraffa some differences strike the eye. However, their importance should not be overrated. Von Neumann assumes constant returns to scale. Sraffa, on the other hand, stresses that in his analysis "no such assumption is made"; he adds however: "If such a supposition is found helpful, there is no harm in the reader's adopting it as a temporary working hypothesis" (Sraffa, 1960, p. v). The different approaches to the question of returns follow

[42] As Joan Robinson (1961, p. 54) succinctly remarked, "we could hardly imagine that, when the workers had a surplus to spend on beef, their physical need for wheat was unchanged."

[43] For an explicit statement by Sraffa on the relative importance of cost of production and utility in explaining relative prices, see the passage quoted from his letter to A. Asimakopulos (Asimakopulos, 1990, p. 342, n. 3; see also Salvadori, 1994). For a similar view, see von Bortkiewicz (1921).

largely from a difference in perspective: while von Neumann is concerned with a uniformly growing economic system and therefore needs this assumption, Sraffa's investigation "is concerned exclusively with such properties of an economic system as do not depend on changes in the scale of production" (ibid., p. v). Hence, unlike von Neumann, Sraffa (for the most part of his analysis) does not specify whether the surplus generated by an economy accumulates or is consumed (unproductively): there are no assumptions regarding saving and investment behavior to be found in his book. Yet there is nothing in Sraffa's approach which, as a matter of principle, would preclude the adoption of constant returns in combination with von Neumann's suppositions regarding saving and investment as working hypotheses, provided these prove useful to study the particular case under consideration. The same holds true with respect to von Neumann's premise of given subsistence wages: Sraffa himself adopts it at the beginning of his investigation and drops it later. Hence with regard to the aspects dealt with so far, the analyses of Sraffa and von Neumann appear to be perfectly compatible with one another. The difference between the two is rather to be seen in the following: whereas von Neumann throughout his paper retains the simplifying assumptions just mentioned, Sraffa makes it clear, sometimes implicitly, that each of them, as well as their combinations, is applicable to particular cases only, while other cases that are of interest to the economist cannot be covered.

Another difference concerns the completeness of detail with which certain phenomena are exposed. Sraffa's argument has rightly been called terse; however, in terms of terseness it does not compare with that of von Neumann. For example, while von Neumann contents himself with the hint that the joint products method is capable of dealing with durable instruments of production, Sraffa devotes a whole chapter to the treatment of fixed capital employing this method (ibid., ch. X, pp. 63–73). He is thus able to demonstrate how powerful this method is: that it is not restricted to the "extremely simplified case" of constant efficiency "but has general validity" (ibid., p. 66); that the method allows one to ascertain correctly the annual charge to be paid for interest and depreciation; and what the results derived imply for the theory of capital. It goes without saying that differences in the degree of comprehensiveness of exposition must not be taken as necessary differences in content.

There remain, however, two closely related issues which appear to indicate differences between the two analyses: (i) while von Neumann adopts the Rule of Free Goods, in Sraffa that rule is never mentioned; (ii) in contradistinction to von Neumann, Sraffa formulates his analysis of joint production in terms of equations rather than inequalities and assumes "that the number of independent processes in the system [is] equal to the number of commodities produced" (ibid., p. 44). This assumption is rationalized in terms of the following argument referring to a two-commodity case: "considering that the proportions in which the two commodities are produced by any one method will in general be different from those in which they are required for use, the existence of two methods of producing them in different proportions will be necessary for obtaining the required proportion of the two products through an appropriate combination of the two methods" (ibid., p. 43, n. 2). (See also the Historical notes to Chapter 8.)

The following remarks might help to clarify the issues under consideration. First, Sraffa, in accordance with the procedure adopted by the classical economists (cf. Section 5), in the case of single production and to some extent also in the case of joint production approaches the theory of value and distribution in two steps. He first analyzes the mathematical properties of a *given* system of production and only subsequently addresses the problem of which system will be chosen by cost-minimizing producers from a set of available alternatives. This approach might be called "indirect." Von Neumann on the other hand is not concerned with investigating the mathematical properties of a given system, rather he tackles at once the problem of the choice of technique from *all* the available alternatives. This approach might be called "direct." As is well known, in the case of single production (and in simple cases involving fixed capital) the two approaches produce exactly the same results; see Chapters 5 and 7. With universal joint production the indirect approach can be elaborated in such a way that it replicates the results obtained with the direct approach, yet in terms of analytical convenience it is inferior to the latter (see Salvadori, 1985). Nevertheless the indirect approach can still be useful when a square cost-minimizing technique is determined, which is necessarily the case in some significant circumstances, but not always (cf. Section 6 of Chapter 8). However, it has to be recognized that Sraffa was wrong in assuming that the number of independent processes in the system is always equal to the number of commodities produced, and that his justification of this assumption in terms of the "requirements for use" is valid only in some circumstances. The fact that these aspects of Sraffa's analysis cannot be sustained must not however be taken, wrongly, to imply the irrelevance of his entire approach.

Sraffa points out that while with single production no price can become negative as a result of the variation of the wage rate between zero and its maximum value, given the system of production, "it may be said at once, however, that this proposition is not capable of extension to the case of joint-products.... The price of one of them might become negative" (ibid., p. 59). Sraffa comments on this possibility as follows:

> This conclusion is not in itself very startling. All that it implies
> is that, although in actual fact all prices were positive, a change
> in the wage might create a situation the logic of which required
> some of the prices to turn negative: and this being unacceptable,
> those among the methods of production that gave rise to such a
> result would be discarded to make room for others which in the
> new situation were consistent with positive prices (ibid.).

This passage is interesting because it witnesses that Sraffa is clear about the fact that the positivity of prices cannot be guaranteed if there is no choice of technique. As to the substance of Sraffa's suggested way out of the impasse arising from the negativity of the price of a joint product, it could be argued that it is tantamount to the *ad hoc* assumption that there is always one or several processes of production which, if adopted, make the phenomenon of negative price disappear. This assumption, as peculiar as it may seem at first sight, is however no more *ad hoc* than the assumption of free disposal. In fact, the latter is equivalent to the assumption that for each process producing a given product there is another process which is exactly identical to the first one except that the product under consideration is *not* produced. (See Section 5 of Chapter 7 and the end of Section 2 of Chapter 8.)

If this interpretation is considered acceptable, then the conclusion is close at hand that there is no fundamental difference separating the analyses of Sraffa and von Neumann.

14

The neoclassical theory of distribution and the problem of capital

The analysis of production, distribution, and relative prices elaborated in this book derives from the contributions of Sraffa and von Neumann which, as has been argued in Chapter 13, can be strictly located in the "classical" tradition. The abandonment of the classical approach and the development of a different theory, which rose to dominance in the wake of the so-called marginalist revolution in the latter part of the 19th century, was motivated, among other things, by the deficiencies of the received labor theory of value. However, in terms of the *method* of analysis adopted the early neoclassical economists, including William Stanley Jevons (1871), Léon Walras (1874), Eugen von Böhm-Bawerk (1889), Knut Wicksell (1893, 1901), and John Bates Clark (1899), essentially followed the classical authors: the concept of "long-run equilibrium" is the neoclassical adaptation of the classical concept of long-period positions (see also Chapter 1).

This chapter is devoted to a brief discussion of major versions of the neoclassical theory of value and distribution. Attention will focus on those versions in which the long-period method of the classical economists is preserved; however, other, that is, more recent, versions will also be dealt with. In order to distinguish the former from the latter, which abandoned the long-period method and the concept of a uniform rate of profit, we shall henceforth call the earlier versions "traditional." Browsing through contemporary literature one sees that traditional neoclassical theory is still used in many fields of economic theorizing. One of the reasons for its popularity appears to be that compared with the other, allegedly more sophisticated, versions, that is, intertemporal and temporary equilibrium theory, it generally allows one to derive clear-cut results that can easily be interpreted. Therefore, a discussion of it appears to be appropriate.

In Section 1 the core of the traditional neoclassical theory of value and distribution will be sketched. Section 2 then distinguishes between the different versions in which that theory was put forward. Section 3 summarizes the critique leveled at the traditional versions of the theory in the famous "Cambridge" controversy in the theory of capital. Section 4 contains a summary of several attempts of varying degrees of sophistication on the part of neoclassical authors to counter the attack. Section 5 provides a critical discussion of the development of modern neoclassical theories, that is, those based on the notions of temporary and intertemporal equilibrium, respectively.

The following discussion will focus on what we consider to be the essentials; the reader interested in a more detailed treatment of the issues under consideration is requested to consult the relevant literature on capital theory, in particular Garegnani (1960, 1970, 1990a), Harcourt and Laing (1971), Harcourt (1969, 1972), Bliss (1975), Burmeister (1980a), Eatwell, Milgate, and Newman (1987), Kurz (1987), and Ahmad (1991).

1. **The core of traditional neoclassical theory**

While the surplus approach of the classical economists conceived of the real wage as determined *prior* to profits and rent, the neoclassical approach aimed to explain all kinds of income *symmetrically* in terms of supply and demand in regard to the services of the respective "factors of production," labor, land, and "capital." It was the seemingly coherent foundation of these notions in terms of *functional* relationships between the price of a service (or good) and the quantity supplied or demanded, elaborated by the neoclassical theory, that greatly contributed to the latter's success.

Historically, neoclassical theory can be shown to derive from a generalization of the theory of rent in terms of land of uniform quality and "intensive" margins to all factors of production, including "capital" (see, in particular, Bharadwaj, 1978). Assume that "corn" can be produced with unassisted labor and land. Variable proportions of the two factors can then be shown as implying equality between the marginal products and the rates of remuneration of the factor services, that is, the wage rate and the rent rate in terms of the product.

In exercises 7.5 and 7.9 of Chapter 10 relationships between the wage rate and the quantity of labor employed were built up in the special cases in which there are either only extensive diminishing returns or only intensive diminishing returns. (A generalization to the case in which there are both extensive and intensive diminishing returns is not difficult; see Kurz and Salvadori, 1992). This relationship is depicted in Figure 14.1 as DD'; it is commonly called the aggregate "demand function" for labor. Confronting this demand function with an aggregate "supply function" of labor, SS' (see Figure 14.1), derived from the optimal choices of utility

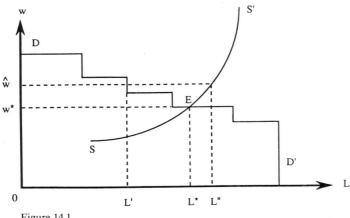

Figure 14.1

maximizing individuals regarding the desired consumption of corn and leisure time (and, consequently, the desired labor time), respectively, for alternative levels of the real wage rate, may then give rise to a constellation such as the one depicted in Figure 14.1, which is familiar from conventional textbooks. In it the downward sloping demand function for labor is intersected by an upward sloping supply function in point E, which gives the equilibrium values of total employment, L^*, and the real wage rate, w^*, in the economy as a whole. With flexible wages point E is assumed to be a center of gravitation. Starting from a level of the wage rate higher than the market clearing level, for example, $w = \hat{w}$, the number of laborers employed would be L' which is smaller than the number of those seeking employment, L''. Unemployed laborers would then start bidding down the real wage until it reaches the level compatible with full employment. Similarly, with an initial wage rate smaller than the market clearing level and hence the demand for labor larger than the supply, landowners, unable to find additional workers at the going wage rate, would start bidding up wages. Assuming other things to be equal, including the amount of land available for the production of corn, in both cases the system would tend toward the equilibrium position E.

Next assume that corn is produced by labor and "capital" consisting exclusively of corn (seed corn), on homogeneous land that is available in unlimited quantities, that is, a free good. With continuously variable proportions between labor and (corn) capital, K, the argument developed for the labor–land case carries over to the present case. Hence a similar equality would hold between the rate of profit (interest), r, and that of wages on the one hand and the marginal products of (corn) capital and

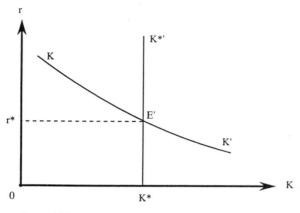

Figure 14.2

labor on the other. Exercise 9.7 of Chapter 2 gives an example of the construction of this relationship. Figure 14.2 illustrates the argument in terms of the "capital market." With (corn) capital in given supply, $K = K^*$, the equilibrium rate of profit would be ascertained at the point where the demand function for capital, KK', derived on the assumption that there is full employment of labor, intersects the horizontal "supply function" $K^*K^{*\prime}$, that is, E' in the diagram with r^* as the equilibrium rate of profit.

This is the analogy between "capital" or land and labor drawn by the early marginalist authors. The question is whether this analogy holds good in cases that are less special than the one in which capital consists exclusively of corn, that is, a commodity homogeneous with the product, and land is not scarce; or the case in which produced means of production do not exist. The answer given by the authors under discussion was in the affirmative. That is, it was contended that the simple case essentially carries over to the general case in which heterogeneous capital goods are used in production and in which land can be in short supply.

Expressing the "quantity of capital" in given supply in value terms is necessitated by the following consideration. Careful scrutiny shows that the advocates of the traditional neoclassical theory of distribution, with the notable exception of Walras (at least until the fourth edition of the *Eléments*; see Subsection 4.2 of Chapter 1), were well aware of the fact that in order to be consistent with the concept of a long-run equilibrium the capital endowment of the economy could not be conceived of as a set of given physical amounts of produced means of production. For, if the capital endowment is given in kind only a short-run equilibrium, characterized by differential rates of return on the supply prices of the various capital goods, could be established by the forces constituting supply and demand. However, under conditions of free competition, which would enforce a tendency toward a uniform rate of profit, such an equilibrium could not be considered, in the words of Hicks (1932, p. 20), a "full equilibrium." Hence the "quantity of capital" available for productive purposes had to be expressed as a *value* magnitude, allowing it to assume the physical "form" suited to the other data of the theory, that is, the endowment of the economy with factors of production other than capital, the technical alternatives of production and the preferences of agents.

Thus the formidable problem for the neoclassical approach in attempting the determination of the general rate of profit consisted in the necessity of establishing the notion of a market for "capital," the "quantity" of which could be expressed *independently* of the price of its service, that is, the rate of profit.[1] Moreover, the plausibility of the supply and demand approach to the theory of distribution was felt to hinge upon the demonstration of the existence of a unique and stable equilibrium in that market (see, for example, Marshall, [1890] 1977, p. 665n.). With the "quantity of capital" in given supply, this, in turn, implied that a monotonically *decreasing* demand function for capital in terms of the rate of profit had to be established.

This inverse relationship was arrived at by the neoclassical theorists through the introduction of two kinds of *substitutability* between capital and labor (and other factors of production): substitutability in consumption and in production. According to the former concept a rise in the rate of profit relative to the real wage rate would increase the price of those commodities, whose production exhibits a relatively high ratio of capital to labor, compared to those in which little capital per worker is employed. This would generally prompt consumers to shift their demand in favor of a higher proportion of the relatively cheapened commodities, that is, the "labor-intensive" ones. Hence in the economy as a whole the capital–labor ratio, or "capital intensity," and the rate of profit are inversely related. The second concept, that is, substitutability in production, we have encountered already in the discussion of the model with corn capital. A rise in the rate of profit (interest) relative to the wage rate would make cost-minimizing entrepreneurs in the different industries of the economy employ more of the relatively cheapened factor of production, that is, labor. Hence, through both routes capital would become substitutable for labor, and for any given quantity of labor employed a decreasing demand

---

[1] In the case of fixed capital the rental price of a capital good includes profits at the going rate plus depreciation to make good the wear and tear of the capital good.

schedule for capital would obtain.[2] Figure 14.2 thus appears to illustrate not only the hypothetical world with corn capital alone, but also the "real world" with heterogeneous capital goods. The conclusion is close at hand that the division of the product between wages and profits can be explained in terms of the "scarcity" of the respective "factors of production": labor and capital, where the latter is conceived as a value magnitude that is considered independent of the rate of profit.

2. Versions of traditional neoclassical theory

We may distinguish between several versions of traditional neo-classical theory. First, there is the *macro*economic version which claims that there is an *aggregate* production function with total labor employed together with the capital stock in existence explaining both total output and its distribution as wages and profits, thanks to the principle of "marginal productivity." Second, there is the *micro*economic version which claims that production functions with capital as an input can be formulated for each single commodity. Finally, since *all* versions of neoclassical theory start from the premise of a given *endowment* of the economy as a whole with a "quantity of capital," we may distinguish between different versions according to which concept of capital endowment is advocated. There are essentially three alternatives, two of which are based on notions of "real" capital, while the third is based on the notion of "value" capital. The three are: (i) capital conceived of as a subsistence fund, that is, the version developed by Jevons and Böhm-Bawerk; (ii) capital conceived of as a set of quantities of heterogeneous capital goods, that is, the version elaborated by Walras; and (iii) capital conceived of as a value magnitude, that is, the version put forward by Wicksell, J. B. Clark, and Marshall.

---

[2] From this it follows that the view frequently to be found in the literature that the premise of substitutability in production is the crucial feature distinguishing the neoclassical approach from other approaches cannot be sustained. It is perfectly possible to set up a model that exhibits all the neoclassical features despite the fact that production in each industry can be carried out in terms of a single fixed coefficients method of production only: substitution in consumption is enough to guarantee that the demand for a factor service is elastic with respect to the price of the service. In the first edition of Walras's *Eléments* (1874), for example, fixed "coefficients de fabrication" were assumed. In this connection it is worth pointing out that in the wake of the "marginalist revolution" attention focused almost exclusively on the sphere of consumption. The reasoning developed there, based on such concepts as "marginal utility," "indifference curve," and "marginal rate of substitution," was later carried over to the sphere of production, with "marginal productivity," "isoquant," and "marginal rate of transformation" as the new, "twin" concepts.

2.1. The aggregate production function

The success of the first version was closely connected with the rise of macroeconomics in the aftermath of the publication of Keynes's *General Theory* (Keynes, *CW*, VII).[3] It was further enhanced by the booming neoclassical theory of growth in the late 1950s (see Solow, 1956, and Swan, 1956). According to this version total output Y, is a function of capital K, and labor L, with the function exhibiting "neoclassical properties," that is,

$$Y = F(K, L),$$

with

$$\frac{\partial Y}{\partial K} > 0, \quad \frac{\partial Y}{\partial L} > 0 \quad \text{and} \quad \frac{\partial^2 Y}{\partial K^2} < 0, \quad \frac{\partial^2 Y}{\partial L^2} < 0.$$

With perfect competition in all markets, the economic system is said to gravitate around a position in which the rate of profit and the real wage rate equal the marginal products of capital and labor, respectively, that is,

$$\frac{\partial Y}{\partial K} = r \quad \text{and} \quad \frac{\partial Y}{\partial L} = w.$$

It should be emphasized that the concept of an aggregate production function meant to describe production in the economy as a whole is of relatively recent origin. It was used, for example, by Cobb and Douglas (1928).[4] Contrary to what is sometimes maintained, it is not to be found in the earlier authors such as John Bates Clark or Eugen von Böhm-Bawerk. These authors, interested as they were in explaining the functioning of a capitalist economy based on the social division of labor, were concerned with the determination of normal income distribution and normal prices. To this effect they rather advocated the concept of capital as a value magnitude to be used in the functions of aggregate supply and demand; some authors assumed in addition that microeconomic production functions that have value capital as an input could be used.

---

[3] It should be noted, however, that contrary to the impression given in many macroeconomic textbooks Keynes himself did not use an aggregate production function.

[4] The *form* of production function suggested by Cobb and Douglas can already be found in the writings of Wicksteed ([1894] 1992, Sections 5 and 7; see also Steedman's introduction, p. 22) and Wicksell ([1896] 1954, part I). This fact does not mean, as is sometimes implied in the literature (see, for example, Jones, 1975, p. 36), that Wicksteed and Wicksell advocated an *aggregate* production function.

2.2. *Capital as a factor of production*

There are two variants of this version. According to the first variant the amounts of heterogeneous capital goods needed in the production of single commodities can be represented by quantities of a single factor capital, conceived of as a value magnitude. According to the second variant a scalar representation of vectors of heterogeneous means of production can be found which is independent of distribution and prices.

(i) Value capital. The alternative methods of production available to produce a certain commodity i in the case in which there is homogeneous land and labor can be described by

$$y_i = f_i(k_i, l_i, b_i), \quad (i = 1, 2, \ldots, n)$$

with y_i as the output of commodity i and k_i, l_i and b_i as the (value) capital, labor and land inputs, respectively. The "marginal products" with respect to each "factor of production" are commonly assumed to be positive and decreasing. The scalar k_i is taken to respresent the "quantity of capital" employed in the production of commodity i, it being understood that it consists of heterogeneous means of production the composition of which is fully adjusted to the quantities employed of the other inputs, land and labor. Thus J. B. Clark distinguished between "capital," which is abstract and permanent, and "capital goods," which are concrete and perishable:

> We may think of capital as a sum of productive wealth, invested in material things which are perpetually shifting – which come and go continually – although the fund abides. Capital thus lives, as it were, by transmigration, taking itself out of one set of bodies and putting itself into another, again and again (Clark, 1899, pp.119–20).[5]

Capital of necessity must change "form" if the proportion in which it is combined with labor changes:

> All that we have said about the change that must take place in the *forms* of capital, when the *amount* of it is fixed and the working force is increasing, applies here, where these conditions are reversed. The steady increase of the capital, if the amount of the labor be fixed, compels a similar change of forms (ibid., p. 183; emphases added).

[5] According to Samuelson (1962) it was particularly J. B. Clark who introduced the "neoclassical fairy tale" in capital theory, based on the notion that capital is some peculiar substance which transmutes itself from one machine form into another like the restless incarnating soul.

These and other passages indicate that the author of *The Distribution of Wealth* entertained the opinion that the "quantity of capital" that can be put in the production function of a single industry could be conceived of as a value magnitude, representing a portion of the "fixed fund of permanent social capital" (ibid., p. 197) available at a given moment of time in the economy as a whole (see also Clark, 1907).

With the amount of capital increasing, other things being equal, its marginal product, or "final productivity," is assumed to fall: "If capital be used in increasing quantity by a fixed working force, it is subject to a law of diminishing productivity" (ibid., p. 48; see also p. 139) – in the same way as the "final productivity" of labor tends to fall with a *ceteris paribus* increase in the employment of labor. Clark concludes: "The principle of final productivity...acts in two ways, affording a theory of wages and of interest" (ibid., p. 187). "Normal" income distribution in conditions of free competition is then defined in terms of a uniform rate of interest throughout the economy r and a uniform wage rate for each kind of labor. Focusing attention on the former, we have

$$\frac{\partial y_i}{\partial k_i} p_i = r, \quad (i = 1, 2, \ldots, n)$$

where p_i is the price of one unit of commodity i. From this equation it also becomes clear why Clark insisted that the theory of distribution and that of value are inseparable (cf. ibid., ch. II): "Prices are at their natural level when labor and capital in one industry produce as much and get as much as they do in any other. Normal prices mean equalized wages and equalized interest" (ibid., p. 16).

Traces of the concept of the "quantity of capital" represented by an amount of value used in the production functions of single commodities can also be found in the writings of Alfred Marshall ([1890] 1977) and Arthur Cecil Pigou (1933). On Clark's theory of capital see also Veblen (1907); on Marshall's theory see Bliss (1990).

(ii) A one-dimensional measure of capital: Time. Other marginalist authors were aware of the deficiency of the above variant and attempted to express the "quantity of capital" as a single magnitude independent of distribution and thus prices.[6] The most important attempt in this respect was that of the Austrian capital theorists, most notably Eugen von Böhm-Bawerk

---

[6] In his controversy with J. B. Clark on the fundamentals of capital theory, Böhm-Bawerk criticized Clark's attempt to differentiate between "true capital" and "capital goods"; in Böhm-Bawerk's view this was "dark, mystical rhetoric" (see in particular Böhm-Bawerk, 1906–7, and Clark, 1907).

([1889] 1891) and Knut Wicksell ([1893] 1954), who sought such a measure of capital in the concept of the "average period of production."[7]

The basic idea underlying the Austrian concept that capital, or rather capital intensity, can somehow be measured by the *time* for which it is invested in a process of production, was anticipated by William Stanley Jevons ([1871] 1965).[8] Referring to the case in which an input of labor in one period yields an output of a consumption good several periods later, the gist of his argument consisted of the concept of a production function for commodity i, $q_i = f_i(T_i)$, where output per unit of labor, q_i, is "some continuous function of the time elapsing between the expenditure of labour and the enjoyment of the results" T_i; this function is assumed to exhibit diminishing returns (ibid., pp. 240–1). Jevons showed that in equilibrium

$$r = \frac{f_i'(T_i)}{f_i(T_i)}.$$

Böhm-Bawerk's concern was with establishing a generalized temporal version of demand and supply theory, the atemporal version of which was identified with Walras's general equilibrium analysis. This involved the appropriate reformulation of the data of the theory. The central elements of his analysis were the concepts of "time preference" and the "average period of production," used in describing consumer preferences and technical alternatives, respectively. As in Jevons, social capital was conceived of as a subsistence fund and was seen to permit the adoption of more "roundabout," that is, time-consuming, methods of production. It was to the concept of the "average period of production" that the marginal productivity condition was applied in the determination of the rate of interest (alias rate of profit).

[7] In *Value, Capital and Rent* Wicksell praised Böhm-Bawerk for having for the first time introduced into the subject the "length of the production period" as "an independent concept, which will presumably prove extremely fruitful" (Wicksell, [1893] 1954 p. 22). As we shall see below (see Subsection 2.3), Wicksell later changed his mind.

[8] For a discussion of Jevons's theory of capital and interest see Steedman (1972). The idea can in fact be traced back even further in the history of economic thought. The time element in production was emphasized, for example, by David Ricardo who played with the idea of reducing all differences between processes of production to differences in the time that elapses between the beginning of a process and the availability of its product; see also Edelberg (1933) and Kurz and Salvadori (1993a, pp. 103–4). The Austrian approach is clearly foreshadowed in the analyses of John Rae (1834) and of the German economists Friedrich von Hermann (1832) and Albert Schäffle (1864). The writings of the latter two were of considerable importance in shaping Böhm-Bawerk's approach to the theory of capital and interest; see on this Hennings (1972) and Kurz (1994b).

The construction of the "average period of production" in Böhm-Bawerk and Wicksell, just like that of the "average time of investment" in Jevons, was subject to the following assumptions:

(i) there is only single production (circulating capital), that is, joint production and fixed capital are set aside;
(ii) there is only a single "original" factor of production, homogeneous labor, that is, land is a free good;
(iii) there is only simple interest, that is, compound interest is set aside.

With wages paid at the beginning of the production period, the "average period of production" of commodity i can be derived as follows. To this effect we make use of the "reduction to dated quantities of labor," dealt with in Section 1 of Chapter 6.

With wages paid *ante factum*, for a given system of production the price equation with compound interest would be

$$\mathbf{p} = w[(1+r)\mathbf{l} + (1+r)^2\mathbf{Al} + (1+r)^3\mathbf{A}^2\mathbf{l} + (1+r)^4\mathbf{A}^3\mathbf{l} + \cdots]$$

or

$$\mathbf{p} = w[(1+r)\mathbf{l}_1 + (1+r)^2\mathbf{l}_2 + (1+r)^3\mathbf{l}_3 + (1+r)^4\mathbf{l}_4 + \cdots], \quad (14.1)$$

where $\mathbf{A}^j\mathbf{l} = \mathbf{l}_{j+1}$ $(j = 0, 1, 2, \ldots)$. With *simple* interest we have instead

$$\mathbf{p} = w[(1+r)\mathbf{l}_1 + (1+2r)\mathbf{l}_2 + (1+3r)\mathbf{l}_3 + (1+4r)\mathbf{l}_4 + \cdots]. \quad (14.2)$$

This can be written as

$$\mathbf{p} = w\left(\sum_t \mathbf{l}_t + r\sum_t t\mathbf{l}_t\right) = w(\mathbf{I} + r\mathbf{T})\mathbf{v},$$

where $\mathbf{v} = \sum_t \mathbf{l}_t$ is the vector of direct and indirect quantities of labor "embodied" in the different commodities, $\mathbf{T}$ is a diagonal matrix which has the "average periods of production" of the different industries on its main diagonal, $t_{ii} = \tau_i$, and

$$\tau_i = \sum_t t\frac{l_{ti}}{\sum_h l_{hi}} = \frac{\sum_t t l_{ti}}{v_i}.$$

It is the weighted average of the periods of time over which the amounts of labor l_{ji}, $j = 1, 2, \ldots$, remain invested until one unit of commodity i is obtained, with the respective amounts of labor serving as weights. By means of this device the Austrian capital theorists thought it possible to replace in each line of production a vector of physically heterogeneous capital goods with a scalar τ_i, which is independent of distribution and prices. "Capital" was thus taken to be reducible to a single variable dimension: the length of time.

Next we come to the different neoclassical conceptualizations of the endowment of an economy with capital. We begin with a brief discussion of the concept of capital as a subsistence fund as it was advocated, among others, by Jevons, Böhm-Bawerk, and the Wicksell of *Value, Capital and Rent* (cf. Wicksell, [1893] 1954).

2.3. Real capital: A fund of subsistence goods

A rather common procedure in the earlier literature, particularly its Austrian variant, was to express the capital endowment of an economy in terms of consumption goods or, more precisely, to conceive of it as a "subsistence fund" in support of the "original" factors of production labor and land, during the period of production extending from the initial expenditure of the services of these factors to the completion of consumption goods. This notion corresponded to the view that capital resulted from the investment of past savings, which, in turn, implied "abstention" from consumption. Thus it appeared to be natural to measure "capital" in terms of some composite unit of consumption goods.

This is clearly expressed by Jevons, who in chapter VII of his *Theory of Political Economy*, entitled "Free and Invested Capital," wrote: "I believe that the clear explanation of the doctrine of capital requires the use of a term *free capital*, which has not been hitherto recognised by economists. By free capital I mean the wages of labor... [in its] real form of food and other necessaries of life. The ordinary sustenance requisite to support labourers of all ranks when engaged upon their work is really the true form of capital" (Jevons, [1871] 1965, pp. 242–3).[9] Similarly, Böhm-Bawerk expressed the view that "in any economical community the supply of subsistence available for advances of subsistence, is... represented by the total sum of its wealth." This is so, Böhm-Bawerk expounded, because "all goods which appear today as the stock or parent wealth of society ... will, in the more or less distant future... ripen into consumption goods, and will consequently cover, for a more or less lengthy time to come, the people's demand for consumption" (Böhm-Bawerk, [1889] 1891, pp. 319, 322).

The idea underlying this concept of capital appears to be the following. Society can be conceived of as possessed of a fund of wage goods that can be used to employ workers to produce consumption goods (including wage goods). The amounts produced are taken to depend, *inter alia*, on the lengths of the (average) periods of production chosen in the different industries. The adoption of more "roundabout" processes is however limited by the given size of the subsistence fund and the real wage rate.

[9] What Jevons calls the "transitory form" of free capital, that is, money wages, need not concern us here.

In order for the composite consumption good to represent "real capital," its composition has to be independent of the rate of interest and the methods of production adopted by cost minimizing producers. However, this condition is generally not met, that is, the "subsistence fund" is not independent of the variables it is supposed, in part, to determine. For example, with a change in the rate of interest relative prices will generally change and, correspondingly, so will the proportions in which commodities are consumed by workers.

Wicksell became aware of the difficulty involved in seeking a measure of real capital in terms of Böhm-Bawerk's "subsistence fund," and by the time of his *Lectures* expressed doubts as to the validity of this concept: "It may be difficult – if not impossible – to define this concept of social capital with absolute precision as a definite quantity. In reality it is rather a complex of quantities" (Wicksell, [1901] 1934, p. 165). With the concept of "real capital" being impossible to define with absolute precision, the idea of seeking a measure of the economy's endowment with capital in terms of a value magnitude was close at hand. Before we investigate whether this indicates a way out of the impasse, we have to turn to another concept of real capital, that is, the one advocated by Walras ([1874] 1954). Since Walras's theory of capital and distribution has already been dealt with in Subsection 4.2 of Chapter 1 we can be very brief.

2.4. Real capital: A vector of heterogeneous capital goods

Walras assumed that the economy's endowment of capital is given in terms of quantities of physically specified capital goods. He emphasized that the vector of capital goods may be any vector whatsoever, that is, it need not be adjusted to, or defined relative to, the other data of the model, namely the pattern of ownership of resources, the preferences of consumers and the technical alternatives from which producers can choose. Setting aside the problems of insurance of durable capital goods, the rate of net income for the ith capital good proper r_i, is

$$r_i = \frac{\pi_i - h_i P_i}{P_i}.$$

$(i = 1, 2, \ldots, l)$, where π_i is the price of the service, P_i is the price of the ith capital good proper, and h_i is the given rate of depreciation. Walras requires that in equilibrium the rates of net income are uniform across all capital goods, that is,

$$r_1 = r_2 = \cdots = r_l = r,$$

where r is the general rate of net income. In addition, according to the "law of cost of production," in equilibrium the cost of production of capital good i, κ_i, equals the price of the capital good:

$$\kappa_i = P_i$$

$(i = 1, 2, \ldots, l)$. Hence, in equilibrium,

$$r = \frac{\pi_i - h_i \kappa_i}{\kappa_i}$$

$(i = 1, 2, \ldots, l)$. However, with an arbitrarily given vector of capital goods proper, there is no reason to presume that the requirement of a uniform rate of net income and that of an equality between the selling price and the cost of production of all capital goods can be satisfied simultaneously. This can be seen in the following way. Assume first that the prices of productive services, and a fortiori also the costs of production of new capital goods, are given and independent of actual outputs of new capital goods. Yet with π_i and κ_i given for each capital good i, the last set of equations will generally not be consistent: the ratio between $(\pi_i - h_i \kappa_i)$ and κ_i cannot be expected to be the same for all capital goods i ($i = 1, 2, \ldots, l$) and equal to r; there will rather be as many different rates of net income as there are different capital goods. Moreover, it cannot be presumed that this inconsistency is removed once the possible effects of variations in the quantities of capital goods produced on the prices of the services and cost of production of capital goods are taken into consideration. The physical composition of the capital stock inherited by the economy may be incompatible with an "equilibrium" as specified by Walras.

In the fourth edition of the *Eléments* Walras noted that his formal analysis is confronted with the difficulty mentioned. He traced the difficulty to the arbitrarily given composition (and size) of the initial capital stock. In the newly inserted §267 of Lesson 28 he writes:

> If we suppose that old fixed capital goods proper...are already found in the economy in [given] quantities...and that their gross and net incomes are paid for at prices determined by the system of production equations and by the rates of depreciation and insurance, it is not at all certain that the amount of savings [S] will be adequate for the manufacture of new fixed capital goods proper in just such quantities as will satisfy the last l equations of the above system. In an economy like the one we have imagined, which establishes its economic equilibrium *ab ovo*, it is probable that there would be *no* equality of rates of net income.... On the other hand, in an economy in *normal* operation which has only to maintain itself in equilibrium, we may *suppose* the last l equations to be satisfied ([1874] 1954, p. 308; the first emphasis is Walras's).

Walras makes clear in this passage that taking the inherited stocks of capital goods as given, then, flukes apart, only a *short-period* equilibrium characterized by unequal rates of net income can be determined. In order to retain the notion of long-period equilibrium in the present framework, it has to be "supposed" that the price equations of the fixed capital goods are satisfied, which is tantamount to assuming that the endowment of the economy with stocks of heterogeneous capital goods is a part of the solution of the system of equations rather than a part of the givens, on the basis of which a solution is sought. In other words, Walras himself arrived at the conclusion that "normal" income distribution and "normal" prices *cannot* generally be explained in terms of the forces of supply and demand. Walras also pointed out how reactions on the part of agents could "correct" the composition of the capital stock and thereby eliminate the internal inconsistency mentioned. The correction requires the production of those capital goods that yield their owners the highest rate of net income, while those items of capital goods which yield lower rates would, if worn out, perhaps not even be replaced (cf. Walras, ibid., p. 481; similarly p. 294). This is discussed by Walras in terms of what he calls a process of *tâtonnement*. In this way the system is said to converge or gravitate toward an equilibrium characterized by a uniform rate of net income.

There do of course exist other neoclassical responses to the finding that an arbitrarily given vector of quantities of heterogeneous capital goods is generally not compatible with a long-run equilibrium. First, there is the option of abandoning the long-period method and with it, in conditions of free competition, the concern with a uniform rate of profit; this alternative will be dealt with in Section 5. Second, there is the option of preserving the long-period method by abandoning Walras's specification of the capital endowment in physical terms and replacing it with the notion of capital as a value magnitude.

2.5. Capital as a value magnitude

The endowment of the economy with a factor called "capital" conceived of as a value magnitude was advocated by several neoclassical authors. The clearest formulation of this version of the theory was put forward by Knut Wicksell.

As we have seen in Subsection 2.2, Wicksell was originally of the opinion that the problem of the heterogeneity of capital goods could be mastered in terms of Böhm-Bawerk's notion of the "average period of production." He, however, became increasingly aware of the fact that once the simplifying assumptions (i)–(iii) (cf. Subsection 2.2) are dropped, the concept can no longer be sustained. For example, with compound interest, that is, starting from equation (14.1) rather than (14.2), there is generally no way of expressing a given set of capital goods as the same magnitude of "capital" whatever the distribution of the social product between wages and profits. Therefore, Wicksell in the *Lectures on Political Economy* abandoned the concept and considered "the total amount of a commodity produced as a function (homogeneous and linear) of all the quantities of labour and land employed (i.e., annually consumed) both *current* and *saved up*" (Wicksell, [1901] 1934, p. 203). He thus postulated a production function for commodity *i*, which in our notation can be written as

$$y_i = f_i(l_{1i}, l_{2i}, l_{3i}, \ldots; b_{1i}, b_{2i}, b_{3i}, \ldots), \quad (i = 1, 2, \ldots, n)$$

where l_{1i} and b_{1i} indicate current services of labor and land, l_{2i} and b_{2i} services in the previous period, etc. In accordance with this view of the capital inputs in production he defined capital and interest as follows:

> *Capital is saved-up labor and saved-up land. Interest is the difference between the marginal productivity of saved-up labor and land and of current labor and land* (ibid., p. 154).

With the wage per unit of labor and the rent per acre paid at the end of the production period (month or year), in *long-period equilibrium* the values of the marginal products of the dated quantities of labor and land are equal to the wage rate and rent rate, *w* and *q*, properly discounted forward, that is,

$$\frac{\partial y_i}{\partial l_{ji}} p_i = w(1 + r)^{j-1} \quad (i = 1, 2, \ldots, n; j = 1, 2, \ldots)$$

$$\frac{\partial y_i}{\partial b_{ji}} p_i = q(1 + r)^{j-1}, \quad (i = 1, 2, \ldots, n; j = 1, 2, \ldots)$$

with p_i as the price of commodity *i* and *r* as the rate of interest. All value magnitudes are expressed in terms of a common numeraire consisting of one or several consumption goods.

Wicksell for simplicity assumed a stationary economy. In equilibrium the total quantity demanded of each factor equals the total quantity of it supplied. The formulation of this condition causes no problem with regard to labor and land, which can be measured in terms of their own physical units. With the quantities of labor *L*, and land *B*, given and independent of the respective rates of remuneration, in equilibrium we have

$$L = \sum_{i=1}^{n} \sum_{j=1}^{\infty} l_{ji}$$

$$B = \sum_{i=1}^{n} \sum_{j=1}^{\infty} b_{ji}.$$

Things are different with regard to capital. In order to be consistent with the notion of a long-period equilibrium, the "quantity of capital" available in the economy at the beginning of the production period K, can be given in value terms only, representing a certain amount of the numeraire commodity. In equilibrium

$$K = w \sum_{i=1}^{n} \sum_{j=2}^{\infty} l_{ji}(1 + r)^{j-1} + q \sum_{i=1}^{n} \sum_{j=2}^{\infty} b_{ji}(1 + r)^{j-1}.$$

The *physical composition* of K in terms of the l_{ji} and b_{ji} is thus a part of the equilibrium solution to the problem of value and distribution rather than one of its data. In this approach the problem of capital is shifted from the conceptualization of the processes of production of single commodities to that of the supply of and demand for "capital" in the system as a whole, that is, to the conceptualization of a market for capital on a par with the markets for labor and land (services).

The ground is now prepared for a summary of the main objections put forward against the different versions of traditional neoclassical theory during the so-called Cambridge controversy in the theory of capital.

3. The critique of traditional neoclassical theory

While, as we shall see in Section 5, inklings to the effect that traditional neoclassical theory does not stand up to close examination are already to be found in earlier debates around the turn of the century and particularly in the 1930s, it was not until the controversy in the 1960s and 1970s that its deficiencies were put into sharp relief.

3.1. The aggregate production function

The macroeconomic version was the target of a criticism put forward in "The Production Function and the Theory of Capital" by Joan Robinson (1953). Her paper was the proper beginning of what has become known as the "Cambridge Controversies in the Theory of Capital" (see Harcourt, 1969, 1972). In the course of investigating the meaning of a production function for total output, Joan Robinson set up what Robert Solow (1963) later dubbed a "pseudo-production function," consisting of the possible positions of equilibrium, corresponding to alternative levels of the rate of profit, given the set of alternative techniques of production. She showed that "there is no meaning to be given to a 'quantity of capital' apart from the rate of profit, so that the contention that the 'marginal product of capital' determines the rate of profit is meaningless" (Robinson, 1970, p. 309). In constructing a "pseudo-production function" she found that over certain ranges of it the technique that becomes eligible at a lower real wage rate (to which a higher rate of profit corresponds) may be less labor-intensive than that chosen at a higher wage rate (to which a lower rate of profit corresponds). This finding contradicted the "well-behaved production function," the popular workhorse of neoclassical macroeconomic theory, which assumes that a lower real wage rate is always associated with a more labor-intensive technique.

Joan Robinson called this finding a "perverse relationship" (Robinson, 1956, pp. 109–10), a "curiosum," and attributed its discovery to Ruth Cohen. Later she stated that this acknowledgment was "a private joke" and added:

> I had picked up the clue from Piero Sraffa's Preface to Ricardo's *Principles* and my analysis (errors and omissions excepted) was a preview of his. When his own treatment of the subject was finally published (Sraffa, 1960), the "Ruth Cohen case" (which I had treated as a *curiosum*) was seen to have great prominence; the striking proposition was established that it is perfectly normal (within the accepted assumptions) for the same technique to be eligible at several discrete rates of profit. It was from this that the sobriquet "reswitching of techniques" was derived (Robinson, 1970, pp. 309–10).[10]

Paul Samuelson (1962), in an attempt to counter Joan Robinson's attack on the aggregate production function, claimed that even in cases with heterogeneous capital goods some rationalization can be provided for the validity of simple neoclassical "parables" which assume that there is a single homogeneous factor called "capital," the marginal product of which equals the rate of return. Samuelson based his defense of traditional theory in terms of the construction of a "surrogate production function" in a model which takes into account heterogeneous capital as in exercises 8.23, 8.24 and 8.26 of Chapter 5: corn is produced with labor and a machine, which is itself produced by labor and the same machine, but for each process to produce corn there is a different machine. In constructing the "surrogate production function," Samuelson, alas, assumed equal proportions of labor to the machine in both sectors of the economy for each technique (cf. ibid., pp. 196–7). This however implied that the two goods could not sensibly be discriminated in the sense that the price of the machine in terms of corn is not affected by changes in income distribution (cf. Section 3 of Chapter 4). By this token the "real" economy with heterogeneous goods was turned into the "imaginary" economy with a

---

[10] It should be noted that the "Ruth Cohen curiosum" as originally introduced by Joan Robinson involved reverse capital deepening rather than reswitching as in the above quotation.

homogeneous output, that is, the "surrogate production function" was nothing more than the infamous aggregate production function. This was shown, among others, by Garegnani (1970).[11] Samuelson (1966a) openly admitted that he was wrong and that what he called the "Ramsey–Clark parable," that is, the aggregate production function, cannot generally be sustained.

In the introduction to her 1953 paper Joan Robinson stressed that "the production function has been a powerful instrument of miseducation" (Robinson, 1953, p. 81). The economic literature published since shows that, strangely enough, it still is.

3.2. Capital as a factor of production

The use of the value of capital as a factor of production alongside labor and land which are measured in terms of their own technical units in the production function of single commodities was already rejected by Knut Wicksell. This implied "arguing in a circle" (Wicksell, [1901] 1934, p. 149), since capital and the rate of interest enter as a cost in the production of capital goods themselves. Hence the value of the capital goods inserted in the production function depends on the rate of interest and will generally change with it.

(i) Arguing in a circle. The vulnerability of any attempt to treat capital as a value magnitude in the definition of the set of technical alternatives available to the economy can be made clear also in the following way. The notion of a production function requires that a single level of output be associated with any given amount of productive resources employed. However, with capital goods represented by their value in the production function, with different levels of the rate of profit the value of the same set of capital goods would generally also be different. This however runs counter to the uniqueness of the relation between output and the amount of productive resources used as input.

The criticism reported is derived from the fact that relative prices, and thus also the prices of capital goods, generally depend on income distribution. It is only in the special case of uniform proportions of labor to circulating means of production in all industries that prices are independent of the rate of profit and are indeed proportional to quantities of labor embodied (see Section 3 of Chapter 4). Following Joan Robinson (1953, p. 95) the dependence of prices on distribution was discussed under the

---

[11] A first version of Garegnani's paper was submitted to the *Review of Economic Studies* in April 1963 and accepted for publication subject to revision shortly afterward; the substantially enlarged final version was submitted in October 1968.

heading of "price Wicksell effects."[12] Even though the phenomenon under consideration had been well known since the classical economists and was referred to by several neoclassical authors also, especially Wicksell (for example, [1901] 1934, pp. 147–51), the earlier authors were not fully aware of the complications involved. In particular, they were of the opinion that with a rise in the rate of profit r, given the system of production, the ratio of prices of any two commodities would *either* stay constant *or* rise *or* fall, throughout the range of variation of r. This opinion was closely related to the hypothesis that the capital–labor or capital–output ratios of the different industries could be brought into a ranking that is independent of distribution. Yet, as Sraffa has shown, this is generally not possible, that is, "the price of a product...may rise or it may fall, or it may even alternate in rising and falling, relative to its means of production" (Sraffa, 1960, p. 15). Therefore, to characterize an industry as "capital intensive" or "labour intensive" in general makes no sense unless the level of the rate of profit is specified at which this characterization is supposed to apply.

Sraffa illustrates his point with reference to the "reduction to dated quantities of labour" (see Section 1 of Chapter 6). The "labour terms" in the series "can be regarded as the constituent elements of the price of a commodity, the combination of which in various proportions may, with the variation of the rate of profits, give rise to complicated patterns of price-movement with several ups and downs" (ibid., p. 37). This is demonstrated by means of an example that figured prominently in the Austrian theory of capital, that is, the maturing of wine and the growing of an oak which eventually is made into a chest. In his reply to a critique by Harrod (1961), Sraffa stresses that this example is a "crucial test" for the marginalist notions of a "quantity of capital" and of an "average period of production" (cf. Sraffa, 1962, p. 478). Indeed,

> the case just considered seems conclusive in showing the impossibility of aggregating the "periods" belonging to the several quantities of labour into a single magnitude which could be regarded as representing the quantity of capital. The reversals in the direction of the movement of relative prices, in the face of unchanged methods of production, cannot be reconciled with *any* notion of capital as a measurable quantity independent of distribution and prices (Sraffa, 1960, p. 38).

[12] See, for example, Swan (1956), Bhaduri (1966), Samuelson (1966a), Robinson and Naqvi (1967), Harcourt (1972, pp. 39–45) and Bliss (1975, pp. 114–7). From the point of view of the history of economic thought this terminology is unfortunate, since the first author ever to analyse in some depth the influence of distribution on relative prices was Ricardo (see, in particular, *Works* I, pp. 30–43).

The radical implication of this result reads: "One can only wonder what is the good of a quantity of capital or a period of production which, since it depends on the rate of interest, cannot be used for its traditional purpose, which is to determine the rate of interest" (Sraffa, 1962, p. 479).

Since the criticism summarized so far in this subsection does not depend on the phenomenon of "reswitching," it might be concluded that the latter is of secondary importance only in the critique of traditional neoclassical theory, despite the almost exclusive attention it received in much of the debate on capital theory. However, to consider this phenomenon "unimportant" is difficult to sustain. In fact, it constitutes a special aspect of the more fundamental deficiency and serves to counter the particular neoclassical claim of a decreasing demand function for capital.

(ii) Reswitching and reverse capital deepening. According to Marshall the applications of the principle of substitution "extend over almost every field of economic inquiry" ([1890] 1977, p. 284). As we have seen in Section 1 above, this principle forms the very basis of the marginalist theory of value and distribution. Hence any criticism of that theory has to deal with the problem of choice from a set of alternatives contemplated by the principle of substitution. In the Cambridge controversy in the theory of capital emphasis was naturally on the problem of the choice of technique rather than that of consumer choice.[13]

Reswitching has been defined in Section 5 of Chapter 5 as a situation in which a technique is cost-minimizing at two disconnected ranges of the rate of profit and not so in between these ranges. The possibility of reswitching of techniques has been investigated in exercise 8.15 of Chapter 3 and in exercises 7.19 and 7.21 of Chapter 5. Samuelson emphasized, "this phenomenon can be called 'perverse' only in the sense that the conventional parables did not prepare us for it" (1966a, p. 578). The implication of the possibility of the reswitching of techniques is that the direction of change of the "input proportions" cannot be related unambiguously to changes of the so-called factor prices. The central element of the neoclassical explanation of distribution in terms of supply and demand is thus revealed as defective. The demonstration that a fall in w (i.e. a rise in r) may lead to the adoption of the less "labor-intensive," that is, more "capital-intensive," of two techniques destroyed, in the minds of the critics of traditional neoclassical theory, the whole basis for the

---

[13] Thus the critique of the marginalist theory does not consist of the denial of the existence of a multiplicity of techniques, as is sometimes maintained in the literature (e.g., Krelle, 1992). It is rather shown that even if several, possibly infinitely many, technical alternatives are admitted traditional neoclassical theory has to be rejected on logical grounds.

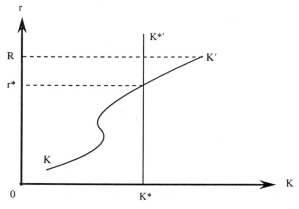

Figure 14.3

neoclassical view of substitution in production. Moreover, since a fall in *w* may cheapen some of the commodities, the production of which at a higher level of *w* was characterized by a relatively low labor intensity, the substitution among consumption goods contemplated by the traditional theory of consumer demand may result in a higher, as well as in a lower, labor intensity. It follows that the principle of substitution in consumption cannot offset the breakdown of the principle of substitution in production.

We talk of "reverse capital deepening" when the relationship between the value of capital (per capita) and the rate of profit is increasing. The possibility of "reverse capital deepening" has been investigated in exercises 6.14 and 6.15 of Chapter 4 and in exercise 8.25 of Chapter 5. The negative implication of reswitching and reverse capital deepening for traditional theory can be illustrated by means of the example of Figure 14.3, in which the value of capital corresponding to the full employment level of labor is plotted against the rate of profit. Obviously, if with traditional analysis we conceived of the curve *KK'* as the "demand curve" for capital, which, together with the corresponding "supply curve" *K*K*'*, is taken to determine the equilibrium value of *r*, we would have to conclude that this equilibrium, although unique, is unstable. With free competition, conceived of, as it is in neoclassical theory, as including the perfect flexibility of the distributive variables, a deviation of *r* from *r** would lead to the absurd conclusion that one of the two income categories, wages and profits, would disappear. According to the critics of traditional neoclassical theory, this result demonstrates all the more impressively the failure of the supply and demand approach to the theory of normal distribution, prices and quantities.

4. Neoclassical responses

It is hardly surprising that the protagonists of the supply and demand approach should have shown so much concern when confronted with the critique. In this section we shall summarize their consecutive responses to the critique. We may distinguish broadly between two types of responses: (i) attempts to defend traditional neoclassical theory and (ii) counter-attacks on the alternative theory from which the criticism had been developed. Historically, the answers belonging to the first type generally preceded those belonging to the second.

4.1. In defense of traditional neoclassical theory

The very first reaction followed Christian Morgenstern's famous dictum that "it cannot be what must not be." In 1965 David Levhari, a student of Paul Samuelson's, claimed to have demonstrated that reswitching was impossible, that is, that systems of production can be ordered according to "degrees of mechanization" (cf. Levhari, 1965). This claim was shown to be false by Luigi Pasinetti, who was encouraged to do so by Piero Sraffa (cf. Baranzini and Harcourt, 1993a, p. 9), in a paper presented at the World Congress of the Econometric Society in Rome in 1965. A revised version of Pasinetti's paper was then published in the November 1966 issue of the *Quarterly Journal of Economics* (Pasinetti, 1966c) together with papers by Levhari and Samuelson (1966), Morishima (1966), Bruno, Burmeister, and Sheshinski (1966), Garegnani (1966), and Samuelson (1966a).[14] Samuelson and Levhari in their joint paper and Samuelson in his "summing up" paper frankly admitted that the no reswitching theorem was wrong. Samuelson also gave some numerical examples which illustrated in simple terms why reswitching and capital reversing are possible. (See also Burmeister and Turnovsky, 1972.)[15]

---

[14] The numerical counterexample provided by Pasinetti in 1965 did not meet all the assumptions underlying Levhari's argument, whereas the one published in 1966 did.

[15] Some authors claimed that there is an analogy between reswitching and the long-known possibility of the existence of multiple internal rates of return. They remarked, quoting the Bible: "there is no new thing under the sun" (Bruno, Burmeister and Sheshinski, 1966, p. 553). However, whereas the phenomenon of multiple internal rates of return is a discovery within the *partial* framework of microeconomic theory of investment, reswitching presupposes a *general* framework. On multiple internal rates of return, see especially Irving Fisher (1930). Interestingly, there are passages in Fisher which indicate that he was aware that prices may vary, possibly in a complex way, with variations in the rate of interest. He contended, however, that this complication is "more intricate than important" (ibid., pp. 170–1).

Since the possibility of reswitching and reverse capital deepening could no longer be denied, doubts were raised as to its empirical importance (see, for example, Ferguson, 1969), thereby insinuating that neoclassical theory was a simplified picture of reality, the basic correctness of which could not be endangered by "exceptions" of the kind analyzed in the capital debate.[16] This sort of reasoning was implicitly dealt with by Sraffa in an oral intervention at the 1958 Corfu conference on the theory of capital. Counterposing the statistician's measure with measurement in theory, which should be able to take into account all possible cases, that is, universally applicable, Sraffa emphasized:

> The theoretical measures required absolute precision.... The work of J. B. Clark, Böhm-Bawerk and others was intended to produce pure definitions of capital, as required by their theories, not as a guide to actual measurement. If we found contradictions, then these pointed to defects in the theory, and an inability to define measures of capital accurately (cf. Lutz and Hague, 1961, pp. 305–6).

Furthermore, it should be clear that attempts to disprove reswitching in terms of wage–profit curves constructed from input–output data for different years (cf. Krelle, 1977, and Ochoa, 1989; see also Petrović, 1991) are fundamentally mistaken. Leaving aside data problems and the conceptual difficulties concerning the required "translation" of empirical "facts" into the categories of the analytical framework, the finding that the *w–r* curves associated with the techniques of 1988 and 1993, for example, do not possess several switch-points cannot be considered an empirical counterexample to reswitching, since the latter refers to the technical knowledge *at a given moment of time*.[17]

Some authors attempted to preserve the traditional neoclassical theory by simply ruling out reswitching and other "perverse," that is, non-conventional, phenomena in terms of sufficiently bold assumptions about available techniques. This route was followed, for example, by Sato (1974). It should come as no surprise that given these assumptions the central neoclassical postulate of the inverse relation between the capital–labor ratio and the rate of profit should re-emerge as "one of the most powerful

[16] Occasionally, reswitching was compared to the "Giffen good" case in consumer theory (cf. Hicks, 1965, p. 154, and Stiglitz, 1974). On the fallacy of this analogy, see Garegnani (1990a, p. 72).

[17] More recently there have been attempts to define and then assess the "probability" of reswitching (or capital reversing) in a given analytical framework; see on this D'Ippolito (1987, 1989) and Mainwaring and Steedman (1993). These attempts are not to be confounded with the applied works referred to above.

theorems in economic theory" (Sato, 1974, p. 355). However, in order to be clear about this move it deserves to be stressed that it was motivated, as one author expressly admits, by the fact that "regular economies" have "desirable properties" (Burmeister, 1980a, p. 124).[18]

Other advocates of the neoclassical approach were conscious of how defective the attempts to avoid reswitching and capital reversing or to play down their importance using the "empirical" route were. Since the phenomenon was irrefutable it had to be absorbed and shown to be compatible with the more sophisticated versions of the theory, that is, those at the "frontier of knowledge" (cf. Hahn, 1975, p. 363). In responses of the second type the criticism of traditional neoclassical theory is therefore generally accepted. Instead of defending what cannot be defended, the alternative classical theory is examined. It is claimed that the latter does not constitute an alternative to the *modern* versions of neoclassical theory, that is, those based on the notions of temporary or intertemporal equilibrium. This was argued by Christopher Bliss (1975), Edwin Burmeister (1980a), and especially by Frank Hahn (1975, 1982). Their responses can be said to follow the motto: "attack is better than defense."

4.2. "General" versus "special" theories

Hahn frankly admitted that the Sraffa-based critique is correct with respect to "many writers whom we regard as neoclassical who have either made mistakes of reasoning or based themselves on special assumptions which have themselves nothing to do with neoclassical theory" (Hahn, 1982, p. 354). He also expressed the opinion that "Sraffa's book contains no formal propositions which I consider to be wrong although here and there it contains remarks which I consider to be false" (ibid., p. 353). However, the main point of Hahn's argument is a different one: "I assert the following: there is not a single formal proposition in Sraffa's book which is not also true in a General Equilibrium model constructed on his assumptions" (Hahn, 1975, p. 362; similarly 1982, p. 353). This has the following implications that Hahn has stressed. First, the criticism of traditional neoclassical theory has no bearing upon General Equilibrium

---

[18] A "regular economy" is defined as one for which the "real Wicksell effect" is always negative (cf. Burmeister, ibid., p. 101), where a "real Wicksell effect" gives the change in the value of capital due to the fact that steady state capital stocks vary with the rate of profit. That is, the value of capital is taken to be inversely related to the rate of profit. The notion of a "regular economy" is also called "a necessary and sufficient condition to preclude paradoxical behavior" (ibid., p. 119). "Such economies exhibit behavior that in some important qualitative respects is similar to that of the standard one-sector model," which in turn is said to be tentatively acceptable "on the basis of empirical evidence" (ibid., p. 101).

theory of the Arrow–Debreu variety.[19] Secondly, it is contended that Sraffa's analysis represents but a "special case" of the latter. Both propositions are ultimately traced back to the fact that in modern General Equilibrium theory the distribution of income is determined in terms of arbitrarily given *physical* endowments of agents. Since the endowment of the economy with capital goods is not given a scalar representation, as in traditional theory, the capital critique is said not to be applicable. Moreover, since in general equilibrium there will generally be as many "own" rates of return as there are different assets in the endowment set, Sraffa's analysis which revolves around the uniformity of rates of profit is said to be concerned with "a very special state of the economy" (ibid., p. 363).

To qualify the analyses of other schools of thought as special cases of one's own analysis is a time-honored device in intellectual controversy amongst economists. Keynes, for example, presented his own theory, which allows for persistent unemployment, as the *General Theory*, implying that the conventional full employment theory is a "special case" (*CW*, VII, p. 3). Representatives of the "neoclassical synthesis" in macroeconomics on the other hand maintained that Keynes's analysis lacks generality, because it is based on special assumptions concerning the flexibility of wages, etc. But does this method carry us very far? While there can be no doubt that in some cases it is appropriate, in others it is not. For example, it is well known that a model of a non-Euclidean geometry can be built up within the axioms of Euclidean geometry. Does this entitle us to consider the non-Euclidean geometry a "special case" of the Euclidean one? Similarly, take the model presented here either in Section 2 or Section 3 of Chapter 10 and assume that matrix $\mathbf{A}$ is zero, vector $\mathbf{l}$ is also zero (that is, there is neither capital nor labor), and matrix $\mathbf{C}$ refers not only to land inputs, but to all inputs. This model is very similar to a neoclassical model in which income distribution is determined by the relative scarcities of the "factors of production." Do we have to conclude from this that neoclassical analysis is a "special case" of "classical" analysis?

There is an obvious way of deciding whether Sraffa's analysis is, or is not, a special case of the Arrow–Debreu model. If it were, it would start from the *same* set of data but impose special restrictions on this set. The set of data, or exogenous variables, on which modern General Equilibrium theory is based are summarized by Hahn in the following definition of what he means by a "neoclassical theory": "I shall call a theory neoclassical if (a) an economy is fully described by the preferences and endowments of

---

[19] In another place Hahn admitted that he himself "every so often slipped into the aggregate version of the neo-classical model" (Hahn, 1972, p. 8).

agents and by the production sets of firms; (b) all agents treat prices parametrically (perfect competition); and (c) all agents are rational and given prices will take that action (or set of actions) from amongst those available to them which is best for them given their preferences. (Firms prefer more profit to less.)" (Hahn, 1982, p. 354). Attention has to focus on element (a), since the other two elements (regarding competition and rationality) are also to be found in classical analysis, with the concept of "free competition" replacing that of "perfect competition." In element (a) we again encounter the data mentioned in Subsection 4.1 of Chapter 1: (i) preferences, (ii) initial endowments (labor powers, lands, capital goods etc.), and the distribution of property rights among agents, and (iii) technical alternatives. As was made already clear in that chapter (and also in Subsection 7.2 of Chapter 13), the main difference between neoclassical and classical theory of value and distribution concerns item (ii), that is, the assumption entertained in neoclassical theory of given endowments of capital goods.

Hahn is thus confronted with the task of showing that Sraffa, very much like modern General Equilibrium theory, starts from given initial endowments, and in addition, very much like a special case of that theory, presupposes a particular composition of those endowments (see also Garegnani, 1990c, pp. 113–5). Yet this cannot be demonstrated for the simple reason that Sraffa, following the classical approach to the theory of value and distribution, develops his analysis in terms of a *different* set of data, thus putting forward a *different* theory. The difficulty of the task Hahn has put to himself can be seen in the way he attempts to tackle it. As to the first aspect of this task, that is, that of discovering *some* assumption about endowments in Sraffa, Hahn simply *claims* that "it cannot be part of the doctrine that you are uninterested whether there [are enough commodities in a given year that can be used as means of production] to meet demand" (Hahn, 1982, p. 365). In the sentence following immediately Hahn admits, however, that his claim is contradicted by Sraffa's analysis: "Yet Mr Sraffa does not consider this matter" (ibid.). Interestingly, this finding does not prompt Hahn to question his "special case" interpretation. It rather makes him seek to establish its correctness adopting a different route: instead of providing direct evidence in support of the claim that Sraffa started from given endowments, he looks out for indirect evidence. He believes to have found it in Sraffa's concern with a uniform rate of profit. Clearly, to impose a uniform rate of profit on a General Equilibrium system would render it overdetermined. Hence, data (i), (ii), or (iii) mentioned above cannot be taken as independent variables. Now it is Hahn's contention that Sraffa's price equations are based on a special proportion between the initial endowments, that is, (ii) is tacitly assumed as being specified accordingly. "So the neoclassical economist who is always happy to consider interesting special cases sets to work to find a proper equilibrium for Mr Sraffa" (ibid.). Combining the familiar assumptions of General Equilibrium theory of given preferences and technical alternatives with the unfamiliar one of a given and uniform rate of profit implies that the composition of the capital stock cannot be taken as independently determined, but must be seen as depending on the givens mentioned: as Hahn emphasizes with regard to the two-commodity illustration of his argument, "we must make one of [the two endowments] into an unknown" (ibid.). This concludes Hahn's attempt to demonstrate that the "special case" interpretation of Sraffa's analysis is correct.

Hahn's interpretation does not stand up to close examination. First, it deserves to be stressed that Sraffa does *not* start from given endowments of capital goods, that is, produced means of production, in order to determine distribution and normal prices. He rather takes as given *gross outputs* and one of the distributive variables. The quantities of the capital goods available in the system are considered as being dependent rather than independent variables. Following the classical economists, he assumes that the capital stocks installed in the different industries are adjusted to these outputs and the given level of the distributive variable, by an appropriate choice of technique, such that these outputs can be produced at minimum costs (see Subsection 2.4 of Chapter 1 and Chapter 13). The tendency toward normal capital utilization and a uniform rate of profit is taken to be the outcome of the working of competition. Sraffa's is a different theory of value and distribution which manages to meet its objective, that is, to determine relative prices and the remaining distributive variable(s) in terms of *these* data. Second, what Hahn thinks is an adequate interpretation of Sraffa's analysis is in fact a reiteration of a finding in older neoclassical authors: as has been seen in Sections 1 and 2 of this chapter, several representatives of traditional neoclassical theory were aware that in order to be consistent with the notion of a competitive equilibrium the capital endowment could only be given in value terms, with the physical composition to be determined endogenously. Hence, ironically, Hahn attributes to Sraffa what Sraffa had identified as the major difficulty of traditional neoclassical theory, that is, that the "quantity of capital" and the distribution of income cannot be ascertained independently of one another.

In the following discussion two further observations on the "special case" interpretation will be provided; the issue will then be briefly taken up again in Subsection 5.5. To claim that the Arrow–Debreu model is general, whereas Sraffa's analysis is special, misses the fact that the former is short-period and the latter is long-period. Thus, in dealing with a "private ownership economy," Debreu (1959, pp. 39 and 78) assumes a *given* number of producers and *given* shares of the profit of the various producers received by consumers. While these assumptions are necessary within the schema of Debreu's short-period theory, there is no room for them in the different schema of Sraffa's analysis.

Duménil and Lévy (1985) (see also Dana, Florenzano, Le Van, and Lévy, 1989) take intertemporal general equilibrium theory as it is and ask whether it is possible to locate in its formalism the concept of "natural" prices, or prices of production, and a uniform rate of profit. They show that under certain conditions, over an infinite horizon, prices in the intertemporal model tend toward "natural" prices as the relative prices progressively stabilize. They conclude:

> What can be conserved in the intertemporal equilibrium is only its asymptotic behaviour position, i.e. *that which coincides with the classical conception of equilibrium*! Therefore, prices of production are not an uninteresting particular case of the neoclassical model. On the contrary, every price described in the neoclassical story which does not correspond to prices of production is totally deprived of any economic significance (ibid., p. 343).

In their view the tracks of "natural" prices are clearly discernible in the neoclassical equilibrium model. They conclude that this undermines the claim that the latter is the general case and the classical long-period theory the special one.[20]

Finally, it should be noted that there is an asymmetry in the way in which Sraffa's analysis is perceived by advocates of General Equilibrium theory and the way in which that theory is perceived by advocates of the Sraffian, that is, "classical," analysis. From the point of view of the former Sraffa's analysis, though correct, is but a "special case" of General Equilibrium theory. Yet from the point of view of the latter, General Equilibrium theory is not only different from Sraffa's analysis but also difficult to sustain. More particularly, it is argued that temporary and intertemporal theory, not differently from traditional neoclassical theory, cannot avoid the problem of capital. We shall come back to this claim toward the end of the following section.

5. Intertemporal and temporary equilibrium

A major motive for breaking away from traditional long-period or "static" theory, as it was then called, shared by Lindahl, Hicks, and Hayek, was its alleged lack of "realism." As Lindahl ([1929] 1939, p. 271) stressed,

---

[20] Comparing the classical notion of gravitation of market prices to "natural" prices and the asymptotic behavior of prices in intertemporal equilibrium theory, Duménil and Lévy contended that the latter could at most be considered "an uninteresting particular case of the classical convergence process" (ibid., p. 343 fn.).

his endeavor was "to bring the theory of price into closer contact with reality." He contended that this necessitated the abandonment of the "static" method and the adaptation of the explanation of prices, including the prices of factor services, in terms of supply and demand to accommodate factors which could no longer be ignored once time is taken seriously. As he stressed with regard to "static" theory, "the possibilities of an analysis of the pricing problem on these lines are somewhat limited. The difficulties here mentioned are associated with the stationary setting of the problem.... Therefore the attempt must be made to build up on this foundation an improved analysis which will have more general validity" (ibid., p. 317). Similarly Hicks, who emphasized that "static" theory neglected important features of the "real world," such as uncertainty and expectations, and thus was "quite incompetent to deal properly with capital and interest" (Hicks, [1939] 1946, p. 116).

5.1. Erik Lindahl

This quest for greater "realism" of economic theory could only have been strengthened by the observation that traditional demand and supply theory was not merely turning a blind eye to the complications posed by time, but was also logically inconsistent. Among the three Lindahl was perhaps best aware of this inconsistency. In a footnote added to the English text of his 1929 paper he pointed out that the received versions of "modern" capital theory "have the disadvantage that the measure of capital is made dependent on the prices of the services invested and on the rate of interest – which belong to the unknown factors of the problem" (Lindahl, [1929] 1939, p. 317).

Following Wicksell, Lindahl was concerned with incorporating the insights of the Austrian theory of capital into the time structure of production in a Walrasian theory of general equilibrium. He proceeded in terms of a sequence of models exhibiting rising degrees of "realism." This sequence was eventually to be crowned by a model capable of portraying, in abstract terms, a "real" economy moving through time. It goes without saying that Lindahl did not achieve this bold aim and openly admitted this.[21] He was, however, convinced that the "dynamic" approach

---

[21] Toward the end of his paper Lindahl ([1929] 1939, p. 348) wrote that his investigation has been brought to a point "at which a further approximation to reality is associated with...considerable difficulties" which he, at the time, felt unable to tackle in a theoretically satisfactory way. These difficulties derived largely from the need to accommodate imperfect foresight and uncertainty in the model. His disenchantment with the achievements of his 1929 paper were also the main impetus for him to write the 1939 paper on "The Dynamic Approach to Economic Theory" (Lindahl, 1939, part I).

to economic problems advocated by him liberated economic theory from a static dead end and shunted it on to the right track.

Lindahl himself did not use the term "intertemporal equilibrium"; yet what he had developed in some parts of his analysis were clearly intertemporal equilibrium models with a finite time horizon. Since these were explicitly based on the assumption of perfect foresight they could represent no more than preliminary steps on the way to a "general dynamic theory" that truly deserved this name.[22] Hence, while it is true, as Debreu (1959, p. 35n) observed, that Lindahl provided "the first general mathematical study" of this sort, its author can most certainly not be accused of having attributed too much importance to it.[23]

In this conceptualization, in accordance with Walras's analysis, the capital stock available at a particular point in time, which is the beginning of the first period of the economy contemplated by Lindahl's theory, is given in kind: "During the initial period in the dynamic process under observation, all existing capital equipment in the community can be regarded as *original*, including any that has actually resulted from the production of earlier periods not covered by the analysis." Hence: "Produced capital goods have the same significance for price formation as true *original* sources of similar kinds" (Lindahl, [1929] 1939, pp. 320–1; emphases added). The importance of the initial conditions for the dynamic behavior of the economy is particularly stressed by Lindahl in his later paper: "The first step in this analysis is *to explain a certain development as a result of certain given conditions* prevailing at the beginning of the period studied. These given conditions must be stated in such a way that they contain *in nuce* the whole subsequent development" (Lindahl, 1939, p. 21).

The study of an intertemporal equilibrium is, as we heard, a first step toward a study of economic change: "Under the assumption that the future is perfectly foreseen, all prices in all periods in the dynamic system thus become linked together in a uniform system. The equilibrium of this system is maintained by the same laws as under stationary conditions. Costs of production and prices coincide, and supply and demand are also equal, both for productive services and for consumption goods." That is, all actions for the entire time-horizon are determined at the beginning of the first period, plans being "pre-reconciled" thanks to the assumption of perfect foresight. Lindahl then comes to speak about the main feature distinguishing an intertemporal equilibrium from a long-period equilibrium,

---

[22] Repeatedly, Lindahl expressed his uneasiness with the assumption of perfect foresight; see Lindahl ([1929] 1939, pp. 285 and 339–40).

[23] It should come as no surprise that Lindahl in the course of his argument introduced also some concept of temporary equilibrium into economic analysis.

or "stationary state"; this concerns the "original" factors, including the capital goods in given supply at the beginning of the first period: "The real difference from the stationary case lies in the circumstance that the primary factors, there regarded as given, are assumed to undergo change from one period to another. In this way a movement arises in the system" (Lindahl, [1929] 1939, p. 330). This movement concerns prices and quantities. As regards prices, Lindahl characterizes the new "dynamic" view of the economic system as opposed to the old "static" one as follows: "while in the stationary case the prices in succeeding periods are equal to the prices in the present period and thus do not introduce any new unknowns into the problem, in the dynamic case they will differ more or less from the prices in the first period" (ibid., p. 319). Correspondingly, the notion of a uniform rate of interest turns out to be generally devoid of any "clear and precise content" (ibid., p. 245).[24] Nevertheless, Lindahl did not think that "static theory" was entirely useless. He maintained rather that the system, if not disrupted by exogenous shocks, would gradually converge to a long-period equilibrium: "If this tendency were alone operative, the community would in time reach stationary conditions" (ibid., p. 331), characterized by a uniform rate of interest throughout the economy.[25] He thus preserved, though in a weak form, the idea underlying the analyses of Walras, Böhm-Bawerk, and Wicksell of the existence of a center of gravitation. As we shall see in the following discussion, the further development of neoclassical theory since the 1930s brought with it the gradual erosion of the received view, still shared by Lindahl, that there is a firm link between a long-period position and the tendency to it.

5.2. John Richard Hicks

According to Hicks (1982, p. 10), Lindahl had exerted a considerable influence on him while working on *Value and Capital* (cf. Hicks, 1939, 1946).[26] "Static theory," Hicks argued, would be applicable, "if we could say that the system of prices existing at any moment depends upon the preferences and resources existing at that moment and upon nothing else." Yet this is not the case: "supplies (and ultimately demands too) are governed by expected prices quite as much as by current prices" (ibid.,

[24] See also the following statement by Koopmans: "The irrelevance-in-principle of the concept of interest to the problem of efficient allocations over time is clearly implied, if not explicitly stated, in Lindahl's penetrating exposition of capital theory" (Koopmans, 1957, p. 114).
[25] It is interesting to note the parallel between the view expressed by Lindahl and that of Duménil and Lévy (1985) (referred to in Section 4).
[26] See also Hicks ([1933] 1980) in which the concept of intertemporal equilibrium is discussed.

pp. 115–16). Hence the economic system had to be conceived of, "not merely as a network of interdependent markets, but as a process in time" (ibid., p. 116). This process, Hicks contended, is best represented as a sequence of temporary equilibria, each temporary equilibrium being dependent on individuals' expectations of the future. Just as in Lindahl, the productive equipment of the economy is assumed to be given in kind. While "the economic problem" was traditionally conceived of, in an atemporal way, as consisting in the allocation of given resources to alternative ends, it now had to be specified explicitly as involving "the allotment of these resources, inherited from the past, among the satisfaction of present wants and future wants" (ibid., p. 130). In such a framework prices are bound to change. While own rates of interest can be defined, they are said to be "of little direct importance for us" (ibid., p. 142).

Hicks's break with traditional neoclassical theory was even more radical than Lindahl's, at least as regards the latter's 1929 article. The concept of the "stationary state" as a position toward which the system is taken to gravitate if not perturbed by a series of exogenous factors of a more or less short-lived nature is rejected on the grounds that "the stationary state is, in the end, nothing but an evasion" (ibid., p. 117). However, it can be questioned that Hicks's dismissal of the time-honored concept of a center of gravitation is warranted. Although Hicks leaves no doubt that the accumulation of some capital goods and the decumulation of others provides the main link between successive periods, his own analysis of this process and its implications for the existence or not of a tendency toward a uniform rate of interest is, at best, incomplete.[27]

5.3. Friedrich August Hayek

For quite some time Hayek's part in the development of the notion of intertemporal equilibrium had not received the attention it deserves. In Bliss's book (Bliss, 1975), for example, which focuses attention on intertemporal and temporary equilibrium models, there is not a single reference to Hayek.[28] One year prior to Lindahl Hayek had published a paper, in German, which for the first time bore the notion "intertemporal equilibrium" (*intertemporales Gleichgewicht*) in its title. Hayek argued that contrary to the received opinion the existence of such "equilibria" is not merely "incompatible with the idea that constant prices are a prerequisite

[27] It is interesting to notice that Hicks later in his career became increasingly skeptical as to the usefulness of the temporary equilibrium method; see, for example, Hicks (1965, p. 66). On Hicks's recantation of the temporary equilibrium method, see Petri (1991).
[28] It was only recently that his contribution to this field was given proper credit (cf. Milgate, 1979, and Huth, 1989).

to an undisturbed economic process, but is in the strictest opposition to it" (Hayek, 1928, p. 37). According to him only few authors had grasped, albeit imperfectly, the "importance of the difference of prices at different points in time"; reference is to Wicksell, Irving Fisher, and Ludwig von Mises (ibid.). Implicit in an intertemporal price system is a multiplicity of commodity-own-rates of interest (ibid., p. 43).

In 1941 Hayek published *The Pure Theory of Capital* in which he elaborated the ideas contained in his earlier article. Although he regarded his analysis as rooted in traditional Austrian capital theory, it is clear that he had effected a major conceptual change both in terms of the object and the method of inquiry: "the explanation of interest will not be the sole or central purpose of the present study, as was the case with most of the similar investigations in the past. The explanation of interest will be an incidental though necessary result of an attempt to analyse the forces which determine the use made of the productive resources" (1941, p. 41). In the new perspective, capital theory had to deal with the problem of intertemporal allocation, the solution of which involved, as a by-product, an answer to the question of distribution. The investigation was concerned "with general equilibria that are not at the same time stationary states" (ibid., p. 15). The capital endowment of the economy could accordingly not be taken as being "a homogeneous substance the 'quantity' of which could be regarded as a 'datum'"; the analysis would rather have to start from "the fuller description of the concrete elements of which it consisted" (ibid., p. 5). As a consequence the central idea, around which traditional capital theory revolved, that "there would be some determinate *in natura* rate of interest" had to be jettisoned: "In fact there would not and could not be one rate of interest" (ibid., p. 35n.).[29]

Despite this and similar statements, the notion of a center of gravitation is not completely eradicated in Hayek's analysis. For example, there are passages in his book in which he stresses that "in so far as we are justified in speaking of a tendency towards equilibrium...[the] endeavour to distribute investment in such a way as to bring the highest return will necessarily bring about a uniform rate of return" (ibid., p. 265–6).

5.4. Gerard Debreu

A total break with the traditional method of analysis and its concern with long-period positions of the economic system characterized

---

[29] It should be noted, however, that the multiplicity of the "own rates of interest" in intertemporal equilibrium is not contradicting the existence of a uniform rate of interest: as is well known, all rates of interest are equal in terms of a common numeraire and equal to the own rate of interest of the numeraire.

by a uniform rate of interest (profit) was finally effectuated in the so-called Arrow–Debreu model, developed by Kenneth Arrow and Gerard Debreu in the 1950s. The *locus classicus* of modern General Equilibrium Theory is Debreu's *Theory of Value* (Debreu, 1959). (See also Malinvaud, 1953.)

Debreu sets himself two tasks: "(1) the explanation of the prices of commodities resulting from the interaction of the agents in a private ownership economy through markets, (2) the explanation of the role of prices in an optimal state of the economy" (ibid. p. ix). Here, our concern will exclusively be with task (1). An "economy" is defined in terms of three sets of data: (i) a given number of consumers, characterized by their consumption sets and their preferences; (ii) a given number of producers, characterized by their production sets; and (iii) total resources (cf. ibid., p. 74). As regards the latter, Debreu specifies: "They include the capital of the economy at the present instant, i.e., all the land, buildings, mineral deposits, equipment, inventories of goods,... now existing and available to the agents of the economy. All these are a legacy of the past; they are *a priori* given" (ibid., p. 75). The property rights as to these resources are also taken as given. Since producers are assumed not to own any resources initially, all resources are owned by consumers.

The abandonment of any concern with the long period in Debreu's analysis is also clearly involved in the assumption of a given and constant number of producers. As is well known, in Marshall the assumption of a given number of firms was entertained only in the short run, but not in the long run. Consequently, in the short run the supply function for any commodity for the economy as a whole equals the horizontally summed up marginal cost functions, whereas in the long run for each quantity supplied by the respective industry the supply price equals the minimum of the average cost function of the single firm.

Commodities are not only specified in terms of their physical characteristics, but also in terms of their date and location of availability. By means of this generalization of the concept of commodity Debreu seeks to accommodate time and space into the model and thus construct a *general* theory: "By focusing attention on changes of dates one obtains, *as a particular case* of the general theory of commodities...a theory of saving, investment, capital, and interest. Similarly by focusing attention on changes of locations one obtains, *as another particular case* of the same general theory, a theory of location, transportation, international trade and exchange" (ibid., p. 32). Debreu assumes that there is only a finite number of distinguishable commodities (ibid.), which implies that the time-horizon of the model is finite. In a note appended to chapter 2 he admits that "there are, however, conceptual difficulties in postulating a predetermined instant beyond which all economic activity either ceases or is outside the scope of the analysis" (ibid., pp. 35–6; see also Malinvaud, 1953).[30] In addition, it is assumed that "the interval of time over which economic activity takes place is divided into a finite number of compact *elementary intervals* of equal length" (ibid., p. 29).

Debreu assumes that there are current markets for *all* commodities, whatever their physical, temporal (within the given time horizon), or spatial specification.[31] Hence, in the "economy" contemplated all trade for the entire time-horizon takes place at the beginning of the first period. If markets were reopened at later dates, then no additional trade would take place. As Arrow and Hahn stressed, the hypothesis that there is a complete set of markets for current goods " 'telescopes' the future into the present" (Arrow and Hahn, 1971, p. 33). Given a set of prices, each agent chooses a plan for all the elementary periods. An equilibrium for a "private ownership economy" requires that all individual plans are, from the initial date onward, mutually consistent for all future dates and compatible with "the capital of the economy at the present instant," that is, initial endowments. Since Debreu assumes free disposal (1959, p. 42), in equilibrium some prices may be zero (in some periods): this concerns goods for which there is a negative excess demand.

Debreu's model exhibits several features that are disquieting. Here we cannot enter into a detailed discussion of these (see, however, Geanakoplos, 1987, Malinvaud, 1987, McKenzie, 1987, and Currie and Steedman, 1990, ch. 7). Some remarks focusing on the problem dealt with in the present chapter must suffice. A major difficulty concerns the treatment of time. "The principal objection to the restriction to a finite number of goods is that it requires a finite horizon and there is no natural way to choose the final period. Moreover, since there will be terminal stocks in the final period there is no natural way to value them without contemplating future periods in which they will be used" (McKenzie, ibid., p. 507). What Debreu in fact assumes in his formal model is that all economic activity stops at the arbitrarily given terminal instant, that is, resources existing at the end

---

[30] The study of intertemporal models with an infinite time horizon was begun by Bewley (1972).

[31] In the final chapter of his book, Debreu tries to cope also with the problem of uncertainty by generalizing the notion of commodity still further: a contract for the transfer of a commodity now includes in addition the specification of "an event on the occurrence of which the transfer is conditional." Debreu adds: "This new definition of a commodity allows one to obtain a theory of uncertainty free from any probability concept and formally identical with the theory of certainty developed in the preceding chapters" (ibid., p. 98). The theory makes use of Arrow's concept of "choices of Nature." In the following discussion we shall set aside this aspect.

of the time-horizon have *zero* value. Because of the recursive structure of the model, all economic activities decided in the initial instant are derived with regard to the final period, since it would make no sense to transfer resources from the last but one period to the last one.

As regards the instant from which the economy is analyzed, that is, the "present instant," the question arises whether there has been no economic activity prior to that date. Debreu's answer is in the negative: the economy is not created "now;" it is rather assumed that, for the purpose of analyzing the economy's future development, the legacy of the past is exclusively *and* completely reflected in the amounts of resources inherited and the distribution of private ownership of these resources. In particular, it is assumed that there are no commitments carrying over from the past that constrain the agents' present decisions. This implies, of course, that the logic of the model does not extend to the past, because otherwise Debreu would have to admit that at some dates in the past agents entered into contracts referring to dates that are still in the future.

As we have seen, earlier neoclassical authors, most notably Walras, were concerned with the long- and short-run equilibrium relationships between the prices of durable capital goods and the prices of their services, that is, the rates of return on different kinds of capital goods, and whether the short-run relationships gravitate toward some long-run relationship characterized by a uniform rate of return throughout the economy. To this effect Walras proposed an explicit *tâtonnement* procedure which he conjectured converged to long-period equilibrium. These concerns are not present in the Arrow–Debreu model. It is not even asked how the economy is supposed to get to equilibrium. The notion of equilibrium is simply one of simultaneous clearing of all markets; there is no discussion of any adjustment process when defining equilibrium. As Currie and Steedman (1990, p. 147) pointed out,

> it is not meaningful to think in terms of rates of return at all in the context of the Arrow–Debreu economy. This follows not from the "generality" of the model but from the assumption that *all* transactions take place at the present instant. Meaningful asset equilibrium conditions – involving uniformity in appropriately defined rates of return – can be established for models which allow for changes in relative prices over time but *only* for those models with spot markets at each date, since, in such models, ownership of a durable good is a way of transferring wealth over time. In contrast, in the Arrow–Debreu model, the notion of transferring wealth over time has no real meaning.

Hence, in the Arrow–Debreu analysis, as opposed to that presented by

Walras with its long-period orientation, general equilibrium cannot be thought of as a "center of gravitation."

Obviously, to take the capital endowment as given in kind implies that only "short-period" equilibria can be determined. Because firms "prefer more profit to less" (Hahn, 1982, p. 354) the size and composition of the capital stock will change. Thus, major factors which general equilibrium theory envisages as determining prices and quantities are themselves subject to quick changes. This, in turn, makes it difficult to distinguish them from those accidental and temporary factors, which, at any given moment of time, prevent the economy from settling in a position of equilibrium.

More important, the fast variation in relative prices necessitates the consideration of the influence of future states of the world on the present situation. The assumption that all intertemporal and all contingent markets exist, which has the effect of collapsing the future into the present, can be rejected on grounds of realism and economic reasoning (see, for example, Bliss, 1975, pp. 48 and 61). In addition, there is the following conceptual problem (see Schefold, 1985). If in equilibrium some of the capital stocks turn out to be in excess supply these stocks assume zero prices. This possibility appears to indicate that the expectations entrepreneurs held in the past when deciding to build up the present capital stocks are not realized. Hence, strictly speaking we are faced with a *dis*equilibrium situation because otherwise the wrong stocks could not have accumulated. Therefore, the problem arises how the past or, more exactly, possible discrepancies between expectations and facts influence the future.

5.5. Temporary and intertemporal equilibrium and the problem of capital

We may conclude this section by way of summarizing what we consider to be the main features of intertemporal and temporary equilibrium models, as far as the problem of capital and interest is concerned. We begin with a discussion of temporary equilibrium.

Temporary equilibrium models are characterized by a seemingly complete evaporation of the concept of capital. Markets exist only for the exchange of commodities at the present date. Supply and demand determine present prices at which individual plans are mutually consistent, given the initial data which include individual agents' expectations about future prices.[32]

---

[32] A weakness of the theories of temporary equilibrium concerns the necessarily arbitrary choice of hypotheses about individual price expectations. Indeed, as Burmeister stressed, "all too often 'nearly anything can happen' is the only possible

Nothing guarantees that these expectations will be realized, so that individual plans will be revised as actual prices are found to differ from what was anticipated. In each single period capital goods cannot be seen differently than natural resources inherited from the preceding period which earn their proprietor a rent if and only if they are scarce. However, while it is true that in these models the concept of capital as a *stock* magnitude has been dispensed with, the concept of capital as a *flow* magnitude is still there. To see this, we have to leave the capital market and turn to the investment-savings market.

Similarly in intertemporal models, in which the problem of capital is also seemingly removed from the scene: the capital goods available at the beginning of the first period have the character of "primary" factors of production and can thus be treated on a par with scarce natural resources, such as land. The income a capital good yields its owner is again similar to the rent of land. These capital goods, together with the other primary factors, are used to produce consumption goods and new means of production in correspondence with intertemporal preferences of consumers, coping with the ever present problem of scarcity as best as possible, given the initial endowments and the available technical alternatives. As offsprings of rent-yielding assets the newly produced means of production bear the stamp of their origin and are also rent-yielding factors. Some uneasiness about the treatment of produced means of production and the asymmetric treatment of the past and the presence in intertemporal equilibrium models is expressed by Geanakoplos:

> The assumption of a finite number of commodities (and hence of dates) forces upon the model the interpretation of the economic process as a one-way activity of converting given primary resources into consumption goods. If there is universal agreement about when the world will end, there can be no question about the reproduction of the capital stock. In equilibrium it will be run down to zero.... One certainly cannot speak about the production of all commodities by commodities (Sraffa, 1960), since at date zero there must be commodities which have not been produced by commodities (Geanakoplos, 1987, p. 122).

What can at most be said is that along the avenue leading from original factor services to consumption goods, intermediate goods will emerge

---

unqualified conclusion" (Burmeister, 1980a, p. 215). Moreover, the stability properties of this kind of equilibrium are unclear, since small perturbations caused by accidental factors may entail changes in expectations, which define that very equilibrium.

which gradually transmute themselves into final goods. To all appearances, the problem of capital is again successfully circumnavigated.

Yet as with temporary equilibrium, these appearances are deceptive. As Malinvaud pointed out in his entry "Intertemporal Equilibrium and Efficiency" in *The New Palgrave* (cf. Malinvaud, 1987), "it is now realized that the rate of interest is related in a very complex way to the many exogenous determinants of equilibrium and that changes of relative prices, which are associated with changes of interest, may be responsible for paradoxical effects" (ibid., p. 960). This admitted, the challenge to inter-temporal equilibrium theory posed by these findings is right away played down using the (infamous) "empirical" route (cf. Section 4 above): "The significance of these various negative theoretical results should of course [!] not be overstated. While reflecting the basic complexity of the relationship between the full system of discounted prices and its determinants, the results do not prove that 'pathological cases' are often empirically relevant" (ibid., p. 960).

To see more clearly why the modern versions of neoclassical theory are not immune to the criticism of the traditional neoclassical notion of "capital" (as summarized in Section 3), a few additional considerations may prove useful. In this context it is worth mentioning that it was particularly Garegnani (most recently 1990a, 1993) who argued that, the fact that capital is resolved into a set of physical factors notwithstanding, the modern versions cannot evade the problem of capital. First, recall that the demand and supply functions for capital, a stock, in the older theories were assumed as operating over time through a sequence of demand functions for gross investment confronted with supply functions for gross savings, that is, flows. The interest elasticity of these demand functions for investment was seen as reflecting the interest elasticity of the demand for capital as a stock. Once this is understood, "it also becomes clear that the difficulties associated with the demand for 'capital' in the traditional long-period versions have to be present also in the contemporary short-period versions of the theory" (Garegnani, 1990a, p. 60). For these short-period versions cannot do without (gross) investment and (gross) saving functions, that is, functions which refer to "capital" in its "free" form. In equilibrium investment equals savings, that is, the aggregate demand for the outputs of means of production equals the aggregate supply. However, there is no guarantee that the equilibrium is stable. With reswitching and capital reversing there is no reason to presume that with a fall (rise) in the effective rate of interest investment demand will increase (decrease). In short, the presence of these phenomena would be reflected in a multiplicity of equilibria, one or several of which would be unstable. However, as was argued in Section 3 with regard to "perversely" shaped, that is, upward sloping, factor-demand functions, this possibility would question the validity of the entire economic analysis in terms of demand and supply.[33]

The above considerations should have made clear the following. First, there is no presumption that the neoclassical theories of intertemporal or temporary equilibrium are "general," whereas the classical theory is "special." The truth is that these theories are *different*: while the former are short-period, the latter is long-period. Secondly, although in the modern neoclassical theories there is no single "quantity of capital" representing the endowment of the economy with produced means of production, the problem of capital is not avoided: it reappears in the investment-savings market and is reflected in the instability of equilibrium. Finally, the modern versions of the demand and supply approach are beset with several methodological and conceptual difficulties which raise serious doubts about their usefulness.

---

[33] The above considerations also show the futility of Solow's attempt, inspired by Fisher (1930), to avoid the problem of capital in terms of the concept of the "social rate of return" which gives the ratio of the present value of the additional stream of future income generated by investment and that investment; see Solow (1963, 1967). For a criticism of that concept, see Pasinetti (1969).

15

On some alternative theories of distribution

In the previous chapter we have seen how the neoclassical theory of distribution attempts to explain all distributive variables in terms of a single principle: that of the (relative) scarcity of labor(s), land(s), and capital. We have also seen the difficulties in which the different versions of that theory got entangled. In this chapter some non-neoclassical approaches to the theory of distribution will be summarized. Attention will focus on the determination of the real wage rate and the rate of profit. It will be assumed that land of the best quality abounds and that labor is homogeneous. (For a discussion of the case of scarce land(s) and heterogeneous labor, see Chapters 10 and 11, respectively.)

Before we begin with our overview, it is useful to recall that the criticism of the neoclassical theory of distribution has shown that the concept of "normal position," or "long-period equilibrium," is incompatible with a symmetric treatment of all distributive variables in terms of demand and supply. This is indeed reflected in one way or another by the theories sketched in this chapter, in which one of the two distributive variables is treated as a residual. Depending on which of the two variables is determined independently and which is considered a residual, the theories may be grouped as follows: (i) those that attempt to determine the real wage rate; and (ii) those that attempt to determine the rate of profit. The theories of distribution advocated by the classical economists, especially Adam Smith, David Ricardo, and Karl Marx, come under the first category; these theories will be sketched in Section 1. The so-called post- (or neo-) Keynesian theories of distribution and also the monetary explanations of the rate of profit come under the second category; these theories will be dealt with in Sections 2 and 3, respectively.[1] Section 4 contains some historical notes.

[1] The following discussion will concentrate on what we consider to be the main aspects of the respective theories. It is not claimed that the investigation of these theories is exhaustive.

1. **Classical approaches to the theory of distribution**

In this section two major classical approaches to the explanation of the real wage rate will be summarized: the one advocated by Adam Smith, which may be called an early version of a "bargaining," "contract," or "conflict theory," and that of David Ricardo, which centers around the Malthusian "Law of Population." Finally, we shall briefly deal with Marx's theory of distribution, which explains the gravitation of wages to some socially and historically given level of "subsistence" in terms of the labor displacing effects of technological change and the ensuing tendency toward an excess supply of labor. It is indeed a characteristic feature of all these approaches that the labor market is conceived of as reflecting a fundamental asymmetry between the respective parties, workers and capital owners, which is detrimental to the former.

1.1. Adam Smith

The conflict over the distribution of income between "workmen" and "masters," that is, capitalists (and landlords), is described by Smith in chapter VIII of book I of *The Wealth of Nations*, "Of the Wages of Labour," as follows: "What are the common wages of labour, depends every where upon the contract usually made between those two parties, whose interests are by no means the same. The workmen desire to get as much, the masters to give as little as possible. The former are disposed to combine in order to raise, the latter in order to lower the wages of labour" (*WN*, I.viii.11). Smith continues: "It is not, however, difficult to foresee which of the two parties must, upon all ordinary occasions, have the advantage in the dispute, and force the other into a compliance with their terms." Three factors are singled out as of the greatest importance in the distribution conflict: (i) the size of the respective party, which is taken to be the main aspect deciding the ease or difficulty with which a combination can be formed; (ii) legal and political factors favoring one of the parties to the detriment of the other; and (iii) the role of private property in such conflicts. Smith expounds:

> The masters, being fewer in number, can combine much more easily; and the law, besides, authorises, or at least does not prohibit their combinations, while it prohibits those of the workmen. We have no acts of parliament against combining to lower the price of work; but many against combining to raise it. In all such disputes the masters can hold out much longer. A landlord, a farmer, a master manufacturer, or merchant, though they did not employ a single workman, could generally live a year or two upon the stocks which they have already acquired. Many workmen

could not subsist a week, few could subsist a month, and scarce any a year without employment. In the long-run the workman may be as necessary to his master as his master is to him; but the necessity is not so immediate (*WN*, I.viii.12).

These observations on the asymmetry of the relation between the two parties might lead one to conclude that the "masters" could reduce the wages to whichever level they wanted. Yet this is not so. There is, Smith explains, "a certain rate below which it seems impossible to reduce, for any considerable time, the ordinary wages even of the lowest species of labour" (*WN*, I.viii.14). He adds: "A man must always live by his work, and his wages must at least be sufficient to maintain him. They must even upon most occasions be somewhat more; otherwise it would be impossible for him to bring up a family, and the race of such workmen could not last beyond the first generation." Smith decides, wisely, to "not take upon me to determine" (*WN*, I.viii.15) the exact level of the "natural" wage defined in terms of "subsistence." The latter concept is indeed an intricate one; it cannot be given a purely physiological interpretation; it involves social and historical elements: for example, in the chapter on wages Smith repeatedly refers to the principles of "common humanity" valid in a particular society as a factor affecting the minimum level of wages.

Smith draws the reader's attention to "certain circumstances...which sometimes give the labourers an advantage, and enable them to raise their wages considerably above this [minimum] rate" (*WN*, I.viii.16). The circumstances referred to are characterized by a rapid growth of the demand for labor due to a rapid accumulation of capital, in which the emerging "scarcity of hands occasions a competition among masters, who bid against one another, in order to get workmen, and thus voluntarily break through the natural combination of masters not to raise wages" (*WN*, I.viii.17). From this Smith draws the following inference:

> It is not the actual greatness of national wealth, but its continued increase, which occasions a rise in the wages of labour. It is not, accordingly, in the richest countries, but in the most thriving, or in those which are growing rich the fastest, that the wages of labour are highest (*WN*, I.viii.22).

Hence, in Smith's view the wages of labor are governed by the general "circumstances of society" (*WN*, I.viii.40), that is, whether it is in a "progressive," a "stationary," or a "declining" state. "In the progressive state ... the condition of the labouring poor, of the great body of the people, seems to be the happiest and the most comfortable. It is hard in the stationary, and miserable in the declining state" (*WN*, I.viii.43).

Interestingly, Smith is of the opinion that the supply of labor is regulated by the demand for labor. He draws an analogy between the multiplication of animals and that of the inferior ranks of people. About the former he writes: "Every species of animals naturally multiplies in proportion to the means of their subsistence, and no species can ever multiply beyond it" (*WN*, I.viii.39). A similar principle is said to govern the multiplication of men: the "liberal reward of labour," by enabling workers to provide better for their children, adjusts the labor force

> as nearly as possible in the proportion which the demand for labour requires.... It is in this manner that the demand for men, *like that for any other commodity*, necessarily, regulates the production of men; quickens it when it goes on too slowly, and stops it when it advances too fast. It is this demand which regulates and determines the state of propagation in all the different countries of the world (*WN*, I.viii.40).

Hence, in Smith's view the real wage rate depends first and foremost on the rate of capital accumulation: wages are higher, the more rapidly capital accumulates. As to the impact of high and rising real wages on the rate of profit, it would seem that nothing definite can be said, given Smith's opinion, expressed toward the end of the chapter on wages, that "the same cause... which raises the wages of labour, the increase of stock, tends to increase its productive powers, and to make a smaller quantity of labour produce a greater quantity of work" (*WN*, I.viii.57). Capital accumulation, by promoting the division of labor, induces technological and organizational change which is reflected in a growing productivity of labor. Whether or not the rate of profit will tend to fall, one is therefore inclined to think, depends on the relative speed with which wages and labor productivity increase. However, surprisingly, in chapter IX of book I, "Of the Profits of Stock," Smith comes up with a definite answer. He introduces the chapter in the following terms: "The rise and fall in the profits of stock depend upon the same causes with the rise and fall in the wages of labour, the increasing or declining state of the wealth of the society; but those causes affect the one and the other very differently" (*WN*, I.ix.1). He adds:

> The increase of stock, which raises wages, tends to lower profit. When the stocks of many rich merchants are turned into the same trade, their mutual competition naturally tends to lower its profit; and when there is a like increase of stock in all the different trades carried on in the same society, the same competition must produce the same effect in them all (*WN*, I.ix.2).

This explanation of a falling tendency of the rate of profit in terms of "competition" does not stand up to examination. First, since Smith generally presupposes free competition, a fall in profitability cannot be traced back to an intensification of competition entailed by capital accumulation. Second, Smith erroneously tries to carry an argument that is valid in a partial framework over to a general framework. A shift of capital from one trade to another, other things being equal, will tend to reduce the rate of profit obtained in the latter (and increase it in the former); this mechanism was referred to by Smith in his explanation of the "gravitation" of market prices to "natural" prices (see Subsection 2.1 of Chapter 1). However, an increase in the economy's capital stock as a whole need not have an adverse effect on the general rate of profit. It all depends on how the real wage rate and the technical conditions of production are affected in the course of the accumulation of capital. This objection was already formulated by Ricardo (*Works* I, ch. 21), to whose analysis we now turn.

1.2. David Ricardo

To determine the laws which regulate the distribution of income, is, according to Ricardo, "the principal problem in Political Economy" (*Works* I, p. 5). The "natural price of labour" is specified by Ricardo as "that price which is necessary to enable the labourers, one with another, to subsist and to perpetuate their race, without either increase or diminution.... The natural price of labor, therefore, depends on the price of food, necessaries, and conveniences required for the support of the labourer and his family" (ibid., p. 93). It is Ricardo's contention that with the "progress of society" the natural price of labor tends to rise, since the fall in the price of manufactures due to improvements in machinery and a better division of labor is more than compensated by a rise in the price of necessaries due to diminishing returns in agriculture. Ricardo emphasizes that the natural price of labor should be conceived of in terms of a social and historical subsistence level:

> It is not to be understood that the natural price of labor, estimated even in food and necessaries, is absolutely fixed and constant. It varies at different times in the same country, and very materially differs in different countries. It essentially depends on the habits and customs of people.... Many of the conveniences now enjoyed in an English cottage, would have been thought luxuries at an earlier period of our history (ibid., pp. 96–7).

The "market price of labour" is the price which is actually paid for it. It may deviate from the natural price but tends to gravitate toward the latter. However, Ricardo argues that "notwithstanding the tendency of wages to conform to their natural rate, their market rate may, in an improving society, for an indefinite period, be constantly above it" (ibid., pp. 94–5). As the above quotation shows, if such a constellation prevails for some time it is even possible that "custom renders absolute necessaries" what in the past had been considered comforts or luxuries, that is, the natural wage is driven upward by persistently high levels of the actual wage rate. Hence, the concept of "natural wage" in Ricardo is a flexible one and must not be mistaken for a physiological minimum of subsistence.

Wages are seen as depending on two circumstances: (i) the "supply and demand of labourers," and (ii) the "price of the commodities on which the wages of labour are expended" (ibid., p. 97). Focusing attention on the former, the demand for labor is governed by the accumulation of capital,[2] the supply of labor by the "Malthusian Law of Population." As a result of extensive and intensive diminishing returns on land, "with every increased portion of capital employed on it, there will be a decreased rate of production." In contradistinction, "the power of population continues always the same." Hence there is a tendency of population "pressing against the means of subsistence" (ibid., pp. 98–9). Ricardo concludes:

> In the natural advance of society, the wages of labor will have a tendency to fall, as far as they are regulated by supply and demand; for the supply of labourers will continue to increase at the same rate, whilst the demand for them will increase at a slower rate. ... I say that, under these circumstances, wages would fall, if they were regulated only by the supply and demand of labourers; but we must not forget, that wages are also regulated by the prices of the commodities on which they are expended (ibid., p. 101).

We may conclude by saying that according to Ricardo as a result of a long-run tendency toward an excess supply of labor, real wages are seen to be oscillating around a socially and historically given level of subsistence. Profits are a residual income based on the surplus product left after the used up means of production and the wage goods in the support of workers have been deducted from the social product (net of rents). As Ricardo emphasizes: "Profits in fact depend on high or low wages, and on nothing else" (Ricardo, *Works* II, p. 252; similarly pp. 264–5).

---

[2] In chapter 31, "On Machinery," of the third edition of the *Principles*, Ricardo clarifies that it is the accumulation of the "circulating" and not the "fixed" capital that governs the growth of demand for labor (cf. *Works* I, p. 395). See also Jeck and Kurz (1983).

1.3. Karl Marx

In Marx's theory of wages we find both elements of Smith's conflict theory and Ricardo's view of a tendency toward an excess supply of labor. However, such a tendency is explained differently by Marx. It is the labor-saving bias of technological change that leads to the emergence of an "industrial reserve army of the unemployed."[3] In chapter XXV, "The General Law of Capitalist Accumulation," of volume I of *Capital* we read:

> Taking them as a whole, the general movements of wages are exclusively regulated by the expansion and contraction of the industrial reserve army, and these again correspond to the periodic changes of the industrial cycle. They are, therefore, not determined by the variations of the absolute number of the working population, but by the varying proportions in which the working-class is divided into active and reserve army, by the increase or diminution of the relative amount of the surplus-population, by the extent to which it is now absorbed, now set free (Marx, [1867] 1954, p. 596).

The size of the industrial reserve army is in turn governed by the accumulation of capital and the prevailing form of technological change that is channeled into the economy with the new means and methods of production. Hence income distribution, that is, the real wage rate, can, in the last instance, be considered determined by the pace of accumulation. This is expressed by Marx as follows: "To put it mathematically: the rate of accumulation is the independent, not the dependent, variable; the rate of wages, the dependent, not the independent, variable" (ibid., p. 581).

It is interesting to see that essentially the same idea, that is, the pace of accumulation governs the distribution of income between wages and profits, was advocated, in one form or another, by Michal Kalecki (cf. in particular Kalecki, 1971) and authors such as Nicholas Kaldor (1955–6) and Joan Robinson (1956) who pioneered the post-Keynesian theory of growth and distribution. However, while Kalecki and Joan Robinson take a position similar to Marx, namely, that labor is normally less than fully employed both in the short and in the long run, Kaldor explicitly assumed that a long-run theory, or theory of growth, should be based on the hypothesis of full employment (and full capacity utilization) (cf. Kaldor,

---

[3] In the chapter "On Machinery" Ricardo himself discussed a case in which a particular form of technological change entails the displacement of workers which are not immediately absorbed, as the theory of automatic compensation, to which Ricardo had once ascribed, maintained. Marx's theory of the "reserve army of the unemployed" can be considered a radicalization of Ricardo's opinion; see Kalmbach and Kurz (1986b).

1960, p. 12). In the following section we sketch the post-Keynesian theory. Kalecki's contribution, which is essentially short run, that is, concerned with the trade cycle, will be touched upon in the Historical notes.

2. The post-Keynesian theory of growth and distribution

The main idea underlying the post-Keynesian theory of growth and distribution is that of savings adjusting to an independently given investment, via the redistribution of income between wages and profits or classes of income recipients. The adjustment of savings to investment, rather than the other way round, is seen to be the central message of Keynes's *General Theory*, published in 1936 (cf. Keynes, *CW*, VII). Yet if there are no margins of spare capacity and no unemployed workers, Keynes's principle of effective demand no longer governs, via the multiplier, the level of output as a whole, the overall degree of capital utilization and the volume of employment, but rather the relationship between money wages and money prices, that is, the distribution of income.

We shall first, in Subsection 2.1, provide a simple analytical exposition of post-Keynesian theory. (For a more complete analysis, see the references in the Historical notes.) We shall then, in Subsections 2.2 and 2.3, deal with the technological relationship between the capital–output ratio and the rate of profit in the cases of single and joint production, respectively.

2.1. An analytical exposition

There are two social classes: workers and capitalists. Workers' earnings comprise wages (W) and profits (P_w) as interest on loans to capitalists. Capitalists receive only profits (P_c). Workers' and capitalists' savings (S_w and S_c, respectively) are defined by the following linear functions

$$S_w = s_{ww}W + s_{pw}P_w$$
$$S_c = s_c P_c.$$

It will also be assumed that

$$0 < s_{ww} \leqslant s_{pw} < s_c < 1.$$

Furthermore, steady-state growth is assumed. Then workers' and capitalists' capitals grow at the same rate g. That is, the following constraints hold:

$$s_{ww}W + s_{pw}P_w = gK_w \tag{15.1}$$

$$s_c P_c = gK_c, \tag{15.2}$$

where K_w is workers' capital loaned to the capitalists, and K_c is capitalists' own capital ($K_w + K_c = K$).

If it is assumed that the rate of interest and the rate of profit coincide, then $P_c = rK_c$ and $P_w = rK_w$. If, moreover, $K_c > 0$, then the rate of profit is immediately obtained from equation (15.2):

$$r = \frac{g}{s_c}. \tag{15.3}$$

This equation is known as the "Cambridge equation." If $K_c > 0$, equation (15.1) merely serves the purpose of determining the capital shares $((K_w/K)$ and $(K_c/K))$ via the (K_w/W) ratio. In fact, from equation (15.1) we obtain

$$\frac{K_w}{W} = \frac{s_{ww}}{g - s_{pw}r}.$$

Therefore

$$\frac{K_w}{K} = \frac{W}{K} \frac{K_w}{W} = \frac{1 - rv}{v} \frac{s_{ww}}{g - s_{pw}r},$$

where v is the capital–output ratio. Hence, $(K_w/K) \leqslant 1$ if and only if

$$\frac{1}{v} \leqslant r + \frac{g - s_{pw}r}{s_{ww}} \tag{15.4}$$

Let us now investigate the case in which $K_c = 0$. Equation (15.2) is satisfied whatever r is and $K_w = K$ since capitalists have disappeared. Therefore, equation (15.1) determines a relationship between $(1/v)$ and r:

$$\frac{1}{v} = r + \frac{g - s_{pw}r}{s_{ww}}. \tag{15.5}$$

The above analysis is presented diagrammatically in Figure 15.1, where the horizontal axis gives the rate of profit r and the vertical axis the output–capital ratio $(1/v)$. The 45° line OD cuts the first quadrant in two parts: only above the line OD are wages positive $(W > 0)$; along OD wages vanish $(W = 0)$. Curve AD represents equation (15.5). Because of inequality (15.4), capitalists' capital is positive only below curve AD. Line BC represents equation (15.3). Steady-state growth is only feasible either along the segment AD or along the segment BC.

Taking into consideration the technological relationship between v and r, a long-run equilibrium exists whenever the technological relationship cuts segment AD or segment BC. If this relationship meets BC at C, then only capitalists earn income. If it cuts AD (point B included) then there is a one-class long-run equilibrium in which capitalists' capital equals zero. A two-class long-run equilibrium is only possible if the technological relationship cuts the segment BC excluding the extreme points B and C.

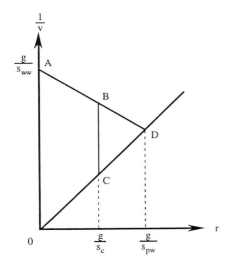

Figure 15.1

Hence a two-class economy exists if and only if the technological relationship satisfies the following inequalities

$$\frac{s_{ww}}{s_c + s_{ww} - s_{pw}} < \frac{g}{s_c} v^* < 1,$$

where $((g/s_c), v^*)$ is a point of the technological relationship.[4]

2.2. The technological relationship: Single production

The technological relationship mentioned in the previous subsection is a correspondence, $v \in V(r)$, since at the levels of the rate of profit

[4] For the sake of completeness a condition for the existence of an odd number of equilibrium solutions – hence at least one – for a one-class (workers') economy can be given:

$$\left[\frac{s_{ww}}{v_0} - g \right] [g - s_{wp}R] > 0,$$

where $(0, v_0)$ is a point of the technological relationship between v and r. The above inequality can be written as

$$\min\left(\frac{s_{ww}}{v_0}, s_{wp}R \right) < g < \max\left(\frac{s_{ww}}{v_0}, s_{wp}R \right),$$

where (s_{ww}/v_0) is the saving per unit of capital if the whole income is distributed to the workers as wages, and $s_{wp}R$ is the saving per unit of capital if the whole income is distributed to the workers as profits.

which are switchpoints (see Section 5 of Chapter 5) there is a range of values v can assume. Such a relationship depends on (i) the technology, (ii) the growth rate, (iii) workers' consumption habits, (iv) workers' saving habits, and (v) capitalists' consumption habits. It is built up in the following way on the assumption that single production prevails.

As we have seen in Chapter 5, for a given rate of profit r lower than the maximum one, R, there is a cost-minimizing technique $(\mathbf{A}, \mathbf{l})$, where $\mathbf{A} = [a_{ij}]$ is the material input matrix and $\mathbf{l} = (l_1, l_2, \ldots, l_n)^T$ is the labor input vector. If more than one cost-minimizing technique exists – which is the case at the switchpoint levels of r – let us apply the following procedure to each cost-minimizing technique. The price vector $\mathbf{p}$ is determined as in Chapter 4 and the intensity vector $\mathbf{q}$ is determined (cf. Subsection 1.7 of Chapter 4) by the equation

$$\mathbf{q}^T = (1 + g)\mathbf{q}^T \mathbf{A} + \frac{[W + (r - g)K_w]}{\mathbf{b}_w^T \mathbf{p}}\mathbf{b}_w^T + \frac{(r - g)K_c}{\mathbf{b}_c^T \mathbf{p}}\mathbf{b}_c^T, \tag{15.6}$$

where $W = w\mathbf{q}^T\mathbf{l}$, $K_w = s_{ww}/(g - s_{pw}r)(w\mathbf{q}^T\mathbf{l})$, $K_c = \mathbf{q}^T\mathbf{A}\mathbf{p} - s_{ww}/(g - s_{pw}r)$ $(w\mathbf{q}^T\mathbf{l})$, and workers consume commodities in proportion to vector $\mathbf{b}_w^T$, whereas capitalists consume commodities in proportion to vector $\mathbf{b}_c^T$. (It is not excluded that $\mathbf{b}_w^T$ and $\mathbf{b}_c^T$ are functions of vector $\mathbf{p}$.) If r is a switchpoint, then vector $\mathbf{p}$ is still uniquely determined, but for each cost-minimizing technique a vector $\mathbf{q}$ can be calculated. Then

$$v = \frac{\mathbf{q}^T\mathbf{A}\mathbf{p}}{\mathbf{q}^T(\mathbf{I} - \mathbf{A})\mathbf{p}} \equiv \frac{\mathbf{q}^T\mathbf{A}\mathbf{p}}{w\mathbf{q}^T\mathbf{l} + r\mathbf{q}^T\mathbf{A}\mathbf{p}}.$$

At a switchpoint more than one vector $\mathbf{q}$ can be determined, and therefore more than one v. In this case $V(r)$ coincides with the range limited by the possible values of v. Otherwise, $V(r) = \{v\}$. Obviously, $V(r)$ depends on s_{ww}, s_{pw}, and $\mathbf{b}_c^T$ unless $\mathbf{b}_c^T \equiv \mathbf{b}_w^T$ or $r = g$ (that is, $s_c = 1$).

The technological relationship $v \in V(r)$ is utilized in order to determine: (i) the capital shares in the case in which two classes exist; (ii) whether one or two classes exist; and (iii) the rate of profit if only workers exist. Obviously, if capitalists do not exist, that is, $K_c = 0$ and $K_w = K = \mathbf{q}^T\mathbf{A}\mathbf{p}$, then s_{ww}, s_{pw}, and $\mathbf{b}_c^T$ do not matter in determining the technological relationship. It is possible to prove that these data may be excluded from the construction of the technological relationship when it is utilized in determining whether one or two classes exist. This can be relevant with respect to two facts. First, in comparative static analysis the technological relationship can remain unchanged if the workers' saving habits or the capitalists' consumption habits change. Second, from a theoretical point of view, whether one or two classes exist is independent of capitalists' consumption habits: it will be proved that, provided $g < s_c R$, two classes exist if and only if

$$s_{ww}w + s_{pw}\frac{g}{s_c}k^* < gk^*, \tag{15.7}$$

where k^* is the capital per unit of labor of the subsystem producing the consumption basket of workers and w is the wage rate. Provided $g < s_c R$, the interpretation is that a two-class economy exists if and only if the one-class economy cannot save enough to sustain growth at rate g and at rate of profit (g/s_c).

To see this, it is first worth recalling that equation (15.6) was considered in Subsection 1.7 of Chapter 4. We just need to add to that analysis that

$$\theta = \frac{s_{ww}}{g - s_{pw}r}. \tag{15.8}$$

In the subsection referred to it was shown that capitalists' capital is not negative if and only if inequality (4.21) holds, that is, if and only if

$$\mathbf{b}_w^T[\mathbf{I} - (1+g)\mathbf{A}]^{-1}\left[\mathbf{A}\mathbf{p} - \frac{s_{ww}w}{g - s_{pw}r}\mathbf{1}\right] \geqslant 0. \tag{15.9}$$

Inequality (15.9) can be stated as

$$\frac{1}{\bar{v}} \leqslant r + \frac{g - s_{pw}r}{s_{ww}},$$

where

$$\bar{v} = \frac{\mathbf{b}_w^T[\mathbf{I} - (1+g)\mathbf{A}]^{-1}\mathbf{A}\mathbf{p}}{w\mathbf{b}_w^T[\mathbf{I} - (1+g)\mathbf{A}]^{-1}\mathbf{1} + r\mathbf{b}_w^T[\mathbf{I} - (1+g)\mathbf{A}]^{-1}\mathbf{A}\mathbf{p}}$$

is the capital–output ratio relative to the subsystem producing the consumption basket of workers. Thus, the relationship between $\bar{v}$ and r plays the same role as the relationship between v and r in determining whether capitalists exist or not.[5] Finally, by defining

$$k^* = \frac{\mathbf{b}_w^T[\mathbf{I} - (1+g)\mathbf{A}]^{-1}\mathbf{A}\mathbf{p}}{\mathbf{b}_w^T[\mathbf{I} - (1+g)\mathbf{A}]^{-1}\mathbf{1}}$$

---

[5] A more intuitive argument could be the following. Assume that

$$\frac{1}{\bar{v}} \leqslant r + \frac{g - s_{pw}r}{s_{ww}},$$

then there would be a two-class economy if capitalists consume the same and taking into account the fact that $r = (g/s_c)$, inequality (15.7) is immediately obtained from inequality (15.9).

It is possible to show that if fixed capital is introduced into the picture, then there is no other complication than that concerning the positivity of capitalists' capital. But if general joint production is allowed for, then the problem of the choice of technique, as we have seen in Chapter 8, cannot be separated from the determination of quantities produced.

2.3. *The technological relationship: Joint production*

The analysis of the case of joint production in which the capitalists' capital is positive has been provided in Section 5 of Chapter 8. Here we need to add to that analysis that θ is defined by equation (15.8). Moreover, if we want to take into account the case in which the capitalists' capital is nought, then we have to consider not only the model dealt with in Section 5 of Chapter 8, but also the model obtained from model (8.8) of that chapter when $\mathbf{d}$ in equation (8.8c) is

$$\mathbf{d}^T = g\mathbf{x}^T\mathbf{A} + \frac{\mathbf{x}^T[\mathbf{B} - \mathbf{A}]\mathbf{p}}{\mathbf{b}_w^T\mathbf{p}}\mathbf{b}_w^T$$

and the rate of profit is *not* given, *but* it is determined by the equation

$$\frac{s_{ww}}{g - s_{pw}r}\mathbf{x}^T\mathbf{l} = \mathbf{x}^T\mathbf{A}\mathbf{p}.$$

A solution to this model will not be provided here.

3. **On monetary explanations of the rate of profit**

The starting point of the recent developments of a monetary theory of distribution within the classical tradition is a hint given by Sraffa in section 44 of his book. He pointed out that

> the rate of profits, as a ratio, has a significance which is independent of any prices, and can well be "given" before the prices are fixed. It is accordingly susceptible of being determined from outside the system of production, in particular by the level of the money rates of interest (Sraffa, 1960, p. 33).

commodities in the same proportions as workers. Let capitalists' consumption pattern now pass smoothly from the workers' consumption basket to their own: the output–capital ratio can rise or fall, but it cannot fall below the 45° line; neither can it rise above the segment AD (see Figure 15.1). The former fact is obvious since $r < R$, the latter would imply the existence of a capitalists' consumption basket such that the relationship between $(1/v)$ and r would cut the segment AD at B, that is, the existence of a one-class economy would hold. Hence a contradiction. A similar argument holds if $(1/\bar{v}) > r + (g - s_{pw}r)/s_{ww}$.

Sraffa left it at that, that is, did not provide an explanation of the origin and the precise meaning of this hint (cf. Panico, 1988a). Several authors (cf., for example, Nuti, 1971, and Dobb, 1973) expressed the opinion that Sraffa's idea could be an appropriate starting point for an investigation of the complex problems of interaction of real and monetary phenomena. Other authors were concerned with working out the analytical foundations of the relationship between the rate of profit and the rate(s) of interest and with tracing reflections of this relationship in the earlier literature on money and income distribution. In this section we shall focus attention on the analytics of the problem under consideration; remarks on its history will be found in the historical notes.

In the literature there are essentially two competitive mechanisms contemplated for substantiating Sraffa's hint. The more direct mechanism is the following one. The general rate of profit is composed of two elements: (i) the long-term rate of interest which represents the "pure" remuneration of capital; and (ii) the normal profit of enterprise which can represent both the compensation of the "risk and trouble" of employing capital in a given line of production, or sector, and profit due to some "degree of monopoly" in that sector. Taking the normal profit of enterprise to be given and constant, that is, independent of the long-term rate of interest, it follows that (lasting) changes in the latter will bring about corresponding changes in the general rate of profit (cf. Pivetti, 1987, pp. 874–5). Since interest payments are a component of costs and since prices tend to be equated to normal unit costs (inclusive of profits), lasting changes in the rate of interest eventually result in changes in money prices. With money wages taken as given, these changes in money prices involve contrary changes in real wages. Hence a rise (fall) in the long-term rate of interest brings about a parallel rise (fall) in the rate(s) of profit via a fall (rise) in the real wage rate.

This argument can be supplemented with the analysis of the own rates of interest introduced by Sraffa in 1932 (Sraffa, 1932). Sraffa's analysis was referred to by Keynes in chapter 17 of the *General Theory* (cf. Keynes, *CW*, VII) and then by Kaldor (1939, 1960). According to this analysis, competitive market forces will direct investment toward those assets with the highest own rates of interest. This will establish a tendency toward uniform own rates of interest that will determine: (i) the structure of interest rates; (ii) the relationship between these rates and the rate(s) of profit; and (iii) the portfolio structures of wealth owners (cf. Panico, 1988b).

The other competitive mechanism that has been suggested to explain why lasting changes in the rate of interest will cause corresponding changes in the rate(s) of profit assumes that the banking sector, like the industrial sectors, has to earn at least the general rate of profit on the own capital which is anticipated as being required to carry on the banking activity. Changes in the interest rates affect the revenues (interest received on bank loans) and the costs (interest paid on deposits and bank loans, profits on the capital advanced) of both the banking and the industrial firms. In competitive conditions this entails adjustment processes which tend to restore conditions of equilibrium between revenues and costs in all sectors and set some constraints linking the movements of the rates of interest and the rate of profit (see Panico, 1980, 1988b).

This version of the monetary explanation of the general rate of profit starts from the hypothesis that the banking sector is a basic sector within the system of production. Next, a distinction is made between the banks' short- and long-term loans to firms, arguing that through the former the banks provide a service to firms that is as necessary to their productive activity as is commercial activity, transportation, insurance, and so on. In this way, the financial services offered by the banks to the firms are treated as inputs of production of the industrial activity, and the payments made for these services directly influence the costs of the industries and the revenues of the banking sector.

The main idea of this approach can be formalized as follows. Let $\mathbf{h}$ be the credit input vector per unit of gross output valued at going prices, that is, the ratio of loans to gross receipts in each industry, i the rate of interest on loans, $\mathbf{u}$ the deposit vector of the industrial sectors, that is, the ratio of deposits to gross receipts, and z the rate of interest on deposits. Assuming single production and adopting the notation used in the other parts of the book, the price equations of the industrial sectors of the economy can be written as follows:

$$\mathbf{p} = (1 + r)\mathbf{A}\mathbf{p} + w\mathbf{l} + i\mathbf{h} - z\mathbf{u}. \tag{15.10}$$

Denoting by $\mathbf{a}_b$ the material input vector of the banking sector, by l_b the corresponding quantity of labor employed, by B the portion of money reserve advanced, by $D = \mathbf{e}^T\mathbf{h}$ total deposits, and by $Q = \mathbf{e}^T\mathbf{u}$ total credits to the industrial sectors, then the banking sector can be represented as follows:

$$iQ = (1 + r)\mathbf{a}_b^T\mathbf{p} + wl_b + rB + zD. \tag{15.11}$$

Finally, the money wage rate is assumed to be given, that is,

$$w = w^*.$$

Note that in the special case in which $z = 0$ and $B = 0$, the matrix of the input coefficients of the industrial sectors can be modified so as to include the inputs of labor and capital goods used in the banking sector. In this case equations (15.10) and (15.11) collapse to

$$\mathbf{p} = (1 + r)\mathbf{A}_B\mathbf{p} + w\mathbf{l}_B,$$

where $\mathbf{A}_B = \mathbf{A} + (1/Q)\mathbf{ha}_b^T$ and $\mathbf{l}_B = \mathbf{l} + (l_b/Q)\mathbf{h}$.

The monetary approach to the theory of distribution has sometimes been considered as an alternative to or even incompatible with that proposed by Kaldor and Pasinetti; see the discussion in Moss (1978, p. 306), Nell (1988), Wray (1988), Pivetti (1988), Pasinetti (1988b), and Abraham-Frois (1991, pp. 197 and 202). However, as Panico (1993) has argued, in a more general framework the two theories of income distribution turn out to be compatible with one another. A characteristic feature of the monetary theory of distribution is that it takes the rate of interest as determined by the monetary authorities irrespective of the overall situation of the economic system under consideration. Yet the "realism" of this hypothesis can be questioned. And even if this were true, there is the question how the other important policy agency, that is, the "government" or those responsible for fiscal policy, act. For example, Kaldor (1958) has argued that the monetary authorities tend to fix the money rate of interest at a specific level, allowing the money supply to adjust. Fiscal policy on the other hand is considered an effective instrument of keeping the economy on a path of steady growth. More specifically, in the case in which the rate of profit corresponding to the existing level of aggregate demand is too low relative to the money rate of interest, the accumulation process would slow down. Fiscal policy could intervene to raise the level of aggregate effective demand and thereby increase the rate of profit to a level that is high enough to guarantee adequate investment activity. In this case the two explanations of the rate of profits apply simultaneously: the rate of profit can be seen to be determined concurrently by the money rate of interest and the growth rate of the system, where the former is fixed by the monetary authorities and the latter by the authorities deciding fiscal policy.

4. Historical notes

4.1. The theories of distribution and growth of the classical economists and Marx have been the object of numerous articles and books. A few references to the literature must suffice. Summary statements and comparisons are provided, for example, by Stigler (1941), Lowe (1954), Walsh and Gram (1980), Garegnani (1984), and Eltis (1984). Cannan's classic book (Cannan, 1917) focuses attention on English political economy from 1776–1848. Studies of Adam Smith's theory of distribution and growth are provided, among others, by Lowe in Skinner and Wilson (1975),

Gehrke (1990), Jeck (1990), and Negishi (1993); see also Hollander (1973b, chs. 5 and 6). Ricardo's analysis is dealt with by Sraffa (1951), Samuelson (1959), Pasinetti (1960), Casarosa (1974, 1978), Hollander (1979), Caravale and Tosato (1980), Morishima (1989), and Peach (1993); on Morishima's interpretation, see also Kurz and Salvadori (1992). On Marx's theory, see Samuelson (1957), Morishima (1973), Steedman (1977a), Morishima and Catephores (1978), and Goodwin (1982); see also the discussion of Marx's theory of accumulation in Steindl (1952, ch. XIV).

4.2. In the post-Keynesian literature the idea that the long-term rate of accumulation determines the distribution of income is frequently traced back to the so-called widow's cruse parable in Keynes's *Treatise on Money*:

> If entrepreneurs choose to spend a portion of their profit on consumption..., the effect is to *increase* the profit on the sale of liquid consumption goods by an amount exactly equal to the amount of profits which have been thus expended.... Thus, however, much of their profits entrepreneurs spend on consumption, the increment of wealth belonging to entrepreneurs remains the same as before. Thus profits, as a source of capital increment for entrepreneurs, are a widow's cruse which remains undepleted however much of them may be devoted to riotous living (Keynes, *CW*, V, p. 125).

While in the *Treatise* an excess of investment over saving is reflected in a change in the general price level only, given the level of output and employment, Kalecki in his early contributions, that is, prior to Keynes's *General Theory*, developed essentially the same idea but allowed for quantity adjustments (cf. Laski, 1987). He stressed that investment "finances itself" (Kalecki, 1954, pp. 49–50) via changes in economic activity and total profits. By assuming that workers consume all their wages while capitalists consume only a fraction of their profits, Kalecki (1938, p. 76) arrived at the conclusion that total profits are equal to investment plus capitalists' consumption. In a subsequent paper, he interpreted this equality by saying that it is capitalists' "investment and consumption decisions which determine profits, and not the other way round" (Kalecki, 1942, p. 259). However, both Keynes's analysis in the *General Theory* and Kalecki's are predominantly short-period.

A selection of Kalecki's most important articles on the theory of economic dynamics is available in Kalecki (1971). Feiwel (1975), Sawyer (1985), and Laski (1987) provide summary statements of Kalecki's works. Kalecki's approach was further developed by Josef Steindl (1952, 1990).

The works of Kalecki and Steindl were major sources of inspiration for authors such as Rowthorn (1980b, 1982), Dutt (1984, 1990), Asimakopulos (1988), and Skott (1989); see also Lavoie (1992) and Kurz (1990d, 1992c, 1994a). Much of the literature in which a Kaleckian approach is adopted is macroeconomic. Among those contributions that deal with Kalecki's microtheory of distribution and pricing, the following deserve mentioning. The internal coherence of Kalecki's consecutive approaches to the theory of price and income distribution is scrutinized by Basile and Salvadori (1984–5); see also the subsequent discussion in the *Journal of Post-Keynesian Economics*. Steedman (1992) points out a set of difficulties in the received Kaleckian mark-up price theory; see also the subsequent discussion in the *Review of Political Economy*.

4.3. The post-Keynesian theory of growth and distribution was first proposed by Kaldor (1955–6). Kaldor called his new theory "Keynesian," even if, he stressed, Keynes had never developed it himself. The theory is derived from the principle of the multiplier, which, according to Kaldor, can be "alternatively applied to a determination of the relation between prices and wages, if the level of output and employment is taken as given, or the determination of the level of employment, if distribution (i.e., the relation between prices and wages) is taken as given" (Kaldor, 1955–6, p. 94). Kaldor's original presentation is characterized by a distinction of groups of income-earners, whose saving habits are homogenous within each group and are differentiated among the groups. Kaldor made a distinction between wage-earners and profit-earners, noting that the propensity of the first group to save can be assumed smaller than that of the second group simply as a consequence of the fact that the bulk of profits accrue in the form of company profits and a high proportion of these profits are put to reserve (see Kaldor, 1955–6, p. 95 fn.). In a later contribution Kaldor (1966, pp. 310–11) confirmed his intention of referring to a situation in which profits were generated by companies with a high propensity to save (i.e. a high quota of undistributed profits to favor self-finance). Kaldor's saving function, therefore, is

$$S = s_\omega W + s_\pi P,$$

where S is the saving of a given economy, and W and P are total wages and total profits. Since, in equilibrium, planned saving equals planned investment and since wages plus profits equal the national income, it is possible to write

$$I = (s_\pi - s_\omega)P + s_\omega Y,$$

where I is net investment and Y is net national income. Finally, because of "the 'Keynesian' hypothesis that investment, or rather, the ratio of investment to output, can be treated as an independent variable" (Kaldor, 1955–6, p. 95),

$$\frac{P}{Y} = \frac{1}{s_\pi - s_\omega} \frac{I}{Y} - \frac{s_\omega}{s_\pi - s_\omega}. \tag{15.12}$$

The rate of profit is then obtained by multiplying equation (15.12) by the output–capital ratio, which Kaldor (1955–6) assumed to be constant with respect to changes in distribution:

$$\frac{P}{K} = \frac{1}{s_\pi - s_\omega} \frac{I}{K} - \frac{s_\omega}{s_\pi - s_\omega} \frac{Y}{K}, \tag{15.13}$$

where I/K is the growth rate.

4.4. Already in the 1930s Kaldor had analyzed the relationship between the rate of profit and the rate of growth (see Kaldor, 1937). However, he did not think at that time of reversing the causal link between the former and the latter variable. A "great deal of stimulus" to move in this direction was provided, according to Kaldor (1955–6, p. 94 fn.), by a paper published by Kalecki (1942) and by some discussions he had with Joan Robinson on her then forthcoming book *The Accumulation of Capital* (Robinson, 1956). The links with the Kaleckian aphorism that "capitalists earn what they spend, and workers spend what they earn" are clearly apparent in the special case in which $s_w = 0$ since equations (15.12) and (15.13) become:

$$\frac{P}{Y} = \frac{1}{s_p} \frac{I}{Y},$$

$$\frac{P}{K} = \frac{1}{s_p} \frac{I}{K}.$$

4.5. In contradistinction to Kaldor, Pasinetti (1962) regarded steady growth analysis "as a system of necessary relations to achieve full employment" (Pasinetti, 1962, p. 267), thus avoiding any reference to the working of actual economies. Besides, he dealt with *classes* (capitalists and workers) rather than with *income groups*, suggesting the use of the following saving functions which assume that the propensity to save out of the profits earned by the capitalist class differs from the propensity to save out of the profits earned by the working class:

$$S_w = s_w(W + P_w),$$
$$S_c = s_c P_c.$$

Further, Pasinetti explicitly introduced the dynamic equilibrium conditions, according to which capitalists' and workers' capital, like all variables changing through time, must grow at the same rate as the economy as a whole. In addition, he pointed out that, since those who save out of wages must receive a part of the profit as interest for what they lend to capitalists, it is necessary to specify the relationship between the rate of interest and the rate of profit in steady growth in order to determine the rate of profit. He maintained that "in a long-run equilibrium model, the obvious hypothesis to make is that of a rate of interest equal to the rate of profit" (Pasinetti, 1962, pp. 271–2).

4.6. Equation (15.3) is a direct consequence of the assumption that the rate of interest is equal to the rate of profit and is totally independent of any assumption on worker's saving habits. This assumption, though clearly stated by Pasinetti (1962, p. 272), has not always been properly taken into account. Samuelson and Modigliani (1966a, p. 269), for instance, failed to mention it when presenting the "Pasinetti Theorem." The same failure can be found in the Introduction to Volume 5 of Kaldor's *Collected Economic Eassays* (Kaldor, 1978, p. xv) and in more recent literature. Marglin (1984, p. 121), for instance, claims that the "Cambridge equation" was obtained by lowering the propensity to save on the profit "that accrues to workers from s_c to s_w." He does not mention at all Pasinetti's assumption of equality between the rate of interest and the rate of profit.

The fact that Kaldor obtained a different result for the rate of profit (see equations 15.3 and 15.14) calls for an explanation. Pasinetti (1962) suggested that Kaldor had slipped on the simple truism that people who save accumulate capital and then obtain profit. But Samuelson and Modigliani (1966a) remarked that "there need not be a 'logical slip' in the Kaldorian model, as long as it is assumed that the propensity to save out of income from capital is s_c whether that income is received by capitalists or by workers. This hypothesis, which may or may not be empirically sound, is certainly not logically self-contradictory." Following this remark, Gupta (1977) and Mückl (1978), rectifying Maneschi (1974), clarified that, if the rate of interest is equal to the rate of profit, the saving habits in Kaldor's analysis require that

$$s_w W K_c = 0,$$

where s_w is the saving ratio out of wages; and Fazi and Salvadori (1981) have shown that if the rate of interest is lower than the rate of profit, then the Kaldorian model is perfectly consistent (see also Fazi and Salvadori, 1985, and Salvadori, 1991). This means that even if Kaldor's formulation of the theory does not need to specify the relationship between the rate of interest and the rate of profit in order to determine the latter, nevertheless a two-class economy with Kaldorian saving functions can exist in long-run equilibrium only if the rate of interest is lower than the rate of profit. This is the reason why in the text it has been assumed $s_{pw} < s_c$.

In subsequent writings, Pasinetti himself (1974, 1983) and other authors (Laing, 1969; Balestra and Baranzini, 1971; Moore, 1974; Gupta, 1976; Fazi and Salvadori 1981, 1985; and Salvadori, 1988b, 1991) examined the implications for post-Keynesian theory of a rate of interest lower than the rate of profit, meaning by that a ratio of workers' profits to their capital lower than the ratio of total profits to total capital. This assumption makes it possible that capitalists and workers hold shares and bonds in different proportions and that the rates of return on these assets are different.

4.7. The "Pasinetti theorem" gave rise to a large debate which turned around the limits of Pasinetti's result. See Meade (1963, 1966), Meade and Hahn (1965), Samuelson and Modigliani (1966a, 1966b), Pasinetti (1964, 1966a, 1966b, 1974), Kaldor (1966), and Robinson (1966). Meade (1963) and Samuelson and Modigliani (1966a) deserve the credit for having drawn attention to the case in which $K_c = 0$, and therefore to the problem of the existence of a two-class economy.

4.8. The possible alternative between the saving functions advocated by Kaldor and Pasinetti suggests that a more general formulation including them as special cases can be found. Chiang (1973) introduced the threefold savings ratio model adopted in the text. This model has also been utilized by Maneschi (1974), Gupta (1976), Pasinetti (1983), and others. Fazi and Salvadori (1985) have presented a formulation where workers' and capitalists' savings are defined by the following general functions:

$$S_w = F(P_w, W),$$
$$S_c = G(P_c).$$

More recently, Salvadori (1991, appendix) has proposed a formulation which also considers the capitalists' and workers' wealths as arguments of the saving functions:

$$S_w = F(P_w, W, K_w),$$
$$S_c = G(P_c, K_c).$$

4.9. The neoclassical participants in the debate often assumed that the technological relationship built up in subsection 2.2 has all the properties generated by a typical neoclassical production function. Kaldor (1955–6, p. 98) assumed that the capital–output ratio is constant with respect to the rate of profit.[6] Franke (1985) and Salvadori (1988b) clarified some

---

[6] Kaldor did not deny that the capital–output ratio can vary with the rate of profit. He however expressed his conviction "that technical innovations ... are far more influential on the chosen v than price relationships" (1955–6, p. 98 fn.)

aspects concerning the construction of this technological relationship. (They also added some remarks on the case in which there is joint production.) Morishima (1964, 1969) was perhaps the first economist who inserted Pasinetti's saving functions in a von Neumann-type model. This route was then followed by people interested in generalizing post-Keynesian theory of distribution in order to take into account joint production and fixed capital. Bidard and Hosoda (1985), Bidard and Franke (1987), and Salvadori (1980, 1988c) worked out this problem under different assumptions on technology and consumption habits.

4.10. As we have seen in note 4.3, Kaldor's starting point was the observation that there were two notions of the multiplier, corresponding to two different routes along which savings could be generated. In the short run, on which Keynes focuses attention, fluctuations in investment demand are reflected in fluctuations in output and the overall degree of capacity utilization, that is, savings are generated via changes in the level of income. Yet in the long run, with which post-Keynesian theory concerns itself, it is contended that there are no margins of spare capacity to accommodate higher levels of investment demand, that is, savings are generated via changes in the distribution of income. The upshot of the post-Keynesian approach is the so-called Cambridge equation. According to the conventional interpretation of this equation it establishes a direct link between the normal rate of profit r (and thus the real wage rate) and the rate of accumulation g, that is, the ratio between net investment and the value of the capital stock. A rise (fall) in the incentive to accumulate is seen as bringing about a rise (fall) in the rate of profit and thus a fall (rise) in the real wage rate via a rise (fall) of money prices relative to the money wage rate. In this view it is an exogenously given incentive to invest, and thus, via the multiplier, effective demand, that exerts a permanent influence on income distribution.

However, as has been pointed out by Garegnani (1992), Kurz (1990e, 1994a) and others, the interpretation of the "Cambridge equation" as a generalization of Keynes's principle of effective demand to the long run is difficult to sustain. If the rate of profit referred to in the equation is to be the "normal" or "general" rate, conceived of, as it commonly is, in terms of the full adjustment of productive capacity to effective demand, then the rate of accumulation in the equation cannot, except by a fluke, be the *actual* rate of accumulation. For, with the level of investment given independently, there is no reason to presume that productive capacity will be utilized at that level which, in conditions of free competition, cost-minimizing producers desire to realize. The rate of accumulation g, referred to in the equation, therefore rather corresponds to that level and composition of investment per unit of capital in existence which, if realized, *would* result in a degree of utilization of productive capacity as desired by entrepreneurs. We may call this rate the *rate of capacity investment*. Since the concept of the normal rate of profit and that of the rate of capacity investment cannot be defined independently of each other, the latter cannot be taken to "determine" the former.

If, on the other hand, the rate of accumulation referred to in the equation is the *actual* rate, then, flukes apart, the corresponding rate of profit cannot be the "normal" or "general" one: it is rather the sum of profits actually obtained during the period under consideration divided by the capital stock in existence evaluated at some given prices, that is, what may be called the "realised" rate of profit (cf. Robinson, 1962). Whichever interpretation is adopted, the "Cambridge equation" cannot be said to settle the question as to the factors governing normal income distribution.

4.11. For a collection of essays devoted to the post-Keynesian theory of distribution and growth, see Panico and Salvadori (1993, see also their introduction). The debate on post-Keynesian models has been surveyed by Harcourt (1972, ch. 4), Baranzini (1988), and Ahmad (1991, ch. 13).

4.12. Both Adam Smith and David Ricardo advocated the view that the rate of interest is subordinate to the rate of profit, that is, governed by the factors determining the latter: the real wage rate and the socially dominant technical conditions of production; see, for example, Smith (*WN*, II.iv.8) and Ricardo (*Works* I, p. 363). However, the opposite view is also to be found in the early literature. The idea of a "conventional" determination of the rate of interest can be traced back far in the history of our subject. It is, for example, spelled out by Joseph Massie in his *Essay on the Governing Causes of the Natural Rate of Interest* (1750). In the 1820s several authors pointed to the possibility that factors which are independent of the rate of profit, for example, the risk preference of asset holders and the intensity of the government demand for loanable funds, can affect the interest rate. It is possible that, in developing these positions, Joplin (1823, 1832), Tooke (1826), and J. S. Mill (1844) were influenced by the sharp variations in the interest rate which occurred during and after the Napoleonic wars.[7] These variations in the interest rate were considered the result of the policy followed to finance the government debt rather than the consequence of a change in the conditions of production implying a higher level of the rate of profit. The presence of these positions in the literature of the time was emphasized by Gilbart, one of the most influencial

---

[7] For an analysis of Joplin's position on this problem, see Caminati (1981). Moreover, note that Mill's essay *On Profit and Interest*, published in 1844 (Mill, 1844), was written in 1829–30.

writers of the nineteenth century on monetary issues (cf. Gilbart, 1834). He concluded that "it appears reasonable to suppose that the rate of interest may have regulated the rate of profit, instead of the rate of profit regulating the rate of interest" (Gilbart, 1834, p. 17).

Other elements supporting these positions were provided in the subsequent writings of Tooke (1838, 1840, 1844), Fullarton (1845), Wilson (1845), and Mill ([1848]1965); see Panico (1988b) and Pivetti (1985, 1991).

4.13. Marx put forward a theory of value which was close to Ricardo's. As his unfinished notes published by Engels as volume III of *Capital* (cf. Marx, [1894] 1959) show, he also developed the view, derived from his study of the British monetary theory and policy, that powerful pressure groups operating in the financial markets can affect the interest rate permanently through the introduction of financial innovation and through their influence on state intervention regulating the legal and institutional arrangements of the markets. Yet Marx did not succeed in integrating these two lines of thought in a coherent theoretical scheme; see also Panico (1980).

4.14. Keynes in the *General Theory* (*CW*, VII, chs. 13 and 14) emphasized the need to develop a theory of the rate of interest based on "conventional" elements as an alternative to the traditional notion of a "natural" rate of interest which he deemed erroneous. The formation of the "common opinion" as to the future level of this rate was put in the center of the stage. According to Keynes, this "common opinion" is mainly influenced by the conduct of the monetary authorities, which, in turn, is affected by monetary and historically relative factors, rather than by a unique set of factors determining the "natural" rate of interest. On possible links between the positions of Keynes and Sraffa, see Garegnani (1979, p. 81).

Mathematical appendix

This mathematical appendix provides proofs of some theorems in advanced linear algebra and the theory of linear programming. It is assumed that the reader knows the basics of linear algebra as they are presented, for example, in Hadley (1961), Schneider and Barker (1968), or Hoffman and Kunze (1971). In the proofs given the use of parts of mathematics other than linear algebra has been avoided as much as possible; however, it is assumed that the reader knows the language of set theory and some elements of calculus when these concepts are mentioned in the statements to be proved. The idea of requiring the reader to know only some linear algebra in order to be able to read this book was suggested by the teaching experience of one of us: to provide some more advanced linear algebra as a side dish is rather convenient, whereas this simply cannot be done for calculus or topology unless one refrains from providing complete proofs. In our opinion such a procedure would be difficult to defend from a didactical point of view since it leads students into mistaking mathematics for a kind of cookbook in which ready-made recipes can be found, while it should rather be seen as a logical tool developed to master issues too complex to be treated in ordinary language. Due to limitations of space we will not expound basic linear algebra here. However, for the sake of simplifying references, the first section of this appendix provides a list of definitions and results in set theory and basic linear algebra. The reader must know these concepts in order to comprehend fully the book (putting to one side for the moment the few statements which mention concepts of calculus).

The remainder of the appendix consists of three sections. Section 2 provides some Theorems of the Alternative relative to the existence of solutions of systems of linear equations or of linear inequalities. Section 3 is dedicated to Perron–Frobenius Theorems for nonnegative matrices.

492

Section 4 deals with the theory of linear programming, no element of computational linear programming being provided.

A.1. Basic concepts

This section is divided in nine subsections. The first two subsections present definitions relative to sets and numerical sets only. The last seven subsections present both definitions and results related to elementary linear algebra. Our major concern is with covering all concepts and results which are utilized in the main text and in the remainder of this appendix, and not with the completeness of the issues: several, even important, concepts which are not mentioned in the main text and are not relevant for the understanding to those that are, will not be considered at all. The reader who is interested in the proofs of the results presented in this section is asked to consult any of the books mentioned in the introductory passage to this appendix. The reader who has no knowledge of linear algebra is strongly recommended to do so.

A.1.1. Sets

A set[1] is simply a collection of things which are called the *elements* of the set. The set is thought of as a single object and is denoted by a capital letter, A, B, etc. If x is an element of A we also say that x *belongs to* A, and in formulas we write $x \in A$. Conversely, $x \notin A$ means that x *does not belong to* A. A set is determined by its elements, which means that a set A is fully described by describing all the elements of A; for example, $\{1, 2, 3\}$ is the set consisting of numbers $1, 2, 3$. Sets are often described as subsets of other sets satisfying a given property. For example, denoting the set of natural numbers by $\mathbb{N}$, the set $\{1, 2, 3\}$ can be described as

$$\{x \mid x \in \mathbb{N}, x \leqslant 3\}$$

or, for the sake of simplicity,

$$\{x \in \mathbb{N} \mid x \leqslant 3\}.$$

The symbol on the left-hand side of "$\mid$" stands for a typical element of the set, whereas on the right-hand side of "$\mid$" there is a property which this typical element satisfies.

Sets A and B are *equal*, $A = B$, if and only if every element of A is an element of B and every element of B is an element of A. Set B is a *subset*

---

[1] The word "set" is not italicized since this is not a definition of *set* which is presented here as a primitive concept.

of set A, $B \subseteq A$ or $A \supseteq B$, if every element of B is an element of A. Obviously $A \supseteq A$; moreover,[2]

$$(A \subseteq B \text{ and } A \supseteq B) \Leftrightarrow A = B.$$

A conventional set, to be thought of as a "set with no element," is considered a subset of each set. This set is called *empty set* and is denoted by $\varnothing$. If A and B are sets, then the *intersection*, $A \cap B$, is the set of all elements which belong to both A and B, that is,

$$A \cap B = \{x \mid x \in A \text{ and } x \in B\}.$$

If sets A and B have no element in common, $A \cap B = \varnothing$, they are called *disjoint*. The *union* of sets A and B, $A \cup B$, is the set of all elements which belong either to A or to B (or to both), that is,

$$A \cup B = \{x \mid x \in A \text{ or } x \in B\}.$$

If B is a subset of A, the set of the elements of A which do not belong to B, $\{x \in A \mid x \notin B\}$, is called the *complement of B in A*.

A.1.2. Numerical sets

The set of natural numbers has been denoted as $\mathbb{N}$. The sets of integer, rational, and real numbers are denoted, respectively, as $\mathbb{Z}, \mathbb{Q}, \mathbb{R}$. The set $\mathbb{N} \cup \{0\}$ is sometimes denoted as $\mathbb{N}_0$. These as well as all their subsets are *numerical sets*. Obviously,

$$\mathbb{N} \subseteq \mathbb{N}_0 \subset \mathbb{Z} \subseteq \mathbb{Q} \subseteq \mathbb{R}.$$

Let A be a numerical set. An element of A larger than any other element of A is the *maximum* of A (formally expressed: max A). Similarly, an element of A smaller than any other element of A is the *minimum* of A (formally expressed: min A). The set

$$\{x \in \mathbb{R} \mid 1 < x < 5\}$$

has no minimum and no maximum. It is then convenient to define[3]

$$\inf A = \begin{cases} \max\{x \in \mathbb{R} \mid x \leqslant y, \forall y \in A\} & \text{if } \{x \in \mathbb{R} \mid x \leqslant y, \forall y \in A\} \neq \varnothing, \\ -\infty & \text{if } \{x \in \mathbb{R} \mid x \leqslant y, \forall y \in A\} = \varnothing. \end{cases}$$

---

[2] In formal language the sign $\Rightarrow$ is used between two statements as an abbreviation for "implies." Analogously, if two statements are equivalent, we put the sign $\Leftrightarrow$ between them.

[3] In formal language the sign $\forall$ is used as an abbreviation for "each." Analogously, the sign $\exists$ is used as an abbreviation for "some," which is supposed to exist. Sentences of the type "$\exists \ldots : \ldots$" are to be read as: "There is (are) ... such that ...."

$$\sup A = \begin{cases} \min\{x\in\mathbb{R}\,|\,x \geqslant y, \forall y \in A\} & \text{if} \quad \{x\in\mathbb{R}\,|\,x \geqslant y, \forall y \in A\} \neq \varnothing, \\ +\infty & \text{if} \quad \{x\in\mathbb{R}\,|\,x \geqslant y, \forall y \in A\} = \varnothing, \end{cases}$$

Obviously, each numerical set A has both $\inf A$ and $\sup A$. Moreover,

$$(\inf A = \min A) \Leftrightarrow (\inf A \in A),$$

$$(\sup A = \max A) \Leftrightarrow (\sup A \in A).$$

The set of all numbers falling between two numbers is the *interval*, or the *range*, between those two numbers. If A is an interval and $\inf A \in A$, then A is *closed on the left*, otherwise it is *open on the left*. Similarly, if $\sup A \in A$ ($\sup A \notin A$), then A is *closed* (*open*) *on the right*. An interval which is closed (open) on both sides is called simply *closed* (*open*). In order to simplify notation, a closed interval between a and b is denoted by brackets

$$[a, b] := \{x \in \mathbb{R}\,|\,a \leqslant x \leqslant b\}$$

and the corresponding open interval is denoted by parentheses:

$$(a, b) := \{x \in \mathbb{R}\,|\,a < x < b\}.$$

Similarly for intervals closed on one side and open on the other:

$$[a, b) := \{x \in \mathbb{R}\,|\,a \leqslant x < b\}, (a, b] := \{x \in \mathbb{R}\,|\,a < x \leqslant b\}.$$

A.1.3. Vector spaces

An *n-vector* (or simply *vector* if no doubt can arise) $\mathbf{x}$ is an ordered set of n real numbers $x_1, x_2, \ldots, x_n$. The number x_i is called the *ith coordinate*, the *ith component*, or the *ith element* of $\mathbf{x}$. The following notation will be used in this and in the following two subsections:

$$\mathbf{x} = (x_1, x_2, \ldots, x_n).$$

The *zero vector*, $\mathbf{0}$, is a vector whose components are all 0. The *ith unit vector*, $\mathbf{e}_i$, is a vector whose ith component is 1, all other components being 0. The vector whose components are all 1 is called the *sum vector*, and is denoted by $\mathbf{e}$. In this context real numbers are called *scalars* to emphasize that they are defined by *one* magnitude.

If $\mathbf{x} = (x_1, x_2, \ldots, x_n)$ and $\mathbf{y} = (y_1, y_2, \ldots, y_n)$ are vectors, then their *sum*, $\mathbf{x} + \mathbf{y}$, is

$$\mathbf{x} + \mathbf{y} = (x_1 + y_1, x_2 + y_2, \ldots, x_n + y_n).$$

If $\mathbf{x} = (x_1, x_2, \ldots, x_n)$ is a vector and λ is a real number, then the *product of vector $\mathbf{x}$ by scalar λ*, $\lambda\mathbf{x}$, is

$$\lambda\mathbf{x} = (\lambda x_1, \lambda x_2, \ldots, \lambda x_n).$$

If $x = (x_1, x_2, \ldots, x_n)$, $y = (y_1, y_2, \ldots, y_n)$, and $z = (z_1, z_2, \ldots, z_n)$ are vectors, and λ and μ are scalars, the following properties hold:

(i) $(x + y) + z = x + (y + z)$ (the sum is associative);
(ii) $x + y = y + x$ (the sum is commutative);
(iii) $x + 0 = x$ (the zero vector is neutral with respect to the sum);
(iv) for any x there is a z such that $x + z = 0$ (existence of the negative);
(v) $\lambda(x + y) = \lambda x + \lambda y$ (the product is distributive with respect to the sum of vectors);
(vi) $(\lambda + \mu)x = \lambda x + \mu x$ (the product is distributive with respect to the sum of scalars);
(vii) $\lambda(\mu x) = (\lambda \mu)x$ (the product by a scalar is associative);
(viii) $1x = x$.

The set of all n-vectors, with the operations "sum" and "product by a scalar" as defined above, is called the *real vector space of dimension n* and is denoted $\mathbb{R}^n$. Indeed, the above properties (i)–(viii) can be taken as axioms for a definition of an abstract vector space.

A.1.4. Linear combinations and related issues

Let $x_1, x_2, \ldots, x_t$ be t vectors in $\mathbb{R}^n$. Vector $x \in \mathbb{R}^n$ is a *linear combination of vectors* $x_1, x_2, \ldots, x_t$ if and only if there are t scalars $\alpha_1, \alpha_2, \ldots, \alpha_t$ such that

$$x = \alpha_1 x_1 + \alpha_2 x_2 + \cdots + \alpha_t x_t.$$

The set of all linear combinations of vectors $x_1, x_2, \ldots, x_t$ is a *subspace* of $\mathbb{R}^n$. This subspace is said to be *spanned by vectors* $x_1, x_2, \ldots, x_t$. The sum of two elements of a subspace is an element of the same subspace and the product of an element of a subspace by a scalar is an element of the same subspace. Properties (i)–(viii) of the previous subsection also hold.

Vectors $x_1, x_2, \ldots, x_t$ in $\mathbb{R}^n$ are *linearly dependent* if and only if there are t scalars $\alpha_1, \alpha_2, \ldots, \alpha_t$, not all zero, such that

$$\alpha_1 x_1 + \alpha_2 x_2 + \cdots + \alpha_t x_t = 0.$$

If vectors $x_1, x_2, \ldots, x_t$ in $\mathbb{R}^n$ are not linearly dependent, that is, if

$$\alpha_1 x_1 + \alpha_2 x_2 + \cdots + \alpha_t x_t = 0 \Rightarrow \alpha_1 = \alpha_2 = \cdots = \alpha_t = 0,$$

then they are *linearly independent*. Vectors $x_1, x_2, \ldots, x_t$ in $\mathbb{R}^n$ are linearly dependent if and only if one of them is a linear combination of the others. Two linearly dependent vectors are also said to be *proportional*.

Vectors $x_1, x_2, \ldots, x_t$ in subspace V constitute a *basis* for subspace V if they are linearly independent and span the whole subspace V. All bases for subspace V consist of the same number of vectors. Such a number is called the *dimension of subspace* V: in symbols, $\dim(V)$. If $\dim(V) = s$, each s linearly independent vectors in V constitute a basis for V. Analogously, vectors $x_1, x_2, \ldots, x_t$ in $\mathbb{R}^n$ constitute a *basis* for $\mathbb{R}^n$ if and only if they are linearly independent, and span the whole space $\mathbb{R}^n$. A basis for $\mathbb{R}^n$ consists of exactly n vectors $(t = n)$. If n vectors in $\mathbb{R}^n$ are linearly independent, they constitute a basis for $\mathbb{R}^n$.

A.1.5. Linear transformations

Let V and W be two vector spaces (which may be equal). Then a *transformation* f *of* V *into* W is determined when there is a rule or formula which assigns an element of W to each element of V. The element of W assigned to the element x of V is called the *image* of x under f and is denoted as $f(x)$. A *linear transformation* T *of* V *into* W is a transformation of V into W such that

(i) $T(x + y) = T(x) + T(y), \forall x, y \in V$,
(ii) $T(\lambda x) = \lambda T(x), \forall x \in V$ and $\forall \lambda \in \mathbb{R}$.

A transformation T of $\mathbb{R}^n$ into $\mathbb{R}^m$ is linear if and only if there is an array of $n \cdot m$ numbers organized in m rows and n columns

$$\begin{bmatrix} a_{11} & a_{12} & \cdots & a_{1n} \\ a_{21} & a_{22} & \cdots & a_{2n} \\ \cdot & \cdot & \cdots & \cdot \\ \cdot & \cdot & \cdots & \cdot \\ \cdot & \cdot & \cdots & \cdot \\ a_{m1} & a_{m2} & \cdots & a_{mn} \end{bmatrix} \tag{A.1}$$

such that

$$T(x) = \left(\sum_{i=1}^{n} a_{1i}x_i, \sum_{i=1}^{n} a_{2i}x_i, \ldots, \sum_{i=1}^{n} a_{mi}x_i \right).$$

An array (A.1) is an $m \times n$ *matrix*, or simply a *matrix* if no doubt can arise; it is regarded as a single object and is denoted by a bold capital letter, for example, A, B, etc. Sometimes we will denote matrix A as $[a_{ij}]$, where a_{ij} is a typical element of A, specifically that on the ith row and the jth column. A matrix whose number of columns is equal to the number of rows is called *square*, otherwise it is *rectangular*. An $n \times n$ matrix is also called a square matrix of *order* n. If $A = [a_{ij}]$ is an $n \times n$ square matrix the elements a_{ii} $(i = 1, 2, \ldots, n)$ constitute the *main diagonal* (or simply the *diagonal*) of matrix A. A matrix all of whose off-diagonal elements are zero $(a_{ij} = 0$ for $i \neq j)$ is a *diagonal matrix*. A matrix all of whose elements above (below) the main diagonal are zero ($a_{ij} = 0$ for $i > j$ ($a_{ij} = 0$ for $i < j$)) is said to be *lower* (*upper*) *triangular*.

In the following, vectors will be denoted as matrices consisting of one column:

$$\mathbf{x} = \begin{bmatrix} x_1 \\ x_2 \\ \vdots \\ x_n \end{bmatrix},$$

and a linear transformation T will be represented either by $T(\mathbf{x})$ or by $\mathbf{Ax}$.

The *identity transformation* of $\mathbb{R}^n$ is the linear transformation of $\mathbb{R}^n$ into itself such that the image of $\mathbf{x}$ is $\mathbf{x}$ itself. It is represented as $\mathbf{Ix}$, where $\mathbf{I}$ is a diagonal matrix whose elements on the main diagonal are all 1. Matrix $\mathbf{I}$ is called *identity matrix*.

If $\mathbf{Ax}$ and $\mathbf{Bx}$ are linear transformations of $\mathbb{R}^n$ into $\mathbb{R}^m$, the transformation $T(\mathbf{x}) = \mathbf{Ax} + \mathbf{Bx}$ is linear and can be represented as $\mathbf{Cx}$, where $[c_{ij}] = [a_{ij} + b_{ij}]$. Matrix $\mathbf{C} = (\mathbf{A} + \mathbf{B})$ is called the *sum* of matrices $\mathbf{A}$ and $\mathbf{B}$. The sum of matrices is commutative and associative:

$$\mathbf{A} + \mathbf{B} = \mathbf{B} + \mathbf{A},$$
$$\mathbf{A} + (\mathbf{B} + \mathbf{C}) = (\mathbf{A} + \mathbf{B}) + \mathbf{C} = \mathbf{A} + \mathbf{B} + \mathbf{C}.$$

If $\mathbf{Ax}$ is a linear transformation of $\mathbb{R}^n$ into $\mathbb{R}^m$ and $\mathbf{Bx}$ is a linear transformation of $\mathbb{R}^m$ into $\mathbb{R}^r$, then the transformation of $\mathbb{R}^n$ into $\mathbb{R}^r$ $T(\mathbf{x}) = \mathbf{B}(\mathbf{Ax})$ is linear and can be represented as $\mathbf{Cx}$, where

$$[c_{ij}] = \left[\sum_{k=1}^{m} b_{ik} a_{kj} \right].$$

Matrix $\mathbf{C} = \mathbf{BA}$ is called the *product* of matrices $\mathbf{B}$ and $\mathbf{A}$. The product of matrices is *not* commutative even when $n = r$, whereas it is associative and distributive with respect to the sum:

$$(\mathbf{AB})\mathbf{C} = \mathbf{A}(\mathbf{BC}) = \mathbf{ABC},$$
$$\mathbf{A}(\mathbf{B} + \mathbf{C}) = \mathbf{AB} + \mathbf{AC},$$
$$(\mathbf{A} + \mathbf{B})\mathbf{C} = \mathbf{AC} + \mathbf{BC}.$$

The identity matrix is sometimes called the *unit matrix* since

$$\mathbf{IA} = \mathbf{AI} = \mathbf{A}.$$

Note that if $\mathbf{A}$ is of dimension $m \times n$, then the first $\mathbf{I}$ is of dimension $m \times m$ and the second $\mathbf{I}$ of dimension $n \times n$.

Let $\mathbf{A}$ be a square $n \times n$ matrix. Define the *powers* of $\mathbf{A}$

$$\mathbf{A}^0 = \mathbf{I}, \quad \mathbf{A}^1 = \mathbf{A}, \quad \mathbf{A}^2 = \mathbf{AA}, \quad \mathbf{A}^k = \mathbf{AA}^{k-1}, \quad k = 3, 4, 5, \ldots .$$

If $\mathbf{Ax}$ is a linear transformation of $\mathbb{R}^n$ into itself and if there is a transformation $T(\mathbf{x})$ such that

$$T(\mathbf{Ax}) = \mathbf{x}, \quad \forall \mathbf{x} \in \mathbb{R}^n,$$

then $T(\mathbf{x})$ is linear and is represented as $\mathbf{A}^{-1}\mathbf{x}$. If $T(\mathbf{x})$ exists, it is unique and matrix $\mathbf{A}^{-1}$ is called the *inverse* of $\mathbf{A}$. If the inverse of $\mathbf{A}$ exists, $\mathbf{A}$ is *invertible* or *nonsingular*, otherwise it is *noninvertible* or *singular*. If $\mathbf{A}$ and $\mathbf{B}$ are both $n \times n$ and invertible, the following equalities hold:

$$\mathbf{A}^{-1}\mathbf{A} = \mathbf{AA}^{-1} = \mathbf{I},$$
$$(\mathbf{A}^{-1})^{-1} = \mathbf{A}$$
$$(\mathbf{AB})^{-1} = \mathbf{B}^{-1}\mathbf{A}^{-1}.$$

If $\mathbf{Ax}$ is a linear transformation of $\mathbb{R}^n$ into $\mathbb{R}^m$ and λ is a scalar, the transformation $T(\mathbf{x}) = \lambda(\mathbf{Ax})$ is linear and can be represented as $\mathbf{Bx}$, where $[b_{ij}] = [\lambda a_{ij}]$. Matrix $\mathbf{B} = \lambda\mathbf{A}$ is called the *product of matrix* $\mathbf{A}$ *by scalar* λ. The following properties hold:

$$\lambda(\mathbf{A} + \mathbf{B}) = \lambda\mathbf{A} + \lambda\mathbf{B},$$
$$\lambda(\mathbf{AB}) = (\lambda\mathbf{A})\mathbf{B} = \mathbf{A}(\lambda\mathbf{B}) = \lambda\mathbf{AB},$$
$$(\lambda\mathbf{A})^{-1} = \lambda^{-1}\mathbf{A}^{-1} \quad \text{if } \mathbf{A} \text{ is square and invertible.}$$

Let $T(\mathbf{x}) = \mathbf{Ax}$ be a linear transformation of $\mathbb{R}^n$ into $\mathbb{R}^m$. Then the following sets are defined:

$$\operatorname{Im} T = \{\mathbf{y} \in \mathbb{R}^m \mid \exists \mathbf{x} \in \mathbb{R}^n \colon \mathbf{y} = T(\mathbf{x})\},$$
$$\operatorname{Ker} T = \{\mathbf{x} \in \mathbb{R}^n \mid T(\mathbf{x}) = \mathbf{0}\}.$$

$\operatorname{Im} T$ is called the *image* of T and it is a subspace of $\mathbb{R}^m$. $\operatorname{Ker} T$ is called the *kernel* of T and it is a subspace of $\mathbb{R}^n$. Moreover

$$\dim(\operatorname{Im} T) + \dim(\operatorname{Ker} T) = n. \tag{A.2}$$

$\operatorname{Im} T$ is the vector space spanned by the columns of matrix $\mathbf{A}$ and $\dim(\operatorname{Im} T)$ equals the number of linearly independent columns of matrix $\mathbf{A}$. It is proved that the number of linearly independent columns of a matrix equals the number of linearly independent rows of the same matrix: this number is the *rank* of that matrix. Hence

$$\operatorname{rank}(\mathbf{A}) = \dim(\operatorname{Im} T), \tag{A.3}$$

$$\operatorname{rank}(\mathbf{A}) \leqslant \min\{m, n\}.$$

A.1.6. *Transposing and partitioning matrices*

For any $m \times n$ matrix $\mathbf{A}$ the $n \times m$ matrix $\mathbf{B}$ characterized by $b_{ij} = a_{ji}$ is called the *transpose* of $\mathbf{A}$ and is denoted as $\mathbf{A}^T$. The following properties hold:

$$(\mathbf{A}^T)^T = \mathbf{A},$$
$$(\mathbf{A} + \mathbf{B})^T = \mathbf{A}^T + \mathbf{B}^T,$$
$$(\mathbf{A}\mathbf{B})^T = \mathbf{B}^T \mathbf{A}^T,$$
$$(\mathbf{A}^T)^{-1} = (\mathbf{A}^{-1})^T \quad \text{if } \mathbf{A} \text{ is square and invertible,}$$
$$(\lambda\mathbf{A})^T = \lambda\mathbf{A}^T.$$

In the previous subsection it has been stated that vectors will always be represented as matrices with a single column, that is, as *column vectors*. The transpose of a (column) vector $\mathbf{x}, \mathbf{x}^T$, is a *row vector*. If $\mathbf{x}$ and $\mathbf{y}$ belong to $\mathbb{R}^n$, $\mathbf{x}^T\mathbf{y} = \mathbf{y}^T\mathbf{x}$ is the *inner product* of $\mathbf{x}$ and $\mathbf{y}$. If $\mathbf{x}^T\mathbf{y} = 0$, vectors $\mathbf{x}$ and $\mathbf{y}$ are called *orthogonal*.

A matrix is sometimes represented as a row vector of its column vectors or as a column vector of its row vectors, that is, for matrix (A.1) we can write

$$\mathbf{A} = (\mathbf{a}_{*1}, \mathbf{a}_{*2}, \ldots, \mathbf{a}_{*n}) = \begin{bmatrix} \mathbf{a}_{1*}^T \\ \mathbf{a}_{2*}^T \\ \vdots \\ \mathbf{a}_{m*}^T \end{bmatrix}, \tag{A.4}$$

where

$$\mathbf{a}_{*j} = \begin{bmatrix} a_{1j} \\ a_{2j} \\ \vdots \\ a_{mj} \end{bmatrix}, \quad \mathbf{a}_{i*} = \begin{bmatrix} a_{i1} \\ a_{i2} \\ \vdots \\ a_{in} \end{bmatrix}.$$

Analogously, it is sometimes convenient to represent matrix $\mathbf{A}$ as

$$\mathbf{A} = (\mathbf{B}, \mathbf{C}) \text{ or } \mathbf{A} = \begin{bmatrix} \mathbf{D} \\ \mathbf{E} \end{bmatrix}, \tag{A.5}$$

where $\mathbf{B}$ ($\mathbf{C}$) is the $m \times s$ ($m \times (n-s)$) matrix made up by the first s (last $n-s$) columns of $\mathbf{A}$, where $s < n$, and $\mathbf{D}$ ($\mathbf{E}$) is the $t \times n$ (($m-t) \times n$) matrix made up by the first t (last $m-t$) rows of $\mathbf{A}$, where $t < m$. Matrices $\mathbf{B}, \mathbf{C}, \mathbf{D}$, and $\mathbf{E}$ are also called *submatrices*. More generally, it is sometimes convenient to represent the $m \times n$ matrix $\mathbf{A}$ as an $s \times t$ matrix of submatrices:

$$
\begin{bmatrix}
\mathbf{A}_{11} & \mathbf{A}_{12} & \cdots & \mathbf{A}_{1t} \\
\mathbf{A}_{21} & \mathbf{A}_{22} & \cdots & \mathbf{A}_{2t} \\
\cdot & \cdot & \cdots & \\
\cdot & \cdot & \cdots & \cdot \\
\cdot & \cdot & \cdots & \\
\mathbf{A}_{s1} & \mathbf{A}_{s2} & \cdots & \mathbf{A}_{st}
\end{bmatrix}. \tag{A.6}
$$

Representations of matrix $\mathbf{A}$ of the types (A.4)–(A.6) are called *partitions* of matrix $\mathbf{A}$. Submatrices on the same row of a partition have the same number of rows and submatrices in the same column of a partition have the same number of columns. The sum of the numbers of the rows of the submatrices in the same column of a partition of $m \times n$ matrix $\mathbf{A}$ equals m and the sum of the numbers of the columns of the submatrices on the same row of a partition of $m \times n$ matrix $\mathbf{A}$ equals n. Sometimes we will denote matrix $\mathbf{A}$ as $[\mathbf{A}_{ij}]$ where $\mathbf{A}_{ij}$ is a typical submatrix of $\mathbf{A}$.

It is possible to sum two partitioned $m \times n$ matrices by adding the corresponding submatrices provided that they are partitioned in the same way. It is also possible to multiply the $m \times n$ partitioned matrix $\mathbf{A} = [\mathbf{A}_{ik}]$ and the $n \times s$ partitioned matrix $\mathbf{B} = [\mathbf{B}_{kj}]$ by the rule

$$
\mathbf{C}_{ij} = \sum_k \mathbf{A}_{ik}\mathbf{B}_{kj},
$$

where $[\mathbf{C}_{ij}] = \mathbf{C} = \mathbf{AB}$ provided that the columns of $\mathbf{A}$ are partitioned in the same way as the rows of $\mathbf{B}$.

Let the square $n \times n$ matrix $\mathbf{A} = [\mathbf{A}_{ik}]$ be partitioned in such a way that submatrices $\mathbf{A}_{ii}$ are square; then matrix $\mathbf{A}$ is called *upper block triangular* if

$$
i < k \Rightarrow \mathbf{A}_{ik} = \mathbf{0}
$$

and *lower block triangular* if

$$
i > k \Rightarrow \mathbf{A}_{ik} = \mathbf{0}.
$$

An upper-block-triangular matrix which is also lower block triangular is called *block diagonal*. A block-triangular matrix $\mathbf{A}$ is invertible if submatrices $\mathbf{A}_{ii}$ are invertible.

A.1.7. Determinants, minors, and the inverse of a (square) matrix

Let $\det(\mathbf{A})$ denote a real number associated with the $n \times n$ matrix $\mathbf{A}$ such that

(i) for each row i of matrix $\mathbf{A}$

$$
\det\left(\begin{bmatrix} \mathbf{a}_{1*}^T \\ \vdots \\ \mathbf{a}_{i-1*}^T \\ \mathbf{x}^T + \lambda \mathbf{y}^T \\ \mathbf{a}_{i+1*}^T \\ \vdots \\ \mathbf{a}_{n*}^T \end{bmatrix}\right) = \det\left(\begin{bmatrix} \mathbf{a}_{1*}^T \\ \vdots \\ \mathbf{a}_{i-1*}^T \\ \mathbf{x}^T \\ \mathbf{a}_{i+1*}^T \\ \vdots \\ \mathbf{a}_{n*}^T \end{bmatrix}\right) + \lambda \det\left(\begin{bmatrix} \mathbf{a}_{1*}^T \\ \vdots \\ \mathbf{a}_{i-1*}^T \\ \mathbf{y}^T \\ \mathbf{a}_{i+1*}^T \\ \vdots \\ \mathbf{a}_{n*}^T \end{bmatrix}\right),
$$

(ii) $\det(\mathbf{A}) = 0$ if two rows of matrix $\mathbf{A}$ are identical,

(iii) $\det(\mathbf{I}) = 1$.

It is proved that for each matrix $\mathbf{A}$ there is one and only one real number satisfying properties (i)–(iii). The real number $\det(\mathbf{A})$ is the *determinant* of matrix $\mathbf{A}$. Many other equivalent definitions of the determinant can be found in the literature. The following further properties hold:

(iv) $\det(\mathbf{A}^T) = \det(\mathbf{A})$,

(v) property (i) with respect to each row of matrix $\mathbf{A}$ holds also with respect to each column of matrix $\mathbf{A}$,

(vi) $\det(\mathbf{A}) = 0$ if two columns of matrix $\mathbf{A}$ are identical,

(vii) if $\mathbf{A}$ and $\mathbf{B}$ are both $n \times n$, $\det(\mathbf{AB}) = \det(\mathbf{A})\det(\mathbf{B})$,

(viii) $\det(\mathbf{A}) \neq 0$ if and only if $\mathbf{A}$ is invertible,

(ix) $\det(\mathbf{A}) = -\det(\mathbf{B})$ if $\mathbf{B}$ is obtained from $\mathbf{A}$ by interchanging two rows (columns),

(x) $\det(\mathbf{A}) = \det(\mathbf{B})$ if $\mathbf{B}$ is obtained from $\mathbf{A}$ by adding column (row) j multiplied by a scalar to column (row) i ($j \neq i$),

(xi) $\det(\mathbf{A}) = 0$ if and only if the columns (rows) of $\mathbf{A}$ are linearly dependent.

Let $\mathbf{B}$ be an $m \times n$ matrix. Let $\mathbf{C}$ be a matrix obtained from $\mathbf{B}$ by eliminating $(m - r)$ rows and $(n - r)$ columns. The determinant of $\mathbf{C}$ is a *minor of $\mathbf{B}$ of order r*. If $\mathbf{A}$ is a square $n \times n$ matrix the *complementary minor of its element a_{ij}* is the minor of order $n - 1$ obtained by eliminating the ith row and the jth column from $\mathbf{A}$ and is denoted as M_{ij}. The scalar

$$A_{ij} = (-1)^{i+j} M_{ij}$$

is the *cofactor of a_{ij}*. The following properties hold:

(xii) $\displaystyle\sum_{i=1}^{n} a_{ij} A_{ij} = \sum_{j=1}^{n} a_{ij} A_{ij} = \det(\mathbf{A})$,

(xiii) $\displaystyle\sum_{i=1}^{n} a_{ih} A_{ij} = \sum_{j=1}^{n} a_{kj} A_{ij} = 0 \quad h \neq j, \quad k \neq i.$

The *adjoint* of $\mathbf{A}$, in symbols $\mathrm{adj}(\mathbf{A})$, is the $n \times n$ matrix $\mathbf{C}$, where $c_{ij} = A_{ji}$, the cofactor of a_{ji} in matrix $\mathbf{A}$. An immediate consequence of properties (xii) and (xiii) is that if $\mathbf{A}$ is invertible, then

$$\mathbf{A}^{-1} = \frac{1}{\det(\mathbf{A})} \mathrm{adj}(\mathbf{A}).$$

Let $\mathbf{B}$ be an $m \times n$ matrix and let s be the greatest of the orders of the nonzero minors of $\mathbf{B}$. (If $\mathbf{B} = \mathbf{0}$, we take $s = 0$.) It is proved that $s = \mathrm{rank}(\mathbf{B})$. As a consequence if $\mathbf{A}$ is a square $n \times n$ matrix, $\mathbf{A}$ is invertible if and only if $\mathrm{rank}(\mathbf{A}) = n$. Finally, if $\mathbf{A}$ is a triangular matrix, $\det(\mathbf{A})$ equals the product of the elements on the main diagonal. Similarly, if $\mathbf{A}$ is a block-triangular matrix, $\det(\mathbf{A})$ equals the product of the determinants of submatrices on the main diagonal.

Let $\mathbf{A}$ be a square $n \times n$ matrix and $\mathbf{B}$ be a square submatrix of it; then the minor of matrix $\mathbf{A}$ $\det(\mathbf{B})$ is a *principal minor* if the elements on the diagonal of matrix $\mathbf{B}$ are also elements on the diagonal of matrix $\mathbf{A}$. Obviously, $\det(\mathbf{A})$ is a principal minor of $\mathbf{A}$. The *decreasing principal minors* of $\mathbf{A}$ are the determinants of the matrices obtained from $\mathbf{A}$ by deleting the last s rows and the last s columns ($s = 0, 1, \ldots, n-1$). All the decreasing principal minors of $\mathbf{A}$ except $\det(\mathbf{A})$ are also called the *decreasing proper principal minors* of $\mathbf{A}$.

A.1.8. Systems of linear equations

Let $\mathbf{A}$ and $\mathbf{b}$ be an $m \times n$ matrix and an m-vector, respectively. Then

$$\mathbf{Ax} = \mathbf{b} \tag{A.7}$$

is a *system of m linear equations in n unknowns*. System (A.7) is also called a *vector linear equation* or simply a *linear equation* (when no confusion is possible). Any vector $\mathbf{y}$ such that $\mathbf{Ay} = \mathbf{b}$ is a *solution* of equation (A.7). Matrix $\mathbf{A}$ is sometimes referred to as the *coefficient matrix*, vector $\mathbf{x}$ as the *unknown vector*, and vector $\mathbf{b}$ as the *given vector*. Equation (A.7) is sometimes referred to as

$$\mathbf{x}^T \mathbf{B} = \mathbf{b}^T,$$

where, obviously, $\mathbf{B} = \mathbf{A}^T$. If $\mathbf{b} = \mathbf{0}$, equation (A.7) is a *system of m homogeneous linear equations in n unknowns*, or a *homogeneous vector linear equation*, or a *homogeneous linear equation*.

If equation (A.7) has a solution, it is called *consistent*. Equation (A.7) is consistent if and only if $\mathbf{b}$ is a linear combination of the columns of matrix $\mathbf{A}$, that is, if and only if

$$\mathrm{rank}([\mathbf{A}, \mathbf{b}]) = \mathrm{rank}(\mathbf{A}).$$

Further results on the existence of a solution to a linear vector equation are presented in Section A.2 of this appendix.

Let $T(\mathbf{x}) = \mathbf{Ax}$ be a linear transformation and $\mathbf{z} \in \mathrm{Ker}\, T$. If $\mathbf{y}$ is a solution to equation (A.7), then also

$$\mathbf{y} + \lambda \mathbf{z} \quad \lambda \in \mathbb{R}$$

is a solution to equation (A.7). In general, if $\mathbf{z}_1, \mathbf{z}_2, \ldots, \mathbf{z}_t$ constitute a basis for Ker T, then $\mathbf{w}$ is a solution to equation (A.7) if and only if there exist t scalars $\lambda_1, \lambda_2, \ldots, \lambda_t$ such that

$$\mathbf{w} = \mathbf{y} + \lambda_1 \mathbf{z}_1 + \lambda_2 \mathbf{z}_2 + \cdots + \lambda_t \mathbf{z}_t.$$

Vector $\mathbf{z}$ belongs to Ker T if and only if $\mathbf{z}$ is a solution to the equation

$$\mathbf{Ax} = \mathbf{0}, \tag{A.8}$$

which is called the homogeneous linear equation associated with linear equation (A.7). The zero vector is trivially a solution to equation (A.8). Any other solution is called a *nontrivial solution*. The number of linearly independent nontrivial solutions of equation (A.8) equals $\dim(\mathrm{Ker}\, T)$ and is equal to $n - \mathrm{rank}(\mathbf{A})$ because of (A.2) and (A.3). Obviously, if $\mathrm{rank}(\mathbf{A}) = n$, then equation (A.8) has no nontrivial solution and equation (A.7) has at most one solution.

Let $\mathbf{y}$ be a nontrivial solution to the homogeneous linear equation (A.8). Then $\lambda \mathbf{y}$ is also a solution to equation (A.8). Sometimes a further condition is added in order to determine λ. When this is done we say that this further condition *normalizes* vectors which are solutions to equation (A.8).[4]

A.1.9. Eigenvalues and eigenvectors
Let $\mathbf{A}$ be a square $n \times n$ matrix. Let $\lambda \in \mathbb{R}$ and $\mathbf{p} \in \mathbb{R}^n$ be such that

$$\lambda \mathbf{p} = \mathbf{Ap}, \quad \mathbf{p} \neq \mathbf{0}, \tag{A.10}$$

then λ is a *real eigenvalue* of matrix $\mathbf{A}$ and $\mathbf{p}$ is a *right eigenvector associated with eigenvalue* λ. If λ is an eigenvalue of $\mathbf{A}$, then the set of all vectors $\mathbf{v} \in \mathbb{R}^n$ such that

$$\lambda \mathbf{v} = \mathbf{Av},$$

that is, the kernel of the linear transformation $(\lambda \mathbf{I} - \mathbf{A})$, is a nonzero subspace of $\mathbb{R}^n$, called the *right eigenspace of* λ. It consists of the zero vector and all right eigenvectors associated with λ. Condition (A.10) is

---

[4] The name refers to the concept of *norma*, which has not been mentioned in the book in spite of its importance when topological aspects of linear algebra are considered.

satisfied if and only if $\det(\lambda I - A) = 0$ (cf. Subsection A.1.8). That is, λ is a real eigenvalue of A if and only if λ is a real root of the algebraic equation of degree n

$$\det(\rho I - A) = 0,$$

called the *characteristic equation* for matrix A. Because of the so-called Fundamental Theorem of Algebra, there exist complex numbers $\lambda_1, \lambda_2, \ldots, \lambda_n$ (which need not all be distinct) such that

$$\det(\rho I - A) = (\rho - \lambda_1)(\rho - \lambda_2) \cdots (\rho - \lambda_n).$$

This polynomial in ρ is also called the *characteristic polynomial* for the matrix A, and its roots are called *characteristic roots* or *eigenvalues* of matrix A.[5]

In a similar way *left eigenvectors* associated with real eigenvalue λ are defined by the conditions

$$\lambda x^T = x^T A, \quad x \neq 0,$$

where $x \in \mathbb{R}^n$. This means that x is a right eigenvector of A^T associated with real eigenvalue λ (A and A^T have the same characteristic equation because of property (iv) of Subsection A.1.7 and therefore the same eigenvalues). Analogously, the *left eigenspace of λ* is also defined. Finally, it is easy to check that any right eigenvector of A associated with eigenvalue λ_i is orthogonal to any left eigenvector of A associated with any eigenvalue $\lambda_j \neq \lambda_i$.

If there is an invertible matrix P such that

$$B = P^{-1}AP,$$

the square matrices A and B are *similar*. Similar matrices have the same eigenvalues. Moreover, if x and p are a left eigenvector and a right eigenvector of matrix A, respectively, associated with eigenvalue λ, then $P^T x$ and $P^{-1}p$ are a left eigenvector and a right eigenvector of matrix B, respectively, associated with the same eigenvalue λ.

In Section A.3 of this appendix a number of further properties which hold for one kind of square matrix will be explored in detail. The square matrix under consideration is of particular interest in view of the material presented in this book.

---

[5] The reader familiar with complex numbers will recognize that eigenvalues can be real or complex. For the comprehension of this book the knowledge of complex eigenvalues is not required.

A.2. **Theorems of the Alternative**

A Theorem of the Alternative is a theorem proving the occurrence of one of two mutually exclusive events. The following Theorems A.2.1 and A.2.2 are sometimes referred to in the literature as the *Fredholm Alternative* of Linear Algebra and the *Farkas Alternative*, respectively. The interested reader can find some other Theorems of the Alternative in Gale (1960, pp. 42–9) and in Mangasarian (1969, pp. 27–34).

Theorem A.2.1 (solutions to linear equations). Either the equation

$$\mathbf{x}^T \mathbf{A} = \mathbf{b}^T \tag{A.11}$$

has a solution or the equations

$$\mathbf{A}\mathbf{y} = \mathbf{0}, \quad \mathbf{b}^T \mathbf{y} = 1 \tag{A.12}$$

have a solution; but never both.

Proof. If all the equations (A.11) and (A.12) are consistent, then we obtain from equation (A.11) that

$$\mathbf{x}^T \mathbf{A}\mathbf{y} = \mathbf{b}^T \mathbf{y},$$

which contradicts equations (A.12). Assume now that equations (A.12) have no solution; then[6]

$$\mathbf{A}\mathbf{y} = \mathbf{0} \Rightarrow \mathbf{b}^T \mathbf{y} = 0.$$

Hence matrices $\mathbf{A}$ and $[\mathbf{A}^T, \mathbf{b}]$ have the same kernel. Therefore, because of equations (A.2) and (A.3), they have the same rank. Thus equation (A.11) has a solution (cf. Subsection A.1.8).   Q.E.D.

If $\mathbf{A}$ and $\mathbf{B}$ are two $m \times n$ matrices, the following conventions for inequalities between them are used: $\mathbf{A} \geqq \mathbf{B}$ means $a_{ij} \geqq b_{ij}$, $\forall i, \forall j$; $\mathbf{A} \geq \mathbf{B}$ means $\mathbf{A} \geqq \mathbf{B}$ and $\mathbf{A} \neq \mathbf{B}$; $\mathbf{A} > \mathbf{B}$ means $a_{ij} > b_{ij}$, $\forall i, \forall j$. A $m \times n$ matrix $\mathbf{A}$ will be said to be *nonnegative* (*semipositive*, *positive*) if

$$\mathbf{A} \geqq \mathbf{0} \quad (\mathbf{A} \geq \mathbf{0}, \mathbf{A} > \mathbf{0}),$$

where $\mathbf{0}$ is the $m \times n$ *zero matrix*, that is, a matrix whose elements are all zero.

In Subsection A.1.8 the theory of linear vector equations has been presented (without proofs); in the remainder of this section we will deal with linear inequalities. Let $\mathbf{A}, \mathbf{B}, \mathbf{C}, \mathbf{D}$ be $m \times n, r \times n, s \times n, t \times n$ matrices, respectively, and let $\mathbf{a} \in \mathbb{R}^m, \mathbf{b} \in \mathbb{R}^r, \mathbf{c} \in \mathbb{R}^s, \mathbf{d} \in \mathbb{R}^t$ ($n \in \mathbb{N}; m, r, s, t \in \mathbb{N}_0; m + r +$

---

[6] $\mathbf{A}\mathbf{y} = \mathbf{0}$ and $\mathbf{b}^T \mathbf{y} = \alpha \neq 0$ imply that $\mathbf{A}\mathbf{z} = \mathbf{0}$ and $\mathbf{b}^T \mathbf{z} = 1$ with $\mathbf{z} = \alpha^{-1} \mathbf{y}$.

$s > 0$). If $\mathbf{x} \in \mathbb{R}^n$ satisfies the conditions

$$\mathbf{Ax} > \mathbf{a}, \quad \mathbf{Bx} \geqslant \mathbf{b}, \quad \mathbf{Cx} \geqslant \mathbf{c}, \quad \mathbf{Dx} = \mathbf{d}, \tag{A.13}$$

then $\mathbf{x}$ is a *solution* to the *system of linear inequalities* (A.13). If $t = 0$, then both matrix $\mathbf{D}$ and vector $\mathbf{d}$ disappear. In this case we say that the equation in (A.13) is *void* (as a matter of fact, it does not bind the vector $\mathbf{x}$). Note that the equation in (A.13) may be void as well as one or two of the other three relations. All the following theorems of the alternative involve solutions of linear inequalities.

Theorem A.2.2 (nonnegative solutions of linear equations). Either the equation

$$\mathbf{x}^T \mathbf{A} = \mathbf{b}^T \tag{A.14}$$

has a nonnegative solution or the inequalities

$$\mathbf{Ay} \geqslant \mathbf{0}, \quad \mathbf{b}^T \mathbf{y} < 0 \tag{A.15}$$

have a solution; but never both.

Theorem A.2.2 can easily be proved by using theorems on separating planes, (cf. Franklin, 1980, pp. 56–7). The following proof, taken from Gale (1960, pp. 44–6), uses linear algebraic methods only.

Proof. In order to prove that the two possibilities are incompatible multiply equation (A.14) on the right by $\mathbf{y}$ and the first inequality (A.15) on the left by $\mathbf{x}^T$; a contradiction arises. If equation (A.14) has no solution, then by Theorem A.2.1 there is an $\mathbf{y}$ such that $\mathbf{Ay} = \mathbf{0}$ and $\mathbf{b}^T \mathbf{y} = -1$; hence $\mathbf{y}$ satisfies inequalities (A.15). Suppose then that equation (A.14) has a solution but no nonnegative solution (hence $\mathbf{b} \neq \mathbf{0}$), and proceed by induction on the number of rows of $\mathbf{A}$. If $\mathbf{A}$ consists of one row, let $\alpha < 0$ be a solution of equation (A.14); as a consequence, $\mathbf{A} = \alpha^{-1}\mathbf{b}^T$. Let $\mathbf{y}^* = -\mathbf{b}$; hence

$$\mathbf{b}^T \mathbf{y}^* = -\mathbf{b}^T \mathbf{b} < 0 \quad \text{and} \quad \mathbf{Ay}^* = \alpha^{-1}\mathbf{b}^T \mathbf{y}^* = -\alpha^{-1}\mathbf{b}^T \mathbf{b} > 0.$$

Thus, $\mathbf{y}^*$ is a solution to inequalities (A.15). Now assume that the theorem is true when the number of rows is less than m. Let us partition $\mathbf{A}$ into

$$\mathbf{A} = \begin{bmatrix} \mathbf{B} \\ \mathbf{a}_m^T \end{bmatrix},$$

where $\mathbf{a}_m$ is the last row of $\mathbf{A}$. If equation (A.14) has no nonnegative solution, then neither does the equation

$$\mathbf{u}^T \mathbf{B} = \mathbf{b}^T.$$

Then, by applying the theorem, there is a vector $\mathbf{w}$ such that $\mathbf{Bw} \geqslant \mathbf{0}$ and

$\mathbf{b}^T\mathbf{w} < 0$. If also $\mathbf{a}_m^T\mathbf{w} \geq 0$, then $\mathbf{w}$ satisfies inequalities (A.15) and the theorem is proved. If $\mathbf{a}_m^T\mathbf{w} < 0$, let

$$\mathbf{C} = \mathbf{Bwa}_m^T - (\mathbf{a}_m^T\mathbf{w})\mathbf{B} \quad \text{and} \quad \mathbf{c}^T = (\mathbf{b}^T\mathbf{w})\mathbf{a}_m^T - (\mathbf{a}_m^T\mathbf{w})\mathbf{b}^T.$$

If the equation $\mathbf{z}^T\mathbf{C} = \mathbf{c}^T$ has a nonnegative solution $\mathbf{v}$, then

$$\mathbf{v}^T\mathbf{Bwa}_m^T - \mathbf{a}_m^T\mathbf{wv}^T\mathbf{B} = \mathbf{b}^T\mathbf{wa}_m^T - (\mathbf{a}_m^T\mathbf{w})\mathbf{b}^T,$$

that is,

$$\mathbf{v}^T\mathbf{B} + \frac{\mathbf{v}^T\mathbf{Bw} - \mathbf{b}^T\mathbf{w}}{-\mathbf{a}_m^T\mathbf{w}}\mathbf{a}_m^T = \mathbf{b}^T.$$

Thus vector $[\mathbf{v}^T, -(\mathbf{v}^T\mathbf{Bw} - \mathbf{b}^T\mathbf{w})/(\mathbf{a}_m^T\mathbf{w})]^T$ is a nonnegative solution to equation (A.14). Hence there is a contradiction and $\mathbf{z}^T\mathbf{C} = \mathbf{c}^T$ cannot have a nonnegative solution. Then, by applying the theorem once again, there is a vector $\mathbf{q}$ such that $\mathbf{Cq} \geq \mathbf{0}$ and $\mathbf{c}^T\mathbf{q} < 0$. Now let

$$\mathbf{y} = \mathbf{wa}_m^T\mathbf{q} - (\mathbf{a}_m^T\mathbf{w})\mathbf{q}.$$

Since

$$\mathbf{By} = \mathbf{Cq} \geq \mathbf{0},$$
$$\mathbf{b}^T\mathbf{y} = \mathbf{c}^T\mathbf{q} < 0,$$
$$\mathbf{a}_m^T\mathbf{y} = 0$$

the theorem is proved.   Q.E.D.

Theorem A.2.3 (semipositive solutions of homogeneous equations). Either the equation

$$\mathbf{x}^T\mathbf{A} = \mathbf{0}^T \tag{A.16}$$

has a semipositive solution or the inequality

$$\mathbf{Ay} > \mathbf{0} \tag{A.17}$$

has a solution; but never both.

Proof. In order to prove that the two possibilities are incompatible multiply equation (A.16) on the right by $\mathbf{y}$ and inequality (A.17) on the left by $\mathbf{x}^T$; a contradiction arises. If equation (A.16) has no semipositive solution, then the equation

$$\mathbf{z}^T[\mathbf{A}, \mathbf{e}] = (\mathbf{0}^T, 1)$$

has no nonnegative solution; hence by Theorem A.2.2 there is a vector $\mathbf{y}$

and a scalar α such that

$$\mathbf{Ay} + \alpha\mathbf{e} \geqq \mathbf{0}$$

and

$$\mathbf{0}^T\mathbf{y} + \alpha < 0,$$

that is,

$$\mathbf{Ay} \geqq -\alpha\mathbf{e} > \mathbf{0}. \qquad\qquad\qquad \text{Q.E.D.}$$

Theorem A.2.4 (nonnegative solutions of linear inequalities). Either the inequality

$$\mathbf{x}^T\mathbf{A} \leqq \mathbf{b}^T$$

has a nonnegative solution or the inequalities

$$\mathbf{Ay} \geqq \mathbf{0}, \quad \mathbf{b}^T\mathbf{y} < 0$$

have a nonnegative solution; but never both.

Proof. Theorem A.2.2 implies that either the equation

$$\begin{bmatrix} \mathbf{x} \\ \mathbf{z} \end{bmatrix}^T \begin{bmatrix} \mathbf{A} \\ \mathbf{I} \end{bmatrix} = \mathbf{b}^T$$

has a nonnegative solution or the inequalities

$$\begin{bmatrix} \mathbf{A} \\ \mathbf{I} \end{bmatrix}\mathbf{y} \geqq \mathbf{0} \quad \text{and} \quad \mathbf{b}^T\mathbf{y} < 0$$

have a solution; but never both. That is, either the equation

$$\mathbf{x}^T\mathbf{A} + \mathbf{z}^T = \mathbf{b}^T$$

has nonnegative solutions or the inequalities

$$\mathbf{Ay} \geqq \mathbf{0}, \quad \mathbf{y} \geqq \mathbf{0}, \quad \mathbf{b}^T\mathbf{y} < 0$$

have a solution. $\qquad\qquad\qquad\qquad\qquad\qquad$ Q.E.D.

A.3. Perron–Frobenius Theorems

Eigenvalues and eigenvectors have been introduced in Subsection A.1.9. Subsection A.3.1 is mainly devoted to prove that if $\mathbf{A} \geqq \mathbf{0}$, then at least one eigenvalue is real and nonnegative, there are right (left) eigenvectors associated with the largest real eigenvalue which are semipositive, and some other good properties also hold. If matrix $\mathbf{A}$ is also indecomposable, a concept which will be defined and explored in Subsection A.3.2, some further good properties hold. A classical reference for Perron–

Frobenius Theorems on nonnegative matrices is Gantmacher (1959, ch. XIII). But we will follow Nikaido (1968) more closely here.

A.3.1. *Perron–Frobenius Theorems for nonnegative matrices*

Let $\mathbf{A}$ be a nonnegative $n \times n$ matrix. Let us first prove the following

Theorem A.3.1. If there is a vector $\mathbf{x} \geqq \mathbf{0}$ and a scalar λ such that

$$\mathbf{x}^T[\lambda\mathbf{I} - \mathbf{A}] > \mathbf{0}^T,$$

then $\lambda > 0$, matrix $[\lambda\mathbf{I} - \mathbf{A}]$ is invertible, and

$$[\lambda\mathbf{I} - \mathbf{A}]^{-1} \geqq \mathbf{0}.$$

Lemma A.3.1. If there is a vector $\mathbf{x} \geqq \mathbf{0}$ such that $\mathbf{x}^T[\lambda\mathbf{I} - \mathbf{A}] > \mathbf{0}^T$, then

$$\mathbf{v}^T[\lambda\mathbf{I} - \mathbf{A}] \geqq \mathbf{0} \Rightarrow \mathbf{v} \geqq \mathbf{0}.$$

Proof. It is immediately recognized that

$$\{\mathbf{u}^T[\lambda\mathbf{I} - \mathbf{A}] > \mathbf{0}^T, \mathbf{u} \geqq \mathbf{0}\} \Rightarrow \mathbf{u} > \mathbf{0}, \quad \lambda > 0. \tag{A.18}$$

Then, assume that the lemma does not hold, that is, that there is a vector $\mathbf{v} \not\geqq \mathbf{0}$ such that

$$\mathbf{v}^T[\lambda\mathbf{I} - \mathbf{A}] \geqq \mathbf{0}^T.$$

Let h be such that

$$0 > \frac{\mathbf{v}^T\mathbf{e}_h}{\mathbf{x}^T\mathbf{e}_h} \leqslant \frac{\mathbf{v}^T\mathbf{e}_i}{\mathbf{x}^T\mathbf{e}_i} \quad (1 \leqslant i \leqslant n).$$

Then

$$\mathbf{w} := \left[\mathbf{v} - \frac{\mathbf{v}^T\mathbf{e}_h}{\mathbf{x}^T\mathbf{e}_h}\mathbf{x} \right] \geqq \mathbf{0}$$

and

$$\mathbf{w}^T[\lambda\mathbf{I} - \mathbf{A}] > \mathbf{0}.$$

Hence there is a contradiction since statement (A.18) implies that vector $\mathbf{w}$ is positive, whereas its hth element equals zero. Thus the lemma is proved.   Q.E.D.

Proof of Theorem A.3.1. If $\mathbf{v}$ is a solution to the equation

$$\mathbf{x}^T[\lambda\mathbf{I} - \mathbf{A}] = \mathbf{0}^T, \tag{A.19}$$

then also $-\mathbf{v}$ is a solution, and, by Lemma A.3.1, both $\mathbf{v}$ and $-\mathbf{v}$ are nonnegative. Therefore $\mathbf{v} = \mathbf{0}$ and equation (A.19) has no nontrivial solution. Hence matrix $[\lambda\mathbf{I} - \mathbf{A}]$ is invertible. If

$$[\lambda\mathbf{I} - \mathbf{A}]^{-1} = [\mathbf{z}_1, \mathbf{z}_2, \ldots, \mathbf{z}_n]^T,$$

then $\mathbf{z}_i^T[\lambda\mathbf{I} - \mathbf{A}] = \mathbf{e}_i^T \geqslant \mathbf{0}^T$, and therefore every $\mathbf{z}_i$ is semipositive as a consequence of Lemma A.3.1.　　　　　　　　　　　　　　　　　Q.E.D.

Now let us associate with matrix $\mathbf{A}$ the numerical sets

$$L(\mathbf{A}) := \{\lambda \in \mathbb{R} \mid \exists \mathbf{x} \in \mathbb{R}^n : \mathbf{x} \geqslant \mathbf{0} \text{ and } \mathbf{x}^T[\lambda\mathbf{I} - \mathbf{A}] > \mathbf{0}^T\},$$

$$R(\mathbf{A}) := \{\rho \in \mathbb{R} \mid \exists \mathbf{y} \in \mathbb{R}^n : \mathbf{y} \geqslant \mathbf{0} \text{ and } [\rho\mathbf{I} - \mathbf{A}]\mathbf{y} > \mathbf{0}\}.$$

Then, let us put

$$\lambda^* = \lambda^*(\mathbf{A}) = \inf L(\mathbf{A}), \quad \rho^* = \rho^*(\mathbf{A}) = \inf R(\mathbf{A}).$$

In the following, we will show in particular that $\lambda^* = \rho^*$ and that λ^* is the largest real eigenvalue of $\mathbf{A}$.

Lemma A.3.2.

　　(i) $L(\mathbf{A})$ and $R(\mathbf{A})$ are not empty;
　　(ii) $\lambda^* \geqslant 0, \rho^* \geqslant 0$;
　　(iii) $L(\mathbf{A}) = \{\lambda \in \mathbb{R} \mid \lambda > \lambda^*\}$ and $R(\mathbf{A}) = \{\rho \in \mathbb{R} \mid \rho > \rho^*\}$.

Proof. Clearly $R(\mathbf{A}) = L(\mathbf{A}^T)$. Therefore $\rho^*(\mathbf{A}) = \lambda^*(\mathbf{A}^T)$ and any result for $L(\mathbf{A})$ and $\lambda^*(\mathbf{A})$ gives also a parallel result for $R(\mathbf{A})$ and $\rho^*(\mathbf{A})$. If $\lambda > \max\{\mathbf{e}^T\mathbf{A}\mathbf{e}_j \mid 1 \leqslant j \leqslant n\}$, then $\lambda > \mathbf{e}^T\mathbf{A}\mathbf{e}_j$, for each j. Hence $\mathbf{e}^T[\lambda\mathbf{I} - \mathbf{A}] > \mathbf{0}^T$ and $L(\mathbf{A})$ is not empty. Statement (ii) is a consequence of statement (A.18). Let $\lambda \in L(\mathbf{A})$, let $\mathbf{x}$ be a nonnegative vector such that $\mathbf{x}^T[\lambda\mathbf{I} - \mathbf{A}] > \mathbf{0}^T$, and let the positive real number σ be so small that[7]

$$\mathbf{x}^T[\lambda\mathbf{I} - \mathbf{A}] > \sigma\mathbf{x}^T,$$

that is,

$$\mathbf{x}^T[(\lambda - \sigma)\mathbf{I} - \mathbf{A}] > \mathbf{0}^T.$$

Then $(\lambda - \sigma) \in L(\mathbf{A})$, and $L(\mathbf{A})$ has no minimum. In order to complete the proof of statement (iii) we just need to prove that if $\lambda \in L(\mathbf{A})$ and $\lambda' > \lambda$, then $\lambda' \in L(\mathbf{A})$. Indeed if $\mathbf{x}$ is a nonnegative vector such that $\mathbf{x}^T[\lambda\mathbf{I} - \mathbf{A}] > \mathbf{0}^T$, then

$$\mathbf{x}^T[\lambda'\mathbf{I} - \mathbf{A}] = (\lambda' - \lambda)\mathbf{x}^T + \mathbf{x}^T[\lambda\mathbf{I} - \mathbf{A}] > \mathbf{0}^T. \qquad\qquad \text{Q.E.D.}$$

---

[7] Let $\mathbf{y}^T := \mathbf{x}^T[\lambda\mathbf{I} - \mathbf{A}] > \mathbf{0}^T$, and let the real number $\mu \ (>0)$ be larger than $\mathbf{x}^T\mathbf{e}_j / \mathbf{y}^T\mathbf{e}_j$ $(1 \leqslant j \leqslant n)$ and $\sigma = 1/\mu$. Then $\mathbf{y}^T > \sigma\mathbf{x}^T$.

Lemma A.3.3. λ^* is a nondecreasing function of every entry of matrix $\mathbf{A}$, namely,

$$\lambda^*(\mathbf{A}) \leqslant \lambda^*(\mathbf{A} + \Delta\mathbf{A})$$

for each $n \times n$ matrix $\Delta\mathbf{A} \geqslant \mathbf{0}$.

Proof. For any $\lambda \in \mathbb{R}$, $\mathbf{x} \geqslant \mathbf{0}$, and $\Delta\mathbf{A} \geqslant \mathbf{0}$ the inequality $\mathbf{x}^T[\lambda\mathbf{I} - (\mathbf{A} + \Delta\mathbf{A})] > \mathbf{0}^T$ is equivalent to $\mathbf{x}^T[\lambda\mathbf{I} - \mathbf{A}] > \mathbf{x}^T\Delta\mathbf{A} > \mathbf{0}^T$. Therefore $L(\mathbf{A} + \Delta\mathbf{A}) \subseteq L(\mathbf{A})$ and hence

$$\inf L(\mathbf{A} + \Delta\mathbf{A}) \geqslant \inf L(\mathbf{A}).\qquad\text{Q.E.D.}$$

Lemma A.3.4. For all $\lambda > \lambda^*$ or $\lambda > \rho^*$, the matrix $[\lambda\mathbf{I} - \mathbf{A}]$ is invertible and $[\lambda\mathbf{I} - \mathbf{A}]^{-1} \geqslant \mathbf{0}$.

Proof. It is an immediate consequence of Theorem A.3.1 because of the definition of λ^*.\qquad Q.E.D.

Lemma A.3.5.

    (i) $\exists \mathbf{p} \geqslant \mathbf{0}: [\lambda^*\mathbf{I} - \mathbf{A}]\mathbf{p} = \mathbf{0}$,
    (ii) $\exists \mathbf{q} \geqslant \mathbf{0}: \mathbf{q}^T[\rho^*\mathbf{I} - \mathbf{A}] = \mathbf{0}^T$.

Proof. Assume that statement (i) does not hold; then there is a vector $\mathbf{z}$ such that

$$\mathbf{z}^T[\lambda^*\mathbf{I} - \mathbf{A}] > \mathbf{0}^T$$

because of Theorem A.2.3. If $\mathbf{z} \geqslant \mathbf{0}$, then $\lambda^* \in L(\mathbf{A})$ and Lemma A.3.2 is contradicted. Let $\lambda^\circ > \lambda^*$ be so close to λ^* that[8]

$$\mathbf{z}^T[\lambda^\circ\mathbf{I} - \mathbf{A}] > \mathbf{0}^T.$$

Since $\lambda^\circ \in L(\mathbf{A})$, Lemma A.3.4 applies and $[\lambda^\circ\mathbf{I} - \mathbf{A}]^{-1} \geqslant \mathbf{0}$. Hence $\mathbf{z} > \mathbf{0}$ and a contradiction is obtained. The proof of statement (ii) is similar.\qquad Q.E.D.

Lemma A.3.6. Let λ_s be a real eigenvalue[9] of matrix $\mathbf{A}$; then $\lambda^* \geqslant |\lambda_s|$ and $\rho^* \geqslant |\lambda_s|$.

---

[8] Let $J = \{1 \leqslant j \leqslant n \mid \mathbf{z}^T\mathbf{e}_j < 0\} \neq \varnothing$ and let

$$0 < \varepsilon < -\frac{\mathbf{z}^T[\lambda^*\mathbf{I} - \mathbf{A}]\mathbf{e}_j}{\mathbf{z}^T\mathbf{e}_j}\quad\text{(each } j \in J).$$

Then, $\lambda^\circ = \lambda^* + \varepsilon$.

[9] The reader familiar with complex numbers will easily recognize that the lemma is still valid when λ_s is complex; in this case $|\lambda_s|$ is the modulus of λ_s and $\mathbf{x}^*$ is the vector each of whose components is the modulus of the corresponding element of $\mathbf{x}$.

Proof. Let **x** be a left eigenvector associated with λ_s, let **x*** be the vector each of whose entries is the absolute value of the corresponding element of **x**, and let x_j be the jth element of **x**. Since

$$|\lambda_s||x_j| = |\lambda_s x_j| = \left| \sum_{i=1}^n x_i a_{ij} \right| \leqslant \sum_{i=1}^n |x_i| a_{ij},$$

we have that

$$|\lambda_s| \mathbf{x}^{*T} \leqslant \mathbf{x}^{*T} \mathbf{A},$$

that is,

$$\mathbf{x}^{*T}[|\lambda_s| \mathbf{I} - \mathbf{A}] \leqslant \mathbf{0}^T.$$

If $|\lambda_s| > \lambda^*$, then $[|\lambda_s| \mathbf{I} - \mathbf{A}]^{-1} \geqslant \mathbf{0}$ and $\mathbf{x}^* \leqslant \mathbf{0}$. Hence there is a contradiction. In a similar way it is proved that $\rho^* \geqslant |\lambda_s|$. Q.E.D.

Theorem A.3.2.[10] Let **A** be a nonnegative square matrix. Then

(a) **A** has a nonnegative real eigenvalue;
(b) no real eigenvalue of **A** can have an absolute value larger than the largest real eigenvalue, λ_m;
(c) at least one right eigenvector and one left eigenvector associated with λ_m are semipositive;
(d) $[\lambda \mathbf{I} - \mathbf{A}]^{-1} \geqslant \mathbf{0}, \forall \lambda > \lambda_m$;
(e) λ_m is a nondecreasing function of each of the elements of matrix **A**.

Proof. λ^* and ρ^* are nonnegative real eigenvalues of **A** (cf. Lemmas A.3.2 and A.3.5) and therefore $\lambda^* \geqslant \rho^* \geqslant \lambda^*$ because of Lemma A.3.6. Hence $\lambda^* = \lambda_m = \rho^*$. This proves statements (a), (b) (cf. Lemma A.3.6), (c) (cf. Lemma A.3.5), (d) (cf. Lemma A.3.4), and (e) (cf. Lemma A.3.3). Q.E.D.

Theorem A.3.3. Let **A** be a semipositive square matrix, and let λ_m be its largest real eigenvalue. Let, moreover, $\lambda > \lambda_m$ and $\nu = (1/\lambda)$. Then

(a) $\lim_{k \to \infty} (\nu \mathbf{A})^k = \mathbf{0}$,

(b) $[\mathbf{I} - \nu \mathbf{A}]^{-1} = \lim_{k \to \infty} \sum_{i=0}^{k} (\nu \mathbf{A})^i$,

(c) $[\lambda \mathbf{I} - \mathbf{A}]^{-1} = \frac{1}{\lambda} \lim_{k \to \infty} \sum_{i=0}^{k} \left(\frac{1}{\lambda} \mathbf{A} \right)^i$.

---

[10] The reader familiar with complex numbers will put statement (b) as follows: "No eigenvalue of **A** can be larger in modulus than the largest real eigenvalue, λ_m." (Cf. previous footnote.)

Proof. In order to simplify the notation, let $\mathbf{B} = v\mathbf{A}$. Since $\lambda > \lambda_m = \lambda^*$ there is a vector $\mathbf{x} \geqslant \mathbf{0}$ such that

$$\mathbf{x}^T > \mathbf{x}^T \mathbf{B}.$$

Obviously $\mathbf{x} > \mathbf{0}$. Let $0 < \theta < 1$ and let θ be so close to 1 that[11]

$$\theta \mathbf{x}^T \geqslant \mathbf{x}^T \mathbf{B}. \tag{A.20}$$

Moreover, by multiplying inequality (A.20) by $\mathbf{B}^h$ (for any $h \in \mathbb{N}_0$) we have

$$\theta \mathbf{x}^T \mathbf{B}^h \geqslant \mathbf{x}^T \mathbf{B}^{h+1} \tag{A.21.h}$$

since $\mathbf{B}^h$ is semipositive as is $\mathbf{B}$. Finally we obtain

$$\theta^h \mathbf{x}^T \geqslant \mathbf{x}^T \mathbf{B}^h \tag{A.22.h}$$

for each $h \in \mathbb{N}$. In fact, inequality (A.22.h) holds for $h = 1$ (cf. inequality (A.20)) and if (A.22.h) holds, then inequality (A.22.h + 1) also holds. In order to show this, multiply inequality (A.22.h) by θ. Since $\theta > 0$,

$$\theta^{h+1} \mathbf{x}^T \geqslant \theta \mathbf{x}^T \mathbf{B}^h.$$

Hence by using inequality (A.21.h), inequality (A.22.h + 1) is obtained. Since inequality (A.22.h) holds for each $h \in \mathbb{N}$ and since $0 < \theta < 1$,

$$\mathbf{0}^T = \lim_{h \to \infty} \theta^h \mathbf{x}^T \geqslant \lim_{h \to \infty} \mathbf{x}^T \mathbf{B}^h \geqslant \mathbf{0}^T,$$

that is,

$$\lim_{h \to \infty} \mathbf{x}^T \mathbf{B}^h = \mathbf{0}^T,$$

and this proves statement (a) since $\mathbf{x} > \mathbf{0}$. In order to prove statement (b), consider

$$S_h = [\mathbf{I} - \mathbf{B}][\mathbf{I} + \mathbf{B} + \mathbf{B}^2 + \cdots + \mathbf{B}^h] = \mathbf{I} - \mathbf{B}^{h+1}.$$

Since

$$\lim_{h \to \infty} S_h = \mathbf{I}$$

because of statement (a), statement (b) is proved. Statement (c) is a direct consequence of statement (b). Q.E.D.

Theorem A.3.4. Let $\mathbf{A}$ be a semipositive square matrix $n \times n$, and let λ_m be its largest real eigenvalue. Then $\lambda > \lambda_m$ if and only if all the decreasing principal minors of $[\lambda \mathbf{I} - \mathbf{A}]$ are positive.

---

[11] Since $0 < (\mathbf{x}^T \mathbf{B} \mathbf{e}_i)/(\mathbf{x}^T \mathbf{e}_i) < 1$, let θ be a real number such that $\mathbf{x}^T \mathbf{B} \mathbf{e}_i / \mathbf{x}^T \mathbf{e}_i \leqslant \theta < 1$ $(1 \leqslant i \leqslant n)$.

Proof. Let $\Delta_1 = \lambda - a_{11}, \Delta_2, \ldots, \Delta_n = \det([\lambda\mathbf{I} - \mathbf{A}])$ be the decreasing principal minors of $[\lambda\mathbf{I} - \mathbf{A}]$. In order to prove the "only if" part let us remark that (cf. the expression for the inverse in Subsection A.1.7 and statement (c) of Theorem A.3.3)

$$\frac{\Delta_{n-1}}{\Delta_n} = \mathbf{e}_n^T[\lambda\mathbf{I} - \mathbf{A}]^{-1}\mathbf{e}_n \geqslant \frac{1}{\lambda} > 0.$$

Then, consider the matrix $\mathbf{B}_n$, obtained from $\mathbf{A}$ by eliminating the nth row and the nth column. Since it is still true that

$$\exists \mathbf{x} \geqslant \mathbf{0} \colon \mathbf{x}^T[\lambda\mathbf{I} - \mathbf{B}_n] > \mathbf{0}^T$$

then

$$\frac{\Delta_{n-2}}{\Delta_{n-1}} = \mathbf{e}_{n-1}^T[\lambda\mathbf{I} - \mathbf{B}_n]^{-1}\mathbf{e}_{n-1} \geqslant \frac{1}{\lambda} > 0.$$

By iteration we obtain that all Δ's have the same sign, and since Δ_1 is positive, all of them are positive. In order to prove the "if" part, let us remark that the theorem is true if $n = 1$. Then we prove that if the theorem is true for $n = s - 1$ it is true for $n = s$. In order to simplify the notation, let

$$[\lambda\mathbf{I} - \mathbf{B}_{s+1}] = \begin{bmatrix} \lambda\mathbf{I} - \mathbf{B}_s & -\mathbf{b}_s \\ -\mathbf{d}_s^T & \lambda - a_{ss} \end{bmatrix},$$

where matrix $\mathbf{B}_i$ ($i = s, s+1$) is obtained from $\mathbf{A}$ by eliminating all rows and columns from the ith to the nth, vector $\mathbf{b}_s$ is constituted by the first $s - 1$ elements of the sth column of $\mathbf{A}$, and vector $\mathbf{d}_s$ is constituted by the first $s - 1$ elements of the sth row of $\mathbf{A}$. Since $\Delta_1, \Delta_2, \ldots, \Delta_{s-1}$ are positive, we obtain from the theorem that $\lambda\mathbf{I} - \mathbf{B}_s$ is invertible and its inverse is semipositive. Moreover[12]

$$\Delta_s = \Delta_{s-1}\{(\lambda - a_{ss}) - \mathbf{d}_s^T[\lambda\mathbf{I} - \mathbf{B}_s]^{-1}\mathbf{b}_s\},$$

and since both Δ_s and Δ_{s-1} are positive, we obtain that

$$\beta := (\lambda - a_{ss}) - \mathbf{d}_s^T[\lambda\mathbf{I} - \mathbf{B}_s]^{-1}\mathbf{b}_s > 0.$$

Hence we can choose a scalar $\varepsilon > 0$ such that $\beta > \varepsilon\mathbf{e}^T[\lambda\mathbf{I} - \mathbf{B}_s]^{-1}\mathbf{b}_s$. Let

$$\mathbf{z}^T := \mathbf{d}_s^T[\lambda\mathbf{I} - \mathbf{B}_s]^{-1} + \varepsilon\mathbf{e}^T[\lambda\mathbf{I} - \mathbf{B}_s]^{-1}$$

---

[12] Since $\begin{bmatrix} \mathbf{I} & \mathbf{0} \\ -\mathbf{CA}^{-1} & \mathbf{I} \end{bmatrix}\begin{bmatrix} \mathbf{A} & \mathbf{B} \\ \mathbf{C} & \mathbf{D} \end{bmatrix} = \begin{bmatrix} \mathbf{A} & \mathbf{B} \\ \mathbf{0} & \mathbf{D} - \mathbf{CA}^{-1}\mathbf{B} \end{bmatrix}$,

$\det\left(\begin{bmatrix} \mathbf{A} & \mathbf{B} \\ \mathbf{C} & \mathbf{D} \end{bmatrix}\right) = \det(\mathbf{A})\det(\mathbf{D} - \mathbf{CA}^{-1}\mathbf{B}).$

and

$$\alpha := (\lambda - a_{ss}) - \mathbf{z}^T \mathbf{b}_s.$$

Then $\mathbf{z} \geqslant \mathbf{0}, \alpha = \beta - \varepsilon \mathbf{e}^T [\lambda \mathbf{I} - \mathbf{B}_s]^{-1} \mathbf{b}_s > 0$, and

$$\begin{bmatrix} \mathbf{z} \\ 1 \end{bmatrix}^T [\lambda \mathbf{I} - \mathbf{B}_{s+1}] = \begin{bmatrix} \mathbf{z} \\ 1 \end{bmatrix}^T \begin{bmatrix} \lambda \mathbf{I} - \mathbf{B}_s & -\mathbf{b}_s \\ -\mathbf{d}_s^T & \lambda - a_{ss} \end{bmatrix} = \begin{bmatrix} \varepsilon \mathbf{e} \\ \alpha \end{bmatrix}^T > \mathbf{0}^T,$$

which completes the proof.   Q.E.D.

A.3.2. Perron–Frobenius Theorems for indecomposable semipositive matrices

A semipositive $n \times n$ matrix $\mathbf{A}$ is *decomposable* if it is possible, by interchanging some rows and the corresponding columns, to reduce it to the form

$$\begin{bmatrix} \mathbf{A}_{11} & \mathbf{0} \\ \mathbf{A}_{21} & \mathbf{A}_{22} \end{bmatrix}, \tag{A.23}$$

where $\mathbf{A}_{11}$ and $\mathbf{A}_{22}$ are square submatrices and $\mathbf{0}$ is a zero submatrix. Conversely, a square matrix is *indecomposable* if it is not decomposable.

Submatrices $\mathbf{A}_{11}$ and $\mathbf{A}_{22}$ in (A.23) may themselves be decomposable; so, in general, a decomposable matrix $\mathbf{A}$ may always be reduced to the form

$$\begin{bmatrix} \mathbf{A}_{11} & \mathbf{0} & \cdots & \mathbf{0} \\ \mathbf{A}_{21} & \mathbf{A}_{22} & \cdots & \mathbf{0} \\ \vdots & \vdots & \vdots & \vdots \\ \mathbf{A}_{s1} & \mathbf{A}_{s2} & \cdots & \mathbf{A}_{ss} \end{bmatrix}, \tag{A.24}$$

where $\mathbf{A}_{11}, \mathbf{A}_{22}, \ldots, \mathbf{A}_{ss}$ are indecomposable square matrices not necessarily of the same order (note that the zero matrix of order 1 is indecomposable). Form (A.24) of matrix $\mathbf{A}$ is called its "canonical form."

Lemma A.3.7. Let $\mathbf{A}$ be a nonnegative square matrix. If there is a real number μ and a vector $\mathbf{x}$ such that $\mathbf{x} \geqslant \mathbf{0}, \mathbf{x} \not> \mathbf{0}$, and $\mu \mathbf{x}^T \geqslant \mathbf{x}^T \mathbf{A}$, then matrix $\mathbf{A}$ is decomposable.

Proof. Let us interchange the rows of vector $\mathbf{x}$ in such a way that $\mathbf{x} = [\mathbf{y}^T, \mathbf{0}^T]^T$ where $\mathbf{y}$ is a positive subvector. After rearranging the rows and columns of matrix $\mathbf{A}$ in the same way as for vector $\mathbf{x}$, we obtain

$$\mu \begin{bmatrix} \mathbf{y} \\ \mathbf{0} \end{bmatrix}^T \geqslant \begin{bmatrix} \mathbf{y} \\ \mathbf{0} \end{bmatrix}^T \begin{bmatrix} \mathbf{A}_{11} & \mathbf{A}_{12} \\ \mathbf{A}_{21} & \mathbf{A}_{22} \end{bmatrix} = \mathbf{y}^T [\mathbf{A}_{11}, \mathbf{A}_{12}]$$

which implies that $\mathbf{A}_{12}$ is a zero submatrix since $\mathbf{y}$ is positive.   Q.E.D.

Theorem A.3.5. Let $\mathbf{A}$ be an indecomposable, semipositive, square $n \times n$ matrix, and let λ_m be its largest real eigenvalue. Then:

(a) Any nonnegative eigenvector associated with λ_m is positive, so λ_m has a positive associated eigenvector.

(b) $\lambda_m > 0$.

(c) The right and the left eigenvectors associated with λ_m are unique up to the multiplication by a scalar.

(d) If $\mathbf{z}^T[\lambda\mathbf{I} - \mathbf{A}] \geqslant \mathbf{0}^T$ and $\mathbf{z} \geqslant \mathbf{0}$, then $\lambda > \lambda_m$, $[\lambda\mathbf{I} - \mathbf{A}]$ is invertible, and $[\lambda\mathbf{I} - \mathbf{A}]^{-1} \geqslant \mathbf{0}$.

(e) If $[\lambda\mathbf{I} - \mathbf{A}]^{-1} \geqslant \mathbf{0}$, then $[\lambda\mathbf{I} - \mathbf{A}]^{-1} > \mathbf{0}$.

(f) λ_m is an increasing function of each of the elements of matrix $\mathbf{A}$.

Proof. Statement (a) is a direct consequence of Lemma A.3.7 and statement (c) of Theorem A.3.2. If $\lambda_m = 0$, then statement (a) implies that $\mathbf{A} = \mathbf{0}$: this proves statement (b). Let $\mathbf{x}$ and $\mathbf{y}$ be two eigenvectors associated with λ_m, and let $\mathbf{x} > \mathbf{0}$; then $\mathbf{x} + \varphi\mathbf{y}$ is still an eigenvector associated with λ_m. Since φ can be chosen in such a way that $\mathbf{x} + \varphi\mathbf{y}$ is nonnegative and not positive,[13] statement (a) is contradicted unless $\mathbf{y}$ is proportional to $\mathbf{x}$; and this proves statement (c). In order to prove statement (d), let $\mathbf{p}$ be a positive right eigenvector associated with λ_m (cf. statement (a)). Then

$$(\lambda - \lambda_m)\mathbf{z}^T\mathbf{p} = \lambda\mathbf{z}^T\mathbf{p} - \mathbf{z}^T\mathbf{A}\mathbf{p} = \mathbf{z}^T[\lambda\mathbf{I} - \mathbf{A}]\mathbf{p} > 0;$$

hence $\lambda > \lambda_m$ and statement (d) is a consequence of statement (d) of Theorem A.3.2. In order to prove statement (e), let

$$\mathbf{v}_i^T = \mathbf{e}_i^T[\lambda\mathbf{I} - \mathbf{A}]^{-1},$$

and then

$$\mathbf{v}_i \geqslant \mathbf{0} \quad \text{and} \quad \lambda\mathbf{v}_i^T - \mathbf{v}_i^T\mathbf{A} = \mathbf{e}_i^T \geqslant \mathbf{0}^T.$$

Hence $\mathbf{v}_i$ is positive because of Lemma A.3.7. Thus $[\lambda\mathbf{I} - \mathbf{A}]^{-1} = (\mathbf{v}_1, \mathbf{v}_2, \ldots, \mathbf{v}_n) > \mathbf{0}$. In order to prove statement (f) let $\Delta\mathbf{A}$ be an $n \times n$ semipositive matrix; then matrix $(\mathbf{A} + \Delta\mathbf{A})$ is indecomposable. Let λ° be the largest real eigenvalue of matrix $(\mathbf{A} + \Delta\mathbf{A})$ and $\mathbf{y}$ an associated positive right eigenvector; that is,

$$\lambda^\circ\mathbf{y} = (\mathbf{A} + \Delta\mathbf{A})\mathbf{y} > \mathbf{0}.$$

---

[13] Since $\mathbf{y}$ is an eigenvector, $\mathbf{y} \neq \mathbf{0}$; moreover, since $-\mathbf{y}$ is also an eigenvector, then, with no loss of generality, at least one element of $\mathbf{y}$ is assumed to be positive. Then

$$\frac{1}{\varphi} := \frac{\mathbf{e}_s^T\mathbf{y}}{\mathbf{e}_s^T\mathbf{x}} \geqslant \frac{\mathbf{e}_j^T\mathbf{y}}{\mathbf{e}_j^T\mathbf{x}} \quad \text{for each } j.$$

Then

$$\lambda^\circ \mathbf{y} \geqslant \mathbf{A} \mathbf{y}.$$

Q.E.D.

Hence $\lambda^\circ > \lambda_m$ because of statement (d).

Theorem A.3.6. Let $\mathbf{A}$ be an indecomposable, semipositive, square matrix; let λ_r be a real eigenvalue of $\mathbf{A}$ different from the largest, λ_m; and let $\mathbf{y}$ be a right (left) eigenvector associated with λ_r. Then $\mathbf{y}$ is not semipositive.

Proof. Let $\mathbf{x}$ be a positive left (right) eigenvector associated with λ_m, then $\mathbf{x}^T \mathbf{y} = 0$ since $\lambda_r < \lambda_m$ (cf Subsection A.1.9). This proves the theorem since $\mathbf{x} > \mathbf{0}$.

Q.E.D.

Theorem A.3.7. Let $\mathbf{A}$ be an indecomposable, semipositive, square $n \times n$ matrix, and let λ be a real eigenvalue of it. Then λ is the largest real eigenvalue of matrix $\mathbf{A}$ if and only if all the decreasing proper principal minors of $[\lambda \mathbf{I} - \mathbf{A}]$ are positive.

Proof. Let $\mathbf{B}$ be the matrix obtained from $\mathbf{A}$ by eliminating the last row and the last column, and let $\mathbf{x}^T \equiv (\mathbf{y}^T, \alpha)$ be a left eigenvector of matrix $\mathbf{A}$ associated with λ and $\alpha \geqslant 0$. Then

$$\mathbf{y}^T [\lambda \mathbf{I} - \mathbf{B}] = \alpha(a_{n1}, a_{n2}, \dots, a_{n,n-1}).$$

If λ is the largest real eigenvalue of $\mathbf{A}$, then vector $\mathbf{y}$ and scalar α are positive, thus

$$\alpha(a_{n1}, a_{n2}, \dots, a_{n,n-1}) \geqslant \mathbf{0},$$

and, as a consequence of statement (d) of Theorem A.3.5, the largest real eigenvalue of matrix $\mathbf{B}$ is lower than λ; finally, the "only if" part of the theorem is a consequence of Theorem A.3.4. If the decreasing proper principal minors of $[\lambda \mathbf{I} - \mathbf{A}]$ are positive, then matrix $[\lambda \mathbf{I} - \mathbf{B}]$ is invertible and its inverse is nonnegative because of Theorem A.3.4 and statement (d) of Theorem A.3.2. Hence vector $\mathbf{y}$ is semipositive. Then the "if" part of the theorem follows from Theorem A.4.6.

Q.E.D.

Let us conclude this section by a further theorem on indecomposable matrices which is utilized in some exercises.

Theorem A.3.8. Let $\mathbf{A}$ be an indecomposable, semipositive, $n \times n$ matrix. Then

$$\mathbf{I} + \mathbf{A} + \dots + \mathbf{A}^{n-1} > \mathbf{0}.$$

Proof. Let $\mathbf{x}$ be a vector such that $\mathbf{x} \geqslant \mathbf{0}$, $\mathbf{x} \ngtr \mathbf{0}$; then vector $\mathbf{x} + \mathbf{A}\mathbf{x}$ has a number of positive entries larger than $\mathbf{x}$ because of Lemma A.3.7. Similarly, if $\mathbf{x} + \mathbf{A}\mathbf{x} \ngtr \mathbf{0}$, then vector $\mathbf{x} + 2\mathbf{A}\mathbf{x} + \mathbf{A}^2\mathbf{x}$ has a number of positive entries larger than $\mathbf{x} + \mathbf{Ax}$. As a consequence vector $\mathbf{x} + \mathbf{Ax} + \mathbf{A}^2\mathbf{x}$ has a number of positive entries larger than $\mathbf{x} + \mathbf{Ax}$. By iterating the argument we obtain that

$$\mathbf{x} \geqslant \mathbf{0} \Rightarrow (\mathbf{I} + \mathbf{A} + \cdots + \mathbf{A}^{n-1})\mathbf{x} > \mathbf{0}.$$

Then the theorem follows by the arbitrariness of $\mathbf{x}$. Q.E.D.

A.4 Linear programming

Linear programming is concerned with the problem of finding the maximum or the minimum of a linear function under linear constraints, a linear constraint being either a linear equation or a linear weak inequality. (In this section, except when explicitly stated otherwise, we will always refer, with no loss of generality, to a minimum problem.) Therefore, a general format of a linear-programming problem is the following:

$$\begin{aligned} \text{Min} \quad & (\mathbf{c}_1^T\mathbf{x}_1 + \mathbf{c}_2^T\mathbf{x}_2) \\ \text{s. to} \quad & \mathbf{A}_{11}\mathbf{x}_1 + \mathbf{A}_{12}\mathbf{x}_2 = \mathbf{b}_1, \\ & \mathbf{A}_{21}\mathbf{x}_1 + \mathbf{A}_{22}\mathbf{x}_2 \geqslant \mathbf{b}_2, \\ & \mathbf{x}_1 \geqslant \mathbf{0}, \end{aligned} \tag{A.25}$$

where vectors $\mathbf{c}_1, \mathbf{c}_2, \mathbf{b}_1,$ and $\mathbf{b}_2$ and matrices $\mathbf{A}_{11}, \mathbf{A}_{12}, \mathbf{A}_{21},$ and $\mathbf{A}_{22}$ are given and vectors $\mathbf{x}_1$ and $\mathbf{x}_2$ are unknown.

A.4.1. Standard and canonical forms

There are two formats of problem (A.25) that are more workable and are called the "standard form" and the "canonical form." In order to transform the problem (A.25) into its standard form, let us introduce two (unknown) nonnegative vectors which are of the same size as subvector $\mathbf{x}_2$ and such that their difference equals $\mathbf{x}_2$; that is, let $\mathbf{z}_1$ and $\mathbf{z}_2$ be nonnegative and such that $\mathbf{z}_1 - \mathbf{z}_2 = \mathbf{x}_2$. Then the problem (A.25) can be stated as

$$\begin{aligned} \text{Min} \quad & (\mathbf{c}_1^T\mathbf{x}_1 + \mathbf{c}_2^T\mathbf{z}_1 - \mathbf{c}_2^T\mathbf{z}_2) \\ \text{s. to} \quad & \mathbf{A}_{11}\mathbf{x}_1 + \mathbf{A}_{12}\mathbf{z}_1 - \mathbf{A}_{12}\mathbf{z}_2 \geqslant \mathbf{b}_1, \\ & -[\mathbf{A}_{11}\mathbf{x}_1 + \mathbf{A}_{12}\mathbf{z}_1 - \mathbf{A}_{12}\mathbf{z}_2] \geqslant -\mathbf{b}_1, \\ & \mathbf{A}_{21}\mathbf{x}_1 + \mathbf{A}_{22}\mathbf{z}_1 - \mathbf{A}_{22}\mathbf{z}_2 \geqslant \mathbf{b}_2, \\ & \mathbf{x}_1 \geqslant \mathbf{0}, \quad \mathbf{z}_1 \geqslant \mathbf{0}, \quad \mathbf{z}_2 \geqslant \mathbf{0}, \end{aligned}$$

that is,

$$\begin{aligned} \text{Min} \quad & \mathbf{d}^T\mathbf{y} \\ \text{s. to} \quad & \mathbf{By} \geqslant \mathbf{a} \\ & \mathbf{y} \geqslant \mathbf{0}, \end{aligned} \tag{A.26}$$

where

$$d = \begin{bmatrix} c_1 \\ c_2 \\ -c_2 \end{bmatrix}, \quad B = \begin{bmatrix} A_{11} & A_{12} & -A_{12} \\ -A_{11} & -A_{12} & A_{12} \\ A_{21} & A_{22} & -A_{22} \end{bmatrix},$$

$$y = \begin{bmatrix} x_1 \\ z_1 \\ z_2 \end{bmatrix}, \quad a = \begin{bmatrix} b_1 \\ -b_1 \\ b_2 \end{bmatrix}.$$

In order to transform the problem (A.25) into its canonical form, let us still consider z_1 and z_2 as nonnegative vectors such that $z_1 - z_2 = x_2$ and let us introduce a nonnegative (unknown) vector v of the same size as vector b_2. Then the problem (A.25) can be stated as

$$\text{Min} \quad (c_1^T x_1 + c_2^T z_1 - c_2^T z_2)$$

s. to $\quad A_{11}x_1 + A_{12}z_1 - A_{12}z_2 = b_1,$

$\quad\quad A_{21}x_1 + A_{22}z_1 - A_{22}z_2 - v = b_2,$

$\quad\quad x_1 \geqslant 0, \quad z_1 \geqslant 0, \quad z_2 \geqslant 0, \quad v \geqslant 0,$

that is,

$$\text{Min} \quad d^T y$$

s. t $\quad By = a,$ (A.27)

$\quad\quad y \geqslant 0,$

where

$$d = \begin{bmatrix} c_1 \\ c_2 \\ -c_2 \\ 0 \end{bmatrix}, \quad B = \begin{bmatrix} A_{11} & A_{12} & -A_{12} & 0 \\ A_{21} & A_{22} & -A_{22} & -I \end{bmatrix}, \quad y = \begin{bmatrix} x_1 \\ z_1 \\ z_2 \\ v \end{bmatrix}, \quad a = \begin{bmatrix} b_1 \\ b_2 \end{bmatrix}.$$

Thus, it is always possible to transform the general format of a linear programming problem (A.25) into the standard form (A.26) or into the canonical form (A.27). The canonical form is very useful when one wants to compute a solution of the linear programming problem (A.25), whereas the standard form is useful for determining interesting results relating to the solutions of the linear programming problem without computing them. In this appendix no attempt will be made to compute a solution of a linear programming problem. Consequently, in the following discussion linear programming problems will always be considered in their standard form.

A.4.2. *Duality and related theorems*

Let us consider the linear programming problem

$$\begin{aligned} \text{Min} \quad & \mathbf{d}^T\mathbf{x} \\ \text{s. to} \quad & \mathbf{A}\mathbf{x} \geqslant \mathbf{b} \\ & \mathbf{x} \geqslant \mathbf{0}, \end{aligned}$$
(A.28)

where $\mathbf{A}$ is an $m \times n$ matrix, $\mathbf{b} \in \mathbb{R}^m$, and $\mathbf{d} \in \mathbb{R}^n$. A vector $\mathbf{x}$ satisfying the constraints of the problem (A.28) is said to be a *feasible solution*, whereas a solution of the problem itself is also said to be an *optimal solution*. That is, the set

$$X = \{\mathbf{x} \in \mathbb{R}^n | \mathbf{A}\mathbf{x} \geqslant \mathbf{b}, \mathbf{x} \geqslant \mathbf{0}\},$$

where n is the number of columns of matrix $\mathbf{A}$, is the set of the feasible solutions of the linear-programming problem (A.28), whereas the set

$$X_0 = \{\mathbf{z} \in X | \mathbf{d}^T\mathbf{z} \leqslant \mathbf{d}^T\mathbf{x}, \forall \mathbf{x} \in X\}$$

is the set of the optimal solutions of the linear-programming problem (A.28).

The following Theorem A.4.1 relates the problem (A.28) to the problem

$$\begin{aligned} \text{Min} \quad & -\mathbf{b}^T\mathbf{y} \\ \text{s. to} \quad & -\mathbf{A}^T\mathbf{y} \geqslant -\mathbf{d}, \\ & \mathbf{y} \geqslant \mathbf{0}, \end{aligned}$$

which is better stated as

$$\begin{aligned} \text{Max} \quad & \mathbf{b}^T\mathbf{y} \\ \text{s. to} \quad & \mathbf{y}^T\mathbf{A} \leqslant \mathbf{d}^T, \\ & \mathbf{y} \geqslant \mathbf{0}. \end{aligned}$$
(A.29)

Let

$$Y = \{\mathbf{y} \in \mathbb{R}^m | \mathbf{y}^T\mathbf{A} \leqslant \mathbf{d}^T, \mathbf{y} \geqslant \mathbf{0}\},$$
$$Y_0 = \{\mathbf{z} \in Y | \mathbf{b}^T\mathbf{z} \geqslant \mathbf{b}^T\mathbf{y}, \forall \mathbf{y} \in Y\}$$

be the set of feasible solutions and the set of optimal solutions, respectively, for the problem (A.29).

Theorem A.4.1. Either both problems (A.28) and (A.29) have optimal solutions and the two optimal values are equal, or both have no optimal solutions and at least one of them has no feasible solution. Namely, either

(i) $X_0 \neq \varnothing \neq Y_0$ and $\mathbf{d}^T\mathbf{x}^* = \mathbf{b}^T\mathbf{y}^*$ for $\mathbf{x}^* \in X_0, \mathbf{y}^* \in Y_0$;

or

(ii) $X = \emptyset$ or $Y = \emptyset$, and $X_0 = \emptyset = Y_0$;

but never both.

Lemma A.4.1

(i) $(x \in X, Au \geq 0, u \geq 0, \lambda \geq 0) \Rightarrow x + \lambda u \in X$;
(ii) $(y \in Y, v^T A \leq 0^T, v \geq 0, \lambda \geq 0) \Rightarrow y + \lambda v \in Y$;
(iii) $(x \in X, y \in Y) \Rightarrow b^T y \leq y^T Ax \leq d^T x$.

Proof. The verification of statements (i) and (ii) is trivial. Since $Ax \geq b$ and $y \geq 0$, $y^T b \leq y^T Ax$. Since $y^T A \leq d^T$ and $x \geq 0, y^T Ax \leq d^T x$.   Q.E.D.

Lemma A.4.2. Either there are vectors x and y such that

$$Ax \geq b, \quad y^T A \leq d^T, \quad x \geq 0, \quad y \geq 0, \quad d^T x \leq y^T b, \tag{A.30}$$

or there are vectors u and v such that

$$Au \geq 0, \quad v^T A \leq 0^T, \quad u \geq 0, \quad v \geq 0, \quad d^T u < v^T b, \tag{A.31}$$

Proof. The first alternative can be stated in the following way. There is a nonnegative solution to the inequality

$$\begin{bmatrix} x \\ y \end{bmatrix}^T \begin{bmatrix} -A^T & 0 & d \\ 0 & A & -b \end{bmatrix} \leqq \begin{bmatrix} -b \\ d \\ 0 \end{bmatrix}^T.$$

Because of Theorem A.2.4, this alternative has a solution if and only if there is no solution to the following alternative. There is a nonnegative solution to the inequalities

$$\begin{bmatrix} -A^T & 0 & d \\ 0 & A & -b \end{bmatrix} \begin{bmatrix} v \\ u \\ \lambda \end{bmatrix} \geqq 0, \quad \begin{bmatrix} -b \\ d \\ 0 \end{bmatrix}^T \begin{bmatrix} v \\ u \\ \lambda \end{bmatrix} < 0,$$

which can be stated as

$$Au \geq \lambda b, \quad v^T A \leq \lambda d^T, \quad u \geq 0, \quad v \geq 0, \quad \lambda \geq 0, \quad d^T u < v^T b. \tag{A.32}$$

Inequalities (A.32) coincide with inequalities (A.31) if and only if $\lambda = 0$. The lemma is then proved if it is shown that λ cannot be positive. By multiplying the first inequality (A.32) by v^T and the second by u, we obtain

$$\lambda d^T u \geq v^T Au \geq \lambda v^T b,$$

which contradicts the last inequality (A.32) unless $\lambda \leq 0$.   Q.E.D.

Lemma A.4.3. Both problems (A.28) and (A.29) have optimal solutions and the two optimal values are equal if and only if inequalities (A.30) have solutions. Namely, for $\mathbf{x}^* \in \mathbb{R}^n$ and $\mathbf{y}^* \in \mathbb{R}^n$ the following two statements are equivalent:

(a) $\mathbf{x}^* \in X_0, \mathbf{y}^* \in Y_0$, and $\mathbf{d}^T \mathbf{x}^* = \mathbf{y}^{*T} \mathbf{b}$;
(b) $\mathbf{x}^* \in X, \mathbf{y}^* \in Y$, and $\mathbf{d}^T \mathbf{x}^* \leqslant \mathbf{y}^{*T} \mathbf{b}$.

Proof. Since $X_0 \subseteq X$ and $Y_0 \subseteq Y$, it is immediately obtained that (a) $\Rightarrow$ (b). Let vectors $\mathbf{x}^* \in X$ and $\mathbf{y}^* \in Y$, that is, they satisfy the first four inequalities (A.30). Then because of statement (iii) of Lemma A.4.1 we also have $\mathbf{y}^{*T} \mathbf{b} \leqslant \mathbf{d}^T \mathbf{x}^*$ and therefore

$$\mathbf{d}^T \mathbf{x}^* = \mathbf{y}^{*T} \mathbf{b}, \tag{A.33}$$

because of the last inequality (A.30). From equation (A.33) and statement (iii) of Lemma A.4.1, we obtain that if $\mathbf{x} \in X$, then

$$\mathbf{d}^T \mathbf{x} \geqslant \mathbf{y}^{*T} \mathbf{b} = \mathbf{d}^T \mathbf{x}^*.$$

Then $\mathbf{x}^* \in X_0$. Similarly, if $\mathbf{y} \in Y$, then

$$\mathbf{y}^{*T} \mathbf{b} = \mathbf{d}^T \mathbf{x}^* \geqslant \mathbf{y}^T \mathbf{b}.$$

Then $\mathbf{y}^* \in Y_0$. Hence (b) $\Rightarrow$ (a). Q.E.D.

Lemma A.4.4. If inequalities (A.31) have a solution then neither problem (A.28) nor problem (A.29) has an optimal solution and at least one of them has no feasible solution.

Proof. Let $\mathbf{u} \in \mathbb{R}^n$ and $\mathbf{v} \in \mathbb{R}^m$ be solutions to inequalities (A.31). Then either $\mathbf{d}^T \mathbf{u} < 0$, or $\mathbf{d}^T \mathbf{u} \geqslant 0$. Assume $\mathbf{d}^T \mathbf{u} < 0$; then $Y = \varnothing$ (so $Y_0 = \varnothing$) and $X_0 = \varnothing$. For if

$$\mathbf{y}^T \mathbf{A} \leqslant \mathbf{d}^T, \quad \mathbf{y} \geqslant \mathbf{0},$$

we obtain from the first and the third of inequalities (A.31) a contradiction:

$$0 \leqslant \mathbf{y}^T \mathbf{A} \mathbf{u} \leqslant \mathbf{d}^T \mathbf{u}.$$

If $\mathbf{x} \in X$, from statement (i) of Lemma A.4.1 we have that $(\mathbf{x} + \lambda \mathbf{u}) \in X$ for all $\lambda \geqslant 0$. Hence $X_0 = \varnothing$ since

$$\lim_{\lambda \to \infty} \mathbf{d}^T (\mathbf{x} + \lambda \mathbf{u}) = \mathbf{d}^T \mathbf{x} + \mathbf{d}^T \mathbf{u} \lim_{\lambda \to \infty} \lambda = -\infty.$$

Assume now $\mathbf{d}^T \mathbf{u} \geqslant 0$. Then $\mathbf{v}^T \mathbf{b} > 0$ from the last inequality (A.31). Then $X = \varnothing$ (so $X_0 = \varnothing$) and $Y_0 = \varnothing$. For if

$$\mathbf{A} \mathbf{x} \geqslant \mathbf{b}, \quad \mathbf{x} \geqslant \mathbf{0},$$

we obtain from the second and the fourth of inequalities (A.31) a contradiction:

$$0 \geqslant v^T A x \geqslant v^T b.$$

If $y \in Y$, from statement (ii) of Lemma A.4.1 we have that $(y + \lambda v) \in Y$ for all $\lambda \geqslant 0$. Hence $X_0 = \varnothing$ since

$$\lim_{\lambda \to \infty} (y + \lambda v)^T b = y^T b + v^T b \lim_{\lambda \to \infty} \lambda = \infty.$$

Therefore, in any case, we have $X_0 = \varnothing = Y_0$ and either $X = \varnothing$ or $Y = \varnothing$ (or both).   Q.E.D.

Proof of Theorem A.4.1. Either inequalities (A.31) have a solution or they have not. In the first case Lemma A.4.4 states that both problems (A.28) and (A.29) have no optimal solution and at least one of them has no feasible solution. In the second case we obtain by Lemmas A.4.2 and A.4.3 that both problems (A.28) and (A.29) have optimal solutions and the two optimal values are equal.   Q.E.D.

Theorem A.4.1 has related the problems (A.28) and (A.29) in a clear and significant way. It is then useful to introduce an appropriate way to refer to the relation between these two problems. Problem (A.29) is called the *dual* of problem (A.28). In this case problem (A.28) is called the *primal*. It is easily shown that the dual of the dual is the primal. Theorem A.4.1 can then be stated in the following way.

Theorem A.4.2 (Duality Theorem). The primal has optimal solutions if and only if the dual has optimal solutions. The primal and the dual both have feasible solutions if and only if both have optimal solutions and the two optimal values are equal.

By using the Duality Theorem the following result is easily obtained.

Theorem A.4.3 (Equilibrium Theorem). The feasible solution x of the primal and the feasible solution y of the dual are optimal solutions if and only if

$$y^T e_j = 0 \quad \text{whenever} \quad e_j^T A x > e_j^T b, \tag{A.34a}$$

$$e_i^T x = 0 \quad \text{whenever} \quad y^T A e_i < d^T e_i. \tag{A.34b}$$

Proof. Conditions (A.34) are equivalent to

$$y^T A x = y^T b, \tag{A.35a}$$

$$y^T A x = d^T x, \tag{A.35b}$$

since

$$\mathbf{A}\mathbf{x} \geqslant \mathbf{b}, \quad \mathbf{y}^T\mathbf{A} \leqslant \mathbf{d}^T, \quad \mathbf{x} \geqslant \mathbf{0}, \quad \mathbf{y} \geqslant \mathbf{0}.$$

First suppose that conditions (A.35) hold. Then

$$\mathbf{y}^T\mathbf{b} = \mathbf{d}^T\mathbf{x}.$$

Thus vectors $\mathbf{x}$ and $\mathbf{y}$ satisfy inequalities (A.30), that is, statement (b) of Lemma A.4.3, and the "if" part of the theorem is a consequence of Lemma A.4.3. Conversely, if $\mathbf{x}$ and $\mathbf{y}$ are optimal solutions to the primal and to the dual, respectively, then from statement (iii) of Lemma A.4.1 and from the fact that $\mathbf{y}^T\mathbf{b} = \mathbf{d}^T\mathbf{x}$ (because of Theorem A.4.1) it is immediately obtained that

$$\mathbf{d}^T\mathbf{x} = \mathbf{y}^T\mathbf{A}\mathbf{x} = \mathbf{y}^T\mathbf{b}.$$

Q.E.D.

References

Abraham-Frois, G. (ed.) (1984). *L'économie classique. Nouvelles perspectives*. Paris: Economica.

Abraham-Frois, G. (1991). "Corporate Behavior, Valuation Ratio and Macroeconomic Analysis," in Nell and Semmler (1991), pp. 190–204.

Abraham-Frois, G. and Berrebi, E. (1978). "Pluralité des marchandises étalons: existence et construction," *Revue d'Economie Politique*, **88**, pp. 688–712.

Abraham-Frois, G. and Berrebi, E. (1979). *Theory of Value, Prices, and Accumulation*. Cambridge: Cambridge University Press.

Abraham-Frois, G. and Berrebi, E. (1980). *Rentes, rareté, surprofits*. Paris: Economica.

Ahmad, S. (1991). *Capital in Economic Theory: Neo-classical, Cambridge and Chaos*. Aldershot: Edward Elgar.

Akerlof, G. A. and Yellen, J. L. (eds) (1986). *Efficiency Wage Models and the Labour Market*. Cambridge: Cambridge University Press.

Åkerman, J. G. (1923–4). *Realkapital und Kapitalzins*, part I 1923, part II 1924. Stockholm: Centraltryckeriet.

Anderson, J. (1777a). *Observations on the Means of Exciting a Spirit of National Industry*. Edinburgh: C. Elliot.

Anderson, J. (1777b). *An Inquiry into the Nature of the Corn Laws*. Edinburgh: C. Elliot.

Arena, R. and Ravix, J. L. (eds) (1990). *Sraffa trente ans après*. Paris: Presses Universitaires de France.

Aristotle (1908–52). *The Works of Aristotle*, 12 volumes, ed. by W. D. Ross. Oxford: Clarendon Press. Quoted as *Works*.

Arrow, K. J. (1951). "Alternative Proof of the Substitution Theorem for Leontief Models in the General Case," in Koopmans (1951b), pp. 155–64.

Arrow, K. J. (1989). "Von Neumann and the Existence Theorem for General Equilibrium," in Dore, Chakravarty, and Goodwin (1989), pp. 15–28.

Arrow, K. J. and Hahn, F. H. (1971). *General Competitive Analysis*. San Francisco: Holden-Day.

Asimakopulos, A. (1988). *Investment, Employment and Income Distribution*. Oxford: Polity Press.

Asimakopulos, A. (1990). "Keynes and Sraffa: Visions and Perspectives" in Bharadwaj and Schefold (1990), pp. 331–45.

Auspitz, R. and Lieben, R. (1889). *Untersuchungen über die Theorie des Preises*. Leipzig: Duncker und Humblot.

527

Autume, A. d' (1988). "La production jointe: le point de vue de la théorie de l'équilibre général," *Revue Economique*, **39**, pp. 325–47.

Autume, A. d' (1990). "Le rôle intime de la demande dans la production jointe," in Arena and Ravix (1990), pp. 245–56.

Babbage, C. (1986). *On the Economy of Machinery and Manufactures*, 1st edn 1832; reprint of the 4th edn (1835). New York: Kelley.

Bailey, S. (1825). *A Critical Dissertation on the Nature, Measure and Causes of Value*. London; reprint (1967) New York: Kelley.

Baldone, S. (1974). "Il capitale fisso nello schema teorico di Piero Sraffa," *Studi Economici*, **29**, pp. 45–106. English translation titled "Fixed Capital in Sraffa's Theoretical Scheme" in Pasinetti (1980), pp. 88–137.

Baldone, S. (1980). "Misure invariabili del valore e merce tipo," *Ricerche Economiche*, **34**, pp. 272–83.

Baldone, S. (1987). "Il capitale fisso come specie del genere produzione congiunta: un commento a Neri Salvadori," *Economia Politica*, **4**, pp. 247–58.

Balestra, P. and Baranzini, M. (1971). "Some Optimal Aspects in a Two Class Growth Model with a Differentiated Interest Rate," *Kyklos*, **24**, pp. 240–56.

Baranzini, M. (1988). "Un quarto di secolo di dibattito sulla teoria della distribuzione," in Targetti (1988), pp. 205–28.

Baranzini, M. and Harcourt, G. C. (1993a). "Introduction," in Baranzini and Harcourt (1993b), pp. 1–42.

Baranzini, M. and Harcourt, G. C. (eds) (1993b). *The Dynamics of the Wealth of Nations. Growth, Distribution and Structural Change. Essays in Honour of Luigi Pasinetti*. New York: St. Martin Press.

Baranzini, M. and Scazzieri, R. (eds) (1986). *Foundations of Economics*. Oxford: Basil Blackwell.

Basile, L. and Salvadori, N. (1984–5). "Kalecki's Pricing Theory," *Journal of Post Keynesian Economics*, **7**, pp. 249–62.

Baumol, W. J. and Goldfeld, S. M. (eds) (1968). *Precursors in Mathematical Economics*. LSE Series of Reprints of Scarce Works on Political Economy, No. 19. London: London School of Economics.

Becker, G. (1964). *Human Capital*, 2nd edn 1975. New York: Columbia University Press.

Beer, M. (1939). *An Inquiry into Physiocracy*. London: Allen and Unwin.

Bellino, E. (1993). "Continuous Switching of Techniques in Linear Production Models," *Manchester School,* **61,** pp. 185–201.

Bernholz, P. (1971). "Superiority of Roundabout Processes and Positive Rate of Interest: A Simple Model of Capital and Growth," *Kyklos*, **24**, pp. 687–721.

Betancourt, R. R. and Clague, C. K. (1981). *Capital Utilisation – A Theoretical and Empirical Analysis*. Cambridge: Cambridge University Press.

Bewley, T. F. (1972). "Existence of Equilibrium in Economics with Infinitely Many Commodities," *Journal of Economic Theory*, **4**, pp. 514–40.

Bhaduri, A. (1966). "The Concept of the Marginal Productivity of Capital and the Wicksell Effect," *Oxford Economic Papers*, **18**, pp. 284–8.

Bharadwaj, K. (1970). "On the Maximum Number of Switches between Two Production Systems," *Schweizerische Zeitschrift für Volkswirtschaft und Statistik*, **106**, pp. 409–29.

Bharadwaj, K. (1978). *Classical Political Economy and Rise to Dominance of Supply and Demand Theories*. New Delhi: Orient Longman.

Bharadwaj, K. (1983). "On a Controversy over Ricardo's Theory of Distribution," *Cambridge Journal of Economics*, **7**, pp. 11–36.

Bharadwaj, K. and Schefold, B. (eds) (1990). *Essays on Piero Sraffa: Critical Perspectives on the Revival of Classical Theory*. London: Unwin Hyman.

Bidard, Ch. (1984a). "Choix techniques en production jointe," in C. Bidard (1984b), pp. 186–207.

Bidard, Ch. (ed.) (1984b). *La production jointe: nouveaux débats*. Paris: Economica.

Bidard, Ch. (1986). "Is von Neumann Square?" *Zeitschrift für Nationalökonomie*, **46**, pp. 401–19.

Bidard, Ch. (ed.) (1987). *La rente, actualité de l'approche classique*. Paris: Economica.

Bidard, Ch. (1990). "An Algorithmic Theory of Choice of Techniques," *Econometrica*, **58**, pp. 839–59.

Bidard, Ch. (1991). *Prix, reproduction, rareté*. Paris: Dunod.

Bidard, Ch. and Franke, R. (1987). "On the Existence of Long-Term Equilibria in the Two-Class Pasinetti-Morishima Model," *Ricerche Economiche*, **41**, pp. 3–21.

Bidard, Ch. and Hosoda, E. (1987). "On Consumption Baskets in a Generalized von Neumann Model," *International Economic Review*, **28**, pp. 509–19.

Bidard, Ch. and Salvadori, N. (1993). "Duality between Prices and Techniques," mimeo. A revised version is going to be published in the *European Journal of Political Economy*.

Blaug, M. (1987). "Classical economics," *The New Palgrave. A Dictionary of Economics*, edited by J. Eatwell, M. Milgate, and P. Newman, vol. 1, pp. 434–45. London: Macmillan.

Bliss, C. J. (1975). *Capital Theory and the Distribution of Income*. Amsterdam: North-Holland.

Bliss, C. J. (1990). "Alfred Marshall and the Theory of Capital," in J. K. Whitaker (ed.), *Centenary Essays on Alfred Marshall*. Cambridge: Cambridge University Press, pp. 223–41.

Boggio, L. (1987). "Centre of Gravitation," *The New Palgrave. A Dictionary of Economics*, edited by J. Eatwell, M. Milgate, and P. Newman, vol. 1, pp. 392–4. London: Macmillan.

Boggio, L. (1992). "Production Prices and Dynamic Stability," *The Manchester School*, **60**, pp. 264–94.

Böhm-Bawerk, E. v. (1889). *Kapital und Kapitalzins. Zweite Abteilung: Positive Theorie des Kapitales*. Innsbruck: Wagner. 4th edn 1921, Jena: Fischer. Translation of the 1st edn, see Böhm-Bawerk (1891); of the 4th edn, see Böhm-Bawerk (1959).

Böhm-Bawerk, E. v. (1891). *The Positive Theory of Capital*, London: Macmillan. Translation of the 1st edn of Böhm-Bawerk (1889).

Böhm-Bawerk, E. v. (1906–7). "Capital and Interest Once More," *Quarterly Journal of Economics*, **21**; part I, November 1906, pp. 1–21; part II, April 1907, pp. 247–82.

Böhm-Bawerk, E. v. (1959). *Capital and Interest*, two vols. Translation of the 4th edn of Böhm-Bawerk (1889). South Holland, Illinois: Libertarian Press.

Bortkiewicz, L. v. (1906–7). "Wertrechnung und Preisrechnung im Marxschen System," *Archiv für Sozialwissenschaft und Sozialpolitik*, **23** (1906), pp. 1–50, **25** (1907), pp. 10–51 and 445–88; in the text referred to as essays I, II, and III.

Bortkiewicz, L. v. (1907). "Zur Berichtigung der grundlegenden theoretischen Konstruktion von Marx im 3. Band des 'Kapital'," *Jahrbücher für Nationalökonomie und Statistik*, **34**, pp. 319–35.

Bortkiewicz, L. v. (1921). "Objektivismus und Subjektivismus in der Werttheorie," *Ekonomisk Tidskrift*, **21**, pp. 1–22.

Bortkiewicz, L. v. (1949). "On the Correction of Marx's Fundamental Theoretical Construction in the 'Third Volume of Capital'," in P. M. Sweezy (ed.), *Karl Marx and the Close of His System*. New York: Kelley, pp. 199–221. Translation of Bortkiewicz (1907).

Bortkiewicz, L. v. (1952). "Value and Price in the Marxian System," *International Economic Papers*, **2**, pp. 5–60. English translation of Bortkiewicz (1906–7 II and III).

Bowles, S. and Gintis, H. (1977). "The Marxian Theory of Value and Heterogeneous Labour: A Critique and Reformulation," *Cambridge Journal of Economics*, 1, pp. 173–92.

Bowles, S. and Gintis, H. (1978). "Professor Morishima on Heterogeneous Labour and Marxian Value Theory," *Cambridge Journal of Economics*, 2, pp. 311–14.

Bródy, A. (1970). *Proportions, Prices and Planning*. Amsterdam and London: North-Holland.

Bruckmann, G. and Weber, W. (eds) (1971). *Contributions to the von Neumann Growth Model*, supplement to *Zeitschrift für Nationalökonomie*. New York and Vienna: Springer.

Bruno, M. (1969). "Fundamental Duality Relations in the Pure Theory of Capital and Growth," *Review of Economic Studies*, 36, pp. 39–53.

Bruno, M., Burmeister, E., and Sheshinski, E. (1966). "The Nature and Implications of the Reswitching of Techniques," *Quarterly Journal of Economics*, 80, pp. 526–53.

Burmeister, E. (1974). "Synthesizing the Neo-Austrian and Alternative Approaches to Capital Theory: A Survey," *Journal of Economic Literature*, 12, pp. 413–56.

Burmeister, E. (1980a). *Capital Theory and Dynamics*. Cambridge: Cambridge University Press.

Burmeister, E. (1980b). "Critical Observations on the Labor Theory of Value and Sraffa's Standard Commodity," in L. R. Klein, M. Nerlove, and Sho Chieh Tsiang (eds), *Quantitative Economics and Development: Essays in Memory of Ta-Chung Lin*. New York: Academic Press, pp. 81–103.

Burmeister, E. (1984). "Sraffa, Labor Theories of Value, and the Economics of Real Wage Rate Determination," *Journal of Political Economy*, 92, pp. 508–26.

Burmeister, E. and Kuga, K. (1970). "The Factor-Price Frontier, Duality and Joint Production," *Review of Economic Studies*, 37, pp. 11–19.

Burmeister, E. and Turnovsky, S. J. (1972). "Capital Deepening Response in an Economy with Heterogeneous Capital Goods," *American Economic Review*, 65, pp. 842–53.

Caminati, M. (1981). "The Theory of Interest in the Classical Economists," *Metroeconomica*, 33, pp. 79–104.

Caminati, M. and Petri, F. (eds) (1990). *Convergence to Long-Period Positions*. Special issue of *Political Economy. Studies in the Surplus Approach*, 6.

Campanelli, G. (1982). "W. Whewell's Contribution to Economic Analysis: The First Mathematical Formulation of Fixed Capital in Ricardo's System," *The Manchester School*, 50, pp. 248–65.

Cannan, E. (1917). *A History of the Theories of Production and Distribution in English Political Economy from 1776–1848*, 3rd edn (1st edn 1893), London: King.

Cantillon, R. (1755). *Essai sur la nature du commerce en général*, edited with an English translation by H. Higgs. London 1931: Macmillan.

Caravale, G. A. and Tosato, D. A. (1980). *Ricardo and the Theory of Value, Distribution and Growth*. London: Routledge and Kegan Paul.

Cartelier, J. (1976). *Surproduit et réproduction. La formation de l'économie politique classique*, Paris: Maspero.

Casarosa, C. (1974). "The Ricardian Theory of Distribution and Economic Growth," *Rivista di Politica Economica*, 64, pp. 959–1015.

Casarosa, C. (1977). "Il problema del capitale fisso nel quadro della teoria ricardiana della distribuzione: la soluzione di Bortkiewicz," *Studi Economici*, 32, pp. 79–95.

Casarosa, C. (1978). "A New Formulation of the Ricardian System," *Oxford Economic Papers*, 30, pp. 38–63.

Cassel, G. (1918). *Theoretische Sozialökonomie*, Leipzig: Deichert.

Cassel, G. (1932). *The Theory of Social Economy*, revised English translation of the 5th German edition of Cassel (1918) by L. Barron (1932), New York: Harcourt Brace. Reprint 1967, New York: Kelley.

Champernowne, D. G. (1945). "A Note on J. v. Neumann's Article on 'A Model of Economic Equilibrium'," *Review of Economic Studies*, **13**, pp. 10–18.

Champernowne, D. G. and Kahn, R. F. (1953–4). "The Value of Invested Capital," *Review of Economic Studies*, **21**, pp. 107–111. Reprinted in Robinson (1956).

Charasoff, G. v. (1909). *Karl Marx über menschliche und kapitalistische Wirtschaft*. Berlin: H. Bondy.

Charasoff, G. v. (1910). *Das System des Marxismus: Darstellung und Kritik*. Berlin: H. Bondy.

Chiang, A. C. (1973). "A Simple Generalization of the Kaldor-Pasinetti Theory of Profit Rate and Income Distribution," *Economica*, **40**, pp. 311–13.

Clark, C. W. (1976). *Mathematical Bioeconomics*. New York: John Wiley and Sons.

Clark, J. B. (1899). *The Distribution of Wealth. A Theory of Wages, Interest and Profits*. New York: Macmillan. Reprint 1965, New York: Kelley.

Clark, J. B. (1907). "Concerning the Nature of Capital: A Reply," *Quarterly Journal of Economics*, **21**, pp. 351–70.

Cobb, C. W. and Douglas, P. H. (1928). "A Theory of Production," *American Economic Review, Supplement*, **18**, pp. 139–65.

Colonna, M., Hagemann, H., and Hamonda, O. (eds) (1994). *Capitalism, Socialism, and Knowledge*. Aldershot: Edward Elgar.

Conrad, J. M. and Clark, C. W. (1987). *Natural Resource Economics. Notes and Problems*. Cambridge: Cambridge University Press.

Craven, J. (1979). "Efficiency Curves in the Theory of Capital: A Synthesis," in Patterson and Schott (1979), pp. 76–96.

Currie, M. and Steedman, I. (1990). *Wrestling with Time. Problems in Economic Theory*. Manchester: Manchester University Press.

D'Agata, A. (1981–2). *La teoria ricardiana della rendita fondiaria dopo Sraffa*. Laurea Thesis, University of Catania.

D'Agata, A. (1983a). "The Existence and Uniqueness of Cost-Minimizing Systems in Intensive Rent Theory," *Metroeconomica*, **35**, pp. 147–58.

D'Agata, A. (1983b). "The Existence and Uniqueness of Cost-Minimizing Systems in External Intensive Rent Theory," Catania, mimeo.

D'Agata, A. (1984). "Molteplicità di merci agricole e rendita differenziale estensiva," *Ricerche Economiche*, **38**, pp. 87–94.

D'Agata, A. (1985). "Produzione congiunta e ordine di fertilità," *Economia Politica*, **2**, pp. 245–8.

Dana, R. A., Florenzano, M., Le Van, C., and Lévy, D. (1989). "Asymptotic Properties of a Leontief Economy," *Journal of Economic Dynamics and Control*, **13**, pp. 553–68.

Dantzig, G. B. and Manne, A. S. (1974). "A Complementarity Algorithm for an Optimal Capital Path with Invariant Proportions," *Journal of Economic Theory*, **9**, pp. 312–23.

Dasgupta, P. S. and Heal, G. M. (1979). *Economic Theory and Exhaustible Resources*. Cambridge: Cambridge University Press.

Debreu, G. (1959). *Theory of Value: An Axiomatic Analysis of Economic Equilibrium*. New York: John Wiley and Sons.

Denicolò, V. (1982). "Molteplicità di merci agricole e rendita differenziale in uno schema teorico neo-ricardiano," *Ricerche Economiche*, **36**, pp. 172–98.

De Vivo, G. (1985). "Robert Torrens and Ricardo's 'Corn-Ratio' Theory of Profits," *Cambridge Journal of Economics*, **9**, pp. 89–92.

De Vivo, G. (1986). "Torrens on Value and Distribution," *Contributions to Political Economy*, **5**, pp. 23–36.

De Vivo, G. (1987). "David Ricardo," *The New Palgrave. A Dictionary of Economics*, edited by J. Eatwell, M. Milgate, and P. Newman, vol. 4, pp. 183–98. London: Macmillan.

De Roover, R. (1958). "The Concept of the Just Price," *Journal of Economic History*, **18**, pp. 418–34.

Diewert, W. E. (1982). "Duality Approaches to Microeconomic Theory," in K. J. Arrow and M. D. Intriligator (eds), *Handbook of Mathematical Economics*, vol. II, pp. 535–99. Amsterdam: North-Holland.

D'Ippolito, G. (1987). "Probabilità di perverso comportamento del capitale al variare del saggio dei profitti: il modello embrionale a due settori," *Note Economiche*, **2**, pp. 5–37.

D'Ippolito, G. (1989). "Delimitazione dell'area dei casi di comportamento perverso del capitale in un punto di mutamento della tecnica," in L. L. Pasinetti (ed.), *Aspetti controversi della teoria del valore*. Bologna: Il Mulino, pp. 191–7.

Dmitriev, V. K. (1968). *Essais économiques. Esquisse de synthèse organique de la théorie de la valeur-travail et de la théorie de l'utilité marginale*, edited with an introduction by A. Zauberman. Paris: Editions du CNRS.

Dmitriev, V. K. (1974). *Economic Essays on Value, Competition and Utility*, English translation of a collection of Dmitriev's essays published in 1904 in Russian, edited by D. M. Nuti. Cambridge: Cambridge University Press. Dmitriev's essay on Ricardo's theory of value was originally published in 1898.

Dobb, M. (1973). *Theories of Value and Distribution since A. Smith: Ideology and Economic Theory*. Cambridge: Cambridge University Press.

Dore, M. (1989). "The Legacy of von Neumann," in Dore, Chakravarty, and Goodwin (1989), pp. 89–99.

Dore, M., Chakravarty, S., and Goodwin, R. (eds) (1989). *John von Neumann and Modern Economics*. Oxford: Clarendon Press.

Dorfman, R. (1959). "Waiting and the Period of Production," *Quarterly Journal of Economics*, **73**, pp. 351–72.

Dorfman, R. (1987). "Leontief, Wassily," *The New Palgrave. A Dictionary of Economics*, edited by J. Eatwell, M. Milgate, and P. Newman, vol. 3, pp. 164–6. London: Macmillan.

Dorfman, R., Samuelson, P. A., and Solow, R. M. (1958). *Linear Programming and Economic Analysis*. New York, Toronto and London: McGraw-Hill.

Duménil, G. and Lévy, D. (1984). "The Unifying Formalism of Domination: Value, Price, Distribution and Growth in Joint Production," *Zeitschrift für Nationalökonomie*, **44**, pp. 349–71.

Duménil, G. and Lévy, D. (1985). "The Classicals and the Neo-Classicals: A Rejoinder to Frank Hahn," *Cambridge Journal of Economics*, **9**, pp. 327–45.

Dutt, A. K. (1984). "Stagnation, Income Distribution and Monopoly Power," *Cambridge Journal of Economics*, **8**, pp. 25–40.

Dutt, A. K. (1990). *Growth, Distribution and Uneven Development*. Cambridge: Cambridge University Press.

Eatwell, J. L. (1975). "The Interpretation of Ricardo's *Essay on Profits*," *Economica*, **42**, pp. 182–7.

Eatwell, J. L. (1987). "Walras's Theory of Capital," *The New Palgrave. A Dictionary of Economics*, edited by J. Eatwell, M. Milgate, and P. Newman, vol. 4, pp. 868–72. London: Macmillan.

Eatwell, J. L., Milgate, M., and Newman, P. (eds) (1990). *Capital Theory*. London: Macmillan.

Eatwell, J. L. and Panico, C. (1987). "Sraffa, Piero," *The New Palgrave. A Dictionary of Economics*, edited by J. Eatwell, M. Milgate, and P. Newman, vol. 4, pp. 445–52. London: Macmillan.

Edelberg, V. (1933). "The Ricardian Theory of Profits," *Economica*, **13**, pp. 51–74.

Egidi, M. and Gilibert, G. (1984). "La teoria oggettiva dei prezzi," *Economia Politica*, **1**, pp. 43–61. An English version of the paper titled "The Objective Theory of Prices" was published in *Political Economy. Studies in the Surplus Approach*, **5** (1989), pp. 59–74.

Eltis, W. (1984). *The Classical Theory of Economic Growth.* London: Macmillan.

Erreygers, G. (1990). *Terre, rente et choix de techniques. Une étude sur la théorie néo-ricardienne,* two vols, mimeo. Université de Paris-X-Nanterre.

Erreygers, G. (1994). "Heterogeneous Labour, Scarcity and Choice of Techniques," *Metroeconomica,* **45,** pp. 47–66.

Faber, M. (1979). *Introduction to Modern Austrian Capital Theory.* Berlin: Springer.

Faccarello, G. (1982). "Sraffa *versus* Ricardo: The Historical Irrelevance of the 'Corn-Profit' Model," *Economy and Society,* **11,** pp. 122–37.

Faccarello, G. (1983). *Travail, valeur et prix. Une critique de la théorie de la valeur.* Paris: Éditions anthropos.

Fazi, E. and Salvadori, N. (1981). "The Existence of a Two-Class Economy in the Kaldor Model of Growth and Distribution," *Kyklos,* **34,** pp. 582–92.

Fazi, E. and Salvadori, N. (1985). "The Existence of a Two-Class Economy in a General Cambridge Model of Growth and Distribution," *Cambridge Journal of Economics,* **9,** pp. 155–64.

Feiwel, G. (1975). *The Intellectual Capital of Michal Kalecki.* Knoxville: University of Tennessee Press.

Ferguson, C. E. (1969). *The Neo-Classical Theory of Production and Distribution.* Cambridge: Cambridge University Press.

Filippini, C. (1977). "Positività dei prezzi e produzione congiunta," *Giornale degli Economisti e Annali di Economia,* **36,** pp. 91–9.

Filippini, C. and Filippini, L. (1982). "Two Theorems on Joint Production," *Economic Journal,* **92,** pp. 386–90.

Filippini, L., Scanlon, J., and Tarantelli, E. (1983). "Towards a Linear Model of Non-Homogeneous Labour," in P. Streeten and H. Maier (eds), *Human Resources, Employment and Development, vol. 2: Concepts, Measurement and Long-Run Perspective.* London: Macmillan, pp. 91–105.

Fisher, A. C. (1981). *Resource and Environmental Economics.* Cambridge: Cambridge University Press.

Fisher, I. (1930). *The Theory of Interest.* New York: Macmillan.

Franke, R. (1985). "On the Upper- and Lower-Bounds of Workers' Propensity to Save in a Two-Class Pasinetti Economy," *Australian Economic Papers,* **24,** pp. 271–7.

Franke, R. (1986). "Some Problems Concerning the Notion of Cost-Minimizing Systems in the Framework of Joint Production," *The Manchester School,* **52,** pp. 298–307.

Franklin, J. (1980). *Methods of Mathematical Economics. Linear and Nonlinear Programming, Fixed-Point Theorems.* New York, Heidelberg, Berlin: Springer.

Freni, G. (1991). "Capitale tecnico nei modelli dinamici ricardiani," *Studi Economici,* **44,** pp. 141–59.

Freni, G. (1993). *Sentieri di equilibrio dinamico del livello di produzione e del prezzo di una merce non base che entra nella propria riproduzione.* Istituto Universitario Navale, Naples: mimeo.

Fujimoto, T. (1975). "Duality and the Uniqueness of Growth Equilibrium," *International Economic Review,* **16,** pp. 781–91.

Fujimoto, T. (1983). "Inventions and Technical Change: A Curiosum," *The Manchester School,* **51,** pp. 16–20.

Fullarton, J. (1845). *On the Regulation of Currencies,* 2nd edition. London: John Murray.

Fuss, M. and McFadden, D. (eds) (1978). *Production Economics: A Dual Approach to Theory and Applications.* Amsterdam: North-Holland.

Gale, D. (1960). *The Theory of Linear Economic Models.* New York: McGraw-Hill.

Gantmacher, F. R. (1959). *The Theory of Matrices.* New York: Chelsea.

Garegnani, P. (1960). *Il capitale nelle teorie della distribuzione.* Milan: Giuffrè.

Garegnani, P. (1966). "Switching of Techniques," *Quarterly Journal of Economics*, **80**, pp. 554–67.

Garegnani, P. (1970). "Heterogeneous Capital, the Production Function and the Theory of Distribution," *Review of Economic Studies*, **37**, 407–36.

Garegnani, P. (1973). "Nota Matematica," published as an appendix to the Italian edition of "Beni capitali eterogenei, la funzione della produzione e la teoria della distribuzione" in P. Sylos Labini (ed.), *Prezzi Relativi e Distribuzione del Reddito*. Turin: Boringhieri. (This mathematical note was mentioned but not published in the original English edition of the paper; cf. Garegnani, 1970).

Garegnani, P. (1979). "Notes on Consumption, Investment, and Effective Demand, II," *Cambridge Journal of Economics*, **3**, pp. 63–82.

Garegnani, P. (1982). "On Hollander's Interpretation of Ricardo's Early Theory of Profits," *Cambridge Journal of Economics*, **6**, pp. 65–77.

Garegnani, P. (1983a). "Ricardo's Early Theory of Profit and Its 'Rational Foundation': A Reply to Professor Hollander," *Cambridge Journal of Economics*, **7**, pp. 175–8.

Garegnani, P. (1983b). "The Classical Theory of Wages and the Role of Demand Schedules in the Determination of Relative Prices," *American Economic Review, Papers and Proceedings*, **73**, pp. 309–13.

Garegnani, P. (1984). "Value and Distribution in the Classical Economists and Marx," *Oxford Economic Papers*, **36**, pp. 291–325.

Garegnani, P. (1987). "Surplus Approach to Value and Distribution," *The New Palgrave. A Dictionary of Economics*, edited by J. Eatwell, M. Milgate, and P. Newman, vol. 4, pp. 560–74. London: Macmillan.

Garegnani, P. (1990a). "Quantity of Capital," in Eatwell, Milgate, and Newman (1990), pp. 1–78.

Garegnani, P. (1990b). "On Some Supposed Obstacles to the Tendency of Market Prices Towards Natural Prices," in Caminati and Petri (1990), pp. 329–59.

Garegnani, P. (1990c). "Sraffa: Classical versus Marginalist Analysis," in Bharadwaj and Schefold (1990), pp. 112–41.

Garegnani, P. (1992). "Some Notes for an Analysis of Accumulation," in Halevi, Laibman and Nell (1992), pp. 47–71.

Garegnani, P. (1993). "Sraffa Lecture," Rome, mimeo.

Geanakoplos, J. (1987). "Arrow–Debreu Model of General Equilibrium," *The New Palgrave. A Dictionary of Economics*, edited by J. Eatwell, M. Milgate, and P. Newman, vol. 1, pp. 116–24. London: Macmillan.

Gehrke, C. (1990). "Wachstumstheoretische Vorstellungen bei Adam Smith," in Kurz (1990b), pp. 129–50.

Gehrke, C. and Lager, C. (1993). "Environmental Taxes, Relative Prices and Choice of Technique in a Linear Model of Production," *Metroeconomica*, forthcoming.

Georgescu-Roegen, N. (1951). "Some Properties of a Generalized Leontief Model," in Koopmans (1951b), pp. 116–31.

Georgescu-Roegen, N. (1971). *The Entropy Law and the Economic Process*. Cambridge, Mass: Harvard University Press.

Georgescu-Roegen, N. (1976). *Energy and Economic Myths: Institutional and Analytical Economic Essays*. Oxford: Pergamon Press.

Gibson, B. (1984). "Profit and Rent in a Classical Theory of Exhaustible and Renewable Resources," *Zeitschrift für Nationalökonomie*, **44**, pp. 131–49.

Gilbart, J. W. (1834). *The History and Principles of Banking*. London: Longman.

Gilibert, G. (1981). "Isnard, Cournot, Walras, Leontief. Evoluzione di un modello," *Annali della Fondazione Luigi Einaudi*, **XV**, pp. 129–53.

Gilibert, G. (1987). "Circular Flow," *The New Palgrave. A Dictionary of Economics*, edited by J. Eatwell, M. Milgate, and P. Newman, vol. 1, pp. 424–26. London: Macmillan.

Gilibert, G. (1991). "La scuola russo-tedesca di economia matematica e la dottrina del flusso circolare," in G. Beccatini (ed.), *Le scuole economiche*, Turin: Utet, pp. 387–402.

Giorgi, G. and Magnani, U. (1978). "Problemi aperti nella teoria dei modelli multisettoriali di produzione congiunta," *Rivista Internazionale di Scienze Sociali*, **86**, pp. 435–68.

Goodwin, R. M. (1982). *Essays in Economic Dynamics*. London: Macmillan.

Goodwin, R. M. (1986). "Swinging along the Turnpike with von Neumann and Sraffa," *Cambridge Journal of Economics*, **10**, pp. 203–10.

Goodwin, R. M. and Punzo, L. F. (1987). *The Dynamics of a Capitalist Economy. A Multi-Sectoral Approach*. Boulder, Colorado: Westview Press.

Gray, L. C. (1913). "The Economic Possibilities of Conservation," *Quarterly Journal of Economics*, **27**, pp. 497–519.

Gray, L. C. (1914). "Rent under the Assumption of Exhaustibility," *Quarterly Journal of Economics*, **28**, pp. 466–89.

Groenewegen, P. D. (1969). "Turgot and Adam Smith," *Scottish Journal of Political Economy*, **16**, pp. 271–87.

Groenewegen, P. D. (1971). "A Re-interpretation of Turgot's Theory of Capital and Interest," *Economic Journal*, **81**, pp. 327–40.

Groenewegen, P. D. (1977). *The Economics of A. R. J. Turgot*. The Hague: Martinus Nijhoff.

Guichard, J. P. (1979). *Rente foncière et dynamique sociale*. Université de Nice, mimeo.

Guichard, J. P. (1982). "La rente différentielle intensive, expression d'un processus d'intensification de cultures," in R. Arena et al. (eds), *Etudes d'économie classique et néoricardienne*. Paris: PUF, pp. 115–38.

Gupta, K. L. (1976). "Differentiated Interest Rate and Kaldor–Pasinetti Paradoxes," *Kyklos*, **29**, pp. 310–14.

Gupta, K. L. (1977). "On the Existence of a Two-Class Economy in the Kaldor and Pasinetti Models of Growth and Distribution," *Jahrbücher für Nationalökonomie und Statistik*, **192**, pp. 68–72.

Hadley, G. (1961). *Linear Algebra*. Reading, Mass: Addison-Wesley.

Hagemann, H. and Kurz, H. D. (1976). "The Return of the Same Truncation Period and Reswitching of Techniques in Neo-Austrian and More General Models," *Kyklos*, **29**, 678–708.

Hahn, F. H. (1972). *The Share of Wages in the National Income: An Enquiry into the Theory of Distribution*. London: Weidenfeld and Nicolson.

Hahn, F. H. (1975). "Revival of Political Economy: The Wrong Issues and the Wrong Argument," *Economic Record*, **51**, pp. 360–4.

Hahn, F. H. (1982). "The Neo-Ricardians," *Cambridge Journal of Economics*, **6**, pp. 353–74.

Halevi, J., Laibman, D. and Nell, E. J. (eds) (1992). *Beyond the Steady State*. London: Macmillan.

Harcourt, G. C. (1969). "Some Cambridge Controversies in the Theory of Capital," *Journal of Economic Literature*, **7**, pp. 369–405.

Harcourt, G. C. (1972). *Some Cambridge Controversies in the Theory of Capital*. Cambridge: Cambridge University Press.

Harcourt, G. C. and Laing, N. F. (eds) (1971). *Capital and Growth*. Harmondsworth: Penguin Books.

Harris, D. J. (1973). "Capital, Distribution and the Aggregate Production Function," *American Economic Review*, **63**, pp. 100–13.

Harrod, R. F. (1961). "Production of Commodities," *Economic Journal*, **71**, pp. 783–7.

Hawkins, D. (1948). "Some Conditions of Macroeconomic Stability," *Econometrica*, **16**, pp. 309–22.

Hawkins, D. and Simon, H. A. (1949). "Note: Some Conditions of Macroeconomic Stability," *Econometrica*, **17**, pp. 245–48.

Hayek, F. A. v. (1928). "Das intertemporale Gleichgewichtssystem der Preise und die Bewegungen des 'Geldwertes'," *Weltwirtschaftliches Archiv*, **2**, pp. 33–76. Translated as "Intertemporal Price Equilibrium and Movements in the Value of Money," in Hayek (1984).

Hayek, F. A. v. (1931). *Prices and Production*. London: Routledge and Kegan Paul.

Hayek, F. A. v. (1941). *The Pure Theory of Capital*. London: Routledge and Kegan Paul.

Hayek, F. A. v. (1984). *Money, Capital and Fluctuations. Early Essays*, ed. by R. McCloughry. London: Routledge and Kegan Paul.

Henderson, J. P. (1985). "The Whewell Group of Mathematical Economists," *The Manchester School*, **53**, pp. 404–31.

Hennings, K. H. (1972). *The Austrian Theory of Value and Capital. Studies in the Life and Work of Eugen von Böhm-Bawerk*, Ph.D. thesis, Oxford. Forthcoming Aldershot: Edward Elgar.

Hermann, F. v. (1832). *Staatswirthschaftliche Untersuchungen*. Munich: Fleischmann.

Hicks, J. R. (1932). *The Theory of Wages*. London: Macmillan.

Hicks, J. R. (1933). "Gleichgewicht und Konjunktur," *Zeitschrift für Nationalökonomie*, **4**, pp. 441–55. Translated as "Equilibrium and the Trade Cycle," *Economic Enquiry*, **18** (1980), pp. 523–34.

Hicks, J. R. (1946). *Value and Capital*, 1st edn 1939. Oxford: Clarendon Press.

Hicks, J. R. (1965). *Capital and Growth*. Oxford: Clarendon Press.

Hicks, J. R. (1970). "A Neo-Austrian Growth Theory," *Economic Journal*, **80**, pp. 257–81.

Hicks, J. R. (1973). *Capital and Time: A Neo-Austrian Theory*. Oxford: Oxford University Press.

Hicks, J. R. (1982). *Collected Essays on Economic Theory*, vol. III: *Money, Interest and Wages*. Oxford: Basil Blackwell.

Hicks, J. R. and Weber, W. (eds) (1973). *Carl Menger and the Austrian School of Economics*. Oxford: Oxford University Press.

Hoffman, K. and Kunze, R. (1971). *Linear Algebra*. Englewood Cliffs (New Jersey): Prentice-Hall.

Hollander, S. (1973a). "Ricardo's Analysis of the Profit Rate, 1813–15," *Economica*, **11**, pp. 260–82.

Hollander, S. (1973b). *The Economics of Adam Smith*. Toronto: University of Toronto Press.

Hollander, S. (1975). "Ricardo and the Corn Profit Model: Reply to Eatwell," *Economica*, **13**, pp. 188–202.

Hollander, S. (1979). *The Economics of David Ricardo*. Toronto: University of Toronto Press.

Hollander, S. (1982). "A Reply to Roncaglia," *Journal of Post Keynesian Economics*, **4**, pp. 360–72.

Hollander, S. (1983). "Professor Garegnani's Defence of Sraffa on the Material Rate of Profit," *Cambridge Journal of Economics*, **7**, pp. 167–74.

Hollander, S. (1986). "Comment on Peach," *Economic Journal*, **96**, pp. 1091–7.

Hollander, S. (1993). "Malthus and the Corn-Profit Model." Toronto, mimeo.

Hosoda, E. (1990). "The Relationship between per Capita Consumption and the Growth Rate: A Note," *Cambridge Journal of Economics*, **14**, pp. 331–8.

Hotelling, H. (1931). "The Economics of Exhaustible Resources," *Journal of Political Economy*, **39**, pp. 137–75.

Howard, M. C. (1980). "Austrian Capital Theory: An Evaluation in Terms of Piero Sraffa's *Production of Commodities by Means of Commodities*," *Metroeconomica*, **32**, pp. 1–24.

Huth, Th. (1989). *Kapital und Gleichgewicht. Zur Kontroverse zwischen neoklassischer und neoricardianischer Theorie des allgemeinen Gleichgewichts*. Marburg: Metropolis.

INED (1958). *François Quesnay et la physiocratie*, 2 vols. Paris: Institut Nationale d'Etudes Démographiques.

Jaffé, W. (1971). "Reflections on the Importance of Léon Walras," in A. Heertje et al. (eds), *Schaarste en Welvaart. Festschrift in Honour of P. Hennipman*. Amsterdam: Stenfert Kroese, pp. 87–107. Reprinted in Walker (1983).

Jeck, A. (1990). "Lohn, Preis und Profit im *Wealth of Nations*," in Kurz (1990b), pp. 173–99.

Jeck, A. and Kurz, H. D. (1983). "David Ricardo: Ansichten zur Maschinerie," in H. Hagemann and P. Kalmbach (eds), *Technischer Fortschritt und Arbeitslosigkeit*. Frankfurt: Campus, pp. 38–166.

Jevons, W. S. (1865). *The Coal Question: An Inquiry Concerning the Progress of the Nation, and the Probable Exhaustion of Our Coal Mines*. London: Macmillan. 3rd edn, revised and edited by A.W. Flux, 1906.

Jevons, W. S. (1871). *The Theory of Political Economy*, London: Macmillan. Reprint (1965) New York: Kelley.

Jones, H. G. (1975). *An Introduction to Modern Theories of Economic Growth*. London: Nelson.

Joplin, T. (1823). *Outlines of a System of Political Economy*. London: Baldwin, Cradock and Joy.

Joplin, T. (1832). *An Analysis and History of the Currency Question*. London: James Ridgway.

Kaldor, N. (1937). "Annual Survey of Economic Theory: The Recent Controversy on the Theory of Capital," *Econometrica*, **5**, pp. 201–33.

Kaldor, N. (1939). "Speculation and Economic Stability," *Review of Economic Studies*, **6**, pp. 1–27.

Kaldor, N. (1955–6). "Alternative Theories of Distribution," *Review of Economic Studies*, **23**, pp. 83–100.

Kaldor, N. (1958). "Monetary Policy, Economic Stability and Growth. A Memorandum Submitted to the Committee on the Working of the Monetary System," published in *Essays on Economic Policy I*, pp. 128–53. London: Duckworth, 1964.

Kaldor, N. (1960). "Keynes' Theory of Own Rates of Interest," *Essays on Economic Stability and Growth*, pp. 59–74. London: Duckworth.

Kaldor, N. (1961). "Capital Accumulation and Economic Growth," in Lutz and Hague (1961), pp. 177–222.

Kaldor, N. (1966). "Marginal Productivity and the Macro-Economic Theories of Distribution," *Review of Economic Studies*, **33**, pp. 309–19.

Kaldor, N. (1978). "Introduction," in N. Kaldor, *Further Essays on Economic Theory*, Volume 5 of *Collected Economic Essays*, pp. vii–xxix. London: Duckworth.

Kaldor, N. (1989). "John von Neumann: a Personal Recollection," Foreword in Dore, Chakravarty, and Goodwin (1989), pp. vii–xi.

Kalecki, M. (1935). "A Theory of the Business Cycle," *Review of Economic Studies*, **4**, pp. 77–97.

Kalecki, M. (1938), *Essays in the Theory of Economic Fluctuation*. London: Allen and Unwin.

Kalecki, M. (1942), "A Theory of Profit," *Economic Journal*, **52**, pp. 258–66.

Kalecki, M. (1943). *Studies in Economic Dynamics*. London: Allen and Unwin.

Kalecki, M. (1954). *Theory of Economic Dynamics; An Essay on Cyclical and Long-run Changes in Capitalist Economy*. London: Allen and Unwin.

Kalecki, M. (1971). *Selected Essays on the Dynamics of the Capitalist Economy 1933–1970*. Cambridge: Cambridge University Press.

Kalmbach, P. and Kurz, H. D. (1986a). "Über einige Mißverständnisse des neuklassischen und anderer Ansätze: eine Erwiderung," in E. Hödl and G. Müller (eds), *Die Neoklassik und ihre Kritik. Diskussionsband zu "Ökonomie und Gesellschaft," Jahrbuch 1*, Frankfurt and New York: Campus, pp. 244–78.

Kalmbach, P. and Kurz, H. D. (1986b). "Economic Dynamics and Innovation: Ricardo, Marx and Schumpeter on Technological Change and Unemployment," in H.-J. Wagener and J. W. Drukker (eds), *The Economic Law of Motion of Modern Society*. Cambridge: Cambridge University Press, pp. 71–92.

Kemeny, J. G., Morgenstern, O. and Thompson, G. L. (1956). "A Generalization of von Neumann's Model of an Expanding Economy," *Econometrica*, **24**, pp. 115–35.

Keynes, J. M. (1971–88). *The Collected Writings of John Maynard Keynes*, vols 1–30, managing eds A. Robinson and D. Moggridge, London: Macmillan. In the text referred to as *CW*, volume number, and page number.

Knight, F. (1944). "Diminishing Returns from Investment," *Journal of Political Economy*, **52**, pp. 26–47.

Koopmans, T. C. (1951a). "Alternative Proof of the Substitution Theorem for Leontief Models in the Case of Three Industries," in Koopmans (1951b), pp. 147–54.

Koopmans, T. C. (ed.) (1951b). *Activity Analysis of Production and Allocation*. New York: John Wiley and Sons.

Koopmans, T. C. (1957). *Three Essays on the State of Economic Science*. New York: McGraw-Hill.

Koopmans, T. C. (1974). Contribution to "General Discussion on Past and Future of the von Neumann Model," in Łos and Łos (1974), pp. 3–4.

Krause, U. (1980). "Abstract Labour in General Joint Systems," *Metroeconomica*, **32**, pp. 115–35.

Krause, U. (1981). "Heterogeneous Labour and the Fundamental Marxian Theorem," *Review of Economic Studies*, **68**, pp. 173–8.

Krause, U. (1982). *Money and Abstract Labour. On the Analytical Foundations of Political Economy*. London: Verso.

Krause, U. (1986). "Perron's Stability Theorem for Non-Linear Mappings," *Journal of Mathematical Economics*, **15**, pp. 275–82.

Kregel, J. A. (ed.) (1983). *Distribution, Effective Demand and International Economic Relations*, London: Macmillan.

Krelle, W. (1977). "Basic Facts in Capital Theory. Some Lessons from the Controversy in Capital Theory," *Révue d'Economie Politique*, **87**, pp. 282–329.

Krelle, W. (1992). Review article of P. Garegnani, *Kapital, Einkommensverteilung und effektive Nachfrage*, ed. by H. D. Kurz in collaboration with C. Rühl, Marburg 1989: Metropolis, in *Zeitschrift für Wirtschafts- und Sozialwissenschaften*, **112**, pp. 75–80.

Kurz, H. D. (1976). "Adam Smiths Komponententheorie der relativen Preise und ihre Kritik," *Zeitschrift für die gesamte Staatswissenschaft*, **132**, pp. 691–709.

Kurz, H. D. (1977). *Zur neoricardianischen Theorie des Allgemeinen Gleichgewichts der Produktion und Zirkulation*. Berlin: Duncker und Humblot.

Kurz, H. D. (1978). "Rent Theory in a Multisectoral Model," *Oxford Economic Papers*, **30**, pp. 16–37.

Kurz, H. D. (1979). "Wahl der Technik und Arbeitswertlehre in einem einfachen Modell mit zwei originären Faktoren," *Jahrbuch für Sozialwissenschaft*, **30**, pp. 27–51.

Kurz, H. D. (1986a). "'Normal' Positions and Capital Utilization," *Political Economy. Studies in the Surplus Approach*, **2**, pp. 37–54.

Kurz, H. D. (1986b). "Classical and Early Neoclassical Economists on Joint Production," *Metroeconomica*, **38**, pp. 1–37.

Kurz, H. D. (1987). "Capital Theory: Debates," *The New Palgrave. A Dictionary of Economics*, edited by J. Eatwell, M. Milgate, and P. Newman, vol. 1, pp. 357–63. London: Macmillan.

Kurz, H. D. (1989). "Die deutsche theoretische Nationalökonomie zu Beginn des 20. Jahrhunderts zwischen Klassik und Neoklassik," in B. Schefold (ed.), *Studien zur Entwicklung der ökonomischen Theorie*, vol. VIII, pp. 11–61. Berlin: Duncker und Humblot.

Kurz, H. D. (1990a). "Adam Smith, die Regel der freien Güter und die 'vent for surplus'-Begründung des Außenhandels," in Kurz (1990b), pp. 235–58.

Kurz, H. D. (ed.) (1990b). *Adam Smith (1723–1790) – Ein Werk und seine Wirkungsgeschichte*, 2nd edn 1991. Marburg: Metropolis.

Kurz, H. D. (1990c). *Capital, Distribution and Effective Demand. Studies in the "Classical" Approach to Economic Theory*. Cambridge: Polity Press.

Kurz, H. D. (1990d). "Technical Change, Growth and Distribution: A Steady-State Approach to Unsteady Growth," in Kurz (1990c), pp. 210–39.

Kurz, H. D. (1990e). "Accumulation, Distribution and the 'Keynesian Hypothesis'," in Bharadwaj and Schefold (1990), pp. 396–413.

Kurz, H. D. (1992a). "Contemporary Austrian Capital Theory," Graz, mimeo.

Kurz, H. D. (1992b). "Adam Smith on Foreign Trade: A Note on his 'Vent-for-Surplus' Argument," *Economica*, **59**, pp. 475–81.

Kurz, H. D. (1992c). "Accumulation et demande effective: quelques notes," *Cahiers d'Économie Politique*, **22**, pp. 59–82.

Kurz, H. D. (1994a). "Growth and Distribution," *Review of Political Economy*, **6**, pp. 393–420.

Kurz, H. D. (1994b). "Auf der Suche nach dem 'erlösenden Wort': Eugen von Böhm-Bawerk und der Kapitalzins," in B. Schefold (ed.), *Klassiker der Nationalökonomie*. Facsimile edn of Böhm-Bawerk's *Geschichte und Kritik der Kapitalzins-Theorien* (1884). Düsseldorf: Verlag Wirtschaft und Finanzen, pp. 45–110.

Kurz, H. D. and Salvadori, N. (1986). "A Comment on Levine," *Journal of Post Keynesian Economics*, **9**, pp. 163–5.

Kurz, H. D. and Salvadori, N. (1987). "Burmeister on Sraffa and the Labor Theory of Value: A Comment," *Journal of Political Economy*, **95**, pp. 870–81.

Kurz, H. D. and Salvadori, N. (1992). "Morishima on Ricardo: A Review Article," *Cambridge Journal of Economics*, **16**, pp. 227–47.

Kurz, H. D. and Salvadori, N. (1993a). "The 'Standard commodity' and Ricardo's Search for an 'invariable measure of value'," in Baranzini and Harcourt (1993b), pp. 95–123.

Kurz, H. D. and Salvadori, N. (1993b). "Von Neumann's Growth Model and the 'Classical' Tradition," *The European Journal of the History of Economic Thought*, **1**, pp. 129–60.

Kurz, H. D. and Salvadori, N. (1994a). "The Non-Substitution Theorem: Making Good a Lacuna," *Journal of Economics*, **59**, pp. 97–103.

Kurz, H. D. and Salvadori, N. (1994b). "Choice of Technique in a Model with Fixed Capital," *The European Journal of Political Economy*, forthcoming.

Laing, N. F. (1969), "Two Notes on Pasinetti's Theorem," *Economic Record*, **45**, pp. 373–85.

Landesmann, M. and Scazzieri, R. (1993). "Commodity Flows and Productive Subsystems: An Essay in the Analysis of Structural Change," in Baranzini and Harcourt (1993), pp. 209–45.

Langer, G. F. (1982). "Further Evidence for Sraffa's Interpretation of Ricardo," *Cambridge Journal of Economics*, **6**, pp. 397–400.

Langholm, O. (1992). *Economics in the Medieval Schools*. Leiden: E. J. Brill.

Laski, K. (1987). "Kalecki, Michal," *The New Palgrave. A Dictionary of Economics*, edited by J. Eatwell, M. Milgate, and P. Newman, vol. 3, pp. 8–14. London: Macmillan.

Lavoie, M. (1992). *Foundations of Post-Keynesian Economic Analysis*. Aldershot: Edward Elgar.

Leontief, W. (1928). "Die Wirtschaft als Kreislauf," *Archiv für Sozialwissenschaft und Sozialpolitik*, **60**, pp. 577–623.

Leontief, W. (1941). *The Structure of the American Economy*. Cambridge, Mass.: Harvard University Press.

Leontief, W. (1951). *The Structure of American Economy, 1919–1939: An Empirical Applica-tion of Equilibrium Analysis*, 2nd enlarged edn of Leontief (1941). White Plains, N.Y.: International Arts and Sciences Press.

Leontief, W. (1953). *Studies in the Structure of the American Economy*. New York: Oxford University Press.

Leontief, W. (1966). *Input–Output Economics*. New York: Oxford University Press.

Leontief, W. (1987). "Input–Output Analysis," *The New Palgrave. A Dictionary of Economics*, edited by J. Eatwell, M. Milgate, and P. Newman, vol. 2, pp. 860–4. London: Macmillan.

Leontief, W. (1991). "The Economy as a Circular Flow," English translation of parts of Leontief (1928) with an introduction by P. A. Samuelson in *Structural Change and Economic Dynamics*, **2**, 1991, pp. 177–212.

Levhari, D. (1965). "A Non Substitution Theorem and Switching of Techniques," *Quarterly Journal of Economics*, **79**, pp. 98–105.

Levhari, D. and Samuelson, P. A. (1966). "The Nonswitching Theorem is False," *Quarterly Journal of Economics*, **80**, pp. 518–19.

Lévy, D. (1984). "Le formalisme unificateur du surclassement: valeur, prix, répartition et croissance en production jointe," in Bidard (1984b), pp. 37–51.

Lindahl, E. (1929). "Prisbildningsproblemets uppläggning från kapitalteorisk synpunkt," *Ekonomisk Tidskrift*. Translated as "The Place of Capital in the Theory of Price" and reprinted as Part III of Lindahl (1939).

Lindahl, E. (1939). *Studies in the Theory of Money and Capital*. London: Allen and Unwin.

Lippi, M. (1979). *I prezzi di produzione. Un saggio sulla teoria di Sraffa*. Bologna: Il Mulino.

Łos, J. and Łos, M. W. (eds) (1974). *Mathematical Models in Economics*. Amsterdam and New York: North-Holland.

Łos, J. and Łos, M. W. (1976). "Reswitching of Techniques and Equilibria of Extended von Neumann Models," in Łos, Łos, and Wieczorek (1976), pp. 97–118.

Łos, J., Łos, M. W., and Wieczorek, A. (eds) (1976). *Warsaw Fall Seminars in Mathematical Economics 1975*. Berlin: Springer.

Lowe, A. (1954). "The Classical Theory of Growth," *Social Research*, **21**, pp. 127–58.

Lutz, F. A. and Hague, D. C. (eds) (1961). *The Theory of Capital*. London: Macmillan.

Mainwaring, L. (1984). *Value and Distribution in Capitalist Economies. An Introduction to Sraffian Economics*. Cambridge: Cambridge University Press.

Mainwaring, L. (1991). *Dynamics of Uneven Development*. Aldershot: Edward Elgar.

Mainwaring, L. and Steedman, I. (1993). "On the Probability of Reswitching and Capital Reversing in a Two-Sector Sraffian Model," Manchester, mimeo.

Malinvaud, E. (1953). "Capital Accumulation and the Efficient Allocation of Resources," *Econometrica*, **21**, pp. 233–68.

Malinvaud, E. (1987). "Intertemporal Equilibrium and Efficiency," *The New Palgrave. A Dictionary of Economics*, edited by J. Eatwell, M. Milgate, and P. Newman, vol. 2, pp. 958–62. London: Macmillan.

Malthus, T. R. (1815). *An Inquiry into the Nature and Progress of Rent*. London: John Murray.

Manara, C. (1968). "Il modello di Piero Sraffa per la produzione congiunta di merci a mezzo di merci," *L'Industria*, pp. 3–18. English translation in Pasinetti (1980).

Maneschi, A. (1974). "The Existence of a Two-Class Economy in the Kaldor and Pasinetti Models of Growth and Distribution," *Review of Economic Studies*, **41**, pp. 149–50.

Mangasarian, O. L. (1969). *Nonlinear Programming*. Bombay: Tata McGraw-Hill.

Marglin, S. A. (1984). *Growth, Distribution, and Prices*. Cambridge, Mass.: Harvard University Press.

Marris, R. (1964). *The Economics of Capital Utilisation*. Cambridge: Cambridge University Press.

Marshall, A. (1890). *Principles of Economics*, 1st edn 1890, 8th edn 1920. Reprint, reset (1977), London: Macmillan.

Marx, K. (1954). *Capital*, vol. I. Moscow: Progress Publishers. English translation of *Das Kapital*, vol. I (1867) Hamburg: Meissner.

Marx, K. (1956). *Capital*, vol. II. Moscow: Progress Publishers. English translation of *Das Kapital*, vol. II, edited by F. Engels (1885), Hamburg: Meissner.

Marx, K. (1959). *Capital*, vol. III. Moscow: Progress Publishers. English translation of *Das Kapital*, vol. III, edited by F. Engels (1894), Hamburg: Meissner.

Massie, J. (1750). *An Essay on the Governing Causes of the Natural Rate of Interest*, London. Reprinted and edited by J. Hollander (1912), Baltimore: Johns Hopkins Press.

Matsukawa, S. (1977). "Sir William Petty: An Unpublished Manuscript," *Hitotsubashi Journal of Economics*, **17**, pp. 33–50.

McKenzie, L. W. (1987). "General Equilibrium," *The New Palgrave. A Dictionary of Economics*, edited by J. Eatwell, P. Newman, and M. Milgate, vol. 2, pp. 498–512. London: Macmillan.

Meacci, F. (1994). "Hayek and the Deepening of Capital," in Colonna et al. (1994).

Meade, J. E. (1961). *A Neoclassical Theory of Economic Growth*. London: Allen and Unwin.

Meade, J. E. (1963). "The Rate of Profit in a Growing Economy," *Economic Journal*, **73**, pp. 665–74.

Meade, J. E. (1966). "The Outcome of the Pasinetti-Process: A Note," *Economic Journal*, **76**, pp. 161–4.

Meade, J. E. and Hahn, F. H. (1965). "The Rate of Profit in a Growing Economy," *Economic Journal*, **75**, pp. 445–8.

Meek, R. L. (1962). *The Economics of Physiocracy*. London: Allen and Unwin.

Meek, R. L. (ed.) (1973). *Turgot on Progress, Sociology and Economics*. Cambridge: Cambridge University Press.

Meldolesi, L. (1966). "La derivazione ricardiana di 'Produzione di merci a mezzo di merci'," *Economia Internazionale*, **19**, pp. 612–38.

Menger, C. (1871). *Grundsätze der Volkswirthschaftslehre*, Vienna: Wilhelm Braumüller. 2nd edn edited by Karl Menger (1923), Vienna: Hölder, Pichler und Tempsky.

Menger, C. (1981). *Principles of Economics*, translation by J. Dingwall and B. F. Hoselitz of the 2nd edn of Menger (1871), with an introduction by F. A. von Hayek. New York and London: New York University Press.

Menger, K. (1973). "Austrian Marginalism and Mathematical Economics," in Hicks and Weber (1973), pp. 38–60.

Metcalfe, J. S. and Steedman, I. (1972). "Reswitching and Primary Input Use," *Economic Journal*, **82**, pp. 140–57.

Metcalfe, J. S. and Steedman, I. (1977). "Reswitching, Primary Inputs and the Heckscher–Ohlin–Samuelson Theory of Trade," *Journal of International Economics*, 7, pp. 201–8.

Milgate, M. (1979). "On the Origin of the Notion of Intertemporal Equilibrium," *Economica*, **46**, pp. 1–10.

542   *Theory of production*

Mill, J. S. (1844). *Essays on Some Unsettled Questions of Political Economy*, reprinted 1948. London: London School of Economics.

Mill, J. S. (1965). *Principles of Political Economy with Some of Their Applications to Social Philosophy*, 1st edn 1848, edited by J. M. Robson. Toronto: University of Toronto Press.

Miller, R. E. and Blair, P. D. (1985). *Input–Output Analysis: Foundations and Extensions*. Englewood Cliffs, N.J.: Prentice-Hall.

Mirrlees, J. A. (1969). "The Dynamic Nonsubstitution Theorem," *Review of Economic Studies*, **36**, pp. 67–76.

Mises, L. v. (1933). "Intervention," in L. v. Mises and A. Spiethoff (eds), *Probleme der Wertlehre*, vol. II, *Schriften des Vereins für Socialpolitik*, **183/II**. Munich and Leipzig: Duncker und Humblot.

Miyao, T. (1977). "A Generalization of Sraffa's Standard Commodity and its Complete Characterization," *International Economic Review*, **18**, pp. 151–62.

Montani, G. (1972). "La teoria ricardiana della rendita," *L'Industria*, **3–4**, pp. 221–43.

Montani, G. (1975). "Scarce Natural Resources and Income Distribution," *Metroeconomica*, **27**, pp. 68–101.

Montet, C. (1979). "Reswitching and Primary Input Use: A Comment," *Economic Journal*, **89**, 642–7.

Moore, B. J. (1974). "The Pasinetti Paradox Revisited," *Review of Economic Studies*, **41**, pp. 297–9.

Morgenstern, O. and Thompson, G. L. (1976). *Mathematical Theory of Expanding and Contracting Economies*. Lexington: Lexington Books.

Morishima, M. (1960). "Economic Expansion and the Interest Rate in Generalized von Neumann Models," *Econometrica*, **28**, pp. 352–63.

Morishima, M. (1964). *Equilibrium, Stability and Growth*. Oxford: Clarendon Press.

Morishima, M. (1966). "Refutation of the Nonswitching Theorem," *Quarterly Journal of Economics*, **80**, pp. 520–5.

Morishima, M. (1969). *Theory of Economic Growth*, Oxford: Clarendon Press.

Morishima, M. (1971). "Consumption-Investment Frontier, Wage–Profit Frontier and the von Neumann Growth Equilibrium," in Bruckmann and Weber (1971), pp. 31–8.

Morishima, M. (1973). *Marx's Economics. A Dual Theory of Value and Growth*. Cambridge: Cambridge University Press.

Morishima, M. (1977). *Walras's Economics. A Pure Theory of Capital and Money*. Cambridge: Cambridge University Press.

Morishima, M. (1978). "S. Bowles and H. Gintis on the Marxian Theory of Value and Heterogeneous Labour," *Cambridge Journal of Economics*, **2**, pp. 305–9.

Morishima, M. (1989). *Ricardo's Economics. A General Equilibrium Theory of Distribution and Growth*. Cambridge: Cambridge University Press.

Morishima, M. and Catephores, G. (1978). *Value, Exploitation and Growth*. London: McGraw-Hill.

Moss, S. J. (1978). "The Post-Keynesian Theory of Income Distribution in the Corporate Economy," *Australian Economic Papers*, **38**, pp. 303–22.

Mückl, W. J. (1978). "On the Existence of a Two-Class Economy in the Cambridge Models of Growth and Distribution," *Jahrbücher für Nationalökonomie und Statistik*, **193**, pp. 508–17.

Murphy, A. E. (1986). *Richard Cantillon: Entrepreneur and Economist*. Oxford: Clarendon Press.

Negishi, T. (1993). "A Smithian-Growth Model and Malthus's Optimal Propensity to Save," *The European Journal of the History of Economic Thought*, **1**, pp. 115–27.

Neher, P. A. (1990). *Natural Resource Economics. Conservation and Exploitation*. Cambridge: Cambridge University Press.

Neisser, H. (1932). "Lohnhöhe und Beschäftigungsgrad im Marktgleichgewicht," *Weltwirtschaftliches Archiv*, **36**, pp. 415–55.

Nell, E. J. (1988). "Does the Rate of Interest Determine the Rate of Profit?" *Political Economy: Studies in the Surplus Approach*, **4**, pp. 263–7.

Nell, E. J. and Semmler, W. (eds) (1991). *Nicholas Kaldor and Mainstream Economics: Confrontation or Convergence?* London: Macmillan.

Nemchinov, V. S. (ed.) (1964). *The Use of Mathematics in Economics*, English translation by A. Nove of the Russian original published in Moscow in 1959. Edinburgh: Oliver and Boyd.

Neumann, J. von (1937). "Über ein ökonomisches Gleichungssystem und eine Verallgemeinerung des Brouwerschen Fixpunktsatzes," *Ergebnisse eines mathematischen Kolloquiums*, **8**, pp. 73–83.

Neumann, J. von (1945). "A Model of General Economic Equilibrium," *Review of Economic Studies*, **13**, pp. 1–9. English translation of von Neumann (1937).

Newman, P. (1962). "Production of Commodities by Means of Commodities," *Schweizerische Zeitschrift für Volkswirtschaft und Statistik*, **98**, pp. 58–75.

Nikaido, H. (1968). *Convex Structures and Economic Theory*. New York: Academic Press.

Nuti, D. M. (1971). "'Vulgar economy' in the Theory of Income Distribution," *Science and Society*, **35**, pp. 27–33.

Nuti, D. M. (1973). "On the Truncation of Production Flows," *Kyklos*, **26**, pp. 485–95.

Nuti, D. M. (1987). "Dmitriev, Vladimir Karpovich," *The New Palgrave. A Dictionary of Economics*, edited by J. Eatwell, M. Milgate, and P. Newman, vol. 1, 907–10. London: Macmillan.

Ochoa, E. M. (1989). "Values, Prices and Wage Profit Curves in the US Economy," *Cambridge Journal of Economics*, **13**, pp. 413–29.

O'Connor, M. (1991). "Passing on the Gift: An Input–Output Analysis of the Dynamics of Sustainability," *Working Papers in Economics*, **85**, University of Auckland, New Zealand.

Okishio, N. (1963). "A Mathematical Note on Marxian Theorems," *Weltwirtschaftliches Archiv*, **91**, pp. 287–99.

Orosel, G. O. (1987). "Period of Production," *The New Palgrave. A Dictionary of Economics*, edited by J. Eatwell, M. Milgate, and P. Newman, vol. 3, pp. 843–6. London: Macmillan.

Panico, C. (1980). "Marx's Analysis of the Relationship Between the Rate of Interest and the Rate of Profits," *Cambridge Journal of Economics*, **4**, pp. 363–78.

Panico, C. (1988a). "Sraffa on Money and Banking," *Cambridge Journal of Economics*, **12**, pp. 7–28.

Panico, C. (1988b). *Interest and Profit in the Theories of Value and Distribution*. London: Macmillan.

Panico, C. (1991). "Some Notes on Marshallian Supply Functions," *Economic Journal*, **101**, pp. 557–69.

Panico, C. (1993). "Two Alternative Approaches to Financial Model Building," *Metroeconomica*, **44**, pp. 93–133.

Panico, C. and Salvadori, N. (eds) (1993). *Post Keynesian Theory of Growth and Distribution*. Aldershot: Edward Elgar.

Panico, C. and Salvadori, N. (1994). "Sraffa on Returns," *The European Journal of the History of Economic Thought*, **1**, pp. 323–43.

Parker, R. H. and Harcourt, G. C. (eds) (1969). *Readings in the Concept and Measurement of Income*. Cambridge: Cambridge University Press.

Parrinello, S. (1970). "Introduzione ad una teoria neoricardiana del commercio internazionale," *Studi Economici*, **25**, pp. 267–321.

Parrinello, S. (1983). "Exhaustible Natural Resources and the Classical Method of Long-Period Equilibrium," in Kregel (1983), pp. 186–99.

Parrinello, S. (1994). "The Efficiency Wage Hypothesis and the Representation of the Production Process", in G. C. Harcourt, A. Roncaglia, and R. Rowley (eds), *Income and Employment in Theory and Practice*. London: Macmillan, forthcoming.

Pasinetti, L. L. (1960). "A Mathematical Formulation of the Ricardian System," *Review of Economic Studies*, **27**, pp. 78–98. Reprinted in Pasinetti (1974a).

Pasinetti, L. L. (1962). "Rate of Profit and Income Distribution in Relation to the Rate of Economic Growth," *Review of Economic Studies*, **29**, pp. 267–79.

Pasinetti, L. L. (1964). "A Comment on Professor Meade's 'Rate of Profit in a Growing Economy'," *Economic Journal*, **74**, pp. 488–9.

Pasinetti, L. L. (1965). "A New Theoretical Approach to the Problems of Economic Growth," *Pontificiae Academiae Scientiarum Scripta Varia*, **28**, Proceedings of a Study Week on the Econometric Approach to Development Planning, Vatican City (reprinted Amsterdam: North-Holland), pp. 572–696.

Pasinetti, L. L. (1966a). "The Rate of Profit in a Growing Economy: A Reply," *Economic Journal*, **76**, pp. 158–60.

Pasinetti, L. L. (1966b). "New Results in an Old Framework," *Review of Economic Studies*, **33**, pp. 303–6.

Pasinetti, L. L. (1966c). "Changes in the Rate of Profit and Switches of Techniques," *Quarterly Journal of Economics*, **80**, pp. 503–17.

Pasinetti, L. L. (1969). "Switches of Techniques and the 'Rate of Return' in Capital Theory," *Economic Journal*, **79**, pp. 508–31.

Pasinetti, L. L. (1973). "The Notion of Vertical Integration in Economic Analysis," *Metroeconomica*, **25**, pp. 1–29. Reprinted in Pasinetti (1980).

Pasinetti, L. L. (1974a). *Growth and Income Distribution. Essays in Economic Theory*. Cambridge: Cambridge University Press.

Pasinetti, L. L. (1974b). "The Rate of Profit in an Expanding Economy," in Pasinetti (1974a), pp. 121–46.

Pasinetti, L. L. (1977). *Lectures on the Theory of Production*. London: Macmillan.

Pasinetti, L. L. (ed.) (1980). *Essays on the Theory of Joint Production*. London: Macmillan.

Pasinetti, L. L. (1981a). *Lezioni di teoria della produzione*, 2nd edn. Bologna: Il Mulino.

Pasinetti, L. L. (1981b). *Structural Change and Economic Growth: A Theoretical Essay on the Dynamics of the Wealth of Nations*. Cambridge: Cambridge University Press.

Pasinetti, L. L. (1983). "Conditions of Existence of a Two-Class Economy in the Kaldor and More General Models of Growth and Distribution," *Kyklos*, **36**, pp. 91–102.

Pasinetti, L. L. (1986). "Sraffa's Circular Process and the Concept of Vertical Integration," *Political Economy. Studies in the Surplus Approach*, **2**, pp. 3–16.

Pasinetti, L. L. (1988a). "Growing Sub-Systems, Vertically Hyper-Integrated Sectors and the Labour Theory of Value," *Cambridge Journal of Economics*, **12**, pp. 125–34.

Pasinetti, L. L. (1988b). "Sraffa on Income Distribution," *Cambridge Journal of Economics*, **12**, pp. 135–8.

Patterson, K. D. and Schott, K. (eds) (1979). *The Measurement of Capital. Theory and Practice*. London: Macmillan.

Peach, T. (1984). "David Ricardo's Early Treatment of Profitability: A New Interpretation," *Economic Journal*, **94**, pp. 733–51.

Peach, T. (1986). "Ricardo's Early Treatment of Profitability: Reply to Hollander and Prendergast," *Economic Journal*, **96**, pp. 1105–12.

Peach, T. (1993). *Interpreting Ricardo*. Cambridge: Cambridge University Press.

Pegoretti, G. (1986). *Risorse, produzione, distribuzione*. Milan: Franco Angeli.

Pegoretti, G. (1990). "Offerta di risorse non riproducibili, scelta della tecnica e struttura produttiva," in Quadrio Curzio and Scazzieri (1990), pp. 81–121.

Perri, S. (1990). "The 'Transfer of Value' Approach to Fixed Capital," *Metroeconomica*, **41**, pp. 225–48.

Perrings, C. (1987). *Economy and the Environment: A Theoretical Essay on the Interdependence of Economic and Environmental Systems*. Cambridge: Cambridge University Press.

Petri, F. (1991). "Hicks's Recantation of the Temporary Equilibrium Method," *Review of Political Economy*, **3**, pp. 268–88.

Petrovič, P. (1991). "Shape of a Wage–Profit Curve: Some Methodology and Empirical Evidence," *Metroeconomica*, **42**, pp. 93–112.

Petty, W. (1662). *A Treatise of Taxes and Contributions*. Reprinted in Petty (1986).

Petty, W. (1676). *Political Arithmetick*. Reprinted in Petty (1986).

Petty, W. (1986). *The Economic Writings of Sir William Petty*, edited by C. H. Hull, vols. I and II, originally published in 1899, Cambridge: Cambridge University Press. Reprinted in one volume (1986), New York: Kelley.

Pigou, A. C. (1933). *The Theory of Unemployment*. London: Macmillan.

Pivetti, M. (1985). "On the Monetary Explanation of Distribution," *Political Economy. Studies in the Surplus Approach*, **1**, pp. 73–103.

Pivetti, M. (1987). "Distribution Theory: Classical," *The New Palgrave. A Dictionary of Economics*, edited by J. Eatwell, M. Milgate, and P. Newman, vol. 1, pp. 872–6. London: Macmillan.

Pivetti, M. (1988). "On the Monetary Explanation of Distribution: A Rejoinder to Nell and Wray," *Political Economy. Studies in the Surplus Approach*, **4**, pp. 275–83.

Pivetti, M. (1991). *An Essay on Money and Distribution*. London: Macmillan.

Pollit, B. H. (1990). "Clearing the Path for 'Production of Commodities by Means of Commodities': Notes on the Collaboration of Maurice Dobb in Piero Sraffa's Edition of the 'Works and Correspondence of David Ricardo'," in Bharadwaj and Schefold (1990), pp. 516–28.

Potier, J.-P. (1991). *Piero Sraffa–Unorthodox Economist (1898–1983)*. London and New York: Routledge.

Prendergast, R. (1986a). "Comment on Peach," *Economic Journal*, **96**, pp. 1098–104.

Prendergast, R. (1986b). "Malthus's Discussion of the Corn Ratio Theory of Profits," *Cambridge Journal of Economics*, **10**, pp. 187–9.

Punzo, L. F. (1989). "Von Neumann and Karl Menger's Mathematical Colloquium," in Dore, Chakravarty, and Goodwin (1989), pp. 29–65.

Punzo, L. F. (1991). "The School of Mathematical Formalism and the Viennese Circle of Mathematical Economists," *Journal of the History of Economic Thought*, **13**, pp. 1–18.

Quadrio Curzio, A. (1967). *Rendita e distribuzione in un modello economico plurisettoriale*. Milano: Giuffrè.

Quadrio Curzio, A. (1980). "Rent, Income Distribution, and Orders of Efficiency and Rentability," in Pasinetti (1980), pp. 218–40; reprinted in Quadrio Curzio (1990), pp. 21–47.

Quadrio Curzio, A. (1983). "Primary Commodity Prices, Exhaustible Resources and International Monetary Relations: Alternative Explanations," in Kregel (1983), pp. 142–52.

Quadrio Curzio, A. (1986). "Technological Scarcity: An Essay on Production and Structural Change," in Baranzini and Scazzieri (1986), pp. 311–38.

Quadrio Curzio, A. (1987). "Land Rent," *The New Palgrave. A Dictionary of Economics*, edited by J. Eatwell, M. Milgate, and P. Newman, vol. 3, pp. 118–21. London: Macmillan.

Quadrio Curzio, A. (1990). *Rent, Distribution and Economic Structure. A Collection of Essays*. Milan: Istituto di ricerca sulla Dinamica dei Sistemi Economici (IDSE).

Quadrio Curzio, A. and Scazzieri, R. (eds) (1990). *Dinamica economica e strutturale*. Bologna: Il Mulino.

Quesnay, F. (1972). *Quesnay's Tableau Economique* [1759], edited by M. Kuczynski and R. L. Meek. London: Macmillan.

Rae, J. (1834). *Statement of Some New Principles on the Subject of Political Economy*. Boston: Hilliard Gray and Co.

Raneda, I. J. and Reus, J. A. S. (1985). "Irregular Leontief-Sraffa Systems and Price-Vector Behaviour," University of Alicante, Spain, mimeo.

Remak, R. (1929). "Kann die Volkswirtschaftslehre eine exakte Wissenschaft werden?" *Jahrbücher für Nationalökonomie und Statistik*, **131**, pp. 703–35.

Remak, R. (1933). "Können superponierte Preissyteme praktisch berechnet werden?" *Jahrbücher für Nationalökonomie und Statistik*, **138**, pp. 839–42.

Ricardo, D. (1951–73). *The Works and Correspondence of David Ricardo*, 11 volumes, edited by P. Sraffa with the collaboration in M. H. Dobb. Cambridge: Cambridge University Press. In the text referred to as *Works*, volume number and page number.

Ritschl, A. (1989). *Prices and Production. Elements of a System–Theoretic Perspective*. Heidelberg: Physica-Verlag.

Robinson, J. V. (1933). *Economics of Imperfect Competition*. London: Macmillan.

Robinson, J. V. (1953). "The Production Function and the Theory of Capital," *Review of Economic Studies*, **21**, pp. 81–106.

Robinson, J. V. (1956). *The Accumulation of Capital*. London: Macmillan.

Robinson, J. V. (1959). "Depreciation," *Rivista di Politica Economica*, **49**, pp. 1703–17.

Robinson, J. V. (1961). "Prelude to a Critique of Economic Theory," *Oxford Economic Papers*, **13**, pp. 53–8.

Robinson, J. V. (1962). *Essays in the Theory of Economic Growth*. London: Macmillan.

Robinson, J. V. (1966). "Comment on P. A. Samuelson and F. Modigliani," *Review of Economic Studies*, **33**, pp. 307–8.

Robinson, J. V. (1970). "Capital Theory Up to Date," *Canadian Journal of Economics*, **3**, pp. 309–17.

Robinson, J. V. (1975). "The Unimportance of Reswitching," *Quarterly Journal of Economics*, **89**, pp. 32–9.

Robinson, J. V. and Naqvi, K. A. (1967). "The Badly Behaved Production Function," *Quarterly Journal of Economics*, **81**, pp. 579–91.

Roemer, J. E. (1981). *Analytical Foundations of Marxian Economic Theory*. Cambridge: Cambridge University Press.

Roncaglia, A. (1971). "Il capitale fisso in uno schema di produzione circolare," *Studi Economici*, **26**, pp. 232–45. English translation in Roncaglia (1978).

Roncaglia, A. (1974a). "Labour-Power, Subsistence Wage and the Rate of Wages," *Australian Economic Papers*, **13**, pp. 133–43.

Roncaglia, A. (1974b). "The Reduction of Complex to Simple Labour," *Bulletin of the Conference of Socialist Economists*, **3**, pp. 1–12.

Roncaglia, A. (1976). "Sulle macchine utilizzate congiuntamente," *Studi Economici*, **31**, pp. 127–32.

Roncaglia, A. (1978). *Sraffa and the Theory of Prices*. New York: John Wiley and Sons.

Roncaglia, A. (1982). "Hollander's Ricardo," *Journal of Post Keynesian Economics*, **4**, pp. 339–59, and "Rejoinder," ibid., pp. 373–5.

Roncaglia, A. (1983). "The Price of Oil," *Journal of Post Keynesian Economics*, **5**, pp. 557–78.

Roncaglia, A. (1985a). *Petty: The Origins of Political Economy*. New York: Sharpe.

Roncaglia, A. (1985b). *The International Oil Market*. London: Macmillan.

Roncaglia, A. (1990). "Is the Notion of Long-Period Positions Compatible with Classical Political Economy?" in Caminati and Petri (1990), pp. 103–11.

Rowthorn, R. E. (1980a). "Skilled Labour in the Marxist System," in Rowthorn (1980b), pp. 231–49.

Rowthorn, R. E. (1980b). *Capitalism, Conflict and Inflation. Essays in Political Economy.* London: Lawrence and Wishart.

Rowthorn, R. E. (1982). "Demand, Real Wages and Economic Growth," *Studi Economici,* **18**, 3–54.

Rubin, I. I. (1928). *Essays on Marx's Theory of Value.* Montreal: Black Rose. This is a translation of the third, 1928 edition; the book presumably first appeared in the early 1920s.

Salvadori, N. (1977). "Sulle macchine utilizzate congiuntamente: note ad un dibattito," *Studi Economici,* **32**, pp. 151–67.

Salvadori, N. (1979a). "Sulle macchine utilizzate congiuntamente: una replica," *Studi Economici,* **34**, pp. 75–85.

Salvadori, N. (1979b). "Mutamento dei metodi di produzione e produzione congiunta. Un commento al §96 di 'Produzione di merci a mezzo di merci'," *Studi Economici,* **34**, pp. 79–94.

Salvadori, N. (1979c). *Mutamento dei metodi di produzione e produzione congiunta,* Università degli Studi di Siena, Istituto di Economia, Quaderni dell'Istituto di Economia, **6**, Siena.

Salvadori, N. (1980). "On a Generalized von Neumann Model," *Metroeconomica,* **32**, pp. 51–62.

Salvadori, N. (1981). "Falling Rate of Profit with a Constant Real Wage: An Example," *Cambridge Journal of Economics,* **5**, pp. 59–66.

Salvadori, N. (1982). "Existence of Cost-Minimizing Systems within the Sraffa Framework," *Zeitschrift für Nationalökonomie,* **42**, pp. 281–98.

Salvadori, N. (1983). "On a New Variety of Rent," *Metroeconomica,* **35**, pp. 73-85.

Salvadori, N. (1984). "Le choix de techniques chez Sraffa: le cas de la production jointe," in Bidard (1984b), pp. 175–85.

Salvadori, N. (1985). "Switching in Methods of Production and Joint Production," *The Manchester School,* **53**, pp. 156–78.

Salvadori, N. (1986a). "Il capitale fisso come 'specie' del 'genere' produzione congiunta," *Economia Politica,* **3**, pp. 21–38.

Salvadori, N. (1986b). "Land and Choice of Techniques within the Sraffa Framework," *Australian Economic Papers,* **25**, pp. 94–105.

Salvadori, N. (1987a). "Basics and Non-Basics," *The New Palgrave. A Dictionary of Economics,* edited by J. Eatwell, M. Milgate, and P. Newman, vol. 1, pp. 680–2. London: Macmillan.

Salvadori, N. (1987b). "Il capitale fisso come 'specie' del 'genere' produzione congiunta. Ulteriori precisazioni ed una risposta," *Economia Politica,* **4**, pp. 265–75.

Salvadori, N. (1987c). "Les ressources naturelles rares dans la théorie de Sraffa," in Bidard (1987), pp. 161–76.

Salvadori, N. (1987d). "Non-substitution Theorems," *The New Palgrave. A Dictionary of Economics,* edited by J. Eatwell, M. Milgate, and P. Newman, vol. 3, pp. 680–2. London: Macmillan.

Salvadori, N. (1988a). "Fixed Capital within the Sraffa Framework," *Zeitschrift für Nationalökonomie,* **48**, pp. 1–17.

Salvadori, N. (1988b). "The Existence of a Two-Class Economy in a General Cambridge Model of Growth and Distribution: An Addendum," *Cambridge Journal of Economics,* **12**, pp. 273-8.

Salvadori, N. (1988c). "Fixed Capital Within a von Neumann–Morishima Model of Growth and Distribution," *International Economic Review,* **29**, pp. 341–51.

Salvadori, N. (1990). "Sul prezzo di una merce non base che entra nella propria riproduzione.

Una soluzione dinamica ad un problema lasciato insoluto dall'analisi statica," in Quadrio-Curzio and Scazzieri (1990), pp. 123–42.

Salvadori, N. (1991). "Post-Keynesian Theory of Distribution in the Long Run," in Nell and Semmler (1991), pp. 164–89.

Salvadori, N. (1994). "'Demand' in *Production of Commodities by Means of Commodities*," in G. C. Harcourt, A. Roncaglia, and R. Rowley (eds), *Income and Employment in Theory and Practice*. London: Macmillan.

Salvadori, N. and Steedman, I. (1988). "Joint Production Analysis in a Sraffian Framework," *Bulletin of Economic Research*, **40**, pp. 165–95.

Salvadori, N. and Steedman, I. (eds) (1990). *Joint Production of Commodities*, Aldershot: Edward Elgar.

Samuelson, P. A. (1951). "Abstract of a Theorem Concerning Substitutability in Open Leontief Models," in Koopmans (1951b), pp. 142–6.

Samuelson, P. A. (1957). "Wages and Interest: A Modern Dissection of Marxian Economic Models," *American Economic Review*, **47**, pp. 884–912.

Samuelson, P. A. (1959). "A Modern Treatment of the Ricardian Economy: I. The Pricing of Goods and of Labor and Land Services; II. Capital and Interest Aspects of the Pricing Process," *Quarterly Journal of Economics*, **73**, pp. 1–35 and 217–31.

Samuelson, P. A. (1961). "A New Theorem on Nonsubstitution," in *Money, Growth and Methodology*, Lund Social Science Studies, vol. 20, Lund: C. W. K. Gleerup, pp. 407–23. Reprinted in Samuelson (1966b).

Samuelson, P. A. (1962). "Parable and Realism in Capital Theory: The Surrogate Production Function," *Review of Economic Studies*, **29**, pp. 193–206. Reprinted in Harcourt and Laing (1971).

Samuelson, P. A. (1966a). "A Summing Up," *Quarterly Journal of Economics*, **80**, pp. 568–83.

Samuelson, P. A. (1966b). *The Collected Scientific Papers of P. A. Samuelson*, edited by J. E. Stiglitz, vol. 1. Cambridge, Mass.: MIT Press.

Samuelson, P. A. (1975). "Trade Pattern Reversals in Time-Phased Ricardian Systems and Intertemporal Efficiency," *Journal of International Economics*, **5**, pp. 309–63.

Samuelson, P. A. (1987). "Sraffian Economics," *The New Palgrave: A Dictionary of Economics*, edited by J. Eatwell, M. Milgate, and P. Newman, vol. 4, pp. 452–461. London: Macmillan.

Samuelson, P. A. (1989). "A Revisionist View of von Neumann's Growth Model," in Dore, Chakravarty, and Goodwin (1989), pp. 100–22.

Samuelson, P. A. (1991). "Sraffa's other Leg," *Economic Journal*, **101**, pp. 570–4.

Samuelson, P. A. and Modigliani, F. (1966a). "The Pasinetti Paradox in Neoclassical and More General Models," *Review of Economic Studies*, **33**, pp. 321–30.

Samuelson, P. A. and Modigliani, F. (1966b). "Reply to Pasinetti and Robinson," *Review of Economic Studies*, **33**, pp. 269–302.

Sato, K. (1974). "The Neo-Classical Postulate and the Technology Frontier in Capital Theory," *Quarterly Journal of Economics*, **88**, pp. 353–84.

Saucier, P. (1981). *Le choix des techniques en situation de limitations de ressources*, Ph.D. thesis, Université de Paris-II, mimeo.

Saucier, P. (1984a). "La production jointe en situation de concurrence," in Bidard (1984b), pp. 155–174.

Saucier, P. (1984b). "L'évolution des rentes dans une économie en croissance," in Abraham-Frois (1984), pp. 165–79.

Sawyer, M. C. (1985). *The Economics of Michal Kalecki*. London: Macmillan.

Scazzieri, R. (1987). "Ziber on Ricardo," *Contributions to Political Economy*, **6**, pp. 25–44.

Scazzieri, R. (1990). "Vertical Integration in Economic Theory," *Journal of Post Keynesian Economics*, **13**, pp. 1–15.

Schäffle, A. E. F. (1864). "Bourgeois- und Arbeiter-Nationalökonomie," *Deutsche Vierteljahrs Schrift*, **106**, pp. 245–358.

Schefold, B. (1971). *Mr. Sraffa on Joint Production*, Ph.D. thesis, University of Basle, mimeo.

Schefold, B. (1976a). "Eine Anwendung der Jordanschen Normalform," *Zeitschrift für angewandte Mathematik und Physik*, **27**, pp. 873–5.

Schefold, B. (1976b). "Relative Prices as a Function of the Profit Rate: A Mathematical Note," *Zeitschrift für Nationalökonomie*, **36**, pp. 21–48.

Schefold, B. (1976c). "Reduction to Dated Quantities of Labour, Roundabout Processes, and Switches of Techniques in Fixed Capital Systems," *Metroeconomica*, **28**, pp. 1–15.

Schefold, B. (1978a). "Fixed Capital as a Joint Product," *Jahrbücher für Nationalökonomie und Statistik*, **192**, pp. 415–39.

Schefold, B. (1978b). "Multiple Product Techniques with Properties of Single Product Systems," *Zeitschrift für Nationalökonomie*, **38**, pp. 29–53.

Schefold, B. (1978c). "On Counting Equations," *Zeitschrift für Nationalökonomie*, **38**, pp. 253–85.

Schefold, B. (1980a). "Von Neumann and Sraffa: Mathematical Equivalence and Conceptual Difference," *Economic Journal*, **90**, pp. 140–56.

Schefold, B. (1980b). "Fixed Capital as a Joint Product and the Analysis of Accumulation with Different Forms of Technical Progress," in Pasinetti (1980), pp. 138–217.

Schefold, B. (1981). "Nachfrage und Zufuhr in der klassischen Ökonomie," in F. Neumark (ed.), *Studien zur Entwicklung der ökonomischen Theorie*, vol. I, Berlin: Duncker und Humblot, pp. 53–91.

Schefold, B. (1985). "Cambridge Price Theory: Special Model or General Theory of Value?" *American Economic Review, Papers and Proceedings*, **75**, pp. 140–5.

Schefold, B. (1988). "The Dominant Technique in Joint Production Systems," *Cambridge Journal of Economics*, **12**, pp. 97–123.

Schefold, B. (1989). *Mr Sraffa on Joint Production and Other Essays*. London: Unwin Hyman.

Scherer, F. M. et al. (1975). *The Economics of Multi-Plant Operation. An International Comparisons Study.* Cambridge, Mass., and London: Harvard University Press.

Schlesinger, K. (1935). "Über die Produktionsgleichungen der ökonomischen Wertlehre," *Ergebnisse eines mathematischen Kolloquiums*, **6**, pp. 10–11.

Schneider, H. and Barker, G. P. (1968). *Matrices and Linear Algebra*. New York: Holt, Rinehart and Winston.

Schumpeter, J. A. (1954). *History of Economic Analysis*. New York: Oxford University Press.

Seraphim, H.-J. (1925). *Neuere russische Wert- und Kapitalzinstheorien*, Berlin: de Gruyter.

Seton, F. (1992). *The Economics of Cost, Use, and Value. The Evaluation of Performance, Structure, and Prices across Time, Space, and Economic Systems.* Oxford: Clarendon Press.

Shephard, R. W. (1970). *Theory of Cost and Production Functions*. Princeton: Princeton University Press.

Simmonds, P. L. (1873). *Waste Products and Undeveloped Substances: A Synopsis of Progress Made in their Economic Utilisation during the Last Quarter of a Century at Home and Abroad.* London: Robert Hardwicke.

Skinner, A. S. and Wilson, Th. (eds) (1975). *Essays on Adam Smith*. Oxford: Oxford University Press.

Skott, P. (1989). *Conflict and Effective Demand in Economic Growth*. Cambridge: Cambridge University Press.

Skourtos, M. (1991). "Corn Models in the Classical Tradition: P. Sraffa Considered Historically," *Cambridge Journal of Economics*, **15**, pp. 215–28.

Smith, A. (1976). *The Theory of Moral Sentiments*, 1st edn 1759, Vol. I of *The Glasgow*

Edition of the Works and Correspondence of Adam Smith, edited by A. L. Macfie and D. D. Raphael. Oxford: Oxford University Press. In the text quoted as *TMS*, part number, chapter number, paragraph number.

Smith, A. (1976). *An Inquiry into the Nature and Causes of the Wealth of Nations*, 1st edn 1776, Vol. II of *The Glasgow Edition of the Works and Correspondence of Adam Smith*, edited by R. H. Campbell, A. S. Skinner, and W. B. Todd. Oxford: Oxford University Press. In the text quoted as *WN*, book number, chapter number, section number, paragraph number.

Smith, A. (1978). *Lectures on Jurisprudence*, Vol. V of *The Glasgow Edition of the Works and Correspondence of Adam Smith*, edited by R. L. Meek, D. D. Raphael, and P. G. Stein. Oxford: Oxford University Press. In the text quoted as *LJ*(A) and *LJ*(B), page number, referring to the two reports of Smith's lectures published in the above volume.

Solow, R. M. (1956). "A Contribution to the Theory of Economic Growth," *Quarterly Journal of Economics*, **70**, pp. 65–94.

Solow, R. M. (1963). *Capital Theory and the Rate of Return*. Amsterdam: North-Holland.

Solow, R. M. (1967). "The Interest Rate and the Transition Between Techniques," in C. H. Feinstein (ed.), *Socialism, Capitalism and Economic Growth. Essays Presented to Maurice Dobb*. Cambridge: Cambridge University Press, pp. 30–9.

Solow, R. M. (1970). *Growth Theory: An Exposition*. Oxford: Oxford University Press.

Spaventa, L. (1968). "Realism without Parables in Capital Theory," in *Recherches récentes sur la fonction de production*, Centre d'Etudes et des Recherches Universitaires de Namur.

Spaventa, L. (1970). "Rate of Profit, Rate of Growth, and Capital Intensity in a Simple Production Model," *Oxford Economic Papers*, **22**, pp. 129–47.

Spengler, J. J. (1977). "Adam Smith on Human Capital," *American Economic Review*, **67**, pp. 32–6.

Sraffa, P. (1925). "Sulle relazioni fra costo e quantità prodotta," *Annali di Economia*, **2**, pp. 277–328. An English translation by John Eatwell and Alessandro Roncaglia circulates privately.

Sraffa, P. (1926). "The Laws of Returns under Competitive Conditions," *Economic Journal*, **36**, pp. 535–50.

Sraffa, P. (1930). "A Criticism" and "Rejoinder," contributions to the Symposium on "Increasing Returns and the Representative Firm," *Economic Journal*, **40**, pp. 89–93.

Sraffa, P. (1932). "Dr. Hayek on Money and Capital," *Economic Journal*, **42**, pp. 42–53.

Sraffa, P. (1951). "Introduction," in Ricardo (1951 ssq.), *Works* I, pp. xiii–lxii.

Sraffa, P. (1960). *Production of Commodities by Means of Commodities. Prelude to a Critique of Economic Theory*. Cambridge: Cambridge University Press.

Sraffa, P. (1962). "Production of Commodities: A Comment," *Economic Journal*, **72**, pp. 477–9.

Stackelberg, H. v. (1933). "Zwei kritische Bemerkungen zur Preistheorie Gustav Cassels," *Zeitschrift für Nationalökonomie*, **4**, pp. 456–72.

Steedman, I. (1972). "Jevons's Theory of Capital and Interest," *The Manchester School*, **40**, pp. 31–52.

Steedman, I. (1976). "Positive Profits with Negative Surplus Value: A Reply to Wolfstetter," *Economic Journal*, **86**, pp. 873–6.

Steedman, I. (1977a). *Marx after Sraffa*. London: New Left Books.

Steedman, I. (1977b). "Basics, Non-basics and Joint Production," *Economic Journal*, **87**, pp. 324–8.

Steedman, I. (1979a). *Trade Amongst Growing Economies*. Cambridge: Cambridge University Press.

Steedman, I. (ed.) (1979b). *Fundamental Issues in Trade Theory*. London: Macmillan.

Steedman, I. (1980). "Heterogeneous Labour and 'Classical' Theory," *Metroeconomica*, **33**, pp. 39–50.

Steedman, I. (1982). "Joint Production and Wage-Rent Frontier," *Economic Journal*, **92**, pp. 377–85.

Steedman, I. (1984a). "L'importance empirique de la production jointe," in Bidard (1984c), pp. 5–20. English translation in Salvadori and Steedman (1990), pp. 3–25.

Steedman, I. (1984b). "Natural Prices, Differential Profit Rates and the Classical Competitive Process," *The Manchester School*, **52**, pp. 123–40.

Steedman, I. (1985). "Heterogeneous Labour, Money Wages, and Marx's Theory," *History of Political Economy*, **17**, pp. 551–74.

Steedman, I. (1987a). "Foreign Trade," *The New Palgrave. A Dictionary of Economics*, edited by J. Eatwell, M. Milgate, and P. Newman, vol. 2, pp. 406–11. London: Macmillan.

Steedman, I. (1987b). "Free Goods," *The New Palgrave. A Dictionary of Economics*, edited by J. Eatwell, M. Milgate, and P. Newman, vol. 2, pp. 419–20. London: Macmillan.

Steedman, I. (ed.) (1988a). *Sraffian Economics*, two vols. Aldershot: Edward Elgar.

Steedman, I. (1988b). "Sraffian Interdependence and Partial Equilibrium Analysis," *Cambridge Journal of Economics*, **12**, pp. 85–95.

Steedman, I. (1989). "On Pasinetti's 'G' Matrix," *Metroeconomica*, **40**, pp. 3–15.

Steedman, I. (1992). "Questions for Kaleckians," *Review of Political Economy*, **4**, pp. 125–51.

Steedman, I. (1994a). "'Perverse' Behaviour in a 'One-commodity' Model," *Cambridge Journal of Economics*, **18**, pp. 299–311.

Steedman, I. (1994b). "The Pure Theory of Capital by F. A. Hayek," in Colonna et al. (1994).

Steindl, J. (1952). *Maturity and Stagnation in American Capitalism*. London: Basil Blackwell. 2nd edn with a new introduction by the author (1976), New York and London: Monthly Review Press.

Steindl, J. (1990). *Economic Papers 1941–88*. London: Macmillan.

Stigler, G. J. (1941). *Production and Distribution Theories*. New York: Macmillan.

Stiglitz, J. E. (1970). "Non-substitution Theorems with Durable Capital Goods," *Review of Economic Studies*, **37**, pp. 543–52.

Stiglitz, J. E. (1974). "The Cambridge–Cambridge Controversy in the Theory of Capital: A View From New Haven. A Review Article," *Journal of Political Economy*, **82**, pp. 893–903.

Swan, T. W. (1956). "Economic Growth and Capital Accumulation," *Economic Record*, **32**, pp. 334–61.

Tani, P. (1986). *Analisi microeconomica della produzione*. Rome: NIS.

Thompson, G. L. (1987). "Von Neumann, John," *The New Palgrave. A Dictionary of Economics*, edited by J. Eatwell, M. Milgate, and P. Newman, vol. 4, pp. 818–22. London: Macmillan.

Thünen, J. H. von (1826). *Der isolirte Staat in Beziehung auf Landwirtschaft und National-ökonomie*, 2nd edn (1842), Stuttgart: Gustav Fischer.

Tooke, T. (1826). *Considerations on the State of the Currency*. London: John Murray.

Tooke, T. (1838). *A History of Prices*, vols I and II. London: Longman.

Tooke, T. (1840). *A History of Prices*, vol. III. London: Longman.

Tooke, T. (1844). *An Inquiry into the Currency Principle*. London: Longman; reprinted (1959) London: The London School of Economics.

Torrens, R. (1818). "Strictures on Mr. Ricardo's Doctrine Respecting Exchangeable Value," *Edinburgh Magazine*, October, pp. 335–8.

Torrens, R. (1820). *An Essay on the Influence of the External Corn Trade upon the Production and Distribution of National Wealth*, 2nd edn. London: Hatchard.

Torrens, R. (1821). *An Essay on the Production of Wealth*. London: Longman, Hurst, Rees, Orme, and Brown. Reprint edited by J. Dorfman (1965), New York: Kelley.

Tozer, J. E. (1838). "Mathematical Investigation of the Effect of Machinery on the Wealth of a Community in Which it is Employed, and on the Fund for the Payment of Wages," *Transactions of the Cambridge Philosophical Society*, vol. VI, part III, pp. 507–22. Cambridge: Pitt Press. Reprinted (1968), New York: Kelley.

Tugan-Baranovsky, M. (1905). *Grundlagen des Marxismus*. Leipzig: Duncker und Humblot.

Turgot, A. R. J. (1766a). *Réflexions sur la formation et la distribution des richesses*, in Meek (1973).

Turgot, A. R. J. (1766b). *Reflections on the Production and Distribution of Wealth*. English translation of the *Réflexions* in Groenewegen (1977).

Turgot, A. R. J. (1767). *Observations on a Paper by Saint-Péravy*. English translation of a note published in Groenewegen (1977).

Ulam, S. (1958). "John von Neumann, 1903–1957," *Bulletin of the American Mathematical Society*, **64**, pp. 1–49.

Ure, A. (1835). *The Philosophy of Manufacture*. London: Knight.

Vaggi, G. (1987a). *The Economics of François Quesnay*. London: Macmillan.

Vaggi, G. (1987b). "Natural Price," *The New Palgrave. A Dictionary of Economics*, edited by J. Eatwell, M. Milgate, and P. Newman, vol. 3, pp. 605–8. London: Macmillan.

Vaggi, G. (1988). "The Classical Concept of Profit Revisited," in D. E. Moggridge (ed.), *Perspectives on the History of Economic Thought*, vol. III, pp. 1–9. Aldershot: Edward Elgar.

Van Daal, J. et al. (1985). "On Walras' Model of General Economic Equilibrium," *Zeitschrift für Nationalökonomie*, **45**, pp. 219–44.

Varian, H. R. (1984). *Microeconomic Analysis*, 2nd edn. New York: Norton.

Varri, P. (1974). "Prezzi, saggio di profitto e durata del capitale fisso nello schema teorico di P. Sraffa," *Studi Economici*, **29**, pp. 5–44. English translation titled "Prices, Rate of Profit and Life of Machines in Sraffa's Fixed Capital Model" in Pasinetti (1980), pp. 55–87.

Varri, P. (1976). "Sulle macchine utilizzate congiuntamente: risposta ad A. Roncaglia," *Studi Economici*, **31**, pp. 133–7.

Varri, P. (1979). "Sulla aggregazione di macchine usate congiuntamente nella produzione: risposta a N. Salvadori," *Studi Economici*, **34**, pp. 95–102.

Varri, P. (1981). "Il valore dei residui negli schemi di produzione congiunta," *Giornale degli Economisti ed Annali di Economia*, **40**, pp. 447–64.

Varri, P. (1987). "Il capitale fisso come 'specie' del 'genere' produzione congiunta: alcune precisazioni," *Economia Politica*, **4**, pp. 259–63.

Veblen, T. (1907). "Professor Clark's Economics," *Quarterly Journal of Economics*, **22**, pp. 147–95.

Wald, A. (1935). "Über die eindeutige positive Lösbarkeit der neuen Produktionsgleichungen," *Ergebnisse eines mathematischen Kolloquiums*, **6**, pp. 12–18. (Comments by Schams and Menger, pp. 18–20.)

Wald, A. (1936). "Über die Produktionsgleichungen der ökonomischen Wertlehre (II. Mitteilung)," *Ergebnisse eines mathematischen Kolloquiums*, **7**, pp. 1–6. (Comment by Gödel, p. 6.)

Walker, D. A. (ed.) (1983). *William Jaffé's Essays on Walras*. Cambridge: Cambridge University Press.

Walker, D. A. (1987). "Walras, Léon," *The New Palgrave. A Dictionary of Economics*, edited by J. Eatwell, M. Milgate, and P. Newman, vol. 4, pp. 853–63. London: Macmillan.

Walras, L. (1874). *Eléments d'économie politique pure.* Lausanne: Corbaz. 5th and definitive edn (1924), Paris: F. Richon.

Walras, L. (1954). *Elements of Pure Economics.* London: Allen and Unwin. English translation of the definitive edition of Walras (1874) by W. Jaffé.

Walsh, V. and Gram, H. (1980). *Classical and Neoclassical Theories of General Equilibrium: Historical Origins and Mathematical Structure.* New York and Oxford: Oxford University Press.

Weintraub, E. R. (1985). *General Equilibrium Analysis. Studies in Appraisal.* Cambridge: Cambridge University Press.

Weizsäcker, C. Ch. von (1971). *Steady State Capital Theory.* Berlin, Heidelberg, New York: Springer.

West, E. (1815). *An Essay on the Application of Capital to Land.* London: Johns Hopkins Press.

Whewell, W. (1829). *Mathematical Exposition of Some Doctrines of Political Economy.* Cambridge: J. Smith. Reprinted in Whewell (1971).

Whewell, W. (1831). "Mathematical Exposition of Some of the Leading Doctrines in Mr. Ricardo's 'Principles of Political Economy and Taxation'," *Transactions of the Cambridge Philosophical Society*, pp. 1–44. Reprinted in Whewell (1971).

Whewell, W. (1971). *Mathematical Exposition of Some Doctrines of Political Economy*, reprint of four papers published by Whewell in 1829, 1831, and 1850. New York: Kelley.

Wicksell, K. (1893). *Über Wert, Kapital und Rente nach den neueren nationalökonomischen Theorien.* Jena: Gustav Fischer. English translation as Wicksell (1954).

Wicksell, K. (1896). *Finanztheoretische Untersuchungen nebst Darstellung und Kritik des Steuerwesens Schwedens.* Jena: Gustav Fischer.

Wicksell, K. (1901). *Föreläsingar i Nationalekonomi*, vol. I. Lund: Berlingska Boktrycheriet. English translation in Wicksell (1934).

Wicksell, K. (1923). "Realkapital och kapitalränta," *Ekonomisk Tidskrift*, **25**, pp. 145–80. A review article of G. Åkerman's doctoral dissertation *Realkapital und Kapitalzins*, Lund 1923. English translation titled "Real Capital and Interest" in Wicksell (1934), pp. 258–99.

Wicksell, K. (1934). *Lectures on Political Economy*, vol. I. London: George Routledge and Sons. Translation of Wicksell (1901) by E. Classen and edited, with an introduction, by Lionel Robbins.

Wicksell, K. (1954). *Value, Capital and Rent.* London: Allen and Unwin. Reprinted 1970, New York: Kelley.

Wicksteed, P. H. (1894). *Essay on the Co-ordination of the Laws of Production and Distribution*, revised edition with an introduction by Ian Steedman (1992), Aldershot: Edward Elgar.

Williamson, O. E. (1979). "Transaction-Cost Economics: The Governance of Contractual Relations," *Journal of Law and Economics*, **22**, pp. 233–61.

Williamson, O. E. (1981). "The Modern Corporation: Origins, Evolution, Attributes," *Journal of Economic Literature*, **19**, pp. 1537–68.

Wilson, J. (1845). "Currency and Banking," a series of articles published in *The Economist* from 8 March to 17 May 1845.

Winston, G. C. (1982). *The Timing of Economic Activities.* Cambridge: Cambridge University Press.

Wittmann, W. (1967). "Die extremale Wirtschaft. Robert Remak – ein Vorläufer der Aktivitätsanalyse," *Jahrbücher für Nationalökonomie und Statistik*, **180**, pp. 397–409.

Woods, J. E. (1988). "On Switching of Techniques in Two-sector Models," *Scottish Journal of Political Economy*, **35**, pp. 84–91.

Woods, J. E. (1990). *The Production of Commodities. An Introduction to Sraffa.* London: Macmillan.

Wray, L. R. (1988). "The Monetary Explanation of Distribution: A Critique of Pivetti," *Political Economy*, **4**, pp. 269–73.

Zaghini, E. (1967). "On Non-Basic Commodities," *Schweizerische Zeitschrift für Volkswirtschaft und Statistik*, **103**, pp. 257–66.

Zalai, E. (1980). "Heterogeneous Labour and the Determination of Value," *Acta Oeconomica*, **25**, pp. 259–76.

Zamagni, S. (1987). *Microeconomic Theory. An Introduction*. Oxford: Basil Blackwell.

Zeuthen, F. (1933). "Das Prinzip der Knappheit, technische Kombination und ökonomische Qualität," *Zeitschrift für Nationalökonomie*, **4**, pp. 1–24.

Name index

Subject index

accumulation of capital, 6, 15, 44, 47–8, 69, 383, 459, 470–4, 483–4
  rate of, 47–8, 53, 474, 484, 489–90
advances in production, 39, 47, 178, 413, 438
  in Physiocrats, 208
agriculture, 3, 6, 240, 277, 279, 293, 305, 308–9, 335, *see also* capital, agricultural; profit(s); natural resources; returns to scale, diminishing; surplus, agricultural
allocation of resources, 36, 459
  intertemporal, 372, 460, 458n
  spatial, 308
Alternative, Theorems of the, 492, 506–9
  Farkas, 506
  Fredholm, 99, 506–8
annual charge, 186, 203–4, 209, 261–2, 264, 329, 329n, 376, 386, 424, *see also* depreciation
apprenticeship, 327n, 328n
arbitrage, 372
asset specificity, 338
Austrian approach to production, 164, 176–8, 213–14, 379, *see also* labor, reduction to dated quantities of
automatic compensation of labor displacement, 474n, *see also* machinery

bad, 41
banking sector, 414, 481–2
basic commodity, *see* commodities
Berlin Mathematical Society, 412
bon prix, 38
bounties, 150

Cambridge controversies in theory of capital, 35, 89, 120, 271, 428, 443, 447, *see also* neoclassical theory, and problem of capital
Cambridge equation, 487–90
canonical trinity formula, 309
capacity
  carrying, 353, 357
  laborers' capacity to work, 327
  productive, 204, 489–90

rate of capacity investment, 490
  spare, 475, 489
  utilization, 474, 489
capital
  adjusted in long period, 14
  advanced, 2, 9, 39, 45, 47, 85–7, 208, 382, 387, 402, 482
  agricultural (incorporated in ground), 208, 381
  as factor of production, 434, 445
  as including wages, 54
  circulating, 23n, 25–6, 54, 85, 208, 211, 213, 270, 404, 412, 418, 437, 445
  conceived of as set of heterogeneous commodities, 22, 432, 439, 441, 466
  conceived of as single magnitude, 22, 309, 43–4, 434n, 435n, 443
  conceived of as subsistence fund, 87, 309, 432, 438–9
  conceived of as value magnitude, 35, 153, 432–4, 439, 441, 445
  conceived of as produced means of production, 152
  conceived of as saved-up labor and land, 438, 442
  conceived of as time, 178, 435–7
  constant, 13, 212
  different employments of, 5–6, 14, 321–2, 326, 334–5
  durable, *see* fixed capital
  endowment, 22, 27, 211, 410, 430–2, 438–41, 452–4, 457, 460–4, 467
  fixed, *see* fixed capital
  floating, 8, 369
  formation, 25
  free, 369, 438
  goods proper, 23–5, 439–41
  heterogeneous, 23–5, 55, 152, 176, 210, 310, 334, 337, 404, 412, 430–2, 434, 435n, 437, 441–2, 444–5, 452, 454, 458–9, 463, 465, 482
  human, 327–9, 333–4, 337–8, *see also* labor, skilled
  in one-commodity world, 9, 44, 51–2, 87–8, 310, 389, 429–32

561

568   *Subject index*

matrix (*cont.*)
  output matrix, 133, 137, 139, 179, 189,
    195, 226, 300, 325, 348, 404
  rank of matrix, 167, 172, 182, 238, 499,
    503–4
  reducible, 104
  Sraffa, 123–4
  structural, 394
  sub-matrix, 96, 109, 117, 123, 185, 192,
    501, 503, 516
  vertically integrated technical coeffi-
    cients, *see* vertical integration
means of subsistence, 35–6, 43–4, 178,
  383, 387, 404, 411, 413, 422, 473
mechanization, degree of, 449
mercantilists, 240
methods of production
  aquacultural, 352–4
  available to each single firm, 16–17
  known, 16–17
  new, 6, 150, 242, 400, 402, 474
  not available to other firms, 16
  old, 402–3
  roundabout, 436
mines, 15n, 240, 335, 369–73
monetary authorities, 483, 491
monopoly, 16–17, 372, 409
  degree of, 481
  natural, 336
  price, 306, 336, 371
myopic behavior, 347–8

natural resources, 2, 17, 42n, 58n, 277–8,
  340, 352, 359, 391, 406n, 407n, 409,
  413, 439, 465
  and scarcity, 17, 20, 33, 308–9
  (non) depletable, 15n, 19, 340
  (non) exhaustible, 19, 33,–4, 278, 340–
    1, 357–73
  in short supply, 33
  new deposits of, 340
  (non) renewable, 33–4, 278, 340, 351–7,
    370, 372
  specific to industry, 17
  see also land
necessities of life, *see* means of subsistence
neo-Austrian approach to production,
  214–15
neoclassical fairy tale, 434n
neoclassical theory, 1–2, 14n, 21–2, 26–7,
  35, 41, 55, 179, 213, 269–70, 309, 311,
  338, 379, 393–4, 406n, 410–11, 422,
  488
  and problem of capital, 427–68

characteristic features of, 20, 410–11,
  452
long-period, *see* traditional
modern, 393, 408, 428, 455–67
on fixed capital, *see* fixed capital
on rent of land, 308–9, 311
traditional, long-period, 20–35, 359,
  410–12, 428–48, 466
see also marginalism; supply and
  demand
neoclassical synthesis, 452
newcomers, 16
non-substitution theorem, 2, 22, 26–8, 41,
  151–2, 255, 270, 391
normal price mechanism, 412
numeraire, *see* value, standard of

oil, 340, 357, 360, 366–8
Okishio theorem, 402n
operation of plant and equipment, 204–7,
  213, 269, *see also* capital, utilization
optimal truncation date, 212–14
output–capital ratio, 44, 87, 116, 476,
  480n, 486
output function, 214
output–labor ratio, 44–5, 51, 332, 436
overhead charges, 16

Pasinetti theorem, *see* Cambridge
  equation
perfect foresight, 341, 347, 456n, 457,
  457n
period of production, 1, 438, 447, 544
  average, 213–14, 278, 436–7, 441, 446
  uniform, 43, 178, 413
Perron–Frobenius Theorems, 96, 102,
  118, 239, 509–18
physiocrats, 12, 38, 208, 240, 305, 383
plant, as device to represent joint utilization of new machines, 187, 207–8,
  250–1, 266–8, 270
point input–point output, 177, 214
pollution, 340
post-Keynesian theory, 47, 53, 475–80,
  485–90
price(s)
  adding-up theory of, 3, 7, 10
  convergence of market to natural price,
    1–20, *see also* gravitation
  discounted, 466
  fundamental, *see prix fondamental*
  good, *see bon prix*
  ideal, 36
  independent of final demand, *see* non-
    substitution theorem
  international, 149–50